The Power Structure

The Power Structure

POLITICAL PROCESS IN AMERICAN SOCIETY

ARNOLD M. ROSE

OXFORD UNIVERSITY PRESS

LONDON   OXFORD   NEW YORK

This book is dedicated to
Louis Wirth, teacher and friend

Foreword

For more than twenty-five years Arnold Rose has fused the liberal ethos with the sociological imagination. An intellectual adventure which began in 1940 with his major role in *An American Dilemma* has now reached its intellectual culmination with *The Power Structure*. It might be added that, distinctly unlike most sociologists, Rose's knowledge of the civic culture and the political arena is authentic—an authenticity certified by his service as a representative in the Minnesota legislature and by his relentless defense of civil and academic freedoms in the courtroom no less than the classroom.

This aspect of Arnold Rose's career is not accidentally related to the book before you—since like all good social scientists, Rose has transformed both personal profile and political commitment into scientific sociology. One may take issue with many of the hypotheses and conclusions he has drawn, but one may not easily contest either the sobriety of his intellectual viewpoint or the worth of the man behind it.

One genuine problem might well be that Professor Rose's involvement in politics at the local level tends to reinforce a populist image of government, which, while in fact present in American society, does not necessarily reflect the structural dilemmas of the society at the national, or even more noteworthy, at the international level. Thus, it may be that the degree of civilian control over the military appears greater from the shores of Lake Superior in Minnesota than from the Bay of Guanabara in Brazil. I doubt that the average American, infused as he is with populist values, and oblivious as he often is of overseas commitments, has the same perception of an American military or diplomatic presence as do those peoples who live in the midst of revolutions or counter-revolutions—successful or otherwise, depending on the attitudes of the United States military mission and the financial appraisals of United States trade groups, no less than on the civilian ambassadorial staff.

The attempt of Arnold Rose is clear enough: to effect a reconciliation of power theories by employing the political analyses of the pluralists, from Bentley to Key, and the sociological methods of the elitist school, particularly the contemporary work of Mills and Hunter. That neither of the contrasting schools of macro-political conflict theory will be much satisfied by Rose's analysis is a foregone conclusion, and clearly appreciated by the author himself. One must welcome Rose's calm and dispassionate examination of the available empirical information, and his willingness to speculate on the outcome of each theory in the light of the current discussion between pluralists and elitists. Without work such as his, the discussion could well become part of general ideology rather than part of systematic sociology.

In this connection one of the most telling virtues of Rose's presentation is his appreciation of the generalized state of false consciousness in American society. There is an absence of a true appreciation of the nature of power, which is by no means confined to trade unionists or a proletarian class but extends throughout the business sectors, the political communities, and all of the intermediary classes which constantly examine their own power in evaluating their influence on social events.

I would not take issue with Arnold Rose on his shrewd observations concerning the generalized misconceptions about power, but rather I would emphasize more the actual disparity between the perception of power and the exercise of power. It might be true to say that the understanding of power on the part of big business is as fragile and limited as it is on the part of big unionism. However, from the point of view of social forces and not just social interactions, the actual dominion of power given over to business is considerably more than that given over to labor. This distinction between the perception and the execution of power is precisely what distinguishes pluralists from elitists, the latter being far more concerned with its exercise and the former far more concerned with its perception than is healthy for either. In this sense I view Professor Rose's book as an attempt to get each major theory of power to confront the other with its particular variety of false consciousness.

There is an ever-present confusion in political sociology between statements of fact (such as the existence of diverse and multi-channeled expressions of power in the United States) and judgments about the moral order (such as "the best way to study power in the United States is by examining perceptions or life chances"). It is important to realize that power may be erroneously perceived not only in terms of underestimation but also in terms of exaggeration. Unionists may exaggerate their power. Militarists may overemphasize their war-making potential. In these circumstances, perceptions may stimulate elitist sentiments rather than contribute to the pluralistic framework. Professor Rose's work does a great deal to clarify, or at least to cata-logue, the present confusion between influence and power, between what is perceived and what is actual.

It might well be that there is a qualitative distinction to be made between voluntary community organizations and a bureaucratic na-tional system. From a community point of view, voluntary organiza-tions seem effective and powerful, but from the national perspective these same kinds of organizations often appear impotent. The nature of power, or at least the perception of power, shifts as the levels of analysis alter. Thus, the power structure in the United States may require one kind of examination when viewed in terms of voluntary community organization, while the United States as a power may bring out different features when considered internationally. Although even at the community level I venture to say that the degree of interlocking political-economic control is impressive.

One serendipitous finding made by Rose is the degree to which his empirical researches demonstrate a gap between civics and politics, between perceptions of influence and basic political issues within the nation. It is clear that the United States suffers not so much from power concentrations as from a breakdown in political dialogue re-sulting partly from a celebration of civic activities. The civic culture may not only vary from actual political behavior, but often represents

an antithetical frame of reference. Civics often dulls the political sen-
sibilities of the American public. This fact is clearly evident in Rose's
work.

One of the most impressive facets of Professor Rose's book on the
power structure is its revelation of his intimacy with the nature of
power. The last sections, on Minnesota, Texas, the Kennedy presidential campaign, and the Medicare legislation, represent four case studies
in political sociology. The case study method is often talked about but
too rarely used. In Rose's hands political sociology is not reduced to
cross-tabulating electoral results. He does not suffer from the fallacy
of electoral determinism, of assuming that important political events
are necessarily linked to electoral behavior. Quite the contrary. There
is a strong undertone to Rose's remarks which clearly places him, no
matter how dissatisfied he is with the results of Mills, on the side of
the "classical" tradition, precisely because political sociology comes
to represent the study of social interaction among political men, and
not the study of electoral victories among nonpolitical men.

In this sense the significance of *The Power Structure* is as much
heuristic as theoretical. Chapter XIV may well be considered a guide
for the perplexed liberal and for the confused sociologist. Written in
the optative mood, it forms a basis for social and political action. Perhaps it is necessary to make constant references to democratic values
in order to make good on the various propositions politicians proclaim
to be existential fact. If the hopeful mood generated by Professor
Rose's book produces a self-fulfilling prophesy based on liberal values,
well and good. But if this same mood produces a smug acceptance of
the American political system, both internally and in its effects on the
rest of the world, then I would find this self-fulfilling prophesy more
in the nature of a self-destructive fantasy.

Arnold Rose is a shrewd man. He appreciates and understands these
various dilemmas. That is why his book manages to remain within the
framework of a multi-influence approach without indulging in the kind
of flatulent, self-congratulatory conclusions so often recorded in the
work of those scholars adhering to pluralism.

This is a serious book deserving of attention and argument. If a
political-economic elite theory of American society is to regain favor
among students of the social sciences, the empirical and theoretical

formulations of the multi-influence school as put forward so cogently
by Professor Rose will have to be coped with squarely. Just as Rose
engages in a symbolic dialogue with men like Mills and Hunter, so
too will the future writers on political sociology have to come to terms
in an equally serious dialogue with Arnold Rose's newest effort to
construct a bridge between society and polity—or more to the point—
between sociology and political analysis.

IRVING LOUIS HOROWITZ

Washington University
St. Louis, Missouri
January 1967

Preface

The influence of C. Wright Mills and Floyd Hunter, both on the general public and on academic researchers, has been startling, considering the usual reception given to sociological writings. Their concepts of the "power elite" and the "power structure" apparently drew a gut reaction, and a great number of their readers—from widely varied segments of the population—were prepared to believe their general theme that a relatively small economic elite controls the United States. The theme was not a new one, but Mills gave it an especially sophisticated formulation, Hunter backed it up with statistics, and both gave it an aura of sociological science. Although Hunter published his *Community Power Structure* in 1953, and Mills published *The Power Elite* in 1956, the influence of these works is as strong today as it was a decade ago.

I have always admired Mills—for his willingness to use sociology to analyze significant social issues, for his insights into the relationship between social structure and individual behavior, for his recognition of what is distinctive about social facts, for his contributions to the sociology of knowledge, for his willingness to ignore the rituals and shibboleths of the sociological profession, and for the clarity and pungency of his writing style.[1] But I had to recognize that *The Power Elite* was a caricature of American society. If it were to represent to

[1]For varied evaluations of the thought and work of C. Wright Mills, see *The New Sociology*, ed. by Irving Louis Horowitz (New York: Oxford University Press, 1964). A sympathetic analysis of Mills's political thought is contained in the essay by Ralph Miliband in that volume (pp. 76–87).

lay intellectuals what sociology had to say about the power structure of the United States, it had to be answered. This was brought home to me all the more strongly when one of my associates in a civic-improvement venture urged that we proceed by importuning the "local power elite" rather than by directing our efforts to the city government officials who had jurisdiction over the matter. I felt that my associate had been misguided by Mills and Hunter, enough to jeopardize the possible success of our efforts. Both from my academic knowledge and my practical experience, I felt that Mills was ivory-towered; he had never descended into the realm of social action. He was also too impatient with the tedious processes of research in his drive toward sweeping conclusions.

Some years earlier I had been shocked by the shoddy methodology and unwarranted conclusions found in a study by Floyd Hunter, *Community Power Structure*. Of course, shoddy methodology is not exactly unique to Hunter, and I plead guilty to having used some myself. But the Hunter book seemed to have drawn a considerable following among some sociologists and others, who were intrigued by the pseudo-precision of his technique of research but who knew nothing about his subject matter. Hunter's conclusions about power on the local level were similar to those of Mills on the national level, and their theses had become quite influential among both professional sociologists and the laity. Hunter later extended his approach to the national scene, with which we are more concerned here, in his book *Top Leadership U.S.A.* (1959).

It then occurred to me that I should write a book to show the weaknesses of the Hunter–Mills thesis, and present what I believe to be a more accurate portrait of the power structure of the United States than Hunter and Mills had presented. Of course, I was aware of the many excellent and not-so-excellent critiques of Hunter and Mills, but these were in the nature of essays and book reviews which might argue their case logically but which offered no empirical evidence. (This was in early 1959.)

There were also a few article-length studies which used the research technique of Hunter, but arrived at quite different conclusions, and there were some book-length monographs by political scientists on some particular political decision or some particular pressure group, but these were in the nature of case studies with limited gen-

eralizing ability. The structure of my proposed series of studies began
to take shape in my mind through the year 1959, but it was not until
June 1960 that I was free to begin work.

The research and writing proceeded fitfully during the following
years—interrupted by teaching duties, lecture tours, other researches
and writing, and excursions into the realm of practical politics,[2] from
which I drew many insights invaluable to the research. During those
years, several political scientists published challenging researches
which succeeded in achieving my general aim of presenting a book-
length study of the actual political power structure. These included
Robert A. Dahl's *Who Governs?*, Nelson Polsby's *Community Power
and Political Theory*, Raymond Wolfinger's *The Politics of Progress*,
Edward C. Banfield's *Political Influence*, Robert Presthus's *Men at the
Top*, and R. Bauer, I. Pool, and L. Dexter's *American Business and
Political Policy*. In addition, a brief report of a superior study by
sociologist Linton Freeman and his associates at Syracuse University,
Local Community Leadership, and another by sociologists William V.
D'Antonio and William H. Form, *Influentials in Two Border Cities*,
were published. These and several lesser studies duplicate my general
aim, but they differ in several significant ways. First, they each deal
with one or two cities only, or one issue only, whereas the present
book attempts to cover the United States, and political issues generally. Second, they each present a single, coherent research, whereas
I offer a series of diverse studies, sampling a wide range of subject
matter pertinent to the political power structure. Third, most of their
work is either purely empirical or is guided by political science theory,
whereas I seek to infuse my work with sociological theory and with
insights drawn from participant observation. I do not mean to suggest
that my work is better than theirs; I merely point out that it is different.

This book consists of summaries of the findings of other researchers
and students of the political power structure in the United States, generalizations based on my personal experience and that of politicians
I have interviewed, and systematic surveys of opinions or events in
monograph form. I have tried to give the book a systematic and coherent framework, but the subject matter is too large and complex to
have allowed me much success. Much of the book consists of abbre-

---

[2]I was elected a state representative to the Minnesota legislature in 1962, and was
continuously active in Minneapolis and Minnesota politics from 1958 to 1964.

viated and superficial sketches that hopefully may serve as guides to future research.

The book starts with a contrast between two theories of power in American society, the one that is expounded by Hunter and Mills, and the one that I expound, which is based on the work of many scholars. A series of chapters then take up the political, economic, and other elites, the institutional frameworks in which they operate, and the influence which they exert on the course of American life. A short systematic research concludes this section and provides a bridge to the next section, which contrasts "leaders" and "the mass" in regard to their participation and sense of alienation.

The development and characteristics of modern mass society next draws our attention. Whereas Mills sees the ordinary American people as a passive, largely alienated mass, we find that the forces making them so are increasingly outweighed by new forces turning large segments of American society into active publics. The major expression of the public today we take to be the voluntary association, and the section closes with a chapter summarizing and interpreting the available research on voluntary associations in the United States.

Hunter drew his portrait of the "local community power structure" with a technique of research which has since come to be known as "the reputational approach." Using variations of his method, we seek to achieve another purpose: to delineate the *image* of the power structure as seen by the average American. The picture which emerges proves to be more complicated than Hunter discovered.

The next series of chapters turns to the hard reality of political power. The first of these chapters deals with the political party, the politicians, and the government at the state level. The second deals with the national political party, and its central function of nominating a candidate for the presidency. The third provides a case study of the passage of legislation for the benefit of the public, rather than for the benefit of a specific interest group. The concluding chapter of this section takes up the knotty problems of ethics in politics and of financing political campaigns, problems which Hunter and Mills all but ignore, but which could have provided them with the strongest arguments for their theory. The final chapter attempts to draw the diverse conclusions of the book together in the light of the contrasting theories which opened the study.

This book has been seven years in the making, but its purpose is as relevant today as when it was conceived. Floyd Hunter's ideas still oversimplify the educated man's thinking about the "power structure," and C. Wright Mills's *The Power Elite* has become almost a bible for a younger generation of "new Leftists" who have a deep-seated need to attack a society which they fail to understand. Mills's serious scholarship means little to them; it is his Marxist-Populist image of American society which captivates them. While many valuable criticisms of Hunter and Mills's works have been written, and excellent researches disconfirming their findings have appeared in print since this book was started, another serious effort to correct the distortions perpetuated by Hunter and Mills is perhaps still in order.

Yet criticism is not the sole content or purpose of the book by any means, although it is the vehicle for presenting the hypothesis. The book also tries, in a positive way, to give a comprehensive picture of how political power is structured and developed in the United States and how it is utilized in social action—whether to serve a narrow interest group or a very large segment of the society as a whole. The scope of the subject matter and the coverage of the published literature are broad enough to allow the book to be used as a text in political sociology. Too many sociologists in the past have neglected the study of power, and this book can be offered to undergraduate and graduate students to help them fill out their picture of society.

University of Minnesota   ARNOLD M. ROSE
Minneapolis, Minnesota
January 1967

Acknowledgments

The empirical studies reported in this book were initiated with a grant from the Rockefeller Foundation. Another grant, made to Professors William C. Rogers and Luther Pickrel of the University of Minnesota by The Fund for Adult Education, was used in part to support my research reported in the chapter "Perceptions of Political Power and Influence." The Graduate School of the University of Minnesota provided small sums from time to time to permit completion of the specific researches begun with the Rockefeller funds. The author is grateful for this financial support. Most of the writing was done on his "own time" during summers and in spare time during the regular academic year when he was teaching at the University of Minnesota.

The author also wishes to thank the Free Press for permission to quote in Chapter IV from Morris Janowitz's *The Professional Soldier*.

Research assistance was provided by several of the author's students over the period 1960–65:

Chapter III, "The Economic Elite"—Leonard S. Robins
Chapter VIII, "The Community Power Elites"—Ronald Lee Cohen
Chapter IX, "Perceptions of Political Power and Influence"—Peter Hall

Certain chapters have benefited from a critical reading by the following colleagues:

Chapter X, "Political Structure and Political Influence in Texas"—Professors Hiram Friedsam and H. C. McCleskey
Chapter IX, "Perceptions of Political Power and Influence"—Professors William C. Rogers and Luther Pickrel
The entire book—Caroline B. Rose.
The index was prepared by Ruth Rose Parker.

The author greatly appreciates the contributions of all the above-mentioned.

Contents

Tables

The Power Structure

I
Introduction: Contrasting Theories
of Political Power in American Society

The belief that an "economic elite" controls governmental and community affairs, by means kept hidden from the public, is one that can be traced at least as far back in American history as the political attacks of some Jeffersonians on some Hamiltonians at the end of the eighteenth century. Scarcely any lower-class political movement in the United States has failed to express the theme that the upper classes successfully used nondemocratic means to thwart democratic processes. Perhaps the widest popular use of the theme was achieved by the Populist movement in the decades following 1890. Anarchism and Marxism were imports from Europe that accepted the theme as one of the essential elements of their ideologies.[1] The history of the United States also provides ample factual examples to strengthen credence in the theme. The literature of exposure, especially that of the "muckrakers" in the first decade of the twentieth century, provides details as to how economically privileged individuals and groups illegally bought and bribed legislators,

[1]That the orthodox communist viewpoint regarding power in the United States today is still in terms of dominance by an economic elite was made evident in a series of interviews Walter Lippmann had with Premier Nikita Khrushchev in April 1961. When Lippmann said that decisions regarding foreign policy would be made by President Kennedy, "Khrushchev insisted that the forces behind the President would determine his policy. These forces behind the Kennedy administration he summed up in the one word: Rockefeller." It was also Khrushchev's opinion that Kennedy could not accelerate American economic growth "because of Rockefeller" and then added, "DuPont. They will not let him." (Walter Lippmann, syndicated columns, *Minneapolis Morning Tribune*, April 17, 18, 1961).

judges, and executive heads of government to serve their own desires for increased wealth and power.

The belief is not entirely wrong. But it presents only a portion of relevant reality and creates a significant misimpression that in itself has political repercussions. A more balanced analysis of the historical facts would probably arrive at something like the following conclusion: Segments of the economic elite have violated democratic political and legal processes, with differing degrees of effort and success in the various periods of American history, but in no recent period could they correctly be said to have controlled the elected and appointed political authorities in large measure. The relationship between the economic elite and the political authorities has been a constantly varying one of strong influence, co-operation, division of labor, and conflict, with each influencing the other in changing proportion to some extent and each operating independently of the other to a large extent. Today there is significant political control and limitation of certain activities over the economic elite, and there are also some significant processes by which the economic elite uses its wealth to help elect some political candidates and to influence other political authorities in ways which are not available to the average citizen. Further, neither the economic elite nor the political authorities are monolithic units which act with internal consensus and co-ordinated action with regard to each other (or probably in any other way). In fact there are several economic elites which only very rarely act as units within themselves and among themselves, and there are at least two political parties which have significantly differing programs with regard to their actions toward any economic elite, and each of them has only a partial degree of internal cohesion.[2] On domestic issues, at least, it is appropriate to observe that there are actually four political parties, two liberal ones and two conservative ones, the largest currently being the national Democratic party, which generally has a domestic policy that frustrates the special interests of the economic elite. This paragraph states our general hypothesis, and we shall seek to substantiate it with facts that leave no significant areas of omission. Merely to provide it with a shorthand label, we

[2]The two political parties sometimes agree on almost identical specific pieces of legislation, but mainly in the areas of foreign policy and national defense, practically never in regard to their programs or actions with respect to an economic elite.

shall call it the "multi-influence hypothesis," as distinguished from the "economic-elite-dominance" hypothesis.

These two hypotheses are not to be equated with what in the social science literature is often called the "opposing theories of consensus and conflict." Both hypotheses fall under conflict theory, and the difference is that the multi-influence hypothesis depicts social reality as a far more complex conflict than does the economic-elite-dominance hypothesis. The latter sees conflict merely between a more or less unified elite and largely unorganized "masses," and if by some chain of events the latter could become better organized, conduct the conflict more effectively and *win*, there could ensue a society with a substantial consensus (ranging—in the writings of the varying proponents of the theme—from traditional agrarianism to communism). The multi-influence hypothesis sees conflict as often multilateral, with large proportions of the population often not involved, with the sides changing at least partially from issue to issue, and with consensus being achieved only temporarily and on a limited number of issues (except when naked force imposes an apparent consensus). The multi-influence hypothesis holds this to be true at least for heterogeneous, industrialized societies; it begs the question as to whether its own image or the "consensus theory" is more applicable to small, "primitive" societies.[3]

The distinction between the two hypotheses we are considering is also not to be equated with another distinction found in the social science literature—that between "social force" explanations and "powerful men" explanations. Sociologists generally are inclined to adopt the former and reject the latter, whereas proponents of the economic-elite-dominance hypothesis openly embrace the latter, at least much of the time. For example, Ferdinand Lundberg, the author of one study using the economic-elite-dominance hypothesis,

[3]The functionalists in anthropology have used a consensus theory to explain the societies they typically study. When they, or the functionalists in sociology, use a consensus theory to explain heterogeneous, industrialized societies, our multi-influence hypothesis is opposed to theirs as well as to the economic-elite-dominance hypothesis. But we shall not deal here with the consensus or functionalist theory. I have considered sociological functionalism in three other publications: *The Institutions of Advanced Societies* (Minneapolis: University of Minnesota Press, 1958), ch. 1; "On Merton's Neo-Functionalism," *Alpha Kappa Deltan*, 30 (Spring 1960), 14–17; and "A Current Theoretical Issue in Social Gerontology," *The Gerontologist*, 4 (March 1964), 46–50.

wholeheartedly accepts the "powerful men" explanation in attributing complete power in the United States to "sixty families."[4] C. Wright Mills, the author of a more recent and more scholarly exposition of the economic-elite-dominance hypothesis,[5] is too much of a sociologist and too much of a Marxist to reject "social force" explanations completely. After making the distinction between the two sorts of explanations, which he calls the "drift" and the "conspiracy" explanations, Mills comes out in favor of a combination of both of them, while concentrating on the latter for the purposes of the study in hand. In now presenting the multi-influence hypothesis and the evidence for it, I accept the general need for balance between "social force" and "powerful men" explanations, and even recognize that for a study of political power it might be desirable to stress the "powerful men" explanation. I believe it is necessary to use terms like "elite" and "leaders," and to recognize that the truly active and innovative people in any group activity are relatively few in number (although probably not so few as Lundberg and Mills suggest). But it is not necessary to consider all "powerful men" explanations as "conspiracy" or "secrecy" theories, as Lundberg and Mills do. While it may be true that not everything about power meets the eye, it does not follow that most things that are open to observation are false. Conspiracy and secrecy theories of power are theories based on inference, with very little fact, and their authors justify the absence of facts by stating that the important facts are kept hidden. This assertion might have a degree of plausibility if empirically supported explanations were offered as to the means of linking the conspiracy to the observable facts of power. But the conspiracy theorists who adopt the economic-elite-dominance hypothesis do not offer such explanations as far as the observable facts of political power are concerned. If facts regarding means and processes are not to be offered, then plausible and rational hypotheses must be presented; lacking even these, the social scientist must be skeptical about conspiracy and secrecy theories of power. In sum, in the hypothesis of this book I am willing to admit a large element of a "powerful men" explanation of power, but not much of a "conspiracy" or "secrecy" explanation.

[4]*America's Sixty Families* (New York: Vanguard, 1937).
[5]*The Power Elite* (New York: Oxford University Press, 1956); see esp. pp. 24–7.

The multi-influence hypothesis differs from the economic-elite-dominance hypothesis both in its conception of the elite and in its conception of the masses. The latter hypothesis envisages society as a vast pyramid, with the people of wealth in control at the top. They may or may not be seen as interspersed with a military elite. At a somewhat lower level are said to be their "lieutenants"—politicians, hired managers, small businessmen, and perhaps a few lesser categories who accept the orders of the economic elite and operate the control mechanisms and institutions that manipulate the rest of the society. Still lower are the "local opinion-makers," persons who constitute the mechanisms of control, who respond more or less automatically to the will of their superiors and who have a "grass-roots" following. At the bottom is the great bulk of the population, envisaged in the hypothesis as inert masses deprived of their rights and exploited economically and politically to serve the interests of those on top.[6]

There is also a "contrast-conception," an ideal of what an alternative structure of society would be, envisaged by those who hold the economic-elite-dominance hypothesis: this is of a classless, equalitarian society, in which the dominant groups have been eliminated or merged as equals into the masses, and the masses have been organized into functional groups that have a social structure for operating a society without the present controllers.[7] Those who hold this hypothesis usually imagine that their theoretical opponents are setting forth their own contrast-conception as the present reality and that they are declaring that a society without classes presently exists in order to fool the masses and keep them acquiescent.

[6]There is some difference of opinion as to the nature of the masses among the various proponents of the economic-elite-dominance hypothesis. C. Wright Mills depicts them as inherently passive and disorganized in the American system, completely unable and unwilling to resist their exploitation. The theorists of a communist bent, however, see them constantly resisting and struggling against their exploiters, but unable to take effective action because they have no access to the instruments of control. This theoretical difference is well expressed in the book by the communist theoretician Herbert Aptheker, *The World of C. Wright Mills* (New York: Marzani and Munsell, 1960).

[7]This contrast-conception ranges from the "communist stage" of Marx through the guild socialism of Mills (best expressed in his 1948 book, *The New Men of Power*) to the "social fascism" of some of the latter-day populists like Representative William Lemke of North Dakota, who, with the Catholic priest Charles Coughlin, sought in the mid-1930's to build a political movement around the goal of "social justice."

While there are undoubtedly some among the wealthy who do deny a class system as a means of fooling the "masses" and trying to keep them satisfied with the status quo, this is not the view of most of those who hold the multi-influence hypothesis. The latter hypothesis, which is expounded and empirically supported in the present study, conceives of society as consisting of many elites, each relatively small numerically and operating in different spheres of life, and of the bulk of the population classifiable into organized groups and publics as well as masses. Among the elites are several that have their power through economic controls, several others that have power through political controls, and still others that have power through military, associational, religious, and other controls. While it is true that there are inert masses of undifferentiated individuals without access to each other (except in the most trivial respects) and therefore without influence, the bulk of the population consists not of the mass but of integrated groups and publics, stratified with varying degrees of power. "Integrated groups" are defined as numbers of individuals operating on the basis of common, "traditional" meanings and values, with networks of communication among themselves, with internal divisions of labor in role and function, and resistant to control by any elites who "pressure" them to behave in ways contrary to their common meanings and values. "Publics" are similar, but much less structured internally, more open to ideas from the outside, whether from an elite or from any other idea-generator (including Marxists), and much more specialized in that they have a very small range of common interests about which their members interact. Constituted mainly of integrated groups and shifting publics, as well as of an undifferentiated inert "mass," the bulk of the population is seen as much more differentiated and much less susceptible to control by any elite in the multi-influence hypothesis than in the economic-elite-dominance hypothesis.

Both hypotheses recognize the role of impersonal forces—such as economics and geography—as having significant influence over the course of society, but there is a difference between the hypotheses in how they view the nature and manner of influence of these impersonal forces. The economic-elite-dominance hypothesis holds economic forces as setting the course of history, and at the present time giving predominance to those private owners and managers of the means of production and media of mass communication they call the economic elite. The multi-influence hypothesis recognizes the importance of economic forces but considers that there are also semi-independent forces of social change in technology, cultural contact and conflict, and concrete and diffuse social movements. It further recognizes resistances to social change not only in economic vested interests but also in law and custom and in social structure generally. Both the impersonal forces of social change and of resistance to social change set marked limits to the power of any elite group to control the actions of society. For example, when we later consider the effort, in 1957–65, to institute a federal program for financing medical care through Social Security, we shall see that a most significant new factor that promotes this is improvement in medical technology, which markedly reduces death through acute illness and leaves an increasing number of older people prone to heavy medical expenses through contracting the chronic illnesses. Social movements and elites then come into operation to promote or retard the formation of a federal program, and elements of existing social structure— such as private insurance plans and the committee system of Congress —play their roles in determining the final outcome. Thus, the multi-influence hypothesis holds that each social change or decision occurs in a matrix of social forces and social resistances, of cultural elements and social structures, only some of which are or can be deliberately controlled or manipulated by elites.

While, as we have pointed out, the economic-elite-dominance hypothesis has had a long history, and has had ups and downs of popular acceptance, its recent resurgence is a result of the publication of works by two sociologists. One is Floyd Hunter, who did a study of power structure, first of a single city, then of the entire United States.[8] The other is C. Wright Mills, who wrote a general analysis of elites and social structure in the United States.[9] These books have received

---

[8]*Community Power Structure* (Chapel Hill: University of North Carolina Press, 1953); *Top Leadership, U. S. A.* (Chapel Hill: University of North Carolina Press, 1959).

[9]*The Power Elite.* We shall occasionally make reference to other works by Mills, but it is the one which sets in fullest fashion the economic-elite-dominance hypothesis. Our criticism of this work does not necessarily imply criticism of other works by Mills that do not deal with the political power structure and processes.

both favorable and unfavorable reviews,[10] and the first Hunter study has been favored by a number of replications, some of which come to the same general conclusion that Hunter does while others do not. Our purpose in this book is not primarily to review or even add to the criticisms, but through the presentation of a variety of related empirical researches and observations to demonstrate the inadequacy of the economic-elite-dominance hypothesis which underlies the Hunter-Mills works and to indicate the greater theoretical and empirical viability of the multi-influence hypothesis as an explanation of political power and political processes in American society.

Certainly this book is not the first to set forth or to seek to substantiate the multi-influence hypothesis. It is implicit in many treatises and studies of nineteenth- and twentieth-century social historians and political scientists.[11] Particularly as it concerns political structure and processes, the hypothesis has received explicit formulation and empirical support in the writings of Arthur Bentley, E. Pendleton Herring, E. E. Schattschneider, David B. Truman, and V. O. Key, Jr.[12] We shall follow the lead of these latter writers in concentrating on political processes, but differ from them in following two procedures brought into the analysis of power by Hunter and Mills, respectively: (1) we shall use, among other research techniques, the "modern" technique of survey analysis, and (2) we shall analyze the facts of power, not in a "narrow" political context, but in the broader context of sociology. Thus, our theory and approach approximate

---

[10]Among the best reviews of Mills's *The Power Elite* are those by C. A. Anderson and H. L. Gracey in the *Kentucky Law Journal*, vol. 46, no. 2 (Winter 1958), 301-17; Daniel Bell, "The Power Elite Reconsidered," *American Journal of Sociology*, 64 (November 9, 1959), 238–50; Robert A. Dahl, "A Critique of the Power Elite Method," *American Political Science Review*, 52 (June 1958), 463–9; and Talcott Parsons, "The Distribution of Power in American Society," *World Politics*, 10 (1957), 123–43. Among the best reviews of Hunter's *Top Leadership U.S.A.* are those of C. Arnold Anderson in the *American Journal of Sociology*, 65 (November 1959), 311; and of Robert O. Schulze, in the *Administrative Science Quarterly*, 4 (December 1959), 373–7. See also Robert A. Dahl in *The Journal of Politics*, 22 (February 1960), 148–51. On Hunter's earlier *Community Power Structure*, see Raymond E. Wolfinger, "Reputation and Reality in the Study of Community Power," *American Sociological Review*, 25 (October 1960), 636–44.

[11]For example, Alexis de Tocqueville, *Democracy in America* (1835).

[12]*The Process of Government* (Chicago: University of Chicago Press, 1908); *The Politics of Democracy* (New York: W. W. Norton, 1940); *Party Government* (New York: Farrar and Rinehart, 1942); *The Governmental Process* (New York: Knopf, 1953); and *Politics, Parties and Pressure Groups* (New York: Knopf, 1959).

those of many social historians and political scientists; our analysis and presentation will seem closer to those of Hunter and Mills. This book does not deal with the exercise of economic power in areas of purely economic decision-making. It does deal with the exercise of economic power in areas of political decision-making, to show that the political elite are not mere lieutenants of the economic elite, although the economic elite provide one major influence on the political decisions made. It also shows something of the influence of political decisions on the economic sphere, although this is a minor focus.[13] Its main task is to set forth the multi-influence hypothesis, as summarized earlier in this Introduction, as a viable framework for future researches on the power structure of the United States.

The Hunter and Mills works are here treated together, as they both present the viewpoint which we have labeled the "economic-elite-dominance hypothesis." As we now turn to a specific analysis of the contents and methods of the writings of these two authors, we shall find that they differ markedly. Hunter presents his readers with straightforward empirical research, with few or no theoretical under-pinnings and with interpretations that might be considered naïve. He claims to arrive at the economic-elite-dominance hypothesis because his facts bring him there. Mills, on the other hand, offers his readers a sophisticated and scholarly work; he is fully conscious of his theoretical framework, and he presents facts to support his hypothesis. Both have produced facts, although these facts do not refer to the processes by means of which power is exercised. On the whole, their facts are not contradicted here: our attitude toward the facts produced by Hunter is that he has misinterpreted them; our attitude toward the facts presented by Mills is that he has not balanced them with other equally relevant facts.[14] Hunter claims to present a picture of the power structure; we say he has presented a partial picture of the *image* of the power structure, as held mainly by the subordi-

---

[13]For a consideration of how governmental processes affect economic life in the United States, see such works as Marshall Dimock, *Business and Government* (New York; Henry Holt, 1949); and Robert E. Lane, *The Regulation of Businessmen* (New Haven: Yale University Press, 1954).

[14]Anderson and Gracey (see n. 10) say of the Mills book: "Whether or not its conclusions are valid, they cannot be derived from the data offered. The few bits of new data are handled incautiously. . . . At no time does he examine the precise operations of any single elite in any actual situation."

nates of the economic elite. Mills claims to present a picture of three elites, with the economic elite (and the military elite recently merged with them) superordinate over the political elite, and all three superordinate over an inert mass; we say he has presented only some of the pertinent facts. We shall now present some of the more specific procedures and findings of Hunter and Mills, along with some specific criticisms.

Hunter states his basic assumptions for *Top Leadership, U.S.A.* in succinct form: "At the beginning of this work I assumed that the most influential men in national policy-making would be found residing in the larger cities, manning the larger corporate enterprises, and using their influence to get the government to move according to their interests" (p. 7). While he elaborates on this statement, it provides his basic hypothesis and becomes his main conclusion. His procedures may be summarized as follows:

1. "The first major step was to consult management personnel of the national organizations. I began by calling upon secretaries in the U.S. Chamber of Commerce, the American Medical Association, the American Bankers Association, the American Farm Bureau, the American Meat Institute, the Congress of Industrial Organizations, the National Association of Manufacturers, and the National Federation of Business and Professional Women's Clubs. I moved from these groups and their secretaries to others" (pp. 11–12). This produced a tentative list of 1,093 organizations.

2. Since this was too many to tap for interviews, "With the aid of four other persons who had a working knowledge of national organizations, the list was pared to 106" (p. 13). The 106 included 4 recreational associations, 6 in the category of science and education, 5 veterans' and fraternal associations, 5 in the area of government and civic affairs, 4 women's organizations, 5 associations of lower professional groups, 6 representing organized labor and consumer groups, and 4 representing religious and minority group interests. These 39 apparently represent elites and groups other than economic. Some additional categories are marginal: 4 service club associations (including Rotary and Lions), 3 national foundations, 2 large social welfare organizations (Red Cross and Community Chest), and the

American Arbitration Association. The remaining 57 organizations—a clear majority—represented major economic interests. Thus Hunter begins to create the conditions in his method of research which are bound to lead him to the economic-elite-dominance conclusion.

3. Some official in each of these 106 organizations was polled for the names of the top 20 organizations and for "the names of persons known to [him] who might be considered top policy makers at the national level" (p. 16).

4. "The names of persons given in response to the question of nominating top national leaders provided a basic list of leaders, nearly 500, to whom a questionnaire was eventually addressed and with whom I had a sample of interviews designed to relate the activities of individual leaders to other leaders, and leader groups, in turn, to the development of public policy" (p. 16).

This first list was modified by later nominations. The list is very heavily loaded with the names of industrialists, bankers, and other businessmen. Only the category of political and government leaders will be analyzed here. Of the 500 names only 17 (3.4 per cent) can be considered as being in this category: 5 were on the presidential or presidential-candidate level (Hoover, Truman, Eisenhower, Dewey, Stevenson), 4 were senators (Byrd, Flanders, Knowland, Saltonstall), 2 were governors (Lausche, Shivers), 3 were State Department officials (Herbert Hoover Jr., Herter, Lodge), 1 was a lesser official in the Department of Health, Education and Welfare (Schottiand), 1 was a mayor (Morrison of New Orleans), 1 a reputed city political boss (Arvey). The 5 at the presidential level seem obvious choices; the others represent obvious biases of selection—there were no representatives, no cabinet officers, no active military leaders, no Northern Democrats (except for Arvey and Lausche, the latter a political maverick).

5. As a result of criticism from a political scientist, Hunter felt it was necessary to make some additions to his 1953 list in 1955. "If one were to have added to the list a few names of ranking, elected and appointed politicians, a sprinkling of news editors and columnists, and a few organization secretaries and lobbyists, the core structure of power at the national level would have been more nearly complete" (p. 59).

6. "Determined to have the study of policy-making completely empirical, I took several polls of national leaders to get their own choices of those whom they consider to be their peers."

"Each new poll added a few names to the list, but also many names were dropped in the process."

"The third and fourth polls of national leaders in 1957 and 1958 revealed that a basic core of names continued to be nominated for national leadership positions. In the 1957 and 1958 polls the names of public politicians were included" (p. 195).

7. The final list was "heavily weighted with industrial leaders (23), followed in order by: 15 U. S. Senators, 10 cabinet members, 6 professionals (3 attorneys, 2 professors, 1 scientist), 5 bankers, 5 publishers, 5 Congressmen, 4 assistant cabinet secretaries, 3 labor leaders, 3 military officers, 4 Presidential assistants, 3 transportation executives (2 air, 1 railroad), 2 ambassadors, 2 governors, 3 United States Presidents (2 retired), and 1 each, chief justice of the Supreme Court, communications executive (radio-TV), religious leader, utilities executive, United Nations representative, and the Vice-President of the United States.

"Of those who could be identified by political party affiliation, 20 were Democrats and 50 were Republicans. Most of them were born in the Northeastern quarter or in the Middle West of the country" (p. 199).

The relationship between this final list and the first list of names (see *(3)* above), as far as political leaders is concerned, is impossible to discern. It seems that somewhere along the line, Hunter became aware of political leadership. Nevertheless, "Policy . . . rarely originated in the legislative halls. . . . Legislators acted decisively on policy matters that were originated in one constituency or another by those who were the most active in producing goods and services in society" (pp. 210–11).

8. Additional studies were made in two states (South Carolina and North Carolina) and two industries (textiles and housing). While the specific facts reported do not indicate that the textile industry got much of what it wanted from Congress, this in no way modified Hunter's conclusion that industry controls the politicians.

It should be evident from the above summary of Hunter's method of research that he is not engaged in systematic scientific research, but uses a hit-and-miss sequence of techniques almost all of which have a built-in bias toward the industrial and commercial elite. Except when he deliberately and arbitrarily interjects politicians and a few others into his lists, his techniques lead him to the economic elite. He asks the lower economic elite who the top elite is, and of course the answers refer to the top economic elite. From this inherent bias and from interviews with a sample of the economic elite, Hunter derives an *image* of the national power structure which he confuses with the power structure itself. A brief summary of this image follows:

1. "After concluding the more extensive study, I feel that the membership lists of the National Industrial Conference, the Committee for Economic Development, and the Business Advisory Council provide good starting points for anyone interested in a quick and partial rundown of national leadership. . . . Along with a sprinkling of foreign policy associations and educational bodies, they represent top groupings of national leadership" (p. 33).

2. "The role of the professional in most instances is subordinate to that of one or more lay leaders" (p. 39).

3. Lobbying, especially through personal contacts, with important congressmen, is the way to get any bill accepted by Congress and the President (pp. 34, 55, 64, 79, 180).

4. There are local leaders who are primarily interested in local issues, and are extremely powerful in determining their outcome, but who know little about national issues and have little influence over these (pp. 86, 111–12).

5. "The wielding of power in American community life . . . is a combination of powerful individuals willing that things be done or not done and sometimes getting others to believe they thought of the idea in the first place and wanted to do it all along" (p. 137).

6. "It is also apparent that each major, particular power structure is related directly and indirectly, through its personnel, to every other structure. This is not to say that there is a monolithic power structure in the nation moving in willful accord on every national issue, but it may be said with confidence that various groups of power within the nation are interlocked by persons who can and do communicate core

policy decisions of a particular power structure to key persons of other structures as occasion demands" (p. 138).

7. The image of power is the power structure itself: "From the point of view of the power structure concept, we are dealing here, in part, with a belief system. Because of their observations of acts, positions, or reputations, men begin to believe that power resides in this or that man. Power is imputed to him. He is then observed in the company of others; or, as importantly, he is believed to be in league with others; or, further, it is believed that if he is not consorting with others of his imputed power rank, he could be if he so willed. It is functional to the structured community system of order that men so believe. The man or men, as the case may be, begin themselves to believe their own or others' estimates of themselves and they weigh others in the balance with themselves and others of their kind" (pp. 172–3).

8. Government is secondary—an instrument for the execution of policy, not the formation of policy. "It was abundantly clear that the men interviewed did not think of government officials exclusively as top policy makers in the country. This does not say they did not recognize the important roles played by politicians in the process of getting things done, but universally, government was thought of as an instrument of extending policy rather than a primary source of policy development" (p. 176).

Only the unimportant people in the small towns think political representatives are powerful in getting things done (p. 184).

9. Few in the elite were closely bound up with politics: "The 100 number-one leaders in the research list were not listed in appreciable numbers as members of the national committees of the major political parties, although 15 of them had been members of some political party committee at some stage of their careers. Some of the leaders expressed an interest in one of the two major parties, particularly the Republican party, but by the time they were recognized national leaders they had restricted their activities largely to helping raise political money and to conferring with others on the suitability of national candidates. For the most part, the leaders of the larger enterprises did not wish to put themselves forward as politicians. Although they were policy makers, with rare exceptions they did not

wish to run for public office, and they held themselves superior to the men who seek office" (pp. 207–8).

10. Politicians are ordinary people who attend mainly to the wishes of industrial policy makers: "When stripped of the glamour and aura of publicity that often surrounds them, the men who are elected to public office are quite ordinary men going about tasks prescribed by the society around them. There is a routineness in much that the politician does which grows out of the stability of the political structure and the general climate of opinion in which he operates. Because so much activity in society is related to men who organize working groups, the politician is compelled to understand and be sympathetic to employers and labor union officials who are powerful in determining industrial policy which in turn affects public policy as previously shown. He listens sympathetically, of course, to other groups, but his attention is centered most often on industrial policy makers" (pp. 208–9).

Mills's general thesis is that there is a national power elite which forms a self-conscious integrated unity, and "Insofar as national events are decided, the power elite are those who decide them" (p. 18).

> The people of the higher circles may also be conceived as members of a top social stratum, as a set of groups whose members know one another, see one another socially and at business, and so, in making decisions, take one another into account. The elite, according to this conception, feel themselves to be, and are felt by others to be, the inner circle of "the upper social classes." They form a more or less compact social and psychological entity; they have become self-conscious members of a social class. People are either accepted into this class or they are not, and there is a qualitative split, rather than merely a numerical scale, separating them from those who are not elite. They are more or less aware of themselves as a social class and they behave toward one another differently from the way they do toward members of other classes. They accept one another, understand one another, marry one another, tend to work and to think if not together at least alike. [Page 11.]

The unity of the power elite, however, does not rest solely on psychological similarity and social intermingling, nor entirely on the structural coincidences of commanding positions and interests. At times it is the unity of a more explicit co-ordination. To say that these three higher circles are increasingly co-ordinated, that this is *one* basis of their unity, and that at times—as during the wars—such co-ordination is quite decisive, is not to say that the co-ordination is total or continuous, or even that it is very sure-footed. Much less is it to say that willful co-ordination is the sole or the major basis of their unity, or that the power elite has emerged as the realization of a plan. But it is to say that as the institutional mechanics of our time have opened up avenues to men pursuing their several interests, many of them have come to see that these several interests could be realized more easily if they worked together, in informal as well as in more formal ways, and accordingly they have done so. [Pages 19–20.]

Mills gives the impression of not being consistent in his thesis, however, especially regarding the role of politicians, for he considers them as subordinates to the economic elite (now integrated with the military elite): "What is usually taken to be the central content of politics, the pressures and the campaigns and the congressional maneuvering, has, in considerable part, now been relegated to the middle levels of power" (p. 28). Elsewhere he speaks of the top politicians as the "lieutenants" of the economic elite. His chapter on the political elite (chapter 10) is the shortest in the book, and almost half of it deals with the civil service rather than the superordinate elected or appointed government officials. Even when he deals with the political elite, he considers it to consist only of those in the Executive branch; there are only a few casual references to the Legislative and Judicial branches. Thus, despite Mills's initial reference to three elites, the book portrays the population of the United States as a *single* power pyramid: The economic-military elite are on top, their appointed henchmen plus the politicians form a secondary level of power, and at the large base are the powerless undifferentiated masses (pp. 28–29). This national pattern prevails also in each of the several communities of the United States, at least in the major ones, except that the military may be absent from the local community power structure:

Local society is a structure of power as well as a hierarchy of status; at its top there is a set of cliques or "crowds" whose members judge and decide the important community issues, as well as many larger issues of state and nation in which "the community" is involved. Usually, although by no means always, these cliques are composed of old upper-class people; they include the larger businessmen and those who control the banks who usually also have connections with the major real-estate holders. Informally organized, these cliques are often centered in the several economic functions: there is an industrial, a retailing, a banking clique. The cliques overlap, and there are usually some men who, moving from one to another, co-ordinate viewpoints and decisions. There are also the lawyers and administrators of the solid *rentier* families, who, by the power of proxy and by the many contacts between old and new wealth they embody, tie together and focus in decision the power of money, of credit, or organization.

Immediately below such cliques are the hustlers, largely of new upper-class status, who carry out the decisions and programs of the top—sometimes anticipating them and always trying to do so. Here are the "operations" men—the vice-presidents of the banks, successful small businessmen, the ranking public officials, contractors, and executives of local industries. This number two level shades off into the third string men—the heads of civic agencies, organization officials, the pettier civic leaders, newspaper men and, finally, into the fourth order of the power hierarchy—the rank and file of the professional and business strata, the ministers, the leading teachers, social workers, personnel directors. [Pages 36–7.]

Actually, Mills is not quite as inconsistent about the existence of *three* power elites as he at first appears to be, for later in his book he explains that, in his view, the economic-military elite have taken over the top "command" positions in the political elite. Thus his view is that a political elite might be said to exist, but it is manned and controlled by certain members of the economic-military elites. Nevertheless his initial statement that there are three power elites is quite misleading; it does not reflect his true views, and it allows his thesis to appear more acceptable than it should in view of the facts about the distribution of power.

Mills does not assume that the unity and integration of the power elite rests on elite consciousness or on deliberate co-ordination among all its members. He thus departs from European aristocratic theories of the elite and from conspiracy theories circulated in both Europe and the United States. Nevertheless, Mills's conception of the power elite is that it is more or less integrated and unitary, but he considers this integration and unity to be based on three other factors: "psychological similarity," "social intermingling," and "coinciding interests." The main *empirical* evidence he brings to these points is on "social intermingling"; he offers no data on "psychological similarity" and little on "coinciding interests," but infers that these result from extensive social interaction from childhood on. While our own inclination is to believe that the United States is too large and too heterogeneous to permit the economic leadership to be as integrated, in any of the three respects, as Mills says it is, we shall not present any direct data on these matters. We shall, however, consider how the *political* elite is subject to diverse pressures, to external limitations not subject to control by the economic elite, and to tendencies which on many occasions resist the interests of the economic elite.

But even at this early stage of our analysis we must express our amazement at the rationalistic nature of Mills's interpretation that an economic elite can control American society. In the first place, there are large-scale historical forces—often of an economic character—which constrain, limit, push, and direct any society in ways beyond the control of any segment in it. If Mills was a student of Marx and Veblen, among others, he apparently did not learn his lesson well. The substructure of any society—its geography, technology, economic organization, and basic institutions of family and religion—are only to a very limited extent manipulable by any one group, no matter how powerful or rational it is in the pursuit of its material interests. Related to this, but somewhat more manipulable, are the demands and requirements of that large-scale organization, the government. Perhaps Mills took these as given, and did not feel the need even to mention them.

In the second place, there are cultural values—both on the high plane of ideals and the low plane of everyday norms—which are also subject to only limited manipulation. The "American creed" of liberty, equality, fair play, justice, etc., and the more universal reli-

gious and humanistic ideals are not mere words which can be completely twisted and distorted to serve the interests of any group, even
though man's ability to rationalize them away while pursuing his
individual or sub-group interests is considerable. The everyday norms
of mutual expectations in interpersonal relations set further limits on
rational behavior, and these norms also are internalized by power
elites no less than by the masses. Rational manipulation can take
place within their framework, but not in spite of it, and if Mills
wished to point out the facts of manipulation and the "higher immorality" in American society, he would be required to start from
the general cultural framework of values and norms. Thirdly, there
are the constraints on power, embodied in the Constitution and other
forms of law, that are supported by public opinion in principle if not
always in detail. Powerful leaders can sometimes get around basic
law or change it, but not with ease or speed. In the fourth place,
there are limits on rational pursuit of individual and group interests
imposed by counter-elites (such as civil-rights groups, youth groups,
and trade unions), kinship and friendship loyalties, public opinion,
and voluntary associations. Mills explicitly denies the importance of
these factors in American society, but we shall later adduce evidence
that they are not without significance. Even if Mills were correct on
this last point, we should have to consider his analysis sociologically
inadequate through his neglect of the first three considerations. If the
economic elite uses its power to make decisions for its own advantage
in many instances, it lacks alternatives in other instances, and does
not always behave rationally where there are alternatives.

It is because of the great social imperatives—that is, the physical,
institutional, and cultural forces—that there is a certain similarity of
action among the contending groups within a society (and sometimes
even across national lines). Mills interprets this as the imposition on
the political elites and other "secondary" leaders of the dominant
will of the top economic elite, whereas usually it is nothing more than
the lack of alternatives. That is, when leaders of the major political
parties, or the leaders of the Western nations, or even the leaders of
the United States and the Soviet Union came to an agreement, it is
usually a case of reason bowing to the inevitable, rather than of
lieutenants bowing to a hidden economic elite. Of course, there are
the extremists—said to be at both ends—who refuse to believe this,

and who, if they accede to political power, use that power to fly in the face of the inevitable. They either get smashed or reverse course without any directions from the economic elite. In world affairs we see this in the actions of Communist China; in the United States we see it in the local communities where right-wing extremists have been elected to public office.

Mills accepts the Marxist assumption of "false consciousness" in the masses—arising out of ignorance, apathy, and deliberate distortion (often with the aid of the mass media). He is supported here by much sociological research on anomie in an urbanized and mass culture, voting and non-voting patterns, alienation from work, the effects of the mass media, individualistic forms of social pathology, and the findings of vast body of research since Durkheim's study of suicide (1897). But, as we shall also attempt to show later, Mills's use of the facts of false consciousness in the mass suffers from two defects. First, Mills assumes that it is avoided by the economic elite, whereas the facts show that this is true only in degree. The economic power elite also has contracted some of the "illness" of the mass society. It sometimes deliberately and consciously works against its own interests, although perhaps less frequently than do the lower classes. Even its incidence of mental illness, addiction, and irrational crime is only somewhat lower than that found in the lower classes. Second, there are certain "reactions to the mass society" developing in all strata of American society which can be expected to operate against false consciousness to some extent. For example, mass education has some effect in immunizing people against ignorance and the distortions of the mass media; some voluntary associations bring their members into realistic participation in politics. Mills gives the impression that the inert masses in the United States are the great majority, whereas studies of participation in voluntary associations suggest that they are not over 40 per cent of the population, and are probably slowly decreasing in proportion. Such conditions and trends will be discussed more fully in subsequent chapters.

Mills's rebuttal to arguments about mass participation in voluntary associations and social movements rests on his opinion that such things are not important. This is not only a personal value judgment; it also leads to circular reasoning: the only important things in American life are those things the economic elite successfully seeks;

since the economic elite has shown little interest in the civil-rights movement, either for or against it, then *ipso facto*, the civil-rights movement is not important, even though it involves the social energies and life chances of a sizable minority of the population.

Whereas Hunter says nothing regarding the means by which the economic elite control the government, Mills lists three such means (pp. 165–70 of *The Power Elite*).

He states, first, that the Constitution, particularly since the adoption of the Fourteenth Amendment, gives free rein to the corporate rich to run the economy. I would not basically quarrel with this statement standing alone, for the American economy is overwhelmingly one of free private enterprise and semi-monopoly capitalism, rather than of state capitalism or guild socialism. However, when Mills carries this over to the political realm, he cites only evidence that supports his view: "In virtually every case of [governmental] regulation that we examine the regulating agency has tended to become a corporate outpost" (p. 166).[15] He ignores the numerous and powerful governmental restraints and limitations on corporations—through the power to tax, to license, to set rates in interstate commerce, to control conditions of marketing (of securities as well as of products), to control the accuracy of labeling and advertising, to set the conditions of collective bargaining and the labor contract, and dozens of lesser governmental powers. It is of course true that in some of these areas (particularly rate-setting and licensing), the economic elite has found means of influencing the government administrators, but even here the fact that they must work through the government administrators (appointed by the President with the consent of the Senate) is a limitation on their power. It is simply incorrect to consider that the relation of government to the economy is the same in 1960 as it was in 1860 except insofar as the government today is even more controlled by the interests of the economic elite than it was then— which is Mills's position. The difficulty lies with Mills's contrast-conception, which is one of state capitalism, or guild socialism, or

15To support this statement, Mills cites "Hearings before the Subcommittee on Study of Monopoly Power of the Committee on the Judiciary," House of Representatives, 81st Congress, 1st Sess. Ser. No. 14, Part 2-A (Washington: U.S. Government Printing Office, 1950), pp. 468–9. These hearings show the persistence of business monopolies in the face of antitrust legislation; they do not show that there is no effective regulation and limitation of business and industry in other spheres.

populism; for implicit in his remarks about the lack of government interference with the economy is his belief that the only real alternative to complete private enterprise is complete state or "worker" ownership, control, and operation of the economy.

The second means by which Mills considers that the economic elite controls the government is that of the large political campaign contribution. I agree that this is a major means of influence, though not of control, and I deal with it in Chapter 13. However, Mills pays very little attention to this factor, which could provide the main factual basis for his thesis. I do not know why Mills considers it so unimportant, but I suspect it is probably because he has little understanding of how politics works.

The third means of elite control over government, which Mills considers the most important of all, he states in the following words: "As the corporate world has become more intricately involved in the political order, these executives have become intimately associated with the politicians, and especially with the key 'politicians' who form the political directorate of the United States government" (p. 167). More specifically:

> During World War II they served on innumerable advisory committees in the prosecution of the war. They were also brought into the military apparatus more permanently by the awarding to many businessmen of commissions in the reserve officer corps. All this has been going on for a long time and is rather well known, but in the Eisenhower administration the corporate executives publicly assumed the key posts of the executive branch of the government. Where before the more silent power and the ample contract was there, now there was also the loud voice. [Pages 167–8.]

> During the last three decades, since the First World War in fact, the distinction between the political and the economic man has been diminishing; although the corporation managers have, in the past, distrusted one of their own who stays too long in the political arena. They like to come and go, for then they are not responsible. Yet more and more of the corporate executives have entered government directly; and the result has been a virtually new political economy at the apex of which we find those who represent the corporate rich. [Page 169.]

I understand these and other statements by Mills to mean that the economic elite has taken over control of the Executive branch of the government. But just exactly how they have done that, he does not say. To point to many specific businessman appointments in the Eisenhower Administration does show a major (not exclusive) reliance of a Republican Administration on businessmen. It does not explain the means of control, and it does not prove that the businessman appointees are running the government for the benefit of business. I suspect that businessmen who go to work for the government develop a quite different point of view toward government from that of businessmen who never have government experience. The latter, I would hypothesize, remain largely alienated from, and hostile to, government even when it is in Republican hands. Mills himself acknowledges this when he states that the business elite become suspicious of their colleagues who remain in government service "too long." Part of the businessmen's antagonism to even Republican administrations, I suspect, is toward the permanent top civil servants, but mainly it is due to a lack of understanding of political processes. The Kennedy Administration made some major business appointments too; it made even more appointments of college professors. Despite the facetious observations, this does not mean that Harvard University (or the academic profession in general) has assumed political control of the nation. The activities of the Executive branch suggest that President Kennedy was mainly in control of his businessman and professor appointees. In Chapter 11 the process by which Kennedy achieved the nomination for the presidency is traced. It was a political process, involving very little special dependence on the economic elite.

Mills does not give much consideration to the Congress, and does not claim that any significant number of businessmen have entered the Congress. Rather he holds, without evidence, that Congress is subordinate to the Executive branch and consists of persons who take orders from the economic elite. I do not doubt that a small number of congressmen have been "bought" by the economic elite, and that a larger number have viewpoints identical to those of the economic elite and contrary to the wishes of the majority of their constituencies. But I believe political processes are such that most congressmen are most of the time responsive to the wishes of the majority of their constituents.[16] And I believe, contrary to Mills, that congressional action is important to the outcome of key national issues. I do not claim to "prove" that these statements are correct, nor do I claim that congressmen or other elected officials are mere passive registers of the wishes of their constituencies. I seek in later chapters to illustrate the complexity of political processes, and to show how largely independent they are of controls from the economic elite. I seek to show this for the selection of the political elite in certain states (Chapter 10) and for the passage of a specific piece of federal legislation (Chapter 12). Insofar as the facts presented about the political process in these studies are representative, they do not confirm Mills's portrayal of economic elite control, although they are not inconsistent with a statement that the economic elite has political influence considerably beyond its proportion in the population.

Mills specifies the theories of others to which he is opposed. He considers Ferdinand Lundberg's attribution of power to "America's Sixty Families"[17] as incomplete and partly out-of-date, although based on a fundamental truth. This propertied class, Mills believes, has been merged with the managerial elite "into a new corporate world of privilege and prerogative" (p. 147). This point explains also his criticism of James Burnham's *The Managerial Revolution*.[18] In Mills's view, there is no opposition of ownership and management; rather, these two groups have merged into a new class with continuity of interests from the time when there was no distinct managerial type. In other words, he accepts the theory of economic elitism of Lundberg and Burnham, but denies that the economic elite consists only of the propertied rich or of the executive managers. Mills holds that these two economic elites are really one, which he calls the "corporate rich": "They are a corporate rich because they depend directly, as well as indirectly, for their money, their privileges, their securities,

16If the majority of congressmen do not favor state capitalism or socialism, that is because their constituencies also do not. I speak of the fact of state capitalism or socialism, not the name. A significant minority of congressmen and of the American people probably favor some degree of state capitalism or socialism in fact, though not in name.

17New York: Vanguard, 1937. Mills also criticizes Lundberg on methodological grounds (p. 377).

18New York: John Day, 1941.

their advantages, their powers on the world of the big corporations" (p. 148).

Another predecessor from whom Mills diverges is Robert Brady. Brady's thesis was that (1) in capitalistic societies control over means of production is increasingly centralized within a small number of giant corporations; (2) these corporations set up "peak associations" (like the National Association of Manufacturers) to speak for them on national political policy; (3) business and its peak associations tend to "shake off all popular restraints on such cumulative powers" as they acquire, and eventually they emerge as the controllers of totalitarian states, as in Italy and Germany. Brady believed that war accelerates economic concentration and economic power and feared that the end of World War II would see the United States become a totalitarian state along some fascist line. Mills did not believe that the economic elite was organized in such a conscious way, nor did he believe that it had to transform the state into a totalitarian form, since it more or less achieved its goals by "Madison Avenue" techniques and by controlling the popularly elected political elite. A prosperous economy (in terms of the interests of the economic elite) and the absence of an internal revolutionary threat along communist lines would keep the economic elite from setting up a totalitarian state. It can be seen that Mills follows the general theme of Lundberg, Burnham, and Brady, but has a more complex and sophisticated analysis which leads him to a different image of the way the economic elite controls American society.

Mills is in much more fundamental disagreement with the theories of A. A. Berle[19] and John Kenneth Galbraith.[20] He asserts that Berle believes in a "restraining corporation conscience," that is, a voluntary relinquishment of power on the part of the modern economic elite in the interests of the masses. Mills criticizes Berle by saying he mistakes expedient public relations and a liberal rhetoric of defense for a corporate soul (page 126). This is unfair to Berle, whose chief point is not that corporations have acquired a conscience or soul, but that the economic elite of today is more restricted in the exercise

[19]*The Twentieth-Century Capitalist Revolution* (New York: Harcourt, Brace, 1954).
[20]*American Capitalism* (Boston: Houghton Mifflin, 1952).

of arbitrary economic and political power than it was in the days of the "robber barons." Mills evaluates the power elite and finds its typical member is characterized by "intellectual mediocrity" and "higher immorality." We have no way of comparing the present elites with past ones in these respects, but we doubt that Mills does either. At any rate, it is in this particular characterization that Mills attacks Berle.[21]

Galbraith's thesis is that there are diverse economic interests, which check each other's power in an equilibrium of "countervailing power." Mills has many criticisms of this: (1) economic interests—including unions—are often in fact integrated or in collusion; (2) as Galbraith himself recognizes, "countervailing power" does not work in periods of inflation, when each economic interest seeks to outbid the other in pushing up the price of its product or service; (3) markets do not actually "generate" countervailing powers, except in a few unconcentrated fields such as food supply; (4) government does not in fact help the weaker economic interests. In general, Mills criticizes Galbraith for setting forth a theory which "is more ideological hope than factual description, more dogma than realism" (p. 126). This is somewhat unfair to Galbraith, who presents both facts and a proposal for government policy.

The thesis of the present book has little or nothing to do with the theories of Lundberg, Burnham, Brady, Berle, or Galbraith. It could agree with Mills regarding the limitations of Lundberg, Burnham, and Brady, and, while it is not incompatible with the theories of Berle and Galbraith, its validity is not dependent on the validity of those theories. This book limits itself to the political processes, and considers that Mills has presented so oversimplified a picture of the relation between the economic elite and the political processes as to be false. Specifically, this study presents evidence against the following statements of Mills:

> There is no effective countervailing power against the coalition of the big businessmen—who, as political outsiders, now occupy the command posts—and the ascendant military men —who with such grave voices now speak so frequently in the higher councils.

[21]See Berle's review of Mills's *The Power Elite, The New York Times Book Review*, April 22, 1956, pp. 3, 22.

> While the professional party politicians may still, at times, be brokers of power, compromisers of interests, negotiators of issues, they are no longer at the top of the state.
>
> The executive bureaucracy becomes not only the center of power but also the arena within which all conflicts of power are resolved or denied resolution. Administration replaces electoral politics. [Page 267.]

Implicit in these and other remarks are Mills's political assumptions that (1) voting means little or nothing; (2) there is no significant difference between the two major political parties; (3) the economic-military elite has an interest in all major political issues against the interest of the masses, and that the former interest is always victorious over the latter; (4) the Legislative branch of government is subordinate to the Executive branch. There are other political assumptions of Mills with which we shall not be concerned: ". . . the virtually complete absence of a civil service that constitutes a politically neutral, but politically relevant, depository of brainpower and executive skill, and the increased official secrecy behind which great decisions are made without benefit of public or even Congressional debate" (p. 296).

Mills adopts an economic determinism which we cannot accept. He points to the fact that most congressmen are of upper-class or middle-class origin (p. 248), and assumes that they must therefore reflect the economic interests of businessmen and other members of the economic elite. Even when a congressman does not have an upper-class or middle-class background, he is assumed to take orders from the economic elite. These assumptions neglect the vast amount of social welfare legislation, particularly since the 1930's, and of other legislation designed to protect the interests of the working classes. They neglect the fact that some of the wealthiest of elected government officials have been among those leading in the fight for such legislation. The aristocratic Franklin Roosevelt doubtless represented the interests of the working masses better than his "average man" political opponent of 1936, Alfred Landon; and a similar comparison could be made between the wealthy John Kennedy and his opponent of more nearly average wealth, Richard Nixon. Of course, Mills can consider Landon and Nixon as "lieutenants" of the economic elite, but he cannot get around the fact that Roosevelt, Kennedy, and such other liberal politicians as W. Averill Harriman, Joseph Clark, Herbert Lehman, Stuart Symington, and G. Mennen Williams are members of the upper economic class. It may be true that military leaders have growing power in government circles, but they have not succeeded in getting much of the legislation they have asked for, nor has any President allowed them to speak freely in public. It is not illuminating to be told by Mills that "a small group of men are now in charge of the executive decisions" (p. 231), for there has always been, and must continue to be, leadership in a democracy; this is even part of the definition of "executive." The significant question is in whose interests the political elite acts and whether it is checked by the mass of voters and of interest groups. There is every evidence that the masses of the American people today are better off economically, both absolutely and relatively, than they were in the past, and that this has been largely due to government intervention, supported by the majority of the voters.

It is explicit in Mills's and Hunter's analyses that the elected legislators have no power in and of themselves. At most, they are "lieutenants" who carry out the orders of the economic elite, who—Mills claims—have taken over the direction of the government through appointment to the top policy-making offices in the federal Executive. In fact, a considerable number of statutes originate in the Congress rather than in the Executive branch—more than in European parliamentary regimes—and many of these are responses to the wishes of private pressure groups, including those of the economic elite. Yet, there are also some bills that are originated by the congressmen themselves, sometimes in opposition to the wishes of both the Executive branch and the pressure groups. Congress also controls the purse strings, and the areas of taxation and appropriations involve far more creative opportunities than is generally understood.

Administrations since 1933 have been diligent in efforts to solve social problems, and have sought enabling statutes and appropriations from the Congress, a large number with success, some after a delay, and others with failure. In most cases Congress has "improved" the bills submitted to it by the Executive before passing them, and that has been its chief role. But in some outstanding instances, it has initiated or expanded legislation on its own when it felt the Executive branch was evasive or dilatory. The Civil Rights Act of 1964 and the Medicare Act of 1965 provide examples of liberal legislation enacted by Congress with provisions that went much beyond what the Administration requested. Congress's annual allocation of funds for medical research and often for medical facilities is usually greater than that requested by the President, and in 1965 Congress doubled the educational program for veterans that the President requested, and made a special allocation, that the President did not request, for schools in areas of high federal employment.[22]

There are a number of other general points to be made against the Mills-Hunter thesis which have been touched on only tangentially in the specific researches reported in the main part of this book.

1. The important facts of political power and political influence are not "secret" or "hidden" or "behind the scenes" most of the time. Pressure groups—of which many represent economic interests —and public opinion operate on legislative and executive branches of government. But only a small proportion of federal legislators and executives are "in the control of" an economic elite. At state and local levels, a larger proportion of legislators seek their positions to serve special economic interests, but even when they do, many of their votes are in accord with their ideological conception of what the public interest is.

There is a circularity in Mills's reasoning because of his beliefs that the top economic elite effects its control of American society secretly and that the political elite consists of lieutenants of the commanding economic elite. From these premises he deduces that the *actions* of the political elite are generally the only means by which the wishes and interests of the commanding economic elite can be ascertained by the outside observers, and that the *words* of the political elite are mere window dressing to mislead the masses into voting for them. There are several factual questions at issue here— the extent to which there is a discrepancy between the words and deeds of the political elite, and the extent to which the deeds of the political elite do not reflect the interests and wishes of the public. But aside from these factual questions, there is dubious logic in reasoning that the political elite constantly proves its subordination to the economic elite by its actions, when there is no independent way

22*The New York Times*, April 5, 1966, p. 21.

of ascertaining what the commanding economic elite really wants because of its secret modes of operating. The economic elite in fact does often expound its wishes—in the programs and campaigns of the National Association of Manufacturers, the United States Chamber of Commerce, and more specialized groups such as the American Medical Association. As we shall see in subsequent chapters the President and the majority of the Congress more often go against these programs than support them, although the businessmen are more likely to get their way when they seek narrow economic advantages from the independent regulatory commissions and the military procurement agencies. Are the National Association of Manufacturers, the Chamber of Commerce, and the American Medical Association merely engaging in window dressing to fool the public as to their true wishes when they come out with a program or campaign?

Secrecy in politics has many functions other than the desire to hide the control that may be exercised by the economic elite on the politicians. The New York Reform Democratic party leader, Edward U. Costikyan,[23] says:

> The nature of politics and politicians is to reach decisions privately. This often leads the public to believe that secrecy is a screen to shield wrongdoing. It usually isn't. Generally it shields a desire for privacy, as well as some confusion, and some selfishness.

He acknowledges that the closed doors must usually simply protect a process that cannot function as well at a public hearing, yet he argues that the doors should be opened—at least more than they now are.

> What goes on behind is normally perfectly exposable to the light of day. Only the mystery is destroyed. But, like magicians, politicians like to smile enigmatic smiles after a startling political result. For mystery breeds respect. And respect breeds power. And power is the principal asset and persistent natural goal of the politician.

Thus, the existence of secrecy in some political actions cannot by

23*Behind Closed Doors: Politics in the Public Interest* (New York: Harcourt, Brace and World, 1966), Preface.

itself be taken as evidence that it hides business control of politics. Just how much secrecy there is in politics is an open question on which there is little evidence. Public ignorance of certain actions taken by politicians does not mean that there is secrecy; it often simply reflects the failure of the news media to report actions that were taken openly. Politicians interviewed by this author invariably stated, when asked about the frequency of the decisions they take in secret, that they occasionally found it expedient to act in secret, but that the secret usually "leaked out" in a matter of days or weeks. They all averred that the value of secrecy to them was temporary, and that they assumed, when they took secret actions, that the secret would likely ultimately become public. They also stated that many of the supposedly secret actions they took were not secret at all: newspaper and other mass media reporters were just not present, and when the news releases were finally issued, the reporters excused their own failure to be present by asserting that the decision-making had occurred secretly.

2. Granted there has been a deviation from the principle of "one man, one vote" because legislatures have failed to redistrict (federal court decisions are now changing this situation); because of gerrymandering, legislators still are fairly representative of the ideological distributions of their constituents. Most of the American people are basically conservative, although regularly willing and even anxious to support specific "reforms." Among the masses of the American people, there is a good deal of ignorance about politics and "false consciousness" about their interests. But so also is there among the economic elite. We have sought to illustrate the false consciousness of the economic elite in an analysis of the politics of the Medicare legislation before Congress in the period 1957–65. But in a far more important sense, the economic elite has demonstrated its false consciousness in its ideological commitment to a balanced federal government budget, which during the 1950's reduced the rate of national economic growth and created several economic recessions. It was the federal Executive, in the persons of Presidents Kennedy and Johnson acting on the advice of economists, that adopted governmental measures to create the sustained prosperity of the 1960's which worked to the benefit of the economic elite along with most other sectors of the American society. Similarly, social welfare measures inaugurated

by President Franklin Roosevelt, and sustained and extended by all federal administrations since his, have usually been opposed by large segments of the economic elite (though not by all). Yet they have provided a floor under poverty which has prevented social unrest from reaching revolutionary proportions (particularly during the 1930's) and have also contributed to the total prosperity of the country. The facts would seem to favor a thesis quite different from that of Marx or Mills—that false consciousness is occasionally found in all segments of society, and, in the most important respects, is found in the economic elite more often than in the lower classes.

3. Mills holds that there are practically no ideological or policy differences between the two major political parties. There were occasions in which this seemed to be true before the 1930's, but since then they have been becoming increasingly different. Systematic studies show that party affiliation explains more congressional voting than any other single variable.[24] The divergence between the two major political parties has especially increased since the late 1940's, as a two-party system has developed in the Northern states and as some leading Republicans have challenged the loyalty of many Democratic leaders. Political partisans, such as former Secretary of State Dean Acheson, often express the antithesis of Mills' position on the facts:

> In 1919–20 the attack on the Democrats was savage and malicious. In 1950–52 the ferocity of the Republican attack knew no limits. It went beyond the policies involved and the competence of leaders. It struck at the character and patriotism of those who devised and executed policies. It assaulted institutions of government, and, as in the Bricker Amendment, even government itself. Nor did it stop at the water's edge. It involved the motives and character of nations and peoples associated with us. It is hardly too much to say that the whole conception of trust and confidence, including the confidence of the people in their own judgment, was brought into doubt. . . . When the ignorant are taught to doubt they do not know what they safely may believe.[25]

[24]Julius Turner, *Party and Constituency: Pressures on Congress* (Baltimore: Johns Hopkins Press, 1951); H. Bradford Westerfield, *Foreign Policy and Party Politics* (New Haven: Yale University Press, 1955).

[25]Dean Acheson, *A Democrat Looks at His Party* (New York: Harper, 1955), p. 65.

In the 1960's, the parties have diverged so sharply that the question can be raised whether the national consensus which holds the country together is not in jeopardy. By 1964, the Republican party was largely controlled by a group that considered most Democratic party leaders, and some of its own former leaders, subversives. Up to 1964 there was a coalition in Congress between the majority of the Republicans and the majority of the Southern Democrats, based on opposition to bills favoring civil rights for Negroes and welfare programs for the poor. With the growth of a two-party system in the South and the weakening of the Republican party in the North, as well as the adroit political leadership of President Johnson, this was no longer an effective coalition in the 1964–65 sessions of Congress, and a great number of "reform" bills passed which had previously been vigorously opposed by the majority of the economic elite. The weakening of the congressional "coalition" sharpened the division between the two major political parties, but it is premature to say that the coalition is entirely dead until the South completes its transition to a two-party system on the pattern of the North.

4. Mills and his followers have been critical of those political scientists like Dahl who hold that political power is pluralistic in the United States. Our position is not simply that power is pluralistic in American society, but that the society itself is pluralistic. The different spheres of life do not interpenetrate each other in the way that in India, for example, religious values and institutions permeate the average man's political, economic, family, artistic, educational, and other spheres of life. Or in the way that, in Hitler's Germany, or Stalin's Russia, political values similarly permeated all the other spheres of life. In the United States (and many other countries), practically every person has differentiated roles and values for the various spheres of life, and so power too usually does not significantly cross the boundaries of each sphere in which it is created. As Merton has put it: "Men with power to affect the economic life-chances of a large group may exert little interpersonal influence in other spheres: the power to withhold jobs from people may not result in directly influencing their political or associational or religious behavior."[26]

26Robert K. Merton, "Patterns of Influence: A Study of Interpersonal Influence and of Communication Behavior in a Local Community," in Paul F. Lazarsfeld and Frank N. Stanton (eds.), *Communication Research: 1948–1949* (New York: Harper, 1949), p. 217.

5. Since 1933, Democrats have won the great majority of the elections, naming all the Presidents but one (Eisenhower), dominating all the Congresses but two (1946–48, 1952–54), and electing a considerable majority of the governors and state legislatures. Yet the majority of businessmen have strongly supported the Republican party. Businessmen have not only not dominated the political scene, but have shown an increasing sense of frustration and bitterness at being "left out" in political decisions.

In 1960, the Committee on Economic Development conducted an attitude survey of bankers. One of the findings was that they felt that Congress ignored them and their interests. They pointed to the much lighter controls on their competitors, the savings and loan associations and the credit unions. In their belief this could be attributed to the "fact" that Congressmen were more likely to place their savings in these latter associations than in banks, and that, because of the high rate of bank failures in the early 1930's, banks were still regarded with suspicion—in spite of the many reforms in procedure that banks had made since then.

The brief two years (1952–54) when the Republicans controlled both the presidency and the Congress must have seemed like a "Restoration" for the majority of businessmen, and it was during this atypical period that C. Wright Mills must have written the bulk of *The Power Elite*. But alienation from government increased during the late years of the Eisenhower presidency as the Administration proved unable to achieve any of the major goals of the businessmen. They became even more antagonistic and truculent toward government when President Kennedy forced back the steel price rise, as reported elsewhere in this book, and they went so far as to pull the Business Advisory Council out of its semiofficial relationship to the government. It was not until a politically extremist minority seized control of the majority of the Republican state organizations that a significant group of big businessmen exhibited a desire to take an accommodating position toward the Democrats. Big businessmen worked out a pragmatic relationship with President Lyndon Johnson[27]—which they had refused to do with Presidents Roosevelt, Truman, and Kennedy—but their subordinate role in the Johnson

[27]David T. Bazelon, "Big Business and the Democrats," *Commentary*, 39 (May 1965), 39–46.

Administration was shown by the fact that more welfare and "reform" legislation was passed by the 1964–65 Congress, under Johnson's stimulation, than by any Congress since 1933.[28]

6. Mills contends that the American top elite has a common provenance: He says that they are upper-class people, who attend the same preparatory schools and private colleges, associate with each other throughout their lives, and pass on their power to their offspring. This picture is certainly not true for the top elected government officials. Very few sons of presidents, governors, and congressmen ever achieve top political positions. The men in these positions have the most diverse social origins. Of presidents in the twentieth century, only the two Roosevelts (sixth cousins to each other) were from the upper upper class, and only one came from a very wealthy family (Kennedy, whose family background is *nouveau riche*); Truman, Eisenhower, and Johnson could be said to have come from the lower middle class, and the others had somewhat higher middle-class family backgrounds. The Middle West provided as many presidents as did the East, and the small towns provided more than the opulent cities or suburbs. The majority did not attend the upper-class private schools or colleges. The great majority of the top elected officials of the United States have experienced a considerable amount of upward social mobility in comparison with their parents, not only in prestige and power, but also in education and wealth.

Studies by Newcomer, and by Warner and Abegglen, suggest that there is more social mobility in the economic elite than Mills claims.[29] In Newcomer's sample of big business executives in the early 1950's, 7.5 per cent were sons of workers, as compared to 4.2 per cent for the executives of 1900; in Warner and Abegglen's study of 8,562 businessmen from 1900 to 1950 there was an increase of 8 per cent in the proportion of executives whose fathers were laborers and a

[28]Throughout this book we leave in abeyance the situation before 1933. Certainly a strong case can be made for the thesis that much of the political leadership then was of a like mind with the economic elite. But this does not say that the latter dominated the former, in Mills's terms. An instructive study—both of the pro-business orientation of a dominating political leader and of his personal power independent of any outside influence—is Blair Bolles's political biography of House Speaker Joseph Cannon, *Tyrant from Illinois* (New York: W. W. Norton, 1951).

[29]Mabel Newcomer, *The Big Business Executive* (New York: Columbia University Press, 1955); W. Lloyd Warner and James C. Abegglen, *Big Business Leaders in America* (New York: Harper, 1955).

decrease of 10 per cent in those whose fathers were owners of businesses. But Mills is almost completely wrong about the absence of social mobility among the political elite.

Dwight D. Eisenhower, General of the Armies and President of the United States, appointer of many top-level business executives to the leading decision-making posts in government, must have been considered by Mills a leading member of the power elite. Yet he was one of the few in top decision-making posts who publicly warned against a "military-industrial complex" as a threat to the United States. On the significant occasion of his Farewell Address, this leader of the Establishment seemed to give support to one of C. Wright Mills's central theses:

> In the councils of Government, we must guard against the acquisition of unwarranted influence, whether sought or unsought, by the military-industrial complex. The potential for the disastrous rise of misplaced power exists and will persist. We must never let the weight of this combination endanger our liberties or democratic processes.

Many individuals not persuaded by the scholar Mills were persuaded by the President Eisenhower.[30] Yet a closer reading of Eisenhower's speech shows that he was on a different track than Mills. In the first place, Eisenhower placed the danger in the future; Mills had the economic-military power elite already in control of the nation. Secondly, Eisenhower was arguing for the autonomy of government; Mills identified the government as a tool of the elite. Thirdly, Eisenhower—a leading figure in Mills's elite—was publicly denouncing the threat posed by that presumed elite, whereas Mills held that the members of the elite were like-minded and operated more or less in secret.

It is clear than Eisenhower was worried about the huge size of the armaments industry, and its consequent potential for using its great economic power to influence many areas of government, education,

---

30 I do not know if Mills welcomed Eisenhower's statement. Among those who accepted it as verification of Mills's thesis were Fred J. Cook, *The Warfare State* (New York: MacMillan, 1962); and Marc Pilisuk and Thomas Hayden, "Is There a Military Industrial Complex which Prevents Peace?" *Journal of Social Issues*, 21 (July 1965), 67–117. The latter mentions many others.

and science. In Chapter 3 we shall discuss some of the existing use of that power. Eisenhower may also have been worried about conflict of interest on the part of the nation's military leaders: As direct purchasers from the armaments industry, and as relatively low-paid government servants who could "retire" at an early age, were they not in danger of making decisions influenced by the fact that they could go into high-salaried jobs in one or another munitions firm after they retired? When Eisenhower made his statement, Congress was considering a bill to require retiring military procurement officers to wait two years before accepting a position in one of the supplying firms. But this may not be a long enough waiting period to prevent conflict of interest, and the law could not apply to civilians working for the Defense Department or to military officers not directly engaged in procurement. There were all sorts of ways of unduly influencing a military procurement officer: The military supply firms even set up trade association, called the National Security Industrial Association, which has been in existence since World War II, to enhance their relationships with military leaders. Provision of information and gossip, wining and dining, and other standard techniques of lobbying were used on the military procurement officers. General Eisenhower was concerned about the conflict of interest on the part of his brother officers, and anxious to maintain the tradition of military independence and service.

Yet Eisenhower's conception of his role as President, as a mere enforcer of laws and mediator of the various conflicting forces in the Executive branch, did much to enhance the very dangers he called attention to. It was his successors, Kennedy and Johnson, because they had a conception of the dominant and decisive role of the presidency, who set industry back several times when it sought an inflationary rise in prices, and whose appointed Secretary of Defense, Robert McNamara, maintained his dominance over the military in all matters. These Presidents were political leaders, who saw a superordinate government as the check on any potential military-industrial complex.

There are some successors to Mills who recognize several defects in his analysis, yet hold to his central theme that there is a economic-military power elite which controls American society. Perhaps the most sophisticated of these are Pilisuk and Hayden,[31] who use the Eisenhower term "military-industrial complex," and define it as "an informal and changing coalition of groups with vested psychological, moral, and material interests in the continuous development and maintenance of high levels of weaponry, in preservation of colonial markets and in military-strategic conceptions of international affairs." These authors have at the same time narrowed Mills's conception to make it primarily operative in the fields of defense and foreign affairs (saying nothing about domestic matters), and broadened it to make it an intrinsic part of American culture and social structure.

> Our concept is not that American society contains a ruling military-industry complex. Our concept is more nearly that American society is a military-industrial complex. It can accommodate a wide range of factional interests from those concerned with the production or utilization of a particular weapon to those enraptured with the mystique of optimal global strategies. It can accommodate those with rabid desires to advance toward the brink and into limitless intensification of the arms race. It can even accommodate those who wish either to prevent war or to limit the destructiveness of war through the gradual achievement of arms control and disarmament agreements. What it cannot accommodate is the type of radical departures needed to produce enduring peace (pp. 98–9).

The problem, then, is not so much in a business elite or a military elite, as in "core beliefs" found among most Americans. These include: (1) "Efficacy is preferable to principle in foreign affairs. In practice this means that violence is preferable to non-violence as a means of defense." (2) "Private property is preferable to collective property." 3) ". . . the particular form of constitutional government which is practiced within the United States is preferable to any other system of government." When the attack is on such fundamental aspects of American culture, and the demand is for such a revolutionary set of changes, it is not possible to refute it by marshaling empirical facts about American life. In this book, therefore, we shall confine ourselves to the data which relate to Mills's more specific attack on American society. It should be noted, however, that the

[31]*Op. cit.;* see esp. pp. 91–2, 98–9.

fact that some of the more sophisticated of Mills's successors have felt it necessary to go much beyond his arguments suggests that they find these arguments inadequate.

In sum, the present book provides an empirically based critique of the Hunter-Mills hypothesis that the economic elite acts in a more-or-less unified fashion to control the political processes of the United States. This hypothesis, as we have suggested, is much older than the writings of Hunter and Mills, but never before has it received such careful formulation (as in Mills) or such an attempt at empirical foundation (as in Hunter and his followers). The hypothesis has received excellent scholarly criticism before this book was written, but by political scientists and political philosophers. Since Hunter and Mills are sociologists rather than political scientists, there might be special merit in a criticism by an empirically based sociologist who considers the same wide range of forces that Hunter and Mills consider. We shall oppose the Hunter–Mills economic-elite-dominance hypothesis with a multi-influence hypothesis. In doing so, we shall limit ourselves to a consideration of the political processes, and not concern ourselves with other areas of interest to Hunter and Mills.

PART ONE
The Elites and Power in American Society

We start our substantive chapters with a consideration of the power structures and elites in American society. Taking our cue from C. Wright Mills, we give practically all our attention to the political, economic, and military elites, though with brief consideration of other elites. Our concern with these elites is not in the characteristics of their members as individuals, but in the social structures the elites create to exercise political power.

Our analysis of the political structure is truncated, as we have no wish to review the well-known formal structure of American government, although we consider this extremely important. Rather, our attention is focused on the less well-known *informal* structures used by politicians, both inside and outside of the formal government. This consideration follows a briefer effort to describe the major ways in which the concept of "power" has been used by scholars. The theme of this chapter is taken up again in much more extensive fashion in Part IV of our book; together, these chapters on the political structure constitute the heart of our *refutation* of the economic-elite-dominance hypothesis.

The chapter on the influence of businessmen on government and politics, along with the last substantive chapter in the book on money and ethics in politics, represent our summary of the real evidence *in support of* the economic-elite-dominance hypothesis. Our facts, however, are quite different from those provided by Mills and Hunter. The complexity, lack of comprehensiveness, and often indirectness

41

of the ways in which the economic elite exercise power in politics
and government give stronger support to the multi-influence hypothesis.

The roles of the military and other elites are usually much more
specialized, segmented, and limited, although on occasion they are
very important. There is much less evidence of the collaboration of
the military elite with the economic elite than of the collaboration of
the military elite with the political.

II

Political Elements in Power

A. Definitions of Power and Related Concepts[1]

As with so many concepts in the social sciences, "there is an elusiveness about power that endows it with an almost ghostly quality. . . . We 'know' what it is, yet we encounter endless difficulties in trying to define it. We can 'tell' whether one person or group is more powerful than another, yet we cannot measure power."[2] The disagreement among researchers as to what constitutes power is inseparably linked with the methodological debate to be examined later. In fact Danzger believes that although the primary concern of scholars has been methodological weakness in the study of power, the basis for it is a lack of conceptual clarity: "It is my contention that failure to specify this concept [power] is at present a prime source of difficulty in the study of community power.[3] One need only sample the results from a number of community power studies to observe the complete lack of agreement concerning the nature of power.

Not only has there been a general failure to define concepts, but also a failure to distinguish clearly between several closely related

[1] This section has benefited from an honors paper prepared by Ronald Lee Cohen, under the author's direction.

[2] Herbert Kaufman and Victor Jones, "The Mystery of Power," *Public Administration Quarterly*, 14 (Summer 1954), 205; see also Robert O. Schulze, "The Bifurcation of Power in a Satellite City," in Morris Janowitz (ed.), *Community Political Systems* (Glencoe, Ill.: Free Press, 1961), p. 19.

[3] M. Herbert Danzger, "Community Power Structure: Problems and Continuities," *American Sociological Review*, 29 (October, 1964), 712.

phenomena. Many have exchanged the terms "power," "influence," "control," "authority," "leadership" for each other at will, and in so doing have added considerably to the confusion. Agger uses the terms "power" and "influence" interchangeably because of his "preliminary empirical finding that people tend to use these concepts as identical or equivalent."[4] Nelson Polsby conceives of "influence" and "control" as serviceable synonyms of "power,"[5] and elsewhere refers to members of the power structure as "leaders" engaged in various leadership roles.[6] In an apparent attempt to cover every possible interpretation of this list of terms, Floyd Hunter refers to the "men of authority" in our society as "power and influence leaders."[7]

The two concepts that have been given the most attention are power and influence, and some authors have attempted to distinguish between them. Most of the researchers agree that both terms refer to relationships between persons and/or groups. Rossi[8] conceives power to be a relationship "in which individual A affects the behavior of individual B because B wishes to avoid the sanctions which A would employ if B did not comply with his wishes," and influence, the case in which "B's behavior is affected in the absence of sanctions."[9] Dahl sees influence as a relationship among actors in which "one actor induces other actors to act in some way they would not otherwise act."[10] The most extreme form of influence is coercive influence, which is based on the "threat or expectation of extremely severe penalties or great losses . . . both negative and positive coercion are sometimes included in the term 'power.'" The extent of A's

[4]Robert E. Agger and Daniel Goldrich, "Community Power Structures and Partisanship," *American Sociological Review*, (23 August 1958), 323.

[5]Nelson W. Polsby, *Community Power and Political Theory* (New Haven: Yale University Press, 1963), p. 3.

[6]Nelson W. Polsby, "The Sociology of Community Power: A Reassessment," *Social Forces*, 37 (March 1959), 233; see also Linton C. Freeman, Thomas J. Fararo, Warner Bloomberg, Jr., and Morris H. Sunshine, "Locating Leaders in Local Communities: A Comparison of Some Alternative Approaches," *American Sociological Review*, 28 (October 1963), 791.

[7]Floyd Hunter, *Community Power Structure, A Study of Decision Makers* (Chapel Hill: University of North Carolina Press, 1953, p. 2.

[8]Peter H. Rossi, "Community Decision Making," *Administrative Science Quarterly*, 1 (March 1957), 425.

[9]Ibid.

[10]Robert A. Dahl, *Modern Political Analysis* (Englewood Cliffs, N.J.: Prentice-Hall, 1963), p. 40.

influence is to be measured by the amount of change in B's behavior. In applying such a measure, however, one must recognize certain underlying measures of influence that are thus encompassed: ". . . the amount of change in the position of the actor influenced, the subjective psychological costs of compliance, the amount of difference in the probability of compliance, differences in the scope of the responses, and the number of persons who respond."[11] D'Antonio and Form view power as being composed of two subclasses: authority, based on the position a person holds in a formal hierarchical structure, and influence, "that more subtle phenomenon of power manifested in the willingness of people to obey others who lack formal authority. . . . They obey because they have respect or esteem for or fear of the person, office, group . . . in its extreme form it becomes charisma." Authority and influence are closely related phenomena. Both are necessary for the efficient wielding of power, but the fact that they are rarely in optimum balance creates issues in the distribution of power.[12] Delbert Miller, who approaches the problem in much the same way introduces the term "Top Influential" for those persons who rank highest on this measure, and "Key Influential" for the sociometric leaders among the Top Influentials.[13]

Max Weber's definition of power as "the chance of a man or of a number of men to realize their own will in a communal action even against the resistance of others who are participating in the action"[14] provides the basis for a discussion of the present-day controversy concerning the nature of this most important concept. His use of the

[11] Ibid. pp. 50–51. "Indeed, the State is distinguishable from other political systems only to the extent that it successfully upholds its claim to the exclusive right to determine the conditions under which certain kinds of severe penalties, those involving physical coercion, may be legitimately employed"; also pp. 42–7. For similar discussions see Hunter, *Community Power Structure*, p. 42; Harold Lasswell and Abraham Kaplan, *Power and Society* (New Haven: Yale University Press, 1950), pp. 75–6; Harold Lasswell, Daniel Lerner, and C. Easton Rothwell, *The Comparative Study of Elites* (Stanford, California: Stanford University Press, 1952), p. 11.

[12] William V. D'Antonio and William H. Form, *Influentials in Two Border Cities* (Notre Dame: University of Notre Dame Press, 1965), p. 11.

[13] Delbert C. Miller, "Democracy and Decision-Making in the Community Power Structure," in William V. D'Antonio and Howard J. Ehrlich (eds.), *Power and Democracy in America* (Notre Dame: University of Notre Dame Press, 1961), pp. 47–9.

[14] Hans Gerth and C. Wright Mills (eds.), *From Max Weber: Essays in Sociology* (New York: Oxford University Press, 1946), p. 180.

word "chance" implies that Weber considered that actual realization of one's will was rather incidental to the basic problem of power. To be sure, one must "have a chance" in order to realize one's will, but the two concepts are by no means identical. It may be said that this chance is a necessary but not sufficient condition for realization of will. Much of the contemporary literature has substituted "ability" or "potential" for Weber's "chance," but maintains the distinction between this potential, and actual realization of will. If power is to be defined as a potential, then in a confrontation between two opposing forces, the fact that the ultimate result can be described as a victory for one over the other does not necessarily mean power rested only with the victor; there may have been power in both forces, but the potential of one may have been greater than the other.[15] If on the other hand, power were to be considered as the actual realization of one's will in a confrontation, ultimate victory or defeat would be the only criterion.

Among those who see power as a potential are: Schulze, "power will denote the *capacity* or *potential* of persons in *certain statuses* to set conditions, make decisions, and/or take actions which are determinative for the existence of others within a given social system";[16] Haer, "the term 'power' refers to the ability or authority of individuals or organizations to control, effectively guide, or influence other individuals or groups";[17] and D'Antonio and Ehrlich, "power in its most general sense refers to a capacity or ability to control others and . . . to control the decision-making process."[18] D'Antonio and Ehrlich go on to say that power as a potential for control and as the exercise of control itself are not mutually exclusive: "persons who exercise power must, by definition, have had a power potential, but not all persons who hold potential power do in fact exercise power."[19]

Nelson Polsby has criticized the concept of potential power: "The

---

[15] For example; "His [the Influential's] will may not always prevail, but his views are usually considered before a final decision is reached." D'Antonio and Form, *Influentials*, p. 11.

[16] Schulze, "Bifurcation of Power," pp. 20–21.

[17] John L. Haer, "Social Stratification in Relation to Attitude Toward Sources of Power in a Community," *Social Forces*, 35 (2), (December 1956), 137.

[18] William V. D'Antonio and Howard J. Ehrlich, "Democracy in America: Retrospect and Prospect," in their *Power and Democracy in America*, p. 132.

[19] Ibid.

assertion that any group 'potentially' could exercise significant, or decisive, or any influence in community affairs is not easy to discuss in a scientific manner."[20] The only way to determine whether or not an actor is powerful, according to Polsby, is to observe a sequence of events supposedly attesting to his power: "If these events take place, then the power of the actor is not 'potential' but actual. If these events do not occur, then what grounds have we to suppose that the actor is powerful? There appear to be no scientific grounds for such an assumption."[21] Polsby is here confusing "power as potential" and a "potential for power." The former expression defines power itself as a potential for control; those who have potential have power, whether or not they exercise control. The latter expression, however, implies a definition of power as control—i.e. in order for one to be said to possess power, one must exercise control, the two being more or less synonymous. It is meaningful, as Schulze, Haer, and D'Antonio and Ehrlich maintain, to speak of power as a potential only, then the matter of "actual control" is another problem. These researchers do not say that a person with a potential for control has a power-potential, but that he has power. Furthermore, the fact that Polsby feels "potential for control" is much harder to discuss scientifically than "actual control" should not dismiss the question of potential as a trivial one or one that need not be explored. Indeed, the difficulty Polsby and all other investigators have encountered in dealing with "actual control" in a scientifically competent manner has not prevented them from attempting to examine it.

In a recent book, D'Antonio and Form attempt to discuss this distinction.[22] Power is defined as the ability (i.e. capacity of potential) to control the decision-making process in the community. Then, however, the authors claim that "much of what passes as these phenomena [authority and influence, the two subclasses of power] represents at best a *potential* for control or sometimes only a reputation for control."[23] A restatement of this would read: "Much of what passes as a potential for control represents at best a potential for control." Evidently, they are not sure whether power is best conceived

20Polsby, *Political Theory*, p. 60.
21Ibid.
22D'Antonio and Form, *Influentials*.
23Ibid. pp. 11–12.

as a potential for control or as control itself. If they mean that often a potential or a reputation for control passes for actual control, and that it is necessary to distinguish the two, one could not but agree. Implicit in the term "potential power" is a definition of "power" itself as actual exercise of control.

Robert Dahl also calls attention to the fact that a "potential for control is not equivalent to actual control . . . the actual *political effectiveness* of a group is a function of its potential for control *and* its potential for unity. Thus a group with a relatively low potential for control but a high potential for unity may be more politically effective than a group with a high potential for control but a low potential for unity."[24] He also points to a distinction among past or present influence, probable future influence, and maximum potential influence. For Dahl to speak of potential influence is not redundant, as in the case of D'Antonio and Form above, because he has defined influence as a behavioral change on the part of the person influenced, and thus potential influence is treated as the ability to induce this change. In Dahl's words, "the influence an actor exerts in some sphere of decisions may fluctuate, but it rarely approaches his maximum potential influence in that sector."[25] The two apparent reasons for this are that a high degree of political skill is acquired by only a few actors, and only a few actors deem it worthwhile to exert themselves to their maximum potential.[26] Ehrlich feels that another reason may be that the "sheer fact of the possession of a power-potential or resource may have been sufficient to determine the action of others." The use of potential power may be necessary only when, and if, those who possess it are directly challenged.[27] That people do react to their perception of the power of others is one of

[24]Robert A. Dahl, "A Critique of the Power Elite Model," *American Political Science Review*, 52 (June 1958), 465.

[25]Dahl, *Analysis*, pp. 47, 49.

[26]Ibid.

[27]Howard J. Ehrlich, "Power and Democracy: A Critical Discussion," in William V. D'Antonio and Howard J. Ehrlich (eds.), *Power and Democracy in America*, p. 92. Robert A. Dahl, "Equality and Power in American Society," in the same volume (p. 78), speaks of this anticipatory indirect influence. D'Antonio and Form, *Influentials*, p. 149, speak of indirect influence as characteristic of those people who are not powerful in their own right, but accomplish their goals by having an intimate knowledge of the structure of power.

the rationalizations for using reputations for power as an index of power.[28]

The debate as to how power may best be defined is intimately related to the manner in which its study is approached. Those who define power as a potential have often "centered their attention on producing inventories of those positions in the community which have the necessary attributes for the wielding of influence or power."[29] Because, as demonstrated above, power as potential may differ significantly from the behavior one might associate with power, an index of power as potential must be based on other than behavioral evidence. Rossi points out that such studies "document who within a community controls significant amounts of economic resources," or attempt to determine " 'the leader,' persons at the heads of various private associations or occupying important public offices."[30] Approaches of this type, which hold that "power can be observed empirically," and "suggest as evidence the identical observations which were used as indices of economic or status positions," have been sternly criticized by Polsby.[31] This method presumes that "power is coextensive with class and status," and "as long as we adhere to the notion that power is an empirically separable variable of social stratification, we must reject these [methods] as improper, and search for specific, separate empirical indices by which power can be measured."[32] Indeed, however power is defined, class and status positions do play a large part in attributions of power, and although the three concepts may be closely related, the fact that they

[28]In his discussion of Hunter's *Community Power Structure*, Herbert Danzger comments: "At a number of points Hunter is forced to interject that the votes of the 'informed' informants do not accurately describe the ranking of power in the community because some of the most powerful people prefer not to participate directly in the processes of leadership. As a result their ratings in terms of votes is less than objective measures of power would demand. . . . the leader has power but does not choose to exercise it, because less powerful individuals, who *are* involved in the decision-processes, will effect outcomes in line with his general interests. The preferable research strategy then, is to define power as *potential* capacity for action." Danzger, "Community Power Structure," p. 713.

[29]Rossi, "Community Decision Making," p. 426.

[30]Ibid.

[31]Polsby, *Political Theory*, pp. 103–4.

[32]Ibid.

have been distinguished theoretically would indicate they ought to be measured as distinct phenomena.

Those, on the other hand, who define power as behavior usually look to participation in the decision-making process for their evidence. C. Wright Mills, for example: "Power has to do with whatever decision men make about the arrangements under which they live . . . in so far as such decisions are made, the problem of who is involved in making them is the basic problem of power."[33] Or Bertrand Russell's definition: "The production of intended effects by some men on other men."[34] Or Lasswell and Kaplan: *"Power* is participation in the making of decisions. . . . The making of decisions is an interpersonal process: the policies which other persons are to pursue is what is decided upon. Power as participation in the making of decisions is an interpersonal relation. . . . What is common to all power and influence relations is only effect on policy. What is affected and on what basis are variables whose specific content in a given situation can be determined only by inquiring into the actual practices of the actors in the situation."[35] Even those who see power as potential recognize the decision-making process as that over which the powerful have the potential to exercise control.[36]

It has been pointed out that "if we can . . . define a decision as 'what officials decide' the task of locating leaders would be simple."[37] This is, in effect, what Rossi has done: a community decision is a "choice among several modes of action which is made by an authoritative person or group within the community institutions and

33C. Wright Mills, *Power, Politics, and People,* edited by Irving Louis Horowitz (New York: Oxford University Press, 1963), p. 23.

34Bertrand Russell, *Power: A New Social Analysis* (London: George Allen and Unwin, 1938), p. 25. Writers who have defined power in such a way as to include unintended effects on others are: Felix E. Oppenheim, *Dimensions of Freedom: An Analysis* (New York: St. Martin's Press, 1961), pp. 92–5; J. A. A. Van Doorn, "Sociology and the Problem of Power," *Sociologia Neerlandica,* I (Winter 1962/63), 16–18.

35Lasswell and Kaplan, *Power and Society,* pp. 75–6, 92. See also Daniel Bell, "Is There a Ruling Class in America? The Power Elite Reconsidered," in his *The End of Ideology* (New York: Collier Books, 1962), p. 70; Robert E. Agger, "Power Attributions in the Local Community," *Social Forces,* 34(4), (May 1956), 323; Hunter, *Community Power Structure,* p. 2.

36D'Antonio and Form, *Influentials,* pp. 10–11: "For us the influential is a person who is *capable* of significantly affecting the *decision-making* process of the community."

37Lasswell, Lerner, and Rothwell, *Study of Elites,* pp. 7–8.

of which the goals are the change or maintenance of community-wide institutions or facilities."[38] Unfortunately, "those who are called officials do not always make the severely sanctioned choices, and the severely sanctioned choices are not necessarily made by persons called officials." Lasswell and his associates thus distinguish between "authority," who ought to decide, and "control," who does decide.[39] In all fairness to Rossi, it should be noted that his definition is technically correct, at least in part; officials do "make" community decisions. However, the point being emphasized here is that, in some cases, to describe power relationships in this way would involve gross distortions. It is sometimes the case that decisions of community-wide import are made by persons other than officials, who then merely act to "rubber stamp" the already-arrived-at decision. Perhaps a better way to phrase it would be that in such cases the officials "announce" the decisions. There is a danger in arguing that there are "real" centers of power behind the "apparent" centers of power. This is discussed below as the "fallacy of infinite regression."

Another point of dispute in the analysis of power is its scope: "Failure to recognize that power may rest on various bases, each with a varying scope, has confused and distorted the conception of power itself, and retarded inquiry into the conditions and consequences of its exercise in various ways."[40] Insofar as power can be defined as the extent to which A can cause B to do something B would not otherwise do, scope refers to "those actions by B which are affected by A's exercise of power."[41] The determination of scope is an empirical matter resting heavily on the bases from which power is derived and the instances in which its exercise is attempted.

One rather refreshing attempt to bring some semblance of order to this field has been made by Danzger. He observes that power is often seen as a relationship in which the actor is able to get his way, in which case he has power, or is unable to get his way, in which case he has none. Instead of this, power ought to be described as the "potential available to any actor for obtaining a goal, whether or not

[38]Rossi, "Community Decision Making," p. 417.
[39]Lasswell, Lerner, and Rothwell, Study of Elites, pp. 7–8.
[40]Lasswell and Kaplan, Power and Society, p. 85.
[41]Raymond W. Wolfinger, "Reputation and Reality in the Study of Community Power," American Sociological Review, 25 (October 1960), 638.

this actor can successfully use his potential,"[42] and the situation in which an actor succeeds in carrying out his will despite resistance ought to be termed "dominance." Two elements interact to determine which actor dominates in a conflict: resources and desirability of goal. "If power is considered to be potential *ability* (rather than willingness to effect a favorable outcome, in other words, possession of the requisite means of resources—which in turn provide lines of action), then to determine power we must be able to separate this potential ability from the importance of the goal."[43] A rough but expedient way of determining importance of the goal is to postulate certain key values for different institutional orders, and then assume that for any institutional order a particular goal may be grossly classified as either salient or non-salient; and further assume that a group will extend itself to its full capacity—that is, employ all available lines of action—for salient goals, but will not do so for non-salient goals. Danzger considers two types of goals to be salient: (1) "pure" goals of a particular institutional order, for example, sacredness in religion, hegemony in politics, wealth in economics; and (2) "organizational imperatives," that is, funds, members, physical plants, etc. He then presents a paradigm relating the relative salience of the goal for each of two actors, the outcome of the conflict, and the inference as to relative amounts of power: "This paradigm permits the researcher to give weight—though only in a rough way—to the importance attached to the goal by the actors in a conflict. A separate calculation of power—i.e. lines of action or resources—is then possible."[44] Although this formulation presents many difficulties of its own, for example the determination of a criterion for goal salience and the assignment of actors to institutional orders, it would nevertheless seem to be a definite step in the direction of deliminating and clarifying power relationships.

Our own definition of power is in terms of actual behavior with

[42]Danzger, "Community Power Structure," p. 714. See the above discussion of actual and potential power.

[43]Ibid, p. 715.

[44]Ibid. pp. 715–16. For example, if a goal is salient for both A and B, the fact that one is dominant in a conflict indicates he is only somewhat more powerful. However, if a goal is salient for A but not for B, and B is dominant, it may be inferred that B is much more powerful.

intended effects, in which definition we are more or less in accord
with C. Wright Mills. We would also call attention to the fact that
power has both a supply and a demand side. Historically most
writers on power emphasized the supply side: the existence of some
people or organizations which were able to control others. Recently
it has become fashionable to emphasize the demand side: the requirement of all societies, or organizations, if they are to continue
to exist, to have some means of ordering the relations of men to
achieve at least minimal needs. Just as in economics, where supply
determines price in the short run and demand determines it in the
long run, so the characteristics and techniques of the power elites determine the actualities of power in the short run, but the basic culture
and social structure of a society determine the actualities in the long
run. Both the short run and the long run are important, as each ac-
commodates to the other. In this book we are concerned with the
actualities of power as it exists in both the short run and the long
run, but only in the United States in the years since 1932. In speaking
of the actualities we do not intend to take a strictly behavioristic
position; subjective images and expectations have an influence on and
are part of those actualities (just as they are in the economic pricing
process).

We begin an analysis of power where we believe it is most concentrated—in politics.

B. Power Implications of American Political Structure

Some aspects of the political-governmental complex of power are
very well understood by the American people, while other aspects
are little understood. The formal structure of government, the voting
process, parts of the political campaign, the political alignments of
individuals and groups are explained in secondary school courses
and in this and many other ways they become part of the average
adult's personal experience. But the informal structure and processes
of political parties, the relationship of candidates to political parties,
and the pressures on and motivations of politicians are unfamiliar to
the great majority of the American people. Even educated people—
if they have not taken college courses in "Political Parties" or "Prac-

tical Politics" or have not actively participated in politics—know little about these aspects of politics.[45] This widespread public ignorance plays its role in the ongoing processes of politics, and contributes to popular ideas that there are conspiracies of one sort or another behind political actions or organizations.

While there are a few excellent textbooks and monographs on informal political processes, there is a relative dearth of such literature, when we consider the public interest in politics and its importance in American life. Autobiographical materials written by practicing politicians are surprisingly sparse, perhaps partly because politicians are too busy with their official duties and maintaining themselves in office, perhaps partly because they are unwilling to give away their "trade secrets" or fearful of revealing their own weaknesses and those of their fellow politicians, but also perhaps partly because most politicians believe that the public is so committed to stereotypes that it would not accept an honest analysis by a practicing politician. Partisan attacks for campaign purposes offer some factual information about what goes on in politics; however, they are deficient in that they are one-sided in the partisan sense and in that they are selective, showing only what the attacking politician feels will appeal to the voting public. Only recently have there been published bodies of case materials intended to describe objectively political events and processes.[46]

Most important in preventing the public from becoming fully aware of significant informal aspects of structure and process in politics are stereotypes held by the public itself—and we continue to include the educated layman in our reference to the "public." The public's attention to politics is limited to specialized interests of a group or individual character, and to campaign conflicts which gain public interest in the same way that competitive sports or any other

[45]The traditional emphasis in political science on formal structure and political philosophy, and the modern emphasis on "political behavior" in the sense of voting behavior and other aspects of the psychology of political participation, both neglect the informal aspects of political structure and process with which we are here concerned.

[46]Such as the Eagleton Foundation Series, *Case Studies in Practical Politics*, published seriatim by Henry Holt and Company; and a study edited by Alan F. Westin, *The Uses of Power* (New York: Harcourt, Brace and World, 1962). In citing these, we do not mean to say they are adequate scientific portrayals, but merely that they deal with neglected areas of politics.

conflict spectacles do. These things the public understands well enough. But the processes by which a politician achieves and maintains public office is of little interest to either the average or the educated citizen; yet these processes give the politician the practical knowledge of his constituency which informs him as to which pressures he must accede to if he is to remain in office, and, which pressures he can give a polite brush-off to. The motivations for the public's ignorance and lack of interest in these latter processes deserve to be studied, but—except for a few general remarks—we shall not go into them here. We shall be concerned only with the areas of ignorance themselves and some of their effects on the political process, not with their causes.

The huge amount of coverage devoted to politics by the mass media might give the average citizen the feeling he knows what is going on. Yet the newspapers and other mass media give the public what they think will interest it (or occasionally what they, from a selfish point of view, want the public to know). The politicians themselves are constantly concerned with their "image" in the eyes of their constituencies or their hoped-for constituencies, and give out only information that will enhance that "image." The gaps in public information regarding politics and government thus remain unfilled, and the public stereotypes in these areas are not challenged. Let me suggest what I believe are a few of the important facts about politics not widely understood by the public:

1. The state and local parties are voluntary associations that usually accept into membership all voting citizens who consider themselves members of the party. While it is true that in many states the parties are largely run by small executive committees, the ordinary party member can nearly always gain some influence in the making of his party's decisions and in voting for members of the executive committee. By these means, and because of his access to elected politicians and his services to these politicians, such a self-selected party member has the strongest long-run influence on the politicians—much more than the pressure-group member who importunes the politician on a single issue and does nothing for him but give a campaign contribution now and then.

2. Every elected politician relies on the party organizations, or on

"personal organizations" also largely made up of volunteers, to do several things for him: help get out the vote, which (hopefully) will be largely partisan for him; do the dozens of chores which are part of every political campaign and which get him more votes than the usually "non-partisan" pressure group "endorsement" or than the average campaign contribution; serve as a counterbalance to the numerous special-interest pressure groups (political group pressures are much broader in interest—being community-wide and occasionally even ideological in terms of the party platform).

3. The national party organizations made up of the elected representatives of the state party organizations are very weak in the United States. As a report prepared for the Brookings Institution pointed out, ". . . state party organizations are far more autonomous than state governments. They are united in a national party by rules and customs far less definitely federal than those that unite the states in a national government. Accordingly, a national party convention takes on some of the characteristics of an international conference of delegations from sovereign nations, some of which may be democracies, others autocracies of one sort or another."[47] Congressmen rely directly on their personal organizations and on the district, local, and state party organizations; incumbent presidents use their administrations as their personal political organizations;[48] aspiring presidential candidates have to build up personal organizations and make use of the state party organizations. Thus the national political parties—whose leaders are often quoted and which are often assumed to be centers of power—are in fact almost powerless and functionless, except when they are transformed once every four years and take on the vital and powerful function of nominating a candidate for president.

4. Because of the vital functions of the state and local and personal political organizations, every elected office holder must avoid offending their members, even though they represent a tiny minority of the voting public, at the same time as he tries to create a favorable

[47]Paul T. David, Ralph M. Goldman, and Richard C. Bain, *The Politics of National Party Conventions* (Washington, D.C.: The Brookings Institution, 1960), p. 2.

[48]This is one reason why presidential compaign managers are generally appointed to the cabinet: Farley to Roosevelt's, Hannigan to Truman's, Brownell and Summerfield to Eisenhower's, and Robert Kennedy to Kennedy's.

public "image" both among the special-interest groups and among the unorganized masses.[49] This situation often creates a role conflict of some intensity for some politicians: the party members expect the politicians to be loyal to their party and to its platform, but the pressure groups want the politician to serve their interests, and the public hopes he will be "above politics."

5. Because of the distinction between party organizations and personal organizations, there is also some distinction regarding position on issues between members of a party in the Congress or legislature and the party itself as a voluntary association.[50] There is complete coincidence between these two only in regard to what is known as "organization of the legislature"—that is, the legislators from each of the regular parties (parties as voluntary associations) vote at the beginning of every session for their "leaders," and vote to determine which party shall be designated as majority party or minority party for committee assignments. After that, each legislator may deviate from the "party line," or the party platform, not only insofar as the wishes of his constituency vary from the party line but also insofar as he has a strong personal organization which differs in its position from that of the party organization. This is not to say that party-as-association is not an important factor in determining how a legislator votes. It appears to be, in fact, often the most important influence on his voting, but this is because his personal organization tends to be weak and because his constituency is not organized or usually articulate.[51] An elected officeholder wants to build up a personal organization because it will be more loyal to him than a party organization (which has many public officials to be concerned about) and because it will increase his independence of pressure

[49]This is not only a difficult political problem but an important constitutional one; less so, to be sure, in America, with its weak parties, than in most other democracies. The officeholder must ask himself, "To whom am I responsible; my party or the electorate?" Students of representative government agree that, in the final analysis, the legislator must be responsible to the public, but they would also recognize that party members do and should receive special consideration. See Robert McKenzie, *British Political Parties* (London: William Heinemann Ltd., 1955), esp. p. 583; and Avery Leiserson, *Parties and Politics* (New York: Knopf, 1958), pp. 208–9 and 213–15.

[50]V. O. Key, Jr., *Politics, Parties, and Pressure Groups* (New York: Thomas Y. Crowell, 1958), pp. 703, 367–8.

[51]Julius Turner, *Party and Constituency: Pressures on Congress* (Baltimore: The Johns Hopkins Press, 1951), p. 23.

groups. But he may not be capable of building a personal organization, especially when his local party is strong. In most states, an elective politician needs the party's endorsement at least the first time he runs, because the endorsement gains him the votes of a number of loyal rank-and-file voters.[52] Contrary to the public impression and to the opinion of many pressure groups, elected officials do not take pressure groups too seriously: The pressure groups are really too little concerned with politics and elections, and their resources to reward or punish the official are too meager for him to be worried about most of the time. The elected official who is backed by an effective party or personal organization is fairly free to make his own choices, within the framework of the "party line."

We shall now consider some aspects of national political power that arise out of the foregoing basic facts about informal political structure regardless of whether the public understands them or not. These are not listed in any special order, but all have the effect of limiting the influence of pressure groups—including those of the economic elite—on government.

1. There is often a cleavage, sometimes quite deep, between a state party's representatives in Congress and its representatives in the state administration and legislature. This is not only because one group is oriented toward national issues while the other is oriented toward state issues, but also because the former are physically removed from the state political party and are more likely to have built up a personal political organization to substitute for it.

2. Hundreds of thousands of volunteers and lowly paid personnel who work in a presidential campaign cannot be rewarded materially after the election in most cases. The victorious candidate can reward a small proportion of them with patronage jobs—these numbered about 4000 for the incoming Kennedy Administration in 1961.[53] The President, however, has two motives for not simply passing

---

[52] In 1961 in New Jersey, however, the Republican senator (Clifford P. Case) and most of the Republican congressmen broke from the state party organization to put up their own candidate for governor (James P. Mitchell, former United States Secretary of Labor). Apparently they did so because the regular party organization's candidates had been defeated since 1953. Mitchell won a bitterly fought primary but lost in the equally difficult general election.

[53] *The New York Times*, February 20, 1961, p. 1.

these jobs out among those persons who worked the hardest for his election, even though such persons might again be his best campaign workers in the next election three and a half years thence: Many of the jobs are policy-making positions, for which the President wishes to hire capable and experienced men so as to run an effective administration; The President wishes to get a program through Congress, and one of his pressures on congressmen is to reward them with the power to nominate for federal appointments. Also, the Senate must confirm all major appointments and there is an informal rule in the Senate that a nominee who is "personally obnoxious" to the senator(s) from his home state who is (are) of the same party as the President will not get the appointment (at least if it is below cabinet level). Thus there are diverse factors affecting the dispensation of patronage, and usually the congressmen (especially the senators) of the same party as the President are a very strong influence. The main point, however, is that even the President does not have much high-level patronage to dispense; most of his campaign workers have to be volunteers whose only reward is having a President who comes at least close to supporting their ideological position on issues. The President must usually bow to such influence, if he is not already personally inclined to do so.

3. Committee posts in the Congress are allocated according to seniority. This means that congressmen who face the least opposition in their re-election campaigns, and hence are re-elected again and again, get the most powerful positions. Generally, this also means that committee leadership in the Democratic party tends to be held by Southerners, and in the Republican party by Congressmen from the Midwest and New England, even though these groups practically never form a majority within their respective parties. An example may be seen in the 1963 Congress: In the House of Representatives, 12 of the 21 standing and special committee chairmanships went to Southerners, and in the Senate 11 of the 18 chairmanships went to Southerners.

4. The presidency is so powerful an office that both major parties put a great deal of effort into gaining it for their side. The successful party is usually the one which can gain the support of the largest number of marginal groups and of independent voters. The presidential election thus gives a centripetal influence to the parties—that

is, it pulls them ideologically toward the "center." Yet the most active and committed party members and workers are generally those with an ideology, which is usually to the "right" or "left" rather than the center.[54] Outside the South, the Democratic party tends to pull its elected officials to the left, and the Republican party to the right. Thus the parties tend to act as centrifugal forces, and a strain tends to develop between them and their presidential candidates, especially when the candidate offers himself for the first time.

5. A "center" position in national politics has the best prospects of appealing to the largest number of voters.[55] When the Republicans control the center, they have a better chance of controlling the presidency and putting across their program. When the Democrats control the center, they also have a better chance of controlling the presidency and putting across their program. But the chances of controlling the center are largely a function of the distribution of ideological positions within the party, and the party with the widest range away from center has the poorest chance of controlling the center. At the present time, in the 1960's, this is the Republican party. The leadership of the Republican party is more to the right of its rank-and-file voters than the Democratic leadership is to the left of its rank-and-file voters.[56] The Republican rank-and-file voters are, in fact, closer to the views of the Democratic leaders than to

---

[54]The ideological difference between party leaders and the average voters for the respective parties is demonstrated in a study by Herbert McClosky, Paul J. Hoffmann, and Rosemary O'Hara, "Issue Conflict and Consensus Among Party Leaders and Followers," *American Political Science Review* LIV (June 1960), 406-27.

[55]". . . in politics—as in chess—the man who holds the center holds a position of almost unbeatable strength." Arthur Larson, *A Republican Looks at His Party* (New York: Harper, 1956), p. 19.

[56]McClosky, Hoffman, and O'Hara, "Issue Conflict and Consensus." The findings of this study for the Republican party are confirmed in a series of polls published independently in November 1961. A Washington newsletter, *Human Events*, polled the Republican delegates and alternates to the 1960 convention as to their preferences for the 1964 candidate for President. Replies were received from about half, and showed Goldwater in the lead with 49.3 per cent of the votes, Nixon with 28.1 per cent, Rockefeller with 16.3 per cent, and "Others" or "Undecided" with 6.3 per cent. (*Minneapolis Sunday Tribune*, November 5, 1961, p. 16B.) On the same day, a Gallup poll reported the choice for 1964 among Republican rank-and-file voters across the nation (the choice offered was between Goldwater and Rockefeller). The results were 51 per cent for Rockefeller, 33 per cent for Goldwater, and 16 per cent undecided (*Minneapolis Sunday Tribune*, November 5, 1961, p. 12A). Thus the delegates and alternates were shown to be clearly more conservative than the rank-and-file Republican voters.

those of the Republican leaders. If a party despairs of winning the presidency in the next election, as the Republican party showed signs of doing in 1961 and 1962, it reduces the power of the centripetal force that results from a strong effort to win the presidency. Thus the Republican party was pulled by its active members more and more to the right. This development not only abandoned the powerful center position to the Kennedy-Johnson Administrations,[57] but it threatened to split the party: If the Republican party takes a consistently rightist position on all major issues, the center Republicans will no longer be able to maintain their affiliation with the party. Thus the pull of the Republican party to the right—developing out of the greater activity of the conservative wing, the possibility of gaining support from conservative sections of the South and the abandonment of a serious race for the presidency in 1964—seriously threatens the unity of the party. Since Franklin Delano Roosevelt's tenure, a similar danger has threatened the Democratic party, but this has now been diminished by the party's pre-emption of the center, by the expansion and growth of the party in the West (which has gradually diminished the relative strength of Southerners in the party), and by the movement of some Southern Democrats toward the dominant Northern position in the party on many issues (though mainly excluding civil rights). For the Republican party to win the presidency, its candidate must at least appear to be considerably to the "left" of the party. Insofar as the apparent growth of the Republican party's conservative wing prevents such a candidate from gaining the nomination, the Republicans cannot realistically hope to gain the presidency, and they disrupt the traditional system of each party seeking to control the center.

6. Despite this weakness in the Republican party, it has enjoyed considerable success in measures facing the Congress by virtue of its occasional coalition with Southern Democrats. While many of the latter find their ideological position closer to that of the majority of the Republican party than to that of the majority of their own party, this is only one basis of the coalition of Southern Democrats with Republicans in Congress. The main basis of the coalition is that the

[57]Cf. Walter Lippmann, Syndicated column, *Minneapolis Morning Tribune*, February 4, 1961, p. 4.

Republicans offer the Southerners support against civil rights or other bills favoring Negroes, and in return get Southern support for a certain proportion of their own measures. In the 1961–62 session of Congress, Representative Howard W. Smith (D., Va.)—the leader of the Southern Democratic section of the coalition in the House— could count on at least 40 or 50 of the 99 Democrats from the 11 states of the old Confederacy to join the coalition on most key votes.[58] If all 176 Republicans voted against a liberal bill—which did not always occur—they needed only 43 Southern Democratic votes to prevent its passage. The coalition was not quite as effective in the Senate because of the larger proportion of liberal Republicans in that body. For that 1961 session, a *Congressional Quarterly* report shows that the two factions joined forces on more than 25 per cent of the roll call votes and that the coalition was victorious on 53 per cent of the roll calls it contested. The coalition was more active in that year than in any since 1957, although it was still not the most important political force. It has become smaller since the late 1940's because of the change in Southern Democratic representation and because of President Kennedy's and President Johnson's leadership. This analysis indicates two things: civil rights issues—on which the Southerners take their most vigorous positions in opposition—play a crucial role in dividing the Democratic party and hence in determining the outcome of many congressional votes on other issues; and the coalition operates successfully only occasionally, so that the Democratic party is more cohesive than is generally assumed. If civil rights declines as a legislative issue, and as the Southern states develop a two-party system with the majority of the adults voting, as is now rapidly occurring, the coalition will decline and disappear. By 1964, President Johnson was almost able to render the coalition ineffective, and the Eighty-ninth Congress passed more liberal legislation than did any of its predecessors.

7. The two-party system, despite the divergences that exist within each party, is the dominant fact of American political life. Many political scientists, especially E. E. Schattschneider,[59] have argued convincingly that this is basically due to certain formal constitutional

---

58 *The New York Times*, November 21, 1960, p. 1.
59 *Party Government* (New York: Rinehart, 1942), esp. pp. 65–98.

provisions for voting in the United States: (a) The independent election of the executive (president, governor, mayor) from a constituency of the whole (nation, state, city), and the strong powers given to the executive. This is in contrast to parliamentary systems where the legislature elects the executive and accords him whatever power he has to lead them. In the American system, groups and factions thus feel a need to coalesce to produce the majority of votes needed to elect a chief executive: (b) The election of each legislator by a plurality vote in a single-member district, rather than some form of proportional representation. The latter system, used in many countries outside the United States permits minority parties to pool scattered votes from the whole country or large districts to gain continuous, if small, representation in the legislature. In the American system of voting, the voter will usually be confronted with only two candidates who have any chance of getting elected.

There is probably also a third factor which permits the United States to have a two-party system, and this is more a matter of general culture and social structure than of formal constitutional provisions. This is the fractionization of the American public along many interest lines in addition to class and ideology.[60] The domination of class and class ideology in Europe is such as to divide people sharply along those lines which are specifically relevant to politics. The relatively diversified interests and loyalties of Americans reduce their concerns about politics and help them to compromise their political differences. From a different angle, Lipset makes this same point very well in reference to the working class: "The failure of Canada and the United States to develop a major working-class party, and the relative stability of their democratic systems, may be partially explained by the difficulty of developing a working-class political consciousness where no rigid status groups already exist to create a perception of community. On the European continent, workers were placed in a common class by the value system of the society, and absorbed a political "consciousness of kind" from the

[60]I have sought to explain this relative fractionization in my studies of voluntary associations in the United States, France, and Italy. See *Theory and Method in the Social Sciences* (Minneapolis: University of Minnesota Press, 1954), ch. 3, 4; and "On Individualism and Social Responsibility," *European Journal of Sociology*, II (Summer 1961), 163–9.

social structure. Marxists did not have to teach European workers that they formed a class; the ascriptive values of the society did it for them."[61]

8. There are various devices to thwart democratic political processes in the United States. Among these are:

(a) The failure to redistrict in accord with population changes. This is most serious at the level of the state legislature, where the disparity between the largest and smallest district has run as great as 873 to 1 (in Vermont's lower house, which had not been redistricted since 1793 until the Supreme Court decision of 1962 forced a redistricting.)[62] The effect of the failure to redistrict is to give disproportionate power to the people of farms and villages, at the expense of those of the cities and suburbs.

(b) The use of so-called "non-partisan" ballots, in many cities and in two states (Minnesota and Nebraska). Under this system, candidates run without party designation on the ballot, any number of candidates can run in the primary election, and the two who gain the most votes in the primary run in the general election. This system helps office-holders to camouflage their political and ideological

[61]Seymour Martin Lipset, "Party Systems and the Representation of Social Groups," *European Journal of Sociology*, I (1960), 8. Lipset also gives considerable emphasis to the primary elections in maintaining a two-party system. I do not agree, as there can be other means within a democracy through which factions within a party can contend. Only where there is the List system of voting is the dominant group within a party given a permanent advantage, and thus minority factions are encouraged to break off and form a new party. The United States had a two-party system before it adopted primaries, and it could again abandon primaries in favor of open-party endorsement and still maintain the two-party system. In other words, it is proportional representation, especially under the List system, which encourages a multi-party system in Europe, not the absence of primaries. Incidentally, as Lipset himself points out, France has the equivalent of a primary with its two-ballot system, and yet also has a multi-party system. For a thoughtful discussion of why the United States has a two-party system, see Key, *Politics, Parties*, pp. 224–31.

[62]In March 1962 the United States Supreme Court in the case of *Baker v. Carr*, reversed itself to insist that a state legislature redistrict itself. The consequences of this decision will be tremendous as far as urban-rural representation in state legislatures and Congress are concerned. By the end of 1962, legal action was initiated in at least 35 states to force redistricting; and in 14 of these states the court actions were favorable to redistricting while in 5 states the rural interests won at least a delay. On June 15, 1964, the Supreme Court expanded its ruling, in the case of *Reynolds v. Sims*, to prohibit legislatures from districting one house on the basis of geography rather than population. Efforts to get a constitutional amendment to reverse this were turned back in Congress in 1965 and 1966.

affiliations and even their voting records,[63] and it weakens the political party as a balance to special-interest pressure groups.[64] The candidate who can fool the largest number of voters with a false image of his party identification is usually a conservative, because poorly educated voters are the ones who can most readily be fooled and because they tend to vote liberal when they are informed. Hence, the effect of being able to fool a portion of the voters by means of "non-partisan" ballot is to give disproportionate power to economic pressure groups and to increase the likelihood of conservative control of the non-partisan legislature.[65]

(c) Efforts, especially in machine-dominated states and cities, to restrict party membership to a chosen following loyal to the political leaders.[66] If this policy is too rigid, however, opposition elements can and do organize rival political caucuses and run candidates in the primaries in opposition to the regular party organizations. This happened in the Democratic party in New York after 1960. Until such an opposition is formed, however, the effect of a closed party membership is to give disproportionate power to existing political leaders.

9. While parties seek to piece together a majority, it is easier to manage a small majority than a large one. If a party's majority becomes large, the following disruptive tendencies are likely to occur, according to Schattschneider:[67] Internal disunity develops, and factions break off to test the power of the dominant group. Too many interest groups have claims on the party, and "it is more profitable to share a victory with a narrow majority than it is to partake of

[63]This has been demonstrated in the study of Oliver P. Williams and Charles R. Adrian, "The Insulation of Local Politics Under the Nonpartisan Ballot," *American Political Science Review*, 53 (December 1959), 1052–1063.

[64]This is the conclusion of the report of the Minnesota League of Women Voters, "The Missing Link in Minnesota Government" (Mimeographed, January 1960). The classic statement about the role of the political party as a balance to the special-interest pressure groups is that of Schattschneider, *Party Government*, pp. 191–6.

[65]Arthur Naftalin, "The Failure of the Farmer-Labor Party To Capture the Minnesota Legislature," *American Political Science Review*, 38 (February–March 1944), pp. 71–8.

[66]Reichley demonstrates how this is done in Philadelphia: James Reichley, *The Art of Government: Reform and Organization Politics in Philadelphia* (New York: Fund for the Republic, 1959), pp. 52–3.

[67]*Party Government*, pp. 95–96.

the spoils of victory with a larger number, for the smaller the number of participants the greater will be the share of each." "Interests participating in the venture, but insufficiently rewarded by the victory, may decide to make a more advantageous bargain with the opposition party." For all three reasons, the major American parties hardly ever can or particularly care to claim too many more than a majority of the votes at a general election.

10. In the continual process of seeking to form a majority, each major political party gradually shifts its leading themes, its unifying philosophy, and its "center of gravity" (which is defined as the weighted average of the liberalism-conservatism of its constituent groups). Political parties are among the institutions most adjustive to social forces and social change; if they don't adjust, they decline, because they are tested at every election. Since the 1930's, the Democratic party has been, relatively speaking, the liberal party, except for some of its Southern representatives; the Republican party has been the conservative party, except for some of its East Coast representatives. This division is largely in terms of domestic issues,[68] although it spills over into foreign policy issues when the latter affect matters of spending and taxation, such as foreign aid to underdeveloped countries. The usual domination of domestic considerations over foreign policy considerations in all but the presidential elections gives the Democratic party an advantage, for its tendency to formulate new programs to deal with new domestic problems seems to appeal to the marginal voters whose vote is not determined either by party loyalty or by personality factors. In the presidential elections, the parties have more equal strength because foreign policy issues carry at least equal weight with domestic issues. Republican presidential candidates are likely to gain strength when they emphasize foreign policy issues; Democratic presidential candidates gain strength when they emphasize domestic issues. This seemed to be evident in the Kennedy-Nixon campaign of 1960. It gets minor support from a Gallup poll published in March 1962:[69] While 72

[68]I am not claiming that issues are uppermost in the voters' decision as to which candidate they should vote for. I agree with the political scientists who observe that "traditional voting," "getting out the vote," "personality appeal," "name recognition" and other non-issue factors are dominant. But I do believe that a minority of voters—which often are the marginal group that decides the outcome of an election—are swayed by parties' or candidates' stands on issues.

[69]*Minneapolis Morning Tribune*, March 2, 1962, p. 31.

per cent of the public approved President Kennedy's handling of domestic problems, only 67 per cent approved his handling of foreign policy—despite the fact that the President was devoting the major share of his attention to foreign affairs.

11. There have been revolutionary movements in the United States since the country began, and one of them broke out into one of the bloodiest civil wars known in history until that time. At the beginning of the "Cold War" in the late 1940's, the country once more entered a period of deep internal cleavage. The "leftist" American revolutionaries were demoralized by events in the Soviet Union—a nation they had previously taken as an ideal—and they were further weakened by a combination of economic prosperity—which reduced the popular dissatisfactions from which they formerly drew recruits, and by police powers exerted against them by the government. With the escalation of the unpopular war in Vietnam in 1964, and the frustrations faced by some of those involved in the movement for minority civil rights, the seedbed is perhaps being laid for a revitalized leftist revolutionary movement in the United States.

But the main immediate internal threat to the stability of constitutional American government has come from a "rightist" revolutionary movement.[70] While this threat can also trace its roots back into the nineteenth century, since 1948 it has attained a vigor and organization that makes it a serious one. It calls itself "conservative," and it has indeed attracted a conservative wing, but most of it is revolutionary with the most radical goals for social change. These revolutionaries constitute, at the maximum, 5 per cent of the adult population, but they have organized for effective political action, and even for some paramilitary operations. From about 1950 until the assassination of President Kennedy in 1963, they had the complete co-operation and alliance of most of the conservative leaders of the United States. It was a conservative Vice-President (Richard Nixon) and Attorney General (Herbert Brownell) who implied that ex-President Harry Truman and former Secretary of State Dean Acheson were traitors, and it was the conservative leader of the American Medical Association who called a mild welfare measure

---

[70]Among the leading studies of right-wing extremism in the United States are: Richard Hofstadter, *The Paranoid Style in American Politics* (New York: Knopf, 1965); J. Allen Broyles, *The John Birch Society* (Boston: Beacon, 1964); Daniel Bell (ed). *The Radical Right* (Garden City, N.Y.: Doubleday, 1963).

to provide some hospital care for elderly sick people "socialism that will inevitably lead to Communism." Some business leaders sought to end two decades of "controlled conflict" in their relations with a now bureaucratic labor movement by starting an all-out attack on the basis of union security itself. But most of these conservatives drew back from following the rightist revolutionaries after President Johnson began to put into operation his "consensus" strategy in 1964, and after they saw the Republican national convention in 1964 come under the control of the revolutionary element. Some conservatives—like Senator Karl Mundt (R., S.D.) and Senator Everett Dirksen (R., Ill.)—found themselves under almost as vigorous an attack from the rightist revolutionaries as the liberals were, and this also weakened their opportunistic alliance with them.

But the rightist revolutionaries remain just as vigorous and powerful as they were in 1953, when Senator Joseph McCarthy (R., Wis.) was their spokesman, or in early 1964, when they captured the machinery of the Republican party in most states outside the East. Their ideology is centered on a conspiratorial view of American history and American political power which differs only in minor details from that of the communists, or of the Populists of an earlier generation: The economic elite and the political elite of both parties are joined in a conspiracy to betray the interests and ideas of the great mass of Americans. This sharing of an almost identical conspiratorial view of power and of a common enemy between the extreme right and the extreme left in the United States, despite the fact that they consider each other the ultimate of enemies, suggests that an understanding of their movements must require deep psychological and sociological analysis rather than merely a rational analysis of what they say. But aside from analysis and interpretation, both the extreme right and the extreme left are increasingly posing a threat to the very existence of an orderly society. Neither of them are strong enough or have enough of a positive program to take over the government and run it, but if they acquire a few more supporters, both of them will have the possibility of destroying the existing democratic and constitutional structure of the United States. An extremely heterogeneous society, held together by compromises of diverse group interests, cannot continue to exist if a large proportion of its politically effective members refuse to compromise.

As long as the rightist revolutionaries have a partial control over the Republican party and neither extremist group has any control over the Democratic party, the chance of the Republican party to win elections is reduced. Insofar as the economic elite have chosen to work within the Republican party, their influence on government is thereby reduced.

The facts of political structure we have just reviewed are the main ones taken into consideration by elective officeholders. They must act in accord with these facts in order to be elected or re-elected —in other words, to have political power. None of them relate to any practical way by means of which pressure groups can influence the elective officeholders. In fact, some of these factors—particularly the party and personal political organizations—reduce the influence which pressure groups might have on a democratic government where parties and personal organizations play little role (as in some of the local non-partisan elections). Our analysis of political structure leads us to believe that pressure groups are not the dominant factor in American governmental decision-making[71] although—for reasons to be analyzed in chapters III and XIII—they are an important factor. Some of the factors we have considered here—particularly the rise of right-wing extremists in recent years and their seizure of the machinery of the Republican party in many states—especially reduce the influence of businessmen (the economic elite) as a pressure group. Politicians do not volunteer these interpretations: they are not likely to brag about their freedom to make decisions in accord with party ideology and their purely personal predilections, they are rarely impolite enough to tell anyone who importunes them that they are paying little attention to him, and they feel whatever pressure there is to be real enough. We are here not speaking of the "bought" legislator or the legislator whose personal ideology is fully in accord with that of the economic elite; these will be discussed in a later section. But we conclude that for the majority of elective officials, political considerations of the order we have considered thus far in this chapter necessarily limit any influence on them which comes from an economic elite or from any other pressure group.

[71]This conclusion was also arrived at—using other considerations—by Raymond A. Bauer, Ithiel de S. Pool, and Lewis A. Dexter, *American Business and Public Policy* (New York: Atherton, 1963).

C. Pressure Groups and Lobbyists

The ways in which an economic elite can dominate government are by electing its "own men" to government positions, or by using various influence and pressure tactics successfully on officeholders. The latter techniques are discussed in the next chapter. The net effect of both methods taken together can be ascertained by studies of politicians' behavior and attitudes with regard to special interest groups, not only by the extent to which they specifically favor them but also by the scope which they allow for government action affecting their interests. This is the topic of the present section, and we shall approach it in several ways.

An important study of sources of federal legislation is that by Lawrence Chamberlain.[72] Selecting 90 major bills that became law from 1882 to 1940, Chamberlain traces their origins and development and seeks to assign credit for their final passage. He found that presidential influence was preponderant in 19 instances, congressional in 35 cases, joint presidential-congressional collaboration in 29 cases, while pressure groups could be said to be responsible for only 7. Chamberlain found that presidential effort was of increasing importance in the latter part of the period he studied, and we would guess that this trend has continued since 1940, when Chamberlain closed his study, except for periods when the President has adopted a hands-off policy (as during major portions of the Eisenhower presidency).

A different but equally significant research approach is that by Wahlke, Buchanan, Eulau and Ferguson.[73] They interviewed practically all (474) legislators in four states during the 1957 legislative sessions to ascertain their role orientations toward pressure groups and their agents. On the basis of answers to a series of questions, they classified the legislators into three categories: (1) "Facilitators," who have a friendly attitude toward pressure group activity and relatively much knowledge about it: (2) "Resisters," who have a hostile attitude toward pressure group activity and relatively much knowledge about it; (3) "Neutrals," who have no strong attitude toward,

[72]*The President, Congress, and Legislation* (New York: Columbia University Press, 1946).
[73]John C. Wahlke, William Buchanan, Heinz Eulau, and LeRoy C. Ferguson, "American State Legislators' Role Orientations toward Pressure Groups," *Journal of Politics*, 22 (May 1960), 203–27.

or very little knowledge about, pressure group activity, or both. For the four states (California, New Jersey, Ohio, and Tennessee) taken together, 37 per cent of the legislators were classified as Facilitators, 37 per cent were classified as Neutrals, and 26 per cent were classified as Resisters. In terms of behavior, Facilitators were more inclined than the others to gain the aid of lobbyists in drafting bills and in lining up support for bills. The legislators were also classified as to their economic-interest inclination. It appeared that the pro-business legislators were about equally divided into the afore-mentioned three categories of role-orientation toward pressure groups; the pro-labor legislators tended to be Resisters; those legislators who were neutral as far as economic interests are concerned were the ones most likely to be Facilitators. Thus, while a majority of the legislators were found to be pro-business, the Facilitative legislator who is friendliest to pressure groups tends to be the one who is above or outside group conflicts and defines his role to include the accommodation of group demands.

A study of business representatives in Washington by the Brookings Institution indicated that company officials often had a narrow view of the role of this agent.[74] They regarded him as a mere salesman (of the company's product to the administrators, and of the company's point of view to the legislators or other rule-makers); they seldom asked his advice in formulating the company's point of view on a legislative or other policy matter; they seldom formulated points of view toward broad issues where the company's interest was only tangential (for example, on welfare or even labor legislation—this was left to the Chamber of Commerce or the National Association of Manufacturers, of which they were likely to be members); they rarely offered to help in the lobbying back home, with the friends of the congressmen. In other words, the top company officials tended to regard the company representative in Washington as just another staff member, not as a key element in some "power" they were supposed to exercise in Washington. All these attitudes reduce somewhat the effectiveness of the Washington representative. Occasionally the top company officials themselves came to Washington if the mission were deemed important enough to the company. Of the

[74]Paul W. Cherington and Ralph L. Gillen, *The Business Representative in Washington* (Washington, D.C.: The Brookings Institution, 1962).

200 largest manufacturing concerns, almost 130 maintain full-time Washington representatives. A number of relatively small companies also have Washington offices.

Perhaps the most comprehensive study of national lobbyists is that by Lester W. Milbrath.[75] In addition to providing much information on their sponsors, their characteristics, and their interests, he presents descriptions of their manner of operation. In general, the picture he offers of the lobbyists' approach is that of the "soft-sell." Lobbyists offer congressmen information and do small favors for them rather than argue with them or threaten them with reprisals at the next election. Their contributions to campaign funds are made most circumspectly. Milbrath quotes one lobbyist as typical:

> Every once in a while people in Congress whom we respect get into difficulty during an election and need money. In such a situation we will generally contact our members in the district and ask them to contribute. We also ask each of them to call five other people and try to get them to contribute. We start the ball rolling and then we walk away from it. In most cases the Member does not even know we have gone in to help him. (Why don't you tell him?) We feel he might be embarrassed and we don't want to embarrass him. Generally, we feel that we are in a stronger position if he is not embarrassed. If he gets the impression that whenever we come down to talk to him that we are trying to take advantage of the $2,000 we put into his campaign, he is going to say to us, "Well, you can't own me just because you gave me $2,000," and probably in the long run we would lose more than we would gain by this kind of activity.[76]

In general, campaign contributions are likely to be given to those candidates who already have an outlook favorable to the lobbyists' interests, not to candidates who can be persuaded to vote in a certain way in return for campaign contributions. Much of the work of the Washington business lobbyists has been to try to dissuade congressmen from voting for bills that may hurt their employers' interest, rather than to get congressmen to support the bills that will aid their employers.[77] Thus the record of the National Association of Manu-

---

[75]*The Washington Lobbyists* (Chicago: Rand-McNally, 1963).
[76]Ibid. p. 86.
[77]David B. Truman, *The Governmental Process* (New York: Knopf, 1951), pp. 80, 251.

facturers over fifteen years has been largely a history of successive defensive retreats: witness its ineffective opposition to the Social Security Act, the Securities Exchange Act, the Reciprocal Trade Agreements Act, the Public Utility Holding Company Act, and others. The weakness of the National Association of Manufacturers is further illustrated by the dominant, though largely implicit, assumption underlying most of its propaganda, that the limits upon "business" leadership are due to public "ignorance" or to "false propaganda," which need only "correction" in order to be reversed.[78]

Most of the other studies of lobbying fall into three categories: (1) Descriptions of all the events leading up to the passage (or failure) of a single piece of legislation. Examples are Stephen K. Bailey, *Congress Makes a Law: The Story Behind the Employment Act of 1946*; Earl K. Latham, *The Group Basis of Politics: A Study of Basing Point Legislation* (1965); and some of the case studies in the Inter-University Case Series Program. (2) More general description of the process by which bills are passed, including analyses of the role of the lobbyists. Major studies here are: E. Pendleton Herring, *Group Representation Before Congress* (1929); E. E. Schattschneider, *Politics, Pressures and the Tariff* (1935); B. Zeller, *Pressure Politics in New York* (1937); D. D. McKean, *Pressures on the Legislature of New Jersey* (1938); D. C. Blaisdell, *Economic Power and Political Pressures*, T.N.E.C. monograph no. 6 (1941); Bertram Gross, *The Legislative Struggle* (1953); Dorothy C. Tompkins, *Congressional Investigation of Lobbies* (1956); Donald C. Blaisdell, *American Democracy Under Pressure* (1957); Roland Young, *The American Congress* (1957); Bernard C. Cohen, *The Influence of Non-Governmental Groups on Foreign Policy Making* (1959); Raymond A. Bauer, Ithiel de S. Pool, and Lewis A. Dexter, *American Business and Public Policy* (1963). (3) Descriptions of special interest groups which maintain lobbies in Washington. To be noted here are: Harwood L. Childs, *Labor and Capital in National Politics* (1930); Andrew Hacker, *Politics and the Corporation* (1958); Orville M. Kile, *The Farm Bureau Through Three Decades* (1948); Oliver Garceau, *The Political Life of the American Medical Association* (1941); Luke Ebersole, *Church Lobbying in the Nation's Capitol* (1951). It is to studies such as these that we must turn when we would find out how an economic elite, or a segment of it, relates

[78]Ibid. p. 259.

itself to the political process in the United States. Neither Hunter nor Mills refers to these studies. The studies show varying degrees of success or failure of pressure legislators. While "carrots and sticks" are sometimes successful in lining up legislators, the most effective single activity of lobbyists is to alert and inform legislators regarding issues of concern to the lobbyist. Thus lobbyists are more often successful as influence groups rather than as pressure groups, in the rigorous sense of these terms.

Since the Legislative Reorganization Act of 1946, lobbyists in Congress are required to register and to report quarterly on their expenditures. Some of the larger ones hide some of their expenditures in indirect activities, such as getting their individual members to use some of the collected funds for campaign contributions. They also divide up their work according to specialties so as not to make their expenditures appear so large. But the names of all the big lobbies are readily accessible through quarterly reports in the *Congressional Quarterly Almanac*. They are lobbies of industry, labor, agriculture, the professional societies (medicine, accounting, law, education, etc), women's groups, civil rights and civil liberties groups, veterans and patriotic societies, and peace groups. The ten largest spenders among the 384 lobbies registered during the year 1963[79] were the following:

United Federation of Postal Clerks (AFL–CIO)	$202,997
AFL–CIO (National Headquarters)	145,636
Business Committee for Tax Reduction in 1963	141,786
Co-ordinating Committee for Fundamental American Freedom, Inc.	127,827
National Farmers' Union	123,345
American Farm Bureau Federation	118,284
American Legion	117,275
Committee for Study of Revenue Bond Financing	111,449
United States Savings and Loan League	98,215
International Association of Machinists, District Lodge #44 (AFL–CIO)	93,964

The figures are rounded off to the nearest dollar.

[79] *Congressional Quarterly Almanac*, vol. 20 (Washington, D.C.: Government Printing Office, 1964), pp. 902–10.

In other recent years, the National Education Association, American Medical Association, International Brotherhood of Teamsters, Fluorspar Consumers' Committee, National Federation of Independent Businesses, Brotherhood of Locomotive Firemen and Enginemen, National Housing Conference, American Trucking Association, and the Association of American Railroads have also made the list of ten top spenders among lobbyists. Of those reporting lobby expenditures in the first half of 1962, 149 business groups listed a total of $820,756; 36 government employee and labor groups reported spending $475,542; 44 "citizens groups" reported spending $262,202; 21 farm groups, $211,036; 17 professional groups $170,133; 6 military and veterans groups, $68,195.[80]

Just how successful lobbies are is difficult to demonstrate, as it is impossible to ascertain how Congress would have acted if there had been no lobbies seeking to influence it. An article in the *Congressional Quarterly*[81] states that the various federal employee lobby groups reported spending $182,467 in the first half of 1962, and Congress passed a billion-dollar-a-year pay raise for their members. During the same time period, the American Medical Association reported spending $67,386, and Congress failed to pass the bill to provide medical care for the aged under Social Security which the AMA opposed. (In 1965, the AMA reported spending more than any other single lobby, but Congress passed the bill they opposed.) The U.S. Savings and Loan League reported spending $62,082, and Congress dropped the bill to withhold taxes on interest, but it also passed a provision opposed by the League—one limiting the amount of money that lending associations may transfer to tax-free reserves to cover bad debts. The American Farm Bureau Federation, which reported $59,567 spent on lobbying, was pleased that Congress did not apply the supply-management concept proposed by the Administration to feed grains. The National Farmers Union, spending $48,552, was pleased with congressional approval of a long-term supply-management program for wheat.

This kind of evidence should not be taken too seriously, for—as Cohen asserted after making an intensive study of the effectiveness

---

[80]These figures are taken from an article in the *Congressional Quarterly*, reprinted in the *Minneapolis Sunday Tribune*, October 14, 1962, p. 9B.
[81]Ibid.

of pressure groups in the foreign policy field—"the interest groups themselves seem generally willing to foster the belief that their opinions or actions have in fact had some important effect on policy."[82] Another study concurs in this statement and shows how pressure groups are limited in their effectiveness by counter-pressures, by shortages of money, information, and time, and by a tendency to talk to those already convinced of their position.[83] Still another student summarizes: "No simple, categorical statement can be made about the effect of pressure groups on American democracy. Only one thing is certain: the difficulty of determining the effect."[84] This statement we may also take as a summary of this section.

D. The Making of a Politician

There are certain pressures operating on all politicians that tend to give them some distinctive characteristics in common, despite the tremendous range of character and temperament to be found among them. Of course, not all politicians react in the same way to similar pressures, not only because of personality differences but also because of differences among constituencies. One can find some constituencies in the United States, for example, that seem to prefer scholarly types and others that seem to demand that their representatives be organizers. The exigencies of politics may tend to select one personality type rather than another, but we shall not be concerned here with the individual personalities of politicians. We shall, rather, be concerned with what the inevitable experiences in politics do *to* politicians. In other words, we shall be concerned with the *role* of politicians, recognizing that a tremendous range of personality types can fit this role. In referring to politicians in this section, we shall limit ourselves mainly to elected ones, thus excluding persons who have only been appointed to public office, and shall discuss secondarily those who work in political organizations without running for government office. Elected politicians ultimately determine govern-

---

[82] Bernard C. Cohen, *The Influence of Non-Governmental Groups on Foreign Policy-Making* (Boston: World Peace Foundation, 1959), p. 2.

[83] Bauer, Pool, and Dexter, *American Business*, esp. ch. 28.

[84] Donald C. Blaisdell, *American Democracy Under Pressure* (New York: Ronald Press, 1957), p. 11.

ment policy. This is not to say that appointed officeholders are not powerful, but their power is not final. We shall consider their influence in a later chapter.

Running for public office is a unique experience, although some elections are "walkovers" in which the candidate is not obliged to do much campaigning to win. In a "walkover" the candidate is generally an incumbent in a "safe" district. But even this fortunate type must have a first campaign in which there is a hard struggle to gain the position of incumbent, and this leaves its mark on the politician. Running for public office is not unlike the job of a salesman—when the salesman's product is himself and his expected future actions rather than some material product. In campaigning, the politician's first task is to make himself known to the potential voters—he must develop "name recognition." This is not especially difficult if his name happens to be a recognizable and "good" one, and if he has funds to purchase mass media publicity (billboards, newspaper ads, radio and TV spot announcements, lawn signs, etc.). This promotion of his name tends to make a candidate "objectify" himself—that is, to think of himself in the third person. This is the first stage in the formation of a role for the politician—he thereafter thinks of himself in terms of a certain public image. The image he has of himself as politician may conform to his self-conception, though it need not, but in all cases it is a third-person image. While building name recognition, the politician also seeks to build a favorable image. This can be done with an agreeable personality, the use of humor, taking the "right" side on popular issues, showing a great deal of knowledge about popular issues, and so on. Many successful politicians do not have agreeable personalities; they build public images in terms of integrity, toughness, tenacity, or wisdom. It is one of the public stereotypes that successful politicians have agreeable personalities or are "good campaigners" in the sense that they make friends with a large segment of the electorate.

Since no person can be perfect—in the eyes of the majority of a constituency—in personality, on issues, or in knowledge, the salesmanship consists in hiding the defects while displaying the more attractive features. This is not always done consciously, for the candidate identifies himself with the "third person" he is displaying. At the same time as the candidate camouflages what he thinks might be his deficiencies in the eyes of the public, he must give the impression of holding nothing back. Again, the third-person mechanism comes to his aid, for he can reveal everything about this imaginary third person and build the third person as he goes along. Thus a candidate can lie, and misrepresent himself, without subjectively having the feeling that he is doing these things. Such behavior is not, of course, limited to politicians.

The candidate requires a close circle of friends and helpers. These may come from the party organization, or he builds up a personal organization of volunteers, and—if he has funds—some of them become paid employees even while they are also considered as "friends." These persons not only perform the thousand and one tasks required in a political campaign, but they constantly help the candidate form his third-person image (including his stand on issues and his campaign strategy). One of their chief tasks is to tell him how he is "doing"—what his third-person image looks like to various segments of the public—and if they fail to do that, they are not performing their task well. Candidates running in large constituencies have to rely heavily on the mass media to get their personality and program "across" to the public, and some put themselves in the hands of professional public relations firms to do this more effectively.[85] Such a candidate is in danger of losing touch with reality unless he has close political friends who can periodically tell him what is happening to him politically. Thus the candidate must take criticism constantly from his friends as well as from his foes, and he can do this best if he depersonalizes his politician's role into a third-person image. The candidate also needs his circle of friends for personal reinforcement: in public, he has to take a lot of criticism, hard questioning, and even personal abuse without much negative reaction; among his friends he can react against his opponents and against the general public.

On the other hand, the politician cannot express himself freely even within his circle of friends or the central party organization. He cannot "explode," be sarcastic to the point of unreasonableness, display his weaknesses, or do any of the other things a human being under great pressure generally does. The most important reason is

[85]See Irvin Ross, "The Supersalesmen of California Politics: Whitaker and Baxter," *Harper's Magazine*, 219 (July 1959), 55–64.

that news of such behavior generally leaks out to the press and the public. Secondly, the politician cannot completely trust his party or even his personal organization: They form an association of competing, often aggressive persons, who have individual goals as well as group goals, and may sometimes turn against their political leader because of ambition, disillusionment, or the attractions of another leader. The politician often finds he must balance factors within his party just as he often has to balance competing vested interest groups in the public. While political parties do have ideologies, and their members are generally more issue-oriented than most citizens, organizational and individual interests often get in the way of issues and ideologies. All these things add to the pressure on a politician and add to his feeling that he must insulate himself from his party and his friends, even while he must not show he is doing so. His followers tend to idealize him to some extent, to place him on a pedestal, so to speak, and he often finds that that isolated spot is the safest place to be.

While a political party helps its candidates with endorsement, information about issues, voter registration and get-out-the-vote drives, workers and the other paraphernalia of organization, and sometimes even with money for campaign expenses, certain tensions almost inevitably develop between party and candidate. In the first place, the candidate is likely to believe that the party is not doing enough for him. There is a popular myth that the party "runs" a candidate and has the resources to do so, and a novice candidate is likely to place some credence in this myth. He soon finds that the party, being a voluntary organization, does not have the resources to do everything the candidate expects it to do. That is when he comes to rely more on his own "organization" and on his own personal resources and abilities. Secondly, in any election the party has several candidates to elect to the various offices, and it must allocate its limited resources among them. At any given election, probably most of the party-endorsed candidates will consider this allocation unfair. They evaluate themselves and the office for which they are running more highly than does the party. Thirdly, the party officials have their own vested interests as leaders of a voluntary association. These sometimes come in conflict with the interests of the candidates in getting elected. Fourthly, the party is aware of its role as a continuing organization, with future candidates as well as present ones. The party keeps its eye on the long run; the candidate is inevitably focussed on the short-run, the election at hand which will make or break his personal career. The party often asks a candidate to do something to enhance the "image" of the party; the candidate tends to be mainly concerned with his own "image" and his vote-getting appeal.

Some pressure groups begin to work on a candidate while he is still a first-time candidate, although they are few compared to what he will face once he is in office. The pressure groups will offer him money for campaign expenses, with the implicit—seldom explicit—expectation that he will favor their position once he attains office. Campaign contributions are generally given to those who are already known to favor the group giving the contribution; it is not necessary —and frequently not effective—to ask for a specific commitment. (Political parties occasionally provide some campaign funds, especially for candidates for the higher offices and especially in the Republican party, but mainly they provide workers, campaign materials, endorsement, and information of many types.) Some individual contributions are completely without strings. A candidate gets votes from a pressure group as well as campaign funds, and if a group is large enough it can help a candidate more with its votes than with its funds. Members of a pressure group not only have their own votes and those of their adult family members, they also can give electoral advice to their friends.

The candidate not only has to deal with friends and foes; he also has to deal with the mass, which is somewhat negative to politicians in general. A defeated candidate for Congress writes:

> My impression was that some of the hostile and apathetic re-actions were not personal to me or to Democrats in general but rather to politicians as such. To these persons politics appeared to represent frustration and futility. They seemed to feel that nothing good can come of politics, that much of their troubles and perplexity is caused by acts and omissions of government, and that they would rather not be reminded of this painful and mysterious fact about which they feel they can do nothing.[86]

[86]Stimson Bullitt, *To Be a Politician* (New York: Doubleday, 1959), p. 114.

In talking to the public, and even to the leaders of interest groups, politicians have to learn what Congressman John Brademas (D., Ind.) has called the "calculated ambiguity of political utterance." Even when he is taking a forthright position on a serious political issue, an effective politician learns that he cannot use extreme language. Mills might take this to indicate the "secrecy" by which the economic elite controls the political elite, or the "Madison Avenue techniques" with which all elites approach the public. But it often means nothing more than the unwillingness of a politician to offend his opponents on an issue, since he may need them as allies on another issue. Further, ambiguous language may be a way of developing a face-saving compromise, which must be one of the goals of a democratic politician.

In the excitement of a campaign, candidates often do strange things. They may feel bitter about what they perceive as the inadequate support of their friends and their political party. They tend to become so self-centered that they refuse to help those running on the same slate for other political offices. They may make "deals" with groups which can provide them with extra votes even when those groups stand for programs which the candidate abhors. They may mislead voters about their own positions, and shift their positions to satisfy a greater number of voters (the latter is often done with the hope that the voters will forget their campaign postures). All these things can and do happen. But the frequency with which they occur is often exaggerated, and the psychology behind them is generally misunderstood. It is not that the politician cynically surveys the public and determines rationally what selfish acts will aid him most. Much more often, the candidate is blinded emotionally by the excitement of the game, a game in which his self-conception, his reputation, and his purse are deeply involved and one which lasts not hours but months.

American elections are winner-take-all affairs. Under European proportional representation elections, the losers gain something, and under European parliamentary systems, the chief of the losers becomes leader of the opposition. But in the United States, the loser by a few votes is as badly off as the loser by practically all the votes. The winner is forgiven many of the cynical and vicious things he did in the campaign; the loser's weaknesses are exaggerated, even by his friends. Some of the less-committed friends even turn their support and admiration to the winner. This is not only a function of the single-member constituency and majority-vote system, but it is also partly due to the fact that Americans like a winner, even more than what he stands for. This is true regardless of party and ideology, and partly regardless of the quality and level of the campaign. Richard Nixon, the loser in the close presidential campaign of 1960, is quoted as saying that losing by a few thousand votes is worse than losing by millions, because everyone in his party thinks the candidate would have won if he had only taken their advice or if he had not made that single specific blunder.[87]

The winner not only takes office and power, he also gains prestige, support, and even adulation. After the "honeymoon" period which every winner has, he begins to lose some of the adulation, although incumbents generally retain some advantages of this sort for subsequent elections. He puts behind him some of the irrationality of the campaign. He usually returns to the complex issues, which are in fact seldom all black or white as he said during the campaign. He faces up, one way or the other, to his obligations to those who aided him in the campaign and to campaign pledges or issues. Except for a few extremists who have been elected through sheer demagoguery or through popular revolts, the elected politician feels a pressure to become a moderate because moderation seems to indicate rationality and wisdom and because the center is the safest and strongest place to be. This is a function of the American structure of politics, not of politics in general nor of tendencies of modern politicians, as Stimson Bullitt seems to think:

> Modern politicians have become too moderate in all aspects of conduct and value except narrowness of purpose and willingness to do hard work. Forgetting the limits which bound the golden mean theory, they treat it as a universal, like the candidate for Mayor who promised to tread the line between partiality and impartiality. To put it another way, they fail to apply the theory to itself and so practice moderation to excess.[88]

[87]James Reston, "The Ironies and Contrasts of Politics," *The New York Times,* November 17, 1961, p. 32.

[88]Bullitt, *To Be a Politician.*

According to Richard Crossman, a British Member of Parliament, politicians usually do not like to exercise power. They enjoy the "game" and the importance of politics, and they like the prestige which their potential power gives them. But, "The vast majority of British politicians, like the rest of their fellow creatures, desire success without too much effort and shudder if ever the moment comes when decision is unavoidable and power must be exercised ruthlessly."[89] Crossman goes on to describe the British politician; much of his characterization applies to congressmen in the United States also:

> What makes a British politician? First, a tradition of public service; then a dash of vanity and another of self-importance and, added to these, a streak of rebelliousness, a pleasure in good talk for its own sake, and in gregarious living. These, much more than the desire for personal power, or the qualities of the individual member. But the individual is shaped into his final form by the institution itself. It is Parliament which takes hold of the players, taming the natural dictator and goading on the lazy, and teaches them all the principles which Wm. Amery unerringly picks out as the essence of parliamentary life—that each may shoot his own goals by his own rules, provided that he believes that the game itself is good.[90]

It is difficult in practice to separate actual power from potential power. Politicians in democracies may dislike having to use naked power, and they seek various indirect means of getting their way without it being too obvious that they are doing so, but they know they have potential power which makes these indirect techniques effective, and this they enjoy having.[91] Some who start on the top in politics—like President Eisenhower or Governor Nelson Rockefeller of New York—take a while to learn that if they do not use their considerable power they will not accomplish their goals, and that if they do not use their power, others may exercise it in their stead,

---

[89] R.H.S. Crossman, *The Charm of Politics* (New York: Harper, 1958), p. 3.
[90] Ibid. p. 9.
[91] The social psychology of the congressman in the context of the influences that play on him are admirably analyzed by Lewis A. Dexter in Bauer, Pool, and Dexter, *American Business*, pp. 403–61.

for different goals.[92] The politician is thus pressured into using his political power, albeit usually indirectly. The fact that many active politicians—if they are lawyers by training and hence eligible for judgeships—happily give up legislative and executive posts for calmer judicial ones suggests that the desire for power may be less than the desire for achievement.

> To legislators, congressmen, and holders of administrative offices the lure of the bench is a composite of many things. One is the economic security. Another is the prestige and social status. A third is the relief it offers from the disillusionments and discouragements of political office.[93]

Sometimes congressmen can turn over specific powers to administrative officials in order to diminish the outside pressure on themselves. In recent decades they seem to have done that with some frequency, as in the case of abandoning specific tariff legislation in favor of broad foreign trade legislation.[94]

Thus far we have been talking of the politician as elected officeholder. Behind each officeholder are hundreds, perhaps thousands, of active party members. In some states a significant proportion of these are receivers of patronage, but in other states there is practically no patronage. Very few party offices pay a salary. With a few exceptions for some of the big cities, the political party organizations are voluntary associations, and their members get only the psychological and social rewards of political activity: They are working for their political goals, they can participate in the "game" of politics at close range, they gain some of the fun and excitement of participation, they also have power through their ability to exert influence on the elected politicians. There are not many studies of representative samples of active party members, but we may cite some findings from an excellent study of the elite among them—those elected to national party conventions.[95]

This Brookings Institution survey found that the delegates' incomes were above average ($10,150 median annual income for the Democrats, $10,900 for the Republicans, in 1948), although they

[92]Leo Egan, "Governor in Politics," *The New York Times*, March 21, 1960, p. 20.
[93]Leo Egan, "Vanishing Candidates," *The New York Times*, June 4, 1962, p. 21.
[94]Bauer, Pool and Dexter, *American Business*, p. 45.
[95]David, Goldman, and Bain, *National Party Conventions*.

showed considerable range. In occupation, the delegates are mainly from the self-employed and proprietary categories in the population —those which permit some flexible use of time to devote to party activity.

> Most delegates . . . are active party workers who frequently hold party office at about the range of county chairman or state committee member. . . . The typical delegate appeared to be the kind of individual who devoted much of his time and energy to politics as an engrossing side line, but looked to some other occupation for his principal sources of income, and frequently contributes his own money while doing party work.[96]

About one-sixth of the delegates were high-level current or past public officials. Many of them are "joiners" in other civic and in occupational associations, and some go to national party conventions to represent these interests as well as those of the entire mass of party members and voters.[97] On the basis of their interests, "they help to form and reform the broad lines of the coalitions of which each party is composed."[98] As in most other political situations, "while all the delegates were subject to many influences, for the most part the pressures from one direction were offset by those from another. Most of the uncommitted delegates apparently in the end had to make their own decisions in terms of their own perceptions of the candidates and of the situation, often influenced by majority sentiment in their delegations.[99] The national convention replicates, on a grander scale, the membership and activities of the state party convention, and even of the smaller district and county conventions. A political party is to be understood mainly as a tremendously complex voluntary association, with a unique and most important set of functions. It is the major influence in selecting candidates for public office, an important influence in getting them elected (through volunteer labor and fund raising), and an important influence in setting their politics. The general policy of a party is only formally expressed in its platform and resolutions; much more important are the coalitions of

96David, Goldman, and Bain, *National Party Conventions*, p. 338.
97Ibid. p. 339.
98Ibid. p. 478.
99Ibid. p. 364.

interests invested in the party and the ethos of the membership as a collectivity. Public officials have to make public policy as they carry on their governmental duties day by day, but they seldom stray very far from the general policy formulated by their respective parties.[100]

The career of a politician tends to make him inwardly resourceful and "tough," if he has not already been "selected" by the political process as one who has these characteristics. Yet outwardly the politician, as a vote seeker and as a "broker" for compromises, must appear to be agreeable and even malleable. Every politician has his "real self" and his "third-person image." It is the third-person image which listens sympathetically to the representatives of a pressure group, and which expresses his gratitude for the promise of a vote or a campaign contribution. This third-person image is also adept at giving the representatives of a pressure group, or any constituents, the impression that they are having a great effect on him: He must reward them for their efforts in this way if in no other. And he does reward them in other ways too. He will introduce a bill, or vote "aye" to an amendment to a bill, knowing full well that such a bill and that particular vote will have no relationship to subsequent legislation. He will also help to work out legislative compromises, in which the interest of the pressure group gains something. On the key votes—the ones that make the laws—the politician (except maybe the "bought" one) votes his convictions most of the time. The "real self" of the politician, his self-conception, does not permit him to vote solely in terms of the external pressures very often. And the political structure and processes—considered earlier in this chapter—tend to make the politician's own convictions coincide much more with those of his political party than with those of any special-interest pressure group. That is why all the systematic studies show that party affiliation is the most frequent and best "objective" predictor of how a congressman or legislator votes. Similar statements could be made for the elected officials in the Executive branch.

---

[100]We are here referring to the party for each level of office; for a legislator it is a district, for an alderman it is a ward; for a senator it is a state; only for the President of the United States is it the national political party—which has the weakest organization of all. The public official participates, of course, in the formation of general public policy by his party.

Appendix to Chapter II
Voluntary Associations of Congressmen, 1961

Politicians must be great joiners, for many reasons. Affiliations provide them with channels of personal contact with portions of the electorate, and provide the latter with a sense of personal identity with their public officials. Thus, membership in voluntary associations helps a politician to get elected. Politicians tend to be gregarious. If a person does not like to associate with others, he is highly unlikely to go into politics. An affiliation with some social influence association sometimes provides the extra bit of motivation and self-confidence that leads a man to try for public office.

Each congressman is invited to prepare a short official biography of himself for the *Congressional Directory*, which is widely circulated around the country. Some congressmen write very little about themselves for this publication, preferring less formal publications to let their constituents know about their activities and affiliations. Thus, the *Congressional Directory* cannot be considered as providing a complete listing of the voluntary associations of congressmen, although it is the only single source of such information. The data provided can be used only to indicate the minimum number of affiliations.

The following information has been tabulated from the 1961 *Congressional Directory*. Only 70 per cent of the congressmen furnished information on the voluntary associations with which they were affiliated, aside from their political party. The most frequent specifications are occupational, and the largest category here is some kind of a professional association, mentioned by 59 per cent of the congressmen. Fully 45 per cent of the congressmen indicated that they were members of the American Bar Association. Ten per cent mentioned an affiliation with a businessman's group, and 8.6 per cent mentioned membership in some Chamber of Commerce. Only 1.5 per cent of the congressmen indicated a present affiliation with a trade union. The "service associations," which have a business orientation—such as Rotary, Kiwanis, Lions, etc.—were mentioned by 25 per cent of the congressmen. Only 8.8 per cent mentioned affiliation with a farm organization, which is not much greater than the proportion of farmers in the total population.

Only 40 per cent of the congressmen mentioned their religious affiliation, and only 10 per cent mentioned holding a lay leadership role in their church. Large proportions mentioned membership in social and fraternal organizations: as many as 40 per cent said they were members of some Masonic lodge, and lesser proportions were to be found in the great variety of similar organizations. Over 21 per cent were members of some collegiate social fraternity, and the same proportion acknowledged affiliation with a recreational or athletic association. A full third of the congressmen said they were members of the American Legion, and lesser proportions were members of the several other veterans' organizations (8.8 per cent were in the Armed Forces Reserves).

Thirty-four per cent of the congressmen mentioned some national or local civic or public-affairs organization and a further 11 per cent said they were members of some organization working for the improved health of the population. Membership in an ethnic association was acknowledged by 4.5 per cent of the congressmen.

In his study of United States senators, Donald R. Matthews asked them to list their non-political associations. He found that "The most popular associations are lodges, followed closely by college fraternities, professional associations, veterans' and patriotic groups, and social clubs."[101] Calculating from Matthews's data, we ascertained that the median number of associations reported by Republican senators was 10.2 per senator, whereas Democratic senators had a median of 9.05 associations per senator.

---

[101]Donald R. Matthews, *U. S. Senators and Their World* (Chapel Hill: University of North Carolina Press, 1960), p. 43.

III
The Influence of the Economic Elite
on Politics and Government

A. Introduction: Some Characteristics of the Economic Elite

Throughout this book the thesis is advanced that: (1) There are many power elites, each of which is somewhat specialized in the area in which it exercises its influence. (2) Power elites interlock only temporarily and on limited types of issues, with some issues being determined in a "democratic" fashion by the great voting public when it occasionally mobilizes itself with interest and action on those issues. This position does not ignore the power of the economic elite. Businessmen, and those who generally control the "excess wealth,"[1] constitute a very important elite in our society. They exercise their influence mainly on issues affecting production, occasionally on issues affecting consumption and distribution of wealth, and ordinarily very little on issues that do not effect wealth directly or primarily. This is not to say that they are always successful in determining the outcome of an issue in which they have expressed an interest.

Two other preliminary points need to be made about the economic elite. The first is that they, like the "masses," sometimes have "false consciousness"; that is, they do not always take a position in accord with their rational interests. The Marxists have made much of the

[1]By "excess wealth" we mean that wealth which is not regularly consumed in the short run and is hence reinvested in productive tools to make future wealth. Thus, those who have excess wealth, the economic elite, constitute those who control the instruments of production, including capital but not including labor.

false consciousness of the laboring class, holding that they are frequently deluded by the economic elite into supporting positions not in accord with their rational interests. This is a fact we would not dispute, although we feel that the extent to which it occurs in the United States today is somewhat exaggerated by the Marxists. We would add that, to some extent, they are recording a fact about human beings in general, which therefore applies also to the economic elite, although perhaps less to the economic elite than to other segments of the population not so well-informed on economic issues. The economic elite is occasionally self-deluded and occasionally it is deluded by other elites, particularly by the political elite and by various professional elites.[2] The economic elite is subjected to the same set of power influences that affect the rest of American society, including the ones they themselves control. As Digby Baltzell points out, with only slight exaggeration:

> But it is one of the tragic ironies of modern life and leadership that these skillful manipulators of others may themselves have become the most manipulated segment of the population. It is no accident that the hidden persuaders, who have so little respect for the privacy or dignity of the average citizen, are living in an exurban nightmare of insecurity and sophisticated conformity. While Riesman has a charming way (perhaps an other-directed way?) of qualifying and minimizing the unpleasant implications of many of his insights, surely anyone who takes seriously such blunter books as the *Hidden Persuaders*, the *Organization Man*, or *The Exurbanites* must be impressed and depressed by the other-directed conformity that characterizes the lives of the most talented and ambitious members of America's postwar generation.[3]

Secondly, there are distinct subgroups within the economic elite, although occasionally they can work together in unity and with deliberateness for a common goal.[4] Perhaps especially on economic

[2]Chapter XII, on the efforts to pass a law to provide medical care for older people, will illustrate these points in detail.

[3]E. Digby Baltzell, "The American Aristocrat and Other Direction," in S. M. Lipset and L. Lowenthal (eds.), *Culture and Social Character* (New York: Free Press of Glencoe, 1961), p. 272.

[4]For a consideration of how frequently American business cannot get together on a legislative bill of economic significance, see Raymond A. Bauer, Ithiel de S. Pool, and Lewis A. Dexter, *American Business and Public Policy* (New York: Atherton, 1963), ch. 22.

issues there are divergences of interest; after all, even if it has not always prevailed, there is such a thing as competition. Competition expresses itself in distribution of power and in divergence of political interest as well as in purely economic forms. There is some competition not merely between producers of the same goods, but also between those businessmen who have divergent interests regarding certain institutions and laws. A tariff, for example, might benefit one group of businessmen but hamper another group. Relationships with banks and other financial institutions provide another source of divergence: One group of businessmen might be powerful enough to control or make deals with the bankers, but another group might be in danger of being taken over by them. In general, one of the great cleavages in interest and power that runs through American history is that between the "big" businessmen and the "small" businessmen.[5] In the twentieth century, big business fell into the hands of well-educated managers and specialists such as lawyers, while small businessmen were more likely to remain "self-made men" with lesser education. "Small" businessmen in the twentieth century often consolidated considerable amounts of wealth, but usually retained control in a single family or partnership; big businesses invariably became corporations with a number of important owners, directors, and managers. These differences were expressed in all kinds of political and economic issues, and even though most of the time both groups could find common political interest expressed through the Republican party (after about 1875) there remained a deep cleavage running through the Republican party itself. The split between Robert Taft and Dwight Eisenhower, or between Goldwater and the Scranton-Rockefeller forces are merely the better-known recent examples of this cleavage.[6]

The cleavage between large and small businessmen is only partly related to the cleavage which Baltzell shows to exist between "old

[5] Even in their lobbying with legislators, small businessmen are likely to oppose the big businessmen openly. For example, a letter from the "Independent Bankers of Minnesota," addressed to all Minnesota state legislators (October 1, 1963) states: "Our members feel that economic power, like political power, must be dispersed and diffused throughout our activities on national, state, and local levels." They were specifically opposing a bill to permit branch banking by the larger banks.

[6] The former of each pair tended to favor the small businessmen; the latter favored the big businessmen.

aristocrats" and "new" businessmen.[7] Only the former have the "old school tie" that Mills makes so much of, but they are of declining power. Another cleavage among big businessmen that emerged during the presidential election of 1964 was that along regional lines, between Easterners and Middle Westerners—the former supported President Johnson, the latter remained faithful to the Republican candidate, Goldwater. It is sometimes held by proponents of the economic-elite-dominance hypothesis that there is an interlocking directorate which controls most of the major corporations in the United States and uses the specific managers of each corporation as its tools. Gordon's study[8] shows that corporation executives are largely controlled by their boards of directors, the executives are primarily concerned with prices, costs, competition, laws, and other impersonal variables, and they believe a favorable balance sheet will do most to keep them in the good graces of their directors. Management often controls a majority of the directors, so that interlocking directorates are the exception rather than the rule.

Although business may frequently have as much power over domestic politico-economic issues as groups that have much larger memberships, there is no indication that the "great and crucial" foreign policy decisions of our time are made by and for business.[9] Nor, on the other hand, do the "people" have any great say in them.[10] Instead, it appears that they are formulated by officials in the Executive branch and their advisors in a foreign-policy-making group of experts and then ratified in a general way by public opinion, as expressed by votes for the President. Under the Constitution, of course, the President has exclusive power to formulate foreign policy with the "advice and consent" of the Senate in treaty-making, and with the approval of Congress as a whole in declarations of war. It would appear obvious that only a limited number of people can effectively formulate foreign policy. The decision-makers may have

[7]E. Digby Baltzell, *The Protestant Establishment* (New York: Random House, 1965).

[8]R. Aaron Gordon, *Business Leadership in the Large Corporation* (Washington: The Brookings Institution, 1945).

[9]Minor action of government in support of private business operating internationally—as in the case of the United Fruit Company in Latin America—of course occurs.

[10]See J. David Singer, "Peace Research, Peace Action," *Bulletin of the Atomic Scientists* (January 1965), 14.

business backgrounds, but this is not conclusive or strong evidence that they act to promote the interests of business. Whose interests then do they promote? They promote, in my opinion, their conception of the national interest in foreign affairs. Their foreign policy attitudes are, in fact, probably more "liberal" than those of the masses.[11] The people seem to have "conservative" and set attitudes on foreign policy questions. The function of the mass media here seems to be the unfreezing of previously relevant public attitudes, not the inculcation of a business-oriented foreign policy.[12] The political leaders, in both congress and the Executive, seem able to act and, in fact, do act as "inner-directed" free agents on the key foreign policy questions before the country.[13] Non-governmental liberals who want to influence foreign policy would do better to spend more time trying to influence those men and less time trying, fruitlessly, to persuade "the public."[14]

In this chapter, we shall concentrate on five particular forms of business influence on government. These are important to business primarily for reasons of narrow economic self-interest, not as ideological issues that divide liberals and conservatives. The first of these is business pressure in determining the amount and allocation of government spending. The effect of business in determining the amount of defense spending and the allocation of defense contracts will be analyzed as "the" illustration of this type of influence. It may not be the most typical case, but it is the most important by virtue of its size and the extent to which the defense budget spreads into the economy's private sector. It also is particularly important because the question of military policy is so important for the nation as a whole. The second is the influence that business has on its regulators:

11Ibid. One reason, I think, for the public's "unenlightened" views on questions of foreign policy is its lack of a "reference frame" independent of the mass media. A union-hating paper will not be very persuasive on the subject of unions to a man in a good union, but the average man's only contact with foreign policy issues is through the mass media.

12Ibid. pp. 14–15. I think that Singer's observation that policy-makers filter the information and the interpretation of it that reaches the public, and his observation that the public receives its information from the mass media, should be interrelated. This helps to explain why the majority of the mass media have supported the government on practically every major foreign policy question of the last twenty-five years.

13See Warren Miller and Donald Stokes, "Constituency Influence in Congress," *American Political Science Review* (March 1965), 49, 51 and esp. 56.

14Singer, "Peace Research," p. 14.

a study of business control of the regulatory commissions. This study has pertinence for understanding the limitations of American government controls on business. Third is the important influence that business can exert on government through the use of the "political strike." This is particularly important in determining the distribution of the tax burden at the state and local levels and also poses important questions concerning the use of power in a democratic society. Fourth is the influence business has on government, particularly on Congress, through its approach to the general public by financial influence on the press and other media of mass communication. Fifth is the influence exercised by businessmen through direct participation in government, and through the use of leading public officials as "representatives" of business.

B. The Defense Industries and Government Expenditures for Military Equipment[15]

There is nothing out of the ordinary about the reasons for various defense firms attempting to influence the amount and allocation of defense spending. Their motivation is the same as that of road-contractors trying to influence state and local governments to build roads and give them the available road contracts. Their motivation is money.[16] A defense contract or several defense contracts may mean the difference between prosperity and bankruptcy for a firm. The "landing" of or failure to land a defense contract may also mean the difference between employment and unemployment for a large number of workers and the difference between prosperity and recession in a city or town.[17] Defense "pays."

[15]The following three sections have benefited from a term paper prepared for one of the author's courses by Leonard S. Robins.

[16]See Fred Cook, *The Warfare State* (New York: Macmillan, 1962), pp. 2–3, 23–4, for a general description of the economic importance of defense spending. Cook is a leading advocate of the theory that a more or less secret "military-industrial complex" has a great deal of political influence in the United States. Regardless of this, his demonstration of the economic facts is valuable. Also see a series of three articles by Julius Duscha, "Arms and the Big Money Men," *Harper's Magazine* 228 (March 1964), 39–47; (April 1964), 59–65; (May 1964), 56–62.

[17]By 1963, military spending provided from 10 to 30 per cent of the gross personal income in 12 states. Armaments factories accounted for 20 to 30 per cent of the manufacturing employment in 8 states—Arizona, California, Colorado, Connecticut, Kansas, New Mexico, Utah, Washington. (Richard Harwood, "Pressures Engulf Department of Defense," *Louisville Courier-Journal* and *Minneapolis Morning Tribune*, June 11, 1963, p. 4; this series of articles appeared June 11–15,

The important question we must ask is, "What are the effects of the various business pressures and interests on our defense and military policy?" One important effect of these pressures is to make congressmen "happy" to appropriate money for defense. This effect is increased by the policy of having congressmen announce the awarding of defense contracts to firms in their districts. Election campaigns are waged on the question of which man or party can do better in bringing defense contracts to the district or state.[18] Since it is easier to get a defense contract when there is a large defense budget, congressmen have a great incentive to vote for a large defense budget.

Another important effect of a huge military budget is the creation of a fear of the economic consequences of disarmament. While many individual businessmen and workers would lose their present means of livelihood if military expenditures should be drastically reduced, this does not mean that they could not be accommodated in other economic activities, or that the American economy as a whole would suffer. A considerable number of economists have convincingly demonstrated how the economy could be restored to civilian-goods production without an economic depression.[19] But even if labor and business did agree that there would be no damage caused to the total economy by disarmament, there would still be an adverse economic effect on those specifically engaged in the defense industry. It must be quite easy for those in the defense industry to believe that the United States should not disarm because it cannot trust the Russians.

These effects on the attitudes of congressmen and citizens have, in turn, important effects on the size and composition of our military establishment. They cause both an increase in the level of defense spending and duplication in our weapon systems. Until the Vietnam War became a divisive issue in the United States, no important special interest group opposed money spent for defense; several

---

1963.) Seven million people are directly or indirectly employed on defense industries. In San Diego, 80 per cent of those in industry jobs are working on government contracts; in Seattle the figure is 50 per cent; in Los Angeles it is 33 per cent. (Duscha, "Arms and the Big Money Men," May 1964, pp. 56–62).

18Although these campaigns are sometimes based on the differing amounts the candidates favor spending for defense, the more usual theme concerns who would have the necessary "pull" to get defense contracts for the district.

19See, for example, Emile Benoit and Kenneth E. Boulding (eds.), *Disarmament and The American Economy* (New York: Harper, 1963).

important interest groups favor a high level of defense spending. Under these circumstances, is it any wonder that almost any project favored by the military will be favored by Congress? One must conclude that one reason for the furor aroused in Congress whenever a decision is made to abandon a weapons system or a military base, or to award a contract to one company over another, is "economic."[20] The inevitable result of decisions made in this context is, of course, duplication and waste. A larger number of people can be satisfied by retaining both variations of an airplane, or finding a new purpose for a plant whose weapon is no longer needed, or keeping a military base that might have "marginal" use.[21] It would be silly to excuse the Pentagon by blaming all military waste on these economic considerations, but they should not be underestimated in importance either.

There is much less validity, however, in the more extreme arguments concerning the importance of business influence on military policy. The economic fear of disarmament may contribute to an overly suspicious attitude on the questions of a test ban and disarmament, but it would be unfair and untrue to say that it is the primary cause of the "arms race."[22] The primary cause of our high

[20]The Executive branch can make this type of decision because it has a national constituency rather than a local one. It also receives greater publicity and has greater fiscal responsibility on this subject. It is, in short, good—or at least not bad—politics for the Administration to cut back on certain questionable aspects of defense spending. The same cannot be said for Congress and congressmen.

[21]A good illustration of this point was the Pentagon's decision that the Republic Aviation plant on Long Island could be used for another purpose after the F-105 was discontinued. For a listing of some of the pressures exerted to "save the jobs" at that plant, see Cook, *Warfare State*, pp. 178–179. Nevertheless, Secretary of Defense McNamara was successful in closing several production lines and military bases. "Not until McNamara took over as Secretary of Defense [in 1961] were efforts made to apply a tight check rein on new projects, to insist that weapons be more carefully thought through before being put into production, to prevent duplication among the services, and to break up the close and expensive relationships between the services and the trusted contractors." (Duscha, "Arms and the Big Money Men," April 1964, p. 61.) There was waste, poor planning, little competitive bidding, and congressional pork-barrel tactics, according to Duscha. McNamara reduced the "cost-plus" contracts from 38 per cent in 1961 to 20 per cent in 1964 (they had been only 13 per cent of all defense contracts in 1952).

[22]This is, of course, where Fred Cook goes wrong. See the review of his book by William Chapman, "Alarmist Tract," *The Progressive*, 27 (March 1963), 42–3. Cook implicitly argues that the military-industrial complex created and perpetuates the cold war in order to perpetuate itself. (See Cook, *Warfare State*, pp. 68–72.) Cook assumes the fact of perpetuation from his analysis of the origins of the cold war.

level of defense spending, and especially our refusal to stop atomic testing or disarm, is a real fear of the Russians and the Chinese. This possibly exaggerated fear may be producing an overly militaristic policy, but it is the fundamental cause of our present military and foreign policy. Marginal factors, however, must also be considered, and the economics of the present arms race does encourage its continuance. Because Senator Gerald P. Nye's 1935 "merchants of death" investigation exaggerated the importance of the armaments industry as a cause of international tension,[23] people today feel that all arguments attempting to relate "profits" to "policy" are incorrect.[24]

· The problem is, as has been mentioned, that there are powerful interests in favor of a large defense budget, but none to point out when too much money is being spent or when money is being spent wastefully. There is no "countervailing power"[25] or any adequate representation of the "public interest"[26] (except for Secretary of Defense McNamara) when the "special" or "narrow" interests do not check each other.

If pressures by armaments manufacturers are seen as a factor in keeping up the high level of total military expenditure, this does not prove that any given single manufacturer benefits from the expenditure. The facts show a considerable turnover in the list of "arma-

[23]Even during the 1930's the exaggeration and incorrectness of Nye's conclusions were pointed out by scholars. See, for example, the neglected study by A. Eugene Staley, *War and the Private Investor* (Chicago: University of Chicago Press, 1935), in which it was shown that business was not particularly aggressive in creating the total demand for armaments, however much businessmen may have used pressure to get contracts for their own company.

[24]This illustration also shows some of the dangers of "learning from history." Nye had a point when he said that the munitions industry encouraged lending to the Allies which, in turn, caused Germany to attack our shipping and led to our declaration of war against Germany in 1917. He was wrong, however, in feeling that this information was particularly relevant for the developing international tensions of the 1930's. The same point can, I think, be fairly made against those who argue that our "hard" policies today will prevent our "making the mistakes of the 1930's."

[25]The concept of countervailing power is found in John Kenneth Galbraith, *American Capitalism: The Theory of Countervailing Power* (Boston: Houghton Mifflin, 1952).

[26]For an important discussion of the public interest concept, see Glendon Schubert, *The Public Interest* (Glencoe, Ill.: Free Press, 1960). A key concept involved in the public interest is the "latent pressure group." This is discussed in David Truman, *The Governmental Process* (New York: Knopf, 1951).

ments manufacturers." Pilisuk and Hayden[27] report that between 1940 and 1964, 82 companies dropped out of the list of 100 top defense contractors, and only 36 were more or less able to keep on the list. In terms of industry, Peck and Scherer[28] report that, between the early 1940's and the late 1950's, the percentage of contracts going to the automobile industry dropped from 25 per cent to 4 per cent, while those going to the aircraft companies went up from 34 to 54 per cent, and those going to the electronics industry went up from 9 to 28 per cent. The pressures of technological change seem to be more inexorable than those of specific armaments lobbyists.

C. Business Pressures on the Independent Regulatory Commissions

The independent regulatory commission is a governmental institution that was orginally specifically designed to remove certain subjects from "politics." It was felt that the sensitive decisions required in regulating private enterprise—decisions of both a quasi-legislative and quasi-judicial nature—should be removed from partisan and pressure-group influence.[29] It would be better if these decisions were made by "experts" who have the "technical" competence to make them.[30] These experts could also not be threatened on the political implications of their decisions, for they would be long-term appointees who could not be removed except for cause. The decisions of the independent regulatory commissions would, in short, be in the public interest because they would be made by experts who were above politics.[31]

Have the actions of the independent regulatory commissions met the expectations of their founders? Can the independent regulatory

[27]Marc Pilisuk and Thomas Hayden, "Is there a Military Industrial Complex which Prevents Peace?" *Journal of Social Issues*, 21 (July 1965), 67–117.

[28]M. J. Peck and F. M. Scherer, *The Weapons Acquisition Process* (Cambridge: Harvard University, 1962).

[29]A major study of the varied efforts of government to control business is that by Robert E. Lane, *The Regulation of Businessmen: Social Conditions of Government Economic Control* (New Haven: Yale University Press, 1954).

[30]It should be noted that the "regular" bureaus of the Executive branch also make and always have made decisions of this kind. The only possible difference is and has always been one of degree.

[31]For a similar discussion of the rationale of the independent regulatory commissions, see Marver Bernstein, *Regulating Business by Independent Commission* (Princeton: Princeton University Press, 1955), pp. 27, 36–38.

commissions be considered a success? The answer to both of these questions is probably no. Both the commissions' friends and their enemies say that they have failed to "do the job."[32] Many case studies of the way commissions have made their decisions lead one to the conclusion that narrow pressure-group influence is at least as important in the decisions made by commissions as in those made by the "political" branches of government.[33] These same studies also show that the Executive and Legislative branches of government also attempt to exert and do exert tremendous "extra-legal" pressure on the regulatory agencies.[34] Senator Everett Dirksen of Illinois provided a candid example in 1960:

> Here is Town "A" and there are three applicants for a TV channel. I know every one of them. They are my friends. They vote for me. Some of them may be a little closer than others.
>
> An attorney comes to see me. He is representing Group "X." They are one of the applicants. He says, "Look, we want that television station. Call them up down there. You've got friends down there, haven't you? Call them up and see whether you can't do us some good."
>
> Why, for 26 years my office has been full of attorneys, who come with missions just like that. Now, you see, I can plead the Fifth Amendment, say "I am sorry. I just can't answer your question, I can't make any comment."
>
> He will probably say—"Well, what kind of a friend are you, anyway? Don't you look after your constituents?" So what am I going to say to him? Or am I going to lift the receiver and see what information I get?
>
> These are hard situations and these go on every day. I got

---

[32]They would not, of course, agree on the extent of failure and the remedies for it. For a critical look at the commissions by one sympathetic to them, see United States Senate, Subcommittee on Administrative Practices and Procedures of the Committee of the Judiciary, *The Landis Report* (Washington, D.C.: Government Printing Office, 1960).

[33]Victor Rosenblum, "How to Get into TV," in Alan Westin, *The Uses of Power* (New York: Harcourt, Brace and World, 1962), pp. 193–4, 196–7.

[34]Ibid. pp. 201–2, 207–10. The cases studied are, of course, sensational ones that probably overemphasize the commissioners' weaknesses. The weaknesses they show are, however, widely prevalent.

a half dozen calls over there in my office I've got to make
after a while to some agencies.[35]

The chief weakness of the independent regulatory commissions is
that nobody has an "interest" in the actions of the commissioners
except the businesses the commissions are regulating and—much
less frequently and then often in the interest of business—the other
branches of government. The main group that keeps a constant eye
on the commissions are the various industries that they regulate.
The "controlled" thus control the "controllers."[36] The commissioners
attend the conventions of the industries, are friendly with the leaders
of the industries, and listen to the testimony provided by the directors
and experts of the industries. There is nothing wrong with any of
these things. When they are not matched, however, by equal or nearly
equal activity of other interests, or by the political check of public
attention, they provide an atmosphere in which favoritism can flour-
ish, and it has. This is why effective pressure-group activity is more
inimical to the public interest when applied to the independent regulatory commissions than when applied to the "political" branches of
government, since the latter get some continuous pressure from the
broad-gauged political parties.[37]

The President's Committee on Administrative Management of
1937 recommended that many of the functions of the independent
regulatory commissions be brought back into the Executive branch.[38]
The Committee's recommendations have been generally accepted by
most scholars studying the suject.[39] These experts feel that the public
interest would be better served by bringing business regulation back

---

[35]Ibid. p. 227. Another interesting case of congressional pressure on an administrative body on behalf of a business friend of a congressman turned up in the
congressional hearings on the former Senate Secretary, Robert Baker: See *The New
York Times*, November 18, 1963, p. 16.

[36]Bernstein, *Regulating Business*, pp. 3–5, 73.

[37]Whether the party can be made a sufficiently active instrument to express
effectively the varied interests of the public is discussed by E. E. Schattschneider,
Party Government (New York: Farrar and Rinehart, 1942), pp. 187–94.

[38]President's Committee on Administrative Management, *Report With Special
Studies* (Washington, D.C.: Government Printing Office, 1937), pp. 39–42.

[39]I am not speaking of the exact details here, but of the general conclusion that
there should be more formal Executive authority in the areas currently being
regulated by the commissions. Bernstein, Landis, and Rosenblum would all, I believe,
agree with this view, and I know of no scholars who are specialists in this field
who would disagree.

into politics. There have been cases in which a commission was as much involved in politics as the most politically oriented congressional committee.[40]

Business pressures on the Executive branch are not restricted to the independent regulatory commissions. They are also directed at every branch of the government that makes decisions affecting business—all the way up to the White House. Procurement officers are wined and dined, or they are "friends" of some business executive, even though there are many rules governing all purchasing by government.[41] Bureau and department heads who have been given authority by statute to set regulations that may affect business in one way or another are regularly beset by communications from the affected businesses. The President's power to modify tariffs, within limits set by legislation, makes him the recipient of many pressures from those businesses that are affected.[42] Most of the requests are very specific— to help one business firm or category of business firms make money, often at the expense of other businesses, but more often at the expense of the general public. They do not reflect any "business philosophy" other than that of economic gain. In fact, probably most of them are against the business philosophy of "free competition" and "unregulated private enterprise." The most general these business pressures ever become is in urging governments to "stabilize in currency" or to provide an "easing of credit" (in recent decades, the latter power is mostly controlled by the Federal Reserve Board, which is only semi-governmental). Seldom any more are there requests from business to balance the budget, as Keynesian ideas have been generally accepted by leading businessmen as well as by government officials.

There can be little doubt that the great bulk of business pressures

[40]See, for example, Edward Lamb, *"Trial by Battle": The Case History of a Washington Witch-Hunt* (Santa Barbara, Calif.: Center for the Study of Democratic Institutions, 1964).

[41]A congressional investigation of government stockpiling of strategic materials revealed that a contract with the M. A. Hanna Company for stockpiling nickel was unusually "favorable" to that company. George M. Humphrey, Secretary of the Treasury in President Eisenhower's cabinet from 1953 to 1957, was president of that company, and was a close friend of all the officials who were responsible for the contract and its fulfillment in both the Truman and Eisenhower administrations.

[42]See, for example, *The New York Times*, December 1, 1962, p. 1: "Kennedy Stiffens Oil Import Rules to Aid U.S. Output."

on, and interventions in, government—on both the Executive and
Legislative branches—are simply additional ways of making sales,
increasing the profit margin of sales, obtaining raw materials at lower
cost, or protecting markets. That is, they are purely "economic," and
it is questionable whether most of the businessmen involved have
any conscious conception of affecting public policy. If these efforts
to get a "better deal" from government are thought of in any way
other than as strictly market efforts to get a better deal in dealing
with private suppliers and customers, there is no evidence of it.[43]
But there is the fact that—in addition to sometimes "fleecing" the
public through government as through the market—these business
operations sometimes do create a public policy which favors business
over other segments of the American population.

D. The "Political Strike" by Business against Government

The third topic that will be discussed is the use by business of the
"political strike," by which I mean the threat by businessmen not to
engage in business unless the political authorities take certain actions
that businessmen demand or refrain from taking certain actions
which businessmen disapprove.

The most frequent and obvious use of the political strike by business is the threat to locate elsewhere if the state or local tax structure
is not adjusted in the desired manner. In the state of Minnesota, for
example, the iron mining industry warned—in a threatening manner
—that Minnesota would suffer economically unless the legislature
passed the "Taconite Amendment," which would freeze taxes on
taconite production at their current low rate for twenty-five years.
Nearly every legislature and city council is told that some other state
or city offers a "more favorable" tax climate, and there is a threat to
move one or more businesses to it.

The important point is that it is the threat that counts, not the
exercise of the threat. As long as people think that business might
move, their behavior will, at least in part, be effectively controlled by
business. Generally speaking, state taxation probably has a very
small effect on industrial location, because so many factors enter

---

[43]The books describing top business executives suggest their dominant preoc-
cupation is with business and social interests, not with public policy. See, for
example Osborn Elliot, *Men at the Top* (New York: Harper, 1960).

into business costs, but a laboring or an unemployed man is probably willing to believe "anything" that effects keeping or getting a job.[44] It should also be emphasized that this type of power is not possessed by labor; labor "follows" business, not the reverse. There may also be a legal barrier to the use of the political strike by labor.[45] But the main weakness in the use of any kind of political strike by organized labor is that it could not hide it from the public, and any possible benefits from the strike itself would be nullified by public opposition, including that coming from the rank-and-file membership of the union.[46] We have no data on the effectiveness of the political strike on the action of legislatures and city councils, except to mention that there are known cases in which such threats to move have prevented the rise of business taxes, although there are also known cases in which the bluff was called, and no moves were made.[47]

There has been one outstanding example in recent American history in which a large segment of an industry made good its threat to move to another section of the country if its demands for tax reduction were not met: this was the move of a significant portion of New England's textile industry to the South. In this case, the problem of the old location was as much that of organized labor's demands on the economically unhealthy industry as it was the state governments' demands for taxes. It is not known whether the move helped

[44]On this point, see Harvey Brazer, "Taxation and Industrial Location in Michigan," in William Haber, Eugene McKean, and Harold Taylor, *The Michigan Economy* (Kalamazoo, Mich.: W. E. Upjohn Institute for Employment Research, 1950), pp. 309–10, 323–7.

[45]This might be considered to be the import of Chief Justice Vinson's opinion in the Douds Case. See United States Supreme Court, *American Communications Association v. Douds*, 339 U.S., pp. 382–3, 387–406.

[46]The discussion of proposed legislation to bar James Hoffa, president of the Teamsters Union, from calling a national transportation strike is evidence of this point.

[47]In Minnesota, for example, organized business groups have threatened to move to the South if personal property taxes on business were not removed, the rise in the income tax halted, and a sales tax substituted. These threats began at least as far back as 1954, but the Minnesota legislature—even though usually conservative-dominated—has continued in the old path hated by business up to the time of this writing (1966). In one sense, the business groups have hurt themselves by demanding the whole package and not being willing to compromise on reforms in the personal property tax which could readily be agreed to by an overwhelming majority of the legislature without much controversy. During this period, Minnesota has attracted many more industrial firms than it has lost—because of other economic advantages offered by the state, such as a highly educated and skilled working force.

the industry, for the labor force found in the South, while relatively docile, was much less skilled, and it gradually also became organized into unions. After a brief period of unemployment, the laid-off textile workers of New England found other suitable employment, as shown by the facts that New England's unemployment rate quickly fell to the average for the rest of the country and its average wage level did not fall.

The federal government could readily counter the business threat to move by partially nationalizing taxation. If state income taxes were supported by a federal income tax credit, the states would be far less hesitant about levying or raising state income taxes. The experience with the federal credit on inheritance taxes is evidence for this point.[48] In 1964 the Johnson Administration toyed with the idea of returning some of its income tax revenues to the state governments, to equalize taxes partially among the states and to reduce the tremendous pressure on the state legislatures, which were faced with rapidly rising burdens of education and health and welfare matters, but nothing came of the idea, at least up to 1966.

Another type of business political strike is the threat that business will "lose confidence" if government takes "undesirable" actions. This is not likely to be very effective when the governmental policies referred to are general, since the administration is too identified with general policies to shift readily, but it can be significant when applied to specific governmental policies. The "steel crisis" of 1962 is an important case in which this threat was allegedly exercised. Many people feel that the stock market decline was attributable, at least in part, to business's disapproval of the Kennedy Administration's actions forcing the steel companies to roll back their prices. More pertinent was the earlier action of the steel companies—the breaking of their implied pledge that they would hold the price line if government would induce labor to hold the wage line—because it provides a more specific example of business directly challenging the government.[49]

[48]Governor's Minnesota Tax Study Committee, *Report* (Minneapolis: Colwell Press, 1956), pp. 352–3.
[49]It was the overt challenge to the government implied in the steel companies' decision to raise prices that angered President Kennedy. It raised the issue from one of technical economics to a "crisis of state." On this point, see Carl Auerbach, "Administered Prices and the Concentration of Economic Power," *Minnesota Law Review*, 47, 2 (December 1962), 196.

It will be instructive for us to examine the steel crisis of 1962, since it provides a major example of direct conflict between an important segment of the national economic elite and the leading segment of the national political elite (the President). The main facts of the confrontation are available from detailed reports in *The New York Times*.[50]

The Kennedy Administration had announced a policy of preventing significant inflation by asking all economic groups not to raise prices more rapidly than the continuing rate of increase in productivity per man-hour. Prior to this, there had been a vicious circle in which organized labor periodically had demanded and obtained a rise in wages larger than the slow (in the 1950's) increase in productivity, and shortly afterward the affected industries set their prices up to compensate for more than the increased cost of labor. This resulted in a steady inflation which hurt economic growth, helped keep unemployment high, cut into export sales, caused a continuing outflow of gold, and hurt especially the unorganized segments of the population who have relatively fixed incomes. In the steel industry's collective bargaining of early 1962, the Kennedy Administration intervened successfully (according to its economic estimates) to keep the steelworkers' union's final demands down to a dollar amount which was less than the increase in the steel industry's productivity per man-hour during the preceding year, thus making it economically unnecessary to raise steel prices. A few days after the labor settlement, on April 10, Mr. Roger Blough, president of the United States Steel Corporation, visited President Kennedy and presented to him a copy of a four-page mimeographed press release that was being sent to the newspapers for publication the next morning. It announced a 3½ per cent increase in United States Steel's prices as a "catch-up" resulting from recent increases in costs, particularly labor costs. The President was reported to have been furious because in the earlier labor negotiations it had been agreed that the final and reduced union demands (reduced at the government's insistence) did not make it economically mandatory for the steel industry to raise its prices. The President is reported to have told Mr. Blough that the United States Steel action was both a jeopardy to the Adminis-

[50]The crisis lasted from April 10 to 13, 1962, and the reports are not only in *The Times* for those days, but also summarized in the issue of April 23, 1962.

tration's anti-inflation policy, which had no legal standing but was in the national interest, and a violation of an informal agreement that would make collective bargaining over wages much more difficult in the future.

As soon as Mr. Blough left the White House, the President took a series of steps which amounted to a full-scale attack on the steel companies that had raised, or were about to raise, their prices:

1. He got Senator Estes Kefauver (D., Tenn.) and the Justice Department independently to announce investigations of "possible" collusion—in violation of the antitrust laws—among the companies which were announcing a price increase. Shortly afterwards, the House of Representatives (through Representative Emmanuel Celler) and the Federal Trade Commission also began to work on the antitrust angle. It should be pointed out that the antitrust laws are only rarely enforced, partly because it is very difficult to get evidence of collusion that will satisfy the courts. But the threat of enforcing them would create difficulties for the companies, and there was the possibility that the steel officials involved would personally be fined or imprisoned, or both.

2. He ordered his staff to collect all the pertinent economic information, which he used the next day for a public denunciation of the steel companies' action as damaging to the national interest.

3. He asked Secretary of Commerce Luther Hodges to telephone leading businessmen, especially private customers of United States Steel, to explain the Administration's viewpoint.

4. He investigated the possibility of cutting off some of the steel companies' tax write-offs on new capital investments.

5. Congressional leaders of the Democratic party denounced the steel price increase and talked vaguely of possible legislation to empower the courts to prohibit price increases in basic industries until there had been a "cooling-off" period. Within forty-eight hours, more definite plans were made for possible new control legislation.

6. Contacts were made between members of the Administration and some of the smaller steel companies—collectively producing only 14 to 18 per cent of the output—which had not raised prices immediately following the United States Steel announcement. The purpose of these contacts was to persuade them to hold the line. While this

pressure could not be verbally very blunt, it was soon backed up by announcements of federal government purchasing orders with the companies which held to lower prices.

7. The Democratic National Committee asked Democratic governors to announce support for the President's position, and to request local steel companies to hold the line on prices.

8. F.B.I. agents checked with newspaper reporters who had heard the president of Bethlehem Steel Corporation say, the day before the United States Steel announcement, that there was no need for a price increase. Bethlehem, the second largest steel producer, had followed United States Steel in raising prices, so the statement might be used in an antitrust suit to show that United States Steel had exercised undue influence on Bethlehem.

9. Two leading Republicans, the candidates for governor and senator of Pennsylvania but then still representatives from the state, wired the United States Steel Corporation expressing their opposition to the price increase. There is no evidence that this was done in consultation with the Administration—their action was probably simply a reflection of both gentlemen's personal opinions, and rational campaign strategy. (One of them, William W. Scranton, shortly thereafter became governor of Pennsylvania, and two years later was a candidate for his party's nomination for the presidency).

10. There were implied threats to cancel certain defense contracts.

Less than seventy hours after Mr. Blough had visited President Kennedy with his price rise announcement, Bethlehem rescinded its price rise—apparently in view of the fact that the smaller competitive companies had not raised their prices and that government orders were being shifted to them. The United States Steel officers announced capitulation about two hours later.

This whole incident gave President Kennedy the reputation in the business world of being anti-business, which he later took many concrete steps to dispel. There was erosion of the Administration's anti-inflation policy by the construction workers' unions, which were too numerous and scattered to control as "Big Steel" had been controlled.[51] The steel companies did not raise their prices until about a year later, when the normal increase in productivity made a price increase compatible with the anti-inflation policy.

[51] James Reston's column, *The New York Times*, May 2, 1962, p. 34.

President Lyndon Johnson used the same techniques with the aluminum and the copper industries in 1965[52] that President Kennedy had used with the steel industry in 1962. Johnson got the companies to rescind their price increases immediately, even before he could use the full barrage of techniques available to him, although he did sell stockpiles to force prices down. He, like Kennedy, was less successful in getting the trade unions to cut down their demands for wage increases, but he did succeed in getting the railroad unions and the steel unions to cut short their strikes and engage in collective bargaining instead. Both Kennedy and Johnson were likely to try persuasion with businessmen before they used coercive powers, but they did not hesitate to use coercion to force businessmen to conform to the economic policies favored by the President. The main techniques used were curtailment of government purchases and sales of surplus stocks.[53] It was said that President Franklin Roosevelt discovered early that he was more successful in getting the "cooperation" of businessmen by coercion than by persuasion, and after that did not spend any time in trying to persuade them until World War II made them more amenable to verbal persuasion "for the good of the nation."[54]

The political strike by business could be eliminated by the government only if it took on a more permanent direction and regulation of the economy. This at present would probably be violently opposed by most of the American people. Many believe that this kind of socialism poses a threat to democracy. At present, the major countervailing actions available to government are those employed by President Kennedy in 1962, although a president with stronger support in Congress might make his countervailing actions even more effective than did Kennedy.

In all three types of power exercised by business over government that we have examined in this section, there is evidence both of the real force behind business's actions and of the possibility of government successfully opposing business. Not all federal administration

[52]*The New York Times*, November 11, 1965, p. 1; November 12, 1965, p. 1; November 19, 1965, p. 53ff. Johnson also sold wheat on the open market to keep prices down: *Minneapolis Morning Tribune*, November 24, 1965, p. 21.

[53]*The New York Times*, April 6, 1966, p. 27.

[54]Arthur M. Schlesinger, Jr., *The Politics of Hope* (Boston: Houghton Mifflin, 1963).

or state governments in the past have wished to oppose business, but when they have, the battle seems to have been an even one. It has also been suggested that new devices could be employed by government to counter the pressures of business. One type of business-government conflict needs more attention—that over the enactment of new legislation—and we shall turn to this topic in our case analysis of the struggle over the passage of a bill to provide medical care for the elderly.

E. Business Influence on Government through the Mass Media of Communication and Public Opinion

Business by no means restricts its approach to the government by direct lobbying or other pressures. It also uses the indirect approach through the bosses of the government—that is, the public. Andrew Hacker summarizes:

> Until a few decades ago pressure groups confined themselves, for the most part, to lobbying: direct contact with legislators and, on occasion, administrators. It was felt that if a case were stated privately and persuasively, a law maker would listen to reason and would give his support to one or another side of an issue. More recently, however, pressure politics have taken a more ambitious turn. Working on the assumption that elected officials are responsive to public opinion, groups now seek to arouse favorable sentiment to their cause among the electorate at large with the thought that this grass-roots feeling will be conveyed upward to the politicians. The consequence is that old-style lobbying is supplemented by new-style public relations. The intimate contacts of the capitol cloakroom are bolstered by the practiced techniques of Madison Avenue.[55]

The National Association of Manufacturers publishes vast numbers of pamphlets, directed at nearly every significant reading audience, including high school youth, and irregularly uses billboard campaigns, radio and TV spot announcements, and full programs.[56]

[55]Andrew Hacker, "Pressure Groups," in Alan F. Westin (ed.), *The Uses of Power: 7 Cases in American Politics* (New York: Harcourt, Brace and World, 1962), p. 325.

[56]Marshall E. Dimock, *Business and Government* (New York: Henry Holt, 1953), pp. 83–9.

Individual businessmen occasionally propagandize their employees to vote in a certain way, and on rare occasions they attempt to get their workers to participate in closed letters-to-congressmen campaigns. With the practical disappearance of the company towns and the open ballot, the direct control of votes of workers by their employers has practically disappeared.

One of the most effective approaches of certain businesses to a segment of the public to put pressure on government in its behalf was illustrated by the campaign of the savings and loan associations in early 1962 to avoid increases in federal taxation. The financial institutions had always enjoyed tax privileges as compared to banks, privileges which the Congress was preparing to reduce drastically in 1962. On January 30, 1962, in response to Administration recommendations, the House Ways and Means Committee proposed a large increase in taxes on the associations. The associations used various approaches to Congress, but apparently one of the most effective was to ask their numerous depositors—who enjoyed a higher rate of interest than that paid by banks—to write their congressmen in protest. By February 22, the Committee substituted a much smaller increase in taxation on the associations.[57] Businessmen have often found that the simple technique of writing, phoning, and telegraphing their congressman—and getting a couple of dozen friends to do likewise— is one of the most effective pressures, at least when no opposing group is putting countervailing pressure in the other direction.[58] Letters "To the Editor," published on the editorial page of newspapers, are sometimes written as a matter of deliberate organizational policy, as a more effective way of engaging public attention than a news release.[59] President Kennedy more than once attributed his lack

[57]*The New York Times*, February 23, 1962, p. 11. Some years later, Representative Ancher Nelsen (R., Minn.) charged that a payoff of $100,000 to Robert Baker, then secretary to the Democratic majority caucus in the Senate, was the effective means by which the savings and loan associations obtained what they wished from the Congress. *Minneapolis Morning Tribune*, October 13, 1965, p. 3. In a recent Federal court action Baker stated he had received $99,600 from the executives of the California savings and loan associations to kill the bill, but had given it to the late Senator Robert Kerr (D., Okla.). (*New York Herald Tribune*, Int'nat'l Ed., January 20, 1967, p. 3.) If true, this raises the question whether the payoff or the depositor's letters was most effective in getting what the associations wanted.

[58]See, for example, James Reston's column for *The New York Times* in the *Minneapolis Morning Tribune*, March 9, 1961, p. 4.

[59]Not infrequently a news release will be distorted or rebutted by a reporter or news editor before it appears in print, whereas a short, clear letter to the "editor"

of effectiveness with Congress, despite his high public-opinion-poll ratings, to organized letter-writing campaigns (both directly to congressmen and to "Editors").[60] While this might have been an excuse to gloss over a more fundamental weakness in his relationship with Congress, there can be little doubt that a systematic letter-writing campaign, which is made to appear spontaneous rather than deliberately organized by business interests, if not countered by an opposing letter-writing campaign, can be effective.

The business community has ties of ownership and friendship with the press, as well as the opportunity to exercise cruder pressure on the press through allocation of advertising (although the trend in smaller cities toward having only one newspaper company continues, this pressure is less effective). There can be little doubt that those who own and manage most of the newspapers of the United States are more pro-business than they are supportive of any other segment of the population. In every presidential election campaign, with the exception of that of 1964, at least 80 per cent of the newspapers outside the South that took an editorial stand supported the Republican candidates (although they may also have supported some local Democratic candidate either because they were genuinely favorable to him or because they wished to give the public an impression of being "balanced" and impartial).[61] The chief means by which this partiality is demonstrated is through selection and placement of news, rather than through the older and cruder method of distorting or manufacturing news stories. The *International Teamster*, a monthly

---

will not be changed, although it may stimulate opposing letters. The American Medical Association conducted a nationwide "Letters to the Editor" campaign over several years in its opposition to the bill providing medical care for older people, suggesting to selected physicians that they should write these letters. The AMA's organized opponent on this issue—the National Council of Senior Citizens—also conducted a letter-writing campaign.

[60]*Minneapolis Morning Tribune*, March 16, 1961, p. 2.

[61]In the 1952 presidential campaign, Eisenhower's candidacy was explicitly supported by 67.34 per cent of the newspapers of the country, with a total circulation of over 40 million (or 86 per cent of the circulation). Stevenson's candidacy was supported by 14.52 per cent of the newspapers, with a total circulation of 5.4 million. The remaining 18.14 per cent of the newspapers were undecided or independent up to one week before the election, according to the survey made by *Editor and Publisher* magazine. See *The New York Times*, October 31, 1952, p. 17. In 1960, 731 dailies, representing 71 per cent of the circulation, supported Nixon editorially; while 208 dailies, representing 16 per cent of the circulation, supported Kennedy. *The New York Times*, November 4, 1960, p. 24.

magazine published by the union headed by James R. Hoffa—who has often experienced an unfavorable press—told its readers: "It is a 'controlled' press—controlled by special interest groups which edit or omit news dispatches to suit their purposes. Publications play down news offensive to big business; play up news delightful to big business (such as news knocking labor or tending to weaken the labor movement)."[62] The article went on to illustrate how Hoffa's alleged shenanigans were given front-page attention, whereas the price-fixing violations of the law by the major electrical equipment manufacturers were either reported in small articles on back pages or—in *Newsweek* and *U.S. News and World Report*—not carried at all.

These aspects of bias in the press have received much study, and will be given no further attention here, although they are an important aspect of the power of the economic elite.[63] Another aspect of distortion by the press—the bias of individual reporters toward what they deem "newsworthy"—has been neglected, but since it has little relevance to the power of the economic elite, it will be passed over here. However, it should be noted that certain leading Republican candidates—especially Richard Nixon, in his presidential campaign of 1960 and his California gubernatorial campaign of 1962—have charged that most reporters have been unfavorable to them and have given them a "bad press." If this is true, it would counterbalance for political affairs the bias of the publishers and editors in favor of Republican candidates.

The above refers to the "regular" press—the big daily newspapers and the big weekly and monthly magazines. There is also a smaller press, consisting of "fly-by-night" or irregularly published newspapers, magazines and pamphlets, as well as publications by small groups, such as churches, business firms, unions, and other organizations. While these usually express varied group interests, occasionally they are subsidized by big business interests as part of a political campaign. In 1960 there was widespread publication and distribution of anti-Catholic literature against presidential candidate John F.

[62]*The New York Times,* February 8, 1961, p. 24.

[63]Frank Thayer, *Newspaper Management* (New York: Appleton-Century, 1938); Neil H. Borden, M. I. Taylor, and H. T. Hovde, *National Advertising in Newspapers* (Cambridge: Harvard University Press, 1946); H. A. Innis, *The Press: A Neglected Factor in the Economic History of the Twentieth Century* (London: Oxford University Press, 1949).

Kennedy.[64] Some of this was subsidized by individual big businessmen, perhaps not so much because they were personally anti-
Catholic, but because the material seemed an effective way to defeat
Kennedy. A number of corporations also support the publications
and public-relations of crackpot right-wing extremist organizations.[65]

Another form of press is that which serves primarily the business
community. An outstanding business publication is the *Wall Street
Journal*, which advertises its economic influence thus: "When you
sell America's mightiest million you are taking a mighty step toward
selling America's 184,000,000—anything!"[66] It is not clear whether
this refers solely to control by these million readers of the *Wall Street
Journal* over production and distribution, or whether it refers also to
their setting consumption standards which others adopt voluntarily.

It is difficult to assess the effectiveness of the approach businessmen make to government through influence on public opinion. Probably no more than a tiny segment of the public gets interested
enough in most things businessmen are concerned with to put pressure on their congressmen, unless the issue has wider significance,
and the effect of the business propaganda is to alert the public to its
own interests. Certainly the President of the United States can get
more publicity for his position, at no cost to himself or his party, than
can the entire business community by purchasing time or space from
the mass media. This is almost as true for governors and leading
congressmen, at least on specific issues that capture the public attention. Two general surveys of public opinion will be reported here
regarding the general evaluation made by the public of the treatment
business gets from the Congress.

Businessmen are occasionally heard to say that unions have more
influence on government than does business, and this is a stated
motive for the Chamber of Commerce's effort to get businessmen
involved in politics. The majority of the public does not agree, according to a 1960 national Gallup poll.[67] In that poll, two questions

[64] See, for example, James Reston, column, *The New York Times*, September 14,
1960, p. 40.
[65] Alan F. Westin, "Anti-Communism and the Corporations," *Commentary*, (January 1964), 3–7.
[66] *The New York Times* (advertisement), November 6, 1961, p. 68.
[67] American Institute of Public Opinion, "Labor Believed Less Powerful than
Business," *Minneapolis Morning Tribune*, May 13, 1960, p. 25.

were asked which provided findings indicating that more of the public believes that business has more influence than labor, but wishes labor to have more influence than business:

	"At the present time, which do you think has the most influence on the laws passed in this country—big business or labor?"		"Which do you think should have the most influence?"	
ANSWER	% OF ALL ADULTS	% OF BUSINESS & PROFESSIONALS	% OF ALL ADULTS	% OF BUSINESS & PROFESSIONALS
Business	43	38	14	17
Labor	34	41	29	16
No difference	10	9	46	58
No opinion	13	12	11	9

Of all the occupational categories, businessmen and professionals are the only ones to have a plurality saying that labor has more power than business, but not by much greater a percentage, and they include a significantly larger percentage saying that there ought to be no difference in power.

On the other hand, when questions were asked about the adequacy of legislation to regulate business corporations and labor unions—presumably their unethical practices—a larger proportion of the public said the laws were not strict enough for unions than for corporations.[68]

	"Do you think the laws regulating business corporations are too strict, or not strict enough?" (percentages)	"Do you think the laws regulating labor unions are too strict, or not strict enough?" (percentages)
ANSWER		
Too strict	9	9
Not strict enough	26	42
About right	32	27
Don't know	33	22

[68]George Gallup, "Stricter Labor, Business Laws Urged by Many," *Minneapolis Sunday Tribune*, October 22, 1961, p. 8E.

Somewhat earlier, in 1951, the Survey Research Center of the University of Michigan showed that the public had a general positive attitude toward big business.[69] A quarter of the population showed some concern over big business and were aware that it had an important effect on their lives. Asked to characterize its social effects, the respondents answered as follows:

The good things outweigh the bad things	76%
They seem about equal	2%
The bad things outweigh the good things	10%
Don't know	5%
Confused: evaluation not ascertainable	7%

Mills might regard the small amount of hostility to big business on the part of the American public as evidence of the success of the "Madison Avenue" techniques of big business. An alternative explanation,[70] which would compare this small amount of hostility today with the probably large amount which existed in the heyday of the Populists and the Progressives before World War I, would be based on the following considerations: (1) Big business is relatively weak today, and has not succeeded in holding up social security, welfare, or pro-labor legislation; it has successfully been subjected to various government controls. (2) Small business, rather than big business, has been the main source of the recent opposition to liberal legislation and the principal upholder of conservatism generally (it was the major force behind the two outstanding victories of conservatism in the present generation—the Taft-Hartley Act and the Landrum-Griffin Act), whereas earlier, small business was seen as the heroic deterrent to big business. (3) The conservative small businessman has become the leading ideological opponent of big business. (4) Big business has not proved to be a closed oligarchy, but allows access to its ranks through education.

[69]Institute of Social Research, *Big Business From the Viewpoint of the Public* (Ann Arbor: University of Michigan, 1951).

[70]Adapted from Richard Hofstadter, "Anti-trust in America," *Commentary*, 38 (August 1964), 47–53.

F. Direct Participation by Businessmen in Government and the Use of Public Officials as "Business Representatives."

When American businessmen have moved into governmental activities, it has usually been through appointments to high, or fairly high, level positions in the Executive branch, somewhat more frequently in Republican administrations than in Democratic ones. In recent decades, not many leading businessmen have sought elective office, and when they have—as, for example, George Romney (former president of American Motors Corporation, who became governor of Michigan) or Chester Bowles (former president of the Benton and Bowles advertising company, who later became governor of Connecticut and congressman from that state)—they took on a completely new occupational commitment, in the same way that former professors Paul H. Douglas and John G. Tower left academic life completely for senatorial careers.

Businessmen, like people in almost every other occupation, have often become active in political parties (occasionally running for part-time offices, such as that of state legislator), while retaining their regular occupations. In this capacity they are more likely to retain a primary identification with their business in general, although they may also have a quite divided interest, in business as a livelihood and in politics as an avocation or hobby. Sometime during the 1950's, the United States Chamber of Commerce began to urge businessmen to get active in their political parties, to participate in party activities to the same extent as any other active member, and not simply to make financial contributions to parties and candidates as they always had done. The Chamber of Commerce organized "courses" in dozens of cities, to teach businessmen how to work effectively in political campaigns (including how to do the chores of campaign workers, such as door-knocking, holding candidates' meetings, etc.). It also provided them with information about political issues of major interest to business, giving them the Chamber of Commerce position. The national Chamber of Commerce provided plans and materials for these courses; local Chambers of Commerce organized them, and each year throughout the country thousands of businessmen—mostly at the middle and lower executive levels—took them. The courses were declared to be non-partisan, but it is safe to say that most of the participants leaned toward the Republican party. It is not known how many of the "graduates" of these courses followed them up by participating in political parties or campaigns. But the fact that the Chamber of Commerce made this a major activity for a number of years makes it seem likely that they thought it important. It would hardly be considered so important if business-men were already in control of the political parties or of a majority of public office holders. Speakers at the introductory sessions often pointed out that businessmen had "unfortunately" avoided politics in the past, and stressed that if the business point of view were to be adequately represented in government, businessmen would have to evidence a more active interest in politics.[71]

Local businessmen's groups and specific firms have also encouraged their members to become active in politics. At a joint meeting of the Minneapolis and St. Paul Employers' associations in 1960, members were urged to work for the election of six or seven conservatives in the state House of Representatives.[72] This would make enough difference, they were told, in that body of 135 persons to determine the outcome of a congressional reapportionment in Minnesota which would take place in the next legislature as a result of the 1960 census. The speaker conceded he was suggesting gerrymandering, and justified it by saying that it would halt the rise in federal expendi-tures and taxation. The American Can Company in 1959 announced that it was training its managers throughout the country in the tech-niques of ward and precinct politics, so that they would be better able to propagate the "company's viewpoint" on a number of national issues.[73] A nine-week course was provided so that the trainees would know how to participate effectively in political parties and campaigns and how to communicate the company's views to candi-dates and to the public. The General Electric Company and the Gulf Oil Corporation, among the larger corporations, had already inaugu-rated similar programs.[74] The Ford Motor Company, with the en-

[71]Articles urging businessmen to go into politics were periodically published in business journals. See, for example, Clarence B. Randall, "The Myth of the Wicked Politician," *Dun's Review and Modern Industry*, 75 (March 1960), 48–50. For the philosophy and activities of the Ford Motor Company on this matter, see Thomas R. Reid, "Management Programs to Encourage Political Participation," Papers Presented at the 1960 Spring Meeting, Industrial Relations Research Association, 1960, pp. 645–53.

[72]*Minneapolis Morning Tribune*, May 26, 1960, p. 11.

[73]*The New York Times*, May 21, 1959, p. 16.

[74]Ibid.

dorsement of the United Auto Workers union, engaged in a less partisan effort to get its employees to contribute financially to the party of their choice.

Perhaps the most representative survey of top businessmen's direct and open relationship to politics was that made for *Fortune* magazine in 1959:

"Sixty per cent of over 1,700 say they take no part in raising party funds, half are not even 'informally associated' with state or national party leaders, over 75 per cent are not members of a party organization. The exception to this general indifference are men who might be said to have gone into politics whole hog: 121 got themselves elected to political office, one to Congress. . . . though almost 80 per cent of the group said they are Republican, 8 per cent Democrats, 13 per cent independents, the Republican candidates (Nixon 76 per cent, Rockefeller 11 per cent) were favored by 87 per cent of one group, Democratic candidates by less than 6 per cent."[75]

The effort, in the late 1950's and the early 1960's, to get businessmen into politics resulted in a large number of businessmen-candidates by the time of the 1962 campaign. Perhaps their greatest and most successful effort was at the state legislature level, where service could be part-time. Some of the successful businessman-legislators retained their regular business salaries while serving as low-paid legislators. For higher posts, the only successful candidate in 1962 was George Romney, and it is likely that he was seeking a genuine change of career—as evidenced by his resignation as president of American Motors Corporation—rather than merely seeking to express the business point of view in government. The latter seems to have been the goal of the other leading businessmen candidates in 1962: John M. Briley, general counsel and vice president of Owens-Corning Fiberglas Corporation, filed for the Republican nomination for senator of Ohio to run against Democratic Senator Frank J. Lausche; Crosby Kemper, president of the City National Bank and Trust Company of Kansas City filed for the Republican nomination for senator of Missouri to run against Democratic Senator Edward V. Long. Both were defeated, in a national election in which neither party made notable gains.

[75]"1,700 Top Executives," *Fortune*, 60 (November 1959) 138 ff., at p. 308.

Most of the influence of business on elected government officials, especially those in the Legislative branch, is through *ad hoc* lobbying, campaign contributions, and pressure through some organized group of voters. There are also some rumored cases of "bought congressmen"—that is, congressmen in the regular pay of a single business firm or of an industry federation, whose primary and regular loyalty is to this business element.[76] Significantly, most of the rumors are about certain Southern congressmen, perhaps because they have more uneducated persons, conservatives, and non-voters among their constituents, and because the one-party system formerly prevailing in much of the South gave them a more secure hold on their offices. It is undoubtedly easier to "buy" state legislators than congressmen, especially in some states and especially before reapportionment.[77] Robert Sherrill, writing of some rural Florida legislators, says "The Economic Establishment has used the Pork Chop bloc to oppose progress only because the bloc was already there and willing to be used."

Former congressmen occasionally work as lobbyists, although not exclusively for business interests. They have the extra privilege of being allowed to go onto the floor of the House or the Senate, wherever they served. In 1961, only seven former congressmen registered as lobbyists, and five of these represented business interests.[78]

Probably more important in providing business representation to the national legislature than the "bought" congressmen are those congressmen with business-oriented ideologies. Whether they are former businessmen themselves or not, these congressmen take on the role and ideology of business representatives. Probably few of these receive direct remuneration from business for their services, though probably all have their election campaigns financed in large part by businessmen. Most of these congressmen receive their fees

---

[76]Some open charges of business-politician alliances have been published, but they practically never specify payment to the politician. In an article in *Harper's Magazine*, Louis E. Lomax claims that Witt Stephens, a wealthy businessman in Arkansas, gains economic benefits by alliance with Governor Orval Faubus ("Two Millionaires, Two Senators, and a Faubus," *Harper's Magazine*, 220 (March 1960), pp. 73–86.

[77]See, for example, Robert Sherrill, "Florida's Legislature: The Pork Chop State of Mind," *Harper's Magazine*, 231 (November 1965), 82–97, at p. 97.

[78]*Congressional Quarterly*, reprinted in *The New York Times*, December 26, 1961, p. 22.

through the legal subterfuge of providing extra-governmental services such as through law offices, business services, and speechmaking. "Gifts" in kind, rather than cash, are probably fairly common, but also usually quite modest. Direct cash bribes are probably quite rare, because exposure means almost certain defeat in the next election, and practically all congressmen seem to live on their known incomes. The one known prominent case of attempted bribery in recent years was by the gas and oil industry, offered to Senator Francis Case (R., S.D.) and publicly revealed by him. The instance suggests that other congressmen also receive bribe offers but do not publicize them; yet the fact that Senator Case was shocked enough by the bribe offer to publicize it voluntarily suggests that not many such bribe offers occur. The Senate Majority secretary during the late 1950's and early 1960's, Robert Baker, was accused of having accepted bribes, but there is no evidence that he passed them along to the senators. In any case, bribery is not as important as campaign contributions, conviction, and ideology in motivating congressmen to represent business in their legislative activities.

Most of the business representatives in Congress are Republicans, though more than a few are Southern Democrats. Northern Democrats will often do important favors for business located in their districts, but these are generally specific favors rather than representation of a continuing business interest, and are legitimated by serving to promote the general economic prosperity of the congressman's district or state.[79] An example of this kind of support for a special industry on the part of a Northern Democratic congressman is provided by a Report to his constituents from Senator Eugene J. McCarthy (D., Minn.) of July 7, 1960:

IRON ORE STUDY

The iron ore import study for which I obtained approval of the Senate Finance Committee is of special importance to the economy of the State of Minnesota. At the order of the Finance Committee the United States Tariff Commission must

[79]On the aforementioned gas and oil bill, every single congressman from five states—regardless of political philosophy—voted for the bill. The industry is concentrated in these five states of Arkansas, Kansas, Louisiana, Oklahoma, and Texas. However, the commentator Richard Rovere remarks: "It is doubtful whether anything of this sort has ever before happened in connection with a piece of legislation involving any sizable conflict of economic interests" (*The New Yorker*, November 15, 1956).

study and report within six months the impact of foreign ore imports on our domestic iron ore industry. The Minnesota iron ore industry has been in depressed condition for several years. In 1959 Minnesota production was only 27½ million tons, compared with over 61 million tons in 1957. If the Tariff Commission finds that our foreign iron ore imports and tariff concessions are clearly impairing our domestic industry, it must advise the President to invoke the "escape clause" provisions in the law—withdrawal or modification of our international agreements allowing free importation of iron ore. If the President does not act within 60 days after receiving the recommendations of the Tariff Commission, he must immediately submit a report to the Senate Finance Committee giving his reasons for not taking the recommended action. . . . Senator Humphrey and Congressman Blatnik supported and recommended this order for an import study, and together we have introduced legislation to be considered if the Tariff Commission finds that imports are impairing our domestic iron ore industry.

Perhaps the most important general business representative in Congress in modern times was the late Senator H. Styles Bridges (R., N.H.) who died in 1961 after a senatorial career of over twenty-five years.[80] With great political acumen, he operated from the vantage points of chairman of the Republican Policy Committee, and chairmanship or ranking minority memberships on the Senate committees dealing with appropriations and armed services, and next-to-ranking membership on the aeronautical and space sciences committee. Because he came from a small state, he could have no aspirations for presidential office; because his state was strongly Republican, there was little possibility that he would ever be defeated in an election. Because his operations in the Senate were more likely to be effective if he were not in the public eye, he was not as well known to the national public as many other senators. But "he wielded more power than very many better-known senators." Doris Fleeson goes on to evaluate his influence:

In the larger sense he may be said to have failed. In his 25 years as senator, he never served under any president as conservative or isolationist as he himself was. But the slow

---

[80]Information on Bridges is taken from various Washington sources.

pace of many economic and social measures for which the country seemed to be voting nationally, especially since the depression, was a rough gauge of his influence and operative skill.[81]

The commentator might have gone on to say that, while Bridges did much to slow down liberal legislation, he and his like-minded colleagues failed to stop it. Certainly Bridges's chief reward was the enjoyment of exercising power, and of seeing his convictions reflected in the passage of legislation he favored or the failure of legislation he opposed.

One of C. Wright Mills's most significant bits of factual analysis was the one showing that most of the key positions in the Eisenhower Administration were held by businessmen or corporation lawyers. Mills interpreted this fact as evidence of a trend from some earlier period when most top administrators in government had primarily political backgrounds. The facts do not bear out this interpretation, but are more consistent with an interpretation that businessman dominance was a quirk of the Eisenhower Administration, or that, because the Republicans had been out of power for twenty years, they had no backlog of experienced political administrators to draw from and hence had to turn to business administrators. There were few top business appointees in the Roosevelt–Truman Administrations, except during the Second World War, when a considerable effort was made to bring in skilled administrators from various walks of life to fill the greatly expanded ranks of a government then engaged in an all-out effort to prosecute a war with a degree of involvement such as the country had never before experienced. But even at that time there was every evidence that the businessmen-administrators did not share a common view of government or their role in it. After the war, businessmen left government service to the extent that there was a complaint that the government was in the hands of Truman's cronies. Half of President Eisenhower's first Cabinet was made up of businessmen: Charles E. Wilson, George Humphrey, Sinclair Weeks, Douglas McKay and Arthur Summerfield. Two others—Oveta Culp Hobby and Ezra Taft Benson—had close connections with the business community. Some of these had been active in Republican politics: Summerfield had been national GOP chairman and national committeeman from Michigan. McKay had been elected governor of Oregon. Weeks had also been a national committee member and had served by appointment as a United States senator. The other three in the Eisenhower Cabinet had previous careers primarily in public service. Granting that businessmen were strongly represented in Eisenhower's Cabinet, the anomaly in Mills's argument is that he states that businessmen dominate politics, when in fact no other president and cabinet were so deferential to Congress (a political elite) in the twentieth century.

In the first Kennedy Cabinet, only three had primarily business backgrounds: Robert McNamara (who started as a professional statistician), J. Edward Day (who had also lower-level political activities), and Douglas Dillon (who had also served in the Eisenhower Administration). Also in the Cabinet were three former governors (Orville Freeman, Luther Hodges, and Abraham Ribicoff), one former congressman (Stewart Udall), and one former congressional committee staff director (Robert Kennedy). Dean Rusk came from a career in government and education. Arthur Goldberg had been close to government as legal counsel to the AFL–CIO. Thus there was a significant shift away from the economic elite at the Cabinet level,[82] and the same could be documented even more strongly for the second level of the Kennedy Administration. The economist Seymour E. Harris[83] compared 200 high-level appointments of Eisenhower and Kennedy and came up with the following percentage distribution according to previous occupation:

	KENNEDY	EISENHOWER
Government	47	28
Academic and non-profit organization	18	26
Law	15	11
Business, finance, and insurance	6	36
Other	14	19

[82]There were other shifts in the character of the Kennedy Cabinet. Whereas the religious affiliation of the Eisenhower group was chiefly Episcopalian and Presbyterian (although it included one Catholic and one Mormon), the Kennedy group had but one Episcopalian, and three Presbyterians; it also had two Catholics, two Jews, one Mormon, one Lutheran, and one Methodist. The average Kennedy appointee was about ten years younger than the Eisenhower appointee, better educated, and less wealthy.

[83]Seymour E. Harris, *Economics of the Political Parties* (New York: Macmillan, 1962), p. 25.

That there remained some businessmen in the top levels of the Administration would disturb only a Populist or a Marxist. Businessmen have certain skills in running large bureaucratic operations which few modern presidents would want to dispense with completely. The Johnson Cabinet moved even further away from business representation: While two Cabinet officers (McNamara in Defense and Connor in Commerce) were previously in business, only one had had a leading position there. Three Cabinet officers were primarily associated with education (Rusk in State, Katzenbach in Justice, and Gardner in Health, Education and Welfare); three others were career politicians (O'Brien in the Post Office Department, Udall in Interior, and Freeman in Agriculture); two were practising attorneys (Wirtz in Labor and Fowler in Treasury); and one had been a government administrator (Weaver in Urban Affairs).

G. Business Co-operation with Government in Common Interests

While business and government sometimes clash over issues of private versus public interest, frequently they co-operate with common interests in economic development. The ideology of free enterprise would have business and government each going its own way, with the government's relationship to business largely restricted to maintaining order. In fact, government can improve the economic health and other aspects of the welfare of the entire society by engaging in certain actions that business also particularly wants. The actions of government to aid business in these respects should not be construed as indicating business domination of government, any more than government aid to trade unions, minority groups, older people, and other segments of the population should be construed as domination by those groups over government. In any national society, including socialist ones, public policy often calls for government aid to business.

A simple and obvious instance is provided by urban renewal. A city government should favor urban renewal to improve the health and housing of its poorer citizens, as well as the attractiveness of the city for all citizens, although there are some forms of urban renewal which destroy the social ties of immigrant slum communities.[84] The

[84]Herbert Gans, *The Urban Villagers: Group and Class in the Life of Italian-Americans* (New York: Free Press of Glencoe, 1962).

larger merchants of a city usually find that urban renewal helps their business, although a significant proportion of the smaller merchants directly displaced by the bulldozer cannot relocate satisfactorily.[85] In cities where the bigger businesses are not dominated by an irrational antigovernment ideology,[86] they take a major role in working with the city government—even though it is often controlled by Democrats—for a major urban-renewal project. Notable instances are those of New Haven, Connecticut,[87] and Pittsburgh, Pennsylvania.

A comparable instance at the national level where one group of businessmen works with a liberal Democratic administration to favor a certain public policy, but also in support of their private interests and against the interests of another group of businessmen, is that involving the tariff. President Kennedy, following the foreign trade policies of Roosevelt and Truman, favored a course of trade liberalism. The chief lobby in Congress and the chief advertiser to the public of this policy is the Committee on National Trade Policy, a group of big businessmen whose companies stand to gain by expanded foreign trade. The Committee on National Trade Policies and President Kennedy worked together on legislation, against the interests of those businesses that would benefit from protective tariffs and against congressmen representing the latter interests.[88] President Kennedy also set up a businessmen's committee to help him lobby through Congress the foreign aid bill in 1961—following a precedent set by President Truman—with the interest of the businessmen being the creation of strong foreign markets.[89]

Another even more powerful group of businessmen that met from 1933 to 1961 under nominal White House auspices was the Business Advisory Council. A hundred corporation presidents and board chairmen, including a majority politically hostile to the Democratic administrations, met at least annually in Washington, and offered information and advice to the President and the Secretary of Com-

[85]Basil G. Zimmer, *Rebuilding Cities: The Effects of Displacement and Relocation on Small Business* (Chicago: Quadrangle Books, 1964).

[86]For an instance of this, see "Why a City Turned Down Federal Dollars," *Nation's Business*, 53 (October 1965), 38ff.

[87]Robert A. Dahl, *Who Governs?* (New Haven: Yale University Press, 1961), esp. pp. 115–140.

[88]*The New York Times*, November 21, 1961, p. 13.

[89]William S. White, *Minneapolis Morning Tribune*, May 15, 1961, p. 4.

merce. In 1961, with President Kennedy's approval, Secretary of Commerce Luther Hodges took a tighter hold on the Business Advisory Council than had been customary for previous Secretaries, and decided to publicize its previously semi-secret activities. Partly because of resistance to this and partly because of a more vigorous policy against business mergers, tax loopholes, and inflationary price rises on the part of the Kennedy Administration, the Business Advisory Council broke off its connection with government and became simply the Business Council, meeting annually at different spots in the nation and offering to provide research and advice for any branch of government. At first no government official asked for its help. After the "steel crisis" of 1962, in which President Kennedy got the reputation of being anti-business, he sent his top economic advisors—Chairman of the Economic Advisory Council Walter Heller, Secretary of the Treasury C. Douglas Dillon, and Undersecretary of Labor Willard Wirtz—to attend the meetings of the Business Council, in order to indicate his lack of hostility to big business.

President Kennedy appointed a significant number of Republicans, including businessmen, to top policy-making positions, particularly in the foreign policy field. Among them were Robert McNamara (a businessman who was nominally a Republican, but actually nonpartisan) as Secretary of Defense, C. Douglas Dillon as Secretary of the Treasury, Allen Dulles and later John A. McCone as head of the Central Intelligence Agency, William C. Foster as head of the Arms Control and Disarmament Agency, Lucius D. Clay as diplomatic representative in Berlin, Arthur Dean as disarmament negotiator, and McGeorge Bundy (a Republican without business connections) as special assistant on national security affairs. Democrats with strong business ties were also appointed: Luther Hodges as Secretary of Commerce and Fowler Hamilton as head of the Agency for International Development. Businessmen were displeased with Hodges for his efforts to control the Business Advisory Council, and were opposed to many of the other top appointments in the Kennedy Administration, including Paul R. Dixon as chairman of the Federal Trade Commission, Joseph C. Swidler as chairman of the Federal Power Commission, and Newton N. Minow as chairman of the Federal Communications Commission.[90] Probably history will record the Kennedy Administration as being neither pro-business nor anti-business, but as having a policy in favor of economic development, using techniques favored by advanced economists which most of the more conservative-minded businessmen opposed.[91] Actually the Kennedy and Johnson administrations were far more successful in keeping the economy expanding and generally "healthy" than was the more business-oriented Eisenhower Administration. The gross national product, the net income per capita, and level of employment moved steadily upward from 1961 onward, and there were no recessions. The Democratic administrations were also able to cut taxes, though not reducing expenditures as desired by businessmen, and provided tax incentives for greater private investment in new capital equipment. Presidents Kennedy and Johnson often expressed themselves as friendly to business, unlike Democratic Presidents Roosevelt and Truman, who did not hesitate to attack business openly.

[90]J. A. Livingston, "Is Administration Unfriendly to Nation's Top Businessmen?" *Minneapolis Morning Tribune*, October 9, 1961, p. 6.

[91]William S. White, "President Tries to Get Confidence of Business," *Minneapolis Morning Tribune*, October 23, 1961, p. 4.

Appendix A   Assumptions by Foreign Leaders
Concerning Business Influence
on American Foreign Policy

Many political leaders abroad, at least outside Western Europe, seem to believe that big business controls the United States in large measure. We have already cited former Premier Krushchev's view, in his interview with Walter Lippmann. The eminent foreign correspondent C. L. Sulzberger provides another source of Russian opinion.

"The fact of the matter is that Moscow is stubbornly convinced that the State Department is run by and for the Rockefeller dynasty and that its ultimate objectives are to strangle any and all revolutions and to protect U.S. access to foreign oil.

"Soviet policy makers, believe it or not, insist that The Rockefellers are the dynasty with an overriding interest in foreign policy; actually speaking, their billions are almost entirely tied up with it.

"Apart from the Pentagon, no Government department is as important to them as the State Department. From their point of view, an American diplomat must be, first and foremost, an oil diplomat.

"This fascinating opinion was expressed in a series of Soviet analyses of American, British, French and West German diplomacy. These contend that 'a man without backing in Rockefeller circles has little chance' of getting certain key posts; also that the Rockefellers have their own private policy-making directorate.

"The Governor of New York is acknowledged as 'political chief.' John D. Rockefeller is described as the family's Far East expert. Dean Rusk, former head of the Rockefeller Foundation, was regarded as its U.N. specialist until he became Secretary of State, succeeding those other Rockefeller stooges, Messrs. Dulles and Herter. The conclusion is: 'To draw a line between the State Department and the vast oil-and-atom empire is as good as impossible.' "[92]

The Russian view, of course, is colored by Marxist theory, but perhaps this is also true of neutralist leaders. At the time of the Cuban crisis of 1961, Prime Minister Nehru said to the Indian Parliament, "In my opinion there has been an invasion of Cuba. I cannot see how it could take place without the organization, encouragement and help of the *authorities*—public or *private*—of the United States. I deliberately say so because *sometimes private authorities can go very far* though they cannot go too far without the support of public authority.[93] He was further quoted as saying that there were strong industrial concerns in the United States whose interests were involved. Enrico Mattei, late director of the state petroleum industry of Italy, who was himself something of an *eminence grise* in his country, believed that American foreign policy was directed by American oil companies.[94]

Actually, private American investments abroad have been progressively brought under United States government control, and government has assumed an increasing share of American capital investment abroad, especially in the underdeveloped countries of Asia and Africa. Private business has increasingly been unwilling to undertake the risk of local foreign government expropriation, and American law now provides the incentive of guaranteeing 90 per cent return on expropriated foreign investment, provided the investment is in conformity with American government policy and standards. By far the largest private American investment abroad is in Western Europe and Canada, because of its profitability in these prosperous countries, and those countries place strong controls on these investments. Practically no realistic charges have been made in recent years that private American capital controls the nations of Western Europe. A problem remains regarding long-established

[92]*The New York Times*, October 9, 1961, p. 34. See also C. L. Sulzberger, column, *The New York Times*, May 18, 1960, p. 38.
[93]*The New York Times*, April 4, 1961, p. 5. Italics mine.
[94]C. L. Sulzberger, "Foreign Affairs," *The New York Times*, November 5, 1962, p. 30.

private American investment in certain Latin American countries and its political interference in those countries. But those countries are increasingly bringing foreign investment to toe their political line, often with the support of the United States government.

Appendix B Note on Concentration of Wealth and of Business Control

During the Great Depression and Second World War period, from 1929 to 1949, differentials in wealth and income in the United States were diminishing.[95] Both poor economic conditions and government controls (including rising income taxation) created pressures on upper income brackets, and the new welfare, social security, and labor organization developments of the 1930's as well as the full employment of the 1940's set floors under and pushed upward the lower incomes. But since 1950 there has been a reversal of trend, though wealth differential is not nearly as great in the 1960's as it was during the 1920's or earlier. Automation which has reduced the demand for unskilled labor, the increasing proportion of "unemployables,"[96] the great growth of war industries during peacetime, and the great increase in stock market values are among the major factors now increasing the wealth differential.

The outstanding study of the recent concentration of wealth is that by Robert J. Lampman.[97] In 1956, the richest 1 per cent of American adults held 27 to 28 per cent of the nation's entire personal wealth, which includes all corporation stocks, government and corporation bonds, real estate, mortgages, cash, and insurance. In 1933, the rich-

[95]*National Bureau of Economic Research Report*, February 1960.

[96]Arnold M. Rose, "The New Problem of Large Scale Unemployability," *American Journal of Economics and Sociology*, 23 (October 1964), 337–50.

[97]*The Share of Top Wealth Holders in National Wealth, 1922–56*, prepared for the National Bureau of Economic Research (Princeton: Princeton University Press, 1962).

est 1 per cent held 28.3 per cent of the personal wealth, only a tiny percentage more. The richest 1 per cent in 1956 held 76 per cent of corporation stocks, 11 per cent of all state and local government bonds, 32 per cent of all United States Government bonds, and 12 per cent of all real estate. The return to the level of concentration of wealth found in 1933 occurred entirely after 1949. Yet the proportion of the poor has also declined, and personal savings are much more widely dispersed. In the 1920's, the richest 1 per cent did 44 per cent of the saving; today they do only 15 per cent. Income is much more widely distributed, while wealth has again become concentrated—due to the rise in the values of corporation stocks.

A. A. Berle, whose landmark work with Gardiner C. Means in the 1930's[98] first recorded the major characteristics of ownership and managership in the contemporary economy, has stated that ownership and control is more tightly held now than ever:

> Today approximately 50 per cent of American manufacturing —that is everything other than financial and transportation— is held by about 150 corporations, reckoned, at least, by asset values. If finance and transportation are included, the total increases. If a rather larger group is taken, the statistics would probably show that about two-thirds of the economically productive assets of the United States, excluding agriculture, are owned by a group of not more than 500 corporations. This is actual asset ownership. (Some further statistical analysis is called for if financial corporations be included, for these, of course, double up. One of the largest and most plainly oligarchically controlled corporations in the United States, the Metropolitan· Life Insurance Company, duplicates assets because it holds securities of other corporations.) But in terms of power, without regard to asset positions, not only do 500 corporations control two-thirds of the non-farm economy but within each of that 500 a still smaller group has the ultimate decision-making power. This is, I think, the highest concentration of economic power in recorded history. Since the United States carries on not quite half of the manufacturing production of the entire world today, these 500 groupings—each with its own little dominating pyramid within it—represent

[98]*The Modern Corporation and Private Property* (New York: Commerce Clearing House, Inc., 1932).

a concentration of power over economics which makes the medieval feudal system look like a Sunday School party. In sheer economic power this has gone far beyond anything we have yet seen.[99]

In a study of the 100 largest nonfinancial corporations, First National City Bank of New York Economists found 50 with assets of one billion dollars or more in 1961, compared with 22 in 1950.[100] Interlocking directorates, where they occur in the larger corporations, give them a high degree of cohesiveness. In 1950 the Federal Trade Commission published a study tracing interlocking relationships stemming from the 1000 largest manufacturing corporations in the United States as measured by total assets as of the end of 1946. The pattern of interlocking was found to be both intricate and varied, to be sometimes in violation of the Clayton Act but often quite legal, to be most commonly of the type that linked a seller of goods or services with a buyer thereof, and generally of such a nature as to make possible a decrease in competition. A less comprehensive study in 1947 by the Antitrust Division of the Department of Justice of the directorships held by some 10,000 persons in 1600 leading corporations in industry showed that 1500 of these 10,000 held directorships in more than one company and that among the 1500 approximately 60 held directorships in two or more competing concerns. It is facts like these which provide the substance for discussions of economic power elites. But such facts cannot be used automatically to prove that economic power elites control the political system.

[99] A. A. Berle, Jr., *Economic Power and the Free Society* (Santa Barbara, Calif.: Fund for the Republic, 1947), p. 14.
[100] *Minneapolis Star*, July 7, 1961, p. 11B.

IV

The Military and Other Elites

A. The Changing Role of Military Leaders

One of the main currents in American political thought since the birth of the Republic has been the conviction that civilians should guide the destinies of the American people. From this policy it necessarily followed that the military was to remain politically impotent, and that a standing army, restricted in number, was a necessary evil, and should be expanded only in times of grave national peril. Further corollaries of this policy were: (1) that armies would be raised by the authority of the Congress, not the Executive, although the President is Commander in Chief; (2) that a standing army is a possible threat to democracy; (3) that democratic state militias are to be preferred to the professional forces of the central government; and (4) that the navy is to be regarded as the first line of defense, with the army to be used only after an emergency had arisen.

For the first 150 years of its existence the United States was able to keep the military services small in size during peacetime, and thus the political supremacy of civilians was not a difficult problem. However, shortly after World War II the decision was made to maintain in peacetime, and for the indefinite future, a large standing military establishment with a global system of military bases, in order to meet commitments throughout the world. This decision has brought many problems, raised many questions, and introduced

134

many changes in American political life. The early needs of the nation matched the popular theory of the minor role of the military. Throughout the eighteenth and nineteenth centuries the geographic isolation of the United States from Europe and Asia meant military isolation as well: the nation simply had no need for a large standing army or navy.

After World War II, the changed military technology sharply reduced the protection afforded by the oceans. Equally important in keeping the size of the military up were international agreements for area defense organizations such as NATO and SEATO, involvement in police actions as in Korea 1950–1953), Vietnam (1958–), and the Dominican Republic (1965), and the general international tension prevailing after 1946. Even before the escalation of the Vietnam war (1964), the regular armed forces numbered over 3,000,000. In addition, there are approximately 1,500,000 civilians employed directly by the Department of Defense. Thus the military have become a more salient feature of American life.[1]

A corollary to this change in civil-military relations is the growth of military expenditures in the federal budget. This expenditure grew from $12 billion in 1947 to approximately $45 billion in 1959, before the Vietnam conflict imposed additional costs. By 1963, the military budget was $53 billion, and it was raised another $6 billion with the escalation of the war in Vietnam in 1965. The political changes which this has wrought are considerable: It has brought higher taxes; it has put our economy on a semi-war footing; and it has resulted in more nonmilitary political objectives being sought through the military budget. For instance, each time that there is a widespread concern regarding the possibility of a business recession, considerable pressure is put on the President and the Congress to avoid curtailment of the military budget, because many people fear this would lead to unemployment.[2]

A third change in civil-military relations since World War II has

[1] The earlier literature on the changes associated with World War II is summarized in Social Science Research Council, *Civil-Military Relations: An Annotated Bibliography, 1940–1952* (New York: Columbia University Press, 1954). A more recent but more specialized summary is that by Morris Janowitz and Roger Little, *Sociology and the Military Establishment* (New York: Russell Sage Foundation, 1964).

[2] Herman M. Somers, "Military Policy and Democracy," *Current History*, 26 (May 1954), 299.

been the increased participation of civilian government by military men. This development has come about in two ways, by professional soldiers stepping out of their military roles into civilian posts, and by professional soldiers still in the military service influencing civilian policies by giving advice and information to politically powerful civilians. The penetration of military men into civilian posts not requiring solely military skills took two forms: military occupancy of positions combining military with political functions, and occupancy of civilian posts with exclusively non-military functions.[3] Some examples of positions combining military and political functions are: military governorships of occupied territories such as existed in Germany until 1949 and in Japan until 1952; international military commands such as SHAPE and the United Nations Korean Command; and military advising and training groups in countries receiving American aid.[4] The phenomenon of military officials occupying civilian posts with exclusively nonmilitary functions actually has been going on since the country was founded. However, the scope of this penetration into civilian positions after World War II was greater than ever before. For example, in 1948 it was estimated that 150 military men occupied important policy-making posts in the civilian government.[5] Some of the more important civilian posts occupied by military men in 1948 included General George C. Marshall as Secretary of State, Fleet Admiral George Leahy as advisor to the President, General Walter Bedell Smith as Ambassador to Russia, General Omar Bradley as head of the Veterans Administration, and Major General Lewis B. Hershey as Director of Selective Service. During the Eisenhower Administration, there were in the White House the President himself, General Wilton B. Persons as Assistant to the President, and Brigadier General Andrew J. Goodposter as White House Staff Secretary (preceded by Brigadier General Paul T. Carroll).

The appointment of military men to honorific and political posi-

[3]Samuel P. Huntington, *The Soldier and the State* (Cambridge: Harvard University Press, 1957), p. 355.

[4]Ibid. p. 355.

[5]Richard C. Snyder and Hubert H. Wilson, *The Roots of Political Behavior*, (New York: 1949), p. 557, quoted in Huntington, *Soldier and State*, p. 355.

tions was another peculiar characteristic of the years following World War II.[6] Many of the appointments were designed merely to reward or honor distinguished military commanders of the war. Included in this category would be appointments to serve on the American Battle Monuments Commission, appointments to various ad hoc commissions, and some ambassadorship appointments. The fact that these appointments were more frequent during Truman's Administration than during Eisenhower's was possibly due to the political popularity of military men right after the war,[7] and to Truman's effort to reward distinguished soldiers for their wartime services. The number of appointments of military men to nonmilitary posts declined during the Kennedy and Johnson administrations.

After World War II, the military played a significant role in influencing popular and congressional opinion. Abandoning its traditional policy of aloofness toward politics and civilians, the military became publicity-conscious. According to one writer: "It has established public relations schools, briefed its officer personnel in the ways of selling the service to the people, and developed a variety of propaganda techniques."[8] Another writer has stated: "Military leaders are actively engaged in drafting and promoting legislation; they have an extensive propaganda network that makes carefully planned use of the press, Hollywood, radio, television, and other media; they share in the preparation of the national budget; and in various ways they exercise an influence in civilian organization."[9]

Another way in which the military has influenced public opinion is through the increased use of lobbying. Not only do the armed services lobby, but they also maintain liaison officers who are permanently attached to the armed services committees and who are on hand to advise and assist congressmen.[10] In addition, the military services are able to call upon veterans groups, civic societies, chambers of commerce, etc., for the necessary support sometimes needed

[6]Huntington, *Soldier and State*, p. 358.

[7]Ibid. p. 358.

[8]William R. Tansill, *The Concept of Civil Supremacy over the Military in the United States*, Public Affairs Bulletin No. 94, Library of Congress, February 1951, p. 37.

[9]John M. Swomley, Jr., "The Growing Power of the Military," *The Progressive*, 23 (January 1959), 25.

[10]Tansill, *Civil Supremacy*, p. 38.

to influence Congress through public opinion.[11] The censorship which the armed services have been able to impose is another example of the military influence on public opinion. Through censorship a great deal of information which probably should have been made public has been labeled "secret" and buried from civilian view.[12]

C. Wright Mills interprets the expanded role of the military in American life by emphasizing the fact that they have joined the power elite. He says, "But they are now more powerful than they have ever been in the history of the American elite; they have now more means of exercising power in many areas of American life which were previously civilian domains; they now have more connections; and they are now operating in a nation whose elite and whose underlying population have accepted what can only be called a military definition of reality. Historically the warlords have been only uneasy, poor relations within the American elite; now they are first cousins, soon they may become elder brothers."[13] Mills goes on to say that while military men have become increasingly involved in politics, they have not shed their military background. He also asserts that it is largely through the default of the civilian politicians that the military have been drawn into the higher political decisions.[14] This is done, Mills states, by politicians who wish to legitimatize their policies by lifting them "above politics." Thus politicians are hiding behind the supposed expertise of military men. Another way in which the military enters politics, according to Mills, is through the lack of a really senior professional civil service. It is the absence of a genuine civil service which makes it easier for the military ascendancy to occur.[15]

Mills slurs over the facts that the military are entering high civilian posts only at the invitation of the Congress or the Executive, and that their role has been primarily advisory rather than decision-making. He also neglects the instances in which the military have

[11]Hanson W. Baldwin, "The Military Move In," *Harper's Magazine*, 195 (December 1947), 481–9.

[12]Tansill, *Civil Supremacy*, p. 37.

[13]Ibid. p. 198.

[14]Ibid, p. 200.

[15]For a discussion of why Mills feels there is no genuine civil service see "The Political Directorate," in *The Power Elite* (New York. Oxford University Press, 1959), pp. 225–42.

been sharply reprimanded by their civilian superiors for occasional participation in right-wing extremist activities. When an Air Force manual charged the National Council of Churches with harboring communists, the Air Force had to make public apologies and remove the manual from circulation. Major General Edwin Walker was dismissed from the service in April 1961 for right-wing extremist activity, including "making derogatory public statements about prominent Americans."

Another questionable assumption made by Mills was that military men, especially major generals and above, are all alike: "More than any other creature of the higher circles, modern warlords, on or above the two star rank, resemble one another, internally and externally."[16] On the contrary, American history suggests there are at least two military traditions.[17] One of these traditions is exemplified by men like Zachary Taylor, U. S. Grant, George C. Marshall, Dwight D. Eisenhower, and Omar Bradley; and is characterized by the friendly easygoing soldier who reflects the ideals of a democratic society and insists that the military must take civilian direction. The other tradition is represented by men like Winfield Scott, George B. McClellan, George Patton, and Douglas MacArthur; this type exemplifies the brilliant, arrogant, and dramatic officer who draws his values and behavior from an older, aristocratic heritage and sometimes finds it difficult to subordinate himself to civilian authority. General MacArthur's insubordination to President Truman is the most spectacular example of this type in modern history. Yet it was the same MacArthur who, in 1962, warned of military usurpation of civilian control over the Armed Services, in a speech to army cadets.

Mills could not have been expected to know, in 1956, when *The Power Elite* was published, that the peak use of military leaders in civilian settings occurred during the Truman and first Eisenhower administrations, but that there would be a sharp deflation in their powers after that. Eisenhower himself, in his "farewell speech" in January 1961, warned against an "industrial-military complex," and beginning in 1961, the strongest civilian Secretary of Defense in modern history—Robert McNamara—reimposed civilian decision-

[16]Ibid. p. 195.
[17]See Harry T. Williams, "The Macs and the Ikes: America's Two Military Traditions," *American Mercury*, 75 (October 1952), 32–9.

making on all but the technical aspects of the military operations. Military encroachments on civilian authority have actually been very few, and in all cases they have been pushed back without much difficulty. There is a problem of conflict of interest in military purchasing, which we have examined in the preceding chapter, but this is found in purchasing by all branches of government, and is more significant for the military only because of its huge size, and hence its significance for the economy as a whole. Congress and the civilian heads of the Executive branch have shown themselves constantly alert to the abuses inherent in military purchasing of supplies, and have succeeded in controlling them. The only uncontrolled problem is that legitimate military purchasing constitutes such a large proportion of American business that its shifts have an impact on the health of the economy.

Another perspective which has arisen out of the fear of the increasing use of military men in civilian positions and the increasing role of military men in influencing public opinion is the garrison state hypothesis.[18] This theory, originally stated by Harold D. Lasswell in 1937, was not fully elaborated upon or popularized until after World War II. The concept of the garrison state was derived from an attempt to apply the traditional values of American liberalism to the apparent reality of continuing military crisis. The garrison state theory has three elements: an analysis of twentieth-century international conflicts; a prediction that as a result of permanent warfare there could emerge a particular form of social organization, the garrison state; and a policy assertion that the only possible alternative to the garrison state was a world commonwealth. A definition of the garrison state is supplied by Louis Smith: "A modern totalitarian state in which a rigid discipline, growing out of military ideals and considerations, dominates all aspects of the people's lives. Not necessarily a state ruled by an army, rather a state on a quasi-military footing, with all considerations subordinated to the purpose of attaining national security by the maximization of power."[19] Basic to

18For a discussion of the garrison state hypothesis see Harold D. Lasswell, *National Security and Individual Freedom*, (New York: McGraw-Hill, 1950); and Arthur A. Ekirch, Jr., "Toward the Garrison State" in *The Civilian and the Military*, (New York: Oxford University Press, 1956). Much of my discussion of the garrison state hypothesis is taken from Huntington, *Soldier and State*.

19Louis Smith, "The Garrison State, Offspring of the Cold War," *The Nation*, 177 (December 5, 1953), 461.

Smith's view, as well as Lasswell's, is that the subordination of all other purposes to war and the preparation for war leads to the garrison state. The garrison state requires the centralization of power in the hands of the few, the Executive and the military gaining at the expense of the Legislative branch and the civilian politicians. Also, according to the garrison state hypothesis, technology, science, industry, and labor all become regimented for the purposes of war. In recent years, the main fears of those who write about the dangers of the garrison state are centered on the belief that the military are increasingly pushing foreign policy toward military action.[20]

There is evidence to support the view that the United States is moving in the direction of the garrison state—the already mentioned use of military "expertise," placement of military men into civilian posts, and the increasing trend toward secrecy in government. There is also some evidence to support the thesis that science, technology, labor, and industry are becoming increasingly dependent upon the military. William R. Tansill had this to say about science and technology: "In numerous schools of science and technology, progressively closer working relationships with the armed services have been established. . . . a number of top-flight scientists in our institutions are being lured away by attractive salaries to work exclusively for the military; concomitantly, freedom of research has been sharply curbed by the extensive bans of publication of scientific papers and by the oppressively effective veil of secrecy drawn about most of the projects initiated by government."[21] Herman Somers also observes: "The great bulk of money currently available for scientific research in the universities comes from governmental appropriations, mainly through the Department of Defense and the Atomic Energy Commission. Some of our great institutions of learning are now dependent upon government contracts even for the basic maintenance of their present establishment."[22]

While we can agree that the trends are toward a garrison state, it does not necessarily follow that the garrison state has arrived or that it will arrive. The future depends on whether the United States remains in a continuous state of war or not. The military are not the

[20]See, for example, John M. Swomley, Jr. *The Military Establishment* (Boston: Beacon Press, 1964).

[21]Tansill, *Civil Supremacy*, pp. 34–35.

[22]Somers, "Military Policy," p. 298.

ones building a garrison state thus far, and they may not be the ones to dominate it if it should develop. The Soviet Union, Communist China, and the earlier fascist nations are or were garrison states, and they were not dominated by a military elite, but by a political elite operating through the Executive. If the garrison state should develop in the United States the trends suggest that the political elite would dominate it here also, rather than an economic or military elite.

There was a third perspective which arose after World War II with regard to civil-military relations. This was the political-military fusionist theory.[23] This theory was an attempt to adjust to the fact of enhanced military power. The theory stated that military and political power were much more closely allied in the post–World War II world than they had ever been previously. From here the theory went on to say that it had become impossible to maintain a distinction between political and military functions at the highest levels of government. This theory dominated civilian thinking on administrative problems of civil-military relations. Specifically it manifested itself in two forms. One was a demand that the military leaders incorporate political, economic, and social factors into their thinking. Every view on national policy, it was held, contained both military and nonmilitary aspects which could not be separated.

The second manifestation of the fusionist theory was the demand that military leaders assume nonmilitary responsibilities—the assumption here was that it is impossible to rely upon the political neutrality of military leaders and their simple obedience to government institutions. It was felt that if military leaders assumed nonmilitary functions they would minimize their military professionalism. Both of these demands would transform the military while giving them more power, but if they *are* coming into operation, it is extremely slowly.

There are additional changes in civil-military relations since World War II which should be mentioned in a comprehensive summary even though they have not been discussed by the three sets of theorists just mentioned. One of these was the reorganization of some federal government agencies and the creation of others. The basic

---

23Huntington, *Soldier and State*, pp. 350–54. Professor Huntington's ideas provide the basic source for the statements I shall make for political-military fusionist theory.

legislation in this regard was the National Security Act of 1947. In general, two factors were responsible for this law.[24] The first was the growing realization of the impossibility of rigidly separating the functions of the State Department and the military services. The second was the increasing acknowledgement that the traditional distinction of functions between the military services was not necessary.

Congress did three things in the National Security Act: (1) It created the office of Secretary of Defense and provided for the unification of the armed forces, including an air force on the same level as the army and navy; (2) it created the National Security Council, with the function of formulating and reviewing basic policies of the United States relating to national security; (3) it created the Central Intelligence Agency, which "co-ordinates the intelligence activities of the several governmental departments." What the National Security Act sought to accomplish is well stated by Walter Millis: ". . . the 1947 act sought to create a policy-making system which could determine from time to time, in accordance with the changing realities of the international scene, what sort of military machine might be required. It was an effort at the higher organization and control of the enormous political, economic, psychological and military power generated by the modern state. It was an effort to harness these powers to civilian domination and make them into an effective instrument of policy within the framework of free, popular government."[25]

Aside from those agencies provided for by the National Security Act, others were also created by Congress in response to the changed military needs of the country. One of these was the Atomic Energy Commission, established in 1946. This agency has a government monopoly on the ownership, production, processing, and manufacturing of fissionable materials; it also has charge of the production of atomic weapons. The implications of atomic energy are so far-reaching that Congress decided it would be unwise to place it under control of military men. Instead, authority was given to a five-man Commission, appointed by the President with the consent of the

[24]Jack W. Peltason and James M. Burns, *Functions and Policies of American Government* (Englewood Cliffs, N.J.: Prentice-Hall, 1958), p. 111.

[25]Walter Millis, *Arms and Men*, (New York: Mentor, 1958), p. 281.

Senate. The military aspects of the Commission's work are co-ordinated with the Defense Department by a Military Liaison Committee.

The Office of Defense Mobilization was set up by the President in 1950 under powers granted him by Congress. This agency makes recommendations for the co-ordination of military and civilian resources for war, and for policies insuring adequate reserves of strategic materials.

These changes in the departmental structure of the Executive branch have brought about other changes and problems. Among the more striking changes are the following: (1) the encroachment of the new agencies on the powers of the State Department. In Washington, the National Security Council made decisions which inevitably involved the formation of foreign policy.[26] Overseas, the Central Intelligence Agency took actions which were sometimes unknown even to the American ambassador.[27] (2) The increasing congressional involvement in military policy and administration. Prior to World War II, Congress expressed little interest in military policy, and what interest it did express was focused on the location of army and navy posts, military procurement, military construction, and in general where and for whom military expenditures were to be made rather than for what purposes they were to be made. After World War II, however, Congress became almost constantly occupied with major policy issues affecting the military, such as selective service, universal military training, the size and composition of the Armed forces, and the organization of the defense establishment. (3) The shift in focus of congressional relations with the military from the supply units of the military departments to the professional heads of the services. Prior to 1940, the primary relations were between Congress and the civilian-oriented supply and public-relations officers within the armed forces. This relative lack of interest by Congress in the central military questions permitted the professional military chiefs,

[26]Burton M. Sapin and Richard C. Snyder, *The Role of the Military in American Foreign Policy*, (Garden City, N.Y.: Doubleday, 1954.) This is a general discussion of factors which bring military into foreign policy-making. In the United States decisions which have military implications bring in the military, and some decisions are called purely military. In Great Britain all decisions are ultimately made by civilians.

[27]See the series of articles on the C.I.A. in *The New York Times*, May 2–6, 1966.

in their infrequent contacts with Congress, to act primarily as spokesmen for the Executive branch. After 1945, the focus of congressional-military relations shifted from the technical services to professional heads of the services. This put a severe strain on the relations between Congress and the military; for if Congress was to play a major role in military policy, it required the same professional advice that the President received. This posed a problem for the military, for now they had to make their appeals to both the Executive branch and the Legislative branch and at the same time antagonize neither.

One reason why Congress dealt directly with military officers was because of its distrust of the civilian heads of the military departments. This meant that when the professional military chiefs went before Congress they inevitably undercut the authority of the civilian Secretaries and the President. An early major example of this came in 1949, when navy chiefs fought the Truman Administration's decision to build the B-36 bomber. In 1962 there was an unprecedented invasion of Executive authority by a congressional committee, acting on the advice of certain military leaders. Representative Carl Vinson, Chairman of the House Armed Services Committee, issued a report which included the following statement: ". . . the Secretary of the Air Force, as an official of the Executive branch, *is directed, ordered, mandated, and required* to utilize the full amount of the $491,000,000 authority granted to proceed with production planning and long lead-time procurement for an RS-70 weapon system" (italics mine). This was after Secretary of Defense McNamara had downgraded the RS-70 bomber as inefficient and of limited effectiveness, and had indicated he was not planning to use all the funds which Congress had appropriated; the Secretary's action had numerous precedents, but Chairman Vinson's order was unique in American history. A more spectacular example occurred in 1963 when Secretary of Defense McNamara awarded the TFX contract for supersonic aircraft to the General Dynamics Corporation; the military leaders favored the model produced by the Boeing Company, and congressional leaders (especially the Senate Permanent Investigations Subcommittee) took the position that the military leaders had the better arguments.

Another reason why Congress now deals directly with the military is because, in an atmosphere of "preparedness," there is tremendous pressure placed on Congress not to cut down on real military needs. If the President offers budget requests which are different from those of the professional military leaders, Congress wants to be in a position to find out at first hand why there is a discrepancy.

These changes create a severe strain on the separation-of-powers doctrine. Each branch of the government is jealous of its prerogatives and guards against any encroachments by any other branch. With the emergence of the "preparedness" consideration after World War II, the relations between Congress and the Executive have become worse, at least in the field of military relations. Still, the increasing relationship between Congress and the military does not mean the ascendancy of the military elite over the political elite. Quite the contrary, the military elite are now more exposed than they ever have been to limitations from politics and public opinion. While growing in size due to a more active American foreign policy, they are also becoming more "civilianized."

The major reasons for the increasingly important role of the military in American life have little or nothing to do with alleged efforts of the military to gain power or to an alleged increasing willingness of the economic elite to use them as allies in their own efforts to increase their power. Insofar as the military have had a more salient role in the American scene since World War II, the reasons seem to be the following:

1. The United States has a much more active foreign policy since it emerged from World War II as one of the two leading world powers. The shift from isolationism to internationalism has entailed, among other things, a greater use of military forces. Some of the change has come by necessity: The oceans are no longer wide enough to isolate the United States from her enemies, nor is the British Navy, on which we long tacitly relied, capable of giving us much aid.

2. There has been a tremendous development of military technology, and the need for experts to develop and handle this technology. Politicians are increasingly dependent on scientists and soldiers to advise them on the use of this technology.

3. Some of the newer technology is "secret," and there has been a great increase in secret military information generally. This has meant an increased military and civilian organization for the main-

tenance of secrecy, and a reduction of open debate in Congress, and even in Executive circles, on certain matters.

4. The military has enjoyed increased prestige since just after World War II. As Professor Huntington pointed out: "After World War II many military appointments [to civilian posts] were designed primarily to honor or reward military commanders who had distinguished themselves in the war."[28] The organizational skills and knowledge of foreign affairs of certain military leaders, gained or proved in wartime, were welcomed in the civilian sector. But this factor has declined as World War II and the Korean War have receded into history.

5. The expansion of the federal government, and the inability of the President to induce enough qualified civilians to take on some of the new positions because of the low pay and the possibility of public abuse, have occasioned some reliance on the more available military leaders. Some of the new positions—e.g. directing the building of the vast new superhighways—entail technical skills which certain military leaders possess and which will keep them in a condition of top training as much as their military posts do.

Thus far in this chapter we have considered civilian-military power relations in the context of the larger forces affecting the United States. We now turn to a briefer consideration of how the internal culture and structure of the military affect the power position of the military in the United States, and use as our main guide the only comprehensive study on this topic, Morris Janowitz's *The Professional Soldier*.[29] Janowitz makes a number of points in direct refutation of Mills's thesis that a more or less homogeneous officer caste is now collaborating with big businessmen to become the dominant power elite of the United States.

1. Janowitz points out that the cleavages between the three services—Army, Navy, and Air Force—is so deep as to prevent their collaboration unless forced to it by their civilian heads. He also finds a cleavage of professional philosophies within each service (which he calls "pragmatist" and "absolutist"), that has the same effect. "A

28Huntington, *Soldier and State*, p. 358.
29Morris Janowitz, *The Professional Soldier* (Glencoe, Ill.: Free Press, 1960).

clash of service and professional perspectives has prevented the military from emerging as a unified elite. Social scientists who have asserted that the growth of governmental bureaucracy is certain to produce a monolithic element in the political process will find little support for this thesis in the political behavior of the military establishment."[30] A blatant example of what Janowitz was talking about was made public in late 1963, when the Air Force publicly accused the Army of keeping the Vietnam war going so as to use it for experimenting with air-borne weapons, at an extra expense of $5 billion and in competition with weapons already available to the Air Force. The civilian secretaries of the three services called an unprecedented press conference to deny the validity of the Air Force charges.[31]

2. Janowitz takes Mills to task for claiming that the managerial skills of military leaders necessarily make them co-operative with managers of industry.

> C. W. Mills suggests that contemporary military leaders are like corporation managers, and are even, in a sense, managers who are interchangeable among various types of organization, thus creating a power elite. There is little to be learned from a theory which can be reduced to the simple formula that a manager is a manager, regardless of his organizational environment. . . . the purposes of military organization are profoundly different from those of business organization, and the loyalties and logic of the professional soldier in his managerial capacities are also different. Merely to state that the military elite are managers throws no light on who is recruited into the military, on how military education and a military career fashion the outlook of the professional soldier.[32]

3. Janowitz holds that the professional training and ethos of the military leaders basically isolates them from civilian leaders.

> If the military style of life strives to produce an internally cohesive community, at the same time, it thwarts social in-

---

[30]Ibid. p. 320.
[31]Ronald Robinson, "Pentagon Rumble," *This Week Magazine*, January 5, 1964, p. 6.
[32]Ibid. p. 73–4.

tegration with civilian society. Despite its increased size, and its elaborate organizational alliances with other civilian leadership groups, the military profession and its elite members are not effectively integrated, on a social basis, with other leadership groups. There is little evidence to support the argument that the military forms an integral part of a compact social group which constitutes the power elite. Rather, in fact, the contrary seems to be the case: namely, the political behavior of the military in the United States is still deeply conditioned by its social isolation. Much of the "public relations" efforts of the military have been an effort to gain social access to other, new elites, particularly to scientific and academic circles.[33]

4. Janowitz claims that the American military for the most part are not positively interested in politics, and have a deepseated ignorance of it and a negative attitude toward it. This leads them to hope that politicians and military leaders should avoid mutual interference as much as feasible.

Officers have not fought primarily because of an explicit political ideology. On the contrary, the political interests of the typical officer have been intermittent at best. Only at the higher ranks and among its elite members is there a more sustained concern with the political purposes of the military establishment. "Honor" is the basis of its belief system. . . .[34] From the point of view of democratic requirements, the important issue is not the extent of extremist thought, but rather the lack of understanding and respect for the creative role of the practical politician. A few conspicuous civilian leaders are seen as heroes, but the military shares the civilian image that politicians are an unworthy lot. There is, moreover, little sympathy for the particular qualities required to produce political compromise. There is little appreciation of the fact that a political democracy requires competing pressures.[35]

5. After discussing the evidence that military leaders are appointed

[33] Ibid. p. 204–5.
[34] Ibid. p. 215.
[35] Ibid. p. 251.

to huge-salaried positions in business after their retirement from the armed services, Janowitz points out that most of the positions they took in business after their retirement were not executive ones, but in public relations, so as to influence the direction of purchasing by the functioning military purchasing officers. A few were appointed to honorific positions in industry, with the sole task of presiding over annual meetings of the board of directors. Senator Paul Douglas in 1959 was able to compile a list of 768 former military officers of the rank of colonel, naval captain, and above who were in the employ of the 100 companies and their 153 subsidiaries which, in the period from July 1, 1957 to June 30, 1958, received 74.2 per cent of all military prime contract awards. (In 1962, Representative F. Edward Hebert reported to Congress that there were a total of 251 generals and admirals, plus 1426 field-grade officers, employed by the 72 leading defense contractors.) But of these, Janowitz states that only about a dozen top retired military officers are in the decision-making positions in industry; the rest were in public relations or in specialized staff jobs. Retired officers are much more likely to go into education and civic associations than into industry.

6. Far more important than retirement activities in affecting civil-military relations, Janowitz holds, are the professional military associations—the Air Force Association, the Navy League, and the Combat Forces Association (pp. 374–6). All three service groups have co-opted top status civilians for their advisory board of directors, to permit these associations to serve more effectively as pressure groups on Congress and the President (pp. 382–7). These associations "conform to the pattern typical of other pressure groups which represent professional and occupational specialists. [Their] Activities are highly decentralized; the services and individual officers compete among themselves" (p. 391).

7. Very few retired officers run for political office, and then usually on an extremist ticket, and hence are defeated. The major exceptions are the popular military heroes who run for President, but these have been mavericks within the military and they have been selected by civilians. Military-hero presidents—such as Jackson, Grant, Theodore Roosevelt, and Eisenhower—have been popularly thought of as men of the people, and they stoutly maintained the tradition of civilian superiority over the military.

8. Janowitz summarizes:

> None of the three forms of civilian alliance—post-retirement employment, professional association activities, and direct participation in politics—serves to integrate the military into a unified political force. With few exceptions, post-retirement employment does not link the military professional into the older and well-established financial elite groups; most frequently, he follows in the pattern of the public servant, or the organizational specialist, or the salesman for an industry seeking to expand its government defense contracts. The direct involvement of the military in partisan politics has been too limited to be significant, except to indicate the direction of sentiment and the style of politics that frustration might produce.
>
> The conflicting interests among the military profession are perpetuated in associational life. Each faction, as it bids for public and political support, can best be described as exercising a veto. This negative power reflects the different sources of public support; the Air Force advantage in support by industrial contractors is counterbalanced by the support of the Army's pragmatic point of view by news commentators and specialized opinion leaders; the Navy draws on its special alliances with key congressional leaders.[36]

In other words, the survey of all the relevant facts from within the military profession indicates that Mills's thesis is largely wrong:

> The military profession is not a monolithic power group. A deep split pervades its ranks in respect to its doctrine and viewpoints in foreign affairs, a split which mirrors civilian disagreements. Instead, the military profession and the military establishments conform more to the pattern of an administrative pressure group, but one with a strong internal conflict of interest. It is a very special pressure group because of its immense resources, and because of its grave problems of national security. The military have accumulated considerable power, and that power protrudes into the political fabric of contemporary society. It could not be otherwise. However, while they have no reluctance to press for larger budgets, they

[36]Ibid. p. 392.

exercise their influence on political matters with considerable restraint and unease. Civilian control of military affairs remains intact and fundamentally acceptable to the military; any imbalance in military contributions to political-military affairs —domestic or international—is therefore often the result of default by civilian political leadership.[37]

B. Other Influential Groups and Categories

We can but suggest the range of the indefinitely large number of groups and categories of the population that exert power on the political scene, aside from the political, economic, and military elites that we have already considered. Some of these are dominant and decisive, but only on a single issue—such as the Roman Catholic Church in getting federal aid to private schools—while others are omnipresent but never controlling on any single issue—such as the congressional staff of some 7000 persons. Some operate through direct political pressures—such as the labor movement—while others exert long-range and indirect influence through creation and channeling of popular ideas—such as the syndicated newspaper columnists. Some may seek to influence government directly through lobbying— such as the various organized groups of civil servants, who do so in order to get their salaries raised—while others operate indirectly through efforts to influence popular thought—such as mass social movements like the civil rights movement. Some are large membership groups—such as the American Federation of Labor–Congress of Industrial Organizations—while others are single individuals—such as newspaper and magazine publishers with a definite editorial point of view.[38]

We shall briefly describe a small number of these groups merely to indicate their nature and variability. In thus treating them cavalierly,

---

[37]Ibid. p. viii.

[38]The late Colonel Robert R. McCormick, who controlled the *Chicago Tribune* and the *Washington Times-Herald*, seems to have had a conscious policy of using his newspapers—not only in editorials, but in the news columns as well—to try to create the popular ideas and images that would set a climate of public opinion on political issues in accordance with his own political philosophy. Most publishers try to do the same thing with greater indirection and more restraint. A more typical and influential publisher of the present day was the late Philip Leslie Graham, who controlled the combined *Washington Post* and *Times-Herald* and the news magazine *Newsweek*.

we do not necessarily mean to say they are of lesser importance than the political, economic, or military elites, but that our hypothesis in this book relates much more directly to the latter three elites.

The American Federation of Labor–Congress of Industrial Organizations (AFL–CIO) has a range of political interests at least as broad as that of the economic elite. On some issues—notably, getting governments to spend money for highways and defense industries, which employ much labor—it often finds itself on the same side as segments of the economic elite. On other issues—notably those involving welfare legislation and other bills for the benefit of the underprivileged—it generally finds itself working in opposition to the economic elite. It uses the same technique as business does—lobbying, putting money into election campaigns, putting out publicity to mold public opinion. In addition, it seeks to mobilize its 17,000,000 members to vote for candidates for public office who are likely to support labor-endorsed legislation. It has been fairly successful in most of its political efforts since the 1930's, although it faced hostile Congresses in 1947, 1953, and 1955. The leadership's report to the AFL–CIO convention in 1961 stated that "the American labor movement has changed the face of American politics," and it claimed a 74 per cent victory score in endorsements of congressional candidates in 1960 where "maximum assistance" was given. It listed 15 victories in 19 senatorial races, 14 in 19 gubernatorial contests, and 157 out of 258 endorsements for the House of Representatives. Its team of lobbyists at every level of government had mixed successes and failures, but the successes were frequent enough to justify a constantly growing expenditure of funds on lobbying. It has generally had greater success in obtaining the passage of legislation for the benefit of poor people than for the specific benefit of organized labor. In the 1965 session of Congress, for example, when so much general welfare legislation being sought by the AFL–CIO—such as medicare for the elderly, anti-poverty programs, rent subsidy programs, federal aid to education—was passed, the specific "organized labor" requests were denied: repeal of Section 14b of the Taft-Hartley Act (which permits states to pass anti-closed shop, or "right to work," laws); a rise in the minimum wage; an overhaul of the unemployment compensation laws. Many of the AFL–CIO's affiliated national and international unions—like the United Steelworkers—have their own lobbying programs, as do the national unions not affiliated with the AFL–CIO—like the Teamsters. If the average American and the intellectual are sure that the most effective lobbies are those of businessmen, the businessmen themselves often say that the most effective lobbies are those of the unions.

The top levels of the congressional staff play a significant though not decisive role in the drafting of legislation. The office staff of each congressman serves as his intelligence arm—pulling together the expressed opinions of his constituents and of his local political party, the pressures from lobbyists who have a claim on his attention, the messages from the Executive branch, the wishes of his associates in Congress, etc.—and they help him to work out decisions on how to vote, on what legislation to sponsor, on what other public positions to take. Just as influential are the staffs of congressional committees, especially of the major standing committees. While their task is supposed to be collecting information, they are often asked to advise on policy, especially by less well-informed congressmen. An outstanding example of a powerful staff man was Colin F. Stam, chief of the staff of the Congressional Joint Committee on Internal Revenue Taxation—which consists of the senior members of the House Ways and Means Committee and the Senate Finance Committee—from 1938 until his retirement in 1965. He headed a staff of lawyers, economists, and statisticians that collected the necessary information to allow his political superiors to act on requests for taxation that had come from the President and the Executive branch generally, as well as from other members of Congress. He had the background of a law degree and employment in the Bureau of Internal Revenue Service. In 1927, he joined the congressional committee as assistant counsel, and in 1929 (as counsel) he began a ten-year task of codifying the tax laws, the first time since 1872. When any tax bill was debated in the House or Senate, he usually sat next to the floor manager for consultation when questions arose. Associates and other congressional staff people said he gave committee members his opinion on tax issues freely when asked, and sometimes even when not asked. His tax philosophy was generally conservative and largely oriented toward the interests of business, although this point of view was hard to separate from that of Senator Harry F. Byrd (D., Va.), who headed the Joint Committee during most of Stam's service.

While some congressmen become experts in specialized fields of government in the course of a long service, their real task is to remain amateurs and to become familiar with a wide range of legislation, while continuing to carry on their political—as distinguished from legislative—duties. The staffs are the professionals, whose job it is to learn and to inform in specialized areas. While they are instruments of the congressmen, the latter have to rely on their professional knowledge, and usually welcome their advice on policy matters and matters of strategy. Usually the staff members take pride in their anonymous roles, but occasionally their actions (like those of Roy Cohn of Senator McCarthy's staff, and Bernard Schwartz of the House Interstate and Foreign Commerce Committee) become highly visible. Their anonymity usually permits them to continue in their positions even when their elected superiors change. While they are known for loyalty to their current superiors, it is also understood that they will make their full knowledge and skills available to a new superior. An example, cited by staffmen around Congress, of how their power is exerted publicly is that of Lewis Deschler, parliamentarian of the House for over thirty-five years, in a debate regarding the admission of Alaska to statehood in 1958. Two opponents of the bill, Clarence Cannon (D., Mo.) and Howard W. Smith (D., Va.), raised a point of order that the bill could not be considered because it contained a section carrying an appropriation, and it had not been considered by the Appropriations Committee. If the bill had been recommitted to committee at that late date in the session, it would have died. Speaker Rayburn called on the parliamentarian for selected precedents, and Mr. Deschler was able to come up with decisions by Speakers Carlisle, Reed, and Longworth. Deschler's power resides in his knowledge of parliamentary precedents and the vagaries of rules, and his informed intuitions as to what is possible in Congress and what is not.

The staffmen not only collect information, they usually write the reports signed by the congressmen. There are at least 250 separate committees, subcommittees, special committee, select committees and joint committees in Congress today, and each has a staff. Most of the staff members are named by the chairman and a few named by the minority party. With the consent of their political superiors, they have considerable power to investigate, and if their relationships with their superiors are good, they have the power to suggest. Some of the standing committee staffmen have been in their jobs for a long while, and their reputations within Congress is very high. Besides Deschler and Stam, there is Everard Smith, the chief clerk of the Senate Appropriations Committee, who has been drafting money bills for half a century; Boyd Crawford, the staff chief of the House Foreign Affairs Committee, who has been on Capitol Hill for 34 years; and several others of like vintage and power. Playing a more openly political role are the secretaries of the two parties in the Senate and House who help their respective leaders round up the congressional votes. Robert G. Baker, secretary to the Democratic majority in the Senate, was forced to resign in 1963 when it was alleged that he used his position to aid his personal finances. This case is undoubtedly extremely rare, if only because most staff professionals take a tremendous pride in their integrity.[39]

The top levels of the bureaucracy in the Executive branch are equally powerful in a different way, since they administer the laws rather than help to make them. Some of them have political appointments; others are civil servants.[40] Most are highly educated, and of urban background. They also place a high value on their occupation as public servants, and enjoy the "important life" in the government. While the political appointees are generally of the same political party as the President who appoints them, they are also usually highly qualified for the jobs they hold. Men who already had established careers in public service formed the largest source of political appointments: "Over 80 per cent of all political executives had had some previous federal government experience."[41]

[39]For a detailed analysis of the work of one important committee and its staff, see Thomas B. Curtis, "The House Committee on Ways and Means: Congress Seen through a Key Committee," *Wisconsin Law Review* (Winter 1966), 121–47.

[40]Two valuable recent studies of these are Dean E. Mann, *Federal Political Executives* (Washington: Brookings Institution, 1964), which deals mainly with recruitment; and W. Lloyd Warner, P. P. Van Riper, N. H. Martin, and O. F. Collins, *The American Federal Executive: A Study of the Social and Personal Characteristics of the Civilian and Military Leaders of the United States Federal Government* (New Haven: Yale University Press, 1963), which presents extensive data on characteristics. Unfortunately, neither of these books deal much with procedures by which power is wielded. On the latter subject, see the relevant chapters in Francis E. Bourke (ed.), *Bureaucratic Power in National Politics* (Boston: Little, Brown, 1965).

[41]Mann, *Federal Political Executives*.

The top civil servants in the United States do not formally possess the policy-making function which is found in the French *Conseil d'état*, or in the permanent undersecretaries of ministries in the United Kingdom or Sweden. The American tradition adheres much more closely to the democratic ideal of policy formation by elected politicians or by persons appointed by them. But government—at all levels—has expanded so greatly that it is impossible for the relatively small number of political officials effectively to supervise the vast bureaucracies. The heads of the latter are compelled to make policy decisions, and if their judgments do not irritate too many people, the political officials will not override them. Most statutes passed in the last four or five decades provide for the later formulation of "administrative rules" and for procedures of appealing against them. An elaborate body of administrative law has grown up. The creation of these laws and their application involves vast powers over the lives of ordinary citizens, even though continued abuses are likely to be corrected through the political process.

Bendix[42] traces two themes of bureaucracy, both of which he finds wrong: Governmental bureaucracy is the administrative instrument of its directing (political) officials; governmental bureaucracy is the administrative instrument in the hands of the ruling class (i.e. the economic elite in the United States). Bendix attempts to show that actually the bureaucracy has a good deal of independent power, but at the same time it has little capacity to determine how its power is to be used. Its power arises out of specialized skills, which neither the political or the economic leaders fully know how to use.

Some 500 federal government officials (in 1959) are employed exclusively to make congressional friends and influence legislation, presumably in the interests of the activities of their respective Executive agencies and departments.[43] They serve as lobbyists in most senses of the term, although they are limited in their techniques: they cannot use funds to contribute to a congressman's campaign fund or stimulate a letter-writing campaign to him. One study shows that there is a relationship between satisfactory communications with the

---

[42]Reinhard Bendix, "Bureaucracy and the Problem of Power," *Public Administratration Review*, 5 (Summer 1945), 194–209. For evidence, see M. Kent Jennings, "Public Administrators and Community Decision Making," *Administrative Science Quarterly*, 8 (June 1963), 18–43.

[43]Lester Tanzer, "Ike's Lobbyists," *Wall Street Journal*, June 16, 1959, p. 1.

State Department and a congressman's tendency to vote in favor of the Department's requests, on the part of those congressmen whose party is not in control of the presidency. (Congressmen whose party is in control of the presidency generally vote in favor of Administration requests regardless of whether information service from the Executive departments is regarded as satisfactory or not.)[44]

Most agencies of government operate with almost painful regard for openness. Politicians, the press, even the average citizen, can inquire about their operations at any time and glean a fairly complete picture. A small number of agencies are secret, designated so by Act of Congress or by Executive Order. These are the Central Intelligence Agency, the National Security Agency, the Defense Intelligence Agency, the intelligence services of the Army, Navy, and Air Force, the Atomic Energy Commission, the Federal Bureau of Investigation, and the State Department's Bureau of Intelligence and Research. Most of these—with the major exception of the Federal Bureau of Investigation—are concerned with military and foreign affairs, and so have very little direct contact with the rest of the American people. According to Wise and Ross, these secret organizations together employ 200,000 people and spend $40 billion a a year,[45] but this seems high when considering the total federal budget is just over $100 billion. Because they are secret, it is difficult to find out much about them; the Wise and Ross book is a serious journalistic effort of considerable coverage, and so is the series in *The New York Times* of early May 1966. The Central Intelligence Agency has been the subject of greatest controversy because of the nature and extent of its operations aside from information gathering, and because questions have been raised by political leaders as to whether it is effectively controlled by either the President or by Congress. While top policy leaders in Washington have the power to control the agency, they are often too busy to do so, and the agency occasionally acts on its own policies. In a number of cases this has led to dubious overseas operations. The power exerted is

44James A. Robinson, "Some Effects of Information on State Department-Congressional Relations: The Interdependence of Process and Policy," unpublished paper, Department of Political Science, Northwestern University, May 1960.

45David Wise and Thomas B. Ross, *The Invisible Government* (New York: Random House, 1964).

not directly over the American people, but it affects the American people through international relations.

Of far greater power in government than any group of administrators, in fact of long-range power equal in some ways to that of the President and Congress, is that of the United States Supreme Court. The power of judicial review and of deciding what the Constitution allows any branch of the government to do or not to do confers upon the Court the possibility of determining much of the basic structure and direction of American life. This is especially true when, as in recent years, the majority of the Court has an activist philosophy.[46] The long-range impact on American society of the decisions to broaden the powers of the federal government through the interstate commerce clause of the Constitution, to enforce the Fourteenth Amendment and thereby protect the civil rights of minorities from discrimination by the states, and to require reapportionment of congressional districts and state legislatures to equalize the voting power of urban and rural citizens, cannot be overestimated. The justices—while nominated by the President and confirmed by the Senate—do not represent any special group or class. They follow the professional tradition of the law, and a special tradition developed in the Court itself. At various times, as now, they have been highly responsive to social needs.

It has long been recognized that lawyers are heavily represented among elected officeholders. According to Matthews,[47] while lawyers have seldom constituted much more or less than 0.1 per cent of the American labor force, they have contributed:

[46]In recent decades, Justice Felix Frankfurter was the leader of those advocating the opposite philosophy of judicial restraint, although he often joined the majority in forward-looking decisions—such as those involving civil rights and the extension of scope of the interstate commerce clause. Justice John Marshall Harlan is probably the most consistent advocate of judicial restraint on the Court today. Leadership of the activist majority can be said to be shared by Chief Justice Earl Warren and Associate Justices Hugo Black and William O. Douglas. The influence of some of these men extends beyond the decisions they make in the courtroom. The perceptive newspaper columnist Doris Fleeson said of Justice Frankfurter upon his retirement in 1962: "The Frankfurter influence was tirelessly extended by vote, by talk, by subtle pats of approval and by sheer personal brilliance throughout the whole power structure of Washington." (*Minneapolis Morning Tribune*, August 31, 1962, p. 5).

[47]Donald R. Matthews, *Social Background of the Political Decision Makers* (Garden City, N.Y.: Doubleday, 1954).

68 per cent of all United States Presidents

70 per cent of Presidents, Vice-Presidents and cabinet members, 1877–1934

57 per cent of United States senators, 1949–1951

56 per cent of United States representatives, 1949–1951

28 per cent of state legislators, 1925–1935

Lawyers do not make up a cohesive body in any political group, of course, with the possible exception of when a legislative body is considering some bill relating to the judiciary or to the codification of statutes. Nevertheless, the common influences, that make for the professional socialization of lawyers—such as the traditions and textbooks of law schools, the codes and ideology of the American Bar Association, the rules of courtroom procedures, and so on—must have a great influence on the thinking of the large number of lawyer-politicians. Lawyers—especially the corporation lawyers—are often the leading instruments of the economic power elite as well as the exercisers of the power of that elite. They also have represented minority groups, organized labor, criminals, and others. Lasswell and McDougal summarize the contemporary power of the attorney:

> . . . the lawyer is today . . . the one indispensable advisor of every responsible policy-maker of our society—whether we speak of the head of a government department or agency, of the executive of a corporation or labor union, of the secretary of a trade or other private association, or even of the humble independent enterpriser or professional man. As such an advisor, the lawyer, when informing his policy-maker of what he can or cannot legally do, is in an unassailably strategic position to influence, if not create, policy. . . . For better or worse, our decision-makers and our lawyers are bound together in a relation of dependence or identity.[48]

Floyd Hunter, in his *Community Power Elite*, makes the claim that much of the political power of the local economic elite is exercised through certain closed associations and through appointive advisory boards to state and local governments. Typically, these associations and boards are headed by more or less self-selected

---

[48]Harold D. Lasswell and M. S. McDougal, "Legal Education and Public Policy," in Lasswell, *Analysis of Political Behavior* (London: Routledge and Kegan Paul, 1948), p. 27.

executive committees (sometimes they are elected by all members of the association) who hire a professional director who, in turn, hires a professional staff. The range of activities of these groups is enormous—from Community Chests to governors' advisory councils on aging, to citizens' leagues for reform of urban government (some of these will be discussed in greater detail in a later chapter on voluntary associations). The power of these associations and boards is occasionally considerable, especially in the areas dealing with welfare and civic issues, and it is this power to which Hunter refers. But it has been my experience, and the observation of other American students of government advisory boards and closed association executive committees,[49] that most of the time the power of the boards and committees is actually exercised by the paid directors, if they are at all skilled in interpersonal relations. The directors are professionals, trained in administration or social work, whose expertise and backgrounds are similar to those of top government civil servants, although they usually have more freedom than top civil servants because they are less bound by bureaucratic rules. These directors, sometimes called executive secretaries or executive vice-presidents, set the agenda of the board or commission meetings, provide their nominal superiors with most of the relevant information available to them, make policy recommendations, and execute policy directives adopted by the board or committee. When there are ideological or personality conflicts within the board or committee, the director usually keeps neutral between the factions but he may occasionally be found on the side of the majority faction. The directors often have their own national or regional professional associations, at the meetings of which—among other things—they pass along the lore of how to control their boards or committees while keeping them "happy" (i.e. unaware that they are being controlled). It is a stupid or inexperienced director who cannot control his board, including the economic elite members on it. Thus, the power of the association or advisory committee is usually exercised in large measure by the professional director.

One particular kind of association, also not open to voluntary membership, is the philanthropic foundation. Its director is also usu-

---

[49]For example, Louis Goldstein, "The Social Agency Executive—A Study of Organizational Isolation," unpublished Ph.D. thesis, University of Minnesota, 1960.

ally trained in public administration or social work, although occasionally he may be an educator or even a businessman. His role and powers are similar to those of the directors of the agencies previously considered. The philanthropic foundation is often deemed to be especially powerful in American society because it has funds to give away. But public and congressional criticism of the philanthropic foundations, especially by the Cox and Reece Committees of the United States House of Representatives in the mid-1950's, has tended to make them cautious. Most of them want to retain their tax-exempt status, so they make the great bulk of their contributions to educational institutions and to scientific research—certainly not the avenue for exercising power in the society. Whatever the merits or defects of the philanthropic foundations, they cannot be considered great centers of power in the United States. This is especially true of the national philanthropic foundations, like the ones bearing the names of Ford, Rockefeller, and Carnegie. Some of the local ones are much more powerful—e.g. the Kansas City Association of Trusts and Foundations. Its director of some years, trained as a social worker, has achieved a national reputation for local power. If he has power, it is because power is widely diffused in Kansas City, and he is therefore one power-holder among many. His power is based on knowledge and skill, as is the case with most administrators and directors of boards and voluntary association executive committees. It also exists because his range of interests is broad, and he is thus equipped to relate one segment of the community to another—a skill rarely found among businessmen.

While a longer listing of types of organizations and persons who hold power would soon cover all those who *frequently and regularly* can exercise power in the community and nation, it would take a very long list to cover all those who have *ever* exercised real power on some occasion. Nearly every organization has some capacity for controlling situations outside of itself under certain circumstances, and nearly every member of an organization can move or sway it once in a while. These almost fortuitous exercises of power are not properly part of a serious study of power, however, and we shall leave them with this mention. Too, we can only offer for speculation the long-range power of churches and schools, which mold the ideals and thought-ways of the people. Here we consider not so much the fact that power is diffused and non-concentrated in American society as that it has different orders and dimensions, and that there is competition for it. Our general listing of the sources of power and how it operates in American society has been completed; we now turn to a consideration of the "masses," the allegedly powerless. We shall return to the specific processes by which power is exercised in a later section of this book.

PART TWO
The "Masses" in American Society

C. Wright Mills, after describing the economic and military elite as the dominant powers in American society and the political and associational functionaries as their lieutenants, gives brief attention to the majority of the people. He pictures them as a powerless, manipulated, passive, more or less undifferentiated (as to power) mass.[1] As in our discussion of the power elite, our analysis of the power position of the majority of the American people finds some truth in Mills's characterization, although the reasons we give for the development of the mass society differ somewhat from those of Mills. But we also find that his distinctions are greatly exaggerated and that there have been some notable reactions to the mass society, especially in the past half century. One of the most important of these reactions is the modern proliferation of the institution called the "voluntary association." We hold that those people, not of Mills's "power elite," who participate in voluntary associations of the instrumental type have a considerable power. Most of the other "reactions to the mass society" do not give power to the masses, but they prevent them from being a passive and manipulated mass.

Chapter V below reports the results of a questionnaire survey

[1]Even the Marxists, to whom Mills has a considerable intellectual debt, find his characterization of the masses inadequate. Herbert Aptheker, for example, holds that the masses are powerless, but not passive, and he believes that the voluntary associations of the trade unions and civil-right organizations have the potential for resisting the power elite. See Aptheker's *The World of C. Wright Mills* (New York: Marzani and Munsell, 1960).

165

which shows that association leaders with "power" are not so sharply differentiated from the average American citizen as Mills and Hunter would have us believe.

In Chapter VI we shall offer a description of the mass society and the factors which have created it. The final section of the chapter will take up the reactions against the mass society and suggest a more balanced picture of the American people of today than a characterization of them as a bulk "mass" would allow. The final chapter in this section (Chapter VII) will offer a description of the voluntary association in its many aspects, but with some special attention to its power-conferring functions.

V

Alienation and Participation:
A Comparison of Group Leaders and the "Mass"[1]

There have been many studies of leaders, but the great majority of them deal with them as individuals with certain distinctive psychological characteristics that have caused them to be "selected" as leaders. Leaders may also be seen as group functionaries, who develop certain social characteristics as a result of the influence of the group they lead and of their position in the group. I will seek to test a number of hypotheses about the characteristics of leaders that can be expected to occur because of their role as active participants in groups.[2]

An effort was made to study, as leaders, the presidents of all of the statewide organizations in Minnesota in 1959 that carried on some kind of a program in relationship to the public. These included all organizations recruiting membership throughout the state except: those operating only for the material advantage of their own members; those engaged in purely "expressive" activities—varying from the arts through hobbies to sports; and those that are mainly non–"voluntary" in membership, such as units of government and churches. Most of the organizations included in our sample had social welfare or social reform purposes. The list of organizations

[1]An abbreviated version of this chapter was published in the *American Sociological Review*, 27 (December 1962), 834–8.

[2]The theoretical framework for the hypotheses of the present study has been presented in my essay, "A Theory of the Function of Voluntary Associations in Contemporary Social Structure," in Arnold M. Rose, *Theory and Method in the Social Sciences* (Minneapolis: University of Minnesota Press, 1954).

167

had been developed through several years of operation of the State Organization Service of the University of Minnesota, and included 151 organizations, so that the initial sample consisted of 151 presidents. These were sent questionnaires through the mails and, with one follow-up letter, 71 (or 47 per cent) responded. This proportion of return is not bad for busy people solicited through the mails, but it does not allow for generalization to the total sample or to the whole body of American voluntary association presidents. Thus, the study must be regarded as exploratory in character. While we cannot claim that non-respondents do not differ in some ways from respondents, it should be understood that all respondents are leaders of statewide organizations.

The leaders' responses will be compared with responses to the same questionnaire by a cross section of the married population of the "Twin Cities," selected by a random procedure (every n^{th} case) from the city directories. Men and women were alternated in the cross-section sample. Those who failed to respond to mail solicitation were interviewed in their own homes, so total response was 90 per cent (195 respondents out of the 220 in the original sample). Partly by virtue of the sampling procedure, the group leaders included slightly more males (not statistically significant), more single persons (there being none in the cross section), and therefore fewer with children. Nevertheless, the group leaders were older on the average (none of them being under thirty-five). Differences are reported between the leaders and the cross section only if they are large enough to be statistically significant at the 5 per cent level, except when noted as nonsignificant differences.

Relatively speaking, the group leaders are of the elite. Seventy-five per cent of the group leaders, as compared to 25 per cent of the general population, have at least some college education. Among the group leaders, 52 per cent have professional or managerial occupations, whereas in the general population the proportion is 12 per cent. When asked to rank themselves along a six-category continuum of class, 90 per cent of the group leaders, as compared to 55 per cent of the cross section, ranked themselves as upper-uppers, lower-uppers or upper-middles. All of these differences are highly significant statistically. But they are not categorical differences: the numerical majority of the group leaders are closer to the averages for the general population than they are to the top levels among the group leaders (except possibly in education). Still, groups are likely to select as leaders those who have the educational background, the vocational skills, and the prestige to make them effective leaders. These facts should be well known, yet they have been wrongly used as new evidence of economic-elite domination of group life in American communities.[3]

Participation itself tends to be a "trait"; we hypothesize that the group leaders also participate more than the general population in organizations other than those in which they are leaders. This is found to be true for church membership, although the difference is not statistically significant: 91 per cent of the group leaders, as compared to 85 per cent of the general population, are members of churches.[4] There is no difference in church attendance among those who are church members. Group leaders are more likely to be members of a union or business group than are the individuals in our cross section of the general population, and here the difference is statistically significant: 54 per cent of the group leaders, as compared to 36 per cent of the general population, are members of a union or business group. Group leaders are also more likely to attend meetings of these groups: 28 per cent of the group leaders reported themselves as attending 13 or more meetings a year of their occupational group, as compared to only 8 per cent of the general population. The major reason given for participation in the occupational association by group leaders is "personal benefits": this is stated in an open-answer question by 43 per cent of the group leaders, but by only 22 per cent of the cross section. None of the group leaders give "social pressures" as a reason for belonging.

Group leaders are also more participant in a range of voluntary associations other than those in which they are leaders. Whereas 51 per cent of the group leaders were members of a social club or recreational organization, this was true of only 18 per cent of the cross section. The difference is somewhat less, but still significant, for

[3]See, for example, Floyd Hunter, *Community Power Structure* (Chapel Hill: University of North Carolina Press, 1952).

[4]Only 7 per cent of the group leaders are Catholic, as compared to 20 per cent of the general population. In the heavily Lutheran community of Minneapolis, group leaders were only slightly more likely to be affiliated with the Lutheran church: 34 per cent compared to 28 per cent.

membership in social welfare or social reform organizations: Membership in these kinds of associations was claimed by 24 per cent of the group leaders, as compared to 14 per cent of the cross section. Reflecting this participation were answers to a question asking "How many evenings during the past month (30 days) have you spent with people who are *not* members of your immediate family?" Thirty-two per cent of the group leaders and 20 per cent of the cross section were spending more than 10 evenings during the preceding month with persons outside the family.[5] Group leaders also claim to have more close friends than do persons in the general population. While indicating these various forms of group participation to a greater extent, group leaders are no different from the cross section in the extent to which they feel they are nonconformists: 25 per cent of both samples say they "enjoy being different from other people in [their] behavior."

Another subjective or psychological reflection of social participation is "need inviolacy," or the expression of need to avoid social contact or exposure. This was measured by a six-item scale.[6] Only 13 per cent of the group leaders agreed with any one or more of these items, as compared to 28 per cent of the general population sample.

It is for all the reasons indicated in the preceding paragraphs that we can consider that the group leaders are more socially integrated than the average persons in the general population sample. We hypothesize, further, that they are less alienated from their society and culture in various subjective or psychological ways because of

[5]This question may be ambiguous in that a member of the family (e.g. spouse) may have joined the respondent in some group activity outside the home. The question does not permit a distinction between activity in a voluntary association and attendance at a commercial recreation establishment.

[6]Developed by the author in collaboration with Kenneth E. Clark, Herbert McClosky, and Paul E. Meehl. The items in the scale, to be answered by checking "agree," "disagree," or "can't decide," were:

"I never try to do more than I know I can, for fear of failure."

"I must admit I get very stubborn when people try to find out about my personal affairs."

"The best policy is to keep things to one's self."

"Compared to your own self-respect, the respect of others means very little."

"Nowadays more and more people are prying into things that ought to remain personal and private."

"What a person thinks about politics is nobody else's business."

this social integration. In stating this hypothesis, we again emphasize that we are dealing with statistically significant differences in proportion, not with categorical or qualitative differences. We do not expect, nor do we find, that the general population is alienated or anomic: It is merely true, but nevertheless important to note, that the general population contains a statistically significant larger proportion of alienated or anomic individuals.

A first approach in support of this hypothesis would be to ascertain if group leadership tends to give a person some sense of satisfaction with his power in the community. When asked, "Do you think people like yourself should have more to say about the running of things in this country?", 5 per cent fewer of the group leaders than of the cross section (40 compared to 45 per cent) answered in the affirmative. This is not a statistically significant difference. At the same time, group leaders are somewhat less likely than the general population to indicate that they are manipulated by a power elite: In response to the question, "To what extent do the people who run this country make you do things that you don't really want to do?", 9 per cent of the leaders, as compared to 22 per cent of the cross section, said they felt this way more than "once in a while." While the difference is statistically significant, the proportions are not large. The same pattern emerges in response to the question, "How often do you feel that you are not given the chance to show what you can do?": 3 per cent of the group leaders answered "most of the time," as compared to less than 8 per cent of the cross section. The difference is not significant, and the proportions are small. Thus, in terms of sense of power in the community and feeling of freedom to take independent action, which form one axis of absence of alienation, not many of the two groups of citizens we are comparing exhibit such alienation. Group leaders feel somewhat more integrated into the social structure, but their difference from the cross section of citizens is not great.

In another sense, however, the group leaders are much less alienated than the general population. This is in regard to knowledge of how the social system works. Group leaders are constantly acquiring social knowledge, and using it to lead or control or manipulate a segment of society, no matter how small or specialized. To test this hypothesis concerning their difference from the general population, we did not present respondents with a test of factual social knowledge, because an adequate test would have to be quite extensive, and because to a considerable degree *relevant* social knowledge differs from one person to another according to where he is placed in the social system. Rather, we utilized a seven-item scale designed to measure feelings of bewilderment and confusion.[7] Differences in scores can be measured in a number of ways, but if we take all those who gave at least one answer indicating bewilderment or confusion, we get the largest number who may be said to feel this way. On this basis, the proportion for group leaders was 24 per cent, while for the general population it was 48 per cent. The difference is statistically significant, and the proportions are large (although it should be recalled that our measure encourages large proportions by being based on agreement with any one of seven items indicating bewilderment or confusion).

The same point can be made by comparing responses on a single, direct question. When asked "How well do you feel you understand what is going on in the world today?," 88 per cent of the group leaders, as compared to 65 per cent of the general population, answered either "very well" or "fairly well." Again, the difference is significant, and the proportion indicating lack of understanding ("not very well" or "not well at all") is moderately high (35 per cent) in the general population.

One of the more familiar indices of alienation, which leadership in voluntary associations might be expected to counteract, is a measure of anomie. Leo Srole has developed a five-item scale measuring anomie[8] which has been successfully used in several studies, and

[7]This scale was developed by the author in collaboration with Kenneth E. Clark, Herbert McClosky, and Paul E. Meehl. It consists of the following scale items, to be answered with "agree," "disagree," or "can't decide":

"Nobody really has any very good answers for the problems that face us today."
"All the experts disagree, so how can a person decide what is right?"
"The government is getting too big."
"I don't know who is to blame when things go wrong in the government."
"It is hard for me to discover who deserves the credit for what the government does."
"The world is too complicated now to be understood by anyone but experts."
"I sometimes feel like a tiny cog in a huge machine."
[8]Leo Srole, "Social Integration and Certain Corollaries," *American Sociological*

which was included in our questionnaire. As we would anticipate from our hypotheses and previous findings, the group leaders are significantly less likely to give any indication of anomie than is the cross section: Only 3 per cent of the group leaders agreed with any of the anomie items, as compared to 20 per cent of the cross section. Even so, the percentage of those among the cross section who indicate this slight degree of anomie is not large.

One of the long-noted manifestations of alienation is intergroup prejudice. Stouffer has shown that group leaders are more inclined to support civil liberties than is the general population,[9] and we shall now see that they are also more inclined to support civil rights.[10] On a three-item scale of social distance toward Negroes,[11] 70 per cent of the group leaders, as compared to only 44 per cent of the general population, showed willingness to associate with Negroes in at least two of the three respects. On a separate social distance item, "Negroes should be put on separate jobs from whites," 97 per cent of the group leaders disagreed, as did 77 per cent of the general population. On a series of items regarding Jews, group leaders showed themselves much less anti-Semitic than the general population, as shown in the following tabulation:

Review, 21 (December 1956), 709–16. The items in the Srole anomie scale, to be answered with "agree," "disagree," or "can't decide," are:

"There's little use writing to public officials because often they aren't really interested in the problems of the average man."

"Nowadays a person has to live pretty much for today and let tomorrow take care of itself."

"In spite of what some people say, the lot of the average man is getting worse."

"It's hardly fair to bring children into the world with the way things look for the future."

"These days a person doesn't really know whom he can count on."

[9]Samuel A. Stouffer, *Communism, Conformity and Civil Liberties* (New York: Doubleday, 1955).

[10]We do not say that "upper-class" people in general are less inclined to manifest group prejudices. But the group leaders in our sample are an especially "social integrated" element of the upper class. We would guess that the majority of the upper class are almost as anomic as the average of the other classes. Stember has shown something of the complicated relationhip between prejudice and class position generally. Charles H. Stember, *Education and Attitude Change* (New York: Institute of Human Relations Press, 1961).

[11]A Guttman-type scale with a reproducibility of 98, showing willingness to live with Negroes in the same block, building, and schools.

| | PERCENT DISAGREEING | |
ITEM	GROUP LEADERS	GENERAL POPULATION
"It would be a good idea if more business concerns would refuse to hire Jews."	98.5	77.4
"It would be a good idea to keep Jews out of Christian neighborhoods."	95.5	79.5
"It would be a good idea if Jews were prevented from getting more power in the business world."	83.6	58.0
"In general, Jews should not be allowed to hold high political office."	92.5	68.7

Similarly, on one item regarding Catholics, group leaders showed themselves somewhat less prejudiced than the general population, although the difference is less here probably because the general population sample included a larger percentage of Catholics than did the group leaders sample. In response to the item, "In general, Catholics should not be allowed to hold high political office," 89.6 per cent of the group leaders disagreed, as compared to 72.8 per cent of the general population.

Another hypothesis concerning the effects of high group participation on the individual is that participation in voluntary associations provides a sense of satisfaction with democratic processes. This sense of satisfaction will be measured along two dimensions: responsible action expected of a citizen in a democracy, and belief in the responsiveness of government to the wishes of the people. To get at the action dimension, respondents were asked if they were registered to vote, how often they voted, and how systematically they read the front pages of the newspapers. In all three respects group leaders were significantly more active than the general population.

1. Of the group leaders, 93 per cent, as compared to 77 per cent of the cross section, said they were registered to vote. Since some of the group leaders lived in small suburban municipalities, where registration was not required, whereas all of the cross section lived in cities, where registration was required, the discrepancy is in fact greater than these figures indicate.

2. Of the group leaders, 98 per cent said they voted in "every

single election" or "most of the time," as compared to 83 per cent of the cross section.

3. When asked, "How often do you read the front page of a newspaper carefully?", only 1 per cent of the group leaders, as compared to 10 per cent of the cross section, admitted they did this only "once in a while."

Three questions were asked to tap attitudes as to whether American government is responsive to the wishes of the people. In two of the three questions the differences between group leaders and the general population were large and statistically significant; for the third question the difference was in the expected direction but not large enough to be statistically significant.

1. When asked, "To what extent do the people who run this country care about what ordinary people think or want?", the proportions answering at least "most of the time" were 90 per cent among the leaders and 57 per cent among the cross section.

2. When asked, "To what extent do the people who run this country have at heart the best interest of the United States?", the proportions answering at least "most of the time" were 88 per cent among the leaders and 75 per cent of the cross section.

3. When asked, "How good a job does the government do in representing the interests of the American people?", the proportions answering "a fairly good job" or "a very good job" were 87 per cent among the leaders and 84 per cent among the general population. While this difference is not significant, it is to be noted that the general population here comes up to the high belief in responsiveness of government held by the group leaders, rather than the leaders falling to the relative low level of opinion of the general population on the preceding two items. The lack of discrepancy here is especially interesting in view of the fact that the "government" at the time of the survey was headed by President Eisenhower, and there was a significantly larger proportion of Republicans among the leaders than among the population cross section.

Thus far we have examined the "traits" and attitudes of group leaders insofar as they relate to the social environment. But, as we anticipated from our general theory, there are differential patterns between group leaders and the general population in how they view their own lives. To a significantly greater extent the leaders are satisfied with their careers or occupational choices: 69 per cent of the leaders, compared to 52 per cent of the cross section, would follow the same occupations if they "could go back to age eighteen and start over again." On the other hand, leaders are significantly less likely to be satisfied with what they have achieved in life: In response to the question "Do you think you have done the best you could have done with your life, considering the circumstances?", 83 per cent of the leaders, as compared to 97 per cent of the cross section, answered either "yes, entirely so" or "yes, fairly much so." Apparently, some group leaders have a negative perspective toward their achievements, but not toward their occupations. This mixed attitude toward personal achievement is reflected in answers to a general question concerning life satisfaction, "In general, how satisfied are you with your life?" The proportion responding "very satisfied" or "fairly satisfied" is slightly greater among the group leaders, but not significantly so (82 per cent among the group leaders compared to 76 per cent among the general population).

The dissatisfaction with their achievements among some group leaders is apparently not due to a belief that they have suffered handicaps. In response to the question "How difficult has your life been?", the proportion answering either "not difficult at all" or "not very difficult" is practically identical for the group leaders and the general population (72 per cent and 71 per cent, respectively). A free-response type of question did best in getting at the source of achievement-dissatisfaction among the group leaders. This question was "If you could change yourself over into any kind of person, what kind of person would you want to be?" The answers given most frequently by the leaders were that they wanted to be more aggressive, more active, better educated, and, specifically, better leaders. In other words, the achievement-dissatisfactions of the group leaders were precisely in the area of their group leadership, not in their occupations.

Characteristic of their greater realism and lesser alienation, the group leaders have a clearer and more definite idea about their personal aspirations. In response to the question, "How clear an idea do you have as to what would be best for you?", the proportion responding "a very clear idea" or "fairly clear idea" was 94 per cent among the leaders as compared to 72 per cent among the general population. Similarly, in response to the question, "How sure are you that you know what the best way of living is?", 87 per cent of the leaders, compared to 77 per cent of the general population, said "very sure" or "fairly sure." Another indication that group leaders are positively oriented to their leadership role is that they are significantly likely to say they wished to carry on their present activity when asked, "In general, what would you like to do when you are past sixty-five years old?" Group leaders are more likely to be decided as to what they plan to do when they are past sixty-five than is the general population: 79 per cent of the group leaders, as compared to 64 per cent of the cross section, claim to be decided.

Summary and Discussion

The specific findings of the study, stated briefly, are:

1. The group leaders are better educated, are more likely to have managerial or professional occupations, and are more likely to identify themselves as members of the upper classes, than is the general population.

2. Active participation in voluntary associations is associated with greater participation in other, "secondary" areas of life, such as churches, occupational organizations, and other voluntary associations.

3. Subjectively, group leaders are less likely than the general population to express a need to avoid social contact or exposure. But they are no different in the proportion who say they enjoy being nonconformists.

4. Group leaders are somewhat less likely than the general population to exhibit any signs of being alienated from the society or culture, but neither group has many alienated persons.

a. The group leaders are slightly more likely to have a sense of power in the community and a feeling of freedom to take independent action, but the differences are so slight as to be not statistically significant and the proportions having these feelings are quite large in both groups.

b. The group leaders are much more likely to have social knowledge, and not to have any sense of bewilderment or confusion about the functioning of society.

c. The group leaders are less likely to be anomic, as measured by the Srole scale, but the proportion of anomic individuals is not great in either group.

d. The group leaders are less likely to express any intergroup prejudice.

5. Group leaders manifest more satisfaction with democratic processes, both in that their behavior is more in accord with what might be expected of a citizen in a democracy and in that their attitudes are more likely to include a belief that the government is responsive to the wishes of the people.

6. Group leaders are more likely than the general population to be satisfied with their occupational choice, but are less likely to be satisfied with what they have achieved in life because they believe they have not been active or aggressive enough in their leadership roles. The group leaders are also more likely to have a clearer and more definite idea about their personal aspirations and their future plans.

The findings of this chapter support certain interpretations of social phenomena which, while not original with this author, run contrary to the dominant interpretations of those phenomena. First, we have shown that group leaders are more likely to be socially integrated and less likely to be alienated from the society than the general population. We interpret this in terms of the very participation and activity of the group leaders in the groups of which they are the leaders, rather than in terms of their individual personalities. Since this is a correlational rather than an experimental study, we cannot prove this interpretation, although all our findings are compatible with the interpretation.

Second, our findings do not indicate that the general population is different in kind from the group leaders, such that it could be called an anomic "mass." There are frequently differences between the two groups sufficiently large as to be statistically significant, and no doubt there is a significant minority of the general population which is alienated and anomic. But such persons are still a minority, and do not justify speaking of the population in general as anomic, alienated, or as being a "mass."[12] As all societies must be, in order to function and deserve the name of society, our society is sufficiently integrated so that most of the time its members are able accurately to predict what other members will do under given conditions, in terms of their understanding of the cultural meanings and values.[13] One is justified in characterizing American society, either now or in the latter half of the nineteenth century, as a mass society only insofar as it differs in degree, not in kind, from the more thoroughly integrated societies of isolated preliterate peoples or of those of our own ancestors in the pre-industrial or medieval era.

Third, in accord with the preceding point, leaders or the "elite" of our society are not completely distinguishable from "the mass" in their monopoly of power or their absolute class differentiation.[14] It is true that more of the leaders have more social power than is to be found among the average members of the general population and they have a higher average class position. But our findings are much more compatible with the interpretation that power is somewhat dispersed through the general population and that there is a wide range of class differentiation in the non-leadership general population. Also contrary to Hunter and Mills, there is no evidence in our data that the local leaders studied believe they are manipulated by a higher power elite (only 9 per cent of them said that "people who run this country make you do things you don't really want to do"). And just as many of the local leaders as of the general population (25 per cent) said they "enjoy being different from other people in [their] behavior."

In sum, our interpretation of the data presented in this study is that group leaders are different only in degree and proportion, not in kind or absolutely, from the general population, and that what dif-

[12]My findings are in accord here with a number of recent researches on group participation and extended family contacts. On the basis of these and other studies, Joseph R. Gusfield has formulated a general statement with which my findings are compatible. ("Mass Society and Extremist Politics," *American Sociological Review*, 27 (February 1962), 19–30.) I have elsewhere stated my belief, and have provided evidence for it, that there are an increasing number of social forces *diminishing* the anomic and mass elements in the society: "Reactions to the Mass Society," in Chapter VI.

[13]Arnold M. Rose, "A Systematic Statement of Symbolic Interactionist Theory," in *Human Behavior and Social Processes* (New York: Houghton Mifflin, 1962).

[14]Hunter, *Community Power Structure*, and *Top Leadership, U. S. A.* (Chapel Hill: University of North Carolina Press, 1959); C. Wright Mills, *The Power Elite* (New York: Oxford University Press, 1956).

ferences there are are due to the leaders' more active social participation. Our findings cannot be regarded as definitive because of the limitations of our sample, but they provide suggestive evidence against certain prevalent ideas about differences between leaders and "the mass."

VI
The Mass Society

A. The Problems of the Mass Society[1]

Many of those who probe into current social problems find at their core the separation of the individual and the group. The individual finds it difficult or impossible to communicate satisfactorily with his fellows and consequently cannot orient his own values or put himself into harmony with society. He feels powerless, and to some extent *is* powerless. It was probably Karl Marx who first put part of the problem into a concrete observation and concept. He spoke of "alienation from work"—the factory worker's failure to gain a sense of the meaning of his work as he performed mechanical, repetitive tasks. Prior to the industrial Revolution, the craftsman or the agriculturist performed *whole* tasks of production—from beginning to end—and could see the meaning of his work as he completed a job of production or a harvest.

The great French sociologist, Emile Durkheim, investigated suicide and found its chief modern cause in what he called "anomie."[2] This was a sense of estrangement from the values of the social group, and of separation from its fellowship ("anonymity"). Faris and Dunham, in their brilliant statistical analysis, *Mental Disorders in Urban Areas*,[3] revealed evidence that schizophrenia, the most common type

[1]This and the following two sections appeared in an earlier version in my "Social Problems in the Mass Society," *Antioch Review*, 10 (September 1950), 378–94.

[2]Suicide (Glencoe, Ill.: Free Press, 1951; 1st edition, 1897).

[3]R. E. L. Faris and H. W. Dunham, Chicago: University of Chicago Press, 1939.

of mental disease, was much more likely to be had by those whose life circumstances prevented them from developing close personal ties with their fellows. Robert Cooley Angell, in a study of how *The Family Encounters the Depression*,[4] demonstrated that a major decline of income resulted in family disorganization only when there were few ties of intimacy and understanding between family members to begin with. Social psychologists such as Fromm[5] and Riesman[6] have been interested in the softening of personality under the impact of the mass society. Riesman traces the trend from a "tradition-directed personality," characteristic of the integrated society of the Middle Ages, to an "inner-directed personality," typical of the commercialization and industrialization period from the sixteenth to the nineteenth centuries to the "other-directed personality," characteristic of the present period. The "other-directed personality" is described as seeking always to please other people, even at the sacrifice of other social and personal values. This list of studies could be greatly extended, but the information that these give is enough to indicate a major conclusion of social science research into certain contemporary social problems: These problems in large measure result from the atomization of social groups into mentally isolated individuals.

Political philosophers have seen the same problem in another context, in terms of the meaning of democracy. When modern democratic ideology was being formulated during the eighteenth century, it was recognized to have at least three components: "liberty, equality, and fraternity"—in the terms of the French Revolutionary slogan. The literature of the period contains a good deal of discussion of these terms, and in no case is there any evidence that the writers thought of "liberty" as the sole or even the most important element of democracy. Equality and fraternity were just as important. Yet Western nations have since elevated liberty to the position of being almost equivalent to democracy. Equality is only permitted to squeeze in during an argument, and fraternity is so completely forgotten that the term no longer has any meaning to the average citizen. Yet liberty, with its concomitant individualism, may come to be

[4]New York: Scribner's, 1936.
[5]Erich Fromm, *Man for Himself* (New York: Rinehart, 1947).
[6]David Riesman, with the assistance of Reuel Denney and Nathan Glazer, *The Lonely Crowd* (New Haven: Yale University Press, 1950).

regarded as of no value to people who do not enjoy equality and fraternity. The problem of modern democratic society may be ascribed in large part to the fact that equality—the ideal that all men should have the same status before God and the law and should have the same chances for life success—is given only lip service, and that fraternity—the ideal that every man must respect every other man and feel a sense of responsibility for him—is completely lost. The three ideals together form an integrated system. Lacking one, the others are in danger. Fraternity represented adequate interpersonal communication and the adjustment of the individual to his social group. Its decline, both as a factual component of our culture and as an ideal, is related to the rise of the problems of mass society and the growth of totalitarianism. Liberty, when unaided by fraternity, encourages the individual to be separated from his fellows. This alienation permits power cliques to arise which deliberately kill liberty.

While the loss of fraternity and the growth of an atomized mass in place of a healthy social order have had the ill effects we have noted, there is also a danger in the opposite direction. Many of the current "isms"—not least fascism and anti-Semitism—have their appeal to the masses in terms of their promise to reintegrate the individual into the social order. They hold out to the isolated, anonymous modern man an offer to rejoin society, to regain his sense of social belonging, and to eliminate his conflict of values arising from an unintegrated existence. This is no small offer to the mass man beset by extreme loneliness and mental conflict. It is more than an appeal to security; it is also an appeal to fraternity, although in a narrow and warped sense. For this, modern man is asked to give up only liberty, and frequently he is willing to do so. The result is fascism or communism, or one of their lesser modifications.

The dilemma of the mass man in a Western democracy is whether he can continue to brave the mental terrors of individualism in order to gain its benefits. His dilemma is a choice of *either* liberty *or* fraternity, *either* freedom *or* order. History has a way of developing such dilemmas even when logic does not create the opposition. There is no logical reason why there cannot be a sphere of individual freedom at the same time as there is satisfactory communication between individuals leading to feelings of belonging and social integration. It is in terms of a combination of both of these sets of values

that the democratic political philosopher finds a solution to the problems of the modern mass man.

As early as 1909, Charles Horton Cooley deplored the trend
toward the mass society, toward a "dead level of culture'" in which
every individual was cut in the same mold as every other one, and all
were subjected to the same influences without the opportunity to
discuss these influences adequately. Cooley observed that nationality
groups were declining in the United States, and would no longer provide the diversity of culture that would be essential for culture
growth. He foresaw and advocated the growth of interest groups,
which would develop specific aspects of culture according to their
special interests, abilities, or backgrounds. Cooley was far more democratic than some of our latter-day cultural pluralists who insist that
nationality is the sole basis of cultural diversity and demand that individuals devote all aspects of their life to their nationality group.
Cooley would not only encourage cultural development in all kinds
of groups, including the nationality groups, but would also allow individuals to join these groups on a voluntary basis instead of being
involuntary members on the basis of birth alone. (John Dewey and
Horace Kallen seem to have had much the same sort of ideas as
Cooley in originating the philosophy of cultural pluralism, although
some adherents of that philosophy today have shifted from the original intent.)

Robert E. Park was another outstanding sociologist who was concerned about the trend toward a mass society. Although following
the lead of certain European writers, he was probably the first to give
a clear definition of the mass. His ideas have been extended and
systematized by Herbert Blumer. For Park and Blumer, the mass is
an agglomeration of individuals socially isolated but not physically
isolated from one another. They are subjected to the same influences,
especially those of propaganda, but because of social isolation have
no opportunity for rational discussion of these influences. They are
thus molded by these influences—all in pretty much the same way—
without having any independent individual reactions. Also because
of social isolation, the individuals in a mass society are lonely and
feel a need to belong to some group movement. They are without
loyalties and are weak on ideals, but desire both—at least unconsciously.

The mass is such an unstable and unsatisfying condition of society that it is actually conducive to totalitarianism. But dictatorship provides only superficial satisfaction for the needs created by mass society: While the totalitarian state gives something to the people to belong to, it still keeps people apart and out of communication with each other. No dictatorship can survive if the common people form publics and discuss their situation, their culture, and their ideals. If they did so, they would threaten the dictatorship, or at least prevent it from doing what it wishes to do. Fascism and communism, therefore, set up the strongest barriers to communication among citizens, and yet try to create the illusion that the citizens are fully integrated members of an understanding and protective state. The dictator must subject his people to frequent propaganda and expect them to respond to it directly. Thus every totalitarian state in these days of high average education and easy means of communication must be a mass society, even though it may have a camouflage of stability. The mass society is no more stable under dictatorship than it is under democracy. Modern totalitarianism eventually turns out to be a mirage: while it recruits members in its early stages because it seems to be a way out of the mass society, it becomes an extreme form of the mass society once it has achieved power and is seeking to keep people in line.

B. The Trend from Folk Society to Mass Society[7]

Students of Western society have been aware for some time that there has been a long-run trend since the Middle Ages toward a mass society.[8]

[7] One of the best sources on the trend toward the mass society, and the reaction to it, is Robert A. Nisbet, *Quest for Community* (New York: Oxford University Press, 1953).

[8] We use the term "mass society" in a way different from that of some other sociologists. Duncan and Artis and Hatt use it to refer to the general American society, as distinguished from the local community. (O. D. Duncan and J. W. Artis, "Some Problems of Stratification Research," *Rural Sociology*, 16 (March 1951), 17–29; Paul K. Hatt, "Stratification in the Mass Society," *American Sociological Review*, 15 (April 1950), 216–22.) Bennett and Tumin use it to refer to a type of social organization where large numbers of people use approximately the same cultural practices. (J. W. Bennett and M. M. Tumin, *Social Life* (New York: Knopf, 1948). Brown uses the term "cultural mass" in about the same way—to refer to the common elements of culture in a pluralistic society. (James C. Brown, "Co-operative Group Formation: A Problem in Social Engineering," unpublished.) Ortega represents an old tradition among political scientists and publicists in using the term "mass society" to refer to a political situation in which power is held by

With some exaggeration we can characterize the older society out of which the mass society developed as one based upon the integrated-group mode of relationship or what Redfield calls the "folk society."[9] Before the Industrial Revolution, beginning at the end of the eighteenth century, communities had to be somewhat isolated from each other—because transportation was difficult and the main occupation was farming, which took space—and their members were governed by strong adherence to common meanings and values. In their limited circle people were in adequate communication with each other and they had a strong sense of belonging and of loyalty to the community. Their values were clear to them and were believed to be practical as well as "true." People believed they understood the controlling forces of their society, even though modern scientists know that these beliefs had little relationship to reality. Outside influences may have existed in their experience, but were regarded simply as beyond their ken and had little challenge for them, little meaning in their daily lives.

The trend toward increasing frequency of occurrence of the audience has been due to several causes. The most obvious one has been the invention of a large number of mass media and the development of conditions through which these mass media could have a wide audience. To a considerable extent the mass media force the formation of audiences, and before they existed there was less opportunity for audiences to form. A second influence in the augmentation of the audience has been the decline of the integrated group. With the Commercial and Industrial revolutions came a good deal of geographical mobility, especially from rural to urban areas.[10] Eco-

---

the bulk of the people as distinguished from one in which power is held by an elite group. (José Ortega y Gasset, *Revolt of the Masses*, (London: Allen and Unwin, 1932). Marx and his followers have referred to the "masses" in this way as meaning the bulk of the population as distinguished from a property-owning or intellectual elite. We use the term "mass society" to refer to a social situation characterized by numerous and frequent formation of people into audiences—in which communication is one-way from a leader or propagandist and there is very little interaction among members.

[9]Robert Redfield, *Tepoztlan: a Mexican Village* (Chicago: University of Chicago Press, 1930).

[10]A most important historical description of the initial effects of the Commercial Revolution is Henri Pirenne, *Economic and Social History of Medieval Europe* (London: Kegan Paul, Trench, Trubner, 1936).

nomic influences broke up a very large number of the old communities and placed people in cities, where it is more difficult to form the highly integrated forms of social existence that are possible in isolated rural areas and small villages.

Coincident with this trend has been the breakup or decline of some of the institutions that formerly buttressed much of the value system of medieval European society. The extended family, which gave the whole community a family-like unity and intimacy, is now greatly reduced and has taken on a different form. The Church, which taught, interpreted, and expressed the social values, has declined sharply in influence since the Middle Ages, and here the decline has been more rapid in Western Europe than it has in the United States. The Industrial Revolution also weakened the integrating effect of certain institutions by forcing people to segmentalize their lives to a certain extent. The nuclear family no longer provides economic occupations, the primary source of recreation, or education for the young. There are now specialized institutions where one works, plays, goes to school, etc., and each of these is distinct from the family. This segmentalization, or division of labor in the broader sense of the term, has further broken up the integrated community in which people once lived in a high degree of mutual interaction with one another. While these changes have released individuals from the tyranny of community pressure to a considerable extent, and have opened up the possibility of greater freedom of thought and action in an individualistic sense, they have also opened the way for the audience to substitute for the integrated community.

Most historians have failed, somehow, to tell us what these drastic changes meant to the average citizen. By far the keenest analysis has come from the pen of an economist, Karl Polanyi.[11] He points out that these changes, especially the "almost miraculous" improvement in tools of production, were accompanied by "a catastrophic dislocation of the lives of the common people." Before the Industrial Revolution, most of the ordinary people had a basic economic security. The feudal serf was treated almost as a slave and had a minimum of legal and political rights. But he "belonged" to a plot of land, and no one could force him off it even though he was not the titular owner.

[11]Karl Polanyi, *The Great Transformation* (New York: Farrar and Rinehart, 1944).

The medieval village also had "common land," on which a bare living could be made by sheep raising. The serf and the peasant before the nineteenth century subsisted on an extremely low standard of living, but they felt that there were minimum economic resources on which they could always rely. Then the "enclosure movement" deprived most of them of the use of common land and the Commercial and Industrial revolutions transformed a majority from farmers into workers.

At first the sudden uprooting from the basic security of the land was met in England by a sort of minimum-wage law (the Speenhamland Act) whereby a worker who did not earn the minimum would have his wages supplemented up to the minimum by the government. This was a last gesture at maintaining the old security under the new system of industrial capitalism. It failed to work because employers found they could depress wages below the minimum without starving their workers and because workers found that they could loaf on the job without getting fired and without their total incomes falling below the minimum specified by law. After the law was repealed, in 1834, each worker found himself completely at the mercy of his employer, and each employer has to meet the competition of an impersonal market. Whenever confidence in the employer was shaken, either because of the employer's personal arbitrariness or because he was not competing effectively, there was a drop in the worker's sense of security. Even though the average income per worker rose markedly under industrial capitalism, the feeling of security sagged. Each depression, with successively larger unemployment rates, provided a new blow to the worker's feelings that he was economically safe. This led to personal demoralization on the one hand and the demand for security on the other.

The demand for security took two forms: the organization of trade unions and pressure for laws to provide minimum financial security. The growth of unions and farmers' organizations and the passage of social-security laws, minimum-wage laws, relief laws, and the like have compensated somewhat for the basic economic security previously provided by the land. But many workers are not members of effective unions, the unions do not have complete control over firing, the farmers' organizations do not have complete control over pricing, and social security payments lag behind the rise in the cost of living, so the economic problem of the mass society remains.

A comparable history could be traced for the businessman. During the Middle Ages his production was protected by guilds and his return by a conception of a "just price." These did not make for efficiency or initiative and so kept his financial return low, but they did give security. When the free-enterprise system developed at the end of the eighteenth century, the businessman had more chances to grow very wealthy, but he also had a greater chance to fail. He was now subject to the vicissitudes of cutthroat competition, of depressions, of fashion in demand for his product, of inventions that would make his product quickly obsolete. So he gradually developed monopolistic combines, "fair trade" laws, techniques to suppress new inventions, and so on. But most businessmen have not completely solved their problems of insecurity, as evident in their panicky behavior whenever a depression seems to threaten.

Another aspect of transition from folk society to mass society has been studied by Elton Mayo and his followers.[12] While studying industrial fatigue and spontaneous featherbedding in industrial plants, Mayo found that improvements in such technical conditions as lighting and rest periods helped to increase worker efficiency. The only difficulty with his early experiments was that *everything* helped; in fact, production stayed high even when all the good things were removed. Interviewing the workers revealed that it had been the sympathetic attention given to the workers while the experiment was going on that had the effect, not the mechanical changes. Similar results have been found throughout industry by Golden and Ruttenberg.[13] They show that even pay raises, bonuses, and profit sharing by themselves have seldom, if ever, increased worker output. After extended investigation, the Mayo group came to the following conclusion: When the worker felt he was treated as an impersonal cog in an industrial machine, he did not care much about doing a good job for the employer. But when personal interest was taken in the

[12] Elton Mayo, *Human Problems of an Industrial Civilization* (New York: Macmillan, 1933).
[13] Clinton S. Golden and Harold J. Ruttenberg, *The Dynamics of Industrial Democracy* (New York: Harper, 1942).

problems of the employee, when he was consulted on all matters concerning his job, and when rewards and punishments were given out with strict attention to all factors in the worker's situation, his job morale and efficiency rose.

Viewed historically, the factory system under capitalism did transform most workers into impersonal cogs—labor was regarded as an ingredient in production, just as were materials and capital. The worker consequently felt a loss of individuality; he became one of the sheep portrayed so realistically by Charlie Chaplin in *Modern Times*. As a number rather than a man, he felt little incentive, even when a raise in pay was held out as bait. A study by Professor W. Lloyd Warner and his associates of a strike in a New England city during the mid-1930's revealed that the strike had been building up in the workers' minds for eighty years.[14] The strike occurred in a shoe factory, where—eighty years earlier—machine production had replaced skilled hand production. Workers no longer owned their tools; there was little opportunity to exercise skill; there was no way of knowing how the productive process might next be altered. Ownership changed hands, passing from the enterprising, responsible, paternalistic local employers to an unknown corporation with headquarters in New York. The new bosses were simply well-paid agents for an impersonal power, and they appeared to care little about the workers or their town. There seemed to be little chance of getting ahead, and there could be little pride in work when the workers' jobs were so petty. The strike, out of which developed a union, was simply one manifestation of decades of frustration.

Drucker reports a telling story of an incident that occurred in an airplane factory toward the end of World War II.[15] The factory was playing a crucial role in war production, yet the turnover and absentee rates were very high and the production rate low. The workers were "fed up" with war shortages of consumers' goods, the difficulties of transportation to and from work, the inadequate housing, the confusion of working in a rapidly expanding plant. Government

[14]W. L. Warner and J. W. Low, *The Social System of the Modern Factory. The Strike: A Social Analysis* (New Haven: Yale University Press, 1947).

[15]Peter F. Drucker, *Concept of the Corporation* (New York: John Day, 1946), p. 77.

officials and plant managers grew frantic as output continued to slip and no appeal seemed to work.

Then the Army put on exhibition a war-battered bomber plane that had been produced at that very factory several years earlier. With it came the crew who had flown the bomber on dozens of missions over Germany and who were back in the States for a deserved rest. Members of the crew were "guides" to the plane; the idea was that they would tell the workers about the bombing flights. It was not expected that many workers would stay after hours to see the plane. But the workers came in droves and most of them asked questions. The questions were pretty much of the same pattern. "My job is to do thus-and-so. Would you please tell me where the part I handle is in the plane, and what does it do?" The workers did not know what they were doing! Naturally they did not see their relation to the war effort. When the part on which each worked was pointed out, its function explained, and perhaps an anecdote passed along as to how that part had once been hit or how it protected a flier, the workers were delighted. It sounds incredible to those who have never felt as these workers apparently did, but production immediately jumped. As far as anyone could tell, the bomber exhibit—or, rather, the workers' discovery of the significance of their jobs in the total war effort—was the cause. The specialists had regained a conception of the whole, at least temporarily.

Economists and industrial relations experts such as Polanyi, Mayo, Warner, and Drucker have done a good job of analyzing the shift from folk society to mass society insofar as it is manifested in the economic sphere of life. Sociologists, as we noted earlier, have paid a good deal of attention to the consequences of a mass society, but they have not analyzed the social consequences in historical terms. What happens to the individual, for example, when reaction shifts from the participant form to the passive-vicarious form? At present we can only speculate, but certain hypotheses seem likely. When individuals participate in games or other sociable recreation they are obliged to communicate constantly with each other, and adjust their behavior and attitudes to the other participants. Social bonds grow out of such adjustments and readjustments. But when individuals take their recreation by observing other people play, they are not "interacting," they are not adjusting their behavior and attitudes to those of other people. Of course there is a certain amount of interaction within the audience, especially when the individual comes to the sports event with other people. But, on the whole, the interpersonal relations consist largely of the members of the audience observing the players, the players communicating to one another and to the audience, with the audience having only a minor reaction back on the players and then not as individuals but as a mass. The modern man of middle or lower income has much more time for recreation than did his ancestors, but an increasing proportion of that recreational time is spent in a passive-audience type of situation in which he is not communicating with, learning from, or adjusting to his fellows.

C. Factors in the Trend

Let us be more concrete in examining some of the trends through which the audience has become a more important factor in the life of the modern citizen. In 1790 only 5 per cent of the people of the United States lived in cities; in 1960, 69.7 per cent lived in cities, and the proportion has undoubtedly risen since then. A major adjustment is involved in moving from a rural area to a city, and not enough study has been devoted to the social consequences of this trend, which is still going on. Most urban neighborhoods, especially those in which people with middle and upper incomes live, are not highly integrated in the sense that people know each other and that a common set of stores and other facilities serve all of them. Whereas in rural areas or villages a resident will know all those who live within a radius of several miles, an urbanite may not know his next-door neighbor. There are special occasions in the village when most people will come out at one time and talk to each other—while attending a fair or an auction, or simply while watching the train come through. The absence of these things in the city creates for it a reputation of being cold and unfriendly.

Actually, of course, it is easy to make more friends in the city than in the country, because more people are available and there is a greater possibility of finding those who have congenial personalities. But one makes friends in a different way—by joining a club, a church, a union, or by going to a skating rink or bowling alley. One's friends may be scattered over many parts of a city rather than living close by. For the person who moves from the country to the city it may be difficult to learn that physical closeness of residence is not a necessary basis for association. Consequently, he is lonely and isolated. This is especially significant in view of the fact that many migrants to the city are unattached people rather than family groups, and so do not even have spouses, parents, or children to turn to for companionship. The isolated individual is a member of the audience, not of an integrated society.

The city is heterogeneous, made up of groups of many divergent interests and backgrounds. The diversity, coupled with the large size of the urban population which permits even a well-known individual to walk down most streets unnoticed, creates opportunities for freedom of personal behavior that are rare in villages and that scarcely existed before the great increase in the number of large cities in the nineteenth century.[16] Freedom and diversity have been some of the great attractions of city life, and they have been an essential element in the development of artistic and intellectual activities wherever they have appeared. But freedom imposes a responsibility on the individual to make up his own mind as to what kind of behavior he wishes to engage in. There are fewer standards to which the individual must conform, and the concepts of "right" and "good" are made more relative. To an individual without the training to make up his own mind on such ethical matters, or the strength of character to conform to standards which he thinks proper, freedom may be demoralizing. The demoralized individual is also a member of an audience, not of an integrated society.

The city is also complex, or rather it reflects the complexity of modern life, which impinges on rural areas also. Complexity is confusing to the average individual. Just as industrial relations experts such as Mayo[17] and Drucker[18] have shown that the complexity of machine production confuses the industrial worker and makes him unhappy, so could it be observed that the increasing complexity of

[16]Louis Wirth, "Urbanism as a Way of Life," *American Journal of Sociology*, 44 (July 1938), 1–24.
[17]Mayo, *Human Problems*.
[18]Peter F. Drucker, *The Future of Industrial Man* (New York: John Day, 1942).

other aspects of modern life creates new sources of confusion for most citizens.

In politics, for example,[19] the activities and structures of government are far more complex today than they were a hundred years ago. The government touches the lives of the average citizen at many points. Despite the higher level of formal education, it is probable that the average citizen today has less understanding of the government at those points where it impinges on him. This perhaps explains the widespread belief that corrupt and evil forces have control of the government even when its head—Roosevelt or Eisenhower, for example—may be widely trusted and respected, and even when there is a popular demand that the government engage in a greater number of activities to aid ordinary people). And a rumor, having no basis in fact, that the Jews are widely infiltrated through the government will be widely adopted as a reasonable explanation of why the operations of government are so mysterious. In the integrated group society of pre-modern times, clearly specified powers were known to have control of government and the common people were not supposed to bother their heads with it. In today's democracy, the people are supposed to take responsibility for government, but it has become too complicated for them to understand. So they are confused, and feel alienated from their "government" in some ways (not from their flesh-and-blood president, senator, representative, or Supreme Court justice, however). A confused people form an audience also, not an integrated society.

There are other aspects of modern society that give the individual a sense of insecurity and alienation, and social forces are tending to increase these feelings. We shall merely mention two such aspects here. First, the functions of women have decreased sharply from the day when a woman was a major helpmate to her husband in bread-winning and when she was the chief educator for a large brood of children. The mechanical revolution greatly reduced and simplified household tasks. Yet society imposes no demands that she seek substitute functions. She can try her hand at a paid job or at social-welfare activity, but usually no one says that she must. And so the

---

[19]William Kornhauser, *The Politics of Mass Society* (Glencoe, Ill.: Free Press, 1959).

modern wife, after her youngest child has started school, is partly functionless, which means that she feels a vague but pervasive dissatisfaction and is likely to raise questions to herself about her very reason for existence. Since she has related herself to other people at only marginal points, and since she is uncertain of her own role in society, she is a member of the audience, not of an integrated society.

Second, while the spread of formal education has increased modern man's sophistication, and in one sense has helped him to understand the forces which control him, it has concomitantly increased his skepticism regarding the sources of his information. This would tend to decrease false beliefs if the citizen knew how to secure alternative sources of facts and if he could weigh all the evidence and apply the scientific historian's rules of internal and external criticism. But the education of most people has not proceeded that far. They have learned only up to the point that they believe propagandists are all about them and that few sources of news are to be trusted. Consequently, some people are generally in as bad a fix as the several hundred women who, in early 1946, while there were still war-induced shortages of many consumer goods, waited outside a hosiery store hoping to get a pair of nylons. An hour earlier the proprietor had put up a sign saying "No More Nylons" and had locked his door, as he could not transact other business with hundreds of women milling about in pursuit of nonexistent nylons. A policeman tried to persuade the women to move along. "Really, ladies, there ain't any more nylons today." Responded one of the hopefuls: "I never believe rumors." While this woman had not yet reached the state of bewilderment arrived at when people find out that sometimes it pays to believe signs and sometimes it doesn't, most Americans have arrived at that stage. When people do not know what to believe, and yet feel a need for information, they are members of an audience, not of an integrated society.

While this analysis of contemporary society could be greatly extended, it should be quite clear that folk society has turned into mass society to a considerable extent. Consensus between people on values and ways of behaving hardly exists any longer because tradition and closely knit social structures have been weakened. People have increasingly become mentally isolated from each other, and they are confused by and suspicious of the forces that seem to control them.

D. Reactions against the Mass Society[20]

The subjective feelings of the individuals who make up a mass society are a major force in the creation of new social institutions that modify the mass society. Economic and political pressures may work in the same direction, by creating power vacuums that invite ambitious men to fill them, but often they also require for their effect a popular frame of mind—based on the same subjective feelings characteristic of individuals living in a mass society—that perceives the economic or political force as satisfying a deeply felt need. Whereas a functionalist explanation of social changes would posit a natural tendency in the social structure to create a new equilibrium when the social forces that create the mass society have upset the old equilibrium, we would credit no such power of self-activation to the social structure. We would rather take the problem to the level of mass feelings and interpretations, and also recognize that these often do not work to restore an equilibrium in the social structure. Individuals who are dissatisfied engage in much trial and error that is probably just as often unsuccessful as not in removing the dissatisfaction. Even where it is successful from the standpoint of individual feelings, the result is not necessarily an equilibrium in the social structure.

Let us first tentatively posit the major subjective feelings of the population in a mass society, and then go on to consider the relatively successful processes that have developed to counteract the mass society. When speaking of mass feelings, it is not claimed that most people have all of them or that those who have one feeling also have the others, but simply that significant proportions of the population have each of the feelings in a significant degree so that a majority of the population is characterized by one or more of the mass feelings.

The first and most pervasive is that of loneliness: the mobility, the diminished ties to the extended family and the community, the increased possibility of living one's life independent of an immediate family, the substitution of urban for rural ways of life, the increased dependence on an impersonal economic market and the distant politi-

[20]An earlier form of this section was published in the *Sociological Quarterly*, III (October 1962), 316–30.

cal state—all contribute to a diminished sense of "belonging" and a measurable diminution in the number of primary contacts.

A second mass feeling is what may be called a subjective sense of ignorance: the diminished power of the churches to provide satisfying and convincing explanations of natural and social events is a major factor here. While the average man of today is much more informed in a scientific or rationalist sense than the average man of the era before the introduction of public education, the public schools do not pretend to offer a popular metaphysics. One way of stating the consequences of this is that modern man is better informed but has less of a feeling of understanding, for the facts he learns are less integrated and less interpreted. Also, the knowledge the schools impart serves to throw into question some of the dogmatic metaphysics offered by those churches that still attempt to provide their members with a comprehensive world view. Further, the increased exposure of modern man to a greater variety of social processes than were known by the bulk of the population in pre-industrial days gives modern man a sense that he knows only a small portion of the knowable world. When the knowable world seemed much smaller and simpler, it was easier to get a feeling that one was close to understanding most of what was capable of being understood.

A third mass feeling is that of helplessness and loss of self-control. It might be questioned whether medieval man had any basis for feeling that he had any freedom of choice, even though the doctrine of free will was widely accepted. But in the eighteenth and nineteenth centuries the increasing liberalization of the entire social structure, plus the new possibility for control of nature made available by a rapidly developing science and technology, developed a sense that there were increased possibilities for personal and social control. This was the era when the idea of progress captured men's imaginations. While even in the nineteenth century some factory workers and some writers began to note that machinery was controlling them more than they were controlling machines, this conception of science and technology dominating society has now spread to a larger part of the population. One set of technological innovations alone—those making possible the mass communications—has been especially potent in reducing most people's sense of being able to control their own behavior. Not only is there more propaganda, but people are much more aware that there is propaganda. This awareness might have the *actual* effect of diminishing the influence of propaganda, but people also seem to believe that they are influenced, and hence the greater awareness of increased propaganda can increase their *feeling* that they are controlled. The startling discoveries of modern science have the same effect. When there is talk of nuclear fission and fusion, electronic computers that have human qualities, space travel, strontium-90 that promises living people cancer and their future offspring imbecility, the transmutation of carbon into diamonds, expanding and curved space, and the dozen other topics that make publicized statements by scientists sound more unreal than the Sunday supplements of fifty years ago, the average person tends to acquire a feeling of relative ignorance and helplessness. The ethos of modern positivism—often wrongly identified as the necessary metaphysics of science—stresses determinism, and insofar as this has substituted for the religious and idealist conceptions of free will, modern man also has a reduced sense of self-control.[21]

Along with this feeling of helplessness and loss of self-control has come a loss of the sense of control over one's identity. Man in the mass society tends to feel that he is anonymous, that is, that he does not have an accepted place in the society, that he does not have secure identifications, and that most of the people around him do not know who he is. With the activities of the society increasingly determined by large-scale forces, there is a decline of personally determined goals, which are what gives distinctiveness and personal identity to the individual.[22]

The separation of the controllers of power in our society from the bonds of tradition has probably increased the average man's belief that he is dependent on their power; the modern dictator has much more power than even the "divine right" and "absolute" kings, and the nineteenth-century captain of industry had much more power than any medieval entrepreneur until the state and the trade union

[21]Science itself does not and cannot take a stand on the metaphysical issue of free will versus determinism; we are here referring to the philosophies that claim to interpret the metaphysical and epistemological implications of science.

[22]On the sense of identity in modern society, see Nelson N. Foote, "Identification as the Basis for a Theory of Motivation," *American Sociological Review*, 16 (February 1951), 14–21; Nelson N. Foote and Leonard S. Cottrell, Jr., *Identity and Interpersonal Competence* (Chicago: University of Chicago Press, 1955).

stepped in to limit his power somewhat. Tradition formerly provided a higher law to which even the captains and the kings were subject. Without it, the average man feels much more subject to their whims, even though he himself has also been partially freed from the binding limitations of tradition.

Individuals who make up the mass society also feel economic insecurity. This has already been amply considered from the standpoint of the producer, both the worker and the employer. From the standpoint of the consumer there was the new possibility of suddenly being cut off by a depression from the goods and services which were ordinarily made available by the society. The pre-modern economy limited the access of each class to certain goods and services—for example, the use of expensive and colorful clothing and adornment was limited to the upper classes—but the lower classes were more *certain* of getting the consumers goods to which they were entitled by tradition. The guilds and the manorial lords had obligations to maintain the traditions. The market economy opened great new possibilities of consumers goods, especially for the lower and middle income groups, when mass production was developed. But these could occasionally be taken away when depression and unemployment struck, and hence no certainty of them or identity with them could develop. Also, consumers goods became more influenced by fashion, which offered the current sense of progress and the ultimate realization of goallessness. Fashions in consumers goods, along with other modern social forces, made the average modern man increasingly aware that change does not always mean progress.

Not all of the attitudes instilled by mass society are unpleasant ones. The recognition of opportunity for economic advancement and upward social mobility is attractive when there is little basis in the economic situation for believing that one is economically insecure. The sense of liberation from tradition can be quite exhilarating, especially for people who are creative. The recognition that one is ignorant of most areas of present and potential knowledge gives some strong-minded people a sense of psychological superiority over people who fail to recognize their ignorance. The increased possibilities for privacy and even solitude appeal to those who find close association and control by the integrated society to be stifling. It should be recognized, however, that the forces creating the mass society probably appeal to only a small minority of the total population most of the time, and that most people look to compensating forces to seek to develop compensating structure in the society.

Some of the reactions have been merely confused and emotional. There has arisen, for example, a widespread hatred of city life and a criticism of it in terms of its evils coupled with a desire to return to the "neighborliness" of the country. It may be hypothesized that the city represents—in the minds of these people—the mass structure of society which urbanization has historically fostered. This attitude has contributed also to the fascination for movements that seek to "incorporate" individuals completely and to provide them with channels for communication from which there can be no deviation. Thus the popular reaction to the audience may have dangers for society even more extreme than those created by the audience itself.[23] The mass society we live in today is not and cannot be stable or progressive in an orderly way. It must run to extreme panaceas: to orgiastic and fundamentalist religious movements on the one hand, and to all-explaining, all-dominating dictatorships on the other. Neither of these will solve the problem, since they rely on false explanations and they maintain the audience condition of society in order to perpetuate themselves.

There are those who would get rid of mass society by seeking to return to a folk society. Included among these are the agrarians who would abolish cities and return the populations to farms, the medievalists who would abolish diversity and set up one moral and intellectual authority, the primitivists who would re-establish ancient cultural forms and abolish modern ones. All these people, with their "quest for certainty," see the problems engendered by modern mass society, but do not see the unplanned results of their solutions. The population is now too large and too specialized to return to the farm; the agrarian solution could be achieved only by killing off 90 per cent of the people. The population is now too well educated and too heterogeneous to accept the medievalist solution of setting up one leader to answer all moral and intellectual questions. The popu-

23Paul Massing, *Rehearsal for Destruction* (New York: Harper, 1949); Robert F. Byrnes, *Anti-Semitism in Modern France* (New Brunswick, N.J.: Rutgers University Press, 1950).

lation is too sophisticated and too dependent on and adjusted to modern technology to accept the primitivist solution of abolishing modern culture forms. Short of a catastrophic destruction of most of the people and of our culture it would appear that the majority seems anxious to take advantage of those culture forms. The question facing most people, then, seems not simply to be how to abolish the mass society, but how to eliminate its unhappy consequences while retaining its benefits. A considerable number of social changes in the past fifty years or so have been exactly of this nature. They have been reactions to the mass society in the form of new or changed institutions within the democratic framework rather than in the form of destructive or totalitarian institutions.

It would seem likely that persons feeling the ill effects of mass society would turn first for psychological compensation to science and education. The belief that scientific knowledge is increasing man's understanding of, and control over, nature more than compensates many people for the loss of dogmatic religion. Recognition that knowledge is available to the masses through public education more than compensates many people for skepticism regarding the teachings of religion. Some people even hope that the development of the social sciences, along with increasing public dissemination of their findings and interpretations, will counterbalance the insecurities created by new discoveries in the physical sciences. Hopefully, the spread of knowledge gained from the social sciences will reduce "false consciousness" and increase the individual's control over his social environment, just as the progress of the natural sciences increased society's control over the natural environment. The whole ideology of "progress," which was developing even as the mass society was developing in the eighteenth century and which reached its greatest popularity when mass society forces were most rampant in the nineteenth century, can be seen as a psychological reaction against, or compensation for, the ill effects of the mass society. The appeal of certain mass forms of pseudo-education—such as the Sunday supplement, the vulgarized public lecture, the quiz program, the "believe-it-or-not" column, and science fiction—is not only that they titillate or thrill but also that they seem to provide knowledge, that they do provide psychological compensation for one's feelings of ignorance. People often say they like these things because they "learn something from them." Insofar as there is a demand for serious adult education—through serious but readable books, articles, and radio-TV programs, as well as formal courses—there is even more basis for this psychological compensation.

A second existing institution to which the modern mass man has turned for psychological security is the nuclear family—that is, the family consisting of husband, wife, and children (and occasionally a grandparent). This institution is found throughout most of Western history and in many non-Western societies, even when it sometimes seemed partly submerged by the extended family and the community. Both children and adults—especially women—have generally depended on it for psychological security. The modern features, which we hypothesize are at least partly reactions against the mass society,[24] are a new emphasis on "companionship" between husband and wife and between parents and children. The husband sharing the wife's housework, the wife sharing the husband's job problems, the wife assuming joint control over the family budget and expenditures, both husband and wife seeking to take their recreation together, their increased play with the children, and their efforts to be "pals" with the children—are all modern phenomena.[25] For many adults in our society, the nuclear family provides the only regular source of companionship, the only regular safeguard against loneliness. It thus provides partial compensation for the mass society.

One of the trends mentioned earlier as leading to the mass society was the weakening of the extended family. By comparison with pre-industrial periods, there has certainly been a relative decline of the extended family. But perhaps sociologists like Weber, Park, and Wirth exaggerated the decline, as recent studies suggest that extended family relations are still significantly to be found in contemporary cities. Studies among middle-class residents of Buffalo,[26] Detroit,[27]

24This is not to deny that the modern nuclear family has other causes, but merely to assert that one of its sources of development and strength is the compensation it provides against the mass society.

25E. W. Burgess and H. J. Locke, *The Family: From Institution to Companionship* (New York: American Book Co., 1945).

26Eugene Litwak, "The Use of Extended Family Groups in the Achievement of Social Goals," *Social Problems*, 7 (Winter 1959/60), 179. (Reference to Litwak's unpublished Ph.D. thesis, 1958, pp. 79–81.)

27Morris Axelrod, "Urban Structure and Social Participation," *American Sociological Review*, 21 (February 1956), 13–18.

and Los Angeles,[28] indicate that almost 50 per cent of the respondents saw relatives at least once a week or more often. In San Francisco, another study[29] reported that almost 90 per cent said that some extended-family member was one of their closest friends. In New Haven[30] close to 70 per cent of a sample of middle-class interviewees said that they received a significant amount of aid from some person or persons in their extended family. In Cleveland,[31] these help and service exchanges approached 100 per cent in the middle classes and 92.5 per cent in the working class. In a study of a working-class community in London, England,[32] the extended-family relations were close enough to result in pressures toward living nearby and toward obligations to find jobs for relatives.

The authors of these studies implicitly assume that their findings prove that extended-family relationships have not declined as much as earlier sociologists thought. However, in the absence of earlier or longitudinal studies, the alternative hypothesis can reasonably be entertained that the extended family did deteriorate badly in Western cities toward the end of the nineteenth century and has been reviving somewhat within the last few decades. No direct evidence is known to support this alternative hypothesis, but it is generally known that there is now less rejection of ethnic identification than there was until about 1930, and that shirking family obligations is less likely in periods of extended prosperity than in periods of frequent unemployment. Thus, it is possible that both the older and the newer sociologists are correct, and that the new findings reflect something of a reaction against the mass society.

A third development is relatively new for the bulk of the population, although it had existed in other societies at other times (such as imperial Rome). This is what earlier writers[33] have called the

---

28Scott Greer, "Urbanism Reconsidered," *American Sociological Review*, 21 (February 1956), 22.

29Wendell Bell and Marion D. Boat, "Urban Neighborhoods and Informal Social Relations," *American Journal of Sociology*, 62 (January 1957), 396.

30Marvin B. Sussman, "The Help Patterns in the Middle Class Family," *American Sociological Review*, 18 (February 1953), 27.

31Marvin B. Sussman, "The Isolated Nuclear Family: Fact or Fiction," *Social Problems*, 6 (Spring 1959), 335; see also p. 344 for reference to other studies.

32Michael Young and Peter Willmott, *Family and Kinship in East London* (London: Routledge and Kegan Paul, 1957).

33A. L. Lowell, *Public Opinion and Popular Government* (New York: 1913);

"public." The public is a large, informal, non-contiguous, unintegrated discussion group.

> When any problem arises or when anything happens that con-
> cerns them collectively, members of the public talk the matter
> over, argue it out in such a way that everyone's attitude is
> influenced by everyone else's. That does not mean that the
> resulting "public opinion" is completely unanimous; it simply
> means that every person more or less understands the other's
> point of view and has somehow given it consideration. It also
> does not mean that everyone is considering the same subject
> or pursuing the same line of cultural development; there are
> many publics, each with a different interest, and one may join
> or leave them freely and voluntarily. While there is this
> element of volition in membership, the public—for any specific
> issue—is a definite enough group with adequate communica-
> tion between its members. There is thus no social isolation, no
> sense of loneliness, no unsatisfied longing to belong to some
> group or movement. While all the members of a public are
> subjected to the same influences, including propaganda, the
> influences are conflicting in their effect and are not taken at
> their face value and so are not directly determining. Members
> of a public do not respond directly to outside stimuli as mem-
> bers of an audience do; rather, they evaluate every influence
> to see how it fits in with their knowledge, beliefs, and expecta-
> tions. The public has a culture and a set of ideals with which
> to make these evaluations.[34]

Publics can exist only when tradition is not strong enough to
stifle or stereotype discussion, when geographic mobility of individuals and the division of labor among groups are great enough to
allow people to communicate at least occasionally with others who
are not their constant associates, and when there is a diversity of
opinion and a heterogeneity of interests in the society. Thus, the

---

A. V. Dicey, *Lectures on the Relation Between Law and Public Opinion in England
During the Nineteenth Century* (London: 1914); R. E. Park and E. W. Burgess,
Introduction to the Science of Sociology (Chicago: University of Chicago Press,
1921), pp. 791–6; W. Lippmann, *Public Opinion* (New York: Macmillan, 1922),
and *The Phantom Public* (New York: Macmillan, 1925).

[34] Arnold M. Rose, *Sociology: The Study of Human Relations* (New York: Knopf,
1956), pp. 295–6; 2nd edition (1965), p. 379.

social effects of the Industrial Revolution which helped to create the mass society also created the conditions which make it possible for the public to develop. But the public requires something more: It requires conversation among people who have only secondary relations with each other; hence people must have interests in conversing and there must not be so many structural barriers to conversation that it is stifled. In fact the only difference between the mass and the public is that when people in the mass break their isolation from each other and begin to exchange facts and opinions they are transformed into a public.[35] The psychological state of members of the public is quite different from that of the members of the mass. Because they are conversing with other people they are no longer so lonely; because they exchange facts and opinions they no longer feel so helpless. Because public opinion is much more stable than mass opinion and has a closer correlation to actual behavior, public opinion is likely to translate itself into votes in a political democracy, and thus helps to create political power for the average citizen (whereas voting in a mass society is likely to be a response to the strongest voice in the mass media). The stranger has quick access to the public, which he does not have to the integrated society, and this is important when increasing mobility, characteristic of the mass society, makes strangers of many people much of the time. The formation of publics is thus a reaction to the mass society and it provides psychological compensation for the feelings engendered by the mass society.

A fourth reaction to the modern mass society is the voluntary association, although this institution too has existed at other times and in other societies. Voluntary associations greatly expanded in numbers and membership after the mass society began to have its impact. The voluntary association is simply a public with a more permanent relationship among its members and a more formal structure. It has in common with the public its specialization on one or a few interests, its activity of discussion sometimes leading to social action, the varying involvement of its members, its willingness to consider new and non-traditional arguments and methods (al-

[35]It is conceivable that the public could develop out of the traditional integrated society, but historically in Western society it seems to have arisen out of the coagulation or partial integration of the mass.

though a voluntary association tends to develop traditions of its own), and its reliance on "rational" discussion. More regularized than the public, the voluntary association usually has a stronger psychological effect on its members in counteracting the feelings engendered by the mass society. By providing regular occasions for meeting and offering an excuse for discussing association activities and problems between meetings, the voluntary association reduces loneliness, and attaches the individual to a social circle even though this group is on an interest basis rather than the traditional residential basis. At least the nucleus of a voluntary association is a *Gemeinschaft* (intimate community). By collecting information regarding the subject(s) of its special interest, imparting this to its members, and providing them with opportunities to exchange views regarding the information, the voluntary association reduces the feeling of ignorance—at least on the specialized subject(s) of interest to its members. By attracting or luring persons who are influential or expert with regard to the subject(s) of its specialized interest, by having its members discuss strategy and technique for attaining the organization's goals, by providing an opportunity for its members to observe how group pressure and strategy are translated into achievement of a particular social change in a democracy, the voluntary association contributes to a reduction of the feeling of social helplessness among its members. By providing an opportunity to work on something creative, even if only in a hobby association, the voluntary association offers its members a partial escape from boredom and a sense of uselessness. In these ways the voluntary association counteracts the feelings engendered by the mass society, and it is modern democratic society's substitute for the integrated group of the primitive or folk society.

A relatively minor counteracting force to mass psychology can best be mentioned at this point. This is the hobby, including amateur sports and the "do-it-yourself" activity around the home which in recent years has assumed almost the dimensions of a social movement. It has already been suggested that voluntary associations sometimes are formed around a hobby and the reactive effects of this against the mass society have been noted. But even when a hobby is practiced by unorganized individuals, there are some psychological effects that counteract those created by the mass society. In the first

place, hobbies offer the opportunity to be creative in ways that ordinary people choose to be and can be creative; these thus offer some
reduction in feelings of boredom and uselessness. The "do-it-yourself"
hobbies possibly add slightly to economic security. Hobbies also
occasionally offer some additional points of social contact—between
buyers and sellers of hobby materials, and between hobbyists to
compare techniques and results. Some hobbies—particularly sports—
require that small groups of like-minded people meet together regularly. Such contacts contribute somewhat to the reduction of loneliness and possibly a little to a reduction of the sense of ignorance.
Some hobbies and sports take people out-of-doors a good deal, and
there is probably a feeling among many such hobbyists that they are
communing with nature if not with other people. Hobbies are probably as old as man, but the use of them has no doubt greatly increased in modern times as leisure time has increased, as there has
developed a new emphasis upon consumption, and as hobbies have
been found to be somewhat useful in counteracting the negative
feelings engendered by the mass society.

Allied with the hobby and the voluntary association are certain
limited developments toward the "ruralization" of modern society.
While the main trend has been toward the "urbanization" of rural
society—that is, the extension of mass society to most farming areas
—there have also been such counter developments as the rise of the
intimate suburban community, the creation of certain "garden" residential communities within the urban complex, the popularization of
the summer vacation cabin or "camping" with fairly "primitive"
facilities, the spread of gardening as a hobby for city-dwellers, and
the intensification of the neighborhood voluntary association to such
an extent in some urban communities that they now have an integrated character. Further, the process of shifting from primary to
secondary relationships in the city seems to have been exaggerated
by many sociologists. A sense of identity with the local community in
the city does seem to arise in the modern city, even if not to the same
extent as in the folk society. Friendship groups do develop in the
city, even if not always on a residential basis, but often on an occupational or interest basis. A study by Gregory Stone[36] of a sample

[36]Sociological Aspects of Consumer Purchasing in a Northwest Side Chicago
Community," unpublished M.A. Thesis, University of Chicago, June 1952.

of Chicago housewives indicates that a large proportion do their purchasing with "personality" and "ethical" orientations rather than "rational economic" or "apathetic" orientations, and that this was especially true of those most urbanized—that is, those who were third-generation city dwellers and who had achieved relatively high economic and educational status. The local store is not only a place to shop, it is also a place where one can get to know storekeepers and discuss things with them. There are a good many friendly, primary relationships that develop in the large city, and one can gain a sense of personal identity with an urban neighborhood and even with a city as a whole.[37] This may be increasing as the urban population is more likely to be urban-born rather than migrants displaced from rural and village backgrounds.

Robert Wood, in his study of "suburbia," gives strong support to the thesis that the dweller in metropolis is more likely to live in an integrated community today than he was sixty or seventy years ago. In both a social and political sense, Wood holds, the pre-industrial town is "reappearing" in American suburbs and even cities:

> Historically, a hypothesis which opposes the theory of metropolitan dominance and the breakdown of the small community takes as its point of departure the Victorian city of sixty and seventy years ago. This was the urban settlement most removed from the American prototype and most advanced in the process of communal disintegration. Far more than the city of today, the Victorian city presented a layered, visible "class stratification" and an "open-class pecuniary" society, acquisitive and impersonal. It was in New York, Boston, and Philadelphia in the 1880's and 1890's that social and political communication and consciousness broke down most completely, and that power, economic and political, flowed into the hands of the few. These were the dark decades of humanitarianism and local government, when escape from the city was impossible and civic authority to deal with problems of social welfare reached its lowest ebb. If the comparison is to the New England town, then, the bleak era for community life was a half-century ago, when the individual was most completely alone, swallowed up in the city or left behind in

[37]Joel Smith, William H. Form, and Gregory P. Stone, "Local Intimacy in a Middle-Sized City," *American Journal of Sociology* 60 (November 1954), 276–84.

deserted rural hamlets. The very success of the boss in creating political organization by providing a calculated facsimile of community life in the political ward testifies to the degree to which the old town spirit had disappeared.

If we take the Victorians as a checkpoint, the subsequent development of the metropolis may be interpreted as a process of community creation as easily as it can be seen as a continuation of metropolitan dominance. While, economically, a single regional system of self-sufficiency is appearing, social and political fragmentation of the metropolitan giant is taking place as well. The dispersion of social groups and economic activities vies with concentration as a predominant trend; decentralization opposes centralization, and the forces of segregation in neighborhood residences stand against the forces for absorption. Compared with the American urban community of fifty years ago, the new metropolitan area may well contain many genuine aspects of small town life and small town culture.[38]

There have been special forms of reaction against the economic insecurity created by the mass society. These can be considered under three heads (1) government activity to provide a minimum social security and put brakes on economic depression; (2) the formation of "monopolies" and other structures to hedge against the vicissitudes of the free market; (3) adjustments in the technology of mass production. There are several economic aspects of these three phenomena with which we have no concern, including the question as to whether they are effective in the long run in reducing economic insecurity. Our assumption is simply that they are partially motivated by the desire to reduce economic insecurity. Businessmen have created corporations to limit their liability in case of failure, formed combines to control the market and keep out competitors, entered into agreements to prevent the free use of inventions, distributed their investments so that all would not be likely to go bad at the same time, imposed contracts on their corporations to pay them a secured income for life, and bribed politicians so that control of natural resources and transportation routes would be assured.

[38]Robert C. Wood, *Suburbia: Its People and Their Politics* (Boston: Houghton Mifflin, 1958), pp. 102–3.

Workers have formed or joined trade unions to raise wages, set arbitrary but impartial rules for promotion and lay-off, set restrictions on job entry, pressured politicians into voting for minimum wage laws and old age and unemployment insurance laws, sought to get guaranteed-annual-wage contracts, and developed medical insurance and pension funds. Some of these measures make for economic inefficiency; most of them work against the economic interests of the other group and of consumers, and many of them increase the economic insecurity of those who are not organized, but they *do* increase the economic security of those directly involved—at least in the short run, where they can see it.

While the quest for economic security has undoubtedly been the primary motive for these developments, they have had certain consequences which also limit the psychological effects of the mass society. These have occurred because the businessmen's combines and the workers' unions are also voluntary associations, and have all of the effects of the voluntary association in counteracting the psychology of the mass society. While some union leaders allow very little or no participation on the part of the rank-and-file members in the actual running of the union, there is more participation of other kinds in most unions. At the lowest level of making routine complaints to the employer in the name of the union, most unions allow rank-and-file activity. Most unions have social affairs; all unions distribute membership cards, buttons, labels, and other material symbols which help members to identify with one another; most unions distribute literature to their members which helps them to learn what is going on in the union and even to interpret events in the larger society; some unions have an educational program for their members; some unions encourage their members to serve on committees or as shop stewards; some unions provide aid to their members in dealing with the government (e.g. giving advice regarding income tax or social services, the law, the housing market, and many of the other large impersonal institutions of modern society. There are non-material psychological "rewards" for union membership: seeing the union representatives talk as equals to the boss, reading about occasional union successes in the daily newspapers, referring to other union members and union leaders as "brothers." Businessmen's associations usually provide even more of this sort of thing, especially in those activities which involve actual distribution of power. All such activities—even the purely symbolic ones—help to counteract the psychological concomitants of modern mass society.

Economic alienation has also resulted from increased technological specialization. As writers from Marx to Friedmann and Drucker[39] have pointed out, the trend after the Industrial Revolution was for the worker not to control his tools, not to be able to "see" a complete production process, not to be able to control the pace and "rhythm" of his work, not to have his employer pay attention to his personal needs. While this trend perhaps continues in some countries which are belatedly adopting "American efficiency" techniques in accord with the pre–World War I advice of Frederick Winslow Taylor, in the United States itself at least there is a significant countervailing trend. While the assembly line system of production continues to be used in many factories, it is now often arranged so that the worker can control its speed and skip parts coming to him without damaging the whole system. Automation is bringing a system of production in which the worker avoids "mechanical" jobs and spends his time in the more "creative," less boring jobs of inspection, repair, and adjustment of highly complicated machines. The long-run trend for the skilled worker to be replaced by the unskilled worker has been reversed not only by the small increase in skilled workers but also by the large increase of semi-skilled workers. The American efficiency expert today is usually very much aware—some would say "too much" aware, from the standpoint of the worker's independent political development—of the "human" and the social relations needs of the worker. Factory managers also pay increasing attention to the worker's orientation to the plant and his understanding of the production process. Thus, to a considerable extent, the most recent technological developments and the newer attitudes of "modern" managers have combined to reverse the consequences of alienation caused by the technological revolution of the eighteenth and nineteenth centuries. There is also a long-run trend—called by Colin Clark[40] a shift from secondary to tertiary occupations—from factory

---

[39]Georges Friedmann, *Problèmes Humains du Machinisme Industriel* (Paris: Gallimard, 1946); Georges Friedmann, *The Anatomy of Work* (New York: Free Press of Glencoe, 1961); Peter F. Drucker, *The Future of Industrial Man* (New York: John Day, 1942).

[40]*Conditions of Economic Progress* (London: Macmillan, 1940), pp. 337–73.

work in general to the less boring service, clerical, and professional occupations.

Since one major cause of the mass society was recurring deep economic depression and unemployment, the apparent partial control of this phenomenon by government since 1940 has also tended to limit the mass character of the society. To the extent that the average man believes he will not be cut off from the goods and services made available by the economy, and in fact finds himself claiming an expanding amount of these, he is less likely to feel economically alienated from the society. Another way of looking at this phenomenon is from the political standpoint: The government—through its increased controls over the economy and its increased protection of the individual against economic vicissitudes—has made itself something of a partner of the "little man" in his economic struggle for existence, and while this may reduce economic and other freedoms in the long run, it also reduces modern man's alienation from his government and his society.

We have examined a number of social forces and institutions—mostly modern at least insofar as they have significance for the bulk of the population—which have developed against the historical trend toward the mass society. In the United States, and in such other industrially developed nations as Sweden and Britain, they have perhaps even stopped or reversed the trend. In the past ten or twenty years, there have been complaints against too much integration and too much conformity in these countries. This does not mean that the social problems of the mass society have been solved: there remain the extreme victims of the mass society (the isolated and the unorganized) which the counteracting forces have not reached; there remains the fact that economic recession has not been completely controlled; there remains the fact that the voluntary association, the nuclear family and the other institutions, do not completely counteract, for many of those they partially reach, the feelings of loneliness, ignorance, helplessness, uselessness, and insecurity created by the mass society. Still, these counteracting forces have developed and they have been gaining greater significance.

VII
Voluntary Associations[1]

A. Conditions for Development

A voluntary association develops when a small group of people, finding they have a certain interest (or purpose) in common, agree to meet and to act together in order to try to satisfy that interest or achieve that purpose.[2] Frequently their action requires that they urge other like-minded persons to join them, so that some associations may become very large and extend throughout the whole country. In the United States they have absolutely no formal contact with the government unless they incorporate, which obliges them to conform to certain minor laws of state governments (and unless, of course, they commit an offense against the general criminal law, which is naturally extremely rare). In fact the "due process" clause of the Fourteenth Amendment of the United States Constitution has been interpreted to protect the independence of voluntary associations from state government restrictions, just as the First Amendment has always been interpreted as protecting voluntary associations from federal government restrictions.[3] A good example of the limitation

[1]This chapter is practically the same as Chapter 10 of the author's *Sociology: The Study of Human Relations* (New York: Knopf, 2nd edition, 1965).

[2]Voluntary associations are usually defined so that their purposes do not include profit making for the members. But many voluntary associations do create economic benefits for their members—for example, the consumers' co-operatives or mutual-aid societies that provide sickness or death benefits for members.

[3]David Fellman, *The Constitutional Right of Association* (Chicago: University of Chicago Press, 1963).

on state action occurred in 1958 when the Supreme Court supported the refusal by the National Association for the Advancement of Colored People to open its membership lists to state inspection in accord with an Alabama statute. Mr. Justice Harlan, speaking for a unanimous court, declared that the Alabama statute would limit "the right of members to pursue their lawful private interest privately and to associate freely with others in so doing."[4] In France and Italy, on the other hand, the national government sets certain restrictions on voluntary associations, and sometimes directs the activities of associations whose purposes are for the benefit of the public.[5]

As social structures, voluntary associations have distinct features of formal leadership, specialized activity, rules for operating, place and time of meeting, and so on. An important distinction among them must be specified. Some associations act only to express or satisfy the interests of their members in relation to themselves—these include the recreational and sport associations, the social and hobby clubs, the professional societies, etc., which may be especially numerous in the modern democracies but which are also found in large numbers in all literate and in some preliterate societies. Other associations are directed outward; they wish to achieve some condition or change in some limited segment of the society as a whole. These are rarely found outside the modern democracies, for reasons we shall examine later. The former associations may be called "expressive" groups and the latter "social-influence" or "instrumental" groups—for lack of better terms.[6] It is with the latter type that we are primarily concerned in this chapter.

Since the social-influence groups have a specific and limited pur-

4John Marshall Harlan, "Text of Supreme Court Decision Upholding NAACP in Alabama Case," cited in full in *The New York Times*, July 1, 1958, p. 18.

5Arnold M. Rose, *Theory and Method in the Social Sciences* (Minneapolis: University of Minnesota Press, 1954), ch. IV; Arnold M. Rose, "On Individualism and Social Responsibility," *European Journal of Sociology*, 2 (Summer 1961), 163–9.

6A test of the validity of this distinction, using ratings by both group members and outsiders, has shown that the dichotomy is widely accepted and can be measured. See Arthur P. Jacoby and Nicholas Babchuk, "Instrumental and Expressive Voluntary Associations," *Sociology and Social Research*, 47 (July 1963), 461–71. Sherwood Fox suggests another way of classifying voluntary associations—according to which groups they serve: majoral associations serve major institutions such as business or education; minoral associations serve important minorities, such as women's clubs or hobby clubs; and medial associations mediate between major parts of the population, such as social welfare groups. See David L. Sills, *The Volunteers* (Glencoe, Ill.: Free Press, 1957), p. 79.

pose, they also tend to have a limited life. When the purpose is accomplished, or the need which gave rise to the association changes, the association usually dies. Since change is rapid in the United States, and many social problems get solved while new ones continually arise, the turnover in voluntary associations of the social-influence type is great. Even when an association continues in full vigor, there can be a large turnover in its membership. Members join and leave an association for a great variety of personal reasons, including a belief that the purpose of the association needs, or does not need, to be accomplished.

We may consider briefly the sense in which these associations are voluntary. Voluntary associations are presumably those into which an individual may freely choose to enter and from which he may freely choose to withdraw. But such a statement is a mere tautology: voluntary implies free choice. "Voluntariness" may be placed in a continuum and thus "voluntary" and "involuntary" become polar terms in an ideal-typical dichotomy. There is no clear-cut, realistic line of division between the two. In this sense, the term "voluntary" can only be defined in terms of "involuntary." The mentioned dichotomy implies a psychology: the assumption is that man, a rational creature, in certain circumstances weighs the advantages and disadvantages of joining a certain group or participating in a collective enterprise and, on the basis of the outcome of this deliberation, joins this group. Such a group would be a "voluntary" association. Conversely, an "involuntary" organization would be one which the individual is compelled to be a member of because of external pressures. The involuntary organizations are usually the ones an individual is born into or must join to survive in the society: the state, the family, the economic system, the school system, the church, the army (where conscription is the law), and perhaps others.

As a matter of fact, ignoring the metaphysical implications, there is seldom free will in the psychological sense considered above. Formal and informal means of social control, or social forces, in effect dictate that certain individuals are going to join certain "voluntary" associations. In those cases when the individual does reflect on the advisability of joining an association or participating in a certain sphere of activity, he may not be "free" in his choice because there are overwhelming advantages to one choice or the other which dictate his decision. On the other hand, certain "involuntary" associations may never be joined. For example, the youth may become a tramp (or a perpetual "student") and never join or participate effectively in the great involuntary association of the economic system to provide a living for himself. In a secular order such as our modern, urban, democratic, free-enterprise society, it becomes, in a sense, quite possible for anyone to withdraw from any involuntary association except a jailhouse. One can leave his family, his church, and even his state and the economic system.

This discussion of the logical meaning of "voluntary" and "involuntary" is really not essential to an analysis of voluntary associations. The reason is that "voluntary" associations is a concept (however lacking in precise formulation it might be) in sociology, and in that universe of discourse it has a meaning that cannot be understood from its constituent words. It is evident that the formulations of lists of voluntary associations in various societies would reveal that there are certain universal criteria of involuntary associations (though not of voluntary associations). Thus voluntary acquires a residual meaning. The general criteria of involuntary associations are: (1) when the individual is physically forced to join an association it will be called involuntary; and (2) when the individual is born into the association it will be called involuntary. Like all social phenomena, voluntary associations are not entities that have a place in some ultimately real classification. The term is merely a concept determined both by conventionality and usefulness.

Voluntary associations of the social-influence type are to be found primarily in societies that are urban and democratic in general character. In the Middle Ages of Western society, to exemplify an alternative, when the church and state had resolved their differences, few individuals could be members of any formal organization other than the church and state; and these were coterminous both with each other and with the community.[7] One of the most characteristic

---

[7]There were religious and knightly orders, of course, but these had the same characteristic tendency to be at once a community, a governmental unit, and a religious unit. In the late Middle Ages the guilds developed, but they did so in response to the urbanization and differentiation of society—which we hold to be among the characteristic conditions for the rise of voluntary associations. See Louis D. Hartson, "A Study of Voluntary Associations, Educational and Social, in Europe During the Period from 1000 to 1700," *Pedagogical Seminary*, 18 (1911), 10–31.

features of the shift from medieval to modern times is the rise of groups with specialized interests and divergent activities *within* the community. But not even in all modern communities is there a significant number of voluntary associations. Strictly speaking, in a modern totalitarian society there are no groups but the state (or, more precisely, the party or social movement that controls the state).[8] All the individual's affiliations are determined in some way by the state, and these affiliations exist ultimately to carry out the purpose of the state.

Even within our primarily urban and democratic society we may note wide variations in the complexity and diversity of group struc-tures in any given community. In a relatively homogeneous rural community, at one extreme, most people tend to go to the same church, to be members of the same occupational (agricultural) or-ganization, to participate in the same sociable activities, and to send their children to the same schools. While there are different organiza-tions for the various activities, and while there is some differential participation in the groups according to age and sex, there is still no large number of groups with divergent membership and interest in a homogeneous rural community. There is less likely to be relatively much diversity of interest and attitude among the groups where all the members of the community belong to the same groups. While we need to learn much more regarding the conditions under which voluntary group differentiation develops, we may take it as a close approximation to the facts that the development of voluntary associa-tions, with diverse ideas as to how the society should be changed, occurs primarily in the modern urban democratic society. The term "urban" is to be understood in its sociological sense, not in terms of the census definition: many villages in the United States are urban, and there is a trend toward their becoming more urban. To put our observations in general terms: The existence of a significant number of social-influence associations in the community seems to require that the population be somewhat heterogeneous in background and

[8]The establishment of modern totalitarian regimes has regularly been attended by the destruction or "integration" of voluntary associations, especially those that sought to have some influence on the society—less so of those that were purely expressive, sociable, or recreational in character. The church—which represents a loyalty alien to the state—is likely to become a problem for the totalitarian state, and may even be a source of resistance unless it is assimilated into the state's interest in some way.

interests, and that no one institution, such as the church or state, be successful in dominating the entire life of most individuals.

B. Numbers and Structure[9]

No one knows how many associations there are in the United States, or how many people belong to them. But the number is known for some local communities where special studies have been made, and extrapolating from these would lead us to estimate that there are well over 100,000 voluntary associations in the United States.[10] A count of the voluntary associations—exclusive of the governmental, the specific church-affiliated, and the strictly occupational—in Minneapolis and St. Paul, by the Minnesota Council of Adult Education, turned up some 3000 organizations, of which some 450 were engaged in an effort to influence or educate the adult population. A list of organizations in a small New England city (50,000 inhabitants) prepared by the local council of social agencies included some 300 associations.[11] In 1924 there were almost 3000 voluntary organizations in a group of 140 rural villages.[12] Warner's "Yankee City" (population 17,000) had 357 associations when it was studied in the early thirties.[13] Boulder, Colorado, a city of 12,000, had 245 associations in the early 1940's.[14] In 1935 there were 200 associations among the 7500 Negroes of Natchez, and 4000 associations among the 275,000 Negroes in Chicago.[15]

[9]Except where otherwise specified, the description in the rest of this chapter will be limited to the United States. Where sources are not specified, information comes from an unpublished study of voluntary associations in Minneapolis and St. Paul, conducted by Arnold M. Rose and John E. Tsouderos in 1953 and 1954.

[10]Fox has compiled a list of 5000 *national* associations alone in the United States, but makes no claim that it is complete. Sherwood Dean Fox, "Voluntary Associations and Social Structure," unpublished Ph.D. thesis, Harvard University, December, 1952.

[11]Arnold M. Rose, "Communication and Participation in a Small City as Viewed by Its Leaders," *International Journal of Opinion and Attitude Research*, 5 (Autumn 1951), 367–90.

[12]Edmond deS. Brunner and J. H. Kolb, *Rural Social Trends* (New York: McGraw-Hill, 1933), pp. 102, 244, 372.

[13]W. Lloyd Warner and P. S. Lunt, *The Social Life of a Modern Community*, Yankee City Series, vol. I (New Haven: Yale University Press, 1941).

[14]F. A. Bushee, "Social Organization in a Small City," *American Journal of Sociology*, 51 (1945), 217–26.

[15]Gunnar Myrdal, with the assistance of Richard Sterner and Arnold Rose, *An American Dilemma* (New York: Harper, 1944), pp. 952–5.

A fairly complete study of voluntary associations was made for the city of Detroit in 1951, where 63 per cent of the population belonged to some organization other than a church. About half of those belonging to non-church organizations belonged to two or more. The types of organizations adhered to were as follows: occupational associations, 37 per cent; fraternal and social clubs, 21 per cent; church-connected groups, 9 per cent; athletic and other recreational associations, 8 per cent; youth-serving groups, 8 per cent; welfare organizations, 7 per cent; neighborhood improvement associations, 5 per cent; women's clubs, 2 per cent; political clubs, 2 per cent; community centers, 1 per cent; nationality groups, 1 per cent; other groups, 3 per cent.[16]

Another systematic study was made in Bennington, Vermont (population 8000), in 1947.[17] The proportion belonging to some voluntary association was 64.2 per cent; 24.6 per cent belonged to only one association, 15.9 per cent to two associations, 8.6 per cent to three associations, 15.1 per cent to four or more associations. The last group of 15.1 per cent held 50.7 per cent of the total memberships. In this small town, 20.4 per cent of the memberships were in church groups; 16.8 per cent in fraternal associations; 10.8 per cent in business, civic, service, or improvement associations; 9.5 per cent in "cultural" groups; 9.4 per cent in youth-serving groups; 9 per cent in athletic or hobby groups; 8.5 per cent in sociable groups; 5.5 per cent in professional or scientific groups; 4.9 per cent in military, political, or patriotic groups; 4.2 per cent in co-operative, mutual-benefit, or protective associations; and 2.3 per cent in labor unions. At the time of the study the average duration of membership had been ten years, but of course most persons had not ended their membership at the time of the study. Frequency of attendance per membership averaged .84 times a month for the men and 1.23 times a month for the women.

There have been a few studies of membership in voluntary associations using polling techniques and national samples, but the re-

[16]Detroit Area Study of the University of Michigan, *A Social Profile of Detroit* (Ann Arbor: University of Michigan, 1952), pp. 13–16.

[17]John Carver Scott, Jr., "Membership and Participation in Voluntary Associations," unpublished M.A. thesis, University of Chicago, September 1948.

sults have been so different and the techniques of getting the data so questionable that these studies do not provide reliable information.[18] The National Opinion Research Center in 1955 used a schedule of 136 questions, and the next to the last one was "Do you happen to belong to any groups or organizations in the community here?" From the answers to this question, the authors concluded that only 36 per cent of American adults belong to voluntary associations. Using a less representative sample, the same inadequate procedures of interviewing, but a somewhat more relevant questionnaire, the American Institute of Public Opinion in 1954 found 55 per cent of adult Americans belonging to voluntary associations. Using a still less adequate sample and an equally inadequate questionnaire, but better interviewing techniques, the Survey Research Center at the University of Michigan found that 64 per cent of adult Americans belong to at least one voluntary association. The very discrepancy between the three figures should make us suspicious of all of them, and it cannot be concluded that the true figure is somewhere in between.[19]

There seem to be urban-rural differences in voluntary-association membership although there is no consensus about their direction. The National Opinion Research Center national survey found that more residents of highly urbanized counties belong to organizations than those living in less urbanized but similar areas.[20] On the other hand, Hausknecht, also using national data, finds a larger proportion of members in small communities. He attributes this to the fact that a large metropolitan area offers many alternatives to voluntary associations for leisure time activity. He suggests that membership in a small town group gives the individual a sense of power which also helps to account for the higher rate.[21] A study in Flint, Michigan, showed that 43.1 per cent of those living in the central city belonged to

[18]The studies are first reported in Charles R. Wright and Herbert Hyman, "Voluntary Association Membership of American Adults: Evidence from the National Sample Surveys," *American Sociological Review*, 23 (June 1958), 284–93. A more comprehensive analysis of the same data is Murray Hausknecht, *The Joiners* (New York: Bedminster, 1962).

[19]The breakdowns reported by the authors, for various categories of the population, may have some significance for comparative purposes, but even this is hard to gauge when non-response is obviously so great.

[20]Wright and Hyman, *Voluntary Association*, p. 290.

[21]Hausknecht, *The Joiners*, p. 18.

voluntary associations while only 24.7 per cent of those living in the fringe areas were members.[22]

While the number of associations in a community naturally appears to be a function of the number of inhabitants of that community, this is not entirely the case, for many of the associations are regional or national and have affiliates in small communities as well as large ones, thus raising the relative number of associations in the small communities.[23] Even when the association is national or regional, there tends to be a great deal of local autonomy, with some exceptions, because of the voluntary nature of the membership. The officers of the central or parent body, usually elected by a congress of representatives from the local associations, secure a minimum degree of similarity among the local associations by demanding conformity to a small list of "basic principles." The major exception to this structural principle of complete democracy and local variation is found among the trade unions. The greater degree of centralization and uniformity among trade unions is made necessary by the conflict activity of these associations, but even here the deviation from principle is not great. American unions, especially those that have developed in the American Federation of Labor as distinguished from the Congress of Industrial Organizations, have much more local autonomy than do European unions.

While the relationships of the local affiliates of a national association with each other tend to be democratic, democracy is not always the governing principle *within* the local association. The reason is easy to understand. Some people have more interest, more time, more drive, more ability, than others, and they tend easily to take over control.[24] Any person who wishes to, however, can usually join the

[22]Basil G. Zimmer and Amos H. Hawley, "The Significance of Membership in Associations," *American Journal of Sociology*, 65 (September 1959), 198. In this study, the definition of voluntary association excluded unions, church and church groups, and P.T.A.'s.

[23]In a representative sample of voluntary associations in Minneapolis and St. Paul, 59 per cent had a national affiliation, 11 per cent had a state affiliation, while 30 per cent were purely local.

[24]In the Minneapolis–St. Paul study about half of the top leaders had been in office longer than two years. Sixty-four per cent of them spent more than ten hours a month in association affairs. In Great Britain until recently leaders in most types of voluntary associations came from the upper classes apparently because there was an upper-class tradition of responsibility for leadership and because some upper-class

leadership of most voluntary associations, if he is willing to spend the time and assume the responsibilities. And those who do not wish to become leaders exert an ultimate control over the latter by voting against them at the annual elections or simply by resigning from the association, which—if done by sufficiently large numbers—kills the organization and permits the formation of a new one with the same purpose but with new leaders.

While only a small proportion of the population is very *active* in the associations, a very large proportion—at least in the town and cities—are *members* of the associations. Several studies show, however, that Americans of middle and higher incomes are more likely to join associations than are people of lower income.[25] A study by Bottomore shows that this is true in Great Britain, and a study by Bo Anderson shows that the generalization holds for Sweden also.[26]

------

people gave money to associations in return for being elected to the office of honorary vice-president even though they did not participate in the activities of the association. The situation has been changing, especially since World War II, and an increasing number of functioning leaders are drawn from the middle and lower classes. See Rosalind C. Chambers, "A Study of Three Voluntary Organizations," in D. V. Glass (ed.), *Social Mobility in Britain* (London: Routledge and Kegan Paul, 1954), pp. 385–7.

[25] R. S. and H. M. Lynd, *Middletown* (New York: Harcourt, 1929); Warner and Lunt, *Social Life*, (1941); W. G. Mather, "Income and Social Participation," *American Sociological Review*, 6 (June 1941), 380–84; Herbert Goldhamer, "Some Factors Affecting Participation in Voluntary Associations," unpublished Ph.D. thesis, University of Chicago, 1943; Bushee, "Social Organization" (1945), pp. 217–26; Mirra Komarovsky, "The Voluntary Associations of Urban Dwellers," *American Sociological Review*, 11 (December 1946), 686–98; Scott, "Participation," (1948), pp. 14–18; I. D. Reid and E. L. Ehle, "Leadership Selection in Urban Locality Areas," *Public Opinion Quarterly*, 14 (Summer 1950), 262–84; Floyd Dotson, "Patterns of Voluntary Association Among Urban Working-Class Families," *American Sociological Review*, 16 (October 1951), 687–93; Walter T. Martin, "A Consideration of the Differences in the Extent and Location of the Formal Associational Activities of Rural-Urban Fringe Residents," *American Sociological Review*, 17 (December 1952), 687–94; Odell Uzzell, "Institution Membership and Class Levels," *Sociology and Social Research*, 37 (July–August, 1953), 390–94; John M. Foskett, "Social Structure and Social Participation," *American Sociological Review*, 20 (August 1955), 433; Wendell Bell and Maryanne T. Force, "Social Structure and Participation in Different Types of Formal Associations," *Social Forces*, 34 (May 1956), 35; Wright and Hyman, p. 288; Morris Axelrod, "Urban Structure and Social Participation," *American Sociological Review*, 21 (February 1956), 13–18; John C. Scott, Jr. "Membership and Participation in Voluntary Organizations," *American Sociological Review*, 22 (June 1957), 315–26.

[26] One difference between the Western European and American lower classes is that the former have some tendency to belong to political organizations—probably because their unions urge them to belong to the Labour party. See Thomas B. Bottomore, "Social Stratification in Voluntary Organizations," in D.V. Glass (ed.),

Lower-income people are, however, likely to be attached to a trade union, to a church, and to informal but fairly stable friendship groups (including kin groups) for recreation, and these perform some of the same functions that the more typical voluntary associations perform for other classes.[27]

To a certain extent an association tends to draw members from a limited class range and from a given religious, ethnic, or racial group, so that a given community will have several associations with the same function but with a different composition of membership.[28] Of course some kinds of associations have a narrower class range than do others. Political clubs tend to have a broad class range within a community as a whole, and are an exception to the above-mentioned finding that the higher the class of a person the more likely he is to be a joiner: there is no correlation between income and membership in political clubs (which, as we have seen, are often politically powerful), although there is a religious variation, with Catholics being the most frequent joiners.[29]

Class differences in types of association participated in do not always show the upper class in the most powerful associations. In "Jonesville," a community studied by W. L. Warner, et al.,[30] the strictly upper-class associations were devoted to sociable, recreational, and cultural affairs, and practically none of them exerted much power. The upper-middle-class associations, such as Rotary (which also included some upper-class men), the Woman's Club, the P.T.A., the Red Cross, "grapple with the problems which face all segments of the community every day." Many of these exercised power in the community. The lower-middle-class associations—chiefly lodges, women's auxiliaries, and small informal social groups—are largely

---

Social Mobility, pp. 381–2; Bo Anderson, "Some Problems of Change in the Swedish Electorate," unpublished study, Department of Sociology, Uppsala University, Sweden, 1950.

[27]Dotson, "Patterns of Voluntary Associations"; Nicholas Babchuk and C. Wayne Gordon, *The Voluntary Association in the Slum* (Lincoln: University of Nebraska Press, 1962), p. 116.

[28]Mhyra S. Minnis, "The Relationship of Women's Organizations to the Social Structure of a City," unpublished Ph.D. thesis, Yale University, 1951; August B. Hollingshead, "Trends in Social Stratification: A Case Study," *American Sociological Review*, 17 (December 1952), pp. 679–86.

[29]Robert E. Lane, *Political Life* (Glencoe, Ill.: Free Press, 1959), p. 79.

[30]*Democracy in Jonesville* (New York: Harper, 1949), pp. 137–43.

devoted to "having a good time," and have little political or civic content to their programs. For the upper-lower-class, with fewer associational memberships, the lodges, the American Legion, and particularly the church organizations were the chief sources of affiliation. But they also have little political content and fail "to relate their members to the community." For the lower-lower-class there is very little associational life of any kind; this particular community had few unions. As may be seen, it is the upper-middle-class associations which show concern for the state of the community and conduct activities designed to do something about it.

Other significant differentials in participation have been reported in a variety of studies, although sometimes the conclusions of these studies are at variance with one another. Most of the studies report that more men than women participate in voluntary associations.[31] Participation is related to religious affiliation in that Protestants and Jews are more frequently members of voluntary associations (excepting political clubs) than are Catholics.[32] Married people are more likely to participate than are single persons.[33] There have been a variety of findings concerning Negro and white participation in voluntary associations.[34] One national study finds that the two groups have the same proportion of participation, another comes to the conclusion that whites have more participation, while a third indicates that Negroes participate more. A study of Lincoln, Nebraska, where

[31]Previously cited studies of the following authors report greater participation by men than by women: Lynd and Lynd (p. 527), Brunner and Kolb (p. 262), Warner and Lunt (p. 335), Goldhamer, Komarovsky (p. 685), Scott (pp. 7, 9). Another study reporting greater male participation is G. A. Lundberg, M. Komarovsky, and M. A. McInerny, *Leisure, A Suburban Study* (New York: Columbia University Press, 1934). Authors reporting greater participation by women than by men are Bushee (pp. 220–21), Mather (p. 381). In the working class, the lower-middle, and the upper class, men participate more; in the upper-middle class, more women participate; see Alfred Hero, "Voluntary Organizations in World Affairs Communications," unpublished study prepared for the World Peace Foundation, 1958, pp. 50–51. Under the age of forty years, men participate more, over forty, women do; see Hausknecht, *The Joiners*, pp. 32–33.

[32]Warner and Lunt, *Social Life*, p. 346; Goldhamer, "Factors Affecting Participation," p. 29; Scott, "Membership and Participation," pp. 14–18; Hausknecht, *The Joiners*, p. 52. Komarovsky ("Urban Dwellers," p. 696) found no religious differences.

[33]Komarovsky, "Urban Dwellers," p. 695; Scott, "Membership and Participation," pp. 14–18; Wright and Hyman, "Voluntary Associations," p. 292; Hausknecht, *The Joiners*, p. 35. Goldhamer found this to be true among men, but not among women ("Factors Affecting Participation," pp. 34–35). Bell and Force that marital status had no effect on partcipation ("Social Structure," p. 34).

[34]Hausknecht, *The Joiners*, pp. 51–52.

there is only a small proportion of Negroes, reports that Negroes participate more than do whites.[35] Married couples with one child are less likely to participate than married couples with no children or with two or more children.[36] Newcomers to a community are likely to participate less than do the natives, but within five years of migration to a large city the newcomers are likely to participate as much as anyone else.[37] Home owners are almost twice as likely to belong to voluntary associations as are renters, possibly because owners feel they have more of a stake in the community.[38]

There are several studies reporting on participation in voluntary associations as related to age. These studies generally show that social participation declines at the later ages despite the increased leisure time following upon retirement. In McKain's[39] study, about one-half of those past 65 years of age reported that they gave less time to organizations than they did when they were 50 years of age, and only 1 per cent said that their social activity had increased. Havighurst[40] corroborates this finding and adds to it:

> Formal associations lose attractiveness as age changes from 40 to 70, though not among women until they reach the sixties. Informal groups are most attractive to men in the 50 to 60 group but are equally attractive at all (middle) ages for women.

On the other hand, in Scott's[41] study of a representative sample of adults of the New England town of Bennington, Vermont, there was no consistent relationship between membership and age. Those under

[35]Nicholas Babchuk and Ralph V. Thompson, "The Voluntary Associations of Negroes," *American Sociological Review*, 27 (October 1962), 652.

[36]Scott, "Membership and Participation," p. 18; N. L. Whetten and C. C. Devereux, Jr., *Studies of Suburbanization in Connecticut: I. Windsor, A Highly Developed Agricultural Area*, Storrs Agricultural Experiment Station Bulletin No. 212 (1936).

[37]Basil G. Zimmer, "Participation of Migrants in Urban Structures," *American Sociological Review*, 20 (April 1955), 218–24. Those who are upper class and come from other cities are the quickest to join voluntary associations in their new home community.

[38]Hausknecht, *The Joiners*, p. 47.

[39]W. C. McKain, "The Social Participation of Old People in a California Retirement Community," unpublished Ph.D. dissertation, Harvard University.

[40]R. J. Havighurst, "The Leisure Activities of the Middle-aged," *American Journal of Sociology*, 63 (1957), 152–62, at p. 160.

[41]J. C. Scott, "Membership and Participation."

25 years of age reported an average of 1.75 memberships, those
between 25 and 39 reported an average of 1.46 memberships, those
between 40 and 54 years reported an average of 1.98 memberships,
while those 55 years and older reported an average of 1.48 memberships. Among men alone, membership in voluntary associations did
not fall with age, whereas it did so markedly among the women.
Studies by Goldhamer,[42] by Freedman and Axelrod,[43] and by Anderson and Ryan[44] also correlated age with membership in voluntary
associations. The Goldhamer study indicates that young adults aged
20 to 30 are, among all age groups, least likely to participate. Foskett finds just the opposite, that this young age group participates the
most. He suggests that this is due to the lower average educational
and income level among the elderly.[45] Hausknecht, using national
samples, corroborates Scott's finding that association membership
reaches a peak around age 40.[46]

Participation normally means attendance at general meetings
(from once a week to once a year),[47] attendance at committee
meetings (which convene irregularly, depending on the amount of
activity), and the performance of the activity prescribed by the association. Membership in a single association can take as little or as
much of one's time as one is willing to devote to it. Reasons for participation or non-participation in voluntary associations vary with the
individual as well as with the structure and purpose of the organization. Often upper and middle-class people join organizations to further their careers, to make business connections, or as a mark of
status. Some large, absentee-owned corporations push their employees
into joining community groups so that the company may maintain
a favorable public image and so that it can keep tabs on the organizations to keep them from adopting programs that would work to the

[42]H. Goldhamer, "Factors Affecting Participation."

[43]R. Freedman and M. Axelrod, "Who Belongs to What in a Great Metropolis?"
Adult Leadership, 1 (November 1952), 6–9.

[44]A. Anderson and B. Ryan, "Social Participation Differences Among Tenure
Classes in a Prosperous Commercialized Farming Area," *Rural Sociology*, 8 (1943),
281–90.

[45]Foskett, "Social Structure and Social Participation," p. 435.

[46]Hausknecht, pp. 33–4.

[47]In the Minneapolis–St. Paul study, 13 per cent of the associations had had no
membership meetings during the previous year; 43 per cent had 1 to 3 meetings; 31
per cent had 4 to 24 meetings; 13 per cent had 25 or more membership meetings
during the year.

corporation's disadvantage.[48] Some people, because of their high status in the community, are pressed into participation in fund drives so that organizations can take advantage of the prestige of their names.[49] Middle-class women may join voluntary associations to help in their adjustment to life after their children are grown.[50]

The reasons for not joining voluntary associations or being inactive members are just as varied. Lack of time because of job or family obligations, which our society defines as more important than voluntary association membership, are reasons individuals often give for their inactivity. Also, membership in many organizations may lead to little participation in some of them.[51] Especially among lower-class people, shyness and lack of self-confidence are also important reasons for lack of participation.[52] Those with less education may not understand how voluntary association activity could affect community policies which have a bearing on their lives. The structure of some organizations encourages inactivity. If there is too much bureaucratization, people will lose interest in an organization.[53] The larger the group, the larger the proportion of apathetic members it is likely to have. This is because a large group tends to be more heterogeneous and therefore tends to have less consensus about what group activities should be.[54] Individual personality and status as well as the structure of the group thus have a bearing on whether or not the individual will be an active participant in a voluntary association. Most associations require their members to pay annual dues, which is usually a small amount except in unions and businessmen's associations. The association usually has other sources of income, and each has its effect on the contributors' psychological involvement and on the extent of the association's activities.

1. Solicitation of voluntary contributions from both members and non-members is usually moderately successful in a culture where

<hr>

[48]For example, to push for enlarged welfare programs that would increase taxes; see Roland J. Pellegrin and Charles H. Coates, "Absentee-owned Corporations and Community Power Structure," *American Journal of Sociology*, 61 (March 1956), 415.

[49]Foskett, "Social Structure and Social Participation," p. 437.

[50]Joan W. Moore, "Patterns of Women's Participation in Voluntary Associations," *American Journal of Sociology*, 66 (May 1961), 598.

[51]Sills, *The Volunteers*, pp. 35–6.

[52]Hero, "World Affairs Communications," p. 6.

[53]Sills, *The Volunteers*, p. 331.

[54]Hero, "World Affairs Communications," p. 3.

"philanthropy" is an accepted cultural trait, even among poor people,[55] and where most contributions can be deducted in calculating income taxes. Practically all American cities also have a "Community Fund," which is a voluntary association whose purpose is to collect contributions once a year, from as many citizens as want to contribute or can be pressured to contribute, for the purpose of distributing these funds to "worthy" associations of many types. These community funds are growing in favor because most people do not like to be bothered by many smaller drives, sometimes conducted by obscure organizations.

2. Legacies and special gifts sometimes are given by interested wealthy people.

3. Money-raising events are likely to produce funds even in hard times; these latter operate on the principle of *quid pro quo*: an association will provide a dinner, or sell all sorts of objects at a bazaar or rummage sale (where the merchandise is provided gratis by members), or offer amusement at a card party or carnival. The labor and materials going into these are provided by the members, and the money earned goes into the treasury of the association to carry on its regular work. Some of the bigger associations—and this includes practically all of the national ones—have enough money to hire professional workers to help carry on the functions of the association and, incidentally, to help in the money raising.[56]

The purposes of associations are as diverse as can be imagined.[57] The only thing they have in common is that the purposes are limited, and practically never will an association act for a purpose different from the original one which brought the members together. The reason is easy to understand: people who have one interest in com-

[55]An extensive study by the Russell Sage Foundation in 1950 revealed that contributions to voluntary associations and philanthropic causes of all sorts were part of nearly every family's expenditures, and that the lower-income groups devoted as large a proportion to this purpose as did the middle- and upper-income groups. See Frank Emerson Andrews, *Philanthropic Giving* (New York: Russell Sage Foundation, 1950).

[56]In the Minneapolis–St. Paul study, about half the associations had at least one paid employee; often this was only a clerical worker.

[57]In the Minneapolis–St. Paul study, 43 per cent of the associations had as primary purpose some sort of benefit or activity intended for their own members; 44 per cent directed their activity toward the public at large; 10 per cent were principally engaged in charity or some form of aid to needy individuals; the rest were principally engaged in co-ordinating the activities of other organizations.

mon are not necessarily likely to have another interest in common, and any effort to act on a second purpose is likely to split the association. Thus the association is the opposite of all-encompassing: it does not seek to involve the individual in all his interests or in all aspects of his life. Therefore it is quite the opposite of a family, of some churches and other religious institutions (such as a monastery), or of the Communist party. The specific nature of the purposes of voluntary associations gives to American culture a characteristic which was originally known as "cultural pluralism" (although that term has recently been distorted to refer solely to religious and nationality diversity). In its original meaning—as stated by Dewey, Cooley, and Kallen—cultural pluralism referred to the encouragement of all kinds of group differences characteristic of American life and referred especially to those group differences that one voluntarily chooses to cultivate. Most individuals are encouraged to be "culturally plural" as they are encouraged to belong to several associations with quite different purposes and often with different memberships.

In order to determine some of the social psychological bases for the formation of voluntary associations we may pose the question as to what other means have been used historically to satisfy the two needs for self-expression and satisfaction of interests through collective action. Again, we have to turn to history for a complete answer, but an impressionistic observation would suggest that other historical societies have relied on the family, either the immediate family or the extended family, on the church, or on the community as a whole for the satisfaction of these needs. This leads us to the observation long made by sociologists, that in contemporary American urban society the extended family, the church, and the community are relatively weak social structures and that many people do not belong to them at all. The hypothesis is suggested, then, that because the American extended family, church, and community are weak, each individual is obligated to turn relatively frequently to voluntary associations for self-expression and satisfaction of his interests, if these two needs are to be met at all.[58] If this is the case, the

___

[58]Of course there exist those victims of the mass society who do not get their needs for self-expression and achievement of interests satisfied. For them, the family, church, and community are weak or otherwise unsatisfactory, but they have not joined voluntary associations.

voluntary association would tend to contribute to the democratic character of American society, since strong family systems, churches, and communities tend to be totalitarian in their influence over the individual, whereas voluntary associations distribute and diversify power influence.

If our hypothesis is correct, it is likely that another psychological satisfaction provided in other societies mainly by the immediate family, and secondarily by the extended family, church, and community, is also being inadequately provided by them in our society. This is the provision of a sense of security, which may be thought of as the defense of the individual against reduction of his need satisfaction by outside forces, as distinguished from attainment of satisfaction in a positive sense. That we are on the right track in our psychological analysis of the motives for joining groups has been suggested by several studies of trade unions, reform groups, fraternal organizations, and even churches.[59]

Certain students of the labor movement have attempted to explain the rise and rapid development of trade unions in such a way that their analysis has relevance as a more general hypothesis for explaining the historical proliferation of all kinds of voluntary associations in contemporary society. We have already considered Polanyi's[60] historical analysis of the breakdown of the pre-industrial social system and how it left a gap that unions and businessmen's organizations sought to fill.[61] Tannenbaum[62] goes one step farther than does Polanyi. He holds that the union movement grew up in

---

[59]A by no means exhaustive list of such studies would include Arnold M. Rose, *Union Solidarity* (Minneapolis: University of Minnesota Press, 1952), ch. III, sect. D; Albert Blumenthal, *Small Town Stuff* (Chicago: University of Chicago Press, 1932); William Gellerman, *The American Legion as Educator* (New York: Teachers College, Columbia University, 1938); C. F. Marden, *Rotary and Its Brothers* (Princeton: Princeton University Press, 1935); E. W. Bakke and C. Kerr, *Unions, Management and the Public* (New York: Harcourt, 1948); Charles W. Ferguson, *Fifty Million Brothers* (New York: Farrar and Rinehart, 1937); Noel P. Gist, "Structure and Process in Secret Societies," *Social Forces*, 16 (March 1938), 349–57; Edward D. Starbuck, *The Psychology of Religion* (New York: Scribner's, 1908), pp. 28 ff.; Lundberg, Komarovsky, and McInerny, *Leisure: A Suburban Study;* Sills, *The Volunteers*; E. Wight Bakke, "Why Workers Join Unions," *Personnel*, 22 (July 1945), 37–46.

[60]Karl Polanyi, *The Great Transformation* (New York: Farrar and Rinehart, 1944).
[61]See Chapter VI.
[62]Frank Tannenbaum, *A Philosophy of Labor* (New York: Alfred A. Knopf, 1951).

reaction to the segmentalization as well as the insecurity of modern life to re-establish a "sense of community" which prevailed in pre-industrial times. He views unions as a means of regaining the security, recognition, and self-expression for the worker which had been lost because of the growth of modern capitalism and the Industrial Revolution.

This approach to economic organizations could be applied to other kinds of voluntary associations; the declining influence of the community (and the extended family and the church) resulted in psychological insecurity, segmentalization of personal relations, reduction of intimacy, and alienation from once-powerful values. The voluntary association is a new kind of institution crescively established to fill the gap left by these social changes. Kluckhohn has suggested this in a succinct passage:

> Mass economic upheaval following unprecedented economic growth; lack of attention to the human problems of an industrial civilization; the impersonality of the social organization of cities; the melting pot, transitory geographic residence, social mobility, weakening of religious faith—all of these trends have contributed to make Americans feel unanchored, adrift upon a meaningless voyage. . . . Why are Americans a nation of joiners? In part this is a defense mechanism against the excessive fluidity of our social structure. Because of the tension of continual struggle for social place, people have tried to gain a degree of routinized and recognized fixity by allying themselves with others in voluntary associations.[63]

Another writer sees the voluntary association as a means of correcting inequalities of status in the different spheres of an individual's life. He joins a voluntary association to provide status in areas where he feels he is weak.[64]

Once a voluntary association is formed, it may undergo one of several processes of development. Some associations die shortly after

[63]Clyde and Florence Kluckholm, "American Culture: Generalized Orientations and Class Patterns," Chapter XX of L. Bryson, L. Finkelstein, and R. M. MacIver (eds.), *Conflicts of Power in Modern Culture* (New York: Harper, 1947), pp. 249–50.

[64]S. N. Eisenstadt, "The Social Conditions of the Development of Voluntary Associations—A Case Study of Israel," unpublished manuscript, Eliezer Kaplan School of Economics and Social Science, Hebrew University, Jerusalem, Israel, p. 27.

they are created; others continue indefinitely without developing; still others have a growth in structure and function. Chapin has provided a succinct description of the growing association, emphasizing bureaucratic tendencies:

A group of citizens meet informally to consider some problem or need. After a few conferences, a chairman is selected. As the problem under discussion is broken down into its elements, various committees are appointed: executive, ways and means, publicity, program, survey, etc. Soon the business of calling conferences and notifying interested persons becomes too arduous for volunteer private citizens and the half-time services of an executive secretary is provided. He soon finds it necessary to have a clerk-stenographer. She needs a typewriter, chair, desk, and filing cabinets. Supplies of stationery, postage, telephone, and other items of equipment are purchased. As the work of the new organization, branch, section (or whatever the names of the new unit may be) grows in volume, it is systematized by establishing membership requirements and dues. A constitution and bylaws are adopted at some stage of its development. The organization may be incorporated if it is an independent entity and not a department of some larger whole. A full line of officers may be chosen: Chairman of the Board, President, Vice-Presidents, Secretary, Treasurer, etc. As the funds accumulate and a bank account is established, the Treasurer is bonded and an annual audit is required.

Meanwhile the organization finds more office space necessary. A full-time executive secretary is engaged. Additional clerks are needed. Office equipment is increased by additional typewriters, chairs, desks, filing cabinets, and other equipment. Then an office manager is chosen. As time passes, and the full-time staff grows in size, vested interests in "the job" appear. Some staff persons become more concerned with the perpetuation of their job and guarding their "rights" than in the function and purpose of the organization. Rules and policies are worked out to cover sick-leave allowances, vacation time, termination pay, and pensions. Along with the expansion of staff hierarchy there goes an expansion of committees of all sorts, so that the dignity and status of office take on added prestige and social position is sought for by interested persons. As the length of line organization increases, the problems of communication between different status levels become more acute. All these tendencies are signs that point to the formalization of the organization, which was originally quite innocent of bureaucratic trends and characteristics.[65]

C. Kinds of Voluntary Associations

To consider how the voluntary association relates an individual to the general society, let us enumerate some of the associations to which a middle-class American man and woman in a moderate-sized city might belong. The man might belong to a sports club or hobby club, which helps its members organize teams for playing baseball or basketball, or for providing materials for the hobby. The sports club also has the purpose of putting pressure on the local government to provide fields and houses where these games can be played. If he is a war veteran, the man might belong to one of the big veterans' organizations, which provides many types of non-athletic recreation and entertainment for him. The veterans' organizations also put pressure on government to obtain special privileges for soldiers and veterans, and occasionally the leaders speak on general political subjects. Whether he is a member of a veterans' organization or not, the average middle-income man may belong to a very similar organization known as a "lodge" or fraternal association. This provides recreation, entertainment, and fellowship, and occasionally does a "good deed" for the community as a whole, but seldom puts pressure on government. The fraternal associations are declining somewhat, but a smaller, less formal, type of social club seems to be taking their place.

Our average man is also likely to belong to an occupational group: to a labor union if he is a factory worker, to a trade association if he is a businessman, to a farmers' organization if he is a farmer, to a professional association if he is in one of the free professions. These groups seek to defend the occupational interests and improve the occupational status of their members. In doing so, they oppose each

[65]F. Stuart Chapin, "The Growth of Bureaucracy: An Hypothesis," *American Sociological Review*, 16 (December 1951), 835. Similar observations were made by Charles Perrow, "The Analysis of Goals in Complex Organizations," *American Sociological Review*, 26 (December 1961), 862.

other and even the society as a whole, since they occasionally stop the functioning of the whole occupational group and they often put pressure on government to get laws or administration of laws favorable to the occupation. Only recently have some of them—mainly the unions—expressed any interest in government in general, but even this is very rare: their main concern with government is primarily in relation to improving conditions of work in their particular occupation.

The average man is also likely to belong to some kind of benevolent, social-improvement, or "charitable" association. For people in the lower-income classes, this association is usually connected with the church. In the middle- and upper-income classes, people also tend to belong to one or more such associations organized independently for social-welfare purposes. The activities of the voluntary associations for social welfare are supplementary to those of government. These functions are too numerous to describe adequately, but a few examples will give their general character. One exists to collect money to subsidize intelligent but poor boys and girls at a university. Another collects money to subsidize scientific research on cancer. Another has its members help blind children in after-school hours. Another directs a neighborhood recreational house for children. Another sews sheets for the public hospital. Another works to integrate recent immigrants into American community life. And so on. For each "underprivileged" group there is in nearly every community one or more voluntary associations—whose members are anybody, often including a few "underprivileged"—to assist them.[66] Each of these functions is carried on by the government (federal, state or local), but the association also helps in a supplementary and personal way.

Some of these social-improvement associations shade over into social-reform[67] associations. One of the latter has as its purpose giv-

---

[66]Chambers traces the development in Great Britain of social-service associations. Originally created by the privileged to help the underprivileged, they have—as in the United States—increasingly included some of the lower classes among their members and even leaders. Judging from Chambers's observations, this trend may have developed further in Britain than in the United States. See Chambers, "Three Voluntary Organizations," ch. 14.

[67]The term "social reform" is used here to refer to any kind of social change, regardless of direction or value. While most social-reform associations in the United States would be judged to have mildly "liberal" purposes, some could be said to have "conservative" or "reactionary" purposes.

ing out propaganda to get a better law on procedures governing the adoption of orphan children. Another distributes information about the United Nations and about international affairs for the betterment of international understanding. Another collects money to send a public-school teacher to an annual institute for the modernization of teaching techniques. Another watches the local government to see that tax money is not "wasted." And so on. For every way in which a dozen or more people in the community think the community should be changed there are one or more associations working in some manner for that change. While there are hundreds of thousands of social-reform associations across the country, only a minority of the population belongs to at least one, although some individuals belong to several. In general, there is a connection between one's income level and one's membership in social-reform associations: poor people usually belong to none, and rich people tend to belong to many.

Women belong to somewhat the same type of associations as men do, but there are some differences. Only a third of the women have occupations other than housewife and so are not so likely as men to belong to occupational associations. Very few women belong to sports clubs, veterans' associations, or "lodges," although there exist female counterparts of the men's fraternal associations. Women, however, tend to be more participant than are men in the informal social clubs, the social-improvement associations, and in some kinds of social-reform associations. There is one type of association that many women, but few men, join: the "self-improvement" or "educational" association. Specific examples would be a club that invites speakers to talk on various subjects, a music-appreciation club, a book-reviewing club, or a "recent political-events discussion club." Men have something of this in their service clubs—Rotary, Kiwanis, Lions—but these clubs also have the function of integrating the business and professional interests of a community. In many cities a few men as well as a few women will form musical societies (orchestras, choruses, chamber-music sections, etc.). The participants of all these self-improvement groups come almost entirely from the middle-income groups, and only a minority of even this class is involved.

Young people belong to many types of associations, and these exist for children of eight years of age and upward, of all socio-economic classes. Many are connected with school life, but many others are outgrowths of the church, the local community, or any other institution to which young people may be attached. Children of high-school age will belong to sports groups, scout groups, religious groups, self-educational groups (for example, nearly every high school and college has its "French Club"), sociable or fraternal groups, hobby groups, school or community improvement groups. College students have an even broader range of associations, for these include many of the adult types, many of the children's types, and still others peculiar to American university life. Experiences in these youth associations train some young people for active participation in adult associations.

In addition to the general types of associations mentioned there are special types to which only a small segment of the population belongs. College graduates, for example, may belong to their college alumni associations, which are for the purpose of supporting their old university. Scientists belong to scientific societies, which have some of the characteristics of other occupational associations but are also devoted to the discovery of new knowledge. Last, but not least, those particularly interested in politics may belong to a local club of their political party. Even though only a small proportion of these persons ever run for political office, they provide much of the direction in politics—especially local politics—and much of the detailed work in election campaigns.

D. Some Specific Associations

In order to get a more co-ordinated picture of the voluntary associations, let us examine a few of them in some detail. Our first example is the Parent-Teachers Association (P.T.A.), which is sometimes scorned by sophisticates as being the archetype of an association without power.

The public schools in the United States are usually controlled by locally elected boards of education, and the relatively large funds which they administer are raised through general taxation. Thus the administration of the public schools is part of local government. The principals and teachers of a public school are hired experts, usually employed under civil-service regulation which set standards for hiring and limit reasons for dismissal. The state and federal governments indirectly set some standards through their control over certain of the funds available to the public schools that conform to their standards. Community pressure groups have an influence on the conditions under which the public schools are run just as they have on other branches of government. In some communities teachers form unions to enhance their economic bargaining power and to maintain the standards of their profession.

In this cross-play of power forces on the public schools it is not surprising that voluntary associations of parents would also form to exert some influence on the administration of public schools, especially when certain well-organized pressure groups of a community often wish to reduce school expenditures in order to keep down taxes. Parents of children in the schools have the opposite motivation of wanting to provide a good education for their children, and they find it desirable to organize to form a contrary pressure group. Shortly after the public schools were set up in the United States during the nineteenth century, parent-teachers groups began to form in various communities to obtain what they considered to be the best available education for their children. Today a substantial majority of local communities have parent-teachers associations that are loosely linked together into a national organization. The major activities and powers are local, however, just as the public schools themselves are locally controlled. Thus the parent-teachers associations vary considerably in size, power, and activity from community to community. Perhaps the most important influences of the P.T.A.'s are the least observable ones. Through their mere existence, even if they are dormant, they serve as a counterbalancing force against other pressure groups in the community that might engage in efforts to detract from the effectiveness of education. Second, P.T.A.'s inform their members concerning political issues affecting the schools, and—while the P.T.A.'s do not endorse candidates for the school boards—this political education serves to guide parents and their friends into informed voting for school-board members. P.T.A.'s are thus indirectly often effective instruments in the election of a qualified and sympathetic board in contradistinction to a board composed of just anybody who might wish to run for public office. While the continuing work of the P.T.A.'s is probably not of so great importance as these two major functions, they nevertheless have an impact on the public schools.

It will be instructive to examine the detailed characteristics of a single Parent-Teachers Association (organized in an elementary school district in Minneapolis, Minnesota).

While only about half of the parents of the children in this school are active in the association, and these mostly the mothers rather than the fathers, and while the teachers belong largely because they feel an implicit pressure to do so, the P.T.A. is quite important. The P.T.A. meets once a month (except during the summer) and has a program consisting of a speaker giving an "educational" talk, a discussion of the current problems of the school and of the association, and a social coffee hour for the purpose of acquainting parents and teachers with each other. The discussion is based on the committee reports, for the active work of the P.T.A. is done by its committees, although the membership as a whole has to vote on important projects. During one recent school year this P.T.A. did the following things: the Community Participation Committee successfully petitioned the City Council to provide a "warming house" at the local ice-skating rink, collected a sufficient number of men and dollars to provide the necessary sponsorship for a local Boy Scout troop, and co-operated with the program of the local Neighborhood House (which provides recreation facilities for all people in the neighborhood, regardless of age and class). The Health Committee disseminated information to parents about proper diet, teeth care, and inoculation of children, and debated the advisability of starting a sex-information course at the school. The Political Committee was active in a successful city-wide campaign to get the voters to approve a new bond issue for the schools (which meant higher taxes even for those who had no children). The Human Relations Committee co-operated with a city-wide program to increase understanding among the different races and nationalities in the city (a program directed at the parents as well as at the children). The School Patrol Committee supervised a group of the older children who were granted the privileges of policemen to stop traffic when children were coming to, or leaving, school (in a few communities where the streets are dangerous the parents themselves take turns directing traffic during the hours when children are going to school and coming home). The Hobby Committee encouraged children to have hobbies and has organized a large hobby show to display the products of hobbies of all family members together; this show attracted a great deal of neighborhood attention and encouraged fathers and mothers to help their children with hobbies. The Ways and Means Committee responded to the teachers' appeal for a restroom in the school where they might have coffee or lie down during the day. They organized a large food "bazaar" to which parents freely brought food delicacies that were sold to anyone who would buy them. The money was used to buy floor tiles, curtains, a bed, coffeepot, etc., for the restroom, and some of the men in the P.T.A. volunteered to lay the tiles and paint the old furniture. The previous year this committee raised enough money to buy the school a new motion-picture projector when the old one wore out and the City Board of Education did not have enough money to buy a new one. The Hospitality and Membership Committee welcomed newcomers into the neighborhood, if they had children, and urged them to join the P.T.A. It had teas for the newcomers (and for other mothers whose children are just beginning school) to introduce them to the old-timers. The Music Committee helped the teachers with a music-appreciation program for children.

In general, the P.T.A. will set up a new committee to perform any function that is felt to be needed by enough parents, or by a reliable educational or community leader. Dues for the P.T.A. are only 50 cents a year, but of course parents generally spend additional money on the food bazaar, the scout donations, and other associated activities. As previously mentioned, members give as little or as much of their time as they want to devote to the association. While most parents nominally belong to the association, only about half the mothers and perhaps 5 per cent of the fathers come to the monthly meetings, a good number of these are occasionally active in the committees, and perhaps 2 or 3 per cent are consistently very active (the latter are the "leaders" and are accorded respect and prestige by the community as a whole).

The second type of voluntary-association activity that will be described also illustrates how social change arises from organized effort. Its purpose is to remove race prejudice from American thoughts and actions and to compensate for the hardships faced by minority peoples because of this prejudice. While one of the most important of the associations—the National Association for the Advancement of Colored People (NAACP)—was begun in 1909, and a few others were begun in subsequent years, the main development has come since 1943, and the members of independent associations now reach into the thousands, with perhaps almost a hundred being organized on a national scale with numerous local branches. Such a complex activity—that delves into a central element of American culture—would take volumes to describe adequately;[68] obviously we cannot even scratch the surface of the question in the short space we can devote to it. Our approach will be to make a few general statements about the strategy of the activity and about its effects.

The outside observer might wonder why Negroes and other minorities that are discriminated against have not become disaffected, since they are so relatively underprivileged in the United States. The answer lies partly in the possibility of change through voluntary activity. As the late Walter White, general secretary of the NAACP and an outstanding Negro, put it:

> In America, organizations like the NAACP are free to criticize all that which displeases them—including the government. . . . We prefer to take our chances, and fight to realize our aspiration in the framework of our democracy, whatever may be its faults, for the progress we make is real.

The progress, so defined, is made by those who work for it—that is, the members of the association—and it is a substantial achievement, even if there is much left to challenge the workers. No one who has closely followed the facts of the American race problem up to 1940 would believe that so much social change could be accomplished in the brief period since then.

Each association has had a different strategy, as each has been made up of people with different backgrounds and different conceptions of social structure. The NAACP has taken advantage of the fact that the Constitution of the United States prohibits any discrimination by the government. It has successfully brought a large number of cases of discrimination into the courts, and has thereby established legal precedents that have made the laws and the courts a protection for minority groups. The Urban League has propagan-

[68]The description of the associations which work for the passage of a Fair Employment Practices Act (FEP) alone has required a book: Louis C. Kesselman, *The Social Politics of FEPC: A Study in Reform Pressure Movements* (Chapel Hill: University of North Carolina Press, 1948).

dized businessmen, with considerable success since 1940, to give Negroes a fair chance to secure good jobs, and it is now working to make better homes available to Negroes. The Anti-Defamation League (organized by Jews), the American Jewish Committee, and the National Conference of Christians and Jews have for many years countered verbal attacks on minorities with better verbal defenses and have used various techniques to combat specific discriminations. The American Jewish Congress, the March-on-Washington Committee now disbanded after a short period of great achievement in 1941–42 and again in 1963), the Congress of American Indians, and other groups have used the mass-protest demonstration effectively. The Congress of Racial Equality has borrowed the non-resistance, direct-participation techniques of Gandhi to discourage customers from using restaurants, swimming pools, etc., until those establishments stopped discriminating against minorities. These techniques have been successfully copied by the Southern Christian Leadership Conference, founded by the Rev. Martin Luther King, and by the Student Nonviolent Coordinating Committee. Many organizations— few more successfully than the Japanese American Citizens' League —have maintained lobbies in Congress and the state legislatures. The community associations use a variety of techniques, depending on the situation, the militancy or conservatism of their members, and the means available to private associations. Some of the most successful long-range reforms are being made in the education of youth. Most children are now being taught that prejudice and discrimination are wrong and that equality and fraternity with all groups should be put into concrete practice. Many youngsters have responded positively to this effort: they say and do things in a democratic, equalitarian fashion that shocks their prejudiced parents.

Let us be more concrete by describing the activities of a single association: the Mayor's Council on Human Relations of Minneapolis, Minnesota, as it functioned up to 1963. It was a group of 27 persons selected by the mayor from nominations made by the dominant organized groups in the city (businessmen, the unions, the minority organizations, the League of Women Voters, etc.) and by the older members of the council itself.[69] Once named, the members were

---

[69]This manner of becoming a member of an association is quite unusual. It can be questioned whether the Mayor's Council should be called a voluntary association

completely independent of the mayor as they could not be dismissed by him and they got no funds from the city government. They got funds by contributions from the organization nominating the members, by solicitations of ordinary citizens who favored their activities, and by an annual dinner at which some outstanding community and national leaders spoke to citizens willing and able to pay $10 for admission. Most of the money went to pay the salary of an energetic young man who spent full time with the Council's activities and gave them the benefit of continuous attention and expert knowledge. The rest of the money paid for a secretary and for propaganda that the organization distributed in the community. The members usually met once every two weeks, at lunch, and their committees met at least that often again.

Some of the committees were very active and successful; others were relatively passive. The Housing Committee sought to prevent real estate companies and landlords from refusing to rent or sell houses and apartments to minority persons. The chairman of this committee was himself a leading realtor in the city, and he made some remarkable dents in the prejudice of his fellow realtors. The Health and Hospitals Committee sought to prevent hospitals from segregating minority persons into special rooms and wards, and, through the chairmanship of a woman of strong will, it changed the policies of more than a fourth of the hospitals in the city. The Education Committee had early success in getting the public schools and the university to institute policies of complete non-discrimination in hiring teachers, in making job recommendations, and in securing rooms for students, and to institute an "intercultural education" program. It later worked to improve the teaching of better intergroup attitudes in the elementary and secondary schools—both private and public—and to encourage minority youngsters of ability to secure a higher education (one of the greatest problems is that Negro, Indian, and

---

because the membership is so limited and because of its connection with city government. We have chosen to consider it a voluntary association because: (1) one can easily refuse the appointment or resign at any time; (2) it operates just like any voluntary association where membership is more open; (3) many kinds of voluntary associations put some limitations on membership, although rarely as restrictive as in the case of the Mayor's Council; (4) the governmental connection of the Mayor's Council is fairly nominal.

Mexican children do not get enough encouragement at home to continue at school). The Employment Opportunities Committee helped to obtain the passage of a city law making it illegal to refuse to hire qualified minority persons. Since a branch of the city government then took over the job of stopping discrimination in employment, and since two other voluntary associations had this same interest,[70] the Employment Opportunities Committee disbanded, and all problem cases coming to the Council's attention are turned over to the other associations. The Committee on Churches, although headed by a brilliant and active Japanese-born Episcopalian minister, made little headway in its chief project of getting churches to welcome members of other races. In the Northern states the churches were at first among the most resistant of community institutions to change their non-equalitarian policies with respect to minorities. The Special Problems Committee handled "incidents" as they arose. When it was learned that a policeman had struck a Negro prisoner who was not resisting him, its protest to the chief of police secured a suspension of two weeks (without pay) and a transfer to another district for the offending policeman. When a salesman at a hat store asked a Negro customer to move to the back of the store where she would not be seen, the Council's protest to the manager secured a formal apology and a promise that the incident would not be repeated.

The group instituted a special course of instruction for policemen so that they might know how to handle equitably and without tension all disturbances and crimes involving minority persons. Special committees were set up to handle new problems as they arose. When the United States decided to expand the army in 1950, and the heads of the army (although not of the navy and air force) made clear their intention to retain Negroes in segregated units, the Minneapolis Council set up a committee to work with similar committees from all over the country to protest this racial discrimination. Two of the members flew to Washington at their own expense to interview the Secretary of the Army and the Chief of Staff (the civilian and military chiefs of the army, respectively) in an effort to get them to change

[70]The Urban League (for Negro social welfare) and the Joint Committee on Equal Employment Opportunity (made up of delegates from 75 other community associations which operate by personally talking to employers about discrimination and by encouraging all citizens to indicate to their tradespeople their support of non-discrimination in employment).

their policy. With two other members of the council, later added to
this new committee on Armed Services, they drew up a detailed and
factually based protest and sent it to the United States senator from
Minnesota, with a request that he transmit copies to the Secretary of
Defense and his subordinate chief of the army (the senator not only
did so, but volunteered to provide the council with all information on
future developments). The changes forthcoming from the army were
slow but steady, and the Minneapolis group continued its interest in
this national problem until it was eliminated.

E. Voluntary Associations and the Distribution of Social Power

Power in our society is differentially distributed in several ways. Class
and ethnic group affiliation have long been among the most important traits associated with the holding of power. Classes and ethnic
groups are not, of course, formally organized as such in our society,
and the exercise of power usually requires formal organization. The
formal organizations in our society having a concentration of power
are political institutions, occupational or industrial groups, and what
we have called social-influence associations. The upper class and the
ethnic groups of Western European origin held their power by their
frequent membership in and control of these formal organizations.
Over the last two decades or so the situation has been changing
somewhat. Now a significant proportion of the lower classes is organized into labor unions, an increasing proportion of the middle
class is assuming leadership in the social-influence associations, the
ethnic minorities have organized their own social-influence groups,
and all of these are taking a stronger interest in politics. Thus power
has become more widely distributed through greater participation in
voluntary associations.

Let us consider some examples of the influence of voluntary associations over the community as a whole. There are groups such as
the Farm Bureau Federation which have the ear of many congressmen; there are groups such as the League of Women Voters, which—
by informing their members on a variety of issues—exercise influence
on the political attitudes of many people; there are specialized action
groups such as the American Civil Liberties Union, which bring
cases before the courts and secure judicial precedents for future legal
cases. Groups that attract members mainly for sociable or recrea-

tional purposes, such as the American Legion, also function as political pressure groups. Even the fraternal organizations, which are predominantly sociable in their function, provide an avenue of influence for members who have political interests. In a largely decentralized democracy such as ours, many political activities—in the broad sense of that phrase—take place in non-governmental groups.

Very few of the great number of organizations having informal political power in our society have attracted membership from the lower-income classes. Low-income people have been too poor to pay membership fees, too ignorant to know how to conduct themselves in group settings, or too apathetic to have any interest in organized group activities. As a consequence, members of the lower-income population have not had the power and influence which go with membership in these groups. The pattern of non-participation has not changed significantly in recent years, nor is there any immediate prospect of its changing. Even the rising educational level of lower-income persons, the increasing leisure time available to workers, and the disappearance from the American scene of unassimilated immigrants have not yet resulted in appreciable increases in participation in those voluntary associations that have informal political power.

Lower-income people have been joining labor unions in large numbers since 1935, however, and these associations have had an increasing power. The rank-and-file members control the policies of their unions only in a very broad sense. Most members are apathetic as long as the union gets them economic benefits, and so policy making is left largely in the hands of union leaders. Union leaders come mostly out of the lower-income population, although their incomes are now at the levels of the middle class and occasionally of the upper class. They seek to represent the lower class in the various power associations in the community. For example, when a group is formed to improve the street lighting system of a city or work for more adequate housing or to make certain that legal rights are protected, it is now frequently considered necessary that "labor" be represented. Union leaders influence many voters; hence they are accorded attention by politicians and those seeking to get certain laws passed. Labor leaders find themselves increasingly requested to participate on boards and committees of both voluntary and governmental organizations. While occasionally the person invited is not a functioning union leader but merely a figurehead, while some labor leaders are not democratically elected as heads of their organizations, and while by no means all workers are organized into unions, when labor leaders become representatives in community-wide groups they usually express the workers' points of view.

Thus there are the beginnings of representation of the lower-income classes in a large number of organizations that together make up the informal government of our society. But this is the mere beginning of a trend. The more important observation is still that the large proportion of lowest-income people in our society do not participate in voluntary associations and that they therefore have little contact with persons of other classes and little power in the community as a whole. The lower-income person is effectively, although not legally, segregated in his neighborhood, his church, and possibly his labor union. The situation creates weaknesses in the social structure not only because a large section of the population is not getting the power and personal satisfaction obtainable from social participation, but also because leaders of this very class can gain enormous political power for themselves by representing the huge amorphous lower class in political parties. What might happen, at the extreme, is that the lower-income classes, who are not active in the many voluntary associations (outside of unions and farmers' organizations) that distribute *informal* power in the community will, by virtue of their large numbers, create a *formal* government out of contact with—and therefore hostile to—these voluntary associations. Because the lower class in our society has the characteristics of what we have called an audience or mass, it lends itself to the centralization of power. Such a government—even though democratically selected by universal suffrage— might become so centralized as to be semi-totalitarian.

F. Functions

To consider what the numerous diverse facts about American voluntary associations might mean, we shall suggest some of the functions they perform in the social structure.[71]

[71]This chapter attempts to give a description of voluntary associations only as they have developed in the United States. Certain other democratic nations—Great Britain, Switzerland, and the Scandinavian countries—also have large numbers of voluntary associations which apparently have many of the same characteristics. Even

The power-distributing function. From the standpoint of the society as a whole, as we have seen, they distribute power and are sort of semi-permanent forms of the public in counteracting tendencies toward an audience mode of relationship in our society.[72] Through the voluntary association the ordinary citizen can acquire as much power in the community or the nation as his free time, ability, and inclinations permit him to, without actually going into the government service, provided he accepts the competition for power of other like-minded citizens. A consideration of the varied activities and achievements of the social-influence types of associations would support that. Political power, or influence, in the United States is not concentrated in the government, but is distributed over as many citizens, working through their associations, as want to take the responsibility for power. As Goldhamer says:

> It is precisely this function of expressing and enforcing the wishes of its members that has characterized the activities of many American organizations. In this way these organizations appear to revive once more, in varying degrees, the participation of citizens in the governmental process.[73]

And Oscar Handlin comments:

> Only through the action of non-political, voluntary associations could men check the state's power without directly opposing it. As long as men are free so to act, they cannot be reduced to the blankness of the subjects of totalitarian regimes.[74]

An alternative interpretation of these facts is that Americans par-

---

those democratic countries such as France, that do not have a large part of their citizenry active in social-influence associations, nevertheless tolerate the associations. Thus the description contained in the chapter is by no means unique to the United States, even though our specific information is so limited. The functions claimed for voluntary associations can also be achieved by other social mechanisms. Frenchmen, for example, have other means of gaining understanding of, and satisfaction with, democratic processes, and other means of instituting social change. Actually, as we have already suggested, the voluntary association is often inadequate to fulfill the functions attributed to it, as it often does not incorporate many people and it often functions inefficiently and ineffectively.

[72]See Rose, *Sociology*, ch. 9.

[73]Goldhamer, "Factors Affecting Participation," p. 509.

[74]Oscar Handlin, *The American People in the Twentieth Century* (Cambridge: Harvard University Press, 1954).

ticipate extensively in voluntary associations because they find it difficult or unpleasant to get into politics.

Pressure groups or lobbies are prime examples of voluntary associations functioning to distribute power. The purpose of these groups is to influence legislation and executive action either directly or indirectly. Although the public views lobbying as evil, those connected with the legislative process look upon lobbyists as experts who are often their only source of technical information. Pressure groups tend to have the most influence when public interest on an issue is low. The scope of influence of a given pressure group is limited only to the one area in which the group has an interest or special knowledge.[75]

The orienting function. Those who thus participate become aware of how social, political, and economic processes function in their society. They learn how things are done at least in the limited sphere in which they operate. The voluntary association informs its members on matters occurring in the society at large which affect the association's purpose. This does not make the members satisfied in the sense that they always like what they learn about, but it makes them satisfied in the sense that they understand some of the complex social mechanisms that control them. As society grows more and more complex, the average citizen is usually less and less able to understand the devious controls within it, and this creates dissatisfaction. The voluntary association provides him an avenue for understanding some of the controls, and thus provides him with a degree of social satisfaction. By working in voluntary associations, people also learn exactly what is wrong with the power structure of the society, from the standpoint of their own values, and this gives them something definite to work toward, rather than leaving them with a vague and delusive feeling that, because "something" is wrong, only a complete revolution can change it. In like measure, the opportunity to engage in something creative, even if only in a lobby association, provides a compensation for the deadening effect of working on a simple repetitive task on the modern production line.[76] The association that does

[75]Bernard C. Cohen, *The Influence of Non-Governmental Groups on Foreign Policy Making* (World Peace Foundation, 1959), p. 12.

[76]No one has described this as well as the French sociologist Georges Friedmann (*Problemès Humains du Machinisme Industriel* (Paris: Gallimard, 1946); *Où Va le Travail Humain* (Paris; Gallimard, 1950).

most about this is the trade union, which seems to the worker to provide him with a significant measure of control over his working conditions, gives him a sense of economic and personal security since it protects him from being fired arbitrarily, and even directly provides him some recreations, social-reform activities, and other creative opportunities. Many intellectuals overlook the fact that there are many compensations for, controls over, and satisfactory adjustments to, the monotony of work on the factory production line. Not the least of these is participation in voluntary associations. The present difficulty —which has certainly not been solved in the United States—is that many people do not take advantage of their opportunities, because they do not see that their needs for understanding the "mysterious" social mechanisms and their need for creative activity can be satisfied by participation in the associations. While they are constantly propagandized to join, the propaganda is far from being always successful.

Hausknecht feels that the orienting function of the voluntary association is less important today than it used to be. Since people have more education now, they have a better idea of how society functions. Many volunteer associations do not help members learn about democratic methods since they are democratic in name only. Most church and social organizations, because of the restricted nature of their aims, provide little opportunity to see how society operates. Finally, he points out that even if voluntary associations do help orient the individual to society, those who most need this kind of education, the lower classes who live in the cities, according to his statistics, are least likely to join voluntary associations.[77]

The social change function. The voluntary associations offer a powerful mechanism of social change. As soon as a felt need for some social change arises, one or more voluntary associations immediately spring up to try to secure the change. Not only do they operate directly on the problem, but their attention to it also makes the government concerned about the problem, as a democratic government has to pay attention to the interests of alert voters. It may take decades to effect the change completely, but movement toward that change is likely to occur in small steps all along the way. Sometimes the change is never completely achieved because the needs behind it

[77]Hausknecht, *The Joiners*, pp. 111–12.

disappear or are converted into other needs, but it would be hard to find a need for a specific social change that existed as long as a hundred years ago in the United States and that still exists today substantially unsatisfied. The associations and the other mechanisms of change are thus usually successful in achieving their purposes in the long run.

Sometimes voluntary associations try to block social change emanating from some other source in the society, when their leaders view it as harmful to their members. One example of this might be the resistance of the private child-welfare associations when the government steps into their field.[78]

The social cohesion function. Most voluntary associations act to tie society together and to minimize the disintegrating effects of conflict. While they are themselves sometimes conflict groups, associations practically never carry their conflicts to the extreme of tearing the society asunder. This is largely because some people belong to more than one association. One association starting a serious fight with another risks losing some of its members who are members of or friendly toward the other group. The most serious conflicts come about where there is no overlapping of membership, such as in labor-management disputes.[79]

The function of personal identification. Insofar as the individual lives in a mass society,[80] he tends to feel anonymous and a mere number in the pull and haul of large-scale social forces. The voluntary association often gives him the feeling of identification with some smaller group that he can fully comprehend and influence in major ways. It thus functions as the small rural community used to function. Many members of voluntary associations today find that their memberships and activities in the association help materially to give meaning and purpose to their lives.[81] This effect on these members

[78]Bernice Boehm, "The Voluntary Association and Social Change," unpublished paper prepared for the author's social psychology course in the spring of 1955.

[79]Hans L. Zetterberg, "Voluntary Association and Organized Power in Sweden," Bureau of Applied Social Research, Columbia University (October, 1959), p. 12.

[80]See Chapter VI.

[81]Studies providing some evidence on this point include Arnold M. Rose, "Life Satisfaction of Middle-Class, Middle-Aged Persons," *Marriage and Family Living*, 17 (February 1955), 15–19; Arnold M. Rose, "Group Consciousness Among the Aging," in A. M. Rose and W. A. Peterson (eds.), *Older People and Their Social World* (Philadelphia: F. A. Davis, 1965).

is what is meant by the voluntary association having the function of personal identification.

The function of social and economic advancement. Many people join clubs and other voluntary associations to enhance their social status. As they gain access to the more exclusive clubs, sometimes they gradually relinquish their memberships in the ones that were easiest to get into.[82] In some clubs—especially the social clubs for businessmen and lawyers and the so-called "service clubs," like Rotary, Kiwanis, etc.—a good deal of "business" is transacted, which is important for the economic advancement of the members. Minority group persons—Jews, Negroes, Orientals, etc.—excluded from these clubs sometimes find it difficult to compete with those to whom membership is accorded. Offices in welfare and civic clubs are often considered a testing ground for young potential executives and managers.[83]

A final word about this often-ignored aspect of modern democratic social life. The voluntary association is characteristically a voluntary activity, and to make it anything but voluntary would destroy its basic functions as we have listed them. It is true that informal community pressures occasionally push people into associations that they have no desire to join. Such people, with the few exceptions who change their minds once in the association, are seldom satisfied with, or effective workers in, the association. They neither share the power, understand it, nor effect social change. They are the "paper" members, from whom dues cannot be collected, and they almost invariably drop out of the association. This leads us to a broader observation: there is no value in participation *per se*; it is only when the individual spontaneously feels the need for participation that it performs any of the above functions for him. This implies, further, that the effective voluntary association is one in which not only membership is voluntary, but the type of activity also voluntary in that the members choose their goals and the means for obtaining them. Few things would wreck an association faster than to impose a goal or a means of action on the members. In other words, pluralism of ends and means is a necessary component of voluntarism in democracy.

[82] John R. Seeley, R. Alexander Sim, and Elizabeth W. Loosley, *Crestwood Heights* (New York: Basic Books, 1956).
[83] Unpublished study by Professor Aileen Ross of McGill University.

Even worse than forced participation would be to encourage the individual to participate in a group activity that could not possibly have any effect, because the sources of power in the society were beyond the influence of that association's activity. If, say, all political power were lodged in a government, and the individual citizens were encouraged to be active in associations that were not allowed to influence that government, the individual's frustrations and lack of understanding of the power processes would be compounded. Fortunately for the United States and other Western democracies, participation in the associations is voluntary and the associations are able to compete for their share of real power in the society.

PART THREE
Power in the Local Community

The analysis of voluntary associations and other reactions to the mass society has taken us down to the local level. It is in the cities and towns of America that we can study power most concretely, and this is where it has been most carefully studied. It could probably have been said until the 1930's that state and local government, and other local sources of power, were far more important for the life style and the life chances of individual Americans than anything any national power structure did to or for him. The importance of the local power structure has been significantly eroded since the 1930's—in respects and to a degree which few of the students of community power structure inform us about—but the local setting of power is still not without importance for the individual citizen. Nevertheless, as we report findings of other studies about the community power structure, we must remember that all the decision-making and the potential for power that occurs in the local community is limited by more basic decisions taken on the national level.

Because of the intensity of research effort and the critical analysis which has accompanied the study of the community power structure, we are better able to discern certain issues concerning power and its study on the local level than on the national level. The first chapter in this part of the book will be exclusively concerned with these issues, both methodological and substantive. The second chapter will report a specific piece of research, using one of the methods of research severely criticized in the first chapter, but not for the purpose

253

of getting information about actual power—the goal of other researchers—rather to gain a picture of the "public image" of the
power structure. We do not claim that there is a complete divorce
between actual power and what is popularly thought to be power—
for the mere belief in power helps to create it—but we do not believe
that merely asking people about *any* social phenomenon—the race
problem, crime, the class system, family stability, or whatever—will
give us a full picture of that phenomenon. Nevertheless, our multi-
faceted approach to the popular image of power gives us another
window through which to view power in America.

VIII

Issues in the Study of Local Community Power[1]

A. Methodological Issues

As Linton Freeman and his associates have demonstrated, the method of study of local community power has in large part determined the outcome of the research, and the several approaches identify different groups of actors as powerful.[2] Polsby has remarked that "What social scientists presume to be the case will in great measure influence the design and even the outcome of their research."[3] There is an interrelation of the definition of variables in the research, the actual research strategy, and the outcome of the investigation. The multitude of definitions has led to a number of methods,[4] and a variety of results. In order to compare the outcomes of any two studies, it is imperative that the interrelation and co-determination of

[1]This chapter has relied in part on an honors paper by Ronald Lee Cohen, prepared under the author's direction.
  This is a technical chapter, dealing with methodological and theoretical issues in research at the local community level, which the general reader may prefer to skip.
  [2]Linton C. Freeman, Thomas J. Fararo, Warner Bloomberg, Jr., and Morris H. Sunshine, "Locating Leaders in Local Communities: A Comparison of Some Alternative Approaches," *American Sociological Review*, 28 (October 1963), 797. Although they use the term "leader," it is obvious it refers to the same phenomenon discussed here as "power."
  [3]Nelson W. Polsby, *Community Power and Political Theory* (New Haven: Yale University Press, 1963) p. 6.
  [4]For a description of the various methods see Robert A. Dahl, *Modern Political Analysis* (Englewood Cliffs, N.J.: Prentice-Hall, 1963), pp. 52–3; Peter H. Rossi, "Community Decision Making," *Administrative Science Quarterly*, 1 (March 1957), 425; Linton C. Freeman, *et al.*, "Locating Leaders," pp. 791–8; and Sethard Fisher, "Community-Power Studies: A Critique," *Social Research*, 29(4) (Winter 1962), 449–66.

these three factors be kept constantly in mind. In general there may
be said to be three methods of research in local community power
studies—the positional, the reputational, and the decision-making
approaches—although there are variations within each approach.

The *positional approach* to the study of community power assumes
that "an actor's power is closely correlated with his position in an
official or semi-official hierarchy."[5] This method searches for the
"potential power-offices in the community's institutionalized economic, political, and/or civic structures."[6]

> We can affix the names of the people who occupy these
> offices, and we can say that here are the people who speak
> for the major institutional sectors of the community. There-
> fore, they surely must be the power-holders of this com-
> munity, the people that are most influential in initiating and
> sanctioning policy.[7]

The great advantage of this method is its simplicity. Aside from
the task of defining which positions in the community are "on top,"
this approach presents the researcher with few, if any, procedural
problems; it "employs objective, verifiable social characteristics of
specified individuals," and "assumes that the power structure consists
largely of those persons who belong in some selected social category."[8] This very simplicity, however, also is the basis of the many
disadvantages of positional analysis, which all accrue from "the shaky
assumption on which it rests, for formal position is not necessarily
correlated with power."[9] There is a complete disregard for those not
occupying formal, official positions, and therefore, no distinction
between authority and control.[10] As sociologists have long known,

[5]Dahl, *Analysis*, p. 52.

[6]Delbert Miller, quoted in conversation by Howard J. Ehrlich, "Power and
Democracy: A Critical Discussion," in William V. D'Antonio and Howard J. Ehrlich
(eds.), *Power and Democracy in America* (Notre Dame, Ind.: University of Notre
Dame Press, 1961), p. 99; also Robert O. Schulze and Leonard U. Blumberg, "The
Determination of Local Power Elites," *American Journal of Sociology*, 63 (November
1957), 291.

[7]Quoted from Delbert Miller (see preceding note).

[8]Fisher, "Community-Power Studies," pp. 449–450.

[9]Dahl, *Analysis*, p. 52. "The positional approach also assumes a connection between social position and social behavior, that is, if one knows the former one can
make reliable inferences about the latter" (Fisher, "Community-Power Studies," p.
450).

[10]Harold D. Lasswell, Daniel Lerner, and C. Easton Rothwell, *The Comparative
Study of Elites* (Stanford, Calif.: Stanford University Press, 1952), pp. 7–8.

the informal social structure is often as important as, or more important than, the formal structure.

It should be mentioned that a strict positional analysis is rarely, if ever, employed as the sole method in community power studies, but rather as an adjunct to other methods. In some studies, after the power structure is identified by other means, it is compared with a list of occupants of formal positions to determine the extent of their participation. In other studies, lists of occupants of positions in different institutional sectors are compared to determine the amount of overlap. Finally, the lists are used as a preliminary step in both the reputational and decision-making methods which are discussed below. In any event, formal position is usually regarded as only one of many possible resources in determining an actor's potential for affecting the behavior of others. It is generally assumed that there are also power-holders who do not formally hold office in the major institutions and associations.

Currently the most widely employed approach to the study of community power, and consequently the one subjected to the most penetrating examination and criticism, is the *reputational approach*. In general, the procedure is to "determine community-power structures on the basis of judgments by community members who are considered 'knowledgeable' about community life. These 'judges' select names from lists of potential candidates based on imputed degrees of influence. Those persons most frequently selected according to the given criteria are said to constitute the power structure."[11]

Most of these power-reputation or power-attribution studies stem from the work of Floyd Hunter in Regional City.[12] One of his most severe critics, Nelson Polsby, acknowledges that "the work of Floyd Hunter dominates the contemporary scene,"[13] and all those who use this approach realize their debt to his pioneering work. It is therefore useful to examine the specific manner in which Hunter went about identifying the power structure of Regional City.

[11]Fisher, "Community-Power Studies," p. 451. See also Freeman, *et al.*, "Locating Leaders," p. 793; Raymond W. Wolfinger, "A Plea for a Decent Burial," *American Sociological Review,* 27 (December 1962), 842; Rossi, "Community Decision Making," pp. 427–9; Dahl, *Analysis*, pp. 52–3; Ehrlich, "A Critical Discussion," pp. 99–100.

[12]Floyd Hunter, *Community Power Structure, A Study of Decision Makers* (Garden City, N.Y.: Doubleday, 1963).

[13]Polsby, *Political Theory*, p. 45.

In essence, Hunter's method was simple—if you want to know about power in a community, ask people who are active in the community. Hunter first got "basic lists of power personnel" for Atlanta, Georgia:

> The Community Council in Regional City (Atlanta), a council of civic organizations, provided preliminary lists of leaders in community affairs. The Chamber of Commerce provided business leaders of establishments employing more than 500 employees and of financial houses doing the largest volume of clearances. The League of Women Voters provided lists of local political leaders who had at least major governmental committee chairmanship status. Newspaper editors and other civic leaders provided lists of society leaders and leaders of wealth.[14]

Hunter then created a panel of 14 "judges"—on what basis *they* were selected Hunter does not tell us—and asked for their opinions as to who "were top leaders on each of the lists thus provided."[15] Through the use of these judges, Hunter practically nullifies the usefulness of the previous lists he gathered, except to put some limits on the judges, for it is the judges who select the 40 "top influentials." These in turn were interviewed and asked, "If a project were before the community that required a *decision* by a group of leaders— leaders that nearly everyone would accept—which *ten* on the list of forty would you choose?"[16] By counting the votes that each person received, Hunter designated the 12 highest as the "upper-limits personnel." This was confirmed by constructing a sociogram of the mutual choices made, indicating that the "upper-limits personnel" rarely voted for people outside that group.

Having located the "power personnel" of Atlanta, Hunter proceeded to interview them extensively to determine how this power structure worked.

At the top of the "power structure" in Atlanta, Hunter found, was a small group of men who made the important decisions for the community. "The test for admission to this circle of decision-makers is almost wholly a man's position in the business community in

14Hunter, *Community Power Structure*, p. 261.
15Ibid.
16Ibid. p. 63 (italics Hunter's).

Regional City."[17] These policy-makers initiate policy. Once a policy has been decided at this level, the policy-makers "move out of the picture" and turn the project over to men in the "under-structure" (professionals, association staff, political figures, etc.) who then see that the policy formulated above is executed.[18] On some projects the policy group may "designate" a number of its members to direct its execution.[19]

How is policy made in Regional City? At one point Hunter specifically states that "the popular notion of men plotting behind the scenes is a fictional illusion. . . ."[20] Nonetheless, even with this explicit disclaimer, the picture of policy-making in Atlanta that he paints is very much one of conspiracy and "behind the scenes" activity. For example, Hunter tells us that "The 'top-flight' meetings—those of high policy nature—are held in private clubs or private homes."[21] And, "The fact that the under-structure personnel do not frequent the clubs is in itself one of the subtle exclusion devices. The 'boys' of the Grandview Club are known to make policy decisions within the confines of the club dining rooms which eventually filter down to the community under-structure."[22]

Hunter quotes at length from James Treat, the individual in the "power structure" who was able to "manipulate" the governor of the state.[23] Treat describes how the policy-makers held a meeting at the Grandview Club where one "crowd" initiated the project of an International Trade Council. Treat goes on:

> There is one detail I left out, and it is an important one. We went into that meeting with a board of directors picked. The constitution was all written, and the man who was to head the council as executive was named. . . . a fellow who will take advice.[24]

At this meeting of policy-makers, the details are worked out and money is raised to get the project started. Up to this point the matter

17 Ibid. p. 78.
18 Ibid. p. 98.
19 Ibid. p. 94.
20 Ibid. p. 178.
21 Ibid. p. 16.
22 Ibid. p. 193.
23 Ibid. p. 160.
24 Ibid. p. 171.

has been kept entirely within the circle of decision-makers, as Treat indicates.

> The public doesn't know anything about the project until it reaches the stage I've been talking about. After the matter is financially sound, then we go to the newspapers and say *there is a proposal for consideration*.[25]

Hunter has quoted Treat at length not because he feels this is an exceptional incident, but rather because he feels that Treat's "description is applicable to many similar situations in the community."[26] But it is not only through the use of their wealth that the top leaders are able to initiate policies and have them carried through, for there are few if any who have the power to resist top leaders.

> The method of handling the relatively powerless under-structure is through the pressures previously described—warnings, intimidations, threats, and in extreme cases violence. In some cases the method may include isolation from all sources of support for the individual, including his job, and therefore his income. The principle of "divide and rule" is applicable in the community, as it is in larger units of political patterning, and it is effective.[27]

Largely because Hunter concluded that Atlanta was ruled by a small clique of decision-makers who made community policies from behind the scenes and in their own interests, the "reputational method" was identified with conclusions of a "power elite" (to use C. Wright Mills's term). As a result, criticisms of the reputational method have often been criticisms of findings of "power elites."

In fact, however, while the reputational method may tend to discover "power elites" where there are none, it only does so when the researcher himself is predisposed toward finding a "pyramidal power structure." As the pluralist critics of Hunter have pointed out,[28] there is much evidence in his study to indicate that a cohesive group of policy-makers, who wield most of the power in the community and make all the important decisions, simply does not exist.

[25]Ibid, p. 172 (italics mine).
[26]Ibid. p. 170.
[27]Ibid. p. 241.
[28]See, for example, Nelson W. Polsby, *Political Theory*, pp. 115–56.

In the first place, Hunter's particular use of the reputational method which *tended* to indicate a cohesive ruling elite was a result of Hunter's expectations. Hunter asked his 40 leaders selected by his panel of judges, "If a project were before the community that require *decision* by a group of leaders—leaders nearly everyone would accept—which *ten* on the list of forty would you choose?"[29] Assume for the moment that there are different leaders on different issues as the pluralists suggest. While we do not know how the judges or the top leaders interpreted the question, hopefully we would find on the list the top leaders in different "issue-areas." We now have a list of "key influentials." The problem is whether the people named on this list are influential across the board or whether each person on the list is very influential in one area and not at all in other areas. But by asking the general question as Hunter does, he cannot distinguish between the two structures of leadership and, in fact, by artificially combining the names of these people on one list he presents the illusion of a cohesive elite.

In addition to the panel-of-experts method used by Hunter, other reputational researchers have employed the "snowball" or "cobweb" technique—in which a number of individuals selected at random name the leaders who, in their turn, are interviewed and asked for additional names—and the community sampling method.[30] As mentioned above, the most popular panel-of-experts method employs positional analysis as an intervening step.

The reputational approach introduces a new dimension in the study of power. In addition to power as a potential for control and power as control itself, one must now recognize power reputations as a new, distinct class of variables. The relationship among these three variables is by no means clear, although even reputational researchers, such as D'Antonio and Form, call attention to the importance of the distinction.[31] Power as control is usually determined by examining

[29] Hunter, *Community Power Structure* p. 63 (italics Hunter's).

[30] A. Alexander Fanelli, "A Typology of Community Leadership Based on Influence and Interaction Within the Leader Subsystem," *Social Forces*, 34(4) (May 1956), 333; Schulze and Blumberg, "Local Power Elites," p. 292; Robert E. Agger, "Power Attributions in the Local Community." *Social Forces*, 34(4) (May 1956), 322–31.

[31] William V. D'Antonio and William H. Form, *Influentials in Two Border Cities* (Notre Dame, Ind.: University of Notre Dame Press, 1965), pp. 11–12; J. R. Lawrence, "In the Footsteps of Community Power," *American Political Science*

the decision-making process; power as a potential for control may be determined by locating the person in various formal hierarchies; and power reputations are determined by asking judges who they think is powerful. It should be mentioned that most reputational researchers do not consider the reputation itself as the goal of their study, but as an index of power as either potential or actual control. For example, Hunter uses "power" to describe "the acts of men going about the business of moving other men to act in relation to themselves or in relation to organic or inorganic things,"[32] while D'Antonio and Form define it as the ability to control the decision-making process.[33] Thus reputations for power have been employed as indices of both potential and actual behavior, although many of the researchers confuse the indices with the definition of power they give lip service to when it comes to interpreting their findings.

Where reputations are used as an index of actual behavior, critics argue that it is more meaningful to study the behavior itself. Polsby claims that what is being determined by this method is the identity of those persons who have the reputation for being influential. This reputation can be divided into "the part which is justified by behavior and the part which is not so justified."[34] That is, "asking about reputations is asking at a remove about behavior. . . . It can be cogently argued that the researcher should therefore make it his business to

Review, 55 (December 1961), 819–20; Howard J. Ehrlich, "The Reputational Approach to the Study of Community Power," *American Sociological Review*, 26(6), (December 1961), 927; Raymond E. Wolfinger, "Reputation and Reality in the Study of Community Power," *American Sociological Review*, 25 (October 1960), 636.

[32]Hunter, *Community Power Structure*, p. 2.

[33]D'Antonio and Form, *Influentials*, pp. 11–12.

[34]Nelson W. Polsby, "Three Problems in the Analysis of Community Power," *American Sociological Review*, 24 (December 1959), 796–7. "The problem that has always bothered me about the reputational method is its latent circularity . . . How do you know whether they are influentials? What is the test of it? Do you ask of other people whether they are influential, and how do you test the projections of these other people? This could go on *ad infinitum*. I do not see it as an objective test by which we know whether the people who finally get on his list are influential or not. Speaking rigorously, all we could say would be that [we have] a list of people who have reputations for influence—and we could never say anything more than that, for this is actually all we know." Dahl, quoted in Ehrlich, "A Critical Discussion," pp. 101–2; see also M. Herbert Danzger, "Community Power Structure: Problems and Continuities," *American Sociological Review*, 29 (October 1964), p. 707.

study behavior directly and not rely on second-hand opinions."[35] Where, on the other hand, reputations are used as an index of power thought of as a *potential* of control, such potential must be evaluated alongside other bases for potential, such as formal position.

This distinction is seen by Ehrlich as explaining Wolfinger's criticism of the reputational method which calls attention to the fact that those identified as influential by that method often lose out to comparatively un-influential people when they confront each other in the community. Wolfinger, he maintains, is concerned with the exercise of power, while the reputational approach focuses on potential power. Thus he says, "If it can be demonstrated that this power potential, as determined by the reputational method, is indeed exercised, then presumably Wolfinger and those of us equally concerned, would accept the validity of this approach. Without such demonstration, I must concur with him that the reputational approach may be telling us nothing or very little about the objective structure of power and decision-making in the local community."[36] Wolfinger had noted a "troublesome tendency for the 'bigwigs' depicted as the rulers of Seattle, Atlanta, etc., to be defeated by plebeians who never made the reputational hit parade,"[37] and, in a reply to Ehrlich, argues that this cannot be explained by claiming that the method measures potential, not exercised, power. According to Wolfinger, if the reputational method measures potential rather than exercised power, it requires "not merely that the respondents be accurate observers and generalizers, a task that demonstrably is too much for many of them, but that they be such profound students of politics that they can identify the bases of power in the community and the possession of these resources by the townspeople. This assumption is so clearly fallacious that to explicate it is to disprove it."[38] Reputations for power can indeed be said to describe the *perceived* distribution of power in the local community, and depending on the purposes of the study, this

[35]Polsby, "Three Problems," p. 797. "In the study of community power, as in other areas of sociology, the examination of intentions, reputations, and attributions is to be applauded. The interpretations we assign to these 'meanings' must, however, always be modulated and enriched by our knowledge of the behavior which accompanies them." Nelson W. Polsby, "The Sociology of Community Power: A Reassessment," *Social Forces*, 37 (March 1959), 236.

[36]Ehrlich, "The Reputational Approach," 926–7.

[37]Wolfinger, "A Plea for a Decent Burial," pp. 844–5.

[38]Ibid.

may be useful in helping to describe the local power system. If, for example, it can be shown that the way in which the power structure is perceived helps determine the way in which people react to it, reputations for power will definitely provide a useful variable in the study of power. For example, Vidich and Bensman comment on a dominant leader working behind the scenes in a small town called Springdale. All groups and individuals overestimate his authority, but by this very fact they increase his power since they act on the basis of their estimation.[39]

Few reputational researchers would accept the relegation of the technique to this comparatively minor role in community power studies, and fewer still would agree with Agger that it is "simply a heuristic device at this stage of theoretical development."[40] To accept such a view would leave them open for Wolfinger's criticism that their approach is "little more than a methodologically elaborate variant of the older procedure of asking insiders."[41] However, to then charge, as Wolfinger does, that these researchers believe their method to be "a sufficient tool to study the distribution of political power in a community,"[42] would seem too extreme, for reputational studies have increasingly employed positional and decision-making analyses to supplement their descriptions.

One of the basic assumptions of the reputational method seems to be that power is exercised behind the scenes and that it is next to impossible to obtain an accurate picture of the structure of power by attending to overt behavior. Thus the researcher must rely on the inside information supplied to him by a panel of knowledgeable community members: "The 'real' leaders are always held to be 'behind' whoever is revealed as the community leadership as the result of first-hand digging."[43] For example, Hunter describes men of power in Regional City enforcing their decisions "by persuasion, intimidation, coercion, and, if necessary, force. Because of these elements of compulsion, power-wielding is often a hidden process. The men involved do not wish to become identified with the negative aspects which the

39Arthur J. Vidich and Joseph Bensman, *Small Town in Mass Society* (Princeton: Princeton University Press, 1958), p. 277.

40Agger, "Power Attributions," p. 331.

41Wolfinger, "Reputation and Reality," p. 637.

42Ibid. p. 638.

43Nelson W. Polsby, "Three Problems," p. 797.

process implies."[44] Polsby charges that this assumption of covert leadership often leads researchers "to disbelieve their senses, and to substitute unfounded speculation for plain fact."[45] Another reason the top power-holders may not be directly observable stems from the fact that they may not choose to exercise their power because less powerful individuals, who are involved in the decision-making process, will act in accordance with the general interests of the top power-holders. They may become active only when directly challenged.[46] One danger underlying the assumption that power is exercised covertly is what Robert Dahl has referred to as the "fallacy of infinite regression." If observable behavior is not to be regarded as a reliable index of power, then one must search behind the scenes for centers of power behind the actors who carry out the drama on stage. Once these covert power-holders are identified, by whatever method, the question immediately presents itself whether there may not be other covert power-holders behind these, and others yet behind them, and so on. There would seem to be no way to prevent this infinite regression of power to ever more concentrated covert centers. That this problem is a real one is demonstrated by the fact that Hunter, among others, is at times "forced to interject that the votes of the informed informants do not accurately describe the ranking of power in the community because some of the most powerful people prefer not to participate directly in the processes of leadership."[47] If the judgments of community knowledgeables are incorrect, there must be some standard against which they are being measured, and this standard is all too often provided by the judgment of the researchers himself. Many reputational researchers do accept the judgments of their panels, however, and thus are not subject to this particular criticism.

Critics of the reputational approach have also turned their attention to the question of the validity of the entire panel-of-experts method. Polsby calls into doubt the special expertise of such a panel

[44]Hunter, *Community Power Structure*, p. 24; also Robert O. Schulze, "The Role of Economic Dominants in Community Power Structure," *American Sociological Review*, 23 (February 1958), 7.

[45]Nelson W. Polsby, "Power in Middletown: Fact and Value in Community Research," *Canadian Journal of Economics and Political Science*, 26(4) (November 1960), 602–3.

[46]See Danzger's discussion of salience of goals in Chapter II.

[47]Danzger, "Community Power Structure," p. 713.

in uncovering behind-the-scenes power activity. Schulze and Blumberg compared the judgments of three different panels in "Cibola," Michigan, and discovered a high degree of consensus "as to the overall composition of the local elite of power and influence."[48] According to Polsby, this "effectively denies the panel's special knowledge and renders the test for expertise—assuming the unlikely possibility that one could be devised—moot."[49] A diligent observer would not be beyond compiling a comparable list, by more direct methods, of facts that are apparently not as covert as was assumed.

Danzger suggests comparing the results obtained through reputational analysis with those obtained through other techniques to determine the former's validity. If the findings are similar, it is claimed, the reputational method is validated.[50] Schulze and Blumberg report that the power structure they uncovered by the reputational technique differed significantly from that determined by superordinate position in either the economic or political-civic institutions.[51] On the other hand, Linton Freeman and his associates found that in Syracuse the leaders uncovered by the positional and reputational approaches were essentially the same. These leaders "enjoy the reputation for top leadership" and head "the largest and most actively participating business, industrial, governmental, political, professional, educational, labor, and religious organizations. . . . In view of their formal command over the institutional structure and the symbolic value of their status as indexed by reputation, these individuals may be called the Institutional Leaders of Syracuse."[52]

Herein is demonstrated a dilemma faced by the reputational method. If a reputational analysis yields a power structure similar to that revealed by the positional approach, or for that matter any more direct approach, its critics denounce its claim to expert, inside knowledge, for if it appears that power is not exercised covertly, there is thus no need to employ an indirect method of study. If, however, reputational analysis yields a power structure different from anything determined by more direct methods, its critics claim there is no basis for validation. The absence of an acceptable criterion is characteristic

48Schulze and Blumberg, "Local Power Elites" p. 293.
49Polsby, *Political Theory*, pp. 51–2.
50Danzger, "Community Power Structure," pp. 708–9.
51Schulze and Blumberg, "Local Power Elites," pp. 292–3.
52Freeman, *et al.*, "Locating Leaders," p. 797.

of most, if not all, measures of validity, and thus this is not a short-coming peculiar to the present case. Since the reputational technique claims to divulge information that is inaccessible by direct observation or by more direct methods, it should be expected to yield different results. In comparing their results to those obtained by other methods, and by accepting concurrence of results as a validation of their method, reputational researchers have implicitly denied the special competence their method is supposed to possess.

Another criticism directed at the reputational approach concerns the accuracy with which the judges perceive power relations. Even granting the questionable assumption that panels of experts are necessary to uncover hidden power relations, this criticism questions the judges' ability to "report political phenomena accurately."[53] The most vocal critics of power reputation studies—Dahl, Polsby, and Wolfinger—report that their study of New Haven reveals that "eminent citizens often were ill-informed about policy-making situations in which they had been deeply involved."[54] Their general argument is that "some people distort reality, that some who should know what is going on don't, and that others accept gossip as gospel and pass it on as the latter."[55] D'Antonio *et al.* reply that "it is, of course, equally true that some people do not distort reality, that some do indeed know what is going on and that others can discern gossip from gospel."[56] Ehrlich's rebuttal admits that a sole reliance on reputational methods may yield an inaccurate picture of the power structure, but that other means of research are neither logically nor empirically excluded to those who use the reputational approach: "If it is true that those who have used the reputational method have employed it as the sole source of their data, then this may well be a deficiency in their research design but not in the reputational method *per se*."[57] Another charge, that it is impossible to

[53]Wolfinger, "Reputation and Reality," p. 640; Fisher, "Community-Power Studies," pp. 462–4, 466.

[54]Ibid., pp. 842–43; also Wolfinger, "Reputation and Reality," pp. 641–2; Robert A. Dahl, "Equality and Power in American Society," in William V. D'Antonio and Howard J. Ehrlich, (eds.), *Power and Democracy in America* (Notre Dame, Ind.: University of Notre Dame Press, 1961), p. 76.

[55]William V. D'Antonio, Howard J. Ehrlich, and Eugene C. Erickson, "Further Notes on the Study of Community Power," *American Sociological Review*, 27 (December 1962), 849.

[56]Ibid.

[57]Ehrlich, "The Reputational Approach," p. 926.

tell whether or not the respondent and the researcher share the same definition of power, is certainly not peculiar to this method or this area of study, but applies as well to all areas of social research.[58]

Critics have also charged that the "reputational method is particularly susceptible to ambiguity resulting from respondents' confusion of status and power."[59] As mentioned above, a preliminary positional analysis has accompanied many reputational studies. From these lists of position-holders, such as those Hunter compiled of business, government, civic, and society institutions, the judges select community leaders, and through a further process of self-selection, the list is reduced. It seems odd that a method designed to probe beneath the surface of visible power relations should begin with the persons most visible to any observer, and it is from this list that the powerful are to be drawn. The judges are presented with the lists and instructed, by Hunter, for example, to "place in rank order, one through ten, ten persons from each list of personnel—who in your opinion are the most influential persons in the field designated—influential from the point of view of ability to lead others. . . . If there are persons . . . you feel should be included in the ranking order of ten rather than the ones given, please include them."[60] The implication would seem to be that the lists already contained the names of almost all possible influentials, and upon the statements of the judges would depend only their relative ranking. D'Antonio and Form depart from this aspect of Hunter's technique by providing judges with no lists of names, but asking them only to name the persons they thought most influential in certain areas.[61] If those who appear on reputational lists of influentials are chosen from lists of position-holders, it ought to be no shock that positional and reputational analyses often identify the same persons. Although D'Antonio and Form claim that their judges did not automatically call an individual influential because he had an important office, and tended rather to

[58]Ibid.

[59]Wolfinger, "Reputation and Reality," p. 640; Fisher, *et al.*, "Community-Power Studies," pp. 462–4, 466.

[60]Hunter, *Community Power Structure*, p. 256.

[61]D'Antonio and Form, *Influentials*, pp. 256–7. On their return trip to El Paso and Ciudad Juarez, in an attempt to estimate the stability of the list of influentials obtained three years earlier, D'Antonio and Form presented the judges with the earlier list of influentials and instructed them to add or subtract names. No explanation is given for this change in technique, which may have biased the results. See pp. 265–6 of their book.

evaluate performance, expected performance, and resources and their use, they mention elsewhere their focus on the community's leaders who are "the influentials, the men of high position."[62]

Danzger and Rossi independently note the likelihood of reputational judges basing their estimates on formal position or organizational participation, and Wolfinger claims that the difficulty is further compounded by the low esteem in which labor leaders, municipal officials, and local politicians are held, as well as their usually lower socio-economic status, compared to businessmen and leaders of charitable organizations.[63] If reputational studies reveal nothing more than status hierarchies, then their use in measuring power must wait upon the specification of the relationship between status and power.

Another closely related question pertaining to the reputational technique is the variability of power. Lasswell and Kaplan believe that "political phenomena are only obscured by the pseudo-simplification attained with any unitary conception of power as being always and everywhere the same."[64] Power derives from and rests on many different bases, and critics have charged that the reputational approach is concerned with a general category of community power that is unrealistic. Wolfinger and Polsby claim that the technique assumes a person's power to be equal for all issues, whereas, they assert, it may actually vary according to the issue. In addition, a person may be given a high general power ranking because "he is perceived to be very influential on a particular issue which is either currently important to the community or salient to the respondent."[65] Even in accepting the premise that an individual's power varies with the issue, Ehrlich denies that a general power ranking across all issues is misleading, although he is uncertain as to what it would yield.[66] This criticism loses much of its force when reputational studies are able to report findings of restricted as well as general spheres of influence. D'Antonio and Form, for example, report that business and politics were generally perceived to be independent spheres of

[62]Ibid. pp. 127–8, 1.

[63]M. Herbert Danzger, "Community Power Structure," pp. 710–11; Rossi, "Community Decision Making"; Wolfinger, "Reputation and Reality," p. 640.

[64]Harold D. Lasswell and Abraham Kaplan, *Power and Society* (New Haven: Yale University Press, 1950), p. 92.

[65]Wolfinger, "Reputation and Reality," p. 638; Polsby, "Sociology of Community Power," pp. 232–6.

[66]Ehrlich, "The Reputational Approach," p. 926.

influence,[67] and Delbert Miller finds that "relatively stable groups of leaders are identified with certain institutional sectors of the community through which they express common interest."[68] Certainly, critics cannot claim that the reputational approach is logically denied the possibility of uncovering differing scopes and spheres of influence, although the early studies using this approach were deficient in this regard.

A number of points of dispute have arisen over the length and composition of the list of community influentials compiled by reputational studies and the interpretation of the work of Floyd Hunter in particular. Hunter's rather arbitrary decision to limit the size of the list to 40 in order to reduce it to manageable size is unfortunate because it has often given the reader "the sense of a supreme military headquarters in which forty top strategists arrive at a consensus on what is to be done, and of a series of lesser commanders."[69] Wolfinger charges Hunter with assuming what he set out to prove: "that no more than 40 people were the rulers of Atlanta, possessed more power than the rest of the population, and comprised its 'power structure.' "[70] This seems a rather inflated accusation since it is by no means clear exactly what Hunter meant to say. In the most recent publication employing the reputational approach, D'Antonio and Form *assume* that a small number of persons were crucial in decision-making.[71] Both this and Hunter's study depend on the agreement of judges, which to Polsby is no more than statistical artifact, to determine how many top leaders there are.[72] Both studies also report that they did not identify all the influentials and that some persons so identified may not be influential.[73] This leads Polsby to argue that the efficiency and economy of the reputational method are quite beside the point if it becomes necessary to inquire as to the relationship between the reputational list and the real world: "clearly, all of

[67]D'Antonio and Form, *Influentials,* pp. 67–68.

[68]Delbert C. Miller, "Decision-making Cliques in Community Power Structures: A Comparative Study of an American and an English City," *American Journal of Sociology,* 64 (November 1958), 306; also Agger, "Power Attributions," p. 323.

[69]Herbert Kaufman and Victor Jones, "The Mystery of Power," *Public Administration Quarterly,* 14 (Summer 1954), 205–12.

[70]Wolfinger, "Reputational and Reality," pp. 642–3; also Polsby, *Political Theory,* p. 49.

[71]D'Antonio and Form, *Influentials,* pp. 58–9.

[72]Polsby, *Political Theory,* p. 49.

[73]Hunter, *Community Power Structure,* p. 61; D'Antonio and Form, *Influentials,* pp. 242–3.

the principal actors in specified community decisions will have to be on the lists."[74] D'Antonio and his colleagues disagree, stating that the necessity of having an exhaustive list depends on the use to be made of it. If, for example, the purpose is to measure perceived power or to determine public opinion on a community issue, the exhaustiveness of the list is irrelevant. However, they concur with Polsby that the list itself tells very little, is meant to be only the starting point of the study, and is meant to reveal only a part of the power structure.[75] These researchers—who started by using the reputational method much as Hunter did—finished their last work by coming close to accepting a severely restricted range of application for the reputational method, and subjecting it to the charge that it is nothing more than a report of public opinion on politics.

Another example of the dispute over the nature of power is revealed by Polsby's charge that the names on D'Antonio and Erickson's list of influentials bear rather a fortuitous relationship to the actual exercise of power. The influentials opposed one another on a variety of issues, often bitterly, and there were always influentials on the losing side in a conflict. D'Antonio finds the accusation unwarranted by observing that 23 of 25 key influentials on the list were actually involved in the decision-making process. Exercise of influence for Polsby seems to be actual realization of will in a conflict over a community issue, while for D'Antonio it involves rather participation in the determination of a community decision with an opportunity to realize one's will. Robert Dahl consents to referring to those who appear on the reputation lists as "influentials," but wishes to reserve the term "dominants" for the victors in a conflict.[76]

[74]Nelson W. Polsby, "Community Power: Some Reflections on the Recent Literature," *American Sociological Review*, 27 (December 1962), 838–9. "It has been pointed many times that such a list, even if it is exhaustive and accurate, does not tell us all we need to know in order to make a description of the ways in which community decisions get made. Further, the steps which must be taken to ensure the exhaustiveness and accuracy of such a list render the list itself superfluous. Worse yet, the time and effort associated with putting together a list of this kind directs the attention of researchers away from the problems of describing the political order and toward certifying the list's adequacy. In any event, the question of the adequacy of the list seems to come first."

[75]D'Antonio, *et al.*, "Further Notes," p. 851.

[76]Dahl, quoted in Ehrlich, "A Critical Discussion," p. 110; see discussion of Danzger's distinction between power and dominance above. See also Wolfinger, "A Plea for a Decent Burial," p. 843; For the exchange between Polsby and D'Antonio see Polsby, "Some Reflections," p. 839; and D'Antonio, *et al.*, "Further Notes," p. 851.

D'Antonio and his associates also reply to a further charge by Wolfinger that reputational researchers rarely ask for respondents' perceptions of specific events and prefer not to probe past their general attitudes toward power. Even Hunter's original study examined certain specific issues.[77] Commenting on Hunter's treatment of issues, Rossi states that "the range of issues with which the power structure concerns itself is delimited by example," and since the total set of issues is unspecified, "the impact of the power structure on the life of the community is hard to assess."[78] Polsby also claims that Hunter's choice of issues is extremely biased and based more upon a desire to confirm his theory than on any objective measure.[79] Later, it will be shown that Polsby and others that advocate a decision-making approach face the very same criticism in attempting to provide an objective basis for a choice as to which community decisions to examine.

Much has been written concerning Floyd Hunter's conclusions about the power structure of Regional City. Rarely do two interpreters agree as to exactly what Hunter meant to say. Perhaps the simplest statement of Hunter's conclusions can be found in his own words.

> The top group of the power hierarchy has been isolated and defined as comprised of policy makers. These men are drawn largely from the businessmen's class in Regional City. They form cliques or crowds, as the term is more often used in the community, which formulate policy. Committees for formulation of policy are commonplace, and on community-wide issues policy is channeled by a "fluid committee structure" down to institutional, associational groupings through a lower-level bureaucracy which executes policy.[80]

Hunter presents data that repeatedly emphasize the close relations that hold among those in the top power group, and it is not without reason that many who have read *Community Power Structure* find merit in Herson's statement that "Hunter unveils a structure of community power that is essentially pyramidal, economic, and—given

[77]D'Antonio, *et al.*, pp. 850–51.
[78]Rossi, "Community Decision Making," p. 429.
[79]Polsby, *Political Theory*, p. 54.
[80]Hunter, *Community Power Structure*, p. 111.

the consensus, interaction, and almost total control at the top—monolithic."[81] Hunter explicitly denied presenting anything more than a rudimentary power pyramid: "I doubt seriously that power forms a single pyramid with any nicety in a community the size of the Regional City. There are *pyramids* of power in this community which seem more important to the present discussion than *a* pyramid."[82] Nevertheless, the picture that time and again emerges from Hunter's descriptions is strikingly similar to Herson's characterization. Lane provides an excellent summary of Hunter's most telling "findings:"[83]

> The techniques whereby these dominant families control the political life of the community are intricate and varied. By their leverage over the economic institutions of the community, they can exercise sanctions over many of the civic leaders and professional people in town; they can intimidate workers through the control over their jobs; they control the credit institutions of the community and can influence such matters as admission to a hospital or a mortgage on a house; they generally control the local press and radio; they subsidize the party (or parties) of their choice and hence influence their selection of candidates. . . .
>
> The political organizations are so completely dominated by the power interests (i.e. business elite) . . . that there is little hope of adequate expression being fostered by them at this time.
>
> They control admission to the prestige associations and clubs; they set the patterns of approved behavior and opinion. . . .
> Hunter speaks of the great "silence found in the mass of the citizenry of Regional City."

Some studies following Hunter's method have found a similar condition of monolithic business dominance in the power structure,[84]

---

[81]Lawrence J. R. Herson, "In the Footsteps of Community Power," *American Political Science Review*, 55 (December 1961), 820; see also Delbert C. Miller, "Decision-Making Cliques in Community Power Structures: A Comparative Study of An American and An English City," *American Journal of Sociology*, 64 (November 1958), pp. 299, 307–9. Hunter's findings are directly contradicted in a later study of Atlanta—the city he studied—by M. Kent Jennings: *Community Influentials: The Elites of Atlanta* (New York: Free Press, 1964).

[82]Hunter, *Community Power Structure*, p. 62 (italics Hunter's).

[83]Robert E. Lane, *Political Life* (Glencoe, Ill.: Free Press, 1959), pp. 257–8.

[84]Orrin E. Klapp and L. Vincent Padgett, "Power Structure and Decision-Making in a Mexican Border City," *American Journal of Sociology*, 65(4) (January 1960),

while D'Antonio and Form and Miller suggest a continuum of power structures ranging from a highly stratified business-dominated pyramid to a "ring of institutional representatives functioning in relatively independent roles."[85] The role of the business community will be discussed in more detail later.

Of an even more controversial nature is the question of the relative solidarity and uniqueness of purpose of the top power group, i.e. whether or not it is legitimate to call this group an elite. The term "elite" has been used often throughout the literature on community power and with hardly more precision than in the case of "power." Perhaps the most commonly used meaning is that of a group of persons at the top of the hierarchy. A definition so general and all-inclusive loses a great deal of utility, and some authors have found it necessary to redefine and delimit the term. A more complete discussion follows in a section devoted exclusively to it, but the present topic requires at least a short explanation. Polsby's definition of an elite is a group of persons, always less than a majority, selected by other than majority vote, standing at the apex of the pyramid of community power, and exercising influence over a wide range of community issues.[86] The question becomes, in this context, to what extent have reputational studies revealed the existence of a "power elite" in American communities. It has already been mentioned that although Hunter qualifiedly disavows parts of the definition and nowhere specifically mentions a power elite, many scholars who have read his work have been left with the impression that a power elite was what he meant to imply.

A closely related issue is whether the use of the reputational method necessarily implies the existence of some type of power elite. Polsby asserts that the question reputational researchers put to their informants, essentially, "Who runs this community?" is somewhat like "Have you stopped beating your wife?" in that "virtually any response short of total unwillingness to answer will supply the re-

---

401–2; Schulze and Blumberg, "Local Power Elites," p. 293; Rossi ("Community Decision Making," pp. 429–30) comments that influence based on economic strength is especially effective in certain circumstances, for example on civic associations dependent on voluntary financial contributions.

[85] D'Antonio and Form, *Influentials*, pp. 222–3; Miller, "Decision-Making Cliques," p. 310.

[86] Polsby, *Political Theory*, p. 10.

searcher with a 'power elite' along the lines presupposed" by his theory.[87] D'Antonio, *et al.,* reply that if such were the case, the reputational literature ought be "replete with depictions of American communities as controlled by small, solidary elites."[88] They find, rather, a variety of community power structures suggested by the literature. In rebuttal, Polsby maintains that he, Wolfinger, and Dahl have urged that all matters of existence, shape, durability, and inclusiveness of a community power structure be regarded as empirical questions not subject to *a priori* settlement by definition and denies that he has asserted "that there is a logical relationship between this tendency, a tendency to use the reputational method, and a tendency to discover a power elite."[89] Polsby further remarks that he and his colleagues do not deny the power-elite hypothesis in the abstract, but that their evidence for New Haven contradicts it: "We have, in fact, argued that there is scant evidence to support a conclusion that American communities are run by power elites, and some evidence which tends to refute this conclusion."[90]

Findings from other reputational studies are inconclusive and conflicting as to whether anything approaching an elite is characteristic of the power structure. Schulze and Blumberg, although not mentioning the term "elite," report that their leadership group constituted a "closely knit friendship group with exercised substantial—if not always decisive—control over the community's decisions,"[91] while D'Antonio and Form report that "in a dynamic metropolitan American community, there is little probability that a single co-ordinated power elite controls all the decisions in the community," and their data for El Paso and Ciudad Juarez fail to document the existence of a solidary, unified influence system.[92] Evidently, whether or not Polsby can be said to have made the statement, the use of the reputational technique does not necessarily predispose the researcher to find a power elite.

Two other specific criticisms of the reputational technique made primarily by Wolfinger ought to be mentioned. The charge has been

[87] Ibid. p. 113.
[88] D'Antonio, *et al.,* "Further Notes," pp. 852–3.
[89] Polsby, "Some Reflections," pp. 838–41.
[90] Ibid. p. 841.
[91] Schulze and Blumberg, "Local Power Elites," p. 296.
[92] D'Antonio, and Form, *Influentials,* pp. 222–3, 128–9.

made that the reputational approach assumes and reports a static distribution of power: "Shifting distribution of power, whether the result of elections or of other factors, presents a problem in political analysis which appears to be unsolvable by the power-attribution method."[93] From the different descriptions of power structures that have emerged, this criticism would seem to apply only to specific instances in which the method was employed and thus would not be characteristic of the method itself. For example, Miller, as cited above, envisions a structure into which power holders from different institutional sectors enter and from which they exit according to the issue involved.[94] Elsewhere, Wolfinger charges that Hunter's decision to carry out a "separate (but not equal) study of the Negro subcommunity," results in a picture of segregated power structures whereas recent news reports clearly indicate that "Atlanta Negroes are neither powerless nor isolated from the city's political life."[95] D'Antonio, et al., point out that Hunter's research was carried out from 1951 to 1953, and the Supreme Court school desegregation decision—"which was undoubtedly the springboard for recent Negro protest activities—was not delivered until May 1954."[96] In spite of this, however, his defenders are unable to explain why Hunter virtually ignored the fact that the power holders repeatedly were forced to bargain with other elements in the city, the Negro population included.

The most attractive qualities of the reputational approach are its transportability and its economy of operation: "Like Henry Ford, Floyd Hunter has found the secret of mass production, and today's builder of community power models no longer need build each model over an attentuated time period, beginning labor with a refining of raw materials."[97] Herson feels that an ultimate conclusion as to the merits of reputational studies is, at present, not easily reached: "The power data now being accumulated by Hunter's method ought

[93] Wolfinger, "Reputation and Reality," p. 644.

[94] Hunter also says that "the personnel of the pyramid would change depending upon what needs to be done at a particular time" (p. 66). However, he does seem to imply, as do others who use this approach, that the structure, in this case a pyramid, is relatively fixed.

[95] Wolfinger, "A Plea for a Decent Burial," p. 844.

[96] D'Antonio, et al., "Further Notes," p. 850.

[97] Herson, "In the Footsteps of Community Power," pp. 821, 818–19.

be viewed as a mound of smelter's ore, offering promise of further refinement and use."[98] Wolfinger's evaluation, as might be expected, is less favorable: "Ten years have passed since Floyd Hunter wrote *Community Power Structure*. In this time neither Hunter nor any of his legion of champions and imitators has produced a validation of the reputational method, while its critics have piled up a mass of refutations. We would do well to bury the reputational method and go on to more valid research techniques and more meaningful questions."[99] Those who continue to employ the reputational approach are convinced that questions on methodology are legitimate and that there is no doubt that more needs to be known about the precision, stability, and congruence of the research operations of power studies. However, they claim "the evidence is not yet in. Neither Wolfinger nor Polsby has provided sufficient evidence to warrant Mr. Wolfinger's necrology."[100]

The third approach to the study of community power to be examined here is the *decision-making process* or *issue-analysis* approach. It eschews both position and reputation as effective means of ascertaining the power structure or generalizing about power, and stresses the actual determination of community decisions and the persons involved in making them: "The process of decision-making is recognized as the nucleus of the phenomenon of power and it is this process that is the object of research."[101] Participation in community decisions is not to be equated with power, but the researcher must, rather, weigh the activities of different participants in decisions and then, by means of an operational definition, appraise their relative power. Dahl considers this operationalism, however crude it may be, as the method's greatest advantage, and other researchers have commented on its effectiveness in representing the realities of community power.[102] Although the reputational approach has received a considerable amount of attention and criticism, the decision-making

---

98Ibid. p. 825.

99Wolfinger, "A Plea for a Decent Burial," p. 847; see also Polsby, *Political Theory*, p. 56; Kaufman and Jones, "The Mystery of Power," p. 208.

100D'Antonio, *et al.*, "Further Notes," p. 849; Ehrlich, "The Reputational Approach," p. 927.

101Fisher, "Community-Power Studies," pp. 452–3. Also Rossi, "Community Decision Making," p. 425; and Dahl, *Analysis*, pp. 52–3.

102Dahl, *Analysis*, p. 53; Fisher, "Community-Power Studies," p. 454; Freeman, *et al.*, "Locating Leaders," pp. 792–3.

approach has received comparatively little of either.[103] Among the
more serious difficulties in its application would seem to be its complexity and the resultant necessity of severely limiting the number
and range of issues studied, the exclusion of the researcher from
spontaneous and private discussions concerning power, and the determination of criteria by which decisions are to be chosen for examination.

D'Antonio and Form have pointed out that there is no way to
know whether all important issues become publicized enough for the
researcher to become sufficiently aware of them. In a similar vein,
Fisher suggests that the decision-making process is only one of a
complex, interwoven set of community processes, and that to fully
understand one process requires knowledge of the others. Even if it
were possible to identify most important issues and to become sufficiently acquainted with the process of resolving them, there would
remain the problem of choosing which of the universe of important
decisions are typical, and thus those whose examination would provide a valid basis for generalization to the decision-making process
in general.[104] Dahl believes it impossible to specify the universe of
issues in a community with any great degree of exactness. He suggests selecting sectors of issues, the question of whose importance
would arouse little dissent, and sampling issues from these sectors.
Since it is difficult to know what a representative sample would mean
here, "all that can really be said at the end of the research is that in
these sectors this is the pattern of influence found."[105] However,
unless the issues chosen from a particular sector can be shown to be
representative of that sector, there may be scant evidence for claiming even as much as Dahl does.[106] Dahl continues by saying that it

103D'Antonio, et al., "Further Notes," p. 853.

104Ibid.; D'Antonio and Form, Influentials, p. 131; Fisher, "Community-Power
Studies," p. 454. "The field studies of most complicated decisions have not been very
valuable. The very complexity and apparent uniqueness of the processes they have
unveiled makes generalization going beyond the specific issues studied very hazardous"
(Rossi, "Community Decision Making," p. 436).

105Dahl, quoted in Ehrlich, "A Critical Discussion," p. 105.

106Dahl claims that "once the sector to be examined has been selected, it is
no longer so difficult to choose the specific issues or decisions in a somewhat non-
arbitrary but not entirely defensible way." (Ibid. p. 106.) There has yet to be
devised a method for choosing decisions in much more than an arbitrary manner,
even if the sector has already been determined.

matters little what specific issues are chosen as long as three or four different sectors are concentrated on in order to determine whether or not influence is specialized in relation to different sectors. If this pattern of specialization can be shown to exist, "at least it becomes clear, if nothing else is known, that there isn't a single homogeneous power elite."[107] Delbert Miller charges that no real pattern emerges in decision-making studies because the usual technique has been to examine "given issues that are currently running," which "only takes a little slice out of the power-structure; . . . the only way to get a pattern for a community is to watch a whole series of issues, which takes a very long time," and which no researcher who takes this approach, according to Miller, has yet accomplished.[108] Miller is concerned that "Professor Dahl may be deceived by a spatter of non-salient issues which cannot display the true structure of community power."[109] In fact, however, Linton Freeman and his associates have studied decision-making in 39 issues, carefully selected from a comprehensive list of 250 issues, in Syracuse over a five-year period.[110]

Freeman and his associates have called attention to the fact that the decision-making method often includes individuals who, although present when a decision is made, had little or no impact on the decision. However, "this seems preferable to the likelihood of excluding important influentials."[111] In view of this consideration, as in the case of the reputational technique, the question must be put to the proponents of the decision-making method as to what exactly is the relationship between the list of influentials they provide and the actual wielding of power as they define it.

Perhaps a more fundamental criticism of the decision-making or issues-analysis method is that it selects *controversial* issues or sources of data from which the power of participating groups is to be inferred. It thus ignores the "settled," "institutional," or "noncontroversial" exercises of power, in which it is more than likely that dominant

---

107Ibid.; also Polsby, "A Reassessment," p. 233.
108Miller, quoted in Ehrlich, "A Critical Discussion," pp. 100–101.
109Ibid., pp. 106–7.
110Linton C. Freeman, Warner Bloomberg, Jr., Stephen P. Koff, Morris H. Sunshine, and Thomas J. Fararo, *Local Community Leadership* (Syracuse, N.Y.: Syracuse University College, 1960).
111Freeman, *et al.,* "Locating Leaders," pp. 792–3.

groups have their way without opposition, because no weaker group finds it worthwhile to make an issue when the strong likelihood is that it will lose. Sometimes, of course, noncontroversial decisions reflect real consensus throughout the community, and occasionally they reflect a preponderance of public opinion which no special interest group finds it practical to oppose. But possibly more often, such noncontroversial decisions reflect the community's acquiescence in the strategically planned decisions taken by some powerful groups, at least temporarily cohesive among themselves. This does not say, of course, that the powerful groups are always the economic elite, the top businessmen; they may on occasion be the labor unions, the government administration, a coalition of other "experts," the combined clergy of the community. In any case, there is no "issue"; a policy decision is announced to the public and there is no negative reaction; and there is no contest of forces for the decision-making investigator to investigate. At the extreme, this situation was probably common in the old-fashioned "company town" once ruled by a single business, but the elitist and monolithic character of power in this situation would not be caught by the issues-analyst if he consistently employed his method. More typically, the situation was regularly reflected, until the past five years, in the uncontested relegation of Negroes to subordinate positions in the community; a coalition of white people—often a minority of the total population in Southern communities—were the power elite in this case.

B. Theoretical and Substantive Issues

The methodological issues in the study of local community power shade over into theoretical and substantive issues. Polsby feels that those who use the reputational method implicitly confuse power with social status, and adopt a "stratification theory" of power.[112] He reviews a host of community power studies which he feels explicitly or implicitly subscribe to the stratification theory. The five main assertions of the stratification theory are: (1) the upper class rules in local community life; (2) political and civic leaders are subordinate to the upper class; (3) a single "power elite" rules in the community; (4) the upper-class power elite rules in its own interests; and

[112]Polsby, *Political Theory*.

(5) social conflict takes place between the upper and lower classes.[113] Polsby isolates three weaknesses in these studies which lead to failure to test these propositions empirically. There is, first of all, a tendency to identify, by definition, economic or status elites with power elites. This is a consequence of defining power as the capacity to realize one's will, even over objections, which signifies the stratification writers' "attempt to find some relatively unambiguous set of resources which unfailingly index the capacity successfully."[114] Secondly, there is a tendency to interview mainly businessmen, which is understandable in the light of the expectations of the theory, but is incomprehensive as a device for testing those expectations. Finally, there is the habit of never specifying issues which makes tests of accuracy of responses difficult, if not impossible.[115] Polsby also charges that since the data reported by these studies often contradict the posited hypotheses, the authors are forced to try to save stratification theory by certain after-the-fact explanations. Among these are: the and-also argument, which suggests that occasions on which the theory's expectations are not met are trivial or irrelevant; the lump-of-power assumption, which asserts that power cannnot be exercised by any person or group not defined as being at the top of the status or economic hierarchy; the assumption of covertness, which allows researchers to maintain that behind the scenes things are exactly the opposite of what they appear to be; the balance-of-power assumption, which asserts that an apparently powerless economic elite is "really" powerful because of its strategic position among community groups; and the power-potential allegation, which holds that the economic or status elite could determine community decisions if it so desired, and only refrains from lack of interest.[116] Polsby feels that none of the so-called stratification studies have confirmed any of the five basic propositions and that they were also rejected in his own research in New Haven, where he attempted to avoid the pitfalls of the previous works.

113Polsby, *Political Theory*, pp. 10–11. The studies he reviews are the Lynds's *Middletown* and *Middletown in Transition*; W. L. Warner's *Yankee City* series, and *Democracy in Jonesville*; A. B. Hollingshead's *Elmtown's Youth*; Digby Baltzell's *Philadelphia Gentlemen*; Hunter's *Community Power Structure*; Pellegrin and Coates's study of Bigtown; Schulze's study of Cibola; and Miller's study of Pacific city.
114Ibid. pp. 108–9.
115Ibid. p. 68.
116Ibid. pp. 67–8.

D'Antonio agrees that the evidence compiled is overwhelmingly against the stratification theory as Polsby defines it, and that a number of researchers have been caught in contradiction.[117] However, according to D'Antonio, the stratification theory is better regarded as a product of Polsby's imagination than a theory logically derived from at least the majority of the studies, which were largely empirical in nature without any well-formulated theory behind them: "Indeed, if the authors began their studies with such well-formulated propositions as Polsby implies must have been the case, and if his proposition is correct that this approach 'encourages research designs which generate self-fulfilling prophecies,' then it is hard to explain how these same researchers were able to come up with so much contradictory data—which they faithfully report in their studies!"

Polsby follows his attack with prescriptions for the study of community power that he labels the pluralist theory, and with which he and Robert A. Dahl have become identified. Pluralism is a theory of the power structure in which power is conceived of as dispersed, and different elites are dominant in different issue-areas. The decision-making methods of research is congenial to the pluralist theory. The researcher is to choose issue-areas as the focus of study and should be able to defend his choice of issue-areas as occupying an important place in the life of the community. Furthermore, he ought to study actual behavior, either at first hand or by reconstructing behavior from newspapers, informants, documents, and other sources. Information about reputations, intentions, or evaluations of actors or issues is of immeasurable value in tracing patterns of decision-making. These must always, however, be accompanied by information concerning actual behavior so that the researcher may distinguish fact from myth. The harm in starting with a list of reputed influential persons is in attributing decisive and final significance to the list. Researchers ought to concentrate on the outcome of actual decisions within the community. There is no need and indeed great danger in assuming prematurely that intentions plus resources inflexibly predetermine outcomes.[118] D'Antonio and his associates have protested

117William V. D'Antonio, review of Polsby's *Community Power and Political Theory, in Social Forces,* 42 (March 1964), 375–6.

118Polsby, *Political Theory,* pp. 120–21, 69–70; Nelson W. Polsby, "How to Study Community Power: The Pluralist Alternative," *Journal of Politics,* 22(3) (August 1960), 483–4. See also Freeman, *et al., Local Community Leadership,* p. 792; D'Antonio and Form, *Influentials,* pp. 89–90.

the identification of "pluralism" with the issue-analysis or decision-making approach, and its special restriction to the work of political scientists. They claim that there are enough conceptual problems in this area without "taking on this unnecessary and unwarranted kind of ideological baggage."[119]

The first and most basic assumption of the pluralist approach is that nothing categorical can be assumed about power in any community. It rejects the assumption of the stratification thesis that some person or group necessarily dominates the community. Rather there is, if anything, an "unspoken notion among pluralist researchers that at bottom *nobody* dominates in a town."[120] This statement has led D'Antonio to charge Polsby with predetermining his results, i.e. of using the self-fulfilling prophecy, a charge which Polsby had earlier leveled against all previous research using the reputational method.[121] In contrast to the cataloguing of power bases by stratification theorists, pluralists concentrate on the power process itself. This emphasis leads to two discoveries: (1) there are many more resources than stratification theory takes into account which may be put to use in community decision-making; and (2) resources are employed with greater or less skill. By concentrating on leadership roles, rather than on an actor's ranking within a system presumed to operate hierarchically, pluralists are able to determine the extent to which a power structure exists. Rulership is often found to be characterized by (1) a wide sharing of power among leaders specialized with regard to issue-area; (2) constraints and conditions imposed on decision-making by elites and non-elites themselves, as well as by impersonal outside forces; and (3) uncertainty about the distribution of payoffs in political actions.[122] Because of the expense involved, only a few issue-areas are studied, but as long as these are different, there is usually enough evidence to confirm the pluralist view that "power

119D'Antonio, *et al.*, "Further Notes," pp. 853–4. "On the operational level, even if, in some hypothetical community, all issues called forth different sectors of the community and there was no overlap in personnel in the different issue areas, the conclusion that this was a 'pluralistic' power structure would still be unwarranted. If all the decision-makers shared the same values, then there would be no pluralism at all. Or, if some sectors of the community were never represented in the decision-making councils, we would have, at best, a most limited form of pluralism."

120Polsby, *Political Theory*, p. 113.

121D'Antonio, "Review," p. 376.

122Polsby, *Political Theory*, pp. 119–20, 118–19, 136; Polsby, "The Pluralist Alternative," pp. 482–83.

may be tied to issues," and that "issues can be fleeting or persistent, provoking coalitions among interested groups and citizens ranging in their duration from momentary to semi-permanent." However, the presumption that the existence of a general power elite is improbable does not prevent the uncovering of one.[123] Finally, the presumption that human behavior is governed in large part by inertia leads pluralist researchers to look upon overt activity as a more valid indication of involvement in community decision-making than reputation for leadership.[124] Among the many community power studies discovering a pluralist distribution of power are Dahl's in New Haven,[125] Rossi and Dentler's in Chicago,[126] Banfield's in Chicago,[127] Martin's and his associates in Syracuse,[128] Freeman's and his associates in Syracuse,[129] and Long's in Boston.[130] Perhaps the most comprehensive study is that of Freeman and his associates, who discover no less than nineteen leadership groups active in the thirty-nine issues studied.

The final set of issues to be discussed concerns the men of power themselves, the relations among them, and the legitimacy of their claim to power. Much of the work done in this area has been motivated by a desire to discover the extent to which political realities conform to the popular picture of democracy in American communities. Hunter, for example, claims that there is a line of communication between the governors and the governed—"the situation does not square with the concepts of democracy we have been taught to revere."[131] Bell also has commented on the fact that often even the "interested public feels trapped by an inability to affect community decisions."[132]

The question of democracy turns on the degree of accountability

[123]Ibid. pp. 113–16.

[124]Ibid. pp. 116–17; Polsby, "The Pluralist Alternative," pp. 474–84.

[125]Robert A. Dahl, *Who Governs?* (New Haven: Yale University, 1961).

[126]Peter H. Rossi and Robert A. Dentler, *The Politics of Urban Renewal* (Glencoe, Ill.: Free Press, 1961).

[127]Edward C. Banfield, *Political Influence* (Glencoe, Ill.: Free Press, 1961).

[128]Roscoe C. Martin, *et al., Decisions in Syracuse* (Bloomington, Ind.: Indiana University Press, 1961).

[129]Linton Freeman, *et al., Local Community Leadership.*

[130]Norton Long, "The Local Community as an Ecology of Games," *American Journal of Sociology*, 64 (November 1959), 251–61.

[131]Hunter, *Community Power Structure*, p. 1.

[132]Daniel Bell, "Is There a Ruling Class in America? The Power Elite Reconsidered," in his *The End of Ideology*, (New York: Collier Books, 1962), p. 70.

of governors to the governed rather than on the relative number of leaders or decision-makers; "the discovery that in all large scale societies (and in local communities) the decisions at any given time are typically in the hands of a small number of people affirms a basic fact . . . : government is always government by the few, whether in the name of the few, the one, or the many. . . . A society may be democratic and express itself through a small leadership."[133] The structure of the influence system and the relationship among its component parts, then, is what is to be explained. Nelson Polsby has at times objected to terming the influence system a "structure" because of two inconvenient connotative meanings of the word: that power and the status or class structure of the community are linked in a certain way, and that the power distributions which prevail at the time of the study are so immutable as to be referred to as "structural properties of the community's social life, that is, permanently fixed in some sense." Such faulty meanings appear as basic premises in many sociological studies of community power, according to Polsby, and ought better be regarded as empirical issues to be ascertained in each case.[134] Therefore, he proposes to define a community power structure as "an inventory of leaders classified according to the numbers and kinds of decisions they make, or an inventory of policy-areas classified according to the ways in which policy outcomes are achieved."[135] Such a definition can be seen to be an immediate consequence of Polsby's pluralistic conception of power and the assumptions he makes in dealing with it, both of which were examined earlier.

Robert Dahl has attempted to deal with the distribution of political resources that helps determine the distribution and structure of influence in a political system. For Dahl, a political resource is "a means by which one person can influence the behavior of other persons."[136] There are four basic reasons why political resources are unevenly distributed in the community: (1) some specialization of function (division of labor) in all societies creates different degrees of access to different political resources; (2) inherited differences,

133Lasswell, Lerner, and Rothwell, *Study of Elites,* p. 7.
134Polsby, *Political Theory,* p. 97; and Polsby, "A Reassessment," p. 232.
135Polsby, "Three Problems," p. 800.
136Dahl, *Analysis,* p. 15.

both biological and social, assure differential access to resources; (3) inherited differences in combination with differences in experience produce differences in incentives and goals, which in turn lead to differences in skills and resources; (4) differences in incentives and goals are usually regarded as socially beneficial because it is necessary to equip individuals for different specialties.[137] He cautions that to point out inequalities in the distribution of political influence is not to imply that any particular distribution, the most common example involving a "power elite," is characteristic. Our political systems exhibit characteristics of both democracy and oligarchy. The tendency toward oligarchy is inhibited by the extent to which these inequalities are dispersed rather than cumulative, by the fact that one type of resource is intrinsically no more significant than any other type, by the competitive elections which ensure that elected officials attempt to shape their overt and covert policies to the satisfaction of the electorate, and by the extent to which individuals or groups who are at a disadvantage can employ resources at a high level, develop a high degree of political skill, and combine their individually less powerful resources so that the aggregate is formidable. Almost any person or group has access to some resources which it can exploit to gain influence.[138] Dahl suggests, as does his colleague Polsby, that disillusion with the realities of the American political system has led many investigators to expect that there must be a monolithic structure of some kind, one often run by the evil elements in the community. If one looks for and examines only the evidence that points to a monolith, one is almost surely to find it. Dahl believes that in most American communities there is no single center of power, that, in fact, "there is even a sense in which *nobody* runs the community . . . perhaps this is the most distressing discovery of all: typically a community is run by many different people, in many different ways, at many different times."[139]

Despite the fears of Dahl and Polsby, and despite Herson's charge that sociologists have been slow to exploit the opportunity for formulating a range of structures,[140] D'Antonio and Form state that most

137Ibid. pp. 15–17; and Dahl, "Equality and Power," p. 79.
138Dahl, "Equality and Power," pp. 80, 83–4, 88–9.
139Ibid. p. 75.
140Herson, "In the Footsteps of Community Power," p. 826.

political sociologists feel that current research reveals the presence of many models varying from the "one-man rule to a situation where there is a high degree of fragmentation of power, with no single person or group in control of community decisions."[141] They feel it is possible to envision an evolutionary development in the structure of decision-making as communities move away from patterns of landed aristocracy to industrialization. This development may often be in restructuring community power toward more pluralistic patterns.[142] Peter Rossi distinguishes four types of community power structure, depending on "the kind of political life to be found" in the given community: pyramidal, caucus rule, polylith, and amorphous.[143] He hypothesizes: "In communities with partisan electoral procedures, whose officials are full time functionaries, where party lines tend to coincide with class and status lines and where the party favored by the lower class and status groups has some good chance of getting elected to office, community power structures tend to be polylithic rather than monolithic." Another sociologist, Delbert Miller, identifies five different power-models which range from a pyramidal or family aristocracy, a business-class-dominated clique structure, and an institutional ring or cone where institutional representatives function in relatively independent roles, to a system of segmented power pyramids, such as that represented by the organization of powerful political blocks.[144]

As the literature suggests a variety of power-models in a wide assortment of communities, Herson sees a possibility of creating two typological sets: one for representing the range of power types, and the other for the range of community structures. "Like scales imprinted on a slide rule, these typological sets may then be matched and manipulated and their [putative] relationships hypothesized. . . .

[141]D'Antonio and Form, *Influentials*, p. 89; see also pp. 229–30.
[142]Ibid. pp. 230–31.
[143]Peter H. Rossi, "Power and Community Structure," *Midwest Journal of Political Science*, 4 (November 1960), pp. 390–401, at 394, 398, 399.
[144]Miller, "Democracy and Decision-Making," pp. 63–8; also Fisher, "Community-Power Studies," pp. 458–9. Barth states that "community influence systems vary in their shape from those which are highly integrated and peaked to those with virtually no structure of influence" (Ernest A. T. Barth, "Community Influence Systems: Structure and Change," *Social Forces*, 40 (October 1961), 63). Polsby, among others, has criticized Barth's findings as applying only to a certain type of structure, that of a pyramid. Polsby, *Political Theory*, pp. 62, 66; Polsby, "A Reassessment," p. 234.

And if present data be insufficient to support the supposed relationships, then additional data can be sought and gathered."[145] Those characteristics of the community that have been suggested as determining the type of power structure it exhibits are: the degree of stability in community life, the orientation of community leaders, the community's economic foundations, the relations between the community and other political systems, and dynamics of population growth.[146]

The type of structure that has received the most attention is the pyramid. Although nothing inherent in the "geometry of power" restricts it to a pyramid, it is the most common of the models depicted in the literature. The pyramidal structure consists primarily of "a few persons with disproportionate power at the top, and persons with little or no power at the bottom."[147] Hunter saw the power structure of Regional City as a pyramid: A basic distinction was drawn between the upper structure of power leaders, the under structure of professional personnel, and the broad base of ordinary people. Despite Hunter's attempts to qualify his descriptions, the picture that emerges is one of a business-dominated power structure that directs and controls most of the affairs of the community. Critics have pointed to many instances in which the facts Hunter himself cites question the autonomy of the top power group and the shape of the structure. The role of the alleged decision-makers is limited to the "relatively innocuous task of getting consent." They rarely appeared as leaders of community organizations or executors of policy. These tasks were supposedly delegated downward to those in the understructure. The effectiveness of the leaders did not depend on the initiation of policy, for Hunter states that policy was initiated more often for than by them. They also kept a close watch for what would and would not "go."[148] Kaufman and Jones suggest that, rather than leading the community, these leaders appear to be "*following* a ground-swell of public opinion."[149] They also call attention to Hun-

145Herson, "In the Footsteps of Community Power," p. 827.
146Fisher, "Community-Power Studies," pp. 460–61; Barth, "Community Influence Systems," p. 63; Schulze, "The Role of Economic Dominants," p. 4; Schulze, Bifurcation of Power," pp. 21–2.
147Fisher, "Community-Power Studies," p. 458: Lasswell, Lerner, and Rothwell, *Study of Elites*, p. 13.
148Polsby, *Political Theory*, p. 55.
149Kaufman and Jones, "The Mystery of Power," p. 210; see also pp. 208–11.

ter's underemphasis of the role of organized groups in the substructure, such as the Negroes, and political parties, which occasionally forced the power leaders to bargain and otherwise set limits on their autonomy.

London claims that power is organized primarily through the medium of special-interest groups, which Hunter practically ignores, and that the power of these groups "transcends the wishes, beliefs, attitudes, and opinions of the individuals in them."[150] Also, if those supposedly occupying the top of the power pyramid are restricted to performing only a power-balancing function, as Pellegrin and Coates suggest, their ability to exercise influence is very severely curtailed and their claim to the top of the pyramid can be easily challenged. Kaufman and Jones conclude that if the "sub-structure personnel" can "decide what issues the top leaders will take up, and if, in addition, the leaders are dependent upon them in many technical matters, then we cannot escape the conclusion that the substructure is not only actually making important social decisions but is also in a position to use its technical competence as a factor in bargaining for what it wants."[151] Indeed, if the so-called "sub-structure" is able to control the extent of the "upper structure's" influence, and if the question of democracy turns on the degree of accountability, the fears expressed by Hunter and others may have less of a foundation, and the picture of a pyramidal power structure may be extremely misleading.

Another related controversial problem centers upon the concept of the "elite." As was shown above, the Hunter study, the Lynds's earlier study of Middletown, as well as Warner's and Hollingshead's studies of the same town in Illinois,[152] gave many the impression that a monolithic power structure characterizes the American community, and that at the top of this structure ". . . one particular sector, most probably business, dominates the community, and its influentials and their followers resolve community problems within an integrated set of values and attitudes. Usually the small group of decision-makers are united on all major issues because they share

[150]Jack London, review of Hunter's *Community Power Structure*, in *American Journal of Sociology*, 60(5) (March 1955), 523.

[151]Kaufman and Jones, "The Mystery of Power," p. 209.

[152]W. Lloyd Warner, *et al.*, *Democracy in Jonesville* (New York: Harper 1949); A. B. Hollingshead, *Elmtown's Youth* (New York: John Wiley, 1949).

common values and economic fates.[153] This small group of community decision-makers is commonly referred to as the "power elite," a term used by C. Wright Mills for a supposedly similar phenomenon.

The power-elite or ruling-elite theory has been subjected to vigorous criticism from many quarters. Lasswell, Lerner, and Rothwell see in the concept of the elite a descriptive classification, designating the holders of high positions in a given society: "There are as many elites as there are values," so that in addition to the power, or political, elite, "There are elites of wealth, respect, and knowledge (to name but a few)."[154] According to such a view, the political elite comprises the power holders of a body politic, the top power class.[155] Much the same definition is implied by Schulze and Blumberg when they assume that all communities and societies contain power elites which are somehow specifiable.[156] However, since there is little dispute over the fact that power, or influence, is unevenly distributed through the population, there are consequently always some actors or groups more powerful than others, and thus, according to this definition, a power elite is ever present. Such a conception can hardly be the basis of the vigorous controversy that exists today over the existence of a power elite; the controversy must spring from another, more specific conception.

The most detailed attempt to identify the characteristics of a ruling-elite theory has been made by Robert Dahl.[157] He states that the least that can be expected of this or any other theory is that the burden of proof rests with the proponents and not the critics, and that there be unmistakable criteria by which the theory could be disproved. A ruling-elite theory, at its base, asserts that one group of people in a specific political system exerts some degree of power or influence over others in the system. In order to compare the relative influence of actors, there must be some difference of preferences for various political values according to which the actors can be classified. Furthermore, since in a democracy the majority constitutes a controlling group, and since the model is to represent a ruling-elite system, the members of such an elite group

153D'Antonio and Form, *Influentials*, pp. 88–9.
154Lasswell, Lerner, and Rothwell, *Study of Elites*, p. 6.
155Ibid. p. 13.
156Schulze and Blumberg, "Local Power Elites," p. 291.
157Dahl, "A Critique of the Ruling Elite Model."

must be less than a majority. Dahl excludes from his definition any controlling group that is a "product of rules that are actually followed (that is, 'real' rules) under which a majority of individuals could dominate if they took certain actions permissible under the 'real' rules."[158] The ruling thus emerges as a

> controlling group less than a majority in size that is not a pure artifact of democratic rules. It is a minority of individuals whose preferences readily prevail in cases of differences of preferences on key political issues. If we are to avoid an infinite regress of explanations, the composition of the ruling elite must be more or less definitely specified.[159]

Unless the group proposed as a ruling elite is specified, the hypothesis could not be rejected until it was tested on every possible combination of individuals in the community. However, since the burden of proof rests with the proponents, and since there is no more *a priori* reason to assume the existence of a ruling elite than to assume its absence, the group must be specified.

According to this definition, there are many instances in which a small group of individuals holds the greatest power in the community but cannot be designated a ruling elite. Among the most important of these are those in which (1) the powerful individuals or groups disagree among themselves, (2) their power may be specialized with regard to certain areas of application, (3) the strength of the less powerful in the aggregate may exceed that of the minority of the more powerful, and (4) the decisions made by the powerful may be of routine or trivial consequence to the community.[160] Many attempts have been made in the literature to satisfy the conditions for a ruling elite specified by Dahl. For example, many studies have attempted to document the unity of the proposed elite: "The El Paso influentials, regardless of occupation, shared a common outlook . . . shared a common perception about community problems and how they should be solved . . . and constituted a rather closely knit group in terms of social characteristics and associational activities";[161] "Those persons

---

158Ibid. p. 464.
159Ibid.
160Dahl, *Analysis*, pp. 34–5. Also Polsby, *Political Theory*, pp. 123–4.
161D'Antonio and Form, *Influentials*, pp. 99–100, 102, 91–2.

identified as leaders tend to form a subsystem in which members are linked by a variety of ties ranging from kinship to membership in the same formal community organizations";[162] "There is an *esprit de corps* among certain top leaders . . . frequency of contact makes for community solidarity among the leaders."[163] Many such remarks may be seen as responses to remarks such as that made by Wolfinger that to constitute a ruling group, the members must exhibit cohesiveness as well as power.[164]

Polsby claims that the evidence to date seems to indicate "that elites are freest in their power to commit the resources of the community when decisions are relatively routine and innocuous; other kinds of decision-making . . . seems [sic] to require special consent by citizens who fall outside the small decision-making group."[165] Here one recalls Hunter's remark that often the power-holders sounded out an idea to see what would and would not "go." Furthermore, as Wolfinger has pointed out, supposedly subordinate groups are often able by their aggregate political solidarity to bargain with or even defeat the elite.

Dahl adds three minimum conditions for a test of the ruling elite hypothesis: (1) the proposed elite must be a well-defined group; (2) the preferences of the proposed elite on a sample of key political decisions must be in opposition to those of any other group that may be suggested; and (3) the preferences of the proposed elite must regularly prevail.[166] These conditions have not been met in the past primarily because there are no criteria by which to judge the representativeness of the sample of decisions chosen and no basis for determining the proportion of such decisions on which the proposed elite would have to prevail before asserting that it dominated the community. Although they are thus not rigid tests of the ruling-elite hypothesis, the studies of Miller in Pacific and English Cities, Klapp and Padgett in Tijuana, and D'Antonio and Form in El Paso and

---

[162]Fanelli, "Typology," p. 335.

[163]Hunter, *Community Power Structure*, pp. 73, 17.

[164]Wolfinger, "Reputation and Reality," p. 643; Bell, *End of Ideology*, pp. 55, 63, 73; Fisher, Community-Power Studies," p. 456; Dahl, "A Critique of the Ruling Elite Model," p. 465.

[165]Polsby, *Political Theory*, pp. 128, 53; Dahl, "A Critique of the Ruling Elite Model," p. 467.

[166]Dahl, "A Critique of the Ruling Elite Model," pp. 466, 468–9.

Ciudad Juarez seem to support Dahl's assertion that the available evidence does not support the existence of a ruling elite.[167]

Another of the conditions that must be met in order to legitimate a group's claim to elite status is that its range of power must be sufficient to include a great variety of areas of decision-making. The problem of the scope of power arose under a discussion of the nature of power in general and the extent to which various methods of locating power made provisions for this dimension, and it arises again in connection with the question of elites. Fanelli has remarked that the term "community leader" implies that the person so designated plays a generalized rather than a specialized leadership role, that the person "demonstrates leadership behavior in a variety of situational contexts."[168] Indeed, when respondents are asked to identify "persons of influence," whom "nearly everyone would accept" on "a major project," or who participate in "issues most important to the community," the interpretation most often given to the results is that the group of persons identified lead, or decide, on all matters of importance to the community. However, this is not the only, nor the most plausible, interpretation.[169]

In cases where issues or issue-areas are specified, the results seem to document the existence of specialized rather than generalized categories of influence. For example, Agger: "Perceptions of specialized influence seem to be the general rule in our community within the defined political arenas . . . influence in this community is actually channelized through relatively specific or specialized substructures";[170] Fanelli: "The Bakerville data indicate that leadership roles tend to be specialized and that a possible factor in such specialization is the variation in occupational type among community leaders";[171] and Polsby: "The finding that participants in decision-

[167]Miller, "Democracy and Decision-Making," pp. 59–60; Orrin E. Klapp and L. Vincent Padgett, "Power Structure and Decision-Making in a Mexican Border City," *American Journal of Sociology*, 65(4) (January 1960), 402, 405; D'Antonio and Form, *Influentials*, pp. 145, 220–21. Several of these cities are outside of the United States and therefore are strictly speaking outside the concern of this book.

[168]Fanelli, "Typology," p. 334.

[169]Polsby, "A Reassessment," p. 232.

[170]Agger, "Power Attributions," pp. 324, 326. "One of the major assumptions involved in the model of local power structure now appears in need of revision, to wit: that political behavior, at least on the part of activists, is a general rather than a specialized phenomenon" (p. 331).

[171]Fanelli, "Typology," pp. 334–5.

making are largely specialized to certain issue-areas has been confirmed by data gathered using both the methods prevalent in community power research."[172] Finally Hunter himself mentions that the constituency of the pyramid would change according to the project being acted upon."[173] To examine a variety of issues does not preclude the possibility of finding a group with a generalized scope of influence, but rather allows for this and also for the possibility of finding specialized and limited scopes.

Most of the studies that have discovered a monolithic power structure in which the top power group supposedly exercised influence over a wide range more or less autonomously have also stressed the disproportionate representation of business interests. Stemming in part, perhaps, from the common-sense "piper-payer" thesis and in part from an assumption that "economic value distributions determine other value distributions,"[174] many researchers have attempted to determine the extent of the businessman's participation in the power structure. The early studies of the Lynds in Middletown, Warner and Hollingshead in a small Illinois town, and Hunter in Regional City, and more recently those of Pellegrin and Coates in Bigtown and Miller in Pacific City, have all claimed to find evidence of a pattern of business dominance.[175] The investigations of Form and D'Antonio in El Paso also "yielded data that support the hypothesis of business domination of local government," although these authors are careful to report that the structure of power is far from being monolithic.[176] This tendency toward business predominance has been viewed with great alarm by many, and Robert Schulze offers the opinion that it is often not adequately recognized that "given a business-oriented system of values, economic power has long served as a *legitimate* basis of wider social and political power."[177]

As might well be expected, Dahl and Polsby have repeatedly

[172]Polsby, *Political Theory*, pp. 124, 20–21, 64; Polsby, "Three Problems," p. 799.
[173]Hunter, *Community Power Structure*, p. 66.
[174]Schulze, "Bifurcation of Power," p. 20. "In a democratic-capitalistic system, the control of property and production has constituted a major source of power" (p. 19). See also Polsby, "A Reassessment," p. 233.
[175]Fisher, "Community-Power Studies," pp. 457–8; also Barth, "Community Influence Systems," pp. 59–60.
[176]William H. Form and William V. D'Antonio. "Integration and Cleavage Among Community Influentials in Two Border Cities," *American Sociological Review*, 24 (December 1959), 814; also D'Antonio and Form, *Influentials*, pp. 102–5.
[177]Schulze, "Bifurcation of Power," p. 19.

challenged the validity of these findings, primarily on the basis of the data they gathered in New Haven. Dahl doubts very much whether "businessmen 'dominate' community policies, except perhaps by definition,"[178] while Polsby claims that the Lynds's study in Middletown "may have helped to fix blinders on contemporary students of community power by drawing their attention too exclusively to businessmen," and that "community power exists whether businessmen are centrally involved in its exercise or not."[179]

Banfield's study of how decisions were made in a half-dozen controversial issues in Chicago comes to the conclusion that top businessmen are not so powerful.

> The notion that "top leaders" run the city is certainly not supported by the facts of the controversies described in this book. On the contrary, in these cases the richest men of Chicago are conspicuous by their absence. Lesser business figures appear, but they do not act concertedly: [There are some of them] . . . on . . . [each] side of every issue. The most influential people are the managers of large organizations the maintenance of which is at stake, a few "civic leaders" whose judgment, negotiating skill, and disinterestedness are unusual and, above all, the chief elected officials. Businessmen exercise influence (to the extent that they exercise it at all) not so much because they are rich or in a position to make threats and promises as, in the words of one of them, "by main force of being right."[180]

Banfield says that, in Chicago, "big businessmen are criticized less for interfering in public affairs than for failing to assume their civic responsibilities."[181] Businessmen readily take a stand only when their economic interests are directly involved. But neither does Banfield find that decisions are made by unified political elite with the mayor at their head. Rather, he finds, that the mayor is checked by (1) other governmental and political leaders, often of the opposite party, (2) the courts, and (3) the voters and the neighborhood political leaders who help mobilize them to vote. The mayor, and the powerful organizations, often co-opt advisory committees, with

---

178Dahl, "Equality and Power in American Society," pp. 75–6.
179Polsby, "Power in Middletown," p. 603; Polsby, "Three Problems," pp. 800–801.
180Edward C. Banfield, *op. cit.*, p. 288.
181Ibid. p. 287.

different compositions of members depending on what they hope the committee will recommend. These committees often help to sell a project to the voters, and often include prestigious businessmen. Organizations affected by an issue will use their boards in about the same manner.[182] Top businessmen, then, sometimes play a civic role, but as facilitators, seldom as innovators, except when their direct economic interests are involved. Of course, the big business-man's local influence is not so much directly "exercised" as it is "anticipated," as Peter B. Clark points out.[183] His interests are accommodated, along with those of other power groups and organizations, by the politicians and the experts in the bureaucracies. In civic ventures, (1) the top businessman is useful to other people who seek the prestige and legitimacy that he can lend to their undertakings; and (2) in the process of trying to co-opt him, the civic innovators to some extent anticipate and try to satisfy his wishes.

Apparently what has long been true in Chicago is now developing in smaller cities as they have become more industrialized. Schulze found that as a city grows from an isolated self-contained entity to one interrelated with the larger economy of the country, its power structure changes from a monolithic one dominated by persons possessing great economic power to a bifurcated structure comprising "two critical and relatively discrete power sets, the economic dominants and the public leaders."[184] While Schulze found this to be true for a city that was satellite to a metropolis, Clelland and Form found a similar pattern for an independent city of growing industrial importance.[185] In both cities, the economic dominants have sharply reduced their ties to the political leadership, and to a lesser extent they have also reduced their participation in civic associations, especially in the satellite city, where there is more absentee owner-ship. While community power structures seem to vary somewhat, this is the pattern which is increasingly being revealed for industrial-ized cities, whereas the pattern of economic-elite dominance is

182Ibid. p. 263 note.

183"Civic Leadership: The Symbols of Legitimacy" (unpublished paper, 1960), p. 3.

184Schulze, "Bifurcation of Power," pp. 19–80, at p. 22.

185Donald A. Clelland and William H. Form, "Economic Dominants and Com-munity Power: A Comparative Analysis," American Journal of Sociology, 69 (March 1964), 511–21.

characteristic only of the older, smaller towns and cities. Even in Kent Jennings's study of Atlanta—the same city studied a decade earlier by Hunter—the newer pattern of separation between economic dominants, political leaders, and civic associations influentials seems to hold true.[186]

As to the elitist versus pluralist patterns of community power that emerge from the use of the reputational method and the decision-making (or "issue-analysis") method, respectively, there is an increasing awareness among students that the power structure varies with the type of community. Instead of studying only one community and generalizing from it to power structures generally, recent students have compared two or more communities, and have ranked the communities along an elitist–pluralist continuum. This makes for such perspicacious and balanced studies as those by Presthus,[187] D'Antonio and Form,[188] and Clelland and Form.[189] In general, the older, smaller towns and cities, especially in the South, have an elitist, oligarchic power structure, with the top businessmen in all the important decision-making positions, while the more industrialized cities have a pluralist, competitive power structure, in which the top businessmen are usually less powerful on non-economic issues than are political leaders, professionals of one specialty or another, and association directors and presidents. In both cases, however, decision-making is carried on by a small minority of the population—about 0.3 per cent in Syracuse in the study of Linton Freeman et al., and between 0.4 and 0.6 per cent in the two New York towns studied by Presthus—but in a framework in which the interests of organized groups and the voting public are taken into account. In both cases, some of the major decisions affecting the communities are made outside the communities—by the state and federal governments mainly, by nationally based corporations and trade unions in some cases—although this fact is most often ignored by the investigators of local community power structure.

[186]*Op. cit.* There are no doubt exceptions. It is held, for example, that Dallas is still controlled by its economic dominants. Carol Estes Thometz, *The Decision-Makers: The Power Structures of Dallas* (Dallas: Southern Methodist University Press, 1963).
[187]Robert Presthus, *Men at the Top* (New York: Oxford University Press, 1964).
[188]D'Antonio and Form, *Influentials.*
[189]Clelland and Form, "Economic Dominants."

IX
Perceptions of Power and Influence

The purposes of the study reported in this chapter[1] are not to find out who are the actual leaders and what their characteristics are, as were the purposes of most of the studies cited in the preceding chapter. Our purposes here are, rather, to ascertain the *perceptions* and *images* of who has power and influence among selected groups or categories of the population. We have studied 21 groups. Four of them are cross sections of the general population of two large Minnesota cities (Minneapolis and St. Paul) and two small Minnesota cities (Red Wing and Crookston). The other 17 samples consist of the formal "leaders" in organized groups or in "leadership categories" (for example, a representative sample of persons listed in *Who's Who*). Thus we have used the positional technique to select our leadership samples, but we do not claim they are actually leaders and we are not generalizing about their characteristics; rather we are interested in the characteristics of and differences in their *perceptions* of power and influence. The only claim we can make about their leadership quality is that they are the formal leaders in 17 different organizations or categories. In asking them for their opinions about power and who has it, we use the reputational technique, but

[1]The study was financed largely by a grant from The Fund for Adult Education to Professors William C. Rogers and Luther Pickrel of the University of Minnesota for a public-affairs education program designed to reach "community leaders." Research was needed to define and locate "community leaders," and thus Professors Rogers and Pickrel both stimulated the research and made suggestions for it. Final phases of the work were supported by a grant to the author by the Rockefeller Foundation.

not for the purpose of ascertaining actual power or potential for power, which is how it is usually used.[2]

Data were collected from the samples by means of a mailed questionnaire. In order to check on the basis of non-response, a follow-up mailed questionnaire was used and the response of those who returned their questionnaires after the second request were compared with those who returned them after the first request. It is assumed that any differences between these two would reflect the characteristics of those who did not respond at all. The first request elicited a 31.1 per cent reponse; the second request pulled an additional 19.1 per cent. Table 1 lists the samples and the number responding to the first and second requests.

The distinctive characteristics of the first sample as compared to the second sample, presumably reflecting the bias in our sample due to incomplete returns, are:

1. There are somewhat fewer in the age group 45-65 years and more in/the over-65 age category.

2. There is a slightly higher average educational level. The larger proportion of "college graduates" in the first sample, however, is almost balanced by the larger proportion of "some college" in the second sample.

3. There is a slightly larger number of small businessmen, and a correspondingly smaller number of skilled workers.

4. There is a slightly larger proportion of business organization members and a correspondingly lower proportion of union members. Attendance at meetings of these occupational associations is also somewhat less.

5. There is a slightly larger proportion of Republicans and a correspondingly lower proportion of Democrats.

There are no significant differences between the original and the follow-up samples in regard to sex, marital status, occupational level (the Anderson-Goodenough scale was used to rank occupations and

[2]At least two previous studies used the reputational technique to get at public images of the community power structure rather than at the structure itself: Thomas R. Dye, "Popular Images of Decision-Making in Suburban Communities," *Sociology and Social Research*, 47 (October 1962), 75–83; William H. Form and Warren L. Sauer, "Organized Labor's Image of Community Power Structure," *Social Forces*, 38 (May 1960), 332–41.

it lumps together skilled workers with retail businessmen), self-designated social class, church attendance and denomination, number of close friends in church and in occupational organization, membership in voluntary associations by number and activity, frequency of attendance at church or at voluntary association meetings, frequency of listening to news broadcasts on radio or TV, frequency of voting in public elections. In general, there is little reason to believe that the original and follow-up samples are sufficiently different to indicate an important sample bias due to non-response. The differences listed above might be kept in mind when interpreting the findings, but our interest is more in comparing the samples which are all subject to the same bias of non-response) than in generalizing from any one sample to the universe of all persons with the distinguishing characteristic of the sample. Thus, we can generally consider the possible bias of non-response to be unimportant for our study.

The content of the study and the specific questions used in the questionnaire will be indicated in the report of the findings which follow. An overview of these can be indicated by listing the titles of the subsections:

A. Images of Powerful Groups

B. Images of Influentials in Different Areas of Life

C. Perceived Relative Influence by Local and Cosmopolitan Leaders

D. Perceptions of the Negative Influentials

E. Images of the Unnamed Power Source

F. Varying Conceptions on How to Stimulate Public Interest

G. Social Participations of Alleged Leaders

We recognize a theoretical difference between "influence" and "power," but feel obliged to blur the distinction for purposes of our study of images and perceptions of these social phenomena. Many able political theorists[3] have made a cogent distinction between those who wield the social instruments of *power* to change the lives of others and those who merely have the prestige of knowledge to *influence* those who control these instruments of power. The distinc-

---

[3]For example, William Henry Beveridge, *Power and Influence* (London: Hodder and Stoughton, 1953).

Table 1. Description of Samples

SAMPLES		NUMER OF QUESTIONNARIES		
	NO. SENT OUT	NO. RESPONDING TO ORIGINAL REQUEST	NO. RESPONDING TO FOLLOW-UP REQUEST	TOTAL IN SAMPLE
Cross-section samples (every *n*th case chosen from city directories, alternating men and women)				
Minneapolis	200	27	46	73
St. Paul	200	42	16	58
Red Wing	200	26	30	56
Crookston	200	20	24	44
"Leadership" Samples				
Who's Who in Minnesota (every *n*th case chosen)	300	111	41	152
Presidents of statewide voluntary associations	200	54	40	94
Executive directors of voluntary associations	328	112	58	170
Presidents of the League of Women Voters	148	74	24	98
Presidents of agricultural organizations	168	58	6	64
Agricultural extension agents	180	80	46	126
Business leaders (Governor's Business Advisory Council)	100	25	10	35
Labor leaders (presidents and secretaries of unions)	100	24	14	38
Hennepin County Health and Welfare Council members (referred to as Minneapolis HWC)	52	18	17	35
American Association of University Women officers	69	26	24	50
Minnesota Welfare Conference officers	70	28	23	51
Elected county commissioners (1 from each county)	87	36	29	65
Officers of Minneapolis Chamber of Commerce and Junior C. of C.	80	30	28	58
Minnesota Republican Workshop (women leaders)	56	30	18	48
Minnesota Federation of Women's Clubs officers	100	44	41	75
National Conference of Christians and Jews (Minnesota Round Table)	70	32	21	53
United Nations Association members	76	30	24	54
Totals	2984	927	570	1497

tion is seldom made, however, in the everyday thinking of those who are not political theorists, and since our purpose in this study is to record an aspect of that thinking, it does not seem appropriate to hold to the theoretical distinction. When we ask such questions as "Who could influence you personally to—?" without having ascertained whether or not the respondent is a manipulator of instruments of social power, we cannot be sure whether we are dealing with influence or with actual power. Thus, for the purposes of this study, we feel obliged to ignore the theoretical distinction between influence and power.

Although, as we stated at the outset, our purpose is different from those who study community power, we use a technique of research akin to what has come to be known as the "reputational approach" to the study of community power, associated with the work of Floyd Hunter[4] and his followers. One of the criticisms of the work of Hunter is that he is at least somewhat arbitrary and subjective in the selection of those of whom he asks questions concerning the holders of power. Our study avoids this criticism by studying 21 different groups of respondents, and by being at least as much concerned with the differences among the groups' answers as in their combined answers. Further, of course, we do not claim that these respondent groups lead us to a true picture of community power, but merely to their varied images or perceptions of power. For this purpose the "reputational" approach appears to be most appropriate.

A. Images of Powerful Groups

One of the basic problems for sociology is to distinguish the influence of *facts* from the influence of *images* of facts. There are sociologists who stress one to the neglect of the other—those who find social causation only in certain "social forces" and those who find it only in "definitions of the situation."[5] It is our belief that both of these are important, although in differing degrees in differing situations. In the case of political power, objective forces are probably usually

[4]*Community Power Structure: A Study of Decision Makers* (Chapel Hill: University of North Carolina Press, 1953).

[5]This is the classic conflict in sociology between the followers of Karl Marx and those of Max Weber and Karl Mannheim, and in social psychology between behaviorists (such as J. B. Watson and F. Allport) and symbolic interactionists (such as W. I. Thomas and G. H. Mead).

more significant than public images, although these forces often work through, and capitalize on, certain images. Images as to who holds objective power can as often work against the effective exercise of this power as they work to enhance it. Public images are sometimes true, or have a strong element of truth, but at least as often they are false. True or false, the images have influence themselves, and the sources of real power have to contend with them. Thus, no matter how it is determined who actually holds effective power, it is valuable to ascertain the *images* regarding who holds power.

Our questionnaire filled out by Minnesota "leaders" and a cross section of the urban population included the question, "What groups do you think are most powerful in this country?" The answers were classified into 30 different categories, and we shall now examine the most frequently mentioned of these to ascertain the images of who holds power in the eyes of our respondents. In general, the leadership groups in our sample distributed their responses into more categories than did the average citizens in our cross sections. Whereas it was necessary to utilize 22 categories to accommodate the responses of the voluntary associations' presidents and 20 categories for the responses of the Chamber of Commerce sample, the responses of the Minneapolis cross section fitted into only 11 of these categories, and the St. Paul cross section into only 9 categories. None of the 17 leadership samples gave responses requiring so few categories of perceived powerful groups as did the cross sections of St. Paul (9) and Crookston (10).

Another evidence of the tendency of "leadership" samples to see power dispersed among more different groups than do the "average citizen" samples is the tendency for the leadership samples to give more different responses. The Minneapolis average citizen gave only 1.9 responses (on the average), the St. Paul citizen only 1.7 responses, the Red Wing citizen 2.1 responses, and the Crookston citizen 1.5 responses. On the other hand the United Nations Association leaders gave an average of 3.3 responses, the Chamber of Commerce gave 2.9 responses (as did the AAUW members), and the labor leaders gave 2.8 responses. Only 1 of the 17 leadership samples gave fewer than 2 responses on the average, and this was the county commissioners, who averaged 1.8 responses. From these two pieces of evidence we conclude that the alleged "leaders" perceive power to be more dispersed among different groups than do average citizens.

In practically all of our samples, trade unions are mentioned the most frequently among the perceived power groups. It should be remembered that our survey was conducted in the summer of 1960 when the revelations of the Senate Select Committee on Improper Activities in the Labor or Management Field were still fresh in people's minds, as was the victory of the United Steelworkers in the great steel strike of the winter of 1959–60. Over 50 per cent of the cross sections in three of the four cities studied mentioned "labor" in general or specific trade unions as one of the most powerful groups in the country, and over 60 per cent of each of 16 of the 17 leadership groups studied mentioned these groups. The exceptions were the cross section of St. Paul (the most unionized of the four cities studied, where only 25 per cent mentioned the unions), and the voluntary associations presidents (48.9 per cent of whom mentioned the unions, a figure perhaps high enough not to be considered as a real exception). The labor leaders in our sample themselves mentioned unions as one of the most powerful groups in the country in 63.2 per cent of the cases.

Business generally was mentioned with second frequency as one of the most powerful groups in the country. This was referred to both in such general terms as "corporations," "monopolies," "big business," "industrialists," "management," and "business world," and in more specific terms as "National Association of Manufacturers," "Chamber of Commerce," "insurance companies," "oil companies," and "war supply manufacturers." Some of these terms may be interpreted as friendly or neutral to the groups referred to, and other terms as hostile. Of the four cities sampled, St. Paul had 31.3 per cent of its respondents mentioning one these groups and Red Wing had 28.5 per cent (Minneapolis and Crookston had lower proportions). Of the seventeen leadership groups sampled, all had more than 25 per cent of their respondents mentioning one of these groups. The highest proportions were found among the labor leaders (89.5 per cent) and the UN association (86.6 per cent). Among the business leaders studied, 42.8 per cent mentioned the business groups as one of the most powerful, and the proportion among Chamber of Commerce members was 50.1 per cent. Only 27.6 per cent of the voluntary associations presidents mentioned the business groups as most powerful, and only 28.9 per cent of the *Who's Who* sample did so. Clearly, these latter groups are more similar to the cross section than they are to the business leaders or the labor leaders. That this is not due to the presence of women among the association presidents or the *Who's Who* sample is shown by the fact that the League of Women Voters leaders mentioned business groups as most powerful in 65.3 per cent of the cases, and the AAUW leaders mentioned them in 46.2 per cent of the cases.

Financial interests as distinct from business or industrial interests —including references to "bankers," "capitalists," "Wall Street," "organized finance"—did not receive many mentions. In only 2 of our 21 samples did over 10 per cent mention them: executives of voluntary associations (12.9 per cent) and labor leaders (10.5 per cent).

Another economic category mentioned as one of the most powerful groups in the country are the professionals, including "the American Medical Association," "The American Bar Association," and a few others. This category is mentioned most frequently by the labor leaders (42.1 per cent). A few of our other leadership samples mention the professionals as the most powerful group almost as frequently: Minnesota Welfare Conference (38.5 per cent), Health and Welfare Council (33.3 per cent). In all of the other leadership samples, the proportion mentioning the professionals as a powerful group ranged between 4.8 and 16.5 per cent (the latter proportion is attained by voluntary associations executives). The cross section of average citizens is least likely to attribute power to professional groups: In St. Paul and Crookston no one mentioned them; in Minneapolis the proportion was 5.7 per cent, and in Red Wing it was 7.1 per cent.

The farmers and farm organizations are listed as a most powerful group in the country with notable frequency by the business leaders (28.6 per cent), the National Conference of Christians and Jews (18.8 per cent), and the labor leaders (15.8 per cent). Our three leadership samples mostly from rural areas mention farmers as a powerful group less frequently; agricultural extension agents, with 14.3 per cent; agricultural organizations presidents, with 12.5 per cent; and county commissioners with 5.6 per cent. As might be expected, scarcely anyone in the four city cross sections mentioned farmers or farm organizations as a most powerful group. It should be remembered that the study was conducted in Minnesota, whose legislature was dominated by rural representatives even though the majority of the state's population was now urban.

Religious groups are frequently considered to have great power by certain of our samples. Unspecified religious groups were mentioned as among the most powerful in the country by proportions ranging from 3.6 to 17.1 per cent for the four city cross sections studied. For the leaders of agricultural organizations the corresponding proportion was 25.0 per cent, and for the Chamber of Commerce sample it was 21.4 per cent. The proportions mentioning unspecified religious groups were lower for the remaining 15 leadership samples, ranging down to 6.3 per cent for the National Conference of Christians and Jews sample and 5.6 per cent for the country commissioners sample.

The Catholics were mentioned as a most powerful group by proportions ranging from 9.1 per cent down to zero for the four city cross sections: The city without a single mention of Catholics was St. Paul, which has the highest proportion of Catholics in its population. The highest proportion among the leadership samples mentioning the Catholics as a powerful group were the 20.0 per cent among the UN Association members and the 17.9 per cent among the Chamber of Commerce sample. The highest proportion among the 21 samples mentioning the Jews as a powerful group was 5.7 per cent for the Minneapolis cross section; the other three city cross sections and 16 of the 17 leadership samples did not include a single person mentioning Jews as a powerful group. The only sample to have a significant proportion mentioning the Negroes as a most powerful group in the country was that of the American Association of University Women (with 15.4 per cent saying this).

There was a wide range of proportions among our samples mentioning political parties (both or unspecified) as a most powerful group in the country. The city cross sections' proportions here were: Red Wing (28.6 per cent), Minneapolis (25.7 per cent), St. Paul (12.5 per cent), Crookston (none). There is even greater variation among our leadership samples. As might be expected, the largest proportion mentioning political parties as a most powerful group was found for a political association—the Minnesota Republican Workshop, with 46.7 per cent. Next was the agricultural organizations leaders with 37.5 per cent, followed by the labor leaders with 31.6 per cent mentioning political parties. Lowest proportions were found among the Minnesota Federation of Women's Clubs leaders (4.5 per cent), the county commissioners (11.1 per cent), and the business leaders (11.4 per cent).

Neither the Republican nor the Democratic parties were mentioned separately very often. Only the county commissioners mentioned the Republican party with any frequency (11.1 per cent), and this relatively high proportion perhaps should be considered as counteracting the low proportion in this group mentioning political parties generally. The Minneapolis Health and Welfare Council had the highest proportion (11.1 per cent) mentioning the Democratic party as a most powerful group.

Unspecified political pressure groups and lobbyists were answers given fairly frequently by some of our samples in answer to the question about the most powerful group in the country. The proportion was highest among the UN Association members (33.3 per cent), with the Minnesota Federation of Women's Clubs leaders next (22.7 per cent), followed by the Minnesota Republican Workshop leaders (20.0 per cent). Neither the economic leadership samples nor the general public mention pressure groups and lobbyists with any significant frequency.

Groups controlling the mass media (newspapers, TV and radio) were indicated to be the most powerful in the country with some frequency by the general public in St. Paul (18.8 per cent) and Red Wing (10.7 per cent). Among our leadership samples, the mass media came in for most frequent recognition by the UN Association leaders (20.0 per cent), the Minnesota Federation of Women's Clubs leaders (18.2 per cent), and the League of Women Voters leaders (14.3 per cent). Again we note that the economic leadership samples were not inclined to mention the mass media as powerful.

Educational groups—including scientists, teachers, and educational institutions—are mentioned as most powerful by 18.8 per cent of the National Conference of Christians and Jews sample, 15.4 per cent of the Minnesota Welfare Conference sample, 13.3 per cent of the Minnesota Republican Workshop sample. Lesser, and therefore insignificant, proportions among the other leadership samples and the four city cross sections mentioned educational groups as one of the most powerful.

The only other category mentioned with any notable frequency as a most powerful group in the country was the veterans' groups (including specific mention of the American Legion and the Veterans of Foreign Wars). This was found only among a few of the leadership samples, for the four city cross sections specified veterans' groups with proportions of 4.5 per cent and below. The leadership samples with the highest proportions here are the Minnesota Welfare Conference and the American Association of University Women (with 15.4 per cent among each mentioning the veterans' groups), followed by the Minnesota Republican Workshop and the UN Association (with 13.3 per cent among each).

There were a few other scattered mentions of other groups as being the most powerful in the country, but not frequently enough to be significant. Their absence from practically anyone's list is pertinent to an understanding of public images of the power structure. Fraternal organizations—such as the Masons, Shriners, Knights of Columbus, or any others—are not mentioned with significant frequency by any of our leadership samples or by the four city cross sections.

The UN Association leaders were the only sample to mention the military or the armed forces as a most powerful group, with more than 5 per cent, and they with only 6.7 per cent. The Community Chest, the Red Cross, and other similar social-welfare organizations were listed as most powerful by significant proportions only among the Minnesota Federation of Women's Clubs leaders (22.7 per cent); no one in the four city cross sections mentioned them at all. The highest proportion listing "government" as a most powerful group was found in the Chamber of Commerce sample, with 10.7 per cent; the other samples had proportions here of 7.1 per cent (for the Red Wing cross section) or less. The "United Nations" got only one mention as a most powerful group in all our samples; but since the question asked about "powerful groups in the country" this could not necessarily be said to reflect our respondents' beliefs about the U.N.

"Criminals" were listed as a most powerful group by 9.1 per cent of the Crookston and 7.1 per cent of the Red Wing cross sections, but by no one in the two big city cross sections. Among all the leadership samples, only three respondents called "criminals" one of the most powerful groups in the country. Law-enforcing agencies (police, courts, F.B.I.) were not recorded at all as most powerful groups.

Powerful groups other than those already mentioned were recorded by one to three respondents among all our samples: These included the Parent-Teachers Association, the League of Women Voters, segregationists, McCarthyites, conservatives, communists, subversives, Russians, racket committees, women, students, civic groups, show people, World Federalists, Madison Avenue, large contributors to political parties. A few of our respondents thought there were no "most powerful groups" at all, but only collectivities of unorganized individuals such as voters, "unorganized white-collar workers," "free-thinking people individually," "those who have demonstrated their reliability," "the people when aroused and informed"; or they said "any individual or group can have power," "depends on issue, setting and time."

Sizable proportions of our respondents failed to list any powerful groups, and there is no way of knowing whether they did not think of any, did not think there were any, or simply did not bother to answer the question. These non-respondents constituted 20 per cent of the four city cross sections collectively. The highest proportions among the 17 leadership samples were found among the county commissioners (16.7 per cent), the business leaders (14.3 per cent), and the *Who's Who* sample (12.5 per cent).

We have seen that there are striking differences among the samples studied with respect to the groups they designate as most powerful. This has been most regularly true between the city cross sections and the leadership samples, but there are also significant differences among the various leadership samples. We shall not be able here to recapitulate all the differences among all the leadership samples, but shall merely compare two of them—the voluntary associations presidents and the business leaders. Floyd Hunter specifically, and C. Wright Mills[6] by implication, hold that leaders of voluntary associations either are business leaders or are their lieutenants. Insofar as their images of power groups are concerned, the two samples do not think alike, according to our data. First, the proportion naming labor groups as among the most powerful is 74.3 per cent among the

[6]C. Wright Mills, *The Power Elite* (New York: Oxford University Press, 1956).

business leaders but only 48.9 per cent among the association presidents. Second, the proportion naming business and industrial groups among the most powerful is 42.8 per cent among the business leaders, but only 27.6 per cent among the association presidents. There is also a slight but not statistically significant difference in the proportions naming financial interests (5.7 to 4.3 per cent). The business leaders are much more likely to see the farmers as a powerful group: 28.6 of them mention farmers, as against only 4.3 per cent of the association presidents. The association presidents are more likely than the business leaders to designate political parties as powerful: 23.4 per cent of them mention parties in general (or both major parties) and another 2.1 per cent mention the Democratic party specifically, while among the business leaders only 11.4 per cent mention parties in general and none mentions either specific party alone. The association presidents also more frequently mention religious groups as powerful: 19.1 per cent mention unspecified religious groups, another 6.4 per cent mention the Catholics, and 2.1 per cent mention the Jews; while among the business leaders, only 11.4 per cent mention unspecified religious groups, 5.7 per cent mention the Catholics, and none mention the Jews. In keeping with our earlier finding, that other kinds of groups are less frequently mentioned by anybody as most powerful, there are no other striking differences between the business leaders and the association presidents. But it is clear that business leaders are more likely to mention economic groups as the most powerful, while the association presidents are relatively more inclined to see the political parties and religious groups as most powerful. The average number of powerful groups mentioned is 2.4 per business leader but less than 2.0 per association president (even though a larger proportion of business leaders failed to answer the question—14.3 per cent as compared to 10.6 per cent among the association presidents). It can be concluded that these two groups of "leaders" have somewhat different images of the power structure.

B. Images of Influentials in Different Areas of Life

One of the unresolved disputes among students of community power structure is between those who claim that there is a single pyramid of power, in which a small number of leaders make the important public decisions in all walks of life, and those who hold that power is specialized, so that different leaders are most influential in the varied areas of public life. The outstanding empirical studies exemplifying these divergent points of view are those of Floyd Hunter on the one hand and of Linton Freeman and his associates on the other.[7] The divergent techniques of these investigators may help to explain their different findings. Our own study uses a technique of research similar to that of Hunter, but reaches conclusions similar to those of Freeman. Our study, it must be recalled, makes no claim to locate actual power, but merely presents images or perceptions of power. When we say that our conclusions are more similar to those of Freeman, therefore, we mean that the images reflect a power structure which is somewhat diversified rather than monolithic.

Our major technique asks respondents in our 21 samples to name the individuals "whose opinions would most likely persuade you to accept their point of view," in 7 different subject matter areas. The great majority of those questioned answered for the areas of being influenced in "political matters" and "economic matters," but progressively smaller proportions answered for the remaining 5 areas: "contribute money for a charitable purpose," "contribute money to a political candidate," "attend a political meeting," "that a certain public issue is important enough to study more," and "join an association in a civic purpose." Several explanations for the high rate of non-response in the latter areas are possible: that the respondent would not engage in the activity no matter who tried to influence him to do it, that the respondent could not think who might influence him in these specialized ways, that the respondent did not make the effort to answer the question. In any case, the rates of non-response for many of the samples render unjustifiable any comparative analysis of the responses. Thus our conclusions will refer primarily to the general areas of political and economic matters, for which response is quite high.

The occupations and positions of those named as influentials are of the most varied sort, but the proportions mentioning each of them do not differ sharply from one sample to another.[8] In response to the

[7]Hunter, *Community Power Structure*; Linton C. Freeman, *et al.*, *Local Community Leadership* (Syracuse, N.Y.: Syracuse University, 1960).

[8]For each area of influence, each respondent was asked to list two names. Thus, the maximum total response for each sample is 200 per cent; but many respondents mentioned only one name so the totals are generally considerably under that figure.

question of who could influence the respondent in "political matters," by far the most frequent references were to state and national governmental office holders and candidates.

Table 2 shows the categories of response for the four city cross sections, and it is evident that the overwhelming proportion of responses are in the governmental-political categories. Outside of these, only educational leaders and clergymen are mentioned with any significant frequency. Members of the "economic elite" get very few mentions. There is slightly greater variation in the responses of the leadership samples, as shown in Tables 3 and 4. Still, the largest numbers of them mention persons in the political-governmental field as most influential. Only the business leaders sample—and not even the broader-based Chamber of Commerce sample—recognizes a significant proportion of businessmen as influencing them on political matters, and even they give more weight to persons in the political-governmental area.

Table 2.   Percentages of the four city cross sections mentioning persons in indicated categories who would influence them in "political matters."

	MINNEAPOLIS	ST. PAUL	RED WING	CROOKSTON
Democratic state and national officeholders and candidates	51.4	50.0	10.7	36.4
Republican state and national officeholders and candidates	42.9	0.0	39.3	40.9
Democratic party officials	2.9	6.3	0.0	0.0
Republican party officials	0.0	0.0	0.0	0.0
State legislators	2.9	0.0	7.1	13.6
Local government officials	0.0	0.0	0.0	9.1
Professors and other educational leaders	0.0	12.6	7.1	4.5
Lawyers and judges	2.9	6.3	3.6	0.0
Clergymen	5.7	6.3	3.6	0.0
Doctors and dentists	2.9	0.0	3.6	0.0
Businessmen and bankers	2.9	0.0	0.0	4.5
Farm organization officials	0.0	0.0	0.0	4.5
Friends or fellow workers	5.7	0.0	0.0	0.0
Members of the family	5.7	0.0	0.0	4.5

Table 3. Percentages of economic leaders samples mentioning persons in indicated categories who would influence them in "political matters."

	BUSINESS LEADERS	CHAMBER OF COMMERCE	FARM ORGANIZATION LEADERS	LABOR LEADERS
Democratic state and national officeholders and candidates	15.4	21.5	21.8	42.1
Republican state and national officeholders and candidates	48.6	71.4	53.1	5.3
Democratic party officials	3.9	0.0	0.0	15.9
Republican party officials	11.6	14.3	12.5	0.0
State legislators	3.9	3.6	6.2	0.0
Local government officeholders	0.0	7.2	3.1	0.0
Professors and other educational leaders	3.9	3.6	6.2	5.3
Lawyers and judges	0.0	10.8	3.1	0.0
Clergymen	0.0	7.2	0.0	0.0
Doctors and dentists	0.0	0.0	0.0	0.0
Businessmen and bankers	25.7	7.2	9.3	0.0
Farm organization officials	0.0	3.6	3.1	0.0
Friends and fellow workers	0.0	0.0	3.1	0.0
Members of the family	0.0	0.0	0.0	0.0
Mass media personnel	7.7	0.0	0.0	0.0
Voluntary association executives	0.0	0.0	0.0	0.0
Union officials	0.0	0.0	0.0	10.6
Appointed government officials	3.9	0.0	6.2	0.0

The civic leadership groups listed in Table 4 also mention persons in the political-governmental field most frequently as those who influence them in political matters. The various groups—both civic and economic—differ in their reference to Republicans or Democrats, but when the two parties are combined there is very little difference among the leadership groups in this regard (only the labor leaders stand out by having an unusually high percentage referring to

Table 4. Percentages of civic association leaders samples mentioning persons in indicated categories who would influence them in "political matters."

	VOLUNTARY ASSOCIATION PRESIDENTS	VOLUNTARY ASSOCIATION EXECUTIVES	LEAGUE OF WOMEN VOTERS	MINNESOTA WELFARE CONFERENCE	FEDERATION OF WOMEN'S CLUBS
Democratic state and national officeholders and candidates	17.0	34.1	30.6	53.8	18.2
Republican national officeholders and candidates	51.1	37.6	24.5	38.5	54.5
Democratic party officials	0.0	1.2	2.0	0.0	0.0
Republican party officials	8.5	4.7	4.1	0.0	0.0
State legislators	4.3	2.4	12.2	23.1	18.2
Local government officeholders	4.3	0.0	2.0	0.0	0.0
Professors and other educational leaders	4.3	3.5	20.4	7.7	4.5
Lawyers and judges	4.3	0.0	2.0	0.0	9.1
Clergymen	0.0	0.0	8.2	0.0	4.5
Doctors and dentists	0.0	1.2	0.0	0.0	9.1
Businessmen and bankers	10.6	17.5	0.0	0.0	9.0
Farm organization officials	0.0	0.0	0.0	0.0	0.0
Friends or fellow workers	0.0	4.7	0.0	0.0	0.0
Members of the family	2.1	0.0	8.1	0.0	0.0
Mass media personnel	4.3	7.1	8.1	15.4	9.1
Voluntary association executives	0.0	1.2	12.2	15.4	4.5
Union officials	0.0	0.0	0.0	0.0	0.0
Appointed government officials	0.0	3.5	0.0	0.0	4.5

political-governmental influentials). The economic leaders are slightly more likely than the civic leaders to refer to party officials, and such civic groups as the Minnesota Welfare Conference and the Federation of Women's Clubs are slightly more likely to refer to state legislators than are the other groups reported on. "Businessmen and bankers" are referred to as influentials by 17.5 per cent of the voluntary association executives; this is the highest proportion of references they achieve among the civic leaders samples. Over 20 per cent of the League of Women Voters sample mention professors or other educators, and persons associated with the mass media and voluntary association executives get significant minorities of the samples mentioning them. No other categories of response stand out.

When asked who would influence them in "economic matters," the distribution of answers of the various respondents changes somewhat. The number of respondents to this question from the four city cross sections is too small to be reported reliably. But among the minority who did respond, none gave a majority of their responses in the category of "businessmen and bankers," although that was—by a slight margin—the largest single category for three of the four cities: 17.1 per cent for Minneapolis, 17.8 per cent for Red Wing, and 27.2 per cent for Crookston. The responses were scattered into 20 different categories, with family members, political-governmental leaders, and educational leaders also getting a significant number of responses.

There are significant discrepancies among the four economic leaders samples analyzed in Table 5. The business leaders and the Chamber of Commerce sample list businessmen's and bankers' names with greatest frequency among those who would most likely influence them in economic matters. While such names also crop up frequently in the samples of farm organization leaders and labor leaders, they are superseded among the former by names of professors and other educational leaders, and among the latter by names of public officeholders. Professors and other educational leaders are also mentioned with high frequency by the Chamber of Commerce sample and the business leaders. No other category of influentials gets a noteworthy number of mentions (possibly the 10.7 per cent of the Chamber of Commerce sample mentioning lawyers is a minor exception).

The civic association samples analyzed in Table 6 indicate that businessmen and bankers would influence them most in "economic matters," except for the League of Women Voters leaders, for whom professors and other educators supersede the businessmen and bankers. Professors and other educators are deemed influential by a significant proportion of the other samples also. These data are somewhat surprising, perhaps, in that significant percentages say that state and national officeholders would influence them in economic matters. Comparing Table 6 with Table 4, we find that at least as large a proportion of civic leaders say that government officials would influence them in economic matters as say that businessmen and bankers would influence them in political matters.

The responses thus far have been analyzed in terms of *categories* of influentials. We shall now turn to the individual names volunteered by the respondents. The outstanding fact shown by these data is that there is only a limited tendency for the same name to crop up frequently. Thus, while we have earlier noted that the respondents

Table 5. Percentages of economic leaders samples mentioning persons in indicated categories who would influence them in "economic matters."

	BUSINESS LEADERS	CHAMBER OF COMMERCE	FARM ORGANIZATION LEADERS	LABOR LEADERS
State and national officeholders and candidates	2.9	3.5	3.1	42.1
Party officials	2.9	0.0	0.0	0.0
All other government personnel	0.0	0.0	6.3	0.0
Businessmen and bankers	65.7	64.2	31.3	31.6
Farm organization officials	0.0	0.0	6.3	5.3
Union officials	0.0	0.0	0.0	5.3
Mass media personnel	0.0	0.0	3.1	0.0
Lawyers	2.9	10.7	0.0	0.0
Engineers, accountants, insurance agents	0.0	3.5	3.1	5.3
Professors and other educational leaders	17.1	25.0	62.5	0.0
Clergymen	0.0	0.0	0.0	0.0
Members of the family	0.0	0.0	0.0	10.5
Voluntary association executives	0.0	0.0	3.1	0.0

Table 6. Percentages of civic association leaders samples mentioning persons in indicated categories who would influence them in "economic matters."

	VOLUNTARY ASSOCIATION PRESIDENTS	VOLUNTARY ASSOCIATION EXECUTIVES	LEAGUE OF WOMEN VOTERS	MINNESOTA WELFARE CONFERENCE	FEDERATION OF WOMEN'S CLUBS
State and national officeholders and candidates	17.1	7.1	12.3	0.0	17.4
Party officials	2.1	0.0	0.0	0.0	0.0
All other government personnel	4.2	6.0	4.0	7.7	4.3
Businessmen and bankers	23.4	36.5	28.5	53.9	43.5
Farm organization officials	0.0	0.0	0.0	0.0	0.0
Union officials	0.0	0.0	0.0	0.0	0.0
Mass media personnel	0.0	1.2	2.0	0.0	4.3
Lawyers	0.0	1.2	2.0	7.7	4.3
Doctors	0.0	0.0	0.0	0.0	8.7
Engineers, accountants, insurance agents	4.2	1.2	0.0	0.0	4.3
Professors and other educational leaders	12.7	22.4	34.6	15.4	8.7
Clergymen	0.0	1.2	0.0	0.0	0.0
Members of the family	0.0	2.4	16.2	0.0	0.0
Voluntary association executives	0.0	2.4	4.0	0.0	0.0

most frequently mention persons in the governmental-political field as ones who would influence them in political matters, they do not tend to mention the same individuals. The first column of Table 7 shows that of the 302 names volunteered as ones who would influence the respondents in political matters, 245 (or 81 per cent) are mentioned only once. Only 11 names are mentioned 15 times or more, and these are all top governmental officeholders or candidates for top public office in the state and nation. One name got as many as 127 mentions, but the second name had only 77 mentions. These top 11 political influentials may be considered a political elite, but it is to be noted that they are all public figures who occupy the top spots in the formal political structure. These patterns of response are found with little variation in all the samples, both the cross sections of average citizens and the 17 leadership samples. Unless these respondents are holding something back, they do not perceive an elite of political influence other than the top public officeholders and candidates for the top public offices. The leadership samples as well as the cross sections were inclined to give a large proportion of idiosyncratic responses.

When we turn to the question as to which specific persons are held to be most likely to influence the respondents in economic matters, we find much the same picture. The second column of Table 7 shows that 315 of the 377 names mentioned are mentioned only once. Only 8 names are mentioned 13 times or more. The top-frequency names —with 55 and 43 mentions, respectively—are of two university professors, one an emeritus in agricultural economics and the other an economist. While both men are very active in public life outside the university, it is interesting that they should be regarded as more influential in economic matters than businessmen. The third and fourth names in frequency, however, were of businessmen who had national reputations and are also very active in public life (they were mentioned 28 and 20 times, respectively). The fifth and sixth names were of political officeholders (they were mentioned 17 and 14 times, respectively). It seems clear that our respondents believe a great variety of different persons would influence them most in economic matters, and that the most influential are not necessarily businessmen. There are no significant variations among our 21 samples. In terms of these findings there is no clear-cut perceived economic elite even in matters of economic influence.

While the number of responses varied for each of the other questions, in all cases the overwhelming proportion of the names are mentioned but once. Further, the top-frequency names change with the subject matter of the question, although the names of the top political officeholders crop up most frequently:

1. In response to the question about "persuade me to contribute money for a charitable purpose," 260 of the 309 names mentioned were listed but once. The top-frequency names included 2 clergymen (with 30 and 15 mentions apiece), 1 local TV commentator and newspaper columnist (with 14 mentions), and 1 businessman (with 14 mentions).

2. In response to the question about "persuade me to contribute money to a political candidate," 190 of the 225 names mentioned were listed but once. The top 4 names (with frequencies ranging from 28 down to 10) were all of leading politicians (3 public officeholders and 1 party official).

3. In response to the question about "persuade me to attend a political meeting," 206 of the 244 names mentioned were listed but once. The top-frequency names were all of top public officeholders or party officials (ranging downward from 23 mentions of a congressman).

4. In response to the question about "persuade me that a certain public issue is important enough to study more," 284 of the 351 names mentioned were listed but once. The top-frequency names (with frequencies ranging downward from 31 mentions) were those of 4 political officeholders and the state chairman of the League of Women Voters.

5. In response to the question about "persuade me to join an association in a civic purpose," 326 of the 362 names mentioned were listed but once. Only 1 name came up with any significant frequency, and this was of a businessman with many civic activities (mentioned 14 times).

Another approach made to the question as to what categories of persons are most influential was to ask how each of 50 named persons would influence the respondent's opinion. The question read:

> Here are the names of persons living in Minnesota who have been mentioned on the front pages of the newspapers recently. Please tell how statements about public issues by these persons

would likely influence your opinion, by checking one of the
spaces after each name.

Spaces were placed after each of the 50 names so that the respondent
could answer, "favorably," "neither way," "unfavorably," or "never
heard of him." The names of the prominent persons were chosen with
the following criteria in mind:

1. They figured on the front pages of the newspapers in the three
months preceding the survey.
2. They had been prominent in Minnesota for at least several
years.
3. They represented various areas of life.
The positions of the 50 prominent persons and the categories they
represent are:

Politics, Republican (11 names): the candidate for governor, the
state treasurer, the national committeeman, the district attorney, the
state auditor, president of the Minneapolis School Board (a prominent retired businessman), a congressman, the mayor of Minneapolis,
the mayor of St. Paul, the state party chairman, a leader in the
state senate.

Politics, Democratic (7 names): the governor, the lieutenant governor, a leader in the state Senate, the national committeeman, a
prominent woman leader and former ambassador, the past attorney
general, the state commissioner of administration.

Education (7 names): president of the state university, a prominent retired university professor of political science, coach of the
university basketball team, a professor of agriculture, a professor of
agricultural economics advising the Democratic candidate for President, president of the leading private college in the state and advisor
to the national Republican administration, director of the state board
of education.

Business (5 names): heads of five corporations of national significance, all prominent in statewide civic affairs.

Mass media (5 names): publisher of the Minneapolis daily newspapers, editor of the Minneapolis daily newspaper, publisher of the
St. Paul daily newspapers, two who were both leading Minnesota
newscasters and newspaper gossip columnists.

Table 7. Frequency of mentions of specific names to seven questions about influence.

NUMBER OF MENTIONS	IN POLITICAL MATTERS	IN ECONOMIC MATTERS	IN CONTRIBUTIONS FOR CHARITY	IN POLITICAL CONTRIBUTIONS	IN ATTENDING POLITICAL MEETINGS	IN STUDYING A PUBLIC ISSUE	IN JOINING CIVIC ASSOCIATIONS
1	245	315	260	190	206	284	326
2	22	29	21	19	16	27	23
3	15	10	5	2	9	18	3
4-7	8	12	7	6	6	15	8
8-11	1	3	3	5	2	4	1
12 or more	11	8	4	3	5	3	1
TOTAL NUMBER OF NAMES MENTIONED	302	377	300	225	244	351	362

Agriculture (4 names): heads of all the important farm organizations.

Judiciary (4 names): judges of the federal district and state supreme courts.

Religion (4 names): outstanding clergymen of the Lutheran, Catholic, Presbyterian, and Jewish faiths.

Labor (1 name): state labor leader and lobbyist.

Medicine (1 name): head of internationally famous clinic.

Patriotic Society (1 name): head of Minnesota Daughters of the American Revolution.

Because the last three categories include only one name apiece, data on them cannot be regarded as reliable for the areas of life they represent, and so will not be reported here.

Tables 8 to 11 indicate the responses of the various samples to the names listed in the above categories. The Minneapolis cross section is paralleled only by the business leaders in the high proportion of no answers. It seems evident that a significant proportion of this "average" city population is not familiar with most of the names. There is a high proportion responding favorably only to the names of religious leaders, and these were identified for the respondents in the questionnaire by such prefixes as "reverend" and "bishop." Only the Democratic politicians receive a significant proportion of unfavorable responses from the Minneapolis cross section, and even this proportion is not high (12.7 per cent).

The business leaders respond favorably to the names of the prominent persons in business, religion, Republican politics, education, the judiciary, and the mass media. They are negative mainly toward the Democratic politicians, and secondarily to the agricultural leaders, although for the most part they are not familiar with the latter names. Almost the identical pattern is found in the Chamber of Commerce sample, although there is a much lower proportion of "no answers" among them. A similar pattern of responses is noted for the Minnesota Republican Workshop sample, although here the positiveness toward the Republican politicians and the negativism toward the Democratic politicians is accentuated.

In sharp contrast is the labor leaders sample, who are most positive toward the Democratic politicians and most negative toward the

Republican politicians. (While the labor leaders are more inclined to be positive than negative toward the names of judges, they are the only group with a significant proportion of unfavorable responses toward the judiciary.) Their proportion of negative responses toward businessmen's names is also significant (13.7 per cent). The farm organization leaders sample shows a different pattern of responses: their most favored group is from education, with Republican politicians' and business leaders' names following. The farm organization leaders are most unfavorable to the names of Democratic politicians, and secondly to the names of agricultural leaders. The latter fact illustrates the conflict among farm organizations: Those in one organization are obviously opposed to the leaders of the other organizations.

The women's organizations samples—analyzed in Table 10—have some notable differences among themselves also. The League of Women Voters tends to be more favorable to the Democratic than to the Republican politicians, whereas among the AAUW and the Federation of Women's Clubs samples the opposite is true. The names of clergymen draw favorable responses from all three groups, but the proportions of these favorable responses is considerably greater in the Federation than in the League. The same differential is found in attitudes toward the judiciary. But toward the names of prominent educators, the differential among the three women's groups is much less (although the AAUW is slightly more positive here). The League sample has quite average attitudes toward the names of businessmen, whereas the Federation sample is most favorable. These data for the three women's groups indicate, with remarkable clarity, how women leaders sort themselves out on their attitudes toward persons said to be influential.

The presidents and directors of voluntary associations tend to be quite similar in their responses, except that the directors tend to be somewhat more favorable to the names of Democratic politicians. Both groups tend to respond most favorably to the names of clergymen, and secondarily to those of educators. Like most of the other leadership samples, they are least familiar with the names of agricultural leaders. The Minneapolis Health and Welfare Council sample—who are also leaders of voluntary associations, in the welfare field—are somewhat distinguished by the relatively high

Table 8. How Minneapolis citizens and economic leaders samples would respond to statements on public issues by persons in the indicated categories.
(Percentage Distributions)

	Republican Politics	Democratic Politics	Education	Business	Mass Media	Agriculture	Judiciary	Religion
MINNEAPOLIS CROSS SECTION								
Favorably	19.5	15.9	16.7	16.6	18.3	2.1	19.3	31.4
Neither way	31.2	26.5	23.7	31.4	36.6	18.6	25.0	26.4
Unfavorably	5.2	12.7	2.4	1.1	2.3	1.4	3.6	5.0
Never heard of him	17.7	17.6	30.2	21.7	17.1	48.6	24.3	13.6
No answer	26.4	27.3	27.0	29.2	25.7	29.3	27.8	23.6
TOTAL PERCENT	100.0	100.0	100.0	100.0	100.0	100.0	100.0	100.0
BUSINESS LEADERS SAMPLE								
Favorably	34.0	7.8	33.1	42.9	28.0	5.7	32.9	40.0
Neither way	26.5	23.3	20.8	29.1	36.0	17.9	27.1	21.4
Unfavorably	6.2	31.8	2.9	1.7	5.1	10.7	4.3	2.1
Never heard of him	7.3	4.5	12.7	2.3	2.9	31.4	8.6	6.4
No answer	26.0	32.6	30.5	24.0	28.0	34.3	27.1	30.1
TOTAL PERCENT	100.0	100.0	100.0	100.0	100.0	100.0	100.0	100.0
FARM ORGANIZATION LEADERS SAMPLE								
Favorably	40.6	13.8	44.6	36.3	29.4	15.6	32.8	33.6
Neither way	27.8	33.5	20.1	26.9	33.8	21.1	32.0	29.7
Unfavorably	3.4	30.4	4.9	0.6	3.1	21.1	0.8	1.6
Never heard of him	10.8	5.8	15.2	18.1	17.5	22.7	17.2	18.8
No answer	17.4	16.5	15.2	18.1	16.2	19.5	17.2	16.3
TOTAL PERCENT	100.0	100.0	100.0	100.0	100.0	100.0	100.0	100.0

Table 9. How selected leadership samples would respond to statements on public issues by persons in the indicated categories.

(Percentage Distributions)

	Republican Politics	Democratic Politics	Education	Business	Mass Media	Agriculture	Judiciary	Religion
CHAMBER OF COMMERCE SAMPLE								
Favorably	30.8	9.2	32.7	51.4	24.3	1.8	35.7	50.9
Neither way	40.3	32.7	22.4	33.6	37.1	10.7	27.7	22.3
Unfavorably	7.8	40.8	2.6	0.7	15.0	13.4	2.7	4.5
Never heard of him	15.9	13.3	38.8	12.9	20.0	67.9	28.6	18.8
No answer	5.2	4.0	3.5	1.4	3.6	6.2	5.3	3.5
TOTAL PERCENT	100.0	100.0	100.0	100.0	100.0	100.0	100.0	100.0
MINNESOTA REPUBLICAN WORKSHOP SAMPLE								
Favorably	53.9	8.6	42.9	53.3	34.7	10.0	26.7	45.0
Neither way	24.8	32.4	22.9	40.0	49.3	13.3	38.3	33.3
Unfavorably	12.1	57.1	3.8	0	5.3	16.7	5.0	3.3
Never heard of him	7.3	1.9	27.6	4.0	9.3	56.7	28.3	16.7
No answer	1.9	0.0	2.9	2.7	1.4	3.3	1.7	1.7
TOTAL PERCENT	100.0	100.0	100.0	100.0	100.0	100.0	100.0	100.0
LABOR LEADERS SAMPLE								
Favorably	3.3	63.2	21.1	3.2	13.7	19.7	23.7	22.4
Neither way	18.7	21.1	25.6	37.9	38.9	7.9	35.5	35.5
Unfavorably	48.8	4.5	1.5	13.7	8.4	6.6	10.5	0.0
Never heard of him	17.2	6.0	38.3	33.7	28.4	52.6	19.7	31.6
No answer	12.0	5.2	13.5	11.5	10.6	13.2	10.6	10.5
TOTAL PERCENT	100.0	100.0	100.0	100.0	100.0	100.0	100.0	100.0

Table 10. How women's organization leaders would respond to statements on public issues by persons in the indicated categories.

(Percentage Distributions)

	Republican Politics	Democratic Politics	Education	Business	Mass Media	Agriculture	Judiciary	Religion
LEAGUE OF WOMEN VOTERS SAMPLE								
Favorably	22.1	29.7	32.9	23.7	21.2	4.6	18.9	31.6
Neither way	34.9	36.4	29.4	43.7	49.0	17.3	35.2	38.3
Unfavorably	18.2	18.1	1.7	2.4	9.0	2.0	0.5	7.1
Never heard of him	19.9	11.4	31.2	23.3	16.7	68.9	39.3	17.3
No answer	4.9	4.4	4.8	6.9	4.1	7.2	6.1	5.7
TOTAL PERCENT	100.0	100.0	100.0	100.0	100.0	100.0	100.0	100.0
FEDERATION OF WOMEN'S CLUBS SAMPLE								
Favorably	42.6	17.5	35.7	47.3	32.7	6.8	37.5	58.0
Neither way	29.8	33.1	26.0	26.4	36.4	22.7	35.2	21.6
Unfavorably	6.2	27.9	1.9	0.0	1.8	10.2	1.1	4.5
Never heard of him	10.3	6.5	18.8	17.3	16.4	38.6	15.9	9.1
No answer	11.1	15.0	17.6	9.0	12.7	21.7	10.3	6.8
TOTAL PERCENT	100.0	100.0	100.0	100.0	100.0	100.0	100.0	100.0
AMERICAN ASSOCIATION OF UNIVERSITY WOMEN SAMPLE								
Favorably	32.2	19.8	39.6	29.2	30.8	0.0	23.1	42.3
Neither way	32.9	29.7	23.1	41.5	29.2	11.5	26.9	28.8
Unavorably	10.5	35.2	2.2	0.0	6.2	5.8	1.9	3.8
Never heard of him	21.7	13.2	29.7	26.2	33.8	80.8	44.2	21.2
No answer	2.7	2.1	5.4	3.1	0.0	1.9	3.9	3.9
TOTAL PERCENT	100.0	100.0	100.0	100.0	100.0	100.0	100.0	100.0

Table 11. How voluntary association leaders would respond to statements on public issues by persons in the indicated categories (percentage distributions).

	Republican Politics	Democratic Politics	Education	Business	Mass Media	Agriculture	Judiciary	Religion
PRESIDENTS OF VOLUNTARY ASSOCIATIONS SAMPLE								
Favorably	32.7	13.1	35.3	28.5	21.3	3.2	31.4	37.8
Neither way	36.4	41.6	26.4	37.9	41.3	29.3	30.9	33.5
Unfavorably	6.8	22.8	2.4	1.7	6.0	8.0	2.1	3.2
Never heard of him	14.1	12.5	24.3	20.9	22.1	45.7	25.0	15.4
No answer	10.1	10.0	11.6	11.0	9.3	13.8	10.6	10.1
EXECUTIVE DIRECTORS OF VOLUNTARY ASSOCIATIONS SAMPLE								
Favorably	30.4	25.9	32.4	32.2	24.2	8.8	29.4	40.6
Neither way	32.8	35.6	28.2	35.5	44.5	24.7	34.4	37.1
Unfavorably	15.2	22.7	4.4	3.8	9.6	8.8	3.8	5.9
Never heard of him	13.3	7.2	25.2	18.6	14.4	45.0	23.2	9.7
No answer	8.3	8.6	9.8	9.9	7.3	12.7	9.2	6.7
MINNEAPOLIS HEALTH AND WELFARE COUNCIL SAMPLE								
Favorably	17.2	31.7	36.5	46.7	33.3	8.3	38.9	38.9
Neither way	52.5	31.7	31.7	28.9	40.0	22.2	33.3	41.7
Unfavorably	18.2	25.4	6.3	13.3	11.1	11.1	8.3	8.3
Never heard of him	8.1	4.8	20.6	6.7	13.3	50.0	11.1	0.0
No answer	4.0	6.4	4.9	4.4	2.3	8.4	8.4	11.1
MINNESOTA WELFARE CONFERENCE SAMPLE								
Favorably	19.6	19.8	28.6	36.9	16.9	9.6	25.0	40.4
Neither way	38.5	29.7	30.8	29.2	46.2	15.4	28.8	30.8
Unfavorably	16.8	35.2	2.2	6.2	7.7	1.9	1.9	1.9
Never heard of him	15.4	13.2	27.5	20.0	21.5	61.6	32.8	15.4
No answer	9.7	2.1	10.9	7.7	7.7	11.5	11.5	11.5

proportions of unfavorable responses they make. They are most positive toward the names of businessmen, and secondarily to clergymen, judges, and educators. The Minnesota Welfare Council sample is more neutral, and includes a slightly higher proportion of persons who have not heard of the names listed in our questionnaires.

C. Perceived Relative Influence by Local and Cosmopolitan Leaders

Since Robert K. Merton[9] distinguished between "locals" and "cosmopolitans" among community leaders, there have been many studies to indicate their relative degree and manner of influence.[10] None of these studies has inquired into people's own conceptions as to whether they are more influenced by locals or by cosmopolitans, and so a question on this was included in our Minnesota survey. The question read "Are you more likely to be influenced on public issues by persons who live in your neighborhood than by the so-called 'prominent persons' in the state?" This question may not always get at the exact distinction between locals and cosmopolitans, but it seemed preferable to other possible wordings in simple terminology. It is not claimed that the answers reveal the *true* sources of influence, but they do suggest who people *believe* are influencing them.

Table 12 shows the answers for the four city cross sections in our sample. In all four cases, respondents were more likely to feel they are influenced by prominent persons than by persons living in their neighborhood. This seems to be somewhat more true in the large cities of St. Paul and Minneapolis than in the small cities of Red Wing and Crookston.

The tendency to think of oneself as more influenced by prominent persons than by neighbors is found in all 17 of our leadership samples. But the variation is considerable. The rural leaders are relatively much more likely to see themselves as influenced by neighbors, whereas some of the highly cosmopolitan urban leaders do not see themselves influenced by neighbors at all. The answers of

[9]"Patterns of Influence," in P. F. Lazarsfeld and F. Stanton (eds.), *Communications Research 1948–1949* (New York: Harper, 1949).
[10]For a summary of such studies, including the major study on the topic, see Elihu Katz and Paul F. Lazarsfeld, *Personal Influence* (Glencoe, Ill.: Free Press, 1955).

Table 12. Relative Influence by Locals and Cosmopolitans, for Four City Samples.

(Percentages)

	MINNEAPOLIS	ST. PAUL	CROOKSTON	RED WING
More influenced by neighbors	9.7	6.8	10.7	13.6
More influenced by "prominent persons"	58.4	56.9	35.7	40.9
"It depends"	29.2	32.9	42.9	45.5
No answer	2.7	3.4	10.7	0.0
TOTAL	100.0	100.0	100.0	
				100.0
Number of cases	(73)	(58)	(56)	(44)

Table 13. Relative Influence by Locals and Cosmopolitans, for Four Leadership Samples.

(Percentages)

	COUNTY COMMISSIONERS	AGRICULTURAL EXTENSION AGENTS	UN ASSOCIATION	MINNEAPOLIS HEALTH AND WELFARE COUNCIL
More influenced by neighbors	22.2	17.5	0.0	0.0
More influenced by "prominent persons"	27.8	44.4	73.3	77.8
"It depends"	50.0	34.9	20.0	11.1
No answer	0.0	3.2	6.7	11.1
TOTAL	100.0	100.0	100.0	100.0
Number of cases	(65)	(126)	(54)	(35)

two samples of each of these two types are presented in Table 13.

The rejection of dominant influence by neighbors is so strong in the urban leadership samples that the variation has to be noted by comparing the relative proportions who answer "it depends" rather than of those who answer "more influenced by neighbors." Here we note a considerable variation. The labor leaders and the Federation of Women's Clubs leaders are more willing to acknowledge conditional influence ("it depends") of neighbors than are the Chamber of Commerce and business leaders: the proportions giving the response "it depends" is 47.4 and 54.5 per cent for the first two groups, but only 14.2 and 17.1 per cent for the last two groups. Thus we see that perception of leadership as local or cosmopolitan is graded, and various segments of the population can be placed on a continuum in this regard.

D. Perceptions of The Negative Influentials

Influence is negative as well as positive. When a public figure or official advocates a certain position on a public issue he may stir up antagonism as well as support. To get at this kind of negative influence, our questionnaire included the following request:

> Please name some persons in Minnesota whose opinions on public issues and problems might persuade you to *oppose* their point of view.

This was followed by spaces for 4 names and their positions (to help us identify the persons mentioned). The responses were classified into 22 categories. The various samples covered in our survey gave a different number of responses to the question. In general, the cross sections gave fewer responses than did the leadership sample: Whereas the Red Wing and Crookston samples averaged only 1.50 mentions per respondent (and the St. Paul sample 1.56 and the Minneapolis sample 1.68), the Minnesota Republic Workshop averaged 4.27, the Chamber of Commerce 2.57, the Federation of Women's Clubs 2.45, and the labor leaders 2.42. A large number of respondents—particularly in the four city cross sections—mentioned no names at all. This may have been through laziness, but it could just as well have been that they could not think of anyone who would influence them negatively. The proportions of non-respondents ranged from 68.8 per cent for St. Paul down to 45.5 per cent for Crookston among the four cities. They ranged from 56.3 per cent for the National Conference of Christians and Jews down to 7.7 per cent for the American Association of University Women, among the 17 leadership samples.

The political and governmental areas of life contained by far the largest proportions of persons to whom negative influence was attributed. At the time of the survey (summer 1960), the national administration was Republican: Minnesota's governor, two senators, and four of the nine representatives were Democrats;[11] the mayors of the state's two largest cities were Republicans. We shall see that officials of both political parties receives frequent mention as negative influentials. Party posts are relatively important in Minnesota, and both the two leading party chairmen at the time of the survey were widely known and controversial figures. Since the classification was derived from the names listed by the respondents, and more than one name in the same category could be mentioned by one respondent, it is possible to have more than 100 per cent response to a given category,[12] and even a figure under 100 per cent would not refer to proportion of respondents. To avoid this misleading way of reporting the data, we shall refer to number of mentions per respondent.

The Democratic political leaders are more frequently rejected than are the Republicans. The number of mentions of Democratic state and national officials per respondent among the four city samples ranged from 0.71 for Minneapolis down to 0.13 for St. Paul. Among the 17 leadership groups, the Minnesota Republican Workshop was high with 2.27 mentions per respondent, followed by the Chamber of Commerce sample with 1.46, the *Who's Who* sample with 1.10, the officers of agricultural organizations with 1.00. Very low were the Minnesota Welfare Conference with 0.23, the UN Association with 0.20, and the League of Women Voters with 0.10.

In general, Republican national and state officeholders received fewer mentions as negative influentials than did the Democrats. Exceptions included the St. Paul cross section (0.19 for the Republicans as compared to 0.13 for the Democrats), the League of Women Voters (0.20 for the Republicans as compared to 0.10 for the Democrats), and the labor leaders (0.74 for the Republicans as compared to zero for the Democrats).

Democratic *party* officials were not nearly so frequently mentioned as negative influentials, but there were 0.10 mentions per business leader, and 0.08 mentions per president of voluntary association. Loca! Democratic public officials also were seldom men-

[11]In Minnesota, the Democratic party is called the Democratic-Farmer-Labor party.

[12]The theoretical maximum would be 400 per cent. This could occur if all respondents in a given sample mentioned four names in the same category. The Minnesota Republican Workshop sample totaled 426.7 per cent, which meant that some of them used more than the four spaces offered.

tioned, with the high being in the Chamber of Commerce sample
(0.08 mentions) and in the Minnesota Welfare Conference sample
(0.08 mentions).

Republican *party* officials came in for more mentions as negative
influentials than did the Democrats: There were 0.13 mentions per
respondent in the St. Paul cross section and 0.11 in the Minneapolis
cross section. For the leadership samples, high proportions making
criticisms come from the labor leaders with 0.68 mentions, the
League of Women Voters with 0.33 mentions, the UN Association
with 0.33 mentions, and the Minnesota Welfare Conference with
0.31 mentions. In all samples, even the Minnesota Republican Workshop and the business leaders, the number of mentions of Republican
party officials as negative influentials was greater than for the Democratic party officials. Particularly salient was one Republican party
leader. Local Republican public officials were, like their Democratic
counterparts, seldom mentioned.

State legislators, who in Minnesota are often indistinguishable by
political party because there is a nonpartisan ballot, are significantly
regarded as negative influentials. The largest number of mentions of
legislators per respondent is found in the League of Women Voters
sample (0.51). Close behind is the Minnesota Republican Workshop, with 0.47 mentions. Considerably lower, but still significant, is
the number of mentions by the UN Association (0.27), by the labor
leaders (0.26), and by the Minnesota Welfare Council (0.24).
Lowest number of mentions of legislators as negative influentials is
found among the business leaders (0.03) and among the agricultural
extension agents (0.03). The four city cross sections' mentions are
also so low as to be insignificant, probably indicating that average
Minnesotans are not much aware of state legislators.

Newspaper and other mass media personnel are referred to as
negative influentials by high proportions in certain samples. In the
four city samples, the highest number of mentions per respondents
was for the St. Paul cross section (0.25), closely followed by the
Crookston (0.23). There is probably some local reason for this, as
the other two city samples had absolutely no mentions. Among the
17 leadership samples, a significant number of mentions per respondent of mass media persons as negative influentials is found
among labor leaders (0.16) and the Minnesota Republican Workshop (0.13).

Trade union officials are mentioned significantly as negative influentials by the Chamber of Commerce sample (0.29), by the business leaders (0.26), by the Minneapolis Health and Welfare Council (0.22), by the American Association of University Women (0.15), by the Minnesota Welfare Conference (0.15), and by the Minnesota Republican Workshop (0.13). Businessmen are mentioned significantly as negative influentials by the UN Association sample (0.33), by the labor leaders (0.21), by business leaders themselves, (0.20–sic) and by the League of Women Voters (0.14). Farm organization leaders are significantly thought of as negative influentials by the following samples in our survey: agricultural extension agents (0.35), officers of agricultural organizations themselves (0.19–sic), the Crookston cross section (0.14), and presidents of voluntary associations (0.11).

Professors and other educators came in for negative mention by a significant number of officers of agricultural organizations (0.13), and the Minnesota Republican Workshop (0.13). No other category of professionals received significant mention as negative influentials. The only group significantly to mention national public figures (other than governmental figures, already mentioned) as negative influentials was the labor leaders (0.11 mentions per respondent).

Scattered and non-significant mentions were made of clergymen, judges, other professional people, non-elected state officials, and civic organization leaders as negative influentials.

From the data presented it is evident that conspicuousness is a main factor in creating negative influentials. It is of course true that practically no sports or entertainment figures were mentioned as persons who could negatively influence the respondents. But such persons seldom state opinions on public issues, which is what the question refers to. Political and governmental figures, as well as those who express opinions in the mass media (columnists, editors, commentators) are the ones who are most frequently mentioned as negative influentials. Among the political figures those on the state level, rather than the local level, were most frequently mentioned, but perhaps this was a function of the time at which the survey was undertaken (summer 1960—when Eisenhower was president, Freeman was governor, and Humphrey and P. K. Peterson were senatorial candidates). Negative influentials were almost as likely to be found among persons in one's own category as among persons in other

categories. Comparing this section with those on the positive influentials, we see that a public figure can be both a strong positive and
a strong negative influential at the same time.

E. Images of the Unnamed Power Source

One of the characteristics of the individual who is alienated from his
society is that he is unable to identify or to name the forces that
control him. In casual conversation, the pronoun "they" appears
without referent whenever the alienated individual speaks of some
social influence or determinant he does not understand. This unnamed force (or forces) is believed to control him or something he
is interested in. Often it is perceived as malevolent: often it lacks
legitimacy except insofar as all powers are thought to be legitimate
simply because they are powerful; sometimes it is assumed to be
merely natural or inevitable.

In an effort to get some empirical information on perceptions of
the unnamed power source or sources in our society, the following
question was included in the questionnaire distributed to our 21
selected samples:

> It is sometimes said that "*they* control things," "*they* get things
> done," "*they* get things their way," and so on. Who are *they*
> in such statements?

A sizable proportion of the respondents did not answer the question,
but it is not known whether non-response means the denial of the
existence of "they," or such a deep acceptance of "they" that the
respondent cannot articulate who "they" might be, or mere laziness
in the face of the question. Our four city cross sections of the general population showed a non-response to the question varying from
15.8 per cent for Minneapolis to 46.4 per cent for Red Wing. All
but one of the seventeen leadership samples had a non-response
ranging from zero per cent for the Minneapolis Health and Welfare
Council and the American Association of University Women to 21.7
per cent for the *Who's Who* sample; the one exception was that of
the county commissioners, 44.4 per cent of whom did not respond to
the question.

There were others who rejected the question in a reasonable

fashion. They said: "There is no such 'they,' " "figments of imagination," " 'they' is a word used by lazy, apathetic, unintelligent, unin-
formed people," "Scapegoaters use 'they.' " Only small proportions
of the respondents were inclined to give one of these answers, except
in some of the leadership samples. High proportions were found in
the sample of League of Women Voters presidents (28.6 per cent),
Chamber of Commerce members (25.0 per cent), and American
Association of University Women presidents (23.1 per cent).

Another category of response which practically denies any specific
meaning to the notion of "they" includes the following answers:
"The in-group as seen by the out-group," "the opposition," "the
other people." Significant proportions of the labor leaders (15.8 per
cent), the American Association of University Women (15.4 per
cent), the League of Women Voters presidents (12.2 per cent),
and the business leaders (11.4 per cent) gave this kind of response.

All of the other respondents projected some meaning of their
own, into the "they" concept, although some respondents obviously
answered in terms of who they thought *others* meant by "they." This
projected meaning varied greatly among the samples and within every
sample. We used 27 categories into which to classify the answers.
The *Who's Who* sample used 21 of them, thereby showing little
tendency to think alike, whereas the UN Association members used
only 7 categories. The inclination to project is perhaps shown by the
number of responses given to the questions: The voluntary association executives were low with just one answer per person; the
Chamber of Commerce sample was high with two answers per average respondent.

We shall report on only the categories which elicited the most
frequent response. The meaning which the largest proportion of
people think of as "they" is "the politicians" (sometimes expressed
as "political parties"). But there was considerable variation among
our samples in giving this response. The highest proportions were
found for the St. Paul cross section (40.0 per cent) and for the
agricultural organization presidents (32.3 per cent), whereas the
lowest proportions mentioning politicians were found among the
Red Wing cross section (3.6 per cent) and the voluntary association
executives (8.2 per cent). Economic leaders were relatively little inclined to identify "they" with politicians: Only 10.7 per cent of the

Chamber of Commerce sample did so, 8.6 per cent of the business leaders, and 15.8 per cent of the labor leaders. Our only sample of political party people is the Minnesota Republican Workshop, 26.7 per cent of whom considered the meaning of "they" to be politicians.

A closely related category which received a significant number of responses was that of "government" (including the responses "high officials," "elected officials," and "heads of government"). Among the four city cross sections, Crookston was high here with 18.2 per cent using this category to define "they"; Minneapolis followed with 13.2 per cent. Among the leadership samples, only one showed any significant number who identified government with "they"—this is the League of Women Voters presidents, with 10.2 per cent.

The next most frequent response is almost as vague as the "they" concept itself. We may call this category the "power elite" response, which term some respondents actually used. Other answers classified here are: "those in power," "small powerful minority," "the insiders," "leadership," "organizers," "ambitious people," "influential and prominent people," "active and successful people." This category claimed the responses of 38.5 per cent of the Minnesota Welfare Conference sample ranging down to 4.8 per cent for the St. Paul cross section.

Business and business groups (sometimes specifically "N.A.M." and "C. of C.") were the definitions assigned to "they" by a significant proportion in several of our samples. The National Conference of Christians and Jews (with 25.0 per cent), the county commissioners (with 16.7 per cent), and the Chamber of Commerce sample (with 21.4 per cent) most frequently gave "business" or business groups as their answer. Labor leaders included about the same proportion (21.1 per cent) as did the business leaders (20.0 per cent). Also significantly high proportions with this answer came from the Minneapolis cross section (18.4), and the agricultural organization leaders (16.1 per cent). Probably a closely linked category of response is that which identifies "they" with "the rich people," the "higher economic groups." The Minnesota Republican Workshop (with 20.0 per cent) and the Minneapolis cross section (with 13.2 per cent) were the two samples which gave this response with significant frequency.

None of the other categories could be said to have attracted frequent response. But significant minorities mentioned the following:

1. *Labor leaders and labor unions.* The Chamber of Commerce sample was high here, with 28.5 per cent identifying "they" as organized labor. Also high here were the county commissioners (22.3 per cent), and the National Conference of Christians and Jews sample (18.8 per cent). The labor leaders sample itself was fairly high here, with 15.8 per cent of them giving "labor" or "labor unions" as the meaning of "they."

2. *"The people," "we," "ourselves," "the public."* This category of definition of "they" was given by 13.6 per cent of the Minnesota Federation of Women's Clubs leaders and by 10.6 per cent of the presidents of voluntary associations, but not in significant numbers by other samples.

3. *"Minority groups."* This was mentioned by 12.5 per cent of the National Conference of Christians and Jews sample, but not significantly by any other sample.

4. *Church groups, welfare groups, and social clubs* (a category referring to voluntary associations of various types). This category received a significant proportion of the response only from the Minnesota Federation of Women's Clubs sample (18.2 per cent).

5. *"Pressure groups" and "lobbies."* This category was mentioned by 15.4 per cent of the Minnesota Welfare Conference sample, 13.3 per cent of the UN Association sample, and 13.3 per cent of the Minnesota Republican Workshop, but only by non-significant proportions of the other samples.

It is as important in studying images of the power structure to know who "they" are *not,* as it is to know who "they" are supposed to be. The following groups were mentioned by at least one respondent but not by any significant proportion of any of our 21 samples:

Farmers

Professional persons or organizations

Women

Teenagers

Apparently these are either too innocent or too powerless to be identified as "they." But it may be somewhat surprising that the following groups were not mentioned by any significant proportion of our samples:

Mass media
Bureaucrats, government administrators
Criminals and gangsters
Communists
Jews
Catholics

Hypotheses can be found in the sociological literature linking each of these latter groups with the nameless power source which the alienated individual typically is said to fear. There is no evidence for this from our study, except for a stray individual here and there in our varied samples. Of course, only our cross sections may be expected to include alienated individuals.

F. Varying Conceptions on
How To Stimulate Public Interest

Different leadership groups are in a different position to stimulate interest in public issues. Executives of the large voluntary associations, for example, have a different approach to the public than do business leaders. Their statements concerning how they would stimulate public interest should reveal something about their conception of their leadership roles. In our survey of four city cross sections and 17 leadership groups in Minnesota, we asked the question, "What would you suggest doing to get people in your neighborhood interested in public issues?" The question was put in terms of "people in your neighborhood" in order to hold constant the feelings the respondents might have about different social classes. There is an implication in the question that the "people" referred to are not sufficiently interested in public issues. While the question asks about techniques or procedure, many of the answers are couched in terms of the impossibility of doing anything to stimulate public interest. Perhaps it could be said that leadership groups who are inclined to think that nothing can be done to encourage public interest are less likely to be effective than leadership groups who have many ideas about technique, even if not all the suggested techniques prove workable.

A large proportion of all four city cross sections failed to answer the question. Since this population contains a large proportion of people who are themselves uninterested in public issues and who are themselves never in leadership roles, this non-response is not surprising.[13] The proportions of non-response have a narrow range, from 36.4 per cent for Crookston to 43.8 per cent for St. Paul. The proportion of non-responders among the 17 leadership groups ranges from a high of 38.9 per cent for the county commissioners and 36.8 per cent for the labor leaders to a low of zero per cent for the Minnesota Republican Workshop and 6.7 per cent for the UN Association. Business leaders are in striking contrast to labor leaders: only 17.1 per cent of them are non-responders (as are only 14.3 per cent of the Chamber of Commerce sample).

One category of response is that "nothing can be done," "people are just apathetic." This was rarely given by the four city cross sections (ranging down from 6.3 per cent for St. Paul to zero per cent for Crookston). Most leadership samples were also very low here, but we note that 13.4 per cent of the UN Association gave this response, as did 12.2 per cent of the League of Women Voters presidents. A similar category of response implies that little can be done to arouse people's interest in public issues, but phrases it in facetious or "tough" terminology: "drop a bomb," "lower wages," "have a crisis." This response was practically never given by the cross section samples, but it was given by 15.4 per cent of the Minnesota Welfare Conference sample and by 11.1 per cent of the Minneapolis Health and Welfare Council sample (and by lesser proportions of the other leadership samples).

Some respondents felt that people are already sufficiently interested in public issues and that enough is already done to stimulate their interest. Among the four city cross sections, St. Paul was again high here, with 12.5 per cent giving this answer. Among the 17 leadership samples, only the National Conference of Christians and Jews had a significant proportion giving this response (12.5 per cent).

One of the most frequently mentioned techniques for stimulating people's interest in public issues was by use of small discussion groups—in the forms of study clubs, coffee hours, seminars. High proportions mentioning this approach were found among the Minnesota Republican Workshop group (66.7 per cent), the UN Asso-

---

[13]The proportion of non-responders is considerably higher for this question than for surrounding questions, also of the "free response" type.

ciation (33.3 per cent), the American Association of University Women and the Minnesota Welfare Conference (each 30.8 per cent). Only small proportions of the four city cross sections (the highest was 10.7 per cent for Red Wing), of the agricultural organization leaders (6.3 per cent) and of the labor leaders (5.3 per cent) gave this response.

Another highly personal approach to getting people interested in public issues is by personal conversation and door-to-door canvassing. This was rarely mentioned by anyone in the four city cross sections. It was mentioned by 20.0 per cent of the Minnesota Republican Workshop and of the UN Association, by 19.2 per cent of the voluntary associations presidents, and by 18.8 per cent of the agricultural organization leaders. It was rarely mentioned by the labor leaders, by the agricultural extension agents, or by the Minnesota Federation of Women's Clubs.

Another frequently suggested technique was to use the mass media with various forms of publicity. The highest proportions mentioning this were found among the American Association of University Women and the Minnesota Welfare Conference (each with 30.8 per cent), and among the labor leaders (with 26.3 per cent). It is perhaps noteworthy that the labor leaders were much more inclined to mention the mass media than to mention small groups; this was not found in any other sample.

Urging people to join civic associations—such as the P.T.A., the League of Women Voters, the Chamber of Commerce, labor unions, neighborhood associations—was mentioned as a technique of developing interest in public issues by significant proportions of some of our samples. Noteworthy here are the League of Women Voters presidents (20.8 per cent) and the American Association of University Women (15.4 per cent). None of the labor leaders or the members of the Minneapolis Health and Welfare Council mentioned this approach.

Educational means—getting people better educated in general or having them participate in adult education classes or public forums with lectures and debates—were suggested by other leadership groups as among the better means of stirring up interest in public issues. Small proportions of the four city cross sections mentioned these techniques, varying from a high of 22.7 per cent of the

Crookston sample to a low of 7.2 per cent of the Red Wing sample. Many references to some educational approach were found among the Minneapolis Health and Welfare Council leaders (33.3 per cent), the American Association of University Women (30.8 per cent), the National Conference of Christians and Jews (25.1 per cent), the agricultural extension agents (28.5 per cent), and the agricultural organization leaders (21.8 per cent). Least inclined to suggest an educational approach were the Chamber of Commerce sample (10.7 per cent), the UN Association (6.7 per cent), and the executives of voluntary associations (6.0 per cent).

The use of political means—getting people to register and vote, or getting them to join a political party—was explicitly mentioned by small but significant proportions in only two leadership groups: the business leaders (11.5 per cent), and the presidents of voluntary associations (8.5 per cent). Perhaps surprisingly, the only political group in our 17 leadership samples had few mentions of this (the Minnesota Republican Workshop—6.7 per cent). Nor did the reference to political means come at all frequently from the four city cross sections. Activity in and by local government, similarly, was seldom mentioned as a means of stirring people's interest in public issues.

Nor was the use of churches and church groups mentioned with any significant frequency by any group. The highest proportion among our 21 samples was the League of Women Voters, with 6.1 per cent.

A scattering of other techniques was given by an occasional respondent here and there. But, in general, as we have seen, the suggestions that were made most frequently to stimulate interest in public affairs were related to the use of small groups and of the mass media. The large non-response and the responses indicating that nothing could be done, suggest a fairly widespread pessimism about the possibility of getting people further interested in public affairs.

G. Social Participations of Alleged Leaders

The social participations of our seventeen samples of formal leaders would be expected either to provide some of the sources of their information and beliefs, or to serve as channels for their influence

on other people, or both. In presenting information about this, we are
not claiming that our samples include true leaders and that we are
therefore giving some information about the character of leadership
in Minnesota. Rather, we present the information to suggest the
sources of the images and perceptions revealed in the preceding
pages of this chapter, and to indicate how these people relate to
others in the society. Facts are presented here about the participations
of our samples of leadership groups in churches, in occupational
groups, in voluntary associations; and about their contacts with
newspapers, magazines, radio and TV. It is not claimed, of course,
that our small samples of selected alleged leadership groups in Minnesota are representative of leaders throughout the United States.

Most of the persons in our 17 leadership groups are church attenders. But there are some groups in which the proportion of non-
attenders is significant: labor leaders (15.8 per cent), League of
Women Voters presidents (10.2 per cent), business leaders (8.6 per
cent), presidents of voluntary associations (8.5 per cent), executives
of voluntary associations (8.2 per cent). Of the four city cross
sections studied, Minneapolis also had a significant proportion of
non-attenders (11.4 per cent). If *regular* attendance be defined as
more than 40 visits to church in a year, or a statement that church
attendance is "regular," not all of the leadership groups may be said
to have high proportions of regular attenders: These include the
business leaders (only 25.1 per cent of whom are regular attenders),
the Chamber of Commerce sample (32.1 per cent), Minneapolis
Health and Welfare Council (33.3 per cent), UN Association (35.7
per cent), League of Women Voters presidents (45.4 per cent), and
the Minnesota Welfare Conference (46.2 per cent). Most of the
leadership groups have a large number of "close friends" in the
church they attend, but a few do not: 61.6 per cent of American
Association of University Women officers have five or fewer friends
in church; the figure for the UN Association is 50.0 per cent, for the
League of Women Voters presidents 45.5 per cent, for the Chamber
of Commerce sample 42.8 per cent, for the business leaders 37.5
per cent. This is in contrast with the greater number of friends in
church claimed by the average citizens in the four city cross sections:
In Red Wing only 14.8 per cent claim 5 or fewer friends, and in the
highest case (St. Paul) the figure is 37.4 per cent. At the other end

of the scale are the groups where at least 25 per cent claim to know "practically everyone" in their church: the county commissioners (41.2 per cent), the *Who's Who* sample (34.3 per cent), the National Conference of Christians and Jews (33.3 per cent), the agricultural extension agents (30.6 per cent), the presidents of voluntary associations (30.2 per cent), the agricultural organization presidents (29.0 per cent).

To get at membership in occupational associations, a question in the survey asks "Are you a member of a union, business, or professional group?" As might be expected, the leadership groups composed of women have the lowest proportions affiliated with occupational organizations. They are followed by the four city cross sections. Among the remaining leadership groups, the ones with the highest attendance at meetings of occupational organization are the labor leaders (with 36.8 per cent attending all business and committee meetings), the agricultural extension agents (36.1 per cent), the Chamber of Commerce sample (28.0 per cent). The groups with the highest proportions claiming to know "practically all" the members of their occupational organization are the agricultural extension agents (62.3 per cent), the Minnesota Welfare Conference sample (61.5 per cent), the presidents of agricultural organizations (58.3 per cent), and the Chamber of Commerce sample (50.0 per cent).

The other voluntary associations our respondents belong to were classified into nine categories. The proportion with membership in each of them is shown for selected leadership groups in Table 14. It is apparent that there is a considerable range in the type of affiliation. The category which includes the largest proportion of affiliates is the sociable one, which includes fraternal organizations, card-playing clubs, and many others. There is considerable similarity between the business leaders and the farm organization leaders. Probably the category of association which offers the greatest opportunity for influence on public issues is the one we have labeled "political or social reform." In addition to some of the groups listed in Table 14, this category has a significant proportion of affiliations in the Minnesota Federation of Women's Clubs (31.8 per cent), the National Conference of Christians and Jews (25.0 per cent), and—of course—the UN Association (100.0 per cent) and the League of Women Voters (100.0 per cent), which belong in the category itself.

Table 14. Proportion belonging to nine categories of voluntary associations, for selected leadership groups.

CATEGORIES OF VOLUNTARY ASSOCIATIONS JOINED	PRESIDENTS OF VOLUNTARY ASSOCIATIONS	EXECUTIVES OF VOLUNTARY ASSOCIATIONS	AMERICAN ASSOCIATION OF UNIVERSITY WOMEN	MINNESOTA REPUBLICAN WORKSHOP	BUSINESS LEADERS	LABOR LEADERS	PRESIDENTS OF AGRICULTURAL ORGANIZATIONS
Community or social-welfare	19.1	16.5	76.9	40.0	11.4	15.8	15.6
Church-affiliated	17.0	7.1	38.5	6.7	2.9	5.3	9.4
Political or social-reform	8.5	9.4	61.5	100.0	0.0	5.3	3.1
Educational	17.0	9.4	15.4	13.3	0.0	5.3	9.4
Artistic	8.5	0.0	0.0	6.7	0.0	0.0	0.0
Family and child oriented	31.9	20.0	30.8	53.3	11.4	26.3	18.8
Sociable	59.6	50.6	100.0	73.3	100.0	63.2	78.1
Veterans'	8.5	12.9	0.0	0.0	2.9	26.3	0.0
Hobby	23.4	12.9	7.7	13.3	22.9	10.5	21.9

Another category which may offer considerable opportunity for influence is the one called "community or social welfare." In addition to some of the groups listed in the table, the leadership groups with large proportions of their members in associations of this category include the Minnesota Federation of Women's Clubs (100.0 per cent), the Minneapolis Health and Welfare Council (67.7 per cent), the UN Association (60.0 per cent), and the League of Women Voters (34.7 per cent).

When asked how many of the members of their voluntary associations could be called close friends, the proportions of the various leadership samples answering "practically all" varied considerably. While this is partly a function of the size of their association, it may be surprising that the proportion was only 8.2 per cent among the presidents of the League of Women Voters, only 18.2 per cent in the Minnesota Welfare Conference, and only 23.1 per cent in the UN Association. The proportions are high for the National Conference of Christians and Jews (100.0 per cent), the Minnesota Federation of Women's Clubs (68.2 per cent), the county commissioners (66.7 per cent), the business leaders (58.8 per cent), and the presidents of agricultural organizations (58.6 per cent).

A question was asked in the survey as to which newspapers and magazines were read "regularly," "occasionally," and "once in a great while." The Minneapolis newspapers were the most widely read through the state: 94.1 per cent of the Minneapolis cross section said they read one of them regularly, as did 40.9 per cent of the Crookston sample, 35.7 per cent of the Red Wing sample, and 25 per cent of the St. Paul sample. Another 9.1 per cent of the Crookston sample, and 7.1 per cent of the Red Wing sample, read the Minneapolis *Sunday Tribune* regularly. Regular readership of the St. Paul newspapers was claimed by 62.5 per cent of the St. Paul sample, but only by tiny proportions in the other three cities. The Red Wing sample read its local newspaper in greater proportion (85.7 per cent), as did the Crookston sample (81.8 per cent). Practically no one in the city cross sections read out-of-state newspapers.

In the leadership samples, high proportions of regular readership of the Minneapolis newspapers were found among the Minneapolis Health and Welfare Council (88.7 per cent), Minnesota Federation of Women's Clubs (86.4 per cent), UN Association (80.0 per cent),

Minneapolis Chamber of Commerce (75.0 per cent), and the presidents of voluntary associations (74.5 per cent). There are some leadership groups which include a significant proportion reading the national or international newspapers: UN Association—(40.0 per cent), the National Conference of Christians and Jews (37.5 per cent), the American Association of University Women (23.1 per cent), the Minneapolis Health and Welfare Council (22.2 per cent), and the League of Women Voters (16.3 per cent).

Occupational newspapers and magazines were much less frequently read. Except for a few executives of the voluntary associations, the only leadership sample that had any respondents who read the labor press regularly was the labor leaders (57.9 per cent). Perhaps surprisingly, practically none of the respondents in the four city cross sections mentioned reading the labor press. The proportions regularly reading the farm journals were insignificant except for the agricultural extension agents (49.2 per cent), the agricultural organization leaders (34.4 per cent), the county commissioners (27.8 per cent), the *Who's Who* sample (11.2 per cent), and the Crookston cross section (9.1 per cent). Business newspapers and journals were somewhat more frequently read: by 57.1 per cent of the business leaders, 50.0 per cent of the National Conference of Christians and Jews, 46.4 per cent of the Chamber of Commerce sample, 24.3 per cent of the *Who's Who* sample, 18.8 per cent of the agricultural organization presidents, 17.0 per cent of the presidents of voluntary associations. For the four city cross sections, the proportions ranged from 13.6 per cent for Crookston down to 3.6 per cent for Red Wing. Professional journals had a high proportion of regular readers only among the Minnesota Welfare Council (30.8 per cent), the American Association of University Women (23.1 per cent), the Minnesota Health and Welfare Council (22.2 per cent), and presidents of voluntary associations (17.0 per cent). Church publications had a significant proportion of regular readers in the Crookston cross section (27.3 per cent), the Minneapolis cross section (14.7 per cent), the executives of voluntary associations (14.1 per cent), the Minnesota Welfare Conference (23.1 per cent), the Minnesota Federation of Women's Clubs (13.6 per cent) and the Minnesota Republican Workshop (13.3 per cent). Other organizational publications had a significant proportion of regular readers among the UN

Association leaders (13.3 per cent) and the League of Women Voters' leaders (10.2 per cent).

Among the general magazines, those with mixed contents—like the Saturday Evening Post, Life, Look, Reader's Digest—attract the largest proportions of regular readership. The proportions for the four city cross sections range fom 56.3 per cent for St. Paul to 40.9 per cent for Crookston. The highest proportions of regular readership of these magazines were found among the Minnesota Republican Workshop (86.7 per cent), the Minnesota Federation of Women's Clubs (68.2 per cent), the Minneapolis Health and Welfare Council (66.7 per cent), and the presidents of voluntary associations (55.3 per cent).

News magazines have a high proportion of regular readers among the Chamber of Commerce sample (60.9 per cent), the Minnesota Republican Workshop (60.0 per cent), the business leaders (57.1 per cent), the National Conference of Christians and Jews (56.3 per cent), the *Who's Who* sample (53.3 per cent), the Minnesota Federation of Women's Clubs (45.5 per cent), the League of Women Voters (40.8 per cent), and the presidents of agricultural organizations (40.6 per cent). The range for the four city cross sections is from 26.5 per cent for Minneapolis down to 13.6 per cent for Crookston.

Magazines of political, social, and cultural commentary are scarcely read at all by the general population in the four city cross sections. The proportion of regular readership of these magazines is fairly high among the following leadership samples: the UN Association (60.0 per cent), the Minnesota Republican Workshop (46.7 per cent), the American Association of University Women (46.2 per cent), and the League of Women Voters (32.7 per cent).

Entertainment and hobby magazines are very popular with the general population: Proportions of regular readers range from 44.1 per cent for Minneapolis to 25.0 per cent for Red Wing. High proportions are found in the following leadership samples: the Minnesota Federation of Women's Clubs (50.0 per cent), the League of Women Voters (36.7 per cent), the Chamber of Commerce (35.7 per cent), and the presidents of voluntary associations (34.0 per cent).

Most of our respondents in all samples said they listened "regu-

larly" to news broadcasts on TV or radio. Among the four city cross
sections, the proportion was highest for St. Paul (93.8 per cent) and
lowest for Red Wing (71.4 per cent). Many of those in the leadership groups did not listen regularly, however. The proportion of regular listeners among the Minneapolis Health and Welfare Council
members was only 44.4 per cent, among the Chamber of Commerce
sample it was only 53.5 per cent, and among the business leaders
71.4 per cent. Groups with very high proportion of regular listeners
were the Minnesota Federation of Women's Clubs (95.5 per cent),
the Minnesota Welfare Conference (92.3 per cent), and the labor
leaders (89.5 per cent). Most of those who did not listen "regularly,"
did listen "occasionally."

A question was asked in our survey about frequency of voting in
elections. Among the four city cross sections, the proportion saying
they voted in "every single election" ranged from 68.5 per cent for
Minneapolis down to 46.4 per cent for Red Wing. Among the 17
leadership groups, high proportions voting every single election were
found among the Minnesota Republican Workshop (100.0 per cent),
the UN Association (100.0 per cent), the *Who's Who* sample (96.0
per cent), the labor leaders (94.7 per cent), the county commissioners (94.4 per cent), the Minneapolis Health and Welfare Council (88.9 per cent), the League of Women Voters presidents (87.7
per cent), the business leaders (85.7 per cent), the presidents of
voluntary associations (80.7 per cent), and the executives of
voluntary associations (77.7 per cent). Leadership groups with
under 70 per cent saying they voted "every single election" included
the Minnesota Welfare Conference (38.5 per cent), the agricultural
extension agents (46.1 per cent), and the Chamber of Commerce
sample (60.1 per cent). Most of those who did not vote "every single
election" did vote "most of the time."

Party affiliation was inquired about in terms of usual voting behavior, and the possible answers permitted an "independent" and
"other" response, as well as Republican and Democratic. Among the
four city cross sections, the proportion usually voting Republican
ranged from 57.1 per cent for Red Wing to 25.0 per cent for St. Paul
(Crookston was 54.5 per cent Republican, Minneapolis 34.3 per
cent). The proportion usually voting Democratic was 43.9 per cent

for St. Paul, 37.2 per cent for Minneapolis, 31.8 per cent for Crookston, and 17.9 per cent for Red Wing. Most of the respondents in the 17 leadership samples tended to vote Republican. The Minnesota Republican Workshop, of course, voted 100 per cent Republican. The business leaders followed with 85.7 per cent, then the *Who's Who* sample with 75.5 per cent, the Minnesota Federation of Women's Clubs leaders with 72.7 per cent, the officers of agricultural organizations with 71.9 per cent, the presidents of voluntary associations with 65.9 per cent, the Chamber of Commerce with 64.2 per cent, the American Association of University Women with 61.5 per cent, the agricultural extension agents with 54.0 per cent, and the National Conference of Christians and Jews with 50.1 per cent. The only groups to have a larger proportion of Democratic voters than of Republican voters are the labor leaders (89.5 per cent Democratic to zero per cent Republican) and the UN Association (33.3 to 26.7 per cent). The Minnesota Welfare Conference was evenly divided at 46.2 per cent acknowledging their affiliation to both the Republican and Democratic parties, and the county commissioners evenly divided at 33.3 per cent. Some groups had a higher proportion voting Republican than Democratic, but a majority claiming neither party affiliation: the executives of voluntary associations (49.4 per cent Republican to 23.5 per cent Democratic), the League of Women Voters (46.9 to 32.6 per cent), the Minneapolis Health and Welfare Council (44.4 to 22.2 per cent).

This section has been heavy with facts, but interpretation would add little. The facts indicate a considerable range among the leadership samples in most of their participations and their contacts with the mass media, and some differences between these samples and the four city cross sections.

H. Perceptions of Power and Influence: Summary and Discussion

One of the crticisms of Hunter's books on this subject is that he did not study actual decision-making (except for one minor case history of the textile tariff, which did not support his general thesis) but rather ascertained the characteristics of those reputed to have power. Our research also studies images of and opinions about power, with somewhat different questions and procedures, but arrives at conclusions opposed to those of Hunter. Ours is a questionnaire and interview study of a representative cross section of the adult population of four cities in Minnesota (Minneapolis, St. Paul, Red Wing, and Crookston), and of the leadership of 17 different groups or categories in the same state. We do not claim, as does Hunter, that our findings indicate anything about *actual* power or potential for power, but merely about *perceptions* of power. Perceptions of power may not tell us anything about actual power and decision-making, but they offer significant data in their own right if cautiously interpreted. The leadership samples in our study are arbitrarily chosen, and are biased in favor of the "economic elite," just as Hunter's samples are, but still the conclusions are contrary to his.

One section of the study is based on questions as to which groups the respondents believe are the most powerful ones in the nation. The conclusions concerning these "images of powerful groups" are:

1. The leadership samples gave significantly different answers, indicating that their images of powerful groups were far from identical. Singled out for special contrast were the presidents of voluntary associations and the business leaders. Hunter's study found them to be very similar in their statements as to the locus of power, but ours found the former emphasizing political parties and churches, and the latter emphasizing economic groups (including unions and business).

2. The leadership samples gave more answers and distributed their answers into more categories than did the cross sections. On this basis it can be said that leaders perceive power to be more dispersed than do average citizens.

3. In general, the group that was declared to be most powerful was the "unions," which was named by over 50 per cent of the four cross section samples, and by over 60 per cent of 16 of the 17 leadership samples (including the sample of labor leaders themselves). In general, the group getting second most numerous mentions as "The most powerful group" was "business." While the four cross section samples had very low proportions mentioning this group, it was mentioned by over 25 per cent of all 17 leadership samples. The third ranking category in number of mentions received

was professional groups—such as "doctors" and "lawyers"—which were similarly mentioned more frequently by the 17 leadership samples (especially the union leaders) than by the cross sections.

4. There was considerable diversity among the samples in the frequency of mentions of "political parties." The one political leadership sample (Minnesota Republican Workshop) mentioned it most frequently (46.7 per cent), and the Federation of Women's Clubs leadership sample mentioned it least frequently (4.5 per cent). The Red Wing cross section mentioned it most frequently (29 per cent); the Crookston cross section mentioned it least frequently.

5. Lesser, but significant, proportions of many of our 21 samples mentioned as most powerful the farmers and farm organizations, the political pressure groups and lobbies, and the mass media.

6. Scarcely mentioned at all as powerful groups are: fraternal and veterans' organizations, the military, the government, criminals, law-enforcement agencies, communists, conservatives (including McCarthyites).

The data for this study were collected in the summer of 1960; it is believed that if the data were collected at another time, the rankings of all the groups might be considerably different.

In another series of questions the respondents were asked to indicate what specific persons, and categories or groups, influenced them most in specified ways.

1. The samples did not vary much, on the average, in response to these questions, but individual respondents within each sample did vary considerably: About 80 per cent of the persons listed as influential were named only once by our entire sample. Only a very small number of influentials were named by 12 or more of our respondents, and these were practically all top government officeholders.

2. Still, there was noteworthy variation in the named influentials (and their positions) according to whether the question asked about influence in political matters, in economic matters, in studying a public issue, in making a contribution to a charity or to a political party, etc. Different persons are thus perceived as influential in different areas of life.

3. For influence in the political matters, all of the top-frequency

names mentioned were in the governmental-political walks of life. Some mentions were made of educators and clergymen, very few mentions were made of economic leaders (either business or union leaders). The only sample to mention businessmen as influential here, with any significant frequency, were the business leaders themselves, but even they gave more mentions to those in the governmental-political field.

4. For influence in the economic field, the samples showed somewhat different results. Businessmen's and bankers' names provided the largest single category of response, but not necessarily forming a majority, for 3 of the 4 cross sections, for the business leaders and Chamber of Commerce samples, and for most of the civic leaders samples. The farm organization leaders most frequently named educators, as did the League of Women Voters presidents. The union leaders sample most frequently mentioned public officeholders. For all the samples of civic leaders, a higher proportion said that government officeholders would influence them in economic matters or said that businessmen and bankers would influence them in political matters. Putting all the 21 samples together for the question on "influence me in economic matters," the two top names mentioned were those of professors, the third and fourth names were those of Minnesota businessmen with national reputations, and the fifth and sixth names were those of top elected officeholders.

5. All respondents were asked to indicate how they would respond to 50 specifically named persons concerning opinions on public issues. The cross section samples showed a high non-response here, probably indicating that they were not familiar with the names; the clergymen were identified by title and the general public was most favorable to them. The other samples exhibited great variation in their responses. Even the three samples of women's organizations were not at all alike in their responses. The business leaders sample were most positive to the names of businessmen, but the civic association presidents were most positive to the names of clergymen and educators, while the labor leaders were most positive to the names of Democratic politicians, and the farm organization leaders were most positive to the names of educators and Republican politicians.

A question was asked about the relative influence of national and local figures. As might be expected for such a general question, a majority of all samples said they would be more influenced by national figures. But the differences in the proportions among the samples were significant. The cross section in the two smaller cities said they were more likely to be influenced by local figures than were the cross sections in the two larger cities. The same was true for the leadership samples: those from rural areas and small towns were relatively more likely to say they would be more influenced by local leaders than by national figures.

One question asked the respondents to name the persons whose opinions would likely influence them to take the opposite opinion. In general, the results for these "negative influentials" were very similar to the results for the positive influentials already reported. Top governmental officeholders were mentioned most frequently as negative influentials, and these were the same persons mentioned most frequently as influentials. The leadership samples mentioned more names here than did the cross sections. Different categories came out high as negative influentials, for the different leadership samples: Prominent mass media personnel received a top frequency of mentions by labor leaders and the Minnesota Republican Workshop sample; prominent businessmen were also frequently mentioned by labor leaders and by leaders in the United Nations Association; union leaders got frequent negative reference by businessmen in our sample (also by the Hennepin County Health and Welfare Council); farm organization leaders were negatively perceived by other farm organization leaders and by agricultural extension agents.

A question was asked about "they"—the unnamed power source. Many refused to answer the question, or specifically denied the existence of "they." For those who did respond to the question, the most frequent definition was "the politicians" or "government officials." The second most frequent definition was some kind of reference to a "power elite"—referring to hidden economic leaders. The third most frequent definition was a reference to a specific businessmen's organization (for example, the N.A.M. or the Chamber of Commerce). Mentioned by only one or two respondents, but no significant percentage, were: the mass media, government administrators (bureaucrats), criminals or gangsters, communists, Jews, or Catholics.

The respondents were asked to suggest how public interest in civic issues would be stimulated. The cross sections of the four cities

had little to offer here. Non-response was also very high among the
labor leaders (36.8 per cent) and the county commissioners (38.9
per cent). In some leadership samples, there were significant proportions saying "nothing can be done" or giving semi-facetious answers
which meant that nothing can be done ("start a fire," "drop a
bomb"). In only one leadership sample did a significant proportion
answer that nothing more *need* be done. The concrete suggestions
for increasing public interest were, in descending order of proportions mentioning them: small discussion groups, personal conversation in door-to-door canvassing, mass-media appeals, encouraging
people to join civic associations, educating people better, getting
people to be active politically. The specific leadership samples advocating each approach are described in the main report; we need
note here only that there was considerable divergence among the
leadership samples as to the approaches most frequently advocated.

The main report also analyzes the social participation of the
samples, so that information is available concerning the possible influence on, and the possible influence of, these people. In general,
there is a considerable range among the leadership samples in the direction and extent of their participation and in their contact with the
mass media.

The picture that emerges from this study is of a highly diversified,
highly specialized and fractionated, image of power and influence
structure in Minnesota. This picture, it must be recalled, emerges
from verbal statements reporting opinions and images, not from
observation of actual decision-making or other forms of everyday
behavior. There is little support for a theory that an economic elite,
openly or secretly, has the reputation of controlling people's opinions
and decisions (except that this opinion is found, to a slight extent,
among business leaders themselves). If any group has ascendancy
in our respondents' minds, it is the top political office-holders
of both political parties, but they are almost as likely to be
thought of as negative influentials as they are to be thought of as
positive influentials. A political elite is even more often defined as
the "unnamed power source" than is an economic elite. But there
is no evidence of a tendency to think of a political power elite as a
single group; at the very least they are divided into the two major
political parties. The only evidence from this study that supports any

of the leading hypotheses of Hunter and Mills is that the "mass" of the people—represented by our four cross sections—is rather inarticulate regarding power and influence over them, and hence may have poorly formed conceptions of how power and influence function in American society. On the other hand, while the leadership samples are much more articulate, and hence their conceptions are clearer cut, this does not mean that they are necessarily more accurate.

PART FOUR
The Political Power Structure and How it Functions

The first part of this book sought to examine various elites in the holding of political power in the United States. The second part took up the masses—the allegedly powerless—whom we sought to show were not completely without power. The third part of the book examined the local community power structure with a main concern for certain issues, methodological and substantive, that divided the students of power structure. There we also got a view of the public image of power, with all its insights and distortions.

In this final section of the book we return to the realities of power. Here we are less interested in the makers and wielders of political power than we are in its processes and instruments. The political party and "politics" are the direct instruments of political power along with the processes of government. Thus our first chapter deals with state politics, using only one state to provide an example—recognizing that each of the 50 states has its own unique politics and political party structure. Our second chapter deals with the national political party, which practically does not exist in the United States, except for its quadrennial manifestation of nominating a candidate for President—which is what is analyzed in our chapter. The third chapter takes up the political processes involved in the passage of an important piece of federal legislation, in which we see strong conflict between the economic elite and the masses of the American people. The final chapter in this part of the book deals with the weaknesses in our political system—the necessity of acquiring a campaign fund, bribery and conflict of interest, and inadequate participation in political processes.

X
Political Structure and
Political Influence in Texas

We turn now to consideration of political structure and political influence at the state level, using Texas as an illustration. No claim is made that Texas is typical of the 50 American states, but it will be used simply to provide a case study of state politics. The economic elite will be seen as an important influence, but by no means the only important influence.

A. Political Structure

Texas has long been usually considered—at least until the election of Republican Senator John Tower in 1961—to be a one-party state of the familiar Southern type. Yet its division into party splinters, each with a distinctive ideology, is at least as great as in any other state. There is a good deal of shifting, and even some overlapping, among these political groups, but they are distinct enough to be identified readily. The Republican party is small, and its contemporary organization is recent, but it has at least two major wings—sometimes called conservative and liberal, sometimes named after its national heroes at different times, Taft–Eisenhower, Goldwater–Nixon—and some smaller splinters, including an old-time Negro one. The conservatives are represented by Senator Tower and by ex-Representative Bruce Alger. The liberals are typified by Mrs. Oveta Culp Hobby, publisher of the *Houston Post*.

Splintering in the Democratic party covers nearly the entire range

359

of American political ideologies. On the right wing are two ultra-conservative factions that differ only in their belief as to the extent to which they should support a Republican candidate for President: those typified by former Governor Allan Shivers believe they should do this consistently as a matter of principle; those formerly represented by ex-Senator William Blakley believe they should do this only as a matter of expediency. Both of these groups are considerably more conservative than the liberal Republicans. Somewhat more moderate in the Democratic party, if only because they are more opportunistic in wanting to gain support from the rest of the party, are several factions, each of which is a unity because it has had an outstanding officeholder as leader (such as former Governor Price Daniel and Attorney General Waggoner Carr). These factions occupy what might be called the "right center" in the Texas spectrum, although they would be considered to be far more conservative if they were in the Northern states.

The true center of the Democratic party was until 1961 somewhat more unified around the dominant personalities of Lyndon Johnson and Sam Rayburn, but it also shifts rapidly in composition and policies, and these two national leaders also captured support from other segments of the party. With the accession of John Connally to the governorship in 1962, he became the leader of the center group in the Democratic party, and probably shifted it more to the right. The "liberals" or "left wing" (in the North they would be called New Dealers, Fair Dealers, or New Frontiersmen, but definitely not "left wing") are in five fairly distinct segments, which sometimes co-operate and often do not. These are, in probable order of voting strength (recognizing that not all the persons belonging to the category vote with the majority in that category): Mexican-Americans, organized labor, Negroes, independent liberals (mostly professionals by occupation), and Roman Catholics following the leadership of Archbishop Robert Lucey of San Antonio (some might consider the last-named group too small to be mentioned with the others, but it usually behaves somewhat independently of the others).

In addition to the two major parties and their various segments, there are small splinter groups at the right and left extremes. One of these that has significant influence is the Constitution party, led by Clarence Manion of Indiana but having more "grass-roots" supporters in Texas than probably any other state (this group finds even the right wing of the Republican party too liberal to work with). Another ultraconservative group is called "Freedom in Action," which seeks to form a coalition of Republicans and right-wing Democrats to co-operate on issues if not on candidates. While it does not nominate candidates and contest elections, it is sufficiently interested in politics to be a potential political faction. The John Birch Society and other right-wing extremist groups are strong in Texas, and some of their members are active in both major political parties. In the 1962 Democratic primary election for governor, Major General Edwin A. Walker, the right-wing extremist, won 10 per cent of the votes.

The traditional sources of conservative support for the Democratic party were most of the rural areas and small towns, although it should be recognized that white rural Texans and other rural Southerners who migrate to Texas' large cities often remain conservative in their new homes. Texas was, until the 1930's, predominantly a rural state, although its rate of urbanization has been one of the fastest in the nation (of the seventeen largest cities in the nation, three are in Texas). This is reflected in a symbolic political fact. Practically all of the leading holders of public office up to 1960 were of rural origin and official rural residence, but practically all of the serious contenders for the senate seat in the special 1961 election were from the big cities. Not only is urbanization changing the political cast of the state, but so also is a related demographic change: Texas has many more Mexican-Americans, whites of Northern origin, and Negroes today than it did a decade or two ago (although the Negroes are not increasing proportionately). Both urbanization and in-migration are gradually shifting Texas toward greater political extremes. The election of Ralph Yarborough as senator in the special election of 1957 marked the first time in several decades that an acknowledged and consistent liberal won in a state-wide election.[1] John Kennedy won the majority of the state's votes in the 1960 presidential race, and it seems likely that other liberal candidates will win statewide elections

[1]This was perhaps an electoral "accident" in part: Texas election laws did not yet provide for a run-off election in special elections in 1957, and Yarborough won with a minority of 39 per cent of the votes in 1957, beating the conservative Democrat Martin Dies and the Republican Thad Hutcheson. In the regular election of 1958, however, Yarborough won with a straight majority.

in the future. The election of John G. Tower as United States Senator in the special election of 1961 marked an historic victory for conservative Republicanism and foreshadowed the rebirth of a Republican party with a fairly full slate of candidates.

The majority of the Texas state legislature has been predominantly rural and conservative Democratic because of certain features of the state constitution.[2] There are 31 state senatorial districts, but no single county may have more than one of these. Thus, Harris County (which includes the city of Houston) with one senator contains over three times as much population as the average senatorial district, and four to five times as much as the smaller districts. State representatives are elected according to a system by which no county may have more than 7 representatives unless the county has over 700,000 inhabitants, after which it gets an additional representative for each additional 100,000 inhabitants. If one divides the 1960 population (9,579,677) by the number of house seats (150), the average population per representative comes out to be 63,864. Thus a county gets equal representation up to the point when it has about 450,000 inhabitants (7 representatives), but larger counties are under-represented. The largest county, Harris, following the redistricting after the 1960 census, has 12 representatives, or about 103,500 inhabitants per representative, whereas on a proportional basis it would be entitled to 19 representatives. The four largest counties together have 35 representatives, whereas proportional representation would give them 52 or 53 seats.

Until 1966 three other limitations on voting operated, and they should be mentioned here: (1) The poll tax. Texas was one of the last four states to retain a poll tax, which, of course, worked against the poorer voters.[3] (2) The exemption from the poll tax of persons over 60 years of age who lived in counties with fewer than 10,000 inhabitants (those over 60 who lived in counties with more than 10,000 inhabitants did not have to pay poll taxes if they obtained an

[2]For a fuller analysis of election laws, see W. E. Benton, "Suffrage and Elections," *Arnold Foundation Monographs* VII (Dallas: Arnold Foundation, Southern Methodist University, 1960).

[3]The state poll tax was only $1.50 a year (counties were permitted to—and most did—add an additional 25¢), but it was to be paid at least 9 months before the regular election, when it is usually not known who the candidates will be. Hence, the poll tax worked against the less politically involved and poorer voters.

exemption certificate each year.) This provision also gave a special voting privilege to the conservative rural voters. (3) The Legislature's failure to redistrict congressional districts for some 30 years. This gave considerable extra weight to votes from rural areas as far as United States congressmen were concerned.[4] All these restraints on the franchise are being eliminated. The United States Supreme Court's decision in Baker v. Carr forced a redistricting into almost equal voting districts in 1965. In February 1966, a three-judge federal court invalidated the Texas poll tax, under the 1965 federal Voting Rights Act. The court did not find that the poll tax seriously discriminated against Negroes, but that it did interfere with the right to vote. Justice Black of the United States Supreme Court sustained the lower court, and the Texas legislature provided for an additional 15-day registration period in March for those who had not paid their poll tax. Thus Texans will be voting without a poll tax and with equal-sized election districts in 1966, for the first time since 1902.

Texas laws have reflected the conservatism of the legislature. Texas does not have an income tax, and did not acquire a sales tax until 1961, and its property and industrial taxes are relatively low, which means that state services have been meager—especially in view of the great private wealth in the state. Texas has great resources that could be taxed: It is the first state in the nation in the production of oil, gas, cattle, cotton, and many lesser resources. Yet in basic social services the state of Texas ranked first in its caseload per state worker; forty-first in old age pensions, fortieth in public-assistance programs in general (even though almost three-fourths of the funds came from the federal government); fortieth in literacy; and lower in educational services generally.[5] Texas is one of two states that do not regulate telephone service, one of four that do not regulate telegraph service, one of six that do not regulate electric light and power service, and one of nine that do not regulate water service. Texas is the only industrial state without an industrial

---

[4]While the legislature has the first authority to redistrict for legislative positions, a constitutional amendment adopted in the late 1940's provides for a Legislative Redistricting Board which has full authority to redistrict if it is not done by the legislature in the first session after each census. The legislature has not failed to redistrict since the passage of this amendment. But the amendment does not apply to, nor does the Board have jurisdiction over, the districting of congressional seats.
[5]Willie Morris, "Legislating in Texas," *Commentary*, 38 (November 1964), 40–46.

safety law. Automobile inspection is practically non-existent; and a driver does not have to comply with what inspection there is to buy his license plates. In some areas of Texas, a child may get a driver's license at the age of 14.[6] There are many other respects in which rural conservatism is reflected in Texas state statutes.

The growing Republican party draws its strength mainly from the middle and upper classes in the cities and suburbs. Its mainly right-wing leadership has a growing number of widely known personalities, such as Thad Hutcheson, the defeated candidate in the 1957 senatorial election, John Tower, the defeated candidate for the 1960 senatorial election and the victor in the 1961 senatorial election, and Bruce Alger, who was congressman from Dallas County for many years before being defeated in the Johnson landslide of 1964. The Republican party gets many votes for its presidential candidates from persons who vote in the Democratic primaries (and who consider themselves as Democrats in state and local elections), and the state gave its electoral votes to Eisenhower in 1952 and 1956. Texas also voted for Hoover in 1928, but this was mainly because of anti-Catholicism (expressed against Al Smith, the Democratic candidate for President), rather than because of the Republican alignment of the majority of the voters at that time. The shift to Kennedy in 1960 is thus all the more remarkable since he was a Catholic also, and since the Republican party was much better organized and supported in 1960 than ever before. The returning support for the Democratic presidential candidates may be attributed to support for "favorite son" Lyndon B. Johnson and to growing strength of the liberals allied on matters which do not divide them from the center. Some Republicans weaken their party by voting for conservative Democrats in state and local races in regular elections.[7]

[6]The last three sentences are taken from George Fuermann, *Reluctant Empire* (New York: Doubleday, 1957), pp. 262–3. Many of the local governments attempt to regulate the utilities but they are unable to regulate effectively. See also *The New York Times*, May 3, 1962, p. 21.

[7]"The legislature in 1959 attempted a contribution to party loyalty by adding a statutory requirement that persons voting in a primary would have their poll tax receipts stamped with the name of the party. Some Republicans grumbled about having their poll tax receipts stamped "Democrat" when they made their customary trek to the primary, but the results of the 1960 primary suggest that most of them decided to put up with the indignity. Persons who vote in the Democratic primary are barred from the conventions of the Republican party—if the latter officials choose to follow the law—but are legally free to vote for the candidates of either party in the

Despite the aforementioned liberal trend in Texas, it is likely that a Republican could win a state-wide race in the growing polarization of state politics, especially if the victor in the Democratic primaries should be a Mexican-American or a white liberal. In fact a Republican, John G. Tower, did win the 1961 special election for United States Senator, although there were unusual circumstances attending this election. The election was made necessary by the resignation of Lyndon Johnson (who had beaten Tower in 1960, but who in January 1961 resigned to become Vice President of the United States). Seventy-one candidates filed for the election,[8] but only six of these were generally considered to be serious candidates. Three of the serious candidates were liberals, so the liberals by splitting the vote insured their own defeat before the race began. This was the first unusual fact that got Tower through the first go-around (April) of the election. Tower's opponent in the run-off was the conservative Democrat (and appointed incumbent Senator) William A. Blakley.

To the surprise of a great number of people, Tower beat Blakley in the May run-off election. Reasons for this included the facts that: (1) Tower was well known in 1961 since he had run against Lyndon Johnson in 1960 (of course, Blakley was well known too). (2) The Republican party was rapidly developing a strong organization at the grass roots. (3) Tower brought to his active support the very popular names of Barry Goldwater and Dwight D. Eisenhower (he openly rejected Richard Nixon), whereas Senator Blakley and President Kennedy were at odds (there is much evidence that most of Blakley's leading supporters were in the Nixon camp in the 1960 election, and Blakley opposed Kennedy's proposals for legislation during his short term of office as Senator).[9] (4) The Blakley campaign may have been inept. (5) Most important of all was the fact that a good number of liberal Democrats either abstained or voted for Tower in the May run-off, even though Tower was a conservative Republican. Their reasoning seems to have been that Blakley, a Democrat, could

---

general elections." (H. C. McCleskey, "The Texas Political System," unpublished paper prepared for the Department of Political Science, University of Houston, p. 7.)

[8]The sole requirement for filing was payment of a fee of $50.

[9]Kennedy finally gave a formal endorsement to Blakley, but few could suppose there were good relations between them.

demand some federal patronage, whereas if Tower were elected, all federal patronage would go through Yarborough and Johnson). Also, Blakley had some important Senate committee posts, which upon his defeat might go to some more liberal Democrat from another state.[10] Tower would be easier to defeat for re-election in 1966 than would Blakley. Some liberals even decided that it was high time to encourage a two-party system in Texas.[11] Practically no liberal doubted that Blakley's voting record would be just as conservative as Tower's, even though Tower was aligned with the Goldwater (conservative) faction of the Republican party. Certainly the defection of the liberals helped Blakley lose his Senate seat, and this undoubtedly encouraged some conservative Democrats in Texas to move into the increasingly well-organized Republican party.[12]

While liberals, with the notable exception of Senator Ralph Yarborough, are not now in statewide key party or governmental positions, and they have been badly factionalized, their prospects for future victories in the Democratic party are also good. Mexican-American and Negro voters are increasing in numbers, they are scarcely any longer likely to be disfranchised by force, they tend to vote in blocs, and they have a growing political consciousness. The Mexican-Americans now have gained the election of some of their own nationality, notably in the person of Congressman Henry Gonzalez (of Bexar County, which includes San Antonio), Congressman

[10]*Minneapolis Morning Tribune*, April 24, 1961, p. 23.

[11]*The New York Times*, May 27, 1961, p. 24.

[12]Texas Republicans were optimistic enough after the Tower election to predict that they would win another congressional seat in a special election held in November 1961 in Bexar County. They unified behind John Goode, Jr., and emphasized his conservatism rather than his Republicanism, and got ex-President Eisenhower, Senator Barry Goldwater and Senator Tower to campaign in his behalf. The Democratic candidate was Henry B. Gonzalez, because the other major contender—Maury Maverick, Jr.—after some hesitation announced that he would not oppose Gonzalez. Maverick and some other liberals seem to have learned the lesson that splitting the liberal vote means defeat. (Gonzalez had carried Bexar County in the April 1961 senatorial election by a wide margin, mainly because 40 per cent of the voters there are of Mexican descent. See *The New York Times*, June 3, 1961, p. 8.) Johnson campaigned actively for Gonzalez, and Senator Yarborough and Governor Daniel endorsed him. He was elected with 54.4 per cent of the vote. Following the election, Republican National Chairman William E. Miller pointed out: "Involved was a district where it had not been possible to persuade anyone to run as the Republican nominee from 1948 to 1961. Consequently, the fact that Goode was able to win 45 per cent of the total vote is an achievement of considerable proportions." (Quoted in UPI dispatch in the *Minneapolis Morning Tribune*, November 7, 1961, p. 5.)

Eligio de la Garza (of Mission, in south Texas), and county commissioner Albert Pena (also of Bexar County). After the 1960 election the "viva Kennedy" movement was organized into the Political Association of Spanish-Speaking Organizations, and in 1963, this group succeeded in electing a slate of Mexican-Americans as mayor and city council in Crystal City, near the Rio Grande. In 1964, they elected de la Garza to the United States House of Representatives. In 1965, they won in Mathis, a small south Texas town, while losing in Crystal City. The Mexican-Americans are the largest of the liberal factions in the state, and, in a generally factionalized Democratic party, they have a good chance of winning a Democratic primary. Whether or not this would mean winning the general election would depend on whether the normally conservative and middle-of-the-road rural Democrats, of the "brass collar" variety who normally have a strong loyalty to the Democratic party, would stand by the victor in the primary. It was undoubtedly to test these possibilities that Gonzalez ran in the 1961 special election for United States senator. He won only 9.4 per cent of the votes in the first election, placing fifth, which indicates that the Mexican-Americans were not yet sufficiently strong to impose a state-wide candidate on the Democratic party.

The other liberal factions have less voting strength than the Mexican-Americans, but they also are likely to grow. Negroes have been concentrated in rural east Texas, which is quite Southern in its orientation. They are moving to the cities (for example, 22.9 per cent of Houston's population and 19 per cent of Dallas's population was Negro in 1960), where they are more likely to be motivated to vote and where political consciousness is stronger, and their numbers are being augmented by in-migration from the Deep South states. A leading Texas Negro estimates that of the 1,187,125 Negroes in Texas (1960 census), 250,000 to 300,000 voted in 1960, and perhaps as many as 80 per cent of these voted "liberal." These estimates may be somewhat high, but they suggest the trends. While it will perhaps be a while before any Negro runs for any but the lowest public offices, their voting strength is being rewarded with some patronage on both the state and city level.

Organized labor is making slow headway in both union organizing and political organizing drives, but the industrialization of Texas favors its prospects. In the 1961 special election for United States senator, the AFL-CIO endorsed Maury Maverick, Jr., thereby splitting off from the Mexican-American candidate, Henry Gonzalez. Not all of organized labor is liberal: a number of the Fort Worth labor leaders at least support the conservative position in politics. Labor leadership is also quite divided, mainly along the lines of the A.F. of L. and the C.I.O., and the two groups have somewhat different political orientations.

The "independent liberals" and "Catholic liberals" (the latter might be considered a segment of the former except for the fact that they form a semi-cohesive group around a few intimates of the Archbishop of San Antonio and they do not always move politically with independent liberals) include a number of persons with high ability and political devotion. Their efforts have been less directed at party position and organization than at all-out efforts in party conventions and especially in election campaigns for selected liberal candidates, such as Adlai Stevenson, John Kennedy, and Ralph Yarborough. While they are called "liberals" and call themselves that, their ideological range is considerable. In the 1961 special senatorial campaign they divided their support among Gonzalez, Maverick, Representative James Wright, and Attorney General Will Wilson. The division so weakened them that none of these otherwise promising candidates won even in the first go-around of the election. Whatever unity the liberals have lies in their "loyalist" support for the national Democratic party and for Senator Ralph Yarborough. The strength of this group would be much greater if they more frequently sought party and lesser public offices and if they agreed on conditions under which they could compromise their differences on state and local candidates and issues.

For the past several decades, most of the political leadership of Texas has rested in the hands of persons who might properly be called "opportunists" (notable exceptions have been Allan Shivers among the conservatives and Ralph Yarborough among the liberals). The term "opportunist" is not chosen to criticize, but to help explain an important fact about Texas politics: In the extreme segmentalization of Texas politics, most statewide candidates can be successful in winning public office only by piecing together coalitions. These coalitions represent a wide range of interests, which gives the candidate who tries to serve all their interests the appearance of not standing for principles. Further, the coalitions tend to fall apart, as one segment or another is attracted by some rival candidate, with the result that the officeholder who is serious about retaining his office in the next election seeks to form a new coalition, in which the interests he serves are at least somewhat different from those of the old coalition. In other words, most successful state-wide officeholders have to be opportunists because of the absence of a strong Democratic party organization and because the range of ideologies represented in that party is so very great. Some of the leading "opportunists" lean to the right, like former Governor Price Daniel; others lean to the left, like former Senator Lyndon Johnson. Some are rank demagogues, like former Governor W. Lee O'Daniel; others are men with great organizational ability and even party loyalty and integrity on the national scene, like Lyndon Johnson.

Lyndon Johnson's "image" in Texas when he was a senator was considerably different than it is on the national scene (where he served as leader of the Senate Democrats until he was elected Vice President in 1960). The nation's mass media gave the impression that he had tremendous popularity and political appeal in Texas. Actually, he had a certain amount of difficulty in piecing together the appearance of virtual unanimity that gave him the endorsement for presidential candidate at the 1960 Texas Democratic "presidential" convention.[13] Johnson won his first senatorial race in 1948, against Coke Stevenson, by a margin of only 87 votes, and it was uncertain whether or not this was an accurate count. Johnson won the 1960 senatorial election by a vote of 1,306,625 to 926,653, when his rival, John Tower, was relatively unknown and a Republican.

[13]Texas Democrats have two state conventions in presidential years—one to select and instruct delegates to the national convention; the other to elect party officers and endorse candidates for statewide elections. The bulk of the opposition to Johnson at the 1960 presidential convention favored Adlai Stevenson for president. Organized labor was in this group until—it was rumored—national AFL–CIO leaders asked state AFL-CIO leaders to support Johnson because of his and Rayburn's importance in getting congressional support for legislation they desired. The author has no way of verifying this rumor, and does not assert that it is true. Johnson also had some difficulty in getting the support of the Mexican-American leadership. The conflict in the Texas labor group—whether to follow their national leadership or to support their local interests in politics—reflects another facet of the complexity of the political power structure in the United States. Not infrequently, national and local levels of the same voluntary association have opposing interests in politics.

It was hard to find individuals or groups in Texas genuinely enthusiastic about Johnson, although many admired—and continue to admire—his political acumen and general ability. Democrats with strong conservative or liberal loyalties tended to oppose Johnson because he was an "opportunist." Democrats of the center were more favorable to Johnson, but a number of them claimed he betrayed them when he felt obliged to form a new and stronger coalition. Johnson as senator seemed to have little charismatic appeal for the masses, and there were unfavorable stories circulating about him in several parts of Texas. One conservative Democratic political leader claimed that the Democratic state conventions of 1958 and 1960 came very close to public censuring of Johnson, but that national pressure on labor and liberals swung them reluctantly to his support at the last moment.

Johnson's political strength in Texas seems to have been based mainly on four facts: (1) He was able to piece together majority coalitions that were at least temporarily cohesive, and he used his great ability in the federal Congress to serve enough state interests to make these coalitions possible. (2) He concentrated on getting his followers into party office, so that whatever strength there was in the Texas Democratic party organization was not likely to be turned against him, and occasionally it helped him significantly. (3) Johnson used money, his not inconsiderable patronage (even during Eisenhower's presidency), and his personal influence to get voting support from those amenable to such direct means, especially voters in the boss-ridden border counties.[14] (4) He got financial support from some of the wealthiest Texans for his political campaigns. This is extremely important in Texas, where the great distances to be covered by a candidate make campaigning expensive, and where party organization is weak. Conservative candidates generally find it easy to raise campaign funds, because most wealthy people are conservatives, but Johnson was "left of center" for Texas and yet was extremely successful in raising campaign funds. It is likely that his enormous *national* power, and that of his ally, Speaker Sam Rayburn, permitted him to compensate his wealthy supporters for their help by specific measures. Johnson was unusually astute in

[14] The Latin *patron* system prevailing in these largely Mexican-inhabited counties seems to be weakening with economic improvement and political consciousness.

selecting such compensations for conservatives: The only consistent support he gave for conservative bills was for those favoring the oil and gas industry; he also used his influence as majority leader of the Senate to get the Executive branch to take certain administrative actions regarding federal contracts, say, in return for a promise of congressional support on another issue. Johnson avoided supporting conservative legislation in general and thereby avoided getting to be known as a conservative (such as did most of the other Southern senators). Most businessmen and industrialists in Texas tend to think of themselves as conservatives, but they were pragmatic in supporting Johnson, apparently often without strong personal conviction. Johnson's achievement was all the more remarkable in that he had both retained a major state-wide political office in Texas over twelve years and was still strong enough in the national Democratic party to be nominated for the vice-presidency and later for the presidency.

To some extent, the Johnson tradition in Texas has been continued by his protégé, John B. Connally, who resigned a top federal position (Secretary of the Navy) to run for Governor in 1962. Connally followed Johnson's techniques of "center opportunism" and was successful in defeating the liberals' candidate, Don Yarborough, in the primary. The same thing happened in 1964. It was rumored that Johnson quietly used his influence in behalf of Connally in 1962, thus carrying on the feud with Texas liberals. By 1964, however, Johnson had fairly well patched up his relationships with the liberals by strongly supporting his former enemy, Senator Ralph Yarborough, in the latter's successful campaign for re-election. By 1965, even Don Yarborough was praising Lyndon Johnson: "The course he has set for himself and the nation has placed him in the ranks of the truly great Presidents."[15] However, in March 1966 there was evidence of a renewed struggle between President Johnson and the Texas liberals. The state Attorney General, Waggoner Carr, a friend of the President, was seeking endorsement for the Democratic party nomination for United States Senator (against the Republican incumbent, John Tower), and national labor leaders were alleged to be putting pressure on state labor leaders to support him.[16] Instead, the state labor leaders—angered by Carr's refusal to indicate

[15]Quoted in *The New York Times*, March 23, 1965, p. 18.
[16]*The New York Times*, March 4, 1966, p. 54.

whether he would support repeal of Section 14(b) of the Taft-Hartley Act, which allows states to outlaw compulsory unionism—indicated that they were ready to give their full support to Ronnie Dugger, a liberal newspaper editor of Austin, for the United States Senate position. The President was said to be behind the national AFL-CIO pressure. The issue was resolved by Mr. Dugger's pulling out of the Senate race, saying that he had come to this decision himself without any White House influence. He said that if Mr. Carr would avoid the rigid unyielding conservatism of the Texas Democratic party, "my withdrawal ought to help him."[17] In the primary and run-off elections of 1966, all state-wide candidates backed by Governor Connally defeated candidates backed by the liberal–labor coalition. The latter was conspicuously ineffective in getting out the vote, despite the fact that the poll tax had been removed by the courts. After the primary, many liberals continued to work against Carr, believing that if Tower were re-elected he would be no more reactionary than Carr and that he would continue to attract conservative Democrats into the Republican party—leaving the Democratic party to be controlled by the liberals.

If a political leader who is both able and popular should arise in the Texas Democratic party, and see his political opportunity not in the opportunistic type of politics that has been almost necessary until now, but in building a strong party organization, he could transform Texas politics by turning it into a complete two-party system and also retain office as long as he wished while still holding a consistent ideology. That is, a liberal or center man could do this for the Democratic party; a conservative Democrat could do it only for the Republican party at this stage. This assumes that some rank-and-file conservatives who vote Democratic have a strong party loyalty. It would not be difficult to build a strong party organization in Texas: both parties are "open" at their grass-roots—that is, anyone may join and work upward (although sometimes the party leaders have been known to refuse the credentials of a dissident grass-roots group at state conventions).[18] This strategy of building

17*The New York Times*, March 25, 1966, p. 26.
18The chairmen of the precinct and of the county executive committee in the Democratic party are elected by the voters in the primary. The state executive committee is composed of a chairman and vice chairman, plus one man and one woman from each of the state's 31 senatorial districts. The rules provide for selection of the committee members by the state convention, but the tradition has been

a strong Democratic party is apparently being followed by Don Yarborough, who started by facilitating a coalition of all the liberal factions in 1963. But the way is still blocked by Governor Connally, who continues to follow the older strategy of "center opportunism," and was re-elected as Governor in 1964.

The structural changes in Texas voting, forced on the state by the federal government—the reapportionment into practically equal districts in 1965 and the invalidation of the poll tax in 1966—can be expected to have a major impact soon on Texas politics. Of the approximately 6 million adult citizens in Texas, only a little more than 2 million vote, even in presidential election years. This is only about half the proportion found in the Northern states. The main barrier to voting has been the poll tax, which was ruled illegal in February 1966. The Supreme Court also required that the registration period, closed as usual after January 31 for the November elections, be reopened for a fifteen-day period in March. Without the poll tax now, an additional 603,368 persons registered—mostly stimulated by the AFL–CIO.[19] This addition of 25 per cent to the voting list, plus others who might register in future years without the poll tax, might change the face of Texas politics. Because the AFL–CIO claimed most of those newly registered, and Governor Connally made known his displeasure with the court's decision and with the additional fifteen-day registration period, it may be guessed that the liberal Democrats benefited at the expense of the center Democrats. The continuing growth of the Republican party, based on defections from the Democratic party by some conservatives, also suggests that the "center opportunism" strategy will soon fail. Whether the liberal Democrats or the Republicans will benefit the most from the changes remains to be seen.

---

that the two members nominated by a caucus of delegates from the counties in each senatorial district will be selected. However, the governor's faction, which often controls the September state convention, has sometimes rejected some of the caucus nominees (mostly liberals) and forced a substitution by formal convention action. By controlling the state executive committee, the governor's faction also controls its appointed credentials commitee, and this in turn sees to it that the convention itself is stacked in favor of this faction. (The practice of refusing credentials to opposition delegates has not been confined to the state convention; it is often used to perpetuate control of county party machinery and of delegations to the state conventions).

19 *The New York Times*, March 23, 1966, p. 30.

At one time Texas politics was largely rural politics, where conservatives and populists fought a fairly even—if see-saw—battle. Then Texas politics moved into the approximately twenty-five-year period of splintering, as the state was making the transition to industrialization and urbanization, and "center opportunism" was the most effective political strategy. Today Texas politics seems ripe for a true two-party system. Another way of looking at this is that Texas seems to be now completing the transition from being a Southern state to being an American state on the Northern or Western pattern.

B. Sources and Means of Power

An analysis of Texas politics cannot stop with an interpretation of the broad outlines of its informal structure, such as we have just given. Further attention must be given to sources of power, and the means by which power is exercised. We shall continue to restrict ourselves to the state-wide level, neglecting the even more complex county and city levels of politics.

There is one state-wide officeholder who retained his office for six terms, 1949–1961, longer than most other major officeholders. This is the lieutenant governor, Ben Ramsey, who managed to retain office, even though he was not very well known throughout the state, apparently because there was no widespread understanding of the powers of his office. Actually, constitutional provisions and the one-party system gave the office a tremendous power: It is almost completely true to say that no bill can pass the state legislature without the approval of the lieutenant governor, and sometimes he can get a bill through that would otherwise have no chance of passage. This is probably more than could be said for the governor or any other official. The constitutional provisions which give the lieutenant governor this power are: (1) He is automatically the presiding officer of the state senate (this is true in most states). (2) He interprets the rules and recognizes senators in the order in which he wishes to (this is also true in some other states, but his rulings are less likely to be upset by the senate itself in a one-party legislature). (3) He names the members of the committees and their chairmen and he assigns bills to the respective committees (this is rare among the states and is the special source of the lieutenant governor's power in

Texas). The committees decide which bills shall be presented to the Senate as a whole, and in what form. Thus, by naming the committees and assigning bills to them as he wishes, the lieutenant governor can prevent bills from coming up for a vote and can get a bill up for consideration that he favors. This power exercised on behalf of bills strongly favored by certain senators gets him further support from these senators in behalf of legislation he himself favors. Ben Ramsey resigned as lieutenant governor in late 1961 to be appointed to the railroad commission (which also "controls" oil and gas).

The speaker of the state house of representatives exercises comparable formal powers, but since a speaker has served more than one term only three times in Texas history (and it takes a bit of time to build up the obligations to the presiding officer that give him so much positive power), it can be seen that the presiding officer of the state senate is actually more powerful than that of the House. Yet, the powers of the speaker are such that he actually begins to "run" for the job two to four years before he is elected, and often spends $20,000 or considerably more in doing so.[20] In addition to ingratiating himself, in previous sessions, with legislators who are likely to be re-elected to the House, and winning re-election himself, the candidate for Speaker may get involved in other legislative contests— "supporting friends, fostering opposition to unfriendly candidates, helping to raise campaign funds for others, and so on."[21] The lieutenant governor does not have to do the latter things, although his

[20]H. C. McCleskey, of the Department of Political Science, University of Houston, in an unpublished paper on "The State Legislature" states: "The winner of a heated contest for Speaker in 1961 was James Turman, who told a newsman (*The Texas Observer*, September 2, 1960, p. 1) that his campaign for the post would cost $20,000 and that of his opponent "three or four times that much." Presumably Speaker Turman was in a position to estimate accurately his own expenses, if not necessarily those of his opponent. Since it is most unlikely that candidates for Speaker will be able themselves to finance a campaign on the scale indicated, they must rely on assistance from others. Such a situation always raises the question of the motives of those who contribute—and of those who accept the contributions. The same question can, of course, be raised regarding financing of candidacies for other state offices, but the sworn reports required for them at least offer some clues as to the source of the money. No such reports are required from those who seek the speakership. While it is doubtful that the Texas Manufacturers Association, or "organized labor," or the Rural Electric Co-op people, or the "oil and gas lobby" or any of the other groups frequently mentioned play the financial role in speakership contests often imputed to them, one does find it hard under present conditions to separate truth from rumor and innuendo concerning the financing of a bid for the office of Speaker."

[21]Ibid. pp. 7–8.

statewide campaign for re-election is more difficult than the district campaign of the potential speaker. Considering everything, it can perhaps be said that the most powerful person in the Texas state government, over the years 1949–1961, was the lieutenant governor. His strategy was mainly to exercise his power quietly so as not to arouse strong opposition, and he succeeded in avoiding a general public awareness, and an awareness on the part of his potential "liberal" opposition, of his tremendous power. These roles of lieutenant governor and speaker, and the means of access to them, in a largely one-party state as far as the legislature is concerned, almost guarantee that legislative politics will be fairly primitive and reactionary.[22]

Economic interests exercise great political power in Texas. One reason why there are so many lobbyists in Texas[23] is that much of the great wealth that can be made in the state, especially from oil and gas, can be made by state-granted franchises and tax-exemptions. A second reason is that the state is so physically large, and even senatorial districts are so large,[24] that election campaigns are expensive, and the campaign donations more needed.[25] The wealthy interests of Texas can almost insure the retention and enhancement of their wealth with well-placed campaign donations. In this situation, it might be expected that the go-between—the representative of the wealthy interests in dealings with public officials—gains power in his own right. One such lobbyist has a great reputation for power, and while there is no doubt that the objective situation described permits him to have a great deal of power, his power is also partly based on reputation for power. Both the legislators, especially novices, and the informed public consider him to have tremendous power, so that his reputation enhances his power. There is even the myth that he "controlled" Lyndon Johnson when the latter was senator. This lobbyist's power is not exercised solely for the economic benefit of those he "represents": He sometimes does favors

22See Willie Morris, "Legislating in Texas," *Commentary*, 38 (November 1964), 40–46.

23A tabulation of registered lobbyists in 1961 showed over 5000 in Texas, more than in any other state, but this may also in part be due to the broad definition of "lobbyist" in the statute.

24There are only 31 senatorial districts for all of Texas.

25There is little evidence of outright bribery, and none of my interviewees thought that it was a significant factor.

for individuals and groups not employing him; this enhances his reputation further, and creates a fund of favors owed him. This man's power is based on a combination of the wealthy interests he represents (with his consequent ability to contribute to campaign funds), on an assiduously cultivated reputation for power, and on a network of obligations.

In Texas, as in other states, there are lobbyists not representing any economic interest but representing their conception of the general welfare. Insofar as these people use good lobbying tactics—presenting reliable facts, offering to save time for the legislator by digging up special information or getting the view of another public official, avoiding pressing the legislator too hard or threatening him—they can have a positive and sometimes continuing effect on legislation, providing they don't run up against bills which the vested-interest lobbyist is willing to pay campaign funds for. The clever lobbyist uses some combination of the carrot-and-stick approach with legislators, but uses it with such low pressure that the legislator sees the carrot and the stick without the lobbyist mentioning them to him. The lobbyist without campaign funds to contribute finds his carrot in the enhancement of the legislator's reputation through providing a needed public service, and his stick is the detraction from the legislator's reputation through being associated with fraud or misgovernment. Most legislators want to do a "good job," and this can provide leverage for the lobbyist without campaign funds. If this lobbyist can also get large numbers of individually written, non-insulting letters from constituents to their legislators, he also has a great asset.

He who can define a situation for a legislator has the greatest influence on him. The legislator, like every other person, likes to make up his own mind and not be told what to do. But if the situation is so defined for him that he can make up his mind in no other way but that favored by a lobbyist, he has been effectively influenced. This is a subject on which very little systematic study has been expended, and all we have is a few case instances to go on. Certainly the legislator's family and friends (including other legislators) define the situation affecting some bills, but there are many bills regarding which they have no knowledge or strong opinion. What the legislator reads or hears is very important in defining the situation for him—

newspapers, magazine articles, research reports, TV or radio programs, etc. In one respect the newspaper is the least important since the legislator knows its editorial point of view and the slant it may give its news. On the other hand, it is the most important since it is the most persistently read of all sources of information.

A pertinent, clearly written research report is most effective in defining situations for most legislators—if they read them. It is the task of an able lobbyist to get selected research reports to legislators, and somehow cajole them into reading them. Most lobbyists round up research reports of some kind, or write them themselves. Some large organizations—like the United States Chamber of Commerce, the National Association of Manufacturers, the AFL–CIO, the League of Women Voters—have research staffs. In Texas, one of the more important groups conducting research with the primary aim of influencing legislation is the Texas Research League, organized in 1952. Its board of directors and main financers are 71 leading businessmen, industrialists, bankers, and corporation lawyers of the state. They apparently set general policy, but the staff—including some extremely able and technically trained researchers, public relations experts, and attorneys—has a good deal of autonomy in procedures. Some of the staff feel that, while the individual members of the board have a number of selfish interests vis-a-vis government, they do not express these at board meetings, and policy is set only in terms of general philosophy. The reasons alleged for not expressing selfish interests in policy are: the board members do not have exactly common interests; they do not wish to appear to be self-seeking in a large meeting; no sub-group gives the bulk of the financial support. But the members do appear to have a common philosophy which is expressed in selection of topics and general orientation for research and lobbying. The philosophy is directed not only at making government more efficient and less costly, but often at providing more adequate service because industry as well as the individual frequently benefits from adequate government service, even of the welfare type. The League has had considerable influence on Texas legislation and administrative procedures, particularly in the fields of health, welfare, education, and public recreation.[26]

26The Texas Research League, *1960 Annual Report* (Austin, 1961).

Other kinds and sources of influences on the state government include:

1. The administrator (sometimes appointed, sometimes a civil servant) who is in a position to make administrative policy, and to advise the governor, legislators, boards and commissions. Not everyone who is in a position to use influence actually does so; this is particularly true of the administrator who doesn't want to "rock the boat." But the administrator who makes himself indispensable to decisions-makers—by knowing everything about pertinent issues, by knowing the political line-ups, by being willing to do various services for a wide range of people, by being reliable and circumspect, by having new ideas but letting others take the credit for them—actually wields a good deal of power even though the formal organization does not give him that power.[27] There seem to be such administrators in Texas, but to describe them further would be to identify them.

2. An elected official, such as a legislator, can serve a similar role in legislative committees and interim commissions. After a few years of such service his influence is considerably more than that of a legislator who does not work on the committees. The average legislator wants to do a "good job"—that is, an expected job—and avoid scandal. His colleague who can help him achieve these aims is going to be rewarded by support, which means extra influence. This factor is especially significant in the Texas house of representatives where the turnover of membership is very great. In the 1957 session, for example, almost 39 per cent of the representatives were serving their first term, and an additional 23 per cent had served only one previous term.[28]

3. Civic organizations in the big cities are often sponsors of political candidates, even for state-wide office, and do much of the organizing work for their candidates. This unusual activity for civic organization seems to be a result of the political fragmentation we

[27]An unusual example of such governmental power is the career of Benjamin B. Pelham, called "boss of Wayne County" (Detroit, Michigan) from 1916–42. Pelham's role is probably far from unique; what made him unusual was the fact that he was a Negro and therefore the subject of considerable prejudice. See Aris A. Mallas, Jr., "A Biography of Benjamin B. Pelham: A Study in Informal Organization," unpublished M. A. thesis, Wayne University, 1952.

[28]Calculated from *Texas Almanac, 1958–1959,* pp. 363–5.

noted earlier, the weakness of the Democratic party organization, and the high degree of political interest among many Texans coupled with the poll tax which keeps the politically uninterested from voting. Campaigns will sometimes be based on reaching voluntary associations of all sorts, rather than door-to-door or telephone campaigns. Thus, the organization leaders are unusually politically influential in Texas, whereas in most other states they generally avoid partisan politics (or if they become active in politics they do so as individuals rather than in their role as organization leaders).

A most unusual, and powerful, association is the Citizens Council of Dallas, composed of organizational leaders. The journalist, George Fuermann, describes it thus:

> Chartered in 1937 as "charitable" and "educational," its 175 members join for life; professional men are barred and few oilmen have been invited to join. Dallas has a city manager, it elects a mayor and a city council, but the Citizens Council runs the city. Not responsible to the public, the council rarely announces its decisions; only the effect of decisions becomes known. The council's control has been watered since 1949, when *Fortune* wrote about it, but public awareness was not followed by criticism because the council benefits Dallas.
>
> The council has impelled construction of Negro housing projects and a medical center; it instigated a $22,000,000 program to help solve the city's water problem. It sees to it that what it thinks is good for Dallas is accomplished. In spite of its achievements, however, Dallas pays a price for the oligarchy. Large issues are settled without public participation. Because of the council, and the fact that the *News* and the Dallas *Times-Herald* shrink from local contention, Dallas has no stage for public debate, no medium through which issues of public concern can be argued. The hurly-burly of such argument in Houston is unheard of in Dallas, where controversy in public is thought to be unseemly. No issue concerning the public—not even a triviality—is decided in Houston until the people have a say-so.[29]

The above list of influences in Texas politics is not intended to be inclusive, but merely to indicate the nature of those influences which

[29]Fuermann, *Reluctant Empire*, pp. 150–51.

have a somewhat special character in Texas. In other respects, Texas politics are subject to those influences which probably could be found in the majority of states. No two states have the same political structures or forces, and it has been our purpose to examine the contribution Texas makes to the total variety. Texas has been thought of as a state in which economic influences over government have been especially strong, and yet we have seen that government and politics have a great deal of autonomous power. If our analysis has been largely correct, no interpretation of American politics can be made in terms of a limited number of structures and forces—such as a two-party system, pressure groups representing largely economic forces, separation of executive from legislature, the expression of public opinion in voting—which operate throughout the United States. The reality is that all states are special cases, even if Texas is more special than most.

XI
How Kennedy Won the Democratic Nomination[1]

Senator John F. Kennedy, with many handicaps—Catholic religion, unusual youth for a presidential nominee, a legislative rather than an executive background, and not being well known before 1960 to the American public—won the 1960 Democratic nomination for president on the first ballot. As late as December 1959, the political editor of the *Wall Street Journal* gave his analysis that Kennedy had no chance for the nomination. The history of how Kennedy achieved victory at the Democratic National Convention in July 1960 should tell us much about important decision-making at the level of the national political parties. Kennedy and his advisors approached the nomination contest almost as objectively as scientists, and an analysis of what they did should thus provide a contribution to political science.

This author does not claim to know all that went on; some information is probably available only to Kennedy's closest associates and other leading Democrats. But they have not offered a full and

[1] This paper was written in the month following the nomination. Since then, other descriptions of the nomination have become available, notably that of the journalist Theodore H. White, *The Making of the President—1960* (New York: Atheneum, 1961). My description differs from his only slightly and is not as complete as his on the factual level, but I have tried to be more analytic and less detailed. Simply to make the distinction, one might say that his is a work in history, whereas mine is an effort in political science. A more comparable effort, which covers the Republican as well as the Democratic nomination, is that of Paul T. David, "The Record of 1960 in Selecting the Presidential and Vice Presidential Candidates," (Paper delivered at the 1960 annual meeting of the American Political Science Association, September 8–10, 1960).

impartial report and analysis. The author has been active for some years in local Democratic politics and was an alternate delegate to the 1960 Democratic National Convention. Immediately before, during, and after the convention he informally interviewed dozens of party officials and delegates in order to ascertain the pertinent facts. He read a good number of the partial analyses and reports in various newspapers and magazines, and read or heard practically all of the "literature" and speeches given out by the various candidates. While partisan toward the Democratic party, he is a social scientist trained to hold partisanship in check while engaged in objective analysis.

Shortly after he barely lost the vice-presidential nomination in 1956, Senator John F. Kennedy must have made up his mind to make an all-out try for the presidential nomination in 1960, for he began to recruit advisers and workers and to engage in a publicity campaign directed toward making him a national figure. His main early efforts were of two types: speaking at local Democratic political conferences and other meetings around the country and writing for the mass literate public. His shift toward a more consistently liberal voting record in the Senate after 1955 reflects either the acquisition of a liberal philosophy which motivated him to seek the top political office or the recognition that a nationally popular voting record was a necessity for attaining that office.

His main efforts were not directed through the medium of the Senate, however, for he neither took the lead in pressing for a body of legislation (as Senators Johnson and Humphrey did) nor did he recruit a body of congressional supporters. His main efforts were, rather, directed at party leaders and at the general public in various sections of the country. This approach may have been based on observation of the ineffectiveness of Senators Johnson and Humphrey in the 1956 national convention in their efforts to get on the national ticket—for all their prominence in the Senate. His approach of seeking local party and general public recognition and approval—leading him toward entry into the 1960 primaries—was made in the face of Senator Estes Kefauver's failure to gain the 1956 presidential nomination through the use of the primaries. But Senator Kefauver had not effectively sought party leaders' support and had even antagonized a significant section of the Democratic party organization. (Kefauver did this partly by ignoring the state party leaders in his determination to win the primaries and partly through suggesting—in the highly publicized crime committee hearings—that there was a link between organized racketeering and the political organizations; innocent politicians were hurt as much as the guilty by this.) Finally, while Senator Kennedy doubtlessly would have welcomed support from the "elder statesmen" of the party—former President Truman, Mrs. Roosevelt, Adlai Stevenson, Speaker Rayburn, and former Senator Lehman—their sympathies were directed to other potential candidates and he had to count on their ultimate opposition. (Perhaps this did not disturb him when he considered how the favorite of Truman in 1956—Governor Averell Harriman—made little progress toward the nomination, and that, as in 1956, these elder statesmen were not likely to agree.)

In considering his approach, Kennedy obviously kept one very significant fact before him: The nomination is voted on by the delegates to the national convention, not by the general public, the leading legislators, the political philosophers, or the elder statesmen. The national Democratic party is made up of 54 almost independent state (and territorial) Democratic parties, and it was to the leaders in these organizations that Senator John Kennedy directed his main efforts from 1957 onward. In a sense, even his enormous publicity program directed at the general public was subsidiary to his approach to the state party leaders: It was not so much directed at putting pressure on the state party leaders—which is the way Kefauver had used his popular appeal—as at convincing them that he could win the election if nominated. Among Kennedy's weaknesses was the tradition that a person of the Catholic faith could not win a presidential election, and thus he had to make a proved popular appeal part of his pitch to the state party leaders. His entry into only selected state presidential primaries demonstrates this strategy, but this will be considered later.

The state political parties are very diverse in their organization, selection, and leadership. They do not lend themselves to quick generalization. Yet they are central to an understanding of the American political process, for they—in effect—select practically all candidates for public office, including the presidential nominees. The public generally merely chooses between the endorsed candidates of the two major parties; this occurs directly in the case of the presidential office, and indirectly—after a primary election usually confirms as nominees the party-endorsed candidates—in the case of most other public offices. The most important fact leading to Senator Kennedy's nomination was that he directed his best efforts at the leaders of the state political parties, whereas his opponents (with the partial exception of Senator Johnson) did not.

Congressmen, especially senators, are not too important an avenue to the state political parties, because there tends to be a structural antagonism between congressmen and the parties. (There are exceptions, of course, such as Senator Byrd's leadership of Virginia's Democratic party and Senator Humphrey's different kind of leadership of the Minnesota Democratic Farmer-Labor party.) This structural antagonism is based partly on the fact that an already elected officeholder is before the public eye so frequently that he usually does not need the party organization to get re-elected, and the party organization often makes nuisance demands on him that he would rather not be obliged to comply with. So unless an officeholder is planning to try for a higher office covering a large electoral area, he is more likely to build what is called a "personal organization" rather than rely primarily on the regular party organization. Congressmen seldom aspire to a higher office, so they have little need of the party organizations. A second factor in the structural antagonism is the simple fact of physical separation between a congressmen's office and the state organization. What is not daily seen is usually not trusted. Governors are considerably more likely to be heads of their party organizations because of their physical presence in their home state, and even where this is not true in fact they are often accorded nominal headships. The major reason why more governors are not the *de facto* heads of their state parties is not so much their lack of need of the party for renomination, but rather because the vicissitudes of politics usually prevent them from having long tenures in office[2] (Governor Williams of Michigan set an all-time record with his 12 years as governor, but eventually he too was "killed off.")

---

[2]In the 1960 elections, of the 27 governors whose terms were expiring, 13 decided not to run or were prevented from running, and of the remainder who did run only 8 were re-elected. In contrast, of the 34 Senators whose terms were expiring, 5 decided not to run, and of the remainder who did run only one was defeated and 28 were re-elected.

Probably the majority of the state party leaders are persons who make a profession or major avocation of politics, and who seldom ever serve as governors or congressmen. Some hold lesser elective offices, like Mayor Daley of Chicago, but others never run for a political office in their whole lives. Some of them are "bosses," like Carmine DeSapio of New York, but this is a function of their particular local party structure, not the fact of their being leaders in the local party organization. There are various degrees of democracy in the state parties, and some are thoroughly democratic and tolerate no bosses. The interest in politics of some state party leaders benefits their occupations, as in the case of Walter Reuther of Michigan, but many others are active for the pure fun of it or because they have a serious impersonal interest in it. Many of those for whom politics is a hobby, not an occupation, develop skills and knowledge comparable to those of other artists who practice their arts as a hobby.

As indicated, Senator Kennedy made his major bid for the nomination to those who would actually vote on the nomination—the potential delegates to the 1960 Democratic national convention. Sometimes he concentrated on the top state political leaders, the governors, professional "bosses," or merely prestigious state party chairmen—but where he could not get their support, he went after the less formally important people who might be delegates. Thus he worked with Representative Stewart L. Udall in Arizona, Byron White in Colorado, and Jack Beaty in New Mexico, who in turn sought to reach the other rank-and-file potential delegates from their states. In following this approach, Senator Kennedy largely ignored his Senate role (it takes a great deal of time to be an effective senator) and his fellow senators. (Practically the only senator who gave him consistent support in his bid for the nomination was Henry M. Jackson of Washington, and even he influenced few delegates from his home state.) This is in contrast with the pre-1960 strategies of Senators Johnson and Humphrey. Senator Kennedy soon found that the "elder statesmen" were already committed to the other potential candidates, and—speaking in terms of votes at the national convention—did not count for much anyway.

On the other hand, Senator Kennedy's approach to the general public was a positive and vigorous one. He made speeches wherever and whenever he could get an invitation, usually at no charge for his services or his expenses,[3] and scores of published articles appeared over his name. He visited all of the states, many of them repeatedly. His Senate speeches, such as the 1957 speech urging France to get out of Algeria, were often more directed at the general public than at any business pending before the Senate, which probably did not enhance his reputation among his fellow senators. This effort to build a reputation as a popular national figure was obviously intended to overcome his handicaps—in the eyes of the state and social party leaders—as a Catholic and as a young, "immature" man. But he practically never used his popular appeal to intimidate state party officials (as Kefauver had done). Instead he wooed the state party officials by serving them (e.g. as a speech-maker whenever they wanted one); by being friendly to them (e.g. the lowliest party official received a "personal" Christmas card from the Kennedys as early as 1958); by appealing to their concern for party organization rather than issues (he quickly built a personal organization—largely through hiring men of brains and skills—that was quite impressive); and by promising them—or rather hinting at promises to them— that they would be rewarded with party and public offices if he were voted the party's leadership in 1960.[4]

Senator Kennedy's approach to the 1960 presidential primaries was most adroit, and his success was abetted by the errors of his rivals. In general, the primaries have not been important: only 16 states have them, and usually the results are not binding on the delegates selected (and practically never *after* the first ballot). Tradi-

[3]One indication of what Senator Kennedy was doing during 1957–59 is to be found in a news note in the *Minneapolis Sunday Tribune* of April 20, 1958, p. 2UM: "Busiest guy in town next week-end will be Senator John F. Kennedy (D., Mass.). He arrives by plane Friday at 11:27 a.m., has lunch with a few labor leaders, speaks at the University of Minnesota at 1:30 p.m., at Hamline University at 3 p.m. At 4 he'll meet the press for an hour. In the evening he'll address the Mississippi Valley Historical Society at the Pick-Nicollet Hotel. Saturday he will lunch with M. W. Thatcher of the Farmers Union Grain Terminal Association, drop in on the day-long DFL economic conference at the Leamington Hotel and make the principal address at the annual Jefferson-Jackson day dinner give by the DFL party at the Nicollet."

[4]By October 1959 Kennedy was already the front-runner among Democratic county chairmen across the country. A Gallup poll responded to by about half the Democratic county chairmen showed 469 of the 1454 respondents selecting Kennedy as "likely nominee" and 424 of them naming him as their personal preference—a higher number in both instances than for any other candidate (*Minneapolis Morning Tribune*, October 21, 1959, p. 6). At the same time, he was running slightly behind Stevenson in the public opinion polls, but Stevenson was way down—behind Symington—in the county chairmen poll.

tionally the winners in contested primaries do not later get selected as the presidential nomineees by their party conventions. State party leaders usually do not like the primaries: not only do they reduce their influence (primaries open the door to candidates who may have little relationship to the party organizations), but they take up money and effort which party leaders would prefer to devote to the bigger battle with the opposition party. Public opinion is seldom informed or highly interested as early as the spring before an election held in November, and the candidate who has a gimmick to capture a little attention can often win a presidential primary over a candidate who is far more qualified and has far more connections with the party organization that has to get him elected in November. But the primaries do exist, and they have the functions of "preventing the party bosses from thwarting the will of the people," and of suggesting the popular appeal of a potential nominee. The national audience, of politicians even more than of the general public, pay considerable attention to certain local primaries, and thus these primaries have more influence as "straws in the wind" nationally than they have to obtain delegate votes locally. This was the function Senator Kennedy made use of by going into selected primaries: he had to demonstrate that his Catholicism and his youth were no bar to a victory over the Republicans in the November election. In some of the primaries he went into there was no significant opposition (e.g. New Hampshire). He avoided primaries where there was a favorite-son candidate (e.g. Florida), so as to avoid antagonizing the state party leaders (except in Oregon where state law forced his entry, and where the favorite son was a senator not strongly attached to the party organization). He likewise avoided a primary where he could arrange a deal for certain support with the state's political leader without a primary (e.g. Ohio). He avoided a primary or two where it appeared that he would lose (e.g. District of Columbia). He chose to enter only two real contests where he would meet a serious rival—Wisconsin and West Virginia, where Senator Humphrey made the race against him. This was a break his other rivals gave him; their antagonism to, or fear of, the primaries caused them to fail to recognize what a primary victory would do for a candidate who was already favored by many state party leaders, and thus they allowed Kennedy to choose his own battlegrounds. Private polls showed pre-primary strength for

Kennedy in Wisconsin and West Virginia, and Senator Humphrey obliged by serving as the foil. If Humphrey had allowed Kennedy to win in Wisconsin and West Virginia by default, party leaders would continue to wonder whether Kennedy could beat a Republican, and Senator Humphrey's considerable skills might have made a great impression on the delegates at the time of the national convention. But Humphrey was apparently concerned about his lack of national popular reputation (most state party leaders had been ignoring him or were negative toward him) and he has an ebullient confidence in his ability to appeal to voters. Humphrey entered the Wisconsin primary with some funds, some local support and significant support from the Minnesota party across the border. But, more significantly, it can be said that Humphrey entered both primaries without the build-up of three years of local speechmaking, article writing, and conversations with local party leaders, without sufficient funds to purchase space and time in the mass media, and with a weak organization, especially in West Virginia. There may have also been other factors in his defeats, including Kennedy's ability to meet the religious issue head-on in West Virginia and thereby overcome it. Humphrey did not do too badly in Wisconsin (winning 44 per cent of the vote, and 4 out of the 10 districts),[5] but the overwhelming West Virginia defeat (39 per cent to Kennedy's 61 per cent) killed his chances for the presidential nomination. In Wisconsin, Kennedy seemingly demonstrated that some Catholic Republicans would vote for him to offset any possible losses from prejudiced Protestant Democrats. (This proved not to be completely true in the general election, for Kennedy lost Wisconsin to Nixon.) In West Virginia, he seemingly demonstrated that there are not a significant number of Protestant Democrats who would vote against a Catholic candidate per se. (This proved not to be true in the campaign for the general election, but the results of the West Virginia primary gave this impression to the political leaders.) Kennedy took serious risks by running in Wisconsin and West Virginia, but he was fortunate in that his opponent had such significant weaknesses (particularly in West

---

[5]The question can be raised as to whether Humphrey was eliminated by the Wisconsin primary, since he could not "deliver" a neighboring state. For those who thought so, Humphrey's decision to enter the West Virginia primary had significance only to demonstrate whether or not Kennedy would be seriously hampered by his Catholic affiliation.

Virginia). By making Kennedy's supposed major handicap, his Catholic faith, seem politically irrelevant, or possibly even an asset, Humphrey truly made Kennedy the front-runner before the national convention met in July.

Senator Johnson was clearly popular in the South, and had made the proper approaches to the state party leaders in the South and West. He had support from some former New Dealers like Oscar Chapman and Abe Fortas, although these were no longer prominent in politics. He had a small handful of leading political supporters in the East. But he was considered a regional, not a national, candidate, and many thought he would lose the Northern liberals and the Negroes if he were the candidate. If Johnson were to overcome this prejudice, it would have been strategic for him to battle in at least one non-Southern primary—say in West Virginia where the party leaders were reportedly for him. But he missed his chance, and went into the convention as a regional favorite son. Although he had the second largest number of delegates pledged to him (over 400), he never really had much of a chance after he decided not to enter a primary. Kennedy sought to weaken Johnson still more in late May and June 1960 by making an unusual effort to gain a few more votes in the Rocky Mountain states. These few votes were not important in themselves, but they cut into Johnson's territory and made him appear even more as a purely Southern candidate. By the time of the convention it seemed as if Johnson's only role could be to swing enough of his pledged delegates—on a second or later ballot, if there had been one—to a candidate other than Kennedy.

Senator Stuart Symington of Missouri built his candidacy for the nomination on the hope that the convention would deadlock, that none of the leading candidates would be able to get a majority, and that then the convention might turn to him as "everyone's second choice." His assets were a liberal record coupled with a conservative manner, executive experience in both business and government, and the support of former President Truman. But he relied too heavily on Humphrey's being able to stop Kennedy in the primaries, and when that failed Symington's only hope was that Johnson might be able and willing to swing all his Southern and Western support to him.

Adlai Stevenson was in a different position. His national popularity was clear to all, even though some held that his two defeats by

Eisenhower showed that he would lose again to Nixon. Stevenson did not need to enter a primary, but if he wished the nomination, he needed to appeal to uncommitted delegates at least a month before the convention. Many of them greatly admired Stevenson and were not strongly attracted to any other candidate. Most of these went eventually to Kennedy because they were importuned by Kennedy's organization. If Stevenson had sought their support, they likely would have gone to Stevenson. But Stevenson was never a candidate in the eyes of the great majority of the delegates, and his stance before and even during the convention was that he was not a candidate. An organization to make Stevenson the candidate effectively mobilized mass demonstrations in Los Angeles and sent waves of telegrams to the delegates from all over the country, and it got a favorable press due to the efforts of Mrs. Roosevelt and a few others. But it did not get the support of Stevenson himself, who might very well have got enough votes in the uncommitted delegations of Pennsylvania and Illinois, as he did without trying in California, to prevent Kennedy from winning on the first ballot. The mass demonstrations did not help Stevenson, as it was apparent to the delegates that the majority of the demonstrators were teen-agers ("nice kids; they'll be able to vote in about five years," a delegate said sarcastically, while perhaps the biggest demonstration in convention history surged around him). Even his nomination by Senator Eugene McCarthy of Minnesota (widely acclaimed as the best speech of the convention), the greatly applauded appearance of Mrs. Roosevelt in the spectators' balcony, the soul-stirring speech by Senator Lehman to the Minnesota delegation (attended by delegates from several other states), and the last-minute move to Stevenson by Senator Humphrey, did not gain many votes for Stevenson, These things happened too late, and the candidate himself did not support them, except possibly for a few hours on the day before the nomination.

If Stevenson had gone to work to seek delegates during the few weeks before the election, he might have picked up a significant number of votes in the delegations released from their pledge to Humphrey (North and South Dakota, District of Columbia, and scattered votes in nine other states); he would surely have picked up sizable small blocs of delegates in the partially uncommitted states of Pennsylvania, Illinois, Washington; he could have caused a partial bolt in Michigan and perhaps could have done better than he actually did do in California. He might even have done some of these things if he had gone to work during the five days before the nomination when the delegates were together in Los Angeles. If Stevenson had done these things, it seems likely that he could have stopped Kennedy on the first ballot. What would have happened then is purely conjectural. It is possible that the announced shifts to Kennedy of the favorite-son delegates in Kansas, Minnesota, and New Jersey after the first ballot would have convinced enough fairly neutral delegates that Kennedy was so close to the nomination that it would be either useless or foolish to continue the battle, and they would have voted for Kennedy on the second ballot and thus provided the nomination. On the other hand, there were many delegates who voted for Kennedy on the first ballot—particularly in Michigan, Ohio, Maryland, Indiana, and Iowa—who had been under the thumb of their state leaders or who had uneasily compromised in favor of Kennedy because no one else had seemed available, and these were likely to shift away from Kennedy. Johnson would have swung into action on the second or third ballot and withdrawn in favor of either Stevenson or Symington. He had recently openly expressed contempt for Kennedy, and it would have been easier for him to accept a vice-presidency under the more prestigious Stevenson or a role as *eminence grise* behind Symington. With Johnson's support, and the likely defectors having defected, Stevenson probably, and Symington possibly, could have won. Symington's only real chance would have occurred if there had been a deadlock between Kennedy and Stevenson, for he had made few enemies even though he had only scattered supporters outside of Missouri.

Kennedy came into the convention with strengths other than those we have already examined. He had made it completely clear that he was going to fight for a liberal program, which appealed to most delegates from the North and West. No candidate was so influential in pushing for a thoroughly liberal platform as was Kennedy, largely through the instrumentalities of Paul Butler of Indiana, Democratic National Chairman and father of the Democratic Advisory Council, and of Congressman Chester Bowles, chairman of the convention's platform committee. Kennedy brought to the convention with him paid and volunteer staffs of experts to work out the details of a liberal platform (I counted 13 persons on Kennedy's staff working on civil rights alone). While some Northerners doubted Kennedy's sincerity as a liberal, and others did not think highly of his youth, his personality, his family, or his prospects in the general election, they could not fail to be impressed by his efforts in favor of the liberal position. The clearly liberal stance was the most powerful one a candidate could take whose main organized opposition came from the conservative South.

Further, Kennedy had many liberal supporters. Not only were there the more or less anonymous staff liberals, but there were such strong party liberals as Chester Bowles, Averell Harriman, G. Mennen Williams, and Orville Freeman (after Humphrey's defeat) on his side. Almost as impressive to the delegates were the intellectuals who had been for Stevenson until he no longer appeared to be a candidate, like Arthur Schlesinger, Jr., J. Kenneth Galbraith, and Henry Steele Commager.[6] Many delegates observed that Kennedy had been able to attract able supporters and advisors.

Another type of supporter that gave Kennedy much strength was some of the strongest state party leaders of the kind he was making his main pre-convention approach to. First and foremost here were John Bailey, state chairman of Connecticut, and Governor Abraham Ribicoff of that same state. In seeking state party support, Kennedy's Catholicism was a strong asset. Many of the organizational leaders are Catholics, as Catholics tend to work in political parties more than persons of other faiths. Catholics have differences of political opinions among themselves just as do other religious groups, and they probably would not necessarily support a man solely because he is a Catholic, but for one reason. They had been understandably annoyed to hear, again and again, that a Catholic could not be elected President. They had a "minority psychology" at least to the extent that they would have liked to break that tradition. Thus, when a Catholic came along who seemed to have enough popular appeal to break through the bonds of prejudice (Kennedy after the West Virginia primary), they were naturally drawn to him. DeSapio and Wagner of New York, DiSalle of Ohio, Daley of Illinois, Lawrence of Pennsylvania, Brown of California—in fact, practically every leading

---

[6]These were among 16 prominent liberals who formerly supported Stevenson but who issued a public statement in support of Kennedy on June 17, 1960.

Catholic Democrat in the United States, except Eugene McCarthy of Minnesota, was for Kennedy by the time of the national convention. It must be said, however, that Kennedy had to demonstrate popular and delegate strength before he obtained the open support of these top party leaders.

Kennedy turned the disadvantage of being a Catholic into an advantage in another way. He could openly attack some of the unpopular things the Catholic Church is supposed to stand for without any danger of being called anti-Catholic: he was the candidate who came out most vigorously for separation of church and state; he announced that he did not favor federal government aid to parochial schools. Furthermore, he did not merely defend himself against anti-Catholic attacks—as Al Smith had in 1928—but he made a positive attack on prejudice. Some unbiased persons felt that sometimes there was an element of psychological blackmail in Kennedy's approach, of the order "If you're not for me, you're prejudiced" (which did appear in the West Virginia primary). But it created guilty consciences among some conscious anti-Catholics, and in this sense was a healthy influence in American politics: by demonstrating that he was not "a creature of the Pope" in politics, he could forward America another major step along its present course toward the elimination of intergroup prejudice. This had an appeal to many Jewish and Negro delegates, as well as to Catholic delegates.

Since we have mentioned the strengths many delegates saw in Kennedy, it would only be appropriate to recapitulate their views of his possible weaknesses as well. First, it was not clear what Kennedy really stood for. Many of his primary campaign statements were necessarily vague and general. Considering his voting record and other political behavior before 1955, the question was raised as to whether his liberalism was merely opportune, and whether he might revert to his earlier conservatism once he had captured the presidency. Associated with this was the fact that he was so surrounded by public-relations men that even the perceptive laymen could scarcely see "the true Kennedy" among them. However, his opponent, Richard Nixon, was even more strongly characterized by opportunism and by a thick veneer of misleading public relations, so the delegates guessed that the country could properly favor Kennedy on this score. The objection to Kennedy because of his youth was also allayed because Nixon was not much older.

Secondly, Kennedy used some "below the belt" political tactics that did not please those who favor cleanliness and dignity in politics. This dirty work was done by henchmen, but there can be little doubt that it had the approval of the strategic leader himself. The accusation that Humphrey was Teamster Hoffa's man, made in the Wisconsin primary, and that Humphrey was a draft dodger in World War II, made in the West Virginia primary, are examples in point, and other examples from these primaries could be dredged up. At the convention itself, conflicting suggestions of rewards in return for support led to the joke among delegates that there were almost enough Vice-Presidents around to have a convention among them alone. It is a commentary on politicians' vanity that a number of them were convinced that they had a chance for the vice-presidential nomination, "even though Jack did not make any definite commitments." The list includes Herschel Loveless of Iowa, George Docking of Kansas, Orville Freeman of Minnesota, Stuart Symington of Missouri, Gaylord Nelson of Wisconsin, Leroy Collins of Florida, Henry Jackson of Washington, Mennen Williams of Michigan, and perhaps others (it is questionable whether the last two mentioned believed they had a chance, although Jackson invested in some of the paraphernalia of a vice-presidential "campaign"). Finally, while it was expected that the presidential nominee would assume control of the national party organization, some Democrats were shocked by the abrupt abolition of the Democratic Advisory Council immediately after the nomination.

The selection of the actual vice-presidential nominee, Senator Lyndon Johnson, was another significant aspect of convention tactics, although the facts about this will probably never be fully known.[7] It is reported that Kennedy's statement about this was that a selected group of state party leaders advised him to offer this position to his chief opponent, and that Kennedy was greatly surprised when Johnson agreed to give up the powerful majority leadership of the Senate if he could be Vice-President. Some informed persons

---

[7]Since this chapter was originally written, Philip Graham's account of this incident has appeared as an appendix to Theodore H. White's *The Making of the President—1964* (New York: Atheneum, 1965), pp. 407–15.

question Kennedy's surprise, as they report that Johnson had indicated in 1956 he was willing to accept the vice presidency then, and believe this was a way for Kennedy to "get off the hook" with his numerous vice-presidential hopefuls as well as to keep the South from bolting to Nixon as a result of the strong civil-rights plank in the platform. Some have been so unkind as to suggest that it was also a way for Kennedy to get Johnson out of the majority leadership in the Senate, but this is doubtful, for Johnson had the ability and knowledge to be almost as powerful as president of the Senate as he had been as its majority leader.

Another story was that Johnson and Speaker Sam Rayburn demanded the vice-presidential nomination from Kennedy. They are alleged not only to have threatened a bolt by the South, but also a "failure" to enact, in the 1960 extra summer session for Congress, the liberal legislation that Kennedy would have found useful to establish a record for the November election. Even if Johnson did not threaten to use this weapon, it may have crossed Kennedy's mind that a disgruntled Johnson could create serious difficulties for him in the special session of Congress. Certainly Johnson's prestige with Congress would make him an asset as Vice-President as well as in the special session. The puzzling question to most delegates was not so much why Kennedy chose Johnson as why Johnson wanted the job when his power was greater as majority leader of the Senate.[8]

[8]Of course, the power of a majority leader is not as great when the President is of the same party as it is when the President is of the other party. The increasing demands on the office of President, and the increased hazards to the life and health of the President, have elevated the office of the Vice-President, as the country had already seen in the case of Richard Nixon. The Twenty-second Amendment to the Constitution, which limits the presidency to two terms, also creates new opportunities for the Vice-President to become heir apparent. (These changes give further reason why political conventions ought to give closer attention to the choice of Vice-President rather than following the tradition of allowing the presidential nominee to make the choice solely in terms of his personal choice or political expediency.) As Vice-President, Johnson was able to shift from a regional to a national figure. Finally, Johnson was one of the few Southerners who might willingly hasten the slow process of "bringing the South back into the Union." His influence and skill could have a marked effect in getting the South to accept legal equality for the Negro and a more liberal social welfare program. Johnson is quoted in a newspaper report (Los Angeles Times, July·16, 1960, p. 2) as saying to a Negro group, immediately after his nomination, "I think I know something about unjust practices. I have done my level best to make progress with civil rights. I think I have the knowledge and the energy. If you give me the strength, I think in the next four years, you will find you have made more progress than in the last 104 years." Thus Johnson had great prospects of making an unusual mark on history as Vice-President. A final consideration for Johnson might have been his difficulties in Texas politics.

Some Northern liberals—particularly in the Michigan and District of Columbia delegations—were so upset by the selection of Johnson as the vice-presidential candidate that they threatened a floor fight. (They had earlier caucused to promote Humphrey for the post, even though Humphrey announced that he would not accept and favored Freeman instead.) It is doubtful that they could have won against both Kennedy and Johnson, and Walter Reuther and Hubert Humphrey effectively urged them to be realistic and call off the fight.

Two general conclusions need to be drawn from this analysis of the Democratic nominations process in 1960. First, it often costs a great deal of money to get nominated for President today, and the candidate with access to large sums of money—if he is at all skillful and has any appealing qualities—is going to have a better chance at the nomination than one who is equally skillful and has equal personal appeal, or even somewhat more of these latter traits. The possession of money permits a potential candidate to speak without a fee to most significant political gatherings, to finance an effective primary campaign, and to pay for the "research" necessary to prepare publications used to build a favorable public "image." This conclusion would not apply to an incumbent who is seeking renomination, of course, nor would it apply so strongly to someone whose national reputation was built by an incumbent administration or a partisan national press. The money need not be the candidate's own; the candidacy of Dwight Eisenhower for the Republican nomination in 1952 probably cost as much as that of Nelson Rockefeller for the Republican nomination in 1960.

Second, the times seem to call for a man who is "tough" or politically skillful in an organizational sense. Stevenson seems to have had more personal appeal, or "warmth" than did Kennedy, but the latter beat the former. As we said at the outset, it is the delegates, not the people, who select the presidential candidate, and the delegates are more impressed by organization than they are by personal appeal. The great personal appeals of Mrs. Roosevelt, Senator Lehman, Senator Eugene McCarthy, and Stevenson himself had little effect on the decisions of the great majority of the delegates, even though the delegates enjoyed the show and even resented somewhat the pressures of the Kennedy organization. It is also true that the delegates want to nominate a winner and that pre-convention polls of public opinion showed Kennedy and Nixon leading their respective opponents in popularity; but delegates have to guess at popularity after a heated campaign of three months rather than merely ratifying a poll taken before convention time.

It may be an anti-climax to this analysis to report some aspects of the psychology of political conventions. First, conventions are so large and delegations so scattered into different hotels that many delegates are not in effective communication with each other. This was especially serious in the sprawling city of Los Angeles, where some delegations were housed as much as twenty miles away from headquarters (and had to be bussed in only a few times a day) and where public transportation was all but non-existent. It is not possible for 3800 delegates and alternates, not to speak of over a thousand other functionaries who get on the floor of a convention, to carry on a meeting using regular parliamentary procedures. At the Los Angeles convention, the confusion created by these large numbers was compounded by the poor acoustics of the Sports Arena and by the small army of roving TV and newspaper reporters with their odd-looking equipment. The only counterbalance to these barriers to communication would be the setting up of a more or less formal communication and intelligence operation in each delegation. This would need to operate on the floor of the convention as well as in the delegation's caucus rooms.

Second, TV seems to be making conventions less democratic: There is greater effort by political leaders to keep the battles in the hotel rooms and the caucuses, away from the eyes of the public, and there is greater effort to slur over the expression of dissident opinion when it does occur. Many delegates remember the bad public impression made when Senator Dirksen personally attacked Governor Dewey on the Republican convention floor in 1952, and are likely to avoid repetition of this. Political conventions have seldom, if ever, been completely democratic, but the effect of TV will undoubtedly be to make them less so unless the delegates devise ways of transacting some of their more controversial business in committee and caucus rooms. As it is today, the convention assembled is almost a campaign device, rather than an important part of the democratic political process in its own right.

Third, delegates pay little attention to street parades, floor demonstrations, and other direct manifestations of public influence, as they are aware how these are organized and manipulated. This has been so especially since the 1940 Republican convention which responded to the galleries' demands that it nominate Wilkie. On the other hand, some delegates are responsive to telegrams and other communications from known persons in their home states, as most of them are not used to receiving so many communications and are not fully aware how such campaigns can be organized. Fourth, about half the delegates in the 1960 Democratic convention were attending their first national convention, and even some of those who had attended conventions before were not aware of how much they could learn, and how much they could influence, if they went outside the boundaries of their state delegation. One of Kennedy's strengths was that he had one or more staff persons working with nearly every state delegation. Fifth, the delegations—at least from the smaller states—become what sociologists call a "small secondary group" with all the friendships, liaisons, and conflicts that ordinarily develop in such groups. Sixth, in a convention as large, confused and speedily moving as the Democratic one in 1960, even experienced political leaders make gross blunders, and often are prey to the usual irrationalities that man is subject to.

XII

The Passage of Legislation: The Politics of Financing Medical Care for the Aging

The passage of a major piece of legislation offers the student of the political power structure of the United States an opportunity to see how that structure operates in practice. The bill to be followed, from its first introduction in 1957 to its passage in 1965, is the so-called "Medicare" or "Forand" bill, which evoked a major political struggle during those years. The histories of no two bills are alike, but the Medicare bill was one of a major series of proposed statutes in the "public welfare" area that have been passed in the years since 1933, and in many ways it provides us with useful insights into political influence and political power.

A. The Issue and its Contestants

During the years 1958–65, the matter of financing medical care for the aging became a major political issue for the federal Congress and the President. The matter took much congressional time during that whole period (especially of the members of the House Ways and Means Committee); it was one of the leading campaign issues in the 1960, 1962, and 1964 elections; and it was on the President's "must" list for legislation every year from 1961 until the bill was passed in 1965. The division was along the lines most significant for the student of American power structure: on one side stood most of the Republican party,[1] the American Medical Association, allied

[1]For the Republican leadership's position, see *The New York Times*, February 10, 1961, p. 12, and January 29, 1965, p. 13. Votes on the bill by party are reported on subsequent pages of this chapter.

professional groups (such as the American Hospital Association), the U. S. Chamber of Commerce, the National Association of Manufacturers, the American Farm Bureau Federation, and most of the medical or health insurance companies; on the other side stood most of the non-Southern Democratic party,[2] organized labor, many "welfare," civic, and religious organizations, and many organizations composed of older people.[3] Mass opinion was also on this side, insofar as a Gallup public opinion poll conducted in May 1961 could correctly ascertain it. In response to the question "Would you favor or oppose having the Social Security tax increased in order to pay for old-age medical insurance?" the nationwide adult responses were: Favor–67 per cent; Oppose–26 per cent; No opinion–7 per cent.[4] Another Gallup poll, in early 1962, asked respondents to indicate preference for the Forand bill as compared to private health insurance; the percentages for the two plans were 55 and 34 respectively, with the remaining 11 per cent undecided or not answering.[5] Local polls showed substantially the same results.[6]

There were some exceptions in this political line-up. Governor Nelson Rockefeller of New York, Senator Clifford Case of New

[2]For the early and fairly consistent position of the Northern Democrats, see the Senate vote on the Anderson amendment on August 23, 1960; and the statement signed by 30 Governors (mostly Northern Democrats) on June 29, 1960, favoring the Social Security approach.

[3]Among the groups endorsing, by 1960, the Social Security approach to financing health benefits for the aging were the American Public Welfare Association, National Council of Jewish Women, Group Health Association of America, National Council of Churches of Christ in the U.S.A., National Association of Social Workers, American Nurses Association, Americans for Democratic Action, National Farmers Union, National League of Senior Citizens. By November 1963 there were additional endorsements from the United Church of Christ, Council of Jewish Federations and Welfare Funds, Synagogue Council of America, Unitarian-Universalist Fellowship for Social Justice, and the National Catholic Welfare Conference.

[4]Minneapolis Morning Tribune, June 9, 1961, p. 40. Age breakdowns showed slightly larger proportions of the elderly than of younger adults in favor of the proposal. While this was to be expected because the proposal would benefit the elderly, it ran counter to the usual correlation between age and conservatism.

[5]Minneapolis Sunday Tribune, April 1, 1962, p. 16A.

[6]The Minnesota Poll, reported in the Minneapolis Sunday Tribune, June 11, 1961, p. 3E, showed 66 per cent of that state's adults in favor of the latest legislative version of the Social Security approach, with 27 per cent opposed, and 7 per cent giving no answer or qualified answers. An Iowa survey of persons over 60 showed 71 per cent of those living in metropolitan areas in favor of the approach and 51 per cent of those living in non-metropolitan areas; about half of the remainder were uncertain. (W. W. Morris, "A Report on the Iowa Survey of Life After Sixty," Bulletin of the Institute of Gerontology, State University of Iowa, vol. VIII, supplement no. 3, March 1961, pp. 4–5.)

Jersey, and former Secretary of Health, Education and Welfare Marion B. Folsom were prominent Republicans who publicly favored the approach opposed by most of their party. *Business Week* and, temporarily, *Life* magazine, also took this exceptional position in editorials.[7] With these and perhaps a few other exceptions, the "economic elite" showed a solidarity seldom achieved, at least for public observation.

The concrete positions are difficult to describe: they were expressed in somewhat varying forms and changed from time to time. In general, one side—which we may label the "liberals"—favored what came to be known as the Social Security approach or the For-and bill (after the congressional sponsor of the legislative proposal). The original bill had a history in earlier, unsuccessful, legislation, and probably had been written by experts outside the halls of Congress. The specific provisions of this legislative approach varied in proposed coverage, administration, contributory requirements, extent of benefits, and other details. But they all provided that persons covered by Social Security reaching a certain age (62 to 68) would have a significant portion of their hospital, nursing, and diagnostic costs paid for by Social Security taxation (usually specified as one-fourth of 1 per cent of wages, with the wage earner and his employer each paying this amount). None of the early bills covered payments to physicians, and all provided explicitly for free choice of physician by the patient.[8] However, the bill that was finally passed in 1965 provided for an optional insurance to cover doctors' bills.

The position of the other side—which we may label the "economic elite"—varied even more drastically. The leadership in stating the position seemed to be the American Medical Association, although at least at one point in 1961–62 the leadership seems to have passed to a coalition of Senate Republicans, headed by Jacob Javits of New York.[9] In the early stages of the battle, in 1958 and 1959, the posi-

[7]*Business Week*, April 16, 1960; *Life*, April 25, 1960. *Life* reversed itself in an editorial of June 15, 1962 ("Medicine, Yes, But a Bad Bill"), p. 4.

[8]The exclusion of payment of doctors' bills was done so as to avoid the charge that the government was interfering with the free choice of physician. Reports of the McNamara Committee (Senate Subcommittee on Problems of the Aged and Aging) indicated that doctors' bills constituted only about 12 per cent of total medical bills in chronic cases.

[9]Senator Javits ultimately voted for the bill that passed in 1965, whereas the majority of his fellow Republican congressmen did not—indicating either that Senator

tion was that medical care costs of the elderly should be handled by the existing provisions of the Old Age Assistance (OAA) program for the indigent and by private medical insurance for the rest of the population, supplemented by programs arranged by voluntary associations.[10] In June 1960, the AMA shifted its position to favor what eventually became the Kerr-Mills Act, which increased federal contributions to state programs for medical care for indigent old persons on OAA and set up a new category of "medically indigent" persons who would receive government subsidy for medical care if their states implemented the legislation. The medically indigent were variably defined by the separate states, but in general they were intended to be persons who had enough income to support themselves except in regard to unusual medical expenses (each state set up its own means test). Especially after the Kerr-Mills Act was passed by Congress in August 1960, the AMA argued that no further legislation should be considered until the Kerr-Mills Act had a chance for implementation. But in the summer of 1960 the Eisenhower Administration gave support to a bill earlier proposed by Senator Javits, which extended medical coverage much beyond that provided for by the Kerr-Mills bill, while still financing it through general revenues rather than through the Social Security tax and requiring its implementation by the states. In the spring of 1961, Republicans in Congress returned to the Javits bill, implying that the Kerr-Mills Act was insufficient, while still strongly opposing the Social Security or "liberal" approach. In January 1962, the American Hospital Association came out for a "compromise" proposal not favored by the AMA. Thus, there was some open difference of opinion among different groups within the "economic elite," although not on the basic

---

Javits changed his mind, or, more likely, that Republican support for the Javits position in 1960–62 was a matter of expediency so as to make the Republican party appear not to be against any form of medicare.

[10]At one time, decades earlier, the American Medical Association had opposed voluntary group health programs, including group insurance programs. But by 1958 the AMA was holding up these programs as model ways of avoiding governmental programs. An editorial, entitled "Hospitals," *Journal of the American Hospital Association*, December 1949, p. 60, stated: "It is a sad fact that through the 1930's and early 1940's, the American Medical Association did not believe in voluntary sickness insurance, and did almost everything possible to prevent its development." During the debate on the extension of Social Security to the permanently and totally disabled, in 1956, the AMA warned that this would mean socialized medicine. The bill was passed, and no further word was said regarding its being socialized medicine.

issue of opposing compulsory hospital insurance under Social Security.

In a later discussion we shall attempt to explain why the passage of the Kerr-Mills Act in 1960 failed to stop the agitation. At this point, we merely note that the consistent distinction beween the two contesting positions was the attitude, for and against, the use of the Social Security system to finance medical care for the aging. The Kerr-Mills bill finally gained the support of both groups, as a means of financing medical care for the *indigent* aged, even though it was originally opposed by some of the "economic elite" as an extension of federal government activity in the welfare field, and even though it was originally opposed by some of the "liberals" because they said it was a means of delaying the passage of a Forand-type bill. The proponents of the Social Security approach did not regard the Kerr-Mills Act as sufficient to meet the needs of the aging, while the opponents of the Social Security approach regarded it as quite sufficient, or even more than sufficient.

The question may be raised as to why the issue arose just at this time. After all, one might say, there have always been elderly people, and they have always had more than their share of need for medical care. The projected answer considers two sets of factors: changes in the objective situation of the elderly and changes in public attitudes toward the elderly. The main objective change affecting the elderly was the discovery—mainly during the 1940's—of medical means to reduce sharply the acute illnesses (e.g. pneumonia, influenza), thereby lengthening life and exposing the elderly to more chronic illness (e.g. cancer, heart disease, crippling arthritis).[11] The longer period of old age and the much longer periods of illnesses have greatly increased medical bills, at a time when medical costs have risen more sharply than the cost of living generally.[12] Thus, in a sense, there arose a *new*

[11]In the National Health Survey of July 1959 to June 1960, it was found that 77 per cent of the elderly population had one or more chronic illnesses. (U. S. Public Health Service, *Health Statistics from the U.S. National Health Survey*, Series B, No. 31, Table 2.) In the short span of years between 1901 and 1955, according to another study, the proportion of persons who died of some chronic disease after the age of 65 rose from 46 per cent to 81 per cent. (*Statistical Bulletin*, New York: Metropolitan Life Insurance Company, August 1960, pp. 1–3.)

[12]The Consumer Price Index had risen to 126.5 in 1961 from the base of 100 set for 1947–49. Medical care costs had risen in the same period to 156.2, and the constituent element in it of hospital room rates—the main item covered by the Forand bill—had risen to 223.3. (U. S. Department of Health, Education and Welfare, *Health, Education and Welfare Trends*, 1961 edition.) The disparity continued to increase through the early 1960's.

objective problem confronting the elderly as far as financing medical care is concerned. There had also been a more gradual increase in the proportion of the elderly without income from employment, due to the relative decline of the self-employing occupations, the adoption of company rules for compulsory retirement at 65 years, and a changing technology which rendered obsolescent the work skills of many older workers.

These changes in the objective position of the elderly helped to spark public interest in their problems. Developments in the social sciences and in social services also increased public attention to the elderly. During the 1930's some of the elderly themselves for the first time formed an organization to gain government benefits (the Townsend movement), and this type of organization expanded and became diversified during the 1950's. There are now scores of national organizations for the elderly, and thousands of local ones, and while most of them are not primarily political pressure groups, they occasionally pass resolutions in favor of certain legislation. It might fairly be said that a minority of those past 65 today *identify* themselves as members of an aging *group*, and their attitudes bear some resemblance to those of ethnic minority groups insofar as they feel that they have low prestige and are discriminated against.[13] The number of persons with such attitudes is increasing, if we use as evidence the rate of formation of action organizations for the elderly. The desire to help the elderly is spreading among those under 65, if we judge by the increase in programs on aging problems held by voluntary associations, by the attendance at state and regional meetings in 1960 held in preparation for the White House Conference on Aging, and by the attendance at such meetings held since then. Such developments allow us to speak of the formation of a social movement of *aging consciousness*. This movement does not have large dimensions, but it is still new and it is growing. It is undoubtedly a factor in the creation of a political issue over financing medical care for the aging.

Favoring the other side was another history of changing objective conditions and attitudes. The long period of prosperity after 1940,

13Milton L. Barron, "Minority Group Characteristics of the Aged in American Society," *Journal of Gerontology*, 8 (October 1953), 477–82; Arnold M. Rose, Chapters 1 and 2 of *Older People and their Social World*, edited by A. M. Rose and W. A. Peterson (Philadelphia: F. A. Davis, 1965).

the increasing willingness (particularly in the younger generations) to use the services of doctors and hospitals when there is illness, the development of private medical insurance programs—all sharply increased the economic demand for medical services. The number of doctors, hospitals, and other medical facilities has not kept up with the rise of economic demand. Physicians and other persons who were aware of this situation seriously questioned whether a new public program to extend medical services could be met with existing resources, or whether meeting it would not create a deterioration of services to existing clients as well as new public controls on fees, priorities of patients, time spent per patient, etc., that would change the social organization of medical services—thus reducing the freedom of doctors. These persons also said that the great increase in demand would create such long waiting lists that the patients too would have little choice of hospitals and doctors in fact.[14]

Secondly, the continuing economic prosperity and the rising need for medical care by the aged have increased the number of persons purchasing private medical insurance. This insurance can be used to pay medical expenses before the age of 65, but many purchasers buy it mainly to increase their security in old age. The estimates vary considerably as to the number of elderly covered now, and at various periods in the future, by private medical insurance, but the total amount of such insurance business is not negligible, and the creation of a governmental compulsory insurance program for financing medical care for the elderly would cut sharply into this private insurance business. It has been argued that since about half of the elderly had some kind of private medical insurance, and since the proportion was growing,[15] there was no need for an additional general coverage program by the government.

[14]Under Blue Cross and other private hospital-insurance plans, the physicians themselves had often been the ones responsible for sending sick people to the hospital who might just as well have been treated at home, as it was easier for the physician to treat patients in the hospital. The King-Anderson bill (a version of the Forand bill that was under consideration by the Congress in 1961–62) sought to prevent this by offering 300 days of home nursing care in lieu of 90 days in the hospital (or various combinations of the two), so that the patient would prefer to get care at home rather than in the hospital. The Act passed in 1965 did not retain this principle, but it offered a longer period of services in nursing homes and at private homes than it did in the hospital.

[15]A Chamber of Commerce *Special Report* of February 15, 1960 (p. 3), stated that "the health insurance industry now estimates that 60 per cent of our aged wanting and needing hospital insurance will have it by the end of 1960 and about 90 per cent by 1970."

There were other, more specific arguments used by the AMA against the Forand bill. (1) The early Forand-type bills provided hospital and nursing care only for those covered by Social Security, which meant that they would not cover a significant minority of the elderly. (2) The Social Security program benefits those who do not need it financially as well as those who do. (3) The various forms of the Forand bill provided some limitations on the extent of the medical care that could be paid for, regardless of need. (4) The great majority of the elderly say they have no uncared-for medical need. (5) The elderly of today were partially prevented from accumulating savings by the great Depression of the 1930's, but that will not be true for the elderly who reached the peak of their earning power after 1940. (6) The Forand bill violates the principles of Social Security in that some workers would have to pay "in order to provide benefits to others also self-supporting on jobs," in that everyone would be eligible to get maximum benefits rather than getting benefits "geared to what beneficiaries had earned in earlier years when working," and in that benefits would not be paid to beneficiaries in cash "so that each could decide what he wanted to spend his benefit money for."[16]

Finally, and seemingly more important to its proponents than any of the aforementioned reasons for opposing such a governmental compulsory insurance program, if the published statements be used as the criteria, there is the argument known as "the foot in the door." There has been a movement on the part of a small number of the "liberals" and of the leaders of organized labor to obtain national health insurance for all Americans, such as exists in a number of other nations. Most physicians oppose this strenuously as they believe it would place great government controls on doctors and other medical personnel and would destroy the existing "fee for service" and "free choice of physician" system. They label national health insurance "socialized medicine," even though there is in fact a distinction between contributory insurance without federal direction and direct federal payment from general revenues coupled with federal direction —which latter would be an objective definition of socialized medicine. The movement for national health insurance for everyone has no relationship to the aforementioned movement of "aging consciousness," although there can be little doubt that some of the proponents of national health insurance see the extension of Social

16Ibid.

Security to finance medical care for the aging as a first step toward getting national health insurance. This perception of a sequential relationship is agreed to by the opponents of national health insurance; hence the "foot in the door" argument. The opponents of a Forand-type bill believed that if it were passed, the next step would be to extend it to all persons covered by Social Security regardless of age: "Since the costs of Social Security health care benefits would be paid for by heavier social taxes on covered workers and on employers, pressures would inevitably develop to extend these benefits to all these workers and their dependents. After all, workers covered by Social Security would be compelled to foot half the bill."[17] For the great bulk of the "aging-conscious" proponents of the Forand-type bills, however, there was no connection between the limited help they sought for the aged and complete "socialized medicine" of any type for the general population.

As we consider the attitudes of opponents of the Forand bill outside the ranks of the medical profession, the "foot in the door" argument takes on an added significance. They may or may not be opposed to socialized medicine as such, but they see the Forand bill as merely the latest in a whole sequence of welfare measures transforming the economy into a socialist one, and shifting power from individual decision-makers like themselves to the government. For them, the fight against the Forand bill was merely the latest skirmish in a more general war. Interviews with two vigorous opponents of the Forand bill will illustrate this most significant point of view. One was a former governor of a Midwestern state, whom I queried about the reasons for his opposition to the Forand bill. His answer seemed at first startlingly irrelevant: He told me about an occasion some fourteen years earlier when he stood up to a crowd of strikers who marched on the state capitol when he was governor to seek a certain action in their favor. His calm firmness at first quieted them and then dispersed them. The recounting of this story took about fifteen minutes and the ex-governor had no more to say in answer to my question about the Forand bill. I understood his parable to mean that the masses will ever rise to bluster and make unreasonable demands, and that the only proper way to handle such demands was to oppose them with calmness and absolute firmness. The specific demand, he

17Ibid. pp. 2–3.

implied for both cases, is unimportant; the important thing is to demonstrate to the masses that they cannot get what they want by group pressure. If they gain one point by such means, no matter what the point, they have gained a foot in the door toward the general evil of socialism.

The second interview, with a businessman, brought forth a comparable response without any specific query from me. We were talking about the problems of the elderly generally, and he proved to be well informed. The remark I found significant referred to an unspecified "they." He said, "They were working to get public housing a few years ago, and now they have shifted their efforts to get public medical care for the aging. Next year it will be something else." My interpretation of this remark was that he perceived the supporters of one governmental welfare measure to be the same individuals supporting all other governmental welfare measures and that their goal seemed to be a general socialized society. The specific measure was unimportant; what was important was to beat those referred to as "they." The specific measure was only a "foot in the door" toward something generally very undesirable. The AMA itself openly attacked the Forand bill as a first step toward socialism. In a lead article in the *AMA News*, dated March 20, 1961, the following statement was made: "The Socialist party in the United States has launched a nation-wide campaign for socialized medicine in America and has made it clear it supports President Kennedy's proposal for health and medical care through the Social Security program to bring full-blown socialized medicine to this country." The Socialists "intended to use socialized medicine as the springboard to reach that bigger prize—full socialism for the United States."[18] This, of course, is an expression of the "conspiracy" theory of power, which is considered elsewhere in this book. It is to be noted, however, that here the economic elite is the group *using* the conspiracy theory, whereas usually the conspiracy is attributed *to* the economic elite by such writers as Ferdinand Lundberg and C. Wright Mills.

The question may be raised as to whether the positions of either or both groups of contestants were self-defeating in terms of their "real" interests. The demand for the Social Security tax as a means of financing medical care for the aging might be considered irrational

18Quotations from *The New York Times*, March 18, 1961, p. 7.

from the standpoint of those who favor progressive taxation. The Kerr-Mills Act and the Javits bill provided for financing medical care out of general revenues, that is, mainly out of the income tax, which is progressive in that it takes proportionately more money from the wealthy. If the state governments had taken a generous view toward the implementation of the Kerr-Mills Act which some opponents of the Forand approach publicly favored in 1964–65 when it appeared that such an approach would actually be legislated, the Act could actually have gone a long way toward meeting the medical care needs of the elderly and could have resulted in something that could properly be called "socialized medicine" for them. The various forms of the Forand bill, on the other hand, provided for financing medical care out of the Social Security tax, which is regressive in that it is proportional to income only up to $4,800 or $5,200 or $6,600 a year, after which there is no tax. Yet most of those supporting the Forand approach were undoubtedly also advocates of progressive taxation, which makes them inconsistent. They also—inconsistently—did little to get the states to implement the Kerr-Mills Act so as to aid the medically indigent, and they opposed the Javits bill.[19]

There were irrationalities and inconsistencies on the side of the "economic elite" also. In the first place, the same argument about taxation applies in reverse to the high-income people who opposed the Social Security approach: Wealthy people should rationally prefer a program which is paid for by the masses who benefit from the program, rather than largely by themselves. In fact, they favored the government approach which meant higher taxation for themselves— namely, the Kerr-Mills Act and ostensibly the Javits bill. In April 1965, the great majority of Republicans in the House of Representatives voted for the "Byrnes amendment," which provided an extensive program of medical care for the elderly, with about two-thirds of the cost being paid for out of general federal revenues (i.e. the income tax). Secondly, for the insurance companies, the costs of maintaining the elderly in medical insurance drive the insurance rates

[19]It may be that they were aware that there was little real support for the Javits bill. Most of those who gave lip service to the Javits bill apparently merely wished to avoid losing the political support of the aging while they fought the Forand bill. As suggested earlier, this criticism probably does not apply to Senator Javits himself, because he consistently supported the principle of providing hospital and other medical care for the aging, and he ultimately voted for a bill like the Forand bill.

so high that they become uneconomic and even prohibitive for those in the younger and middle-age brackets. Marion B. Folsom, former Secretary of Health, Education and Welfare in President Eisenhower's cabinet and then president of the Eastman Kodak Company, gave this as a major reason for his support of the Social Security approach in 1961.[20] This logic apparently made little impact on his fellow businessmen. Furthermore, while the Forand bill would take some business away from the private vendors of medical insurance, it would provide a windfall for vendors of life insurance: More universal availability of medical care for the elderly would increase the average length of life, thus delaying payments for life insurance. Increasing length of life has provided greatly increased prosperity for life insurance companies in the past and can do so again. The life insurance business is considerably greater than the medical insurance and annuity business together,[21] and should logically outweigh them in the eyes of most insurance companies. In fact, the insurance companies were not swayed by this rational argument, for they almost unanimously opposed the Forand bill.

For physicians, older patients have generally created a payment problem. Most physicians have to lower their fees for elderly people, especially those who get the chronic illnesses which require costly hospital and nursing care, and in some cases they forgo their fees completely for such patients. It would seem rational for physicians to favor a government program that pays most of the costs of hospital and nursing care, and leaves the physicians completely uncontrolled. In fact, the great majority of them vigorously oppose this program, and instead favor a private insurance program which cannot cover a large proportion of the elderly, but does impose limits on fees for the physician who serves patients covered by the private insurance.

Thus, the controversy over the means of financing medical care for the aging took on the aspect of class warfare, in which neither side was operating primarily according to its economic interests. Particularly the opponents of the social security approach chose to

[20]In a widely publicized speech delivered at the White House Conference on Aging, January 12, 1961.

[21]That is, for that portion of it carried by profit-seeking insurance companies, and not including that portion presumably not producing a profit, which is carried by Blue Cross and Blue Shield, both controlled by the hospitals and the doctors.

make the issue a symbol of their relative power in the society, for their political campaign against any form of the Forand bill was very costly, in terms of dollars, effort, and prestige. The economic elite has seldom been so unified and so vigorous in its opposition to a measure sponsored by a popular social movement. The stand it has taken does not reflect its economic interests, as we have demonstrated, and must therefore reflect its ideology (or "principles," to use the more popular term). To this battle for its principles, the economic elite brought a great deal of energy and devotion.

B. Approaches to the Public

Both sides to the controversy used a vast array of printed leaflets, mimeographed releases, newspaper ads, "conferences" and mass meetings, radio and TV programs, and other means of mass communication to influence the attitudes of the public. At least one part of the conflict consisted of a struggle to reach the public mind. The volume of material which was of direct cost to its sponsors was much heavier from the side of the opponents of the Social Security approach. Free publicity, in the newspapers and on radio and TV, was much more balanced in quantity.

The arguments reaching the public may be illustrated from leaflets and advertisements. The major source of paid material in favor of the Social Security approach was at first the American Federation of Labor and Congress of Industrial Organizations (AFL–CIO). The headings of a leaflet entitled "Medical Care for the Aged—A Matter of Right!" may be quoted to illustrate the approach used by this organization: "Social Insurance: Sound Financing with no Means Test," "Broad Benefits are Possible," "Lifetime Protection: the Only Way," "Public Assistance Cannot Do the Job." The criticism by the opponents of the Social Security approach which the proponents sought most fully to answer publicly was the one that private medical insurance could do the job. Not only did they claim that the estimate, made by the Health Insurance Association of America, of 49 per cent covered was exaggerated. They also made these assertions. (1) Costs of medical insurance are high, especially when offered by profit-making companies and especially for low-risk younger persons. (2) New policies were practically unavailable to those past 65 until the battle over the Forand bill became significant, and this availability after 1958 may simply be a political device which would be withdrawn when and if the Forand bill is defeated (there would be no need to withdraw the policies if—as happened—a Forand-type bill was passed, since practically no one would then want to purchase such a basic-care policy. (3) The benefits are inadequate; they quote former HEW Secretary Arthur Flemming (of the Eisenhower Cabinet!): "a large percentage of persons aged 65 and over do not have protection against long-term illnesses, and either cannot obtain protection at rates they can afford to pay, or cannot obtain adequate protection."[22]

The public arguments of the American Medical Association against the social security approach may be quoted from the answer to a question printed in a leaflet entitled "Common Sense Health Care of the Aged: Helping Those Who *Need* Help."

> *Question.* What are the flaws in the Forand-type approach? *Answer.* There are many besides its astronomical cost. To name just a few: (1) It is totally unnecessary. The Kerr-Mills Law will do the job. (2) It would mean poorer, not better health care for the aged, with government employees telling doctors what drugs and treatment they could provide their patients; telling hospitals how to operate; telling nursing homes what they could and could not do. (3) It would lead to the decline, if not the end, of private health insurance, which has made such great strides in recent years. (4) It would mushroom into compulsory national health insurance for every American, as time went by. What would start out as socialized medicine for the aged would eventually become socialized medicine for every man, woman, and child in the country.

Besides the open advertising, various indirect and subtler tactics were used to sway the attitudes of influential segments of the public. The struggles to select and influence the delegates to the White House Conference on Aging (held in Washington, D.C., January 9–12, 1961) may be used to illustrate this approach. The bulk of the delegates to this conference were selected by the governors of the re-

[22]Statement before the House of Representatives Ways and Means Committee, May 4, 1960, p. 2.

spective states (usually on the advice of committees of citizens appointed by the governors) and by the leaders of some 325 national organizations interested in the aging. In the early stages of the preparation for this conference, at the state level, it was not apparent that the conference was going to be used as a forum for debating the merits of the Social Security approach. Rather, attention was focused on the general problems of the aging, and the governors tended to appoint to their advisory committees persons who were interested in these problems. Thus, a number of civic leaders, social welfare workers, and social scientists were appointed, as well as physicians, businessmen, insurance executives, and others. These advisory committees were charged with making recommendations for the welfare of the aging as well as recommendations of names of persons to serve as official delegates.

By early 1960 it was becoming increasingly apparent that the White House Conference on Aging was to become a battleground over the question of the mode of financing medical care for the aging. Pressures were then applied on the governors' advisory committees and on the governors themselves. Judging from oral statements made to me by members of the advisory committees, the pressures came overwhelmingly from the organizations opposed to the Social Security approach. Since my interviews with members of these advisory committees were not systematic or deeply probing, they cannot be said to reveal all the pressures used, but merely to illustrate them.

1. In Missouri, in preparation for the White House Conference an extensive survey was taken of the attitudes and problems of a representative sample of older people. The report included the statement that "some persons over 65 mentioned that they were too old or too ill to qualify for health insurance." A representative of a health insurance company, which offered a partial insurance program for older people, demanded a public "correction" of the statement, which would be also mailed to all the older people in the sample surveyed, because "it left the impression that there was no alternative to medicare."

2. In California, the recommendations to be sent to the White House Conference were voted on by the participants at the various

sections of the state conference on aging. Those opposed to the Social Security approach—mostly physicians—formed a "flying squad" to go from one section to another to vote on any issue being considered by any section that would relate to medical care financing.

3. In Florida, a physician who had been a member of the governor's advisory committee from its inception, and who had voted with his fellow members in favor of all recommendations in support of the Social Security approach and other matters, publicly denounced the report of the committee just as it was about to be released. The chairman of the committee—former United States Senator Harry Cain—stated, in an open letter to Governor Leroy Collins, August 17, 1960, that Dr. Karelas had called him from Gainesville on Wednesday, August 10, to say he had not authored the denunciation. It had been prepared and typed in an office other than his own, and he declared he had been forced into signing it and the letter of transmittal because he feared that to refuse would place his professional career in jeopardy. Cain's letter goes on to document the misrepresentations made in the denunciation.[23]

4. In Illinois, a physician who had indicated his approval of the Social Security approach was withdrawn from the list of delegates by the governor, upon receiving a request to do so from the state medical association.

5. In New Mexico, the entire list of delegates—who had been working as the governor's advisory committee for over a year—was withdrawn by the newly elected governor a week before the White House Conference and replaced with new delegates who had not participated in the state's activities in preparation for the White House Conference.

6. Lesser efforts to cajole or coerce governors' advisory committees in six other states were reported to me.

Both sides used social science research in support of their positions. In fact, there was probably no other issue up to that time on which so many social scientists were quoted, in the Congress and to the public. The proponents of the Social Security approach mainly made

[23]In a public speech on March 19, 1961, HEW Secretary Ribicoff made a general statement that the AMA uses sanctions against doctors who favor the Social Security approach. *Minneapolis Morning Tribune*, March 20, 1961, p. 3.

use of government studies, and publicized them. One of their main sources was the reports of the Senate Subcommittee on Problems of the Aged and Aging (usually called the "McNamara Committee" after its chairman, Senator Pat McNamara of Michigan). These reports included a systematic compilation of data on the incomes, medical needs, insurance coverage, and medical expenditures of the elderly. Some of these data got fairly widespread coverage in public speeches and in the newspapers. A study made by the Department of Health, Education and Welfare was the basis of an article in *Look* magazine in March 1961. It reported that costs of administration of insurance were lower under government Social Security than under Blue Cross, Blue Shield, or any of the commercial companies; that insurance companies had great difficulty in establishing reasonable rates for medical insurance; that the coverage of private medical insurance ranged down to less than a fifth of the total medical costs an aged person might be expected to incur.[24] These and other studies cited by the proponents of the Social Security approach were designed to show: (1) that the overwhelming majority of those past 65 did not have sufficient income or savings to pay for extensive or *major* medical care if they should need it (the proportion was estimated up to 88 per cent, but this of course depends on how "major" is defined); (2) that only a minority of the elderly needed this major medical care, and that therefore the insurance principle ("sharing the costs of the risks") is a good one; (3) that private medical insurance is not adequate to meet the very heavy costs of major medical care and that less than half of the elderly were at that time covered by any amount of medical insurance.

The opponents of the Social Security approach relied particularly on three studies, mainly to demonstrate that only a small minority of the elderly ever needed major medical care, and that therefore a system covering practically the entire population would tend to "socialize" the aging and encourage them to claim medical benefits when they did not really need them. One study widely quoted at first was conducted by the National Opinion Research Center, under the direction of sociologist Ethel Shanas. This carefully designed study showed that, among the non-institutionalized aged 65 and over, only

---

[24] Only about one-fourth of those over 65 with private medical insurance received payment for more than one-half of their hospital bills.

between 10 and 14 per cent thought of themselves as "very sick."[25] On the uncertain assumption that these are the only older people needing extensive medical care, and with the added information that 18 per cent of the "very sick" had private health or hospital insurance and that 37 per cent were on OAA, the AMA took the position that, at most, only 5 to 7 per cent of the total population over 65 years of age had need for extensive medical care who were not already financially helped. The AMA argued from this that it was not justifiable to impose so comprehensive a program as the Forand bill when such a small proportion of the population had need for it.

When Dr. Shanas publicly endorsed the Social Security approach[26] and stated that none of her findings contradicted the need for it, the American Medical Association relied more on a study conducted by James W. Wiggins and Helmut Schoeck, two sociologists at Emory University. The latter study was extensively quoted and denounced in the public press, in sessions of Congress, and in professional meetings such as those of the International Gerontological Congress, the American Sociological Association, and the Society for the Study of Social Problems. Because of the attention given this study— certainly much greater than accorded most sociological studies—and the significant role it played in the political controversy, it will be given detailed attention.

The Wiggins-Schoeck study was financially sponsored by the Foundation for Voluntary Welfare of Burlingame, California, a subsidiary of the William Volker Fund. An AMA spokesman described the Volker Fund's outlook as "conservative."[27] There was also some basis to believe that the study was also sponsored by the American Medical Association, since Professor Wiggins was a consultant to the AMA, and it was the Association which released the report of the study to the newspapers of the country just as it was being presented at the meetings of the International Gerontological

[25]Ethel Shanas, "The 'Very Sick' in the Older Population," *Journal of the Michigan State Medical Society*, 59 (May 1960), 752–3. Also see Ethel Shanas, "How Sick are Older People?," *Journal of the American Medical Association*, January 9, 1960, pp. 169–70.

[26]She was one of the signers of the declaration of a 1960 Democratic party campaign committee called "Senior Citizens for Kennedy."

[27]*The New York Times*, August 15, 1960, p. 11.

Association on August 11, 1960. The newspaper story emphasized the following points:

1. The "vast majority" of the elderly wanted voluntary health programs and only 10 per cent supported "compulsory plans," although 36 per cent would approve the federal government setting up a medical insurance plan for persons over 65 who wanted it.

2. Most of the elderly were in "moderately good financial condition, not hardship cases." Sixty per cent said that if they sold everything they owned and paid all outstanding bills, they would have more than $7,500 in the bank.

3. Of the 1500 persons over 65 years surveyed, 61 per cent considered their health good, 29 per cent thought it was fair, and only 10 per cent thought it was poor.

4. Ninety per cent could think of no personal medical needs not being taken care of.

5. Sixty per cent said they were covered by private voluntary health insurance.[28]

The U.S. Senate was, at the very time of the release of the Wiggins-Schoeck study, considering the Kerr-Mills bill and the Anderson amendment to it (the latter was the most recent version of the Forand bill, and had the support of Senator John F. Kennedy, then the Democratic candidate for President). Several favorable references to the study were made on the floor of the Senate by opponents of the Anderson amendment. Senator Eugene McCarthy (D., Minn.) on August 22, 1960, made a full speech denouncing the Wiggins-Schoeck study as a "poor public opinion poll." He made the following points:

1. The sample surveyed was unrepresentative: Negroes, the institutionalized elderly, and those on Old Age Assistance were deliberately excluded, and 20 per cent of the remainder approached refused to be interviewed. The technique of sampling was the "quota" method, rather than the superior "area probability" method.

2. Elderly people cannot report accurately on the state of their own health. A study by the Commission on Chronic Illness shows a great discrepancy between self-evaluation of medical need and actual

[28]These statements are taken verbatim from *The New York Times* story of August 15, 1960, p. 11, entitled "Aged said to bar U.S. health aid."

medical need as determined by clinical examination of the same persons. The National Health Survey, sponsored by the federal government, showed a much higher proportion of chronic illnesses among the elderly than did the Wiggins-Schoeck survey.

3. Several of the sociologists around the nation listed by Wiggins and Schoeck as collaborating with them to conduct the interviews publicly criticized the techniques used in carrying out the study. Sociologists attending the meeting at which the study was first presented were generally quite critical of it.

A third study made use of by the AMA for propaganda purposes was one conducted by the Survey Research Center of the University of Michigan, which showed that those over 65 had more accumulated assets than those 18 to 44. From this fact the AMA drew the conclusion that "the aged as a group are substantially better off on the average than younger Americans," and that the study led to the "irresistible conclusion" that the King–Anderson proposal "is built on a monstrous fraud."[29] The AMA had equated accumulated assets with ability to pay for medical care, neglecting the facts that few over 65 had much current income and that most had much heavier medical needs than younger adults. The Survey Research Center denied responsibility for the AMA's conclusion, saying it had provided only the raw statistics.

There were other aspects of the campaign led by the AMA to oppose the passage of the Forand bill:

1. Dr Edward R. Annis, a surgeon of Miami, Florida, accepted the full-time job of traveling around the country "educating doctors so they can educate their patients" about government health insurance schemes.[30] Local medical associations had one or more of their members working at the same task. Physicians were given literature and posters (headlined "Socialized Medicine and You") for their offices, and were asked to talk to their patients in opposition to the Forand bill.[31] A public relations firm was hired by the AMA to prepare and distribute this and other material.

2. Under the sponsorship of the National Chamber of Commerce,

[29]*The New York Times*, October 16, 1962, p. 68.
[30]*Minneapolis Morning Tribune*, May 22, 1961, p. 16.
[31]*The New York Times*, February 15, 1961, p. 18.

each local Chamber of Commerce was asked to devote at least one meeting to an explanation of the dangers of the Forand bill. The Chamber of Commerce printed several brochures on the subject and distributed them widely throughout the country. It was also the source of several newspaper releases and of a film strip which was a general attack on the expansion of Social Security legislation since 1935. One of the Chamber's speakers regularly predicted that, "by 1970, 80 to 90 per cent of those who want private health insurance will have it, unless the government steps in with compulsory insurance."

3. The AMA regularly reported the various states' adoptions of the Kerr-Mills Act. On December 31, 1961, it gave out a newspaper release stating that 38 states had passed legislation to qualify for federal matching funds for medical care for the aged. The AMA stated that 27 states had set up new programs, 11 states had expanded existing programs, 9 states had medical aid programs on OAA before the passage of the Kerr-Mills Act, 2 states had "excellent assistance programs at the local level which include medical care," and only one state (Alaska) had no medical care program.[32] This release was misleading; it failed to point out how meager the programs were as enacted by most of the states; how the legislatures were motivated to pass them partly to shift some of the existing state expenses of OAA onto the federal government rather than to expand state medical care programs for the elderly in any material way; and how most states' implementation consisted of extending medical care benefits for those already on OAA, rather than extending benefits to an additional segment of the elderly population which proponents of the Kerr-Mills Act called the "medically indigent." Each side, of course, has charged the other side with misrepresenting its case to the public.

4. The AMA and the Chamber of Commerce sponsored radio and television programs to present a one-sided version of the Forand bill. Perhaps the most ambitious of these involved the actor Ronald Reagan, who later was identified with an extremist conservative political position and in 1966 was elected governor of California. Such programs were to be distinguished from debates presenting

---

[32]*The New York Times*, January 1, 1962, p. 12.

both sides of the issue, offered as a public service by the national networks and the local stations. Newspaper space to advertise its position was also purchased by the AMA, and requests were made to readers to write their senator and representative. In many cases the ads were published over the names of state and county medical societies.

5. The AMA and the Chamber of Commerce encouraged their members to join old people's groups to turn them against the Forand bill, and "talk about the problem" before local civic groups and other organizations to persuade them to join the "cause."[33]

6. The AMA helped sponsor TV entertainment programs to create a more favorable public image of the doctor. The "Dr. Kildare" series was of long standing, but when the struggle over medical care costs to the aging began, the "Dr. Ben Casey" program was added. Both of these programs later became self-sustaining when they attracted regular commercial sponsors.

7. The AMA called on doctors to "lower their fees to aged patients of modest means whether or not the patients carried health insurance. . . . The action was interpreted as another move by the American Medical Association to head off the pending King-Anderson Bill."[34]

8. In January 1962, the AMA announced a new nation-wide Blue Shield program of uniform surgical and medical benefits for persons 65 years of age and over. The program, to cost about $3 a month per person, is more fully described later in this chapter. Since the program is not economically viable from an insurance standpoint, it might also be considered as a move by the AMA to combat the King-Anderson bill, and presumably would be discontinued when the legislative battle was over.

The National Council of Senior Citizens for Health Care Through Social Security (NCSC) was founded in 1961, and it gained new members rapidly through the following years. Soon it became the leading private spokesman supporting bills of the Forand type. It is a co-ordinating organization, combining the efforts of a great variety of other voluntary associations in favor of medical care for the aging, but having their public benefits for the elderly among their

[33]*The New York Times*, February 15, 1961, p. 18.
[34]*The New York Times*, February 6, 1962, p. 33.

goals as well. While its individual and group members, claimed to be 600,000 by late 1962, paid dues to support its lobbying and publicity activities, it is probably correct to say that its main financial supporter was the AFL–CIO. The main techniques used by NCSC to reach the public were as follows: (1) publishing a monthly bulletin called *Senior Citizens News*; (2) conducting mass rallies in the larger cities; (3) sending prominent speakers and staff members to speak at these rallies and at other meetings; (4) encouraging its constituent groups to send mass-signed petitions to their congressman; (5) distributing newspaper releases; (6) organizing the proponents' testimony at public hearings on medical care for the elderly; (7) encouraging older people's groups organized for recreational or other purposes to endorse the current Forand-type bill; (8) encouraging letters "To the Editor" in local newspapers around the country. Its messages were the already mentioned arguments in support of medical care for the aging, as well as attacks on the AMA and its arguments. It also worked for the election of public officials friendly to the Forand-type bills. During its first year of operation, the NCSC claimed to have distributed 1,875,000 pieces of literature, consisting of almost 200 different items.[35] When its main goal of securing passage of a Forand-type bill was achieved in 1965, the NCSC continued its existence as the nationally organized core of a movement to improve conditions for the elderly.

Some of the conflict over the Medicare issue went beyond the intellectual arguments and used distortions, irrelevancies and naked political pressure. We shall not deal here with the occasional personal attacks, partly because it is impossible to get comprehensive or even representative data on them—most of the press was responsible enough not to report them.[36] Still, the topic is difficult to present objectively because some of it was secret or very localized and hence information about it was not available to this author. Also, the very selectivity of the information to be presented may represent partly the bias of the author. It would seem to him that more of the "underhanded" or vicious tactics were used by the opponents of the Forand-type bills than by their proponents.

The proponents did not fully reveal the extent to which the or-

[35]*Report* of the National Council of Senior Citizens for Health Care Through Social Security, April 23, 1962, by Blue Carstenson, Executive Director, p. 6.
[36]*The New York Times*, November 22, 1963, p. 25.

ganized labor movement was behind the effort to pass the bill. The main co-ordinating pressure group was the National Council of Senior Citizens, and it did succeed in gradually attracting the support of hundreds of local and national welfare and "senior citizens" groups after its organization in 1961. But the main organizer of NCSC, and its main financial supporter for much of the period 1961–65, was the AFL–CIO and its constituent international unions. Labor support was never hidden, but the centralness of its direction over NCSC was somewhat camouflaged by the fact that the board of directors was elected by the constituent membership groups of NCSC. This is not to say that the labor leadership distorted in any way the goals of any of the membership groups who desired to get the Forand-type bill passed; but the constituent membership groups by themselves would never have been able to mount the efficient and concerted attack that the well-organized AFL–CIO could. Yet the AFL–CIO could speak more effectively to the non-labor public and to Congress in the name of NCSC than in its own name.

The proponents answered most of the opponents' arguments with facts and relevant counterarguments, but they failed to meet one argument: that there were (and are) insufficient medical facilities, including doctors and nurses, in the United States to meet the demand and need for these medical services by older people once the bill was passed. The proponents were able to bypass this argument because the opponents themselves did not make effective use of it, probably because they thought it would create an unfavorable public image of medical personnel and of the AMA and because they were pressing the opposite argument (which was erroneous) that older people were able to get all the medical services they needed without a Forand-type law (at least after the Kerr-Mills Act was passed in 1960).

The proponents failed to give the Kerr-Mills Act a fair chance to show whether it could meet the needs or not. They nominally favored the Kerr-Mills Act, but lost no opportunity to point out its inadequacies—without attempting to correct them through support of additional state or federal legislation. Probably they felt they did not have to do this, as the AMA put considerable effort into strengthening the operation of Kerr-Mills. The partial failure of the Kerr-Mills approach, during the five years (1960–65) when it operated without a Forand-type law to compete with, shows that the proponents of Forand were correct in their attitude toward Kerr-

Mills, but it can still be said that they never gave Kerr-Mills a fair chance or effective support.

The tactics of the opponents of the Forand approach are much more susceptible of criticism; possibly they engaged in such tactics because they felt their position was weaker. We have already mentioned their openly expressed but false (although undoubtedly sincerely believed) arguments that the Forand approach was socialism, that older people had few medical needs that were not being met, that private medical insurance coverage would soon be complete and comprehensive without bankrupting the insurance companies. We have also mentioned their tongue-in-cheek criticism of the Forand bill as not going far enough to meet the needs of the older people (criticisms which later backfired into improvements of the Forand bill); that it didn't pay for doctors' bills, that it didn't cover those not on Social Security, that the proposed coverages were not comprehensive enough to meet the needs of a chronic patient. These last-named criticisms of the Forand bill were fully justified, but they were not sincerely meant and were used merely as propaganda to turn the public against the bill. We have also mentioned the purely tactical and insincere support which the AMA gave to the Kerr-Mills bill, only after June 1960 when it was a foregone conclusion that the bill would pass. The AMA regularly publicized the increasing number of states that legislatively "implemented" the federal Kerr-Mills law, without mentioning that most of the states provided for very little coverage, and did not even supply enough funds to take care of this small amount of theoretical coverage. Even by 1965, no more than six states had "strong" laws to implement Kerr-Mills, over 90 per cent of the federal funds under Kerr-Mills went to these six states, no more than 1 per cent of the nation's older people received benefits from it in any one year, and administrative costs took up a sizable share of the funds available.[37]

Other questionable practices engaged in by the AMA, by its political arm AMPAC, or by constituent state medical societies, in the effort to prevent passage of a Forand-type bill included:

1. Circulation of a phonograph record in 1963 purporting to be

[37]For factual criticisms of the Kerr-Mills Act in practice, see annual reports of the Senate Sub-Committee on Aging.

a recording of a Steelworkers' union meeting in Pittsburgh, which was shown in court to be a fraud.[38] The union official involved sued for libel, and the AMA—after the Medicare bill was passed—settled out of court for $25,000 and a public apology.

2. At least nine state medical societies passed resolutions of non-compliance with any further Forand-type bill that might in the future be passed by Congress. The national AMA strongly discouraged such resolutions as possible violations of the anti-trust laws, but emphasized that individual physicians could (and by implication should) take such a position.

3. In 1962, the AMA accused HEW Secretary Abraham Ribicoff of "a criminal act" by lobbying for the King-Anderson bill.[39] It also accused President Kennedy of giving out "incorrect information" by saying that the AMA had opposed the Social Security Act and its extensions.[40]

4. The AMA arranged to have Blue Cross and Blue Shield and some other private insurance companies, in 1962–63, offer hospital and medical insurance to older people. Many of the state Blue Cross and Blue Shield programs either quickly withdrew these offers, after advertising them extensively, or raised their rates drastically to avoid bankruptcy.[41] Even when available, these insurance programs were subscribed to by only one-fourth of the elderly, although it was claimed that a majority had them.[42]

5. The AMA attacked the British national health service program —to suggest how badly off the United States would be if it followed the British plan (which the Forand bill would actually not do)—to such an extent that the *British Medical Journal* denounced these attacks as "vulgar, cheap and nonsense . . . misrepresentation."[43]

6. The Erie County (New York) physicians apparently blacklisted a radiologist for supporting the King-Anderson bill,[44] and threats of similar actions were allegedly made in other parts of the country.

[38]*Minneapolis Morning Tribune*, November 22, 1963, p. 1; *The Machinist*, January 23, 1964, p. 4; *The New York Times*, March 12, 1966, p. 13.

[39]*The New York Times*, May 10, 1962, p. 27.

[40]*The New York Times*, May 26, 1965, p. 1; June 6, 1962, p. 1.

[41]*Washington Post*, August 11, 1963; *The New York Times*, December 31, 1963, p. 16; October 17, 1964, p. 1; July 28, 1962, p. 1.

[42]Senate Subcommittee on Aging, *Report* of July 21, 1964; *The New York Times*, November 6, 1962, p. 17.

[43]Editorial in the *British Medical Journal*, July 1962.

[44]*Minneapolis Morning Tribune*, September 27, 1962, p. 8.

7. There was a charge by a newspaperman (reported later in this chapter) that the AMA made a deal with certain tobacco-state congressmen (particularly from Kentucky and North Carolina) that it would not denounce cigarette smoking as hazardous to health if they would vote against Forand-type bills. This report was not proved.

C. The Conflict in Congress

Bills to provide some form of federal assistance to help meet the costs of medical care have been introduced into Congress since the 1930's and the movement for compulsory medical insurance dates back to before World War I.[45] Most of these bills did not distinguish between the elderly and other segments of the population, and they ranged from providing federal subsidy to private medical insurance programs to comprehensive national health insurance. None of these bills passed until the special session of Congress in the summer of 1960 approved Public Law 86-778 (known as the Kerr-Mills Act) which included provisions to increase old age assistance funds to provide some medical services for needy aged persons. We shall not consider the early proposals (except to note that they all had the vigorous opposition of the AMA and most of the economic elite groups and that they all failed in Congress) because most of them were not specifically directed at helping the aging. One or two early bills were restricted to the elderly (notably a bill by Senator Hubert H. Humphrey of Minnesota), but they attracted very little attention. The first bill to propose a federal health program for the aging that attracted much attention was that of Representative Aime J. Forand (D.,R.I.), who introduced it in Congress in August 1957. Forand later made slight changes in the bill, and similar slight changes were proposed in Forand-type bills submitted by at least thirty other representatives and senators. The common characteristics of these bills were that (1) they proposed to aid only the elderly, (2) funds were to be derived from increases in the Social Security tax, (3) payments were to be made to all persons covered, without a means test to determine

45In the original Social Security bill of 1935, there was one line to the effect that the Social Security board should study the problem of health insurance and report to Congress. The opposition was so strong, in the form of telegrams to Congress, that the line was eliminated by the Ways and Means Committee. In 1943, Senator Robert F. Wagner (D., N.Y.) introduced a health insurance bill, and in 1949 the Murray-Wagner-Dingell bill received the strong support of President Truman.

whether the elderly person needed help to pay his medical expenses, (4) only certain medical expenses were covered—notably excluded were payments to physicians, and (5) the patient would have completely free choice of hospital and surgeon (if licensed) and there would be no government interference with hospitals or with the practice of medicine.

Organizations such as the AFL–CIO, which had previously backed comprehensive national health insurance, after 1957 concentrated their efforts on Forand-type legislation. Since many of these organizations were still on record in favor of the more comprehensive form of legislation, the shift in attention was partly tactical—the bill aiding only the elderly had much more public support. In the light of the early legislative history, and of the record of many of the organizations supporting the Forand-type bills the opponents were justified in calling these later bills a "foot in the door" toward socialized medicine. But the Forand-type bills did not in fact provide for socialized medicine, according to any previous definition of socialized medicine, and most of the public did not regard them as such. In opposing all Forand-type bills, the AMA and the other economic-elite organizations were simply continuing their long-standing efforts to prevent the federal government from entering the medical care field. But to large sections of the public, and to many organizations favoring the Forand-type bills, the battle was an entirely new one—the key novelty being that these were the first bills to help the *aging* with medical care. To an outsider, the AMA's perspective appeared to be blinded by an irrelevant history.

The original Forand bill proposed that medical insurance for the elderly be financed by an increase of one-fourth of 1 per cent of insured wages, on both employer and employee, taken by Social Security, and only those covered by Social Security would be eligible for benefits (the self-employed would pay three-eights of 1 per cent of their insured income). Some of the later bills extended coverage to those not under Social Security, but excluded other categories covered by Forand, such as elderly persons who continue to have a wage or salary (this was true of the McNamara bill). Some later bills proposed additional funds from general revenues (that is, mainly the income tax). The original Forand bill, like the general Social Security Act in 1957–1961, proposed that benefits be provided to men over 65, women over 62, and dependents and survivors of insured persons. Some later variations raised the age to 68 years, and cut out dependents and survivors; others cut back the age at which benefits were to begin to 62 years. The original Forand bill proposed that the program be administered by the federal Social Security Administration, but some of the proponents of the Forand approach considered this a modifiable feature (although there has been widespread recognition that the Social Security Administration is efficient and has a relevant administrative mechanism already set up). Under the original Forand bill, beneficiaries were to be insured for up to 60 days of hospital care a year, with the usual hospital services. Nursing-home services also were to be covered if the patient were transferred from the hospital and treated for the same ailment; the maximum period of coverage for combined hospital and nursing-home care was to be 120 days a year. Some later bills provided longer coverage than this, and added home health service.

The original Forand bill provided for coverage of surgical services performed in a hospital and certified as being necessary by a licensed physician, as well as minor or emergency surgery in the outpatient department of a hospital or in a doctor's office. Some later bills did not cover payments for surgical services, or added drug expenses or diagnostic services without the requirement of hospitalization. The original Forand bill provided for no contributory payment by the patient for the period or services covered. Some later bills did provide for contributory payments as a means of preventing irresponsible use of benefits and as a means of spreading out the benefits with the same funds. The numerous later variations on the Forand bill suggest the large amount of attention and work devoted to the proposed legislation by a significant number of congressmen.[46]

The House Ways and Means Committee held hearings on the Forand bill as early as June 1958, but took no action on it until 1960, when it twice rejected it. In February 1959, the Senate created a Subcommittee on Problems of the Aged and Aging (known as the McNamara Committee) which held hearings on all aspects of the problems of the elderly and made a comprehensive series of recommendations for legislation to benefit the aging, which included an

---

[46]Usually each bill was sponsored by more than one congressman.

endorsement of the Forand approach. On March 31, 1960, the House Ways and Means Committee rejected a move to add the Forand bill to an omnibus Social Security revision. The vote was 17 to 8, with all ten Republicans voting to reject (the seven Democrats rejecting included the chairman, Wilbur D. Mills of Arkansas).

The Eisenhower Administration opposed the Forand approach, but delayed coming out with a substitute until May 4, 1960 (apparently the delay was at least partly due to disagreements within Republican ranks as to what the Administration should do, if anything). The liberal Republicans in the Senate were enough disturbed by the administration's inaction to offer a bill of their own, which came to be known as the Javits bill, after its chief author. This bill was submitted on April 7, 1960, and offered an extensive program of medical care to be administered through the states by commercial companies and non-profit groups, paid for out of general revenues and involving a means test. The Eisenhower Administration proposal (which used the term "Medicare Program" apparently for the first time) had these same three features, and added a contributory feature except for those on public assistance. It also made the program optional, even though it provided an upper limit on income for eligibility. At first the Administration's proposal attracted little support; it was said that its only major proponents were Vice-President Richard Nixon and HEW Secretary Flemming,[47] but others agreed that the Administration must counter the Forand bill with something.

Neither the Javits bill nor the Eisenhower plan were acted on by the relevant committees in either the House or Senate. After a second rejection of the Forand bill on June 3, 1960, the majority of the House Ways and Means Committee—led by Chairman Wilbur Mills —came out with the bill that ultimately became the Kerr-Mills Act.[48] This provided for (1) federal contributions up to $12 per case per month to the states which provided medical care in Old Age As-

[47] *The New York Times*, April 1, 1960, p. 1; May 6, 1960, p. 1.

[48] The exact origin of this bill is unclear. It was apparently worked out by Chairman Mills as a modification of the Eisenhower plan. The Eisenhower plan was never presented in the form of a bill but consisted only of the statement of principles made to the House Committee by Secretary Flemming on May 4, 1960. The Kerr-Mills Act differed from the Eisenhower plan mainly in that it left the means test up to the states, and did not have a deductibility provision, enrollment fee, or option of private insurance, but it did have an expenditure ceiling.

sistance grants;[49] and (2) federal contributions to be joined with varying state contributions, if the state adopted the program, to provide a variety of medical care benefits for additional persons who were "medically indigent." The Act was administered by the states; it allowed the states to specify the benefits; and it involved a means test, although liens could not be placed on recipients' property as in the case of OAA. The funds came from general revenues. On June 15, 1960, the AMA House of Delegates, very reluctantly and with some qualifications, voted to endorse the Mills bill—thus removing the last major organizational opposition.[50] This bill was submitted to the House under a "closed rule" which permitted no amendments, and it was passed on June 23, 1960, by the wide margin of 380 to 23. This vote meant that the Eisenhower Administration had accepted the Committee's bill in place of its own bill,[51] and that the liberal Democrats saw it as a first step toward providing health care for the aging (most liberal representatives hoped to see the bill amended by the Senate). The Senate took no action on the bill before it recessed, on July 3, for the national political conventions.

The Democratic platform of 1960 endorsed the Social Security approach, while the Republican platform merely pledged the "development of a health program that will provide the aged needing it, on a sound fiscal basis and through a contributory system, protection against burdensome costs of health care." The Senate reconvened in special session on August 8 and shortly thereafter took up consideration of the House bill (sponsored in the Senate by Senator Kerr of Oklahoma) as well as amendments (known by the name of their chief sponsor, Senator Anderson of New Mexico) which constituted

[49]This simply increased federal grants, first provided for in a law passed in October 1950. By 1960, there were still 8 out of the 54 states and territories which had not taken advantage of the 1950 law to help provide medical payments under OAA. Average medical payments under OAA vary from 44 cents a month in Mississippi to $55 a month in New York; the average for all states was about $15.

[50]The AMA had previously criticized the Eisenhower bill. *The New York Times*, May 6, 1960, p. 1.

[51]In August, 1960, when the Senate was considering the Kerr-Mills bill, Eisenhower also endorsed the Javits bill as an amendment to the Kerr-Mills bill. This may have been a tactical maneuver to oppose the Anderson (Forand) amendment and yet appear to support a more adequate program than the Kerr-Mills bill. Vice-President Nixon was greatly concerned that the Administration support something beyond Kerr-Mills. See statements by Senator Hartke (D., Ind.), Humphrey (D., Minn.), and Javits (R., New York) in the *Congressional Record, Senate*, August 23, 1960, pp. 15949–50-55.

another variation of the Forand bill. As soon as this came up, the House Committee chairmen (Mills of Ways and Means, and Smith of Rules) indicated they would kill any bill which included the Forand approach. This put several senators who favored the Forand approach in a quandary: If they passed the Kerr-Mills bill with the Anderson (Forand) amendment, the whole thing would be killed in the House or by the President, but the Kerr-Mills bill alone provided certain financial benefits to their states which they would not willingly forego. A case in point is that of Senator Russell Long (D., La.), whose state would get a windfall of approximately $12 million a year through the first part of the Kerr-Mills Act, which provided for a federal contribution to state payments for medical care of old age assistance cases.[52] Still other senators reasoned that the Kerr-Mills bill had some intrinsic value—to help OAA cases with medical care —and that this justified its passage without the Anderson (Forand) amendment, whereas if the amendment were passed it would result in the death of the whole measure. Senator Kerr argued on these grounds, while admitting that his bill did not go far enough to meet the needs of the aging.[53] Thus the Anderson amendment lost support from those who would have voted for it as a separate bill on another occasion, and it was defeated by a vote of 51 to 44.[54] Only one Republican, Senator Clifford Case of New Jersey, voted for it, and most of the Southern Democrats voted against it.[55] The Kerr-Mills bill then passed the Senate with only two votes against it,[56] and President Eisenhower signed it into law on September 16, 1960.

[52]See Senator Long's statement in *Congressional Record, Senate,* August 23, 1960, p. 15997. It was this feature which led some critics of the Kerr-Mills bill to refer to it as a "federal aid to the states" bill. Even the second portion of the bill, designed to aid a new category of persons—the "medically indigent" not on OAA—permitted some states to transfer large portions of their OAA medical program to federal expense if they would slightly expand the eligibility for OAA. Massachusetts implemented the Kerr-Mills law to this effect.

[53]*Congressional Record, Senate,* August 23, 1960, p. 15995. Some Republicans did not want to present Eisenhower with a bill he would veto, as that would hurt the Republican party in an election year.

[54]The Javits bill, which now had the support of candidate Richard Nixon, lost by a vote of 67 to 28, and it is doubtful whether many of those voting for it— all Republicans—would have voted for it if they thought it had a chance of passage.

[55]Of the 19 Democrats voting against the Anderson amendment, 18 were from the South.

[56]Those opposed on the final vote were Senator Barry Goldwater of Arizona and Senator Strom Thurmond of South Carolina.

In his presidential campaign, candidate John F. Kennedy made the provision of medical care for the aging through Social Security a key issue, and when Congress opened in January 1961, President Kennedy listed it among the items of "must" legislation. The White House Conference on Aging, bringing thousands of people together in January 1961 from all over the country, also stirred up public interest in the Forand approach, for this became the key item of controversy at the conference.[57] The Kerr-Mills Act, while generally recognized as desirable for those already on OAA, was not deemed sufficient to meet the medical needs of the aging by the advocates of the Forand approach, for the following reasons. (1) About 16 per cent of the elderly were on OAA; the remainder had enough savings or help from offspring to support themselves for their usual needs, but most of them did not have enough to pay for serious or chronic illnesses. The great majority in the latter category were "middle-class" persons, who would be shocked by the thought of going on OAA and who resented a means test. (2) The states, much more limited in their ability to raise tax revenues than the federal government, showed great reluctance to extend the number of persons who would be eligible for benefits under the Kerr-Mills Act, since they had to raise 20 to 50 per cent of the amount themselves and they could not put the usual residence requirements and property liens on the additional beneficiaries.

The Forand approach was presented to the 1961 Congress on February 9 in the form of the King-Anderson bill, named after its co-sponsors, Representative Cecil King (D., Calif.) and Senator Clinton Anderson (D., N.M.). The bill contained the following provisions: (1) increase in Social Security tax of one-fourth of 1 per cent of pay up to $5,000[58] for both employer and employee, with an increase of three-eighths of 1 per cent for the self-employed; (2) administration of the program by the Social Security Administration,

[57]The Income Maintenance Section of the Conference was assigned the topic of "economics of medical care" and this section voted in favor of the Forand approach. A couple of the other 19 sections of the conference also voted in favor of the Forand approach, but the chairman ruled them out of order for lack of jurisdiction. The conference as a whole voted on none of the recommendations approved by its 20 sections.

[58]The insured pay proposal was raised from $4,800 to $5,000 in the 1961 session. When the bill was re-introduced in 1962, the proposed insured pay was raised to $5,200.

with coverage for all those under social security or railroad retirement; (3) full payment of hospital bills for stays up to 90 days for each illness; except that the patient must contribute $10 a day for the first 9 days, with a minimum deduction of $25; (4) nursing-home care from 180 to 300 days a year, depending on how much hospital care had been used that year; (5) hospital outpatient clinic diagnostic services for all costs in excess of $20 a patient; (6) home-visiting-nurse services for up to 240 days a year.

The King-Anderson bill got the support of the Kennedy Administration, and Secretary of Health, Education and Welfare Abraham Ribicoff led the Administration's drive. The opposition also stepped up its offensive against the bill. Non-governmental proponents of the bill joined forces in a "National Council of Senior Citizens for Health Care Through Social Security" (NCSC), which by the close of 1961 claimed a membership of 400,000 elderly persons and 900,000 supporting members of all ages.[59] It appeared that the Senate had sufficient votes to pass the King-Anderson bill, but it could not constitutionally vote on this tax-affected measure before the House did, unless it used the strategem of tacking it on as an amendment to some related bill sent from the House. The Senate avoided doing this so as not to offend the House. In the House, the measure was blocked from consideration by two congressmen: Representative Wilbur D. Mills (D., Ark.), chairman of the Ways and Means Committee, which had jurisdiction over the bill, and Representative Howard Smith (D., Va.), chairman of the Rules Committee, which would have to allow the bill to get onto the floor.

All bills have to be approved by the Rules Committee to get consideration from the House of Representatives;[60] the Rules Committee acts officially as a kind of traffic policeman to allow the House to consider the thousands of bills which the majority of congressmen are against but prefer not to have come up for a vote or to waste House time on. These functions also give the Rules Committee the

[59]The leading organizational backers of the NCSC are listed at the beginning of this chapter. Its first chairman was ex-congressman Aime Forand (Forand had voluntarily retired from his House seat in 1960 on grounds of ill health, but very soon thereafter became active in private efforts to pass Forand-type legislation).

[60]There are some parliamentary devices to get around the Rules Committee, but they are extremely difficult to use when a measure is controversial, which is usually the only kind of measure the committee holds up.

power to kill bills which its own members are against. At the start of the 1961 Congress the Rules Committee consisted of six Democrats which the Kennedy Administration could generally count on as favorable to its proposals, four Republicans whom the Republican leadership had selected over the years to be against liberal legislation, and two Democrats who could be counted on to block liberal legislation. The latter two were the committee's chairman, Howard Smith (D., Va.), and William Colmer (D., Miss.). When the latter two voted with the Republicans, which they almost invariably did on liberal legislation, they could prevent bills from going to the floor of the House for a vote, because the 6–6 tie vote was decided by the vote of the chairman. The new Kennedy Administration decided immediately that its entire legislative program—including the King-Anderson bill—could be killed by the Rules Committee, and therefore it sought to change the composition of the committee. The battle over this was the crucial congressional conflict of 1961. Two strategies were open to President Kennedy: (1) The first was to remove Representative Colmer from the committee on the ground that he and his state had not supported the national Democratic ticket in the 1960 election and that he was therefore not entitled to the privileges of members of the majority party. This was opposed on the grounds that it provoked the South, and that it challenged the principles of seniority and of a congressman's privilege to vote the way he wished to. (2) The second possibility was to ask the House to add three new members to its Rules Committee (two Democrats and one Republican) in the expectation that then the Kennedy Administration could usually command an 8–7 majority. While this proposal went counter to Congress's tradition against committee-packing, it had two powerful supports—that of Speaker Sam Rayburn and that of the patronage and other favors that could be offered by the new Kennedy Administration. The legislative battle—in which the Forand bill was given prominent consideration—was fierce, but eventually the House voted by the narrow margin of 217 to 212 to approve the enlargement of the Rules Committee.[61]

---

[61]The majority consisted of 195 Democrats and 22 Republicans. The minority consisted of 148 Republicans and 64 Democrats, of which 62 came from the eleven Southern states (plus one each from Oklahoma and Missouri). Among the 195 Democrats in the majority, 37 were from the eleven Southern states.

This was only a first step, and not a sufficient one, for Chairman Mills of the House Ways and Means Committee refused to take up the King-Anderson bill. As the 1961 session wore on, it became apparent that the Kennedy Administration was putting its strength behind other bills and allowing the King-Anderson bill to languish. As a face-saving device before the public, the Administration obtained the consent of Chairman Mills to hold public hearings on the King-Anderson bill on the days following July 24. The hearings added nothing to the 1958 and 1959 hearings before the same committee, or to the 1959–60 hearings before the McNamara Committee in the Senate. The 1961 session was adjourned without a vote on the King-Anderson bill in the Ways and Means Committee.

As the 1962 session of Congress opened it seemed more likely that the Kennedy Administration was prepared to push all the way for a vote on the King-Anderson bill. This year was an election year, and there was no doubt that a Forand-type bill had the support of a significant majority of the American people. Secretary Ribicoff set up a "task force" to consider minor compromises that might be made and to work out some details of the bill that had met objection on technical grounds. The Kennedy Administration let it be known that even if the House should vote against the bill, it could go to the country on this issue above all others and thus get more favorable congressmen elected in November 1962. Its task was to get the bill through the Ways and Means Committee and onto the floor of the House. One of the first things President Kennedy did as the 1962 Congress opened was to have a long private talk with Chairman Mills, but Mills subsequently announced his continued opposition to the King-Anderson bill, although he indicated he would support other Administration measures.[62] The President was handicapped by the recent death of Speaker Sam Rayburn, who had given mild support to the Forand bill. The new Speaker, John McCormack (D., Mass.) was more strongly in favor of the King-Anderson bill, but he did not enjoy the prestige and personal power of his predecessor.

The Republican leadership—Representative Charles Halleck (R., Ind.) and Senator Everett Dirksen (R., Ill.)—announced that they

[62]*Minneapolis Morning Tribune*, January 26, 1962, p. 16.

would do their utmost to hold Republican congressmen against the bill (even though they were prepared to allow individual voting on certain other Kennedy "must" legislation). The non-congressional opposition, perhaps feeling their position weakening, or perhaps merely developing a new tactic, publicized some possible compromises. The first was announced by Senator Jacob Javits (R., N.Y.) as early as October 2, 1961, and was submitted by him as a bill to the Senate in the opening days of the 1962 Congress.[63] It was not immediately clear whether Senator Javits had any backing for his new bill from any other opponent of the King-Anderson bill. The Javits bill provided for financing by the Social Security tax, but in addition would protect those not covered by Social Security out of general revenue. Every person over 65 would be protected, so there would be no means test. The bill would permit individuals to elect one of three alternative benefit programs: (1) Full payment for 21 days of hospital care or 63 days of nursing home care (combinations of these would be possible on a ratio of 3 days of nursing home care for each day of hospital care). (2) After the first $250 of costs (to be paid by the beneficiary), 80 per cent of the following costs: 120 days of hospital care; surgical service, drugs, and appliances provided in a hospital; 365 days of nursing-home service less hospitalization days at a ratio of 3 to 1; full visiting-nurse or other home health care benefits. (3) Payments up to $100 a year for premiums on private insurance plans. The Javits plan would be administered by the states or by the Secretary of Health, Education and Welfare if he were unable to conclude an agreement with the states. Aside from details of benefits and greater difficulty of administration through the states, the Javits bill was more "liberal" than the King-Anderson bill in offering medical care for the aging, insofar as it extended benefits to those not covered by Social Security without a means test. Since the Javits bill accepted Social Security financing and the principle of "no means test," it abandoned all that the AMA and the Chamber of Commerce had fought against. It was thus possibly a political "trial balloon," without any backing other than that of Senator Javits himself, supported by other Republicans merely to embarrass the Democratic Administration in its support of the King-

[63]*Minneapolis Morning Tribune*, January 8, 1962, p. 1.

Anderson bill. Senator Javits and his political ally, Governor Nelson Rockefeller of New York, had always favored some kind of government-sponsored medical care for the aging, but never had significant Republican support even though Javits disagreed with the Democratic majority concerning Social Security financing and other provisions. Most of the House Republicans in 1962 said they were supporting a bill first introduced by Representative Frank T. Bow (R., Ohio). This provided for private medical-hospital insurance policies for all persons over 65 years, to be paid for by federal income tax credits. By April 1962, 27 other Republicans had introduced almost identical bills.[64]

Another "compromise" offered by the non-congressional opposition to the King-Anderson bill was sponsored by the Blue Cross Association and the American Hospital Association.[65] It provided for financing by government funds for persons whose income was below a certain level and by the elderly themselves in varying proportions for those whose income was above that level. It did not specify the source of the federal funds—whether from general revenue or the Social Security tax—and left this crucial matter deliberately ambiguous. The program would provide 70 days of hospital accommodations, compared with 90 days under the King-Anderson bill. But more of the charges would be deductible (up to $90 in the King-Anderson bill) and coverage could not be limited to persons under the Social Security system. The program would be administered by the Blue Cross, a private company, rather than by the Social Security Administration. It would involve a means test in ascertaining the amount to be contributed by each participant, and it would provide no assistance for medical costs other than those associated with the hospital. The AMA neither supported nor denounced this plan.

Only a few days later the AMA announced a new private program of medical care for the aging which would also aid its legislative position against the King-Anderson bill. The program was to be offered by the National Association of Blue Shield Plans.[66] Coverage

[64]*The New York Times*, April 9, 1962, p. 11. It is difficult to know whether this was a *bona fide* move, or merely a tactic to draw public support away from the King-Anderson bill, as the Bow bill had no chance of passage.

[65]*The New York Times*, January 4, 1962, p. 31; January 5, 1962, p. 33.

[66]*The New York Times*, January 18, 1962, p. 1.

would cost about $3 a month per person. It would pay the full cost of medical and surgical services for single persons whose annual income was less than $2,500 and for couples whose income was $4,000 or less. Physicians' fees would be fixed by Blue Shield for this low-income group, but would vary by area, and physicians could charge others more if they liked. The spokesman for the doctor-sponsored Blue Shield organization said the plan "would pay for surgery performed in a hospital or doctor's office. It would cover medical care at a hospital or nursing home but not at the patient's residence. The number of visits covered, not yet set, would be thirty to seventy. . . . the plan would provide payments for, among other things, anesthesia, radiation treatments, X-rays and laboratory tests."[67] The 69 Blue Shield programs around the nation were said by this spokesman to cover 3,500,000 persons 65 or over, and apparently the new plan would make the divergent existing plans more uniform. If additional benefits were to be granted the aged, they would have to come from lower fees paid to physicians or from higher costs paid by Blue Shield members under the age of 65.

The Kennedy Administration's reaction was stated by Secretary Ribicoff, who pointed out that the Blue Shield plan would not take care of the principal costs of hospital and nursing home care.[68] The King-Anderson bill, of course, would not pay for doctors' bills, so the Secretary said he could not see how the AMA Blue Shield plan was in any way an answer to the Administration-sponsored proposal. The Secretary did not comment on the earlier compromise proposal of the American Hospital Association–Blue Cross Association, which would be a conceivable substitute for the King-Anderson bill. Nor was there any Administration reaction to the Javits compromise proposal, but the "task force" in the Department of Health, Education and Welfare was no doubt examining the possible compromises.

The House Ways and Means Committee continued to be negative toward the King-Anderson bill all through 1962, and so, on July 17, 1962, it was offered in the Senate as an amendment to the House's public welfare bill. To the dismay of its proponents, the amendment was defeated by a vote of 52-48. President Kennedy and many congressmen made the King-Anderson a major issue in the congressional

67Ibid.
68*Minneapolis Sunday Tribune*, January 21, 1962, p. 13B.

campaign of 1962. So did the AMA, by setting up a political arm, called American Medical Political Action Committee (AMPAC) to provide financial support to friendly congressional candidates who were facing pro-Medicare opponents. The outcome of the battle was not clear-cut: The National Council of Senior Citizens announced after the November 1962 election that 24 to 25 new pro-Medicare congressmen were elected, but that 21 incumbent pro-Medicare congressmen had been defeated. The AMA made no public announcement of how it regarded the outcome of the election. One obvious gain for the proponents of the bill was the elimination of two of the bill's opponents on the House Ways and Means Committee: James B. Frazier (D., Tenn.) through defeat, and Burr P. Harrison (D., Va.) through retirement. When Congress convened in January 1963, it replaced these with two pro-Medicare Democratic congressmen. But there was still not a majority on the committee in favor of the bill: All 10 Republicans remained opposed; 12 Democrats favored the bill, but 3 Democrats opposed it—Chairman Wilbur D. Mills (Ark.), A. Sidney Herlong (Fla.), and John C. Watts (Ky.)[69]—to create a division of 13–12, the majority against.

Nothing of significance happened on the bill in 1963, except that it was broadened to include persons over 65 not on Social Security— allegedly to gain the support of five liberal Republican Senators, including Senator Javits. Chairman Mills allowed a few more desultory "hearings" late in the session, allegedly to allow President Kennedy to "save face." In 1964—with Johnson, a more politically skillful President, in the White House—Chairman Mills offered a "compromise"—a bill to liberalize some aspects of the basic Social Security Act and to raise Social Security payments by 5 per cent, so that recipients could better afford to buy their own private health insurance. In the Senate, the Finance Committee voted for an amendment by Senator Abraham Ribicoff (D., Conn.) to permit Social

[69]Columnist William V. Shannon blamed Watts's opposition to political log-rolling. Representative Watts represents a tobacco-growing district in western Kentucky, and Shannon claimed that "For the past two years the tobacco and AMA lobbyists have had an understanding. If AMA would not condemn smoking as the cause of lung cancer and other disease, the congressmen from the tobacco states would oppose medicare." Watts denied the connection, but it is to be noted that Kentucky provided the only significant number of Democratic votes outside the South against the President's Medicare bill when the House finally voted on it on April 8, 1965. (See *Senior Citizens News*, July 1964, p. 1.)

Security recipients to opt for either a 7 per cent increase in cash payments or a King-Anderson insurance program. On the Senate floor, Senator Albert Gore (D., Tenn.) substituted an amendment to grant Social Security recipients both the 7 per cent increase and the King-Anderson insurance program, and the Senate voted in favor of the Gore amendment, 49 to 44, on September 2. This was the first time in its three opportunities to vote on the measure that the Senate passed a Forand-type bill—a success largely due to President Johnson.[70] In the conference committee there was no agreement, and both Mills's compromise and Gore's amendment were deleted from a Social Security bill which now included only a few trivial changes in the basic law. Both sides were gearing themselves for the 1964 election campaign and its probable implications for the 1965 struggle over Medicare.

D. Connections to Broader Political Issues

The question can be raised as to how a bill can be blocked or voted against in Congress when the majority of the voting public favors it, and there are organized proponents who can publicize the congressmen's voting record. The explanation on one level is simply in terms of the structure of Congress, which allows the chairmen of the Rules and the Ways and Means committees,[71] coupled with enough others on their committees with commitments against a bill, to block it successfully unless a full majority of congressmen can be pressured or persuaded to sign a discharge petition to bring it to the floor for vote.[72] Or, if the other house of Congress should be more favorable, a strategem can be used to get around the committees of the reluctant house. This is to allow the friendly house to pass the controversial bill as an amendment to some irrelevant bill passed by the reluctant house. Then the amended bill goes to conference committee and then to both houses as a whole, without going through the Rules and

[70]*Minneapolis Morning Tribune*, September 6, 1964, p. 4.

[71]These are the names of the relevant committees in the House of Representatives. In the Senate, the Rules committee is very weak, but the Finance committee, then under the chairmanship of Harry F. Byrd (D., Va.), is very strong, and it also sought to block the Forand-type bills.

[72]Congressmen are reluctant to sign discharge petitions, as this bypasses the basic system of committees with which any effective large body must operate, and it opens the possibility of retaliation by the committee against some minor bill sponsored later by one or more of the petitioners.

Ways and Means committees.[73] If the positions of the two houses were reversed—and the Senate having the reluctant committees rather than the House—there would be the additional barrier that the filibuster would more likely be used.[74]

Negative congressional action regarding the Forand-type bills cannot simply be explained by reference to Congress's structure and rules. There were forces of power and opinion that were more significant. While it is true that a large majority of the general public favored the Social Security approach, this may not have been true for every district; thus some congressmen could oppose the measure and be in harmony with their constituencies. Reference to relevant votes—the Senate vote on the Anderson amendment in 1960 and the House vote on the change in the Rules Committee in 1961—indicates that practically all of the opposition came from the majority of the Republicans and a large segment of Southern Democrats; only a very few Northern Democrats would vote against the King-Anderson bill. The majority of the Republicans were identified with the interests of the economic elite, on some measures even against the wishes of the majority of their constituencies when this could be ascertained (as in the case of the King-Anderson bill). Probably most of them had genuine convictions against socialized medicine, and they perceived the Social Security approach to providing medical care for the aging as at least a first step toward socialized medicine and, often, other evils.

The actions of the Southern Democrats have to be explained in a somewhat different way. Some of them had the same ideological

[73]In the case of the King-Anderson bill, since it involved a financing provision, the Constitution required that it first be passed by the House of Representatives before the Senate could consider it. So the stratagem had to take the form of having the Senate pass the King-Anderson bill as an amendment to some other irrelevant tax measure that came from the House. Senator Anderson moved to use this stratagem in January 1962 by asking the Senate Finance Committee to consider the King-Anderson bill concurrently with the House Ways and Means Committee. The Senate committee refused by a vote of 10 to 7, and "Senator Anderson was expected to cite the committee's vote to counter any argument later on the floor that the committee had not had a chance to study the matter." (*The New York Times*, February 1, 1962, p. 12.). Still, this incident indicates that committees are disinclined to bypass their opposite numbers in the other house, possibly for fear of future retaliation.

[74]The filibuster cannot be used under House rules. If the House were to send a tax bill (which the King-Anderson bill is, in part) to the Senate, there would be some pressure on the Senate to consider it—that is, the Senate Finance Committee would be somewhat reluctant to insult their House confreres by ignoring the bill.

position as the majority of the Republicans, and many of them would be Republicans if they represented a majority in a two-party region; their constituencies were as conservative as they were. Undoubtedly some others were "lieutenants" of the economic elite, in C. Wright Mills's sense, as were some of the Republicans. It has been said that the AMA was more influential in the South than in other regions in the country, since the South is less industrialized and its professional men were more likely to constitute the local elite than were its businessmen. This should have made little difference regarding the Forand bill, however, as the businessmen of the North were just as likely as the physicians to be strongly against the bill. More pertinent was the fact that the lower classes in the South were less likely to be informed about political issues, and less likely to vote, leaving the local economic elite, whatever its composition, more influential.

Still more significant was the fact that the South had one overriding concern that colored its reaction to nearly everything else in life—the race problem. While the race problem may seem logically remote from medical care for the aging, there was a connection in Congress. Southern congressmen, whether they were liberals or conservatives on welfare issues, felt obliged to oppose civil rights legislation at the sacrifice, if necessary, of everything else. This has led to the "Coalition": Some Southerners have been willing to trade votes on welfare issues to the Republican majority, in return for votes against civil rights bills. Usually defense and international issues are excluded from this consideration, but nearly every domestic measure in Congress is deeply soaked with the race problem. Except for some Texans and Tennesseans who no longer feel that their constituencies will rise up in horror if Congress passes some moderate civil rights bills, the overwhelming majority of Southern congressmen fight a twofold battle for every single issue faced by a Northern congressman. Even if Southern congressmen prior to 1965 personally favored, and even believed the majority of their constituency favored, a welfare measure such as the Forand bill, they would not necessarily vote for it. They would still feel obliged to propose their "quid pro quo" to the Republican leadership in return for support against civil rights bills. Thus, even a liberal Southern Democrat has been partly under the thumb of the "economic elite," which is vitally concerned about Congress voting against welfare measures but is little concerned with civil rights bills. This was clearly evident in the 1961 Congress when Southern senators agreed to put off consideration of the King-Anderson bill in return for a Republican agreement to vote against a change in Rule 22, the Senate rule permitting filibusters (usually invoked only against civil rights bills).[75] The only surcease for the liberal Southern congressmen occurs when the national Democratic leadership—both the Democratic President, if there is one, and the Democratic heads of Congress—informs him that no civil rights actions will be taken "this year." It was possibly for this reason that President Kennedy did not press for a change in Rule 22 (the "filibuster" rule) in the Senate in 1961; this was done in the hope of getting Southern support on such other critical issues as federal aid to education and foreign aid. Of course, a Democratic president who acts in this way takes a grave risk of losing Northern Negro votes, which are almost essential to getting him re-elected in the next presidential election. Thus, no aspect of domestic politics can be considered on its own merits or even in terms of public opinion until the race problem ceases to be an overriding concern for Southern congressmen.[76] This was achieved to a large extent by the passage of the Civil Rights Act of 1964 and the Voting Rights Act of 1965, since it is difficult to conceive that drastic civil rights legislation affecting the *Southern* race problem would ever be considered necessary in addition to these strong laws.

Just as the South has been hung up on the race problem with regard to such domestic issues as providing medical care for the aging, another segment of the country—sometimes called the "right-wing extremists"—are hung up on what they conceive to be socialism. Here the relationship with the Forand-type bills is more direct, as we

[75]Information from administrative assistants to five senators, each providing the information independently of the others.

[76]From the late 1870's to about 1945, the race problem was not a major factor in American politics, not because it was not a concern to Southern congressmen, but because the Executive and the Northern congressmen had an implicit agreement with the Southerners that there would be no governmental action to reduce discrimination against Negroes. The situation we describe for the present came into existence during the Truman Administration. (For the reasons for its development, see Arnold Rose, "Postscript" to the second edition of *An American Dilemma* by Gunnar Myrdal, with the assistance of Richard Sterner and Arnold Rose (New York: Harper, 1962). It does not seem likely now that the country can go back to the political truce on the race problem prevailing before 1945.

explained earlier in discussing the "foot-in-the-door" argument. The right-wing extremists are those who have regarded the development of welfare legislation since 1933 not as a set of pragmatic governmental responses to a changing technology and society, but as a conspiracy by socialists to kill capitalism and institute socialism or communism. For them, the threat of communism does not lie in the Soviet Union or in "Red" China (as much as they dislike the governments of those countries) but in the trend toward "communists" taking over the United States government.[77] These "communists"— as the right-wing extremists publicly identify them—include most of the Northern Democrats in Congress and the liberal and moderate wings of the Republican party (including ex-President Eisenhower). The right-wing extremists, while few in number, have been able to gain public support during periods of great international threat to the United States from the communist nations, such as during the Korean War and the multiple international crises of 1960–66. A significant portion of the American people does not understand why the strong and wealthy United States cannot contain the territorial expansion and scientific advancement of the communist powers; they become amenable to the "explanation" that "communists" are weakening the United States from within.

The issue of providing medical care for the aging was directly tied up with this. The AMA explicitly stated that the Forand bill was a "foot in the door" toward socialized medicine, and that socialized medicine was a major step toward socialism.[78] Socialism means to many Americans, including the right-wing extremists but many others as well, a weakening of the moral fiber of the American people, a decadence of American society and institutions. Thus, the fight over the Forand proposal was a major expression of a basic conflict within American society. A large portion of the opposition saw it thus, and if the proponents did not, they were partially blind to what was occurring. As the Forand bill (by 1963 called the "Administration's Medicare bill") neared a vote in Congress, the battle lines became more evident. Of course, the outcome of the conflict was not

[77]There seems to be implicit in the right-wing extremist ideology the assumption that the United States can save itself from Russia and China by retirement into international isolation, "Fortress America." The major seeming inconsistency here is that some of these extremists have favored support for Nationalist China and have shown their willingness to engage in all-out war with Red China during the Korean and Vietnamese conflicts.

[78]For example, see *AMA News*, March 20, 1961, p. 1.

to be determined by whether the Forand bill was passed or killed; the battle would then simply shift to another front. But the battle over providing medical care for the aging revealed the basic features of the domestic power conflict in the United States.

The disagreement was not simply over whether American society should do more about providing for the medical needs of the aging, nor even over whether the Social Security Administration was the most effective instrument for doing this. The battle was really over which of the following two popular ideologies should prevail: (1) New social needs and problems, created by vast impersonal social forces, are to be solved by *ad hoc* pragmatic governmental actions in response to the pressures of interest groups and public opinion operating in a multi-interest society. (2) An economic elite, which took the leadership in building the United States up to the strength and prosperity it reached in the 1920's, should re-assert its leadership and insist that major social decisions be made by private individuals and groups (especially those they themselves dominate) rather than by the federal government. Thus, the fight over medical care for the aging was, in one sense, basically between national leadership by a political elite, operating through democratic political processes, or national leadership by an economic elite, operating through private decisions in which wealth and industrial control play an especially weighty role. Since the 1930's the first-mentioned ideology has been in the ascendency—not by intention or design, just as there was little intention or design in the limited role of government before 1930, but because of the pressures created by rapid social change in an industrial society. Due to its declining role, the majority of the economic elite has been becoming more self-conscious of itself as a group, and it has become fearful enough of the trend of legislation to increase its political activities. For this reason, by the 1950's the country witnessed the development of overt conflict between a political and an economic elite, rather than a relatively impersonal division of labor between them which had prevailed earlier.[79] There are few issues

[79] While all sorts of factors enter the political process, on most issues there has probably been agreement between the majority of the political elite and the majority of the public. The economic elite also has a public to back it up on political issues, but in most cases where it is at odds with the political elite, its public is only a minority. No study has been made of the public opposing the Forand bill, but it would certainly include a large number of middle-class persons who were fearful of what they believed to be internal subversion, socialism, and a decline of individual character and traditional institutions.

over which this was more evident than in the case of the Forand bill struggle, partly because of the time at which the controversy occurred and partly because it was brought to the general public as well as to Congress. Thus the analysis of this specific struggle reveals the anatomy of a basic power conflict in the country today.

E. Last Stages of the Political Conflict

The passage of the Administration's Medicare bill in 1965 was almost an anticlimax, although it was symptomatic of the utter rout of the "economic elite" by the "liberal" political elite which occurred in that year. In 1963, the Kennedy Administration had given the same publicly strong, actually weak, support to the measure which it gave in 1961 and 1962. There can be no doubt that the President and his advisors strongly favored the bill, but they apparently felt other measures were more important to get through Congress and so placed the bill relatively low on the list of "must" legislation, aware that Congress was likely to pass only a few items on that list. There is some evidence that President Kennedy—knowing that Medicare was one of the more popular of the measures he was supporting—was planning to make it a major political issue during the 1964 presidential election campaign, and, if he were re-elected, to fulfill his campaign pledge by working very hard for its passage in Congress in 1965.

On November 22, 1963, President Kennedy was assassinated. His successor, President Lyndon B. Johnson, also strongly favored the Medicare bill, but also did not give it top priority in his list of "must" legislation during the 1964 session of Congress. The bill was slightly modified, but still faced the same line-up of proponents and opponents. President Johnson used the Medicare issue during the 1964 presidential election campaign, but did not make it a dominant issue of that campaign. His opponent, Senator Barry Goldwater, opposed the bill, but also did not place it on top of his list of Administration measures to oppose. Negro civil rights, public order, general poverty, foreign policy (especially in Vietnam), and taxes were among the issues that took higher priority than Medicare for both of the leading candidates during the 1964 election. That election provided an unprecedented victory for the Democratic party, including, and not least, President Johnson. Among the Republicans defeated in 1964 were such opponents of Medicare as Representatives Bruce Alger (Texas), Victor A. Knox (Mich.), and Steven Deroonian (N.Y.). The election shifted the balance on the House Ways and Means Committee from 15 Democrats and 10 Republicans to 17 Democrats and 8 Republicans. Thus, there were now enough votes in the committee to release the Medicare bill.

When the Eighty-ninth Congress opened in January 1965, there was a stronger expectation than in previous years that the Administration's Medicare bill—still based on the same features contained in the Forand bill of 1957—was going to pass in some form. It was on the President's list of "must" legislation, perhaps a little higher on the list than it had been during the Kennedy years, although still many steps from the top. Nevertheless, the passage of the bill by Congress in July 1965, offered many surprises. These were of two types: an unusual development characteristic of most items on the President's "must" list for congressional action that year, and unexpected developments unique to the Medicare bill as it was finally passed. The former was the huge number of bills passed by Congress in 1965 on the "recommendation" of the President; not since 1933 at least had there been such a large number of significant bills passed. This was partly the result of President Johnson's skill in congressional relations (already manifest in the 1964 session); of his overwhelming election victory in November 1964, which also helped to elect 58 new Democratic House members who thereupon voted almost uniformly for the President's programs;[80] and of the partial removal of the race issue from the congressional scene by the passage of the Civil Rights Act in 1964, thereby practically removing the basis of the coalition of Southern Democrats with conservative Republicans. Thus, the Administration's Medicare bill was swept through Congress along with practically all the rest of the President's extensive program. While President Johnson tried to dramatize the passage of the bill by flying to Independence, Missouri, and signing it in the office of the octogenarian ex-President Harry Truman, the passage of the bill went relatively unremarked in the nation's press because of the welter of other significant legislation that was passed.

[80]About forty of these had publicly announced their support of the President's Medicare bill.

The surprises connected with the Medicare bill itself in 1965 were: (1) Chairman Wilbur Mills of the House Ways and Means Committee, who had been probably the most effective opponent of the Forand bill since its inception in 1957, reversed himself and became the chief sponsor of the bill. (This undoubtedly had something to do with President Johnson's persuasive powers.) (2) The bill itself, despite the continuing oposition of the AMA and of most of the other groups that had opposed it from the beginning, was significantly augmented in the House Ways and Means Committee, and passed in a form beyond the expectations of its strongest noncongressional proponents. The main new feature was a provision to allow elderly persons to subscribe optionally to insurance providing payment for doctors' bills, upon payment of $3 a month for this insurance; Congress raised Social Security disbursements 7 per cent to more than cover this. Some such provision had been earlier suggested by Senator Javits, but the immediate impetus for it probably came from AMA criticism of the bill, which took the form of calling attention to incomplete coverages in the bill. Thus, the AMA protests against earlier versions of the Forand bill on the false grounds that it involved control over doctors—false because the earlier Forand bills did not provide for payments of physicians and contained a clause prohibiting any government control over physicians or over their selection by the elderly patients—were finally met by a provision in the statutes which undoubtedly *would* involve significant controls over physicians, and this provision was largely the direct result of the AMA's own attack on the bill. Earlier predictions proved correct that the AMA's behavior was like that of the prankster in the folk tale who cried "Wolf, wolf!" when there was no wolf, and therefore no one came to his aid when a wolf did actually appear and had his way with the prankster. The "wolf" for the AMA, of course, was "socialized medicine," which the Forand-type bills until 1964 carefully avoided, but a measure of which was started by the 1965 statute.

The bill did not get through the 1965 Congress without a great deal of opposition and skirmishing. The AMA continued to spend at its previous high rate for advertising and other forms of publicity against the bill. Its chief tactical device was the introduction of a bill —called "Eldercare" to attract popular support—which mainly offered an improvement of the Kerr-Mills Act. It offered fuller medical coverage than did the Administration's Medicare bill, but would be available only to those who could pass a means test, and retained the voluntaristic and state-control features of the Kerr-Mills Act. The Eldercare bill received a significant build-up at first, but support for it collapsed after it became evident that Congressman Mills—backed by President Johnson—was determined to pass a Forand-type bill out of the House Ways and Means Committee. Even Representative Sidney Herlong (D., Fla.), one of the official sponsors of Eldercare, publicly stated that too much was being falsely claimed for it by the AMA,[81] and later he announced that he would vote for the Medicare bill.

When the bill passed the Ways and Means Committee, by a 17 to 8 vote along strict party lines, and came to the floor of the House, the opposition tactic was a motion offered by Representative John W. Byrnes (R., Wis.). He moved to send the bill back to committee to have it delete hospital insurance through Social Security and substitute a comprehensive voluntary insurance program about two-thirds subsidized by the federal treasury. This motion failed by a margin of only 45 votes: the vote was 236 to 191, with only 10 Republicans (6 of them from New York) in the majority voting against the motion. The 63 Democrats voting for the motion were, all but one, from the South.

The next type of opposition was a spontaneous outburst from many groups of doctors, which the AMA itself cautioned against. It took the form of a resolution against co-operating with the Medicare program if it should become law. The grass-roots movement among some doctors began in New Jersey in 1962,[82] but the national AMA succeeded in damping it. A "doctors' strike" would not create a favorable public image, and there was a legal question whether a collusive effort of this type might be a violation of antitrust laws. But in April and May of 1965, at least nine state medical societies passed resolutions of non-compliance with any future Medicare law. It was all the AMA leadership could do to prevent the passage of such a resolution at its own national convention, and it did warn again and again against collusion on the part of doctors, stating that

81 *The New York Times*, March 17, 1965, p. 43.
82 *The New York Times*, May 15, 1962, pp. 21, 35; May 5, 1962, p. 1.

individual non-co-operation was legal, but formal agreement among physicians against co-operation was illegal. These resolutions reflected the frustrations of many physicians and their local leaders as they saw a bill about to pass Congress which, they had been told for many years by their AMA leaders, was "socialized medicine" and represented the end of their freedom as individual businessmen. Even after the bill was passed, the defiant Association of American Physicians and Surgeons urged its 16,500 members not to co-operate in the program.[83] The resolutions seemed to have little influence on public opinion, and were ignored by the Administration.

After a strong Forand-type bill passed the House of Representatives on April 8, 1965, by a vote of 313 to 115 (with the Republicans now split 65 to 73), it met an unexpected hurdle in the Senate Finance committee. Senator Russell Long (D., La.), the Senate Whip and an opponent of the bill, now criticized the House bill as not providing enough hospital, nursing-home and home-visit care for chronically ill persons, and he proposed to extend those benefits considerably. To pay for them, he proposed that each person over 65 contribute, when the benefits were used, according to his or her means. Five liberal Northern Democrats on the committee joined the conservative minority in voting for these amendments, perhaps because of Long's influence, or perhaps because they did not realize that contributions according to means revived the means test as one criterion for benefits, which was anathema to the lay proponents of the Forand-type bills. The National Council of Senior Citizens rallied its supporters throughout the country, and with the aid of the Administration succeeded in getting the committee to reconsider the amendments. A "compromise" was worked out: the controversial "contributions according to means" was eliminated, and the benefits were somewhat extended (not as much as Senator Long advocated), to be paid for by a higher maximum on the salaries from which the Social Security tax would be required (plus a higher contribution from general revenues for those not on Social Security). Thus, once again, the bill expanded benefits for older people as a result of the unsuccessful attacks on its basic principles. Another effort was made to introduce a means test, by Senator Carl Curtis (R., Neb.),[84]

[83] *The New York Times*, August 5, 1965, p. 1.
[84] Senator Curtis called some features of the bill "pure socialism." *Honolulu Advertiser*, July 9, 1965, p. A-5.

when the bill reached the Senate floor. This was defeated by a narrow 51 to 41 vote, and then the bill was passed by the Senate on July 9 by a vote of 68 to 21 (with 11 Republicans for the bill and only 8 Southern Democrats against it). Differences between the House and Senate versions were quickly ironed out in conference committee, and the Congress passed the bill without further debate.

The Medicare statute (Public Law 89-97)—passed by the House on July 27 by a vote of 307 to 116, passed by the Senate on July 29 by a vote of 70 to 24, and signed by President Johnson on July 30— was part of several new extensions of the Social Security Act of 1935, as subsequently amended. We shall mention only those portions of the statute pertinent to Medicare.

1. It applies to all Americans over 65 years of age, whether they are covered by general Social Security or not, after July 1, 1966.[85] This is an extension of the original Forand bill, added after 1962, to meet one of the tongue-in-cheek criticisms of the bill made by its opponents that it did not cover about 20 per cent of the existing older population who were not then eligible for general Social Security or Railroad Retirement payments.

2. For each "spell of illness" during each year, the participant will receive free hospital care for 60 days, including semiprivate accommodations and full hospital services, except for the first $40 (a small deductible to reduce abuse). In addition, the program pays all but $10 daily for an additional 30 days during the same "spell of illness." ("Spells of illness" must be separated by 60 consecutive days to be eligible for coverage.) There is a lifetime limitation of 190 days on payments for treatment in mental hospitals. All of these features are somewhat more generous to the participant than were the provisions of the original Forand bill, and they also were largely responses to criticisms from the opponents of the bill.

3. The program will pay 80 per cent of the cost for diagnostic services for an outpatient during a 20-day period, except for the first $20 for each 20-day period. This is an addition to the original Forand bill.

---

[85]Some employees of the federal government, who are already covered under another law, will not come under the new hospital insurance program, but may apply for medical insurance. Aliens not eligible for Social Security may get both hospital and medical insurance if they have permanent residence status and have resided in the United States for five years.

4. After a hospital stay of 3 days or more, the participant will be eligible to receive free care for 20 days in a skilled nursing home or other extended-care facility, for each "spell of illness." The program will also pay all but $5 daily for an additional 80 days.

5. After a hospital or nursing home stay of 3 days or more, the participant will be eligible to receive up to 100 free visits at home, during each 365-day period, from nurses, physical therapists, or other health workers (except physicians).

6. All of the above are financed by a 3.5 per cent increase in Social Security tax on the first $6,600 of annual pay in 1966 for employee, employer, and self-employed person. There will be periodic increases in this tax beginning in 1967. This is to cover the costs for those on Social Security; for others the funding comes out of general taxation (that is, mainly the income tax).

7. For an additional payment of $3 per month (the federal government adds a like amount out of general taxation), the person over 65 is eligible for medical insurance. This provides full physicians' and surgeon's services; up to 100 home visits per year from any other health worker, with no need for prior hospitalization, in addition to the 100 visits provided by the hospital insurance program; and complete other medical and health services, regardless of where rendered (including diagnostic tests, radiotherapy, surgical dressings, braces, artificial organs, certain ambulance services, iron lungs, etc.). The only services not covered are routine physical check-ups, eyeglasses and eyeglass examinations, dental bills (except for oral surgery), cosmetic surgery, orthopedic shoes, hearing aids, private duty nurses, and custodial care. Drugs are covered under the hospital insurance program, only if furnished in a hospital or extended-care facility, and under the medical insurance program, only if administered by a physician. For all these supplemental services and supplies, the participant pays the first $50 per year, plus 20 per cent of the costs beyond this; that is, the program pays 80 per cent beyond the first $50 annually. This medical insurance program was added to the Medicare bill in 1965, after the opposition proposed "Eldercare"— a revision of the Kerr-Mills Act—as a way of gaining public support against the Administration's Medicare bill. Because the Eldercare bill included doctors' payments (for indigents), the Medicare forces in Congress (now led by Representative Mills) absorbed this popular idea into their own bill and extended doctors' payments in the form

of insurance to everyone. Thus was one of the chief threats to the AMA born out of its own propaganda.

8. A 7 per cent increase in Social Security payments will more than cover the aforementioned $3 monthly payment for the voluntary medical insurance.

9. A whole new program was inaugurated under Title 19. This applies not only to the indigent aged, but also to the blind, the disabled, and to families receiving aid to dependent children (ADC program). The states must take the initiative in this Title 19 program, but if they formulate a plan that meets the high requirements of the law, the federal government will pay 50 to 83 per cent of the medical care costs of these categories of persons who are on welfare programs. There must be standards for the quality of care, and provision is made for checking the actual performance of hospitals, clinics, and doctors. This feature of the new law goes far beyond anything envisioned in the earlier discussion over the Medicare bills, and does involve some aspects that might legitimately be called "socialized medicine." The AMA has not yet attacked it, possibly because it applies only to the indigent, and the AMA since 1960 has declared that it is not opposed to medicare for the indigent, or possibly because the AMA found its opposition was no longer effective. But opposition developed in Congress as the provision was found to cost more than expected, because the states were passing liberal coverage provisions (in New York, families earning less than $6,000 were covered).

It took Congress eight years to pass this law, a somewhat longer time than for most "liberal" statutes with the exception of those dealing with civil rights. But the law that was passed in 1965 was considerably more "liberal" than the bill introduced in 1957 or those discussed in Congress between 1958 and 1964, and there had been a partial victory in 1960 (the Kerr-Mills Act). Also, the period had seen the elimination of a fundamental structural source of opposition to almost any future liberal legislation—namely, the coalition of the majority of Republicans with Southern Democrats based on the latters' need to block civil rights bills[86]—and the reconstitution of the

[86]Indeed, the very basis of political organization in the South was rapidly being transformed: The 1964 election had seen a considerable shift of Southern votes toward Republican candidates, at least on the national level, and it seemed likely that future elections would find the Southern electorate voting along sub-

House Rules and Ways and Means committees more in alignment with the sentiments of the majority of the House membership. While some of the congressional rules frequently used to block liberal legislation—the seniority criterion for appointment to committees, the right of a committee to prevent a bill from reaching the floor, and the filibuster in the Senate—were retained, both houses of Congress showed themselves much more willing to override these rules occasionally. While prediction of congressional action is always foolhardy, these changes suggest that future liberal legislation will have easier going in the Congress than did the Medicare Act of 1965.

The AMA discredited itself to a surprising extent by the character of its fight against Medicare. An article in the *Saturday Evening Post* quotes a congressional aide: "Politically, the AMA lost the pennant. It used to scare hell out of Congress. But the docs yelled 'socialism' once too often, and Congress quit listening to them."[87] A leading medical researcher who headed a nationwide committee to oppose anti-vivisection legislation informed me that his committee was no longer able to use the AMA and practicing physicians to voice the medical researchers' position on this issue—the congressmen did not consider their opinions on legislation reliable, he said. The Executive branch of the government charged with putting the bill into effect—the Department of Health, Education and Welfare—made every effort to be conciliatory toward the AMA by inviting its representatives to sit on committees to set up the regulations for administration of the new law and by providing for "agents"—Blue Shield, Blue Cross, and other private organizations—in each state, rather than the local Social Security offices, to provide the first level of administration, thereby multiplying the cost of administration of the program. The purpose of using private agents was to avoid requiring physicians to send their bills to a government agency. It appeared that most physicians would co-operate with the Medicare program, but some—particularly those associated with the Association of Physicians and

---

stantially the same lines as the Northern electorate. These changes were immediately caused by the passage of the Civil Rights Act of 1964 and the initiation of extensive voting by Negroes; more fundamentally they were caused by economic, political, demographic, and educational changes in the South.

[87] John Bird, "Your Doctor and the A.M.A.," *Saturday Evening Post*, 239 (January 1, 1966), 13–17, 47.

Surgeons—announced that they would refuse to do so; they would continue to send their bills for service only to their patients, and let the patients apply directly for reimbursement to the agent.[88] The public and Congress seemed to regard the battle over Medicare to be finished.

[88]*The New York Times*, March 28, 1966, p. 1.

XIII
Some Problems of Politics: Money, Ethics, and Citizen Participation

A. Money in Politics: Ethical Issues

In this chapter a brief description of two problems will be offered as providing the strongest real evidence in support of the "economic-elite-dominance hypothesis"—although our interpretation of this evidence would not satisfy C. Wright Mills or Floyd Hunter,[1] who are considered to be the leading proponents of the hypothesis. Yet Mills and Hunter scarcely mention these problems, so it cannot be said that our consideration of them is less adequate than theirs. The first problem can be called that of ethics in politics, and the second that of citizen involvement in politics. The two problems are connected, and they are also both related to the central problem of this book—the relative power of the economic and the political elites.

The typical American strongly wants his government to be ethical and equitable. Even the criminal, who is generally recognized as not having been ethical in his dealings with others, becomes unusually enraged and embittered when he believes the police, the courts, or the prison administration is not dealing "fairly" with him.[2] The average citizen believes it is all right for him to commit misdemeanors

[1]See C. Wright Mills, *The Power Elite* (New York: Oxford University Press, 1956); Floyd Hunter, *Top Leadership U.S.A.* (Chapel Hill: University of North Carolina Press, 1959); *Community Power Structure* (Chapel Hill: University of North Carolina Press, 1953).

[2]Gresham Sykes, *The Society of Captives* (Princeton, N.J.: Princeton University Press, 1958); Richard Cloward and Lloyd E. Ohlin, *Delinquency and Opportunity* (Glencoe, Ill.: Free Press, 1960).

or even more serious offenses, such as destroying public property, driving without a license, and cheating on the income tax, but he becomes outraged by evidence of the slightest deviation on the part of public officials. Only the religious leaders of the society are required to toe the ethical line as closely as public officeholders. More than a small amount of self-seeking, favoritism, and even corruption is tolerated in businessmen, labor leaders, and professionals, but the government official is required to be completely equitable and honest. Perhaps this demand for purity exists because the public officeholder is considered to be the custodian of the secular values, just as the religious leader is considered to be the custodian of the sacred values, and in a pluralistic society there is a separation of the sacred and the secular. Perhaps in another type of society—where the sacred and secular are not so separated—the clergy alone suffice to guard the society's ideals, and the political leaders may be permitted to ignore ideal behavior as much as does the average citizen.

But while the American demands purity in his government officials, he does not think they are really pure. He is suspicious of them and cynical toward them, in marked contrast to his attitude toward the sacred leaders. He believes most politicians to be unethical and is not surprised when corruption is occasionally revealed among them, even though as a matter of course he demands their banishment from public life at the slightest sign of deviation from the secular values. Needless to say, this creates a strain on the politician: He is expected and usually forced to adhere much more closely to the laws and to other secular ethical standards than are most citizens, but he must constantly submit to being suspected and even openly accused of deviating from these standards.

His problem is compounded by certain requirements of politics which do not permit him to be always completely ethical and equitable. There are certain conditions of politics and government which tend to force participants in them to deviate from secular ethical standards in order to attain and retain public office. The politician is often pressured by these into behavior which, if it becomes public knowledge, will cost him his position. At the same time he is the object of close public scrutiny and even suspicion, so he has great difficulty in hiding anything.

It may seem that my analysis has placed the politician in an impossible situation, one in which no man could maintain his role as a politician for very long. There is, however, another factor which needs to be brought into the picture, a factor which protects the politician and provides him a camouflage which public scrutiny prevents him providing for himself. This is the public's ignorance of certain facts of politics and acceptance of a series of myths and stereotypes about politics which result in the public being prevented from seeing what is going on before its very eyes. Perhaps no area of life is so little understood by the public as politics, despite the close scrutiny by the mass media. This is so because false preconceptions are widely held among the public. No attempt will be made here to explain why these conditions prevail; attention will instead be focused on showing how they function to extricate the politician from the impossible situation created, on the one hand, by the public demand that he conform to the secular standards, and on the other, by the political facts of life he must conform to in getting elected to public office. Public ignorance and acceptance of certain myths serve to camouflage the very conditions by reason of which politicians are usually obliged to be unethical and yet to which they must submit in order to get elected. While there is intense public scrutiny of all other aspects of their behavior, the very activities in which the politicians are almost necessarily unethical are the ones which the public either chooses not to examine or completely misunderstands.

A first example of this may be found in the fund for campaign expenses. It costs a considerable amount of money to campaign for a contested public office, and the costs are mounting as more reliance is being placed on publicity through the mass media.[3] It costs $3,000

---

[3]Alexander Heard shows that the costs are not rising faster than the increase in population or national income (*The Costs of Democracy* (Chapel Hill: University of North Carolina Press, 1960), pp. 375–80). But these facts are not as relevant for the individual office-seeker as is the fact that he must be beholden to many more interest groups for financial support as the real costs (not merely the dollar costs) of campaigning go up. Heard's book is the best source of information on the costs of political campaigns, and I have relied heavily on it for facts.

Earlier studies of campaign contributions and the costs of campaigning include: Louise Overacker, *Presidential Campaign Funds* (Boston: Boston University Press, 1946); Overacker, *Money in Elections* (New York: Macmillan, 1932); and Overacker, "Presidential Campaign Funds, 1944," *American Political Science Review*, 39 (1945), 899–925. A summary of national and state laws may be found in *Election Law Guidebook*, 1952, Senate Document No. 97, 82nd Cong., 2nd Sess. Two recent inquiries into expenditures in elections are presented in "Investigation into the 1950 Ohio Senatorial Campaign," *Hearings before the Senate Committee on Rules and*

to $5,000 to be elected alderman of a city ward or mayor of a small town. It costs $100,000 or more to be elected mayor of a large city or representative to Congress. The campaign committee working for the election of John V. Lindsay as mayor of New York City reported that they spent a total of $2,539,981.00 on his successful campaign in 1965.[4] The minimum cost for running for the positions of governor or senator is about $75,000. The best estimates, by Professor James K. Pollock of the University of Michigan, are that the presidential campaigns of 1952 collectively cost $140 million, the 1956 campaign $155 million, the 1960 campaign $175 million, and the 1964 campaign $200 million. Clearly these expenses cannot be afforded by the candidate himself, unless he is independently wealthy, and he must get the money elsewhere. Who is willing to give money for campaign expenses, especially when the contribution is not tax-deductible and there is not the same moral sanction behind such giving as there is for "charity"? While political parties and candidates have learned to "raise" small campaign funds from a large number of people, the main support for most campaign funds must come from sizable contributions from a small number of individuals[5] and organizations.[6] Robert E. Lane points out that, although corporations

---

Administration, 82nd Cong., 2nd Sess.; "Senator from New Mexico," *Hearings before the Senate Committee on Rules and Administration*, 83rd Cong. 1st Sess. together with Sub-committee Report on these hearings, 83rd Cong., 2nd Sess.; and "1956 Presidential and Senatorial Campaign Contributions," *Hearings before the Senate Committee on Rules and Administration*, 84th Cong., 2nd Sess., Parts 1 and 2.

[4] *The New York Times*, November 24, 1965, p. 1.

[5] "In federal campaigns it is estimated that 90 per cent of the money comes from less than 1 per cent of the population." (League of Women Voters of Minnesota, *Money in Elections* (Minneapolis: October 1960), p. 3.) In the 1960 campaign, 334 persons contributed $1,600,000 to the Republican national campaign and $1,000,000 to the Democratic. In 1964, because of the rejection by many businessmen who usually voted Republican of the specific candidacy of Barry Goldwater for President, there was a reversal of pattern of giving to the two political parties. Only 25 per cent of the funds given to the Republican National Committee came in gifts of more than $100. By contrast, the Democratic National Committee received over 90 per cent of its money in gifts of more than $100.

[6] In the 1958 election, organized labor committees operating in more than one state gave a total of $1,828,777 to the campaign war chests of candidates. Labor unions cannot legally take funds from their treasuries, but they do ask union members to make "voluntary contributions," which they collect and turn over to candidates, mostly Democrats. Officers of corporations make similar requests of their salaried employees, and these funds more often are given to the campaign fund of the Republicans. (From the *Congressional Digest*, as reported in the *Minneapolis Star*, April 20, 1959, p. 6; and the *Minneapolis Morning Tribune*, July 7, 1963, p. 6B.)

and unions are legally prohibited from making contributions to political parties and candidates, they have ways of getting around the restrictions:

> We said earlier that corporations cannot make gifts to political parties, but this does not mean that they are unable to employ their resources to advance political objectives. In good faith and perfect legality they may:
>
> 1. Pay salaries and wages of officers and regular employees while engaged in political activity.
> 2. Publish opinions and arguments of a political nature, expressed as the views of the corporation, in any house organ or other printed document circulated at the expense of the corporation.
> 3. Purchase radio and television time or newspaper space for the presentation of the corporation's political views.
> 4. Use any other means of expressing the political views of the corporation management, publicly or privately.
> 5. Encourage people to register and vote and disseminate information and opinion concerning public issues without regard to parties or candidates.
>
> And that isn't all. Perhaps without sanction of the law, but with slim chance of legal difficulty, the management of a corporation or trade association may divert funds to political purposes as follows:
>
> 1. Make use of the advertising or entertainment funds of trade associations for political contributions.
> 2. Place advertisements in political publications through public relations firms or advertising agencies. [This was prohibited by congressional statute in 1966.   A.M.R.]
> 3. Make contributions in kind to political candidates (make available to them without pay the use of offices, airplanes, etc.).
> 4. Permit the padding of expense accounts with the understanding that political contributions should be made out of the padded amounts.
> 5. Pay or repay bonuses with the explicit or tacit understanding that part of such remunerations shall be spent in campaign contributions.[7]

[7] *Political Life* (Glencoe, Illinois: Free Press, 1959), p. 59.

In 1966, an amendment to a tax bill was passed which prohibited deduction as a business expense of money used for admission to political fund-raising dinners and the like and for advertising in political publications and program books, but until this law was passed both major parties benefited from these forms of business contributions.

Most "big" contributors to political funds want something for their money; if they do not ask for support for a specific measure, contract, or franchise, then they do expect a general outlook toward the role of government as a whole. Here is a major pressure on the politician. He is not "bought," but his campaign fund is. As long as a candidate accepts money only for his campaign fund, he is not regarded as unethical. But his objectivity and equity as a legislator may be affected nevertheless. Sometimes a lobbyist will make his contribution to the campaign fund for a congressman over several years, and not ask for a favor until he can show the congressman several receipts for contributions made to several of the congressman's campaign committees. Sometimes he will never directly ask for a favor, but leaves it to the politician's supporters to whom the campaign contribution was made to ask for the favor. Sometimes a favor is not specifically requested, but the lobbyist ascertains that the candidate will be favorable to the legislation he seeks before he makes a contribution.[8] The average citizen seldom raises the question as to where the campaign funds come from, or he has the false belief that it does not cost much to campaign or that large sums are readily available for candidates without obligation. His desire for ethical purity in public officeholders is frustrated by his lack of knowledge and his false beliefs concerning campaign financing. The average citizen who would demand the immediate dismissal of an officeholder who accepted a personal bribe blinds himself completely to the contributions for campaign funds and to the motives for them. Nor does he support legislative action that would reduce the importance of the campaign fund or separate the campaign fund from the candidate. A public opinion poll of a cross section of adults in Minnesota

[8]Some of the indirect techniques of lobbyists in making contributions to campaign funds were revealed by a Senate Foreign Relations Committee investigation in 1963 in a case involving a lobby for the Philippine Government. See *Minneapolis Morning Tribune*, April 19, 1963, p. 1.

conducted by the *Minneapolis Star and Tribune* showed that only 19 per cent favored legislation to have the federal government pay part of the costs of presidential election campaigns, while 72 per cent definitely opposed the idea.[9]

The public seldom makes a distinction between a campaign fund and a personal fund of a politician. Some Republican leaders were worried when, during the campaign of 1952, it was revealed that vice-presidential candidate Richard Nixon had a personal fund given to him by well-to-do contributors for his personal use; but this disclosure did not seem to hurt his campaign at all. While a number of other top elected politicians, especially the less wealthy ones, undoubtedly had similar personal funds, the issue was not raised in public again until 1966, when it was publicized by the columnists Drew Pearson and Jack Anderson that Senator Thomas J. Dodd (D., Conn.) had received approximately $100,000 at three fund-raising dinners. This money was used by Dodd for his own personal use, and the only legal question was whether he should have paid income or gift tax on it. Certainly, it was collected in an open way —at open-invitation dinners—and it was doubtful whether those attending the dinner knew or cared that their contributions were destined for a personal fund rather than a campaign fund. The senator declared that his living expenses in Washington exceeded his salary and other personal income, so that he needed these contributions to remain a senator. There were also charges that Dodd unduly aided a lobbyist who had helped to organize the dinners. Despite the considerable publicity given to the affair, it was doubtful whether there were any ethical issues involved other than those which affect every person who runs for public office: funds are contributed to him openly, during campaigns it is difficult to distinguish between campaign expenses and personal expenses, funds left over from campaigns are often used for other purposes, including personal ones; elected officials are more responsive to some lobbyists than to others. The Senate Select Committee on Ethics, under pressure of public and newspaper opinion, agreed to look into the use of the financial contributions. Dodd sued Pearson and Anderson for libel in regard to the charge that he misused the funds and failed to pay

9*Minneapolis Sunday Tribune*, December 3, 1961, p. E3.

income tax on them. But it was doubtful that he could win such a suit, because the Supreme Court handed down a decision in *The New York Times v. Sullivan* (May 1964) which held that a public official can win a libel or slander suit only if the defendant had "actual malice" in addition to making false charges.

A distinction might be made between a wealthy contributor who makes his contribution for the purpose of corruption or purely personal advantage—to gain some personal economic or prestige benefit not forthcoming under the law or under equitable administration—and a wealthy contributor who makes his contribution for power purposes, to see the general course of government go in the direction he wishes. But in both cases the mechanism is the same and the need for ethical, equitable government is equally frustrated. Mills would probably consider the distinction unimportant anyway. We have no way of telling which is the more frequent motivation for a large contribution to a political party or candidate. But we do consider these contributions to the campaign funds of candidates as the major means by which the economic elite can gain some measure of control over the political elite in the United States at the present time.

It was to seek a solution to this problem that President Kennedy, in 1961, set up the Commission on Campaign Costs, with Professor Alexander Heard as its chairman. In creating the commission, Kennedy said that "large financial contributions of those with special interest is highly undesirable." The commission received a variety of drastic proposals, including one from Walter Reuther, president of the United Auto Workers Union, that campaign contributions be limited to $10 a person, with 90 per cent of that returned to the donor as an income tax credit, and with privileges extended to all qualified candidates for federal office of free radio and television time, free mailing privileges, and a federal subsidy to supplement campaign contributions.[10] The commission made a number of recommendations, but only one, which was very modest, got as far as being put into a bill: a permissible deduction of $10 from income reported for federal income tax purposes if the money were contributed in a federal election campaign. There was little public support even for

[10]*Minneapolis Sunday Tribune*, February 11, 1962, p. 14B.

this extremely mild proposal; the lobbyists strongly opposed it; and Congress did not pass a bill to enact it. President Johnson, in his 1966 annual message to Congress, also came out for new legislation to control campaign contributions. Later in that year he offered a bill which would: permit a taxpayer to deduct up to $100 from his taxable income for all political campaign contributions; Require more accurate reporting of campaign gifts to and expenditures by federal candidates, and of other sources of income to officeholders, and require every contribution or expense over $100 to be reported; put a ceiling of $5,000 on the size of a contribution from a single donor to a single federal candidate in a primary or general election; and limit sales of campaign souvenirs to $5 per campaign per person. If passed, this bill would reduce some of the abuses in the present system of campaign financing, but it would not control multiple contributions by members of the same family, effectively limit the rising costs and length of campaigns, control free television and radio time, or eliminate campaign expenditures for questionable purposes.

One motive for making a large contribution to a campaign fund at the national level is to obtain a prestigious appointment. Especially in the case of ambassadorships, it has become customary for the President to make appointments from among wealthy men who have contributed heavily to his campaign fund. There have been many cogent statements why ambassadors should be chosen from among those skilled in diplomacy and familiar with the countries where they are to be stationed.[11] But none of the statements stoops to mention alternative ways of getting large enough campaign funds necessary to elect a President. Their authors ably present the need to have capable ambassadors, but blind themselves to the political reasons for appointing less capable ones. This situation exists on the state level also. Professor James MacGregor Burns (of Williams College in Massachusetts) has charged that large campaign contributions are an accepted way of "buying" judgeships in the Commonwealth of Massachusetts.[12]

Another ethical issue in political fund-raising arises when the "initiative" for the contribution arises from the politician's side rather

---

[11]See for example Charles W. Thayer, "Our Ambassadors," *Harper's Magazine*, 219 (September 1959), 29–35.
[12]See *The New York Times*, November 2, 1962, p. 32.

than from the donor's. That is, either implicit intimations or direct threats are made that, unless contributions are forthcoming, there will be economic reprisals against the potential donor. In Illinois the Republican party chairman was for some time the purchasing agent for the State of Illinois. On the Democratic side, the Democratic National Committee in 1965 published a brochure entitled "Toward an Age of Greatness," which praised the accomplishments of the 89th Congress. It charged $15,000.00 for a full-page advertisement; some 60 companies purchased full pages.[13] While both political parties, on both state and national levels, had long used the technique of the "advertisement" to raise funds, the Democratic National Committee was so embarrassed by the publicity given to this particular brochure that it announced that the funds raised would be used for non-partisan political purposes, such as to assist Negro voting-registration efforts in the South, rather than to help pay off its $2 million debt from the 1964 election campaign or to aid "voter education" in the districts of co-operating Democratic congressmen. Largely as a result of the publicity surrounding this brochure, Congress passed a statute in 1966 prohibiting a company from deducting as a business expense on its income-tax statement any expenditure for admission to political or inaugural ceremonies or functions, or for advertising in a political publication or program book. Such restrictions force the political parties to turn to small individual contributions, which are difficult to obtain, or to seek candidates who are independently wealthy enough to finance most of their own campaigns. Probably neither the "political advertisement" nor its restriction has any effect toward creating influence of the economic elite over the politicians.

We have been noting how the need for money in campaigns partially frustrates the need for ethics in government. Pressures can take many other forms than offering money for political favors: equally important in politics are "establishing contacts," lending influence, providing campaign-workers, sustaining the ego or building morale, and threats to cut off a significant number of votes. These can move a public officeholder to take unethical or inequitable action as much as a money contribution can. The culture defines bribery solely in

[13]*The New York Times*, April 15, 1966, p. 21.

terms of the use of money, but these other offers can operate in exactly the same way. Their saving merit lies in the fact that they are available to be used by persons who do not have access to large sums of money. Because money is necessary for elections, these other offerings can serve as counter-pressures if used by persons who cannot offer money. But pressure is pressure and these influences can also have an important effect on the ethics of the politician, an effect that is again unperceived by the public.

There is also the problem of direct bribing of public officeholders. In 1958, Senator Francis Case of South Dakota revealed that he was offered $5,000 if he would support an oil bill. In 1964, Representative Wright Patman revealed that a House colleague had been offered bank stock "either free or at a cost greatly under the market value."[14] In 1960, Senator John J. Williams (R., Del.) revealed that the maritime industry offered congressmen a free sea-trip for themselves and their families when Congress was considering legislation affecting that industry.[15] But Senator Case publicized the offered bribe and indicated that it was the reason for his voting against the bill; this publicity was probably the cause of the bill's death. Representative Patman also revealed the rejected bribe. And Senator Williams implied that the ship industry's offer was the only significant one made to a whole group of congressmen that he knew of.

Lesser bribes are probably more frequently offered to state legislators and city councilmen than to congressmen, and are probably accepted more often. But the danger of exposure is also significant, with resultant defeat of the accepting legislator at the next election. Tiny "bribes" in the form of free banquets and small gifts are extremely frequent, but they probably have little effect on the voting of any but the petty "hungry" legislator, since they are so easy to obtain that few legislators covet them. Despite the great public outcry upon disclosure of a bribe, it is probable that bribery influences legislation much less frequently in most states than does the "legitimate" campaign contribution. Perhaps, in some states, bribery has become an accepted pattern for a significant proportion of the legis-

14Speech in the House of Representatives, August 5, 1964 (from the *Congressional Record*, 88th Cong., 2nd Sess.).
15*Minneapolis Morning Tribune*, April 6, 1960, p. 4.

lators, but even there more legislators are influenced by the campaign contribution.[16]

Not infrequently, what many people assume to be a bribe is not in fact a bribe. The following incident, which occurred during the 1963 session of the Minnesota state legislature, will illustrate how such a misunderstanding can arise. The legislature has the power to determine the salaries of several categories of state, county, and local government employees, and hence many of these latter form committees to hire professional lobbyists to try to persuade legislators of their need for salary raises. Around the middle of the 1963 session, rumors were circulating that employees of the Hennepin County District Court were paying bribes to legislators in order to get a salary raise that year. The rumors were traced to a typed "bulletin" sent to each court employee, which read as follows:

> Is your Salary Bill actively before the Legislature? It's up to you. Let's Get The Flight Off the Ground! The Wheel that does the squeaking is the wheel that gets the grease! First, we need more grease for the wheels within our organization. Next, we must apply the necessary lubrication over in St. Paul. About 65 per cent of our staff of clerks have shown good faith and contributed to the Lobbyist Fund on which we voted at a regular meeting. WHAT HAPPENED TO THE OTHER 35 PER CENT? Sixty-five per cent participation is like trying to "take off" in a plane with only half of the running gear operating. No time now to drag your feet—the Legislative Session will be all over in about twelve days. As business men and women, we know our bill for a salary increase will not get attention in the Legislature unless we play smart and keep this bill in the active foreground. *Cast your bread on the water and it will come back "buttered." Where else can you invest*

[16]Illinois state senator Paul Simon, as told to Alfred Balk, "The Illinois Legislature: A Study in Corruption," *Harper's Magazine*, 229 (September 1964), 74–91. For an exposure of corruption in Massachusetts state politics, see the three-part article by Anthony Lewis in *The New York Times*, June 19–21, 1961, p. 1ff. Also see the report of the Massachusetts Crime Commission, issued in April 1965, on the corruption of public officials in that state. Fraud in elections and vote-buying are more common. An article on these things in Kentucky indicates that vote-buying is not only in cash and whiskey but also in contributions to charities and churches. See 'A Kentucky Legislator,' "How an Election Was Bought and Sold," *Harper's Magazine*, 221 (October 1960), 33–8.

> *$30.00 and be reasonably sure of a much larger return within a few months*? The Big Boys play the game in the Legislature through experts and lobbyists. We are in the Big League— Let's play ball like a Major League team.

It is easy to understand, from reading this "bulletin," why the court employees thought they were giving bribes by contributing $30.00 apiece to their "committee." There were 39 legislators from Hennepin County who would have been accused of receiving bribes if there had been any, since they were the ones who had to decide on the salaries.

Actually, most of the money went to pay for the salary of the professional lobbyist—whose effectiveness in getting the salaries raised was questionable—although he may have used a small portion of it to pay for an occasional lunch or dinner of some legislator. The legislators were angry and fearful when they saw a copy of the "bulletin"; it convinced many individuals that there was bribery and it might even have convinced a newspaper reporter. They collectively decided to notify the court employees that they must publicly apologize for the "bulletin" and the rumors or else they would not receive their deserved raise that year. Fifty-two employees of the court signed the following apology:

> The undersigned employees of the Hennepin County District Court respectfully state that an unfortunately worded bulletin prepared for only the members of that office was circulated among us under date of March 28, 1963.
>
> That any inference in said bulletin which suggested that members of the legislature were being compensated or lavishly entertained for possible favors or increased salaries or benefits that the employees might be given in the District Court Clerk's Office, from legislation in their behalf, is vehemently denied. Never has the committee or members of this organization contributed money for such purpose.
>
> Fund raising among the employees of the Clerk of District Court has been limited to the minimum necessity for expense of the committee.
>
> The undersigned employees respectfully apologize for the occurrence of the unfortunate situation caused by the bulletin and wish each member of the Legislature to know that not

a single employee ever conceived a bribe or any other emolument was for the members of the legislature.

If a copy of the "bulletin" had not been discovered by a legislator, the legislators would never have known what the source of the rumors that they were receiving bribes was. Or there could have been fund-raising, a lobbyist, and rumors about bribes without the existence of a "bulletin." The public—in this case represented by county employees—is all too prone to assume that politicians take bribes, whether a lobbyist encourages this belief or not.[17]

Between the illegal bribe and the legal campaign contribution as means of influencing government behavior is the "conflict of interest." This occurs when a public official uses his office to affect some decision which benefits him personally. Since 1950, federal officials Lamarr Caudle and Matt Connelly have gone to prison for this. Sherman Adams, Roswell Gilpatric, Jerry Holleman, and Fred Korth have been pressed to resign from their posts for involvements that appeared to be conflicts of interest. Robert Baker, secretary to the Senate Democratic Majority, was alleged to have been involved in several conflicts of interest in 1963–65, and he was forced to resign his position when the allegations were first made public. Baker, of course, was in the Legislative, not the Executive, branch of the government. These are the only significant cases of conflict of interest reaching public attention involving high-level appointed federal government officials, in over fifteen years. Thus the problem seems to be rare, considering the total number of employees that could have been involved. At the lower levels of the federal Executive branch, in the civil service, cases of conflict of interest, like those of bribery, are occasionally discovered, but they also could not be said to be numerous.[18] Considering that conflict of interest is illegal in the Executive and Judicial branches, and that recent Chief Executives have had strong policies against even the implication of it,

[17]While this author was a member of the Minnesota State Legislature in 1963, he received an anonymous phone call from a person saying that bribes were being given to legislators to oppose a certain bill of which the author was co-sponsor. The bill would have eliminated certain unethical practices in one small service industry. Yet no significant opposition to this bill emerged, and the bill was passed. What basis there could have been for the charge of bribery remains a mystery to me.

[18]For an example involving nine employees of the Federal Housing Administration, see *The New York Times*, June 27, 1963, p. 53.

it could probably not be considered as a significant means by which an economic elite could control government.

But the problem is much more serious, relatively speaking, in the case of the elected congressmen. Yet there is no law making conflict of interest on the part of legislators illegal, and it seems to be quite frequent among them. At the heart of the problem is the concept of the legislative role as developed by the nation's founding fathers. The legislator alone—in contrast to the administrator or the judge— was given the right to continue his business or profession while ful- filling his government assignment. It was felt that the legislator's job was a part-time one, that he would better represent his constituency if he remained involved in his local occupation, and his public salary was made lower than that of an administrator or judge at com- parable levels. There have always been rules, formal or informal, against unethical behavior on the part of legislators, but the federal and state constitutions provide that the legislatures themselves shall be the final judge of the qualifications of their own members. In recent years many state legislatures have adopted formal codes of ethics, but conflict of interest involving legislators has nowhere been sharply reduced. Many state legislators, and some congressmen, are closely associated with economic interests, and in a not insignificant number of cases their major reason for being a legislator is to serve these interests. They promote legislation which will financially aid themselves, their friends, their business associates, or their influential constituents, and they intercede with, and sometimes threaten (by their control of budgets), the government departments and the "independent" regulating agencies for the same purposes. This became an issue, for example, in the re-election campaign of Sen- ator A. Willis Robertson (D., Va.), when it was revealed that New York bankers raised a campaign fund of more than $30,000 to aid this chairman of the Senate Banking and Currency Committee, who had recently pushed through a bill to exempt banks from certain provisions of the antitrust laws.[19] Legislators' activities of the type known as "conflict of interest" remain as one of the significant avenues by which certain members of the economic elite can influ- ence legislation and administrative decisions.

[19]*The New York Times*, June 27, 1966, p. 32.

Because congressmen are now employed full-time in their public office, and their salaries have recently been raised to the levels of Cabinet officers, it might be possible to develop statutes and codes of ethics that would progressively control their conflicts of interest. Bills to this effect have already been introduced in Congress, but it would take a massive force of public opinion to get them enacted and enforced. Many congressmen, and possibly an increasing number, voluntarily police themselves regarding conflict of interest. This is not only a matter of personal ethics; it is also a way of avoiding difficulties with the electorate. A charge of conflict of interest, made by an opposing candidate or party, can sometimes defeat a congressman. This may be becoming increasingly true, as a section of the public has become aware of what conflict of interest involves in the Executive branch.

The problem is much more serious in the case of the state and local legislator. His usually remains a part-time job (except in the case of some big-city aldermen), and public salaries are too low for the public to expect able men to eschew private occupations while they hold public ones on a part-time basis. While charges of conflict of interest have occasionally defeated a legislator, the charges are sometimes used falsely, and libel and slander suits are difficult to sustain and their results often come too late to keep a legislator in his seat. The United States Supreme Court decision in the case of *The New York Times* v. *Sullivan* (1964)—which makes it impossible for a public official to win a libel or slander suit except by proving "actual malice" as well as falsity of accusation—will undoubtedly encourage the use of false charges in election campaigns, and thus render weaker the force of public opinion in controlling real cases of conflict of interest. If conflict of interest seems to be diminishing in the federal Congress, there is little evidence that this is also true of state legislatures and city councils. While many of the cases of conflict at the state and local levels involve small sums and a great variety of small economic interests, some of them serve the interests of the economic elite. Some movements to raise the standards of state legislatures—such as those promoted by the League of Women Voters and the Citizens' Conference of State Legislatures—hold some promise for future reform. The basic source of the problem remains the public's confusion of illegal bribery with legal (but unethical) conflicts of interest, and the consequent lack of public support for efforts to create working conditions for legislators in which they will tend to avoid conflict of interest. Conflict of interest has been sharply reduced in the Executive and Judicial branches of most state and city governments during the past half-century, and is now being reduced in the federal Congress; It is thus reasonable to conceive of its being similarly reduced in the state legislatures and city councils.

Another important misconception the public holds about politics which gets in the way of ethics in government is the belief that the processes of government are unimportant, and that the important decisions affecting the nation or the community are made privately by a small group of the economic elite. That is, the very "economic-elite-dominance hypothesis" which we are examining in this book— insofar as it is widely believed by the public—is itself contributory to unethical behavior in government. The average person who holds to this belief is not likely to have read Mills or Hunter for his ideas, but is likely, rather, to have been directly influenced—consciously or unconsciously—by the Populist or Marxist strains in American popular thought. This belief has the effect of distracting the citizen's attention away from politics, or giving him a sense of justification for his unwillingness to concern himself with what goes on in politics. To the extent that this viewpoint prevails in the public, the politician can "ignore the public" in making many decisions and allow the heavy contributors to his campaign fund to make up his mind for him. Thus, the belief is self-fulfilling; insofar as people believe it, it tends to become true. The economic elite certainly do not appear to believe that government is unimportant, for not only are they the source of the large campaign contributions but they also pay heavily to have lobbies represent their interests before legislatures.

But it is also an error to assume that—in the absence of significant public interest in the votes of legislators—the strenuous efforts of the economic elite to influence legislators and legislation proves that they control legislatures. In the first place, there are pressure groups which do not represent the economic elite. Secondly, the legislator bases his decisions on many influences besides those coming from pressure groups. Thirdly, except possibly for those who come from "safe" districts, legislators are very dependent on their party organizations for help in getting re-elected, and the party usually includes so many diverse interests that it serves as a counter-pressure to any single lobby. The fact is that most of the time, legislators vote in accord with their party's position and thus show themselves as not being under the direct control of any single pressure group. More realistic questions about the power of the economic elite would be whether they dominate any political party, and if so whether they are representing only themselves or also large sections of the electorate in the leadership they give to this party.

It is certainly true that public officeholders, especially legislators, often misrepresent themselves to their constituencies. Most voters do not bother to find out on their own how their representatives have voted on most issues, and it is probable that many would be shocked and disturbed to find out. The officeholder usually tries to create an "image" which appeals to the largest number of voters in his district, and this image sometimes has little to do with his votes on legislation. But it is to be expected that during the next campaign his opponent will seek to spike a false image and point to the incumbent's actual voting record. The question of whether the citizen's needs are being represented by the public official again comes down to whether the citizen takes the effort to find out what the official is actually doing, and whether the candidate has the means to get his record and his opponent's record across to the public. The worst sort of misrepresentation by a legislator, and the most effective and unethical form of lobbying, occurs when legislator and lobbyist coincide in the same person. Conflicts of interest in the Executive and Judicial branches of government have been carefully guarded against by statutes and administrative rules, but only slight and ineffective efforts have been made to restrict the equally unethical and dangerous conflicts of interest in the Legislative branch. Some large industries encourage an employee or two to run for the state legislature or city council so that they might have a "built-in" lobbyist with actual power.

Another unusually favorable situation for the economic elite of a community to control local politics by misrepresenting themselves to the public occurs where there are nonpartisan elections. Where the political parties are rendered inoperative by law, the wealthy can use their wealth most effectively to control elections, since there is no other basis of organization to elect the officeholders. This is an historical irony, as it was mainly the Populists who sought to protect the common people against the wicked political parties by instituting the nonpartisan election, the open primary, and other techniques of "direct democracy." All of these techniques, by weakening the major political parties, have left the average citizens—victims of their own political ignorance—open to political control by the economic elite. Williams and Adrian have demonstrated this generally for those cities and towns that have nonpartisan elections,[20] and we shall provide an example from Minneapolis.

Elections for the school board in Minneapolis are nonpartisan, and for a decade or so the only continuing organizations strong enough and interested enough to put up candidates for a school board race were the school janitors' and the teachers' unions, with the backing of other elements of organized labor. The board members thus elected were "built-in lobbyists" for the unions' vested interests, to the detriment of the education of the children and at the expense of the taxpayers. Finally, in 1951, some of the parents' groups and taxpayers' groups formed a Citizens' Committee for an Independent School Board (CCISB) to endorse and support non-labor candidates for the school board. The parents' groups that battled for this goal had a turnover of membership, and within a few years the Citizens' Committee for an Independent School Board was nothing more than an executive committee of five persons, with a part-time paid executive secretary. They continued to operate with relatively large campaign funds from the local economic elite, who were pleased to see the school board out of the hands of the labor unions. The selection of candidates for the school board was made by the executive secretary, with the approval of the five-man executive committee, who were themselves now members of the economic elite, from whom all the campaign funds came. At each election, the old list of the original sponsors of the CCISB was paraded out, and claimed to be the selecting body, but it no longer existed as a functioning group. The voting public was never informed that six people quietly selected the candidates for the school board, and that the election campaign was paid for by the rich people of the city to represent one viewpoint on

[20]Oliver P. Williams and Charles R. Adrian, "The Insulation of Local Politics Under the Nonpartisan Ballot," *American Political Science Review*, 53 (December 1959), 1052–1063.

the school board. Not 1 per cent of the population of Minneapolis knows this. The teachers' union put up a spirited opposition for several elections, but it was labeled as union-controlled, and—with the aid of its own political ineptness—it lost every election. This situation continued until 1963, when the Democratic party began to put up candidates in opposition to the CCISB candidates and won two seats on the seven-man board. While the CCISB continues to control the majority of the board, it is circumspect, in that it selects candidates who are genuinely interested in education, and it does not try to control their specific actions once they are elected to the board. Thus, the board is controlled by the economic elite, by the device of misrepresenting itself to the public, but the public does not suffer from poor schools, since the board members try to do a good job within their limitations.

All that has been said so far boils down to the statement often heard among those who are informed about politics, that the public gets the kind of government it deserves. With few exceptions, the political problems of government are connected to the ignorance of and myths about politics which keep the public from understanding the nature and cause of these problems. Ignorance and myths keep citizens estranged from politics, when the only cure for the ethical problems of politics can come when there is increased participation. The politicians, try as they might, cannot eliminate these ethical problems, for one element in all the problems is the non-participation of any significant number of the citizenry. Merely electing better and abler men to public office, while it may have other advantages, will have little effect on the problems we have considered. Only increased public participation will help.

B. Citizen Participation

This takes us directly to the second problem of this chapter—the need for a citizen of a democratic society to understand generally what is going on in his government and to participate to some degree in its decision-making processes. Whereas most other participations tie him to local, or narrow, highly specialized groups, participation in politics is one of the few ways the average citizen can relate himself to his society as a whole. In a diversified, complex, pluralistic society

—as compared to an integrated, tradition-bound society—it is easy for the average person to lose contact with the ethos and general culture of his society. His needs for understanding the world in which he lives and for having some sense of control of his position in that world tend to be less than satisfied. The only way of satisfying these needs in contemporary society is through increased participation in some nation-wide organization with power, that can both interpret the large-scale events affecting the society and give him some share in dealing with these events. Participation in political organizations can also serve needs for companionship and identification which participation in other kinds of organizations equally well serve. The needs for ethical and equitable politics in a democratic, pluralistic society, and the personal needs of the average citizen thus coincide. They both require increased participation on his part.

It would be utopian to expect that any society could ever have all of its citizens participating actively in politics, with equal opportunity for each to attain public office and equal benefits to each from governmental actions. In a pluralistic society especially, people have diverse interests, and many would prefer activities and involvements other than political ones, under the best of circumstances. Further, government has different degrees of impact on these different interests, so that even a thoroughly equitable government is bound to affect the lives of some of its citizens much more than of others. The satisfaction of needs for political involvement can probably best be met by a minimal participation on the part of most people and intensive participation on the part of an interested minority. This means extending the minimal participation from perhaps 20 per cent of the adult population which is the present situation, to about 80 per cent, and the intensive participation from perhaps 2 per cent to 10 per cent. Lane estimates that party officers, including precinct committeemen, make up 0.25 per cent of the adult population, and that volunteers in any one election never go over 5 per cent.[21] A Gallup poll, reported in the *Minneapolis Morning Tribune* of September 11, 1965 (p. 5), showed that only 16 per cent of a cross section of

---

[21]Lane, *Political Life*, p. 56. For other measurements of political participation, see articles by Morris Rosenberg and by Robert A. Dahl, in Heinz Eulau, *et al.* (eds.), *Political Behavior: A Reader in Theory and Research* (Glencoe, Ill.: Free Press, 1956).

American adults ever served on a jury, only 19 per cent ever wrote to a congressman, and only 16 per cent ever wrote a "letter to the Editor."

The minimal participation should include informing oneself about the candidates and major issues before voting, contributing to campaign funds, and expressing oneself to politicians on issues which one happens to be particularly interested in and informed about.[22] Intensive participation would include, besides the above, membership in a political organization, working in the campaign to elect certain candidates, disseminating information about major issues and candidates, working for the adoption or implementation of some specific governmental program, and perhaps running for public office. It is easy to see how these forms of participation would contribute to serve individual needs for companionship, identification, and subjective understanding of pertinent social forces. It remains for us to examine how this participation would serve the people's needs to have government run ethically and equitably.

What we have called the minimal necessary participation of all (or most) citizens to solve the two problems of ethics and of involvement in government need not be done directly by the citizens; such participation is perhaps most effective when done indirectly through voluntary associations. It is not realistic to expect the average citizen to look up the voting records of his legislators on all the issues that interest or concern him. But it is not unrealistic for members of a voluntary association to discuss public issues that concern them, pass resolutions on these issues, and then have the leaders of the association present the resolution to the congressman or legislators. It is also not unrealistic to have some representative from each voluntary association active in each of the two major political parties, to communicate on occasion the point of view of the association so that this point of view becomes part of the countervailing pressure that political parties regularly put on their candidates through platforms and resolutions. The last-mentioned indirect procedures are more effective ways for the average citizen to participate in govern-

22It is to be noted that our conception of minimal participation in politics goes beyond the informal expressions—which may never be heard by politicians—suggested by Fred E. Katz and Fern V. Piret: "Circuitous Participation in Politics," *American Journal of Sociology*, 69 (January 1964), 367–73.

mental affairs, to help keep his legislators working in his behalf, than the direct avenue of letters or personal visits. Financial contributions to political parties and for candidates can be made directly (both major parties now have door-to-door solicitations annually in a number of areas) or indirectly through some branch of their voluntary associations.

Even a nominal financial contribution from a majority of the citizens—say $1.00 a year—would pay most of the cost of running all the political campaigns.[23] An increase in the number of volunteer workers would reduce the money costs of campaigning. If there were these two forms of increased participation, there would then be no obligation on the elected officeholders to return political favors for large campaign contributions. Even if this sum of money should not quite suffice to pay all campaign costs, the citizens who had made a small contribution would not be likely to tolerate the buying of political favors with large contributions. Simple public awareness of the large costs of campaigning would produce enough pressure to achieve the democrat's dream of getting a significant amount of free publicity for political campaigns. These developments, along with more effective controls on certain types of campaign expenditures,[24] would eliminate the pressure on public officeholders to be inequitable in their public actions.

Without the pressure to collect a large campaign fund, more persons would feel free to run for office. Of course, not all of those offering themselves for candidacy would be meritorious, but it would be expected that a much larger total number of candidates would include a proportionate increase in the number of able candidates.

[23]It has been estimated that $175,000,000 was spent in all of the 1960 campaigns— national, state, county, and municipal. It is not likely that this amount would be spent in non-presidential election years. Herbert E. Alexander, *Financing the Parties and Campaigns* (Washington: The Brookings Institution, 1961).

[24]Present laws on campaign expenditures usually limit the amount a candidate or a political committee can spend. These laws are ineffective because (1) the candidate or his friends organize more than one committee—as many, in fact, as they can get maximum contributions for and which they feel they can use; and (2) many candidates fail to report their contributions, and the law often does not specify who should do the enforcing and how it should be done. In New York City, for example, less than one-sixth of the candidates in the September 1962 primary election filed their "required" pre-primary statement of contributions and expenditures (*The New York Times*, August 29, 1962, p. 17). More effective controls would include prohibition of certain types of expenditures and specification of enforcement procedures.

Well-qualified citizens would no longer be deterred from running for public office by the obstacle of having to accumulate a campaign fund, with the sometimes odious requirement of promising political favors. The increase in the number of potential candidates would make the election and endorsement process by political parties more significant. Participants in this process would gain a greater sense of control over public affairs if the process had more significance and effectiveness, and thus one of the individual needs of the party activist would be better served. The increase in funds passing through the party's coffers would strengthen the parties and help them keep their men in office more responsible.

An increase in public participation, even on the minimal level, would greatly reduce the present unethical practice of many legislators voting one way in the legislature and then trying to present the opposite image to the voters. Following the voting record of legislators is the only effective way of keeping some legislators honest. It would not be necessary for a majority of citizens to follow the development of all legislation. A well-dispersed minority of citizens following specialized legislation that happens to interest them would be enough to spike any false representation that a legislator would try to offer his constituents.

The strong political party—which is characterized, among other things,[25] by having enough members to do a major share of the work in getting candidates elected—can better perform its function of balancing vested-interest pressure groups. The party cannot, of course, be expected to be always pure in working for the public interest since it has its own structural interests to maintain. But it is likely to be much more broadly based than most pressure groups and to be concerned more about the interests of a potential majority of the voting population than of a single vested-interest pressure group. Even in a machine-dominated state, one former legislator reports:

> For every occasion when a party leader asked me for a favor
> that disturbed my conscience, I can think of a dozen times

[25]There are obviously other characteristics of a strong party besides sheer number of members—such as efficient organization, morale of leaders and members, etc.—but they are not pertinent to the discussion in this chapter. Some have been discussed in other chapters.

when the same party leader helped me defend the public interest against the importunities of nonparty pressure groups.[26]

A stronger party can perform this balancing function for its public officeholders more effectively. And a broadly based membership can counteract to a considerable extent the party leader's proclivities to assert and defend the structural interests of the party at the expense of the broader public interest.

Greater public involvement in political processes should give a larger proportion of the citizenry an understanding of the complexities of the political process, and thereby a greater respect for the politicians who have to tread their way through these complexities. There are obviously many non-financial rewards for politicians at present, but the kind of person who goes into politics tends to have an unusually great need for ego-gratification and respect. The blows he must take from critics need to be more than counterbalanced by praise from admirers, else he will either quit politics or stay in solely for financial rewards. Respect and praise are among the most effective devices to keep politicians from cynically seeking financial rewards, which usually involve dishonest behavior. Under the present system we do not reward our politicians with enough respect and praise. It is, of course, necessary to remain ever suspicious of politicians, as the opportunities for corruption are present and corruption cannot be condoned. But respect and praise should not encourage corruption; on the contrary, they should make the politician ashamed to do things that would not merit the praise and respect he has received. Americans tend to weaken the ethics of politicians by showing only suspicion toward them. Summarizing public opinion polls concerning politics as a vocation, Hyman and Sheatsley note that many people:

> . . . took the stand that it was "almost impossible" for a man to go into politics without becoming dishonest. This same reason, incidentally, was advanced by about half of the group who would not like to see their sons enter politics: public service is essentially dishonest and corrupting. Many among those who would favor a political career for their sons explain their attitude by saying that politics is corrupt now and

26Stephen K. Bailey, *Ethics and the Politician* (Santa Barbara: The Fund for the Republic, 1960), p. 7.

honest men are needed to reform it. Yet, when asked whether or not they are satisfied with the way most office holders in their state are handling their jobs, about half the population indicate satisfaction.[27]

It will not be easy to change people's attitudes toward politicians. Ennoblement by the public would tend to make noble-men of them, just as it now tends to do for judges and for the President of the United States. Granting other politicians a higher status would tend to lead them to conform to the public's expectations of persons of high status.

In this chapter we have sought to present and defend the thesis that two political needs in a pluralistic society, for more ethical and equitable behavior on the part of politicians and for a sense of political understanding and influence on the part of ordinary citizens, can best be satisfied together. Greater involvement in politics by ordinary citizens will not only satisfy their personal needs but also provide the only effective cures for two of the major political ills in our democratic, pluralistic society. This is not a recipe for political perfection, of course. Politics is too complex for that. The necessity for speed in making political decisions will by itself reduce the possibility of having completely ethical judgments, for example. What is the correct ethical decision is often far from clear, especially at the limited moment when the decision must be made. Mistakes will be made, and often when the best judgment has been made on one side of an ethical issue, much right will remain on the other side. There are many structural problems in politics not related to the need for ethical and equitable behavior on the part of officeholders, but we have not considered them because they are not related to our central concern with the relative power of economic and political elites.

Special and vested interests are inherent in a pluralistic society, and it is inherent in the democratic process that they have a full and free opportunity to pressure for their narrow and often selfish goals. The economic elites have been within their legal and democratic rights in using practically every technique of influence which they have used to gain their ends in government, even if those techniques

[27]Herbert H. Hyman and Paul B. Sheatsley, "The Current Status of American Public Opinion," in John C. Payne (ed.), *The Teaching Of Contemporary Affairs* (Menasha, Wis.: George Banta, 1951), p. 22.

are often not ethical. We have contended that the most effective way of balancing most of the structural pressures toward unethical behavior and inequitability in government is by greater citizen participation.

XIV
Conclusion

Political power in the United States, like any other social phenomenon, is changing its locus of concentration, its distribution, and its manifestations constantly.[1] Some of the observations and generalizations made in this book will be out of date by the time the reader is able to analyze and criticize them. Recent changes, for example, have occurred in the rural-urban distribution of power in state legislatures, in the strength of the Republican–Southern Democratic "coalition" in Congress, and in the extent to which businessmen are to be found in key positions in the national Administration. Nevertheless, most aspects of power have remained sufficiently stable for a student of the power structure to draw generalizations and to note slow-moving trends. In contrast to the major theses of C. Wright Mills and Floyd Hunter—that there is a secret, hierarchical, and unified power structure in the United States headed by an economic elite, that the political elite occupies only a secondary position in the power structure, and that the masses are apathetic and act in terms of false consciousness of their interests—we would assert the following propositions. Most of them are based on studies reported or summarized in this book; others are based merely on general or participant observation.

1. There is a power structure in every organized activity of American life and at every level—national, regional, state, and

[1] Even from the time the present study was begun, in 1960, until it was sent to the publishers, in 1966, there were so many significant changes that additions, corrections, and qualifications had to be made regularly in the manuscript.

local. Power is the major means used by a large, heterogeneous society to effect or to resist change, and—except in simple face-to-face relations—power is structured, which is to say that there are different roles and role relationships, and a pattern into which these roles and relationships fit.

2. There are varying degrees of relationship and agreement among these varied power structures. They are certainly not unified into a simple power structure, even *within* the categories of the economic and the political, although occasionally semi-permanent liaisons develop among them. Nor are they usually countervailing, because each operates primarily within its own sphere of influence, although countervailing (or check-and-balance) relationships occasionally do occur. The political party power structures—there are at least four major ones on the national level alone—probably have the largest number of relationships with other power structures, both because one of their specific roles is to mediate conflicts and because they have a large degree of control over the bureaucratic machinery of government, which—in turn—monopolizes most of the instruments of organized physical force.

3. Within each power structure, a small number of persons hold the largest amount of power. In community studies, this has been estimated to constitute less than 1 per cent of the population, but such estimates refer to those who lead in community-wide political decisions, and not to power *within* the spheres of business, unions, voluntary associations, schools, churches, etc. While in any sphere of activity there are "leaders," who constitute a tiny proportion of all those affected by the activity, this does not mean that the others have no power whatsoever. Opposition groups occasionally form, and sometimes succeed in overturning the existing elite. In all cases where there are elections, the rank-and-file voters exercise some restraining and modifying power over the elite. Their power is a function of the extent to which they have interacted to create a public opinion, the extent to which the election machinery is honest, and the extent to which voters are equal. Under these criteria, most governmental elections accord a good deal of power to the electorate, most business corporation elections accord practically no power to the electorate, and labor union and voluntary association elections vary between these two poles. But even in government and in actively

democratic trade unions, there is an ever-changing elite which exercises most of the power at any given moment.

4. Each elite manifests its power mainly within its own domain. That is, the strongest powers of businessmen are exercised within their own businesses, and the strongest powers of politicians and public administrators are exercised within government. But particularly the political and economic elites, among all the elites, influence each other's spheres. Especially since the 1930's the government has set various restrictions and controls on business, and has heavily taxed business and the public to carry out purposes deemed to be for the general good—welfare programs, education programs, highways, war and military defense activities, etc. Business leaders use lobbyists, "business representatives" in legislatures, contributions to campaign funds, publicity designed to influence public opinion, the "political strike," and other lesser techniques to influence government. Businessmen influence government more effectively than most non-businessmen—not only because they can afford lobbyists, advertisements and other costly techniques—but also because they are more educated, more knowledgeable, more articulate, and more activist than average citizens. The latter qualities give them an advantage quite compatible with a democratic society.

5. The economic elite has its greatest success in influencing government where there are no counter-pressures—from other sectors of the economic elite, from other non-economic elites, and from public opinion. The result has been that the economic elite has been relatively successful in influencing government purchasing agents and the independent regulatory commissions. This is not quite an accurate way of stating the facts, however, since individual businesses often compete strongly with each other in influencing these factors of government, and there is a considerable turnover in the individual businesses benefited by these sectors of government. In pressuring or appealing to the top levels of the federal administration, to the Congress, or even to many state legislatures (especially outside the South), businessmen have been much less successful since the 1930's. In fact, as far as general legislation is concerned, they have had an almost unbroken series of defeats, although they have succeeded in *delaying* the passage of certain bills for years. Thus, while businessmen have gained certain economic benefits from government, their

typical ideology—in favor of businessman leadership in the society and of a minimum of government activity for the benefit of other segments of the population—has made no progress.[2]

6. While the federal government has been gaining ascendancy over the state and local governments, and while the office of the President has been gaining power at the expense of Congress, it is far from true that the state governments and the Congress are powerless. Rather, it could be said that the "balance of power" doctrine envisaged in the Constitution has come into operation only since 1933, because the federal government (except for military activities) and the presidency (except in wartime) were relatively weak institutions before then. These two trends in political power have reduced the influence of the economic elite, for the federal government is less susceptible to influence from businessmen than are most of the state governments, and the presidency is less susceptible to such influence than are many of the congressmen.

7. In the early 1960's a coalition of several decades' duration between two major political power structures—the conservative leadership of the Republican party and the Democrats in power in most of the Southern states—largely broke down. The Southern Democrats, changing in membership and reduced in number by Republican inroads on their constituencies, drew closer to the Northern Democrats, except publicly over the issue of civil rights. The South was rapidly becoming like the North—in its industrialization, urbanization, patterns of race relations permitted by Negro voting, and development of a two-party system.[3] The Republican party was sharply divided between its conservatives and liberals, on the one hand, and a smaller group of right-wing extremists with a vigorous ideology who seized control of the party's grassroots structures in the majority of states. The extremists—while occasionally ideologically supportive of business—were not as willing to make political

[2] It has been argued that this businessman's ideology represents a "false consciousness"—that is, it claims to represent an economic interest, but is in fact, contrary to the economic interest of businessmen. The factual argument is that businessmen gain most economic benefits when the government actively promotes the welfare and education of even its poorest citizens, when it maintains a regularly unbalanced budget, and when it reduces tariffs—all policies which most businessmen oppose.

[3] The decline in the number of "safe" Democratic House seats has been documented by Raymond E. Wolfinger and Joan Heifetz, "Safe Seats, Seniority, and Power in Congress," *American Political Science Review*, 59 (June 1965), 337–49.

compromises in behalf of business or as willing to trust leading businessmen, as had been the previous conservative leaders of the Republican party. All these developments, coupled with the political skill of President Lyndon B. Johnson, permitted the passage of a great deal of "liberal" legislation in the 1964–65 sessions of Congress—including "Medicare" for the elderly (analyzed in Chapter XII), federal aid to education, the anti-poverty program, tax reduction without a balanced budget, a comprehensive civil rights act, a voting rights act, elimination of national quotas for immigrants, creation of a new Department of Housing and Urban Development, aid to urban mass-transit programs and to highway and city beautification efforts, and a National Foundation on the Arts and Humanities. Further, the President had an unofficial price control policy which worked for a few years to keep major industries from raising prices.

8. In the passage of the above-mentioned legislation, interested economic elite pressure groups were mostly defeated. On the other hand, the major legislation sought by organized labor—repeal of Section 14(b) of the Taft-Hartley Act—was also defeated in the Senate. The one economic elite group that continued to reap major economic benefits from government activity was the armaments and space-exploration supply industries, although the Secretary of Defense made certain decisions on procurement—such as in favor of competitive bidding rather than cost-plus contracts—even in this area which were not favored by the leading manufacturers.

9. Through the Voting Rights Act of the Congress and the *Baker* v. *Carr* and *Reynolds* v. *Sims* decisions of the United States Supreme Court—including the giving of permission to the Attorney General to seek a Court review of the poll tax (which was consequently outlawed by the Supreme Court)—a major democratization of voting for state legislatures was occurring in many states. Both state and local government activities were increasingly influenced by standards set by federal aid programs that covered ever wider spheres.

10. The pattern of legislation at both federal and state levels revealed the emergence of new popular pressure groups with considerable power, partly because of demographic shifts and partly because of growing political consciousness among these groups. These groups are the elderly, a portion of whom are now organized into

many associations, the most politically active of which is the National Association of Senior Citizens; the Negroes, possibly a majority of whom are organized into various civil rights associations and activist churches; and the "resentful disaffecteds," practically all organized into a variety of leftist and rightist extremist organizations, of which the John Birch Society is the largest and the wealthiest. The political organization of voluntary associations representing these three categories of the "masses" provides increasing evidence of a thesis expounded in an earlier section on "Reactions against the Mass Society" (pp. 196-212).

11. The major area of small-group control of national policy remaining in the country was that of foreign policy. The most powerful arm of this small group—namely the President and his official advisers—are quite exposed to the public. But there are secret decision-makers operating in this area also—secret in that their influence and processes of decision-making are not accessible to the public. These decision-makers are the CIA, the foreign policy "experts" in the universities and in such organizations as the Foreign Policy Association and the Council on Foreign Relations, and the military supplies industrialists who exert their influence mainly through the military leaders. The last-named are the ones whom Mills placed at the pinnacle of the power elite in the United States; we identify them rather as one influence among several affecting the nation almost exclusively in the area of foreign policy. We are entirely skeptical about Mills's contention that the other "members" of the economic elite—say, for example, those organized in the Chamber of Commerce—have more influence on foreign policy than the workers organized into trade unions, especially when they engage in shipping boycotts.

12. Despite the fact that the Republican party's ideological move to the right after 1962 left the Democrats securely in command of the center, the program of the Democratic party remained as liberal as it had ever been. This can be seen not only by comparing national party platforms over the years, but by reviewing the legislation supported (and usually passed) by the majority of Democrats in Congress and by the Democratic Presidents Kennedy and Johnson. This can be explained either as a long-run trend—in terms of the increasing strength of voters who favor liberal measures and generally support the Democratic party as the instrument to achieve them—or

as part of a structural cycle. Lipset specifies a version of the latter theory:[4] Republican Presidents seek center support and so force Republican congressmen from safe conservative seats to behave in a more liberal fashion. When a Republican holds the presidency, the Southern contingent of conservative Democrats have more power in their party. Thus, in a Republican presidency, the two congressional parties are not so far apart. But when a Democrat holds the presidency, he pulls his congressmen to the left, to respond to the needs of the greater number of voters there, while the Republican congressmen are free to follow their ideological inclination toward the right, and the two parties are quite far apart. It is difficult to judge from the facts which theory is correct, but this author tends to regard the former theory as more persuasive, especially in view of the decline of differences between South and North. In any case, there has been a significant difference between the platforms and policies of the two national parties at least since 1932,[5] and the difference in the mid-1960's was as great as could be found between democratic political parties anywhere in the Western world. The increasing number of differences between the two major political parties, and the growing ideological framework for those differences, will probably have profound implications for the political future of the United States—but it is still too early to foresee the future development. Nevertheless, from the standpoint of the thesis of this book, we can say that there is little evidence that business is playing any significant role in the development of these trends. Business is a declining influence on the political power structures, except in the narrow area of its relationship to government procurement officials and the independent regulatory commissions—largely because business exerts its strongest efforts on these and because there are few countervailing influences on them, as we pointed out in Chapter III.

13. The public's and the formal leadership's image of the power structure—if we can generalize from a study of the one state of

[4]Seymour Martin Lipset, *Political Man* (New York: Doubleday, 1960), pp. 306–7.
[5]The basic ideological difference between the leadership of the two parties, on the average, has been demonstrated by Herbert McClosky, Paul J. Hoffman, and Rosemary O'Hara, "Issue Conflict and Consensus Among Party Leaders and Followers," *American Political Science Review*, 54 (June 1960), 406–27. The public, also, sees ideological differences between the two parties. See, for example, the report of the Minnesota Poll in the *Minneapolis Sunday Tribune*, November 3, 1963, p. UM2.

Minnesota—does not include many people as seeing the economic elite as all-powerful, although the extent to which they do see business as influential may be somewhat exaggerated in terms of the facts. Judging from their public pronouncements, it is the political extremist—of both the right and the left—whose image of the American power structure includes a conspiratorial and all-powerful role for the economic elite. The extremist groups have different names for this "all-powerful group" but they refer to the same business elite: The "lunatic fringe" rightists call them "the hidden group behind the communists," the more rational extreme rightists call them "the Establishment"; the more rational extreme leftists also call them "the Establishment" or "Wall Street," but are more likely to use the Mills-Hunter terms "the power elite" or "the power structure," while the less rational extreme leftists either use the same terms or refer bluntly to "the big business conspiracy." While it is of considerable interest that the political extremists of both right and left—apparently along with many non-extremist intellectuals influenced by Mills and Hunter—have the same image of the top business elite as being all-powerful, it is of greater importance to note that the majority of the people and of the positional leaders of American organized society do not have this image. We have adduced much evidence in this book that the top business elite are far from having an all-powerful position; that power is so complicated in the United States that the top businessmen scarcely understand it, much less control it; and that since 1933 the power position of businessmen has been declining rather than growing.

14. Because the spheres of their organizations have grown in recent decades, the elites of the federal administration (including the military), of the federal courts, of certain voluntary associations, and of certain education and scientific institutions, have grown more powerful. While on rare occasions they supersede in power the top political elites—as when the United States Supreme Court ordered the state governments to end racial segregation and to reapportion their legislatures in accord with population, or when the same Court declares unconstitutional a federal statute, or when the civil rights associations pressure Congress into voting for a statute as sweeping as the Civil Rights Act of 1964, or when the labor and old-age groups pressure Congress into voting for a statute as sweeping as the Medi-

care Act of 1965 (although both these statutes had the full support of that significant political elite—the President)—the political elites are usually ascendent over them. The political elites control the agencies of force and the instruments of legislation, have considerable access to the mass media, and have the support of public opinion. The political elites—the two major parties, the President, the factions in the houses of Congress, the executives and legislatures of the states and large cities—are not unified of course, and they check-and-balance each other to a considerable extent.

15. While the two major political parties are listed by us as among the most powerful groups in the United States, their structures are quite generally misunderstood by the public and by nonspecialized intellectuals and other leadership groups. They are structured mainly as voluntary associations, with grass-roots elections that range from being wholly democratic to being "controlled" from a self-perpetuating group at the top. In some states (e.g. Texas) they are highly fractionated and schismatic. They are structured on the layer principle: ward or county, municipality, district, and state. They scarcely exist as voluntary associations at the national level—except for the quadrennial national nominating conventions—but they exist in the caucuses of Congress, where they are the most important single influence on congressmen's voting behavior despite the bifurcation within both political parties.

16. While money in the hands of rich people opens special opportunities to democratic political processes—such as through the use of lobbyists, advertisements, and campaign contributions—these processes are by no means closed to poor people. A volunteer campaign worker for a congressman will have more influence on him than most lobbyists, and as much influence on him as a campaign contribution equivalent to the voluntary labor, roughly speaking. The fact that the political party in most states is an open, if not entirely democratic, voluntary association, and the fact that it is the single most important influence on most elected officials, also gives the non-wealthy citizen access to political power often greater than that of the wealthy, but not politically active, citizen. In this context it should be understood that most elected officials, especially at higher levels, are only partially open to pressures of any kind. Practically all congressmen, and probably most state legislators, vote for bills in accord

with their own personal convictions—when they have convictions with regard to specific bills—most of the time. Where they do not have convictions regarding a specific bill, the most important influence on them are the caucus leaders or committee chairmen of their own political party who are representing the party leadership's position. The "personal convictions" factor suggests that the *initial* selection of candidates and the means which they use to get elected to Congress are the two most important links in the chain leading to the passage of bills where influence can be most effectively applied. It is for this reason that we say that voluntary campaign labor, participation in the grass-roots party (as voluntary association), and monetary campaign contributions are the most powerful instruments to influence a legislator (or probably any other elected official).

In sharper summary, the conclusions of this book—in contrast with those of Mills and Hunter—are that power structure of the United States is highly complex and diversified (rather than unitary and monolithic), that the political system is more or less democratic (with the glaring exception of the Negro's position until the 1960's), that in political processes the political elite is ascendant over and not subordinate to the economic elite, and that the political elite influences or controls the economic elite at least as much as the economic elite controls the political elite. To arrive at such conclusions we must in part have a contrast conception: What should the American political power structure be compared to? We believe that Mills has implicitly compared the existing American power structure to some populist or guild socialist ideal, which has never existed and which we believe could never exist considering basic sociological facts —such as the existence of culture, of the value of money to most people, etc. Our implicit comparison in this book has been to any known other society—past or present (with the possible exception of the contemporary Scandinavian countries). We do not say that the multi-influence hypothesis is entirely the fact, or that the United States is completely democratic; we simply say that such statements are more correct for the United States today than for any other society.

While the whole first chapter of this book might be repeated in the summary, we wish merely to repeat in conclusion the statement of the multi-influence hypothesis which has guided the studies reported in this book: Segments of the economic elite have violated democratic political and legal processes, with differing degrees of effort and success in the various periods of American history, but in no recent period could they correctly be said to have controlled the elected and appointed political authorities in large measure. The relationship between the economic elite and the political authorities has been a constantly varying one of strong influence, co-operation, division of labor, and conflict, with each group influencing the other in changing proportion to some extent, and each operating independently of the other to a large extent. Today there is significant political control and limitation of certain activities of the economic elite, and there are also some significant processes by which the economic elite use their wealth to help elect some political candidates and to influence other political authorities in ways which are not available to the average citizen. Further, neither the economic elite nor the political authorities are monolithic units which act with internal consensus and co-ordinated action with regard to each other (or probably in any other way): in fact, there are several economic elites, which only very rarely act as units within themselves and among themselves, and there are at least two (we prefer to think of them as four) political parties which have significantly differing programs with regard to their actions toward any economic elite and each of these parties has only a partial degree of internal cohesion.

The power structure of the United States is indeed so complex that this book only touches on certain aspects of it, rather than providing full empirical evidence for these aspects. We believe, however, that enough empirical documentation has been provided to give basic support to the multi-influence hypothesis as a general statement about what is true of the power structure of the United States.

Index

495